AMERICAN INCOMES

Demographics of Who Has Money

AMERICAN INCOMES

Demographics of Who Has Money

8th EDITION

New Strategist Publications, Inc.
Ithaca, New York

New Strategist Publications, Inc.
P.O. Box 242, Ithaca, New York 14851
800/848-0842; 607/273-0913
www.newstrategist.com

ISBN 978-1-935775-43-0 (hardcover)
ISBN 978-1-935775-44-7 (paper)

Printed in the United States of America

Table of Contents

Tables

Chapter 2.   Men's Income

Men's Income Trends

Men's Incomes, 2010

Chapter 3. Women's Income

Women's Income Trends

Women's Incomes, 2010

Chapter 4. Discretionary Income

Chapter 5. Wealth

Chapter 6. Poverty

Poverty Trends

Illustrations

Men's Incomes, 2010

Chapter 3. Women's Income

Women's Income Trends

Women's Incomes, 2010

Chapter 4. Discretionary Income

Chapter 5. Wealth

Chapter 6. Poverty

Poverty Trends

Poverty, 2010

Introduction

The United States is recovering from the worst economic downturn since the Great Depression. Although the Great Recession is officially over, incomes are still falling, poverty is rising, and net worth has declined. Americans are hurting. As the country adjusts to new economic realities, it is vital to stay on top of these socioeconomic trends. The eighth edition of *American Incomes: Demographics of Who Has Money*, is your map to the changing consumer landscape.

Almost everywhere you look, the numbers are troubling. The $49,445 median household income of 2010 was 7 percent lower than the median of 2000, after adjusting for inflation. Men's median income fell by an even larger 10 percent during those years. Men aged 45 to 54—who are the nation's biggest earners—saw their median income decline by a stomach churning 13 percent, a loss of $6,540. The percentage of people in poverty was much higher in 2010 (15.1 percent) than in 2000 (11.3 percent). Although most households still have some discretionary income to spend after paying taxes and buying necessities, many are using that money to pay down debt rather than go out to eat or shop at the mall. The Federal Reserve Board reports that median household net worth reached a peak of $125,400 in 2007, then fell to $96,000 in 2009 as the stock and housing markets crashed.

As if the recession alone was not enough trouble, the aging of the enormous baby-boom generation out of the peak earning and spending age groups will dampen any economic recovery. Boomer incomes and spending were a big factor behind the economic gains of the past two decades. Boomer retirees are likely to be a drag on the economy of the next two decades. The demographic trends that had been working in our favor are now working against us, making the determination of the real economic status of Americans much more complex. Researchers, businesses, and government policymakers will need to look beyond the averages to determine the trends. *American Incomes: The Demographics of Who Has Money* can help them do just that.

The eighth edition of *American Incomes* explores and explains the economic status of Americans. It looks at household income trends by age, household type, race and ethnicity, education, region of residence, and work status. It examines trends in the incomes of men and women by a variety of demographic characteristics. It includes an analysis of hard-to-get discretionary income figures, produced by New Strategists' statisticians specifically for this book. It provides the latest data on the wealth of American households. The poverty population is also a focus of *American Incomes*.

American Incomes reveals the economic consequences of the many social, technological, and global changes that have transformed the workplace, families, the roles of men and women, and life in the United States. It reveals who is staying even and who is falling behind.

The raw ingredients of *American Incomes* are the massive spreadsheets of socio-economic statistics housed on the government's web sites. Navigating these databases and making sense of them is a challenge for researchers who want to explore and analyze the trends. In some ways, the Internet has made it more time-consuming than ever to get no-nonsense answers to questions about the economic status of Americans. For those with questions, *American Incomes* has the answers. It has the numbers and the stories behind them. Thumbing (or scrolling) through these pages, you can gain more insight into the economic wellbeing of Americans than you could by spending all afternoon surfing databases on the Internet. By having *American Incomes* on your bookshelf or computer, you can get the answers to your questions faster than you can online.

How to use this book

American Incomes is designed for easy use. It is divided into six chapters, each of which provides an abundance of data about Americans and their money. The chapters are Household Income, Men's Income, Women's Income, Discretionary Income, Wealth, and Poverty.

• **Household Income** Chapter 1 examines trends in household income over the past 20 years. It also presents current household income statistics by age of householder, race and Hispanic origin of householder, type of household, and other important demographic characteristics.

• **Men's Income** Trends in men's incomes are examined in Chapter 2. Current income statistics for men are also shown by a variety of demographic characteristics.

• **Women's Income** Chapter 3 examines trends and the current status of women's income, which has become increasingly important to family economic well-being.

• **Discretionary Income** Presented only in *American Incomes*, the hard-to-find statistics in Chapter 4 show that even now most American households have some money to spend after paying taxes and buying necessities.

• **Wealth** The statistics shown in Chapter 5, most of them from the Federal Reserve's one-of-a-kind Survey of Consumer Finances, provide a comprehensive portrait of the assets, debts, and net worth of American households.

• **Poverty** Poverty is on the rise, and Chapter 6 reveals the demographic characteristics of those who are falling behind.

Most of the tables in *American Incomes* are based on data from the March 2011 Current Population Survey (CPS). In this annual survey, the Census Bureau interviews the occupants of about 60,000 households, asking them for their demographic characteristics and their income in the preceding year. The Current Population Survey is the best source of up-to-date, reliable information on the incomes of Americans. While the Census Bureau produces most of the data published here, the tables in *American Incomes* are not reprints of Census Bureau spreadsheets. Instead, each has been individually compiled and created by New Strategist's editors, with calculations designed to reveal the stories behind the statistics. A page of text accompanies most of the tables, analyzing the data and highlighting the trends.

New Strategist's statisticians produced the discretionary income statistics in *American Incomes* using data from the Bureau of Labor Statistics' Consumer Expenditure Survey. These proprietary estimates give researchers a look at how much money households have left over after they pay their bills. The wealth statistics in Chapter 5 are from the Federal Reserve Board's special 2009 update of the 2007 Survey of Consumer Finances, providing a look at how the Great Recession affected household wealth. The Survey of Consumer Finances, taken every three years, provides the most comprehensive and reliable portrait of the wealth of Americans at the household level.

American Incomes contains a comprehensive list of tables to help you locate the information you need. For a more detailed search, use the index at the back of the book. Also at the back of the book is the glossary, which defines the terms commonly used in the tables and text.

American Incomes reveals the reality beneath the business headlines and political clichés, helping you prepare for the economic change that lies ahead.

1

Household Income

Household incomes have diminished not just because of the Great Recession, which began in December 2007 and officially ended in June 2009, but because many Americans never really recovered from the recession of 2001. The $49,445 median household income of 2010 was well below the record high of $53,252 reached in 1999, after adjusting for inflation. Nevertheless, slightly more than one in five households (20.5 percent) had an income of $100,000 or more in 2010, below the peak of 21.9 percent reached in 2007 but well above the 15.6 percent of 1990. Behind the near-record level of affluence is the baby-boom generation's presence in the peak earning age groups. This explains why—despite the Great Recession—median household income in 2010 is still above the level of 1990, after adjusting for inflation.

Typically, householders aged 45 to 54 have the highest incomes. In 2010, householders aged 45 to 54 had a median income of $62,485—26 percent higher than the average household. The median income gap between householders aged 45 to 54 and the average household exceeded 40 percent during most of the 1990s and has fallen steeply along with the incomes of these peak earners. In 2010, the median income of householders aged 45 to 54 barely exceeded the median income of householders aged 35 to 44.

Among householders aged 55 to 64, median income was relatively stable between 2000 and 2010, falling by only 0.4 percent. Behind the stability were two-earner baby-boom couples postponing retirement.

■ As aging boomers remain in the workforce longer, they limit job opportunities for generation X and millennials, reducing incomes in the younger age groups.

Household Income Trends

Richest Households Control Large Share of Income

Top 5 percent of households control more than one-fifth of household income.

A common way to examine the distribution of income in the United States is to divide the total number of households into fifths based on their income and determine how much of total household income accrues to each fifth. This calculation reveals that the nation's richest households are in control of a large share of income.

In 2010, households in the top fifth of the income distribution controlled the 50.2 percent majority of aggregate household income. This is slightly less than the all-time high of 50.5 percent reached in 2006, but well above the 46.6 percent of 1990. The share of income controlled by households in the top 5 percent of the household income distribution rose from 18.5 percent in 1990 to 21.3 percent in 2010—not far from the peak of 22.4 percent reached in 2001.

To get into the elite top 5 percent of households, household income needed to be $180,810 or higher in 2010. This cut-off was $153,224 in 1990—an 18 percent increase after adjusting for inflation.

■ Sixty percent of the nation's households controlled only 26 percent of household income in 2010.

Richest 20 percent of households control more than half the nation's income

(percent of household income accruing to households in the top fifth of the household income distribution, 1990 to 2010)

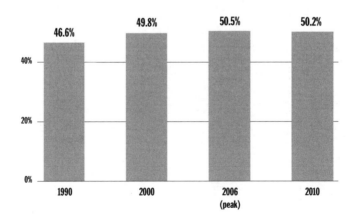

Table 1.1 Share of Aggregate Income Received by Each Fifth and Top 5 Percent of Households, 1990 to 2010

(distribution of aggregate income by household income quintile, 1990 to 2010; in 2010 dollars; households in thousands as of the following year)

	total households	upper limit of each fifth					share of aggregate income					
		bottom fifth	second fifth	third fifth	fourth fifth	lower limit of top 5 percent	bottom fifth	second fifth	third fifth	fourth fifth	top fifth	top 5 percent
2010	$118,682	$20,000	$38,043	$61,735	$100,065	$180,810	3.3%	8.5%	14.6%	23.4%	50.2%	21.3%
2009	117,538	20,791	39,186	62,821	101,651	182,972	3.4	8.6	14.6	23.2	50.3	21.7
2008	117,181	20,974	39,493	63,518	101,508	182,277	3.4	8.6	14.7	23.3	50.0	21.5
2007	116,783	21,337	41,116	65,197	105,156	186,126	3.4	8.7	14.8	23.4	49.7	21.2
2006	116,011	21,666	40,848	64,883	104,930	188,175	3.4	8.6	14.5	22.9	50.5	22.3
2005	114,384	21,419	40,206	64,397	102,420	185,397	3.4	8.6	14.6	23.0	50.4	22.2
2004	113,343	21,338	40,025	63,751	101,580	181,399	3.4	8.7	14.7	23.2	50.1	21.8
2003	112,000	21,320	40,307	64,553	102,980	182,707	3.4	8.7	14.8	23.4	49.8	21.4
2002	111,278	21,713	40,452	64,430	101,824	181,797	3.5	8.8	14.8	23.3	49.7	21.7
2001	109,297	22,131	41,027	65,272	102,833	185,345	3.5	8.7	14.6	23.0	50.1	22.4
2000	108,209	22,689	41,782	66,058	103,525	183,865	3.6	8.9	14.8	23.0	49.8	22.1
1999	106,434	22,423	41,769	65,930	103,678	185,813	3.6	8.9	14.9	23.2	49.4	21.5
1998	103,874	21,528	40,620	64,570	100,188	176,596	3.6	9.0	15.0	23.2	49.2	21.4
1997	102,528	20,859	39,551	62,306	96,846	171,410	3.6	8.9	15.0	23.2	49.4	21.7
1996	101,018	20,435	38,413	60,893	94,116	165,414	3.6	9.0	15.1	23.3	49.0	21.4
1995	99,627	20,456	38,234	59,667	92,514	160,526	3.7	9.1	15.2	23.3	48.7	21.0
1994	98,990	19,532	36,661	58,337	91,421	159,767	3.6	8.9	15.0	23.4	49.1	21.2
1993	97,107	19,267	36,669	57,640	89,597	155,478	3.6	9.0	15.1	23.5	48.9	21.0
1992	96,426	19,185	36,755	57,706	88,321	150,767	3.8	9.4	15.8	24.2	46.9	18.6
1991	95,669	19,657	37,469	57,873	88,612	150,499	3.8	9.6	15.9	24.2	46.5	18.1
1990	94,312	20,215	38,266	58,542	89,276	153,224	3.8	9.6	15.9	24.0	46.6	18.5

Source: Bureau of the Census, Current Population Survey, Historical Tables, Internet site http://www.census.gov/hhes/www/income/data/historical/household/index .html; calculations by New Strategist

Household Incomes Are Falling

Proportion of households with incomes of $100,000 or more is down slightly.

Despite the Great Recession, a substantial 20.5 percent of households still had an income of $100,000 or more in 2010. This figure was below the peak of 21.9 percent reached in 2007, after adjusting for inflation, but it was well above the 15.6 percent of 1990.

One factor behind the significant increase in the proportion of households with incomes of $100,000 during the 1990s was the aging of the baby-boom generation into the peak earning years of 45 to 54. Now boomers are leaving the peak earning age group, reducing household affluence even without the Great Recession.

■ The percentage of households with incomes of $100,000 or more will fall in the years ahead as boomers retire.

More than one in five households has an income of $100,000 or more

(percent of households with incomes of $100,000 or more, 1990 to 2010; in 2010 dollars)

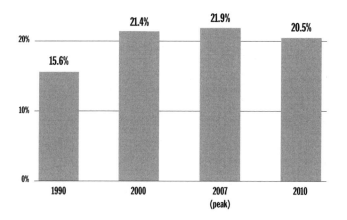

Table 1.2 Distribution of Households by Income, 1990 to 2010

(number of households and percent distribution by income, 1990 to 2010, in 2010 dollars; households in thousands as of the following year)

	total households		under $15,000	$15,000–$24,999	$25,000–$34,999	$35,000–$49,999	$50,000–$74,999	$75,000–$99,999	$100,000–$149,999	$150,000–$199,999	$200,000 or more
	number	percent									
2010	118,682	100.0%	13.7%	12.0%	10.9%	13.9%	17.7%	11.4%	12.1%	4.5%	3.9%
2009	117,538	100.0	12.9	11.8	11.0	14.1	18.0	11.7	12.1	4.6	4.0
2008	117,181	100.0	12.9	11.7	10.8	14.0	17.8	12.0	12.3	4.6	3.9
2007	116,783	100.0	12.5	11.0	10.7	13.7	18.0	12.2	13.0	4.8	4.1
2006	116,011	100.0	12.2	11.2	11.0	14.1	17.7	12.1	12.7	4.9	4.2
2005	114,384	100.0	12.7	11.5	10.7	13.7	18.4	12.0	12.4	4.5	4.2
2004	113,343	100.0	12.9	11.4	11.2	13.9	17.7	12.5	12.1	4.6	3.8
2003	112,000	100.0	12.8	11.6	10.2	14.4	17.6	12.2	12.7	4.5	3.9
2002	111,278	100.0	12.6	11.3	10.3	14.6	17.7	12.7	12.5	4.3	3.8
2001	109,297	100.0	12.2	11.2	10.4	14.5	17.9	12.6	12.5	4.5	4.0
2000	108,209	100.0	11.5	10.9	10.6	14.2	18.4	13.0	12.6	4.8	4.0
1999	106,434	100.0	11.6	11.3	10.6	14.2	18.2	12.8	12.8	4.4	4.1
1998	103,874	100.0	12.4	11.2	10.6	14.3	18.7	12.6	12.5	4.1	3.6
1997	102,528	100.0	13.0	11.6	10.9	14.4	18.8	12.3	11.7	3.9	3.3
1996	101,018	100.0	13.3	12.2	11.1	14.6	18.6	12.6	11.1	3.7	2.9
1995	99,627	100.0	13.4	12.1	10.9	15.2	19.1	12.3	10.9	3.3	2.8
1994	98,990	100.0	14.3	12.5	11.2	15.0	18.7	11.9	10.5	3.3	2.7
1993	97,107	100.0	14.8	12.2	11.2	15.5	18.5	12.0	10.3	3.2	2.4
1992	96,426	100.0	14.5	12.6	10.8	15.5	19.1	12.4	10.0	2.9	2.1
1991	95,669	100.0	14.3	12.1	11.2	15.6	19.4	12.1	10.2	3.1	2.0
1990	94,312	100.0	13.8	11.7	11.0	15.5	20.1	12.3	10.3	3.1	2.2

Source: Bureau of the Census, *Income, Poverty, and Health Insurance Coverage in the United States: 2010, Current Population Reports, P60-239, Internet site http://www.census.gov/hhes/www/income/data/index.html*

Most Age Groups Have Lost Ground since 2000

Householders under age 55 have been hit especially hard.

Median household income fell 7 percent between 2000 and 2010, after adjusting for inflation. House-holders aged 45 to 54 have seen their median income decline by more than twice that amount—down 14 percent, a loss of more than $10,000 since 2000. Householders under age 25 saw their median income fall by a stunning 20 percent during those years. In contrast, the median income of household-ers aged 55 to 64 fell just 0.4 percent during the decade because many are postponing retirement. The median income of householders aged 65 or older climbed 7 percent as labor force participation rates grew among older men and women.

Although median household income was lower in 2010 than in 2000, it was still above the level of 1990 in some age groups. But for householders under age 25 and aged 35 to 54, median household income in 2010 was below the 1990 level. Householders aged 55 or older experienced the biggest growth in median income over the past two decades. Between 1990 and 2010, the median income of householders aged 55 to 64 climbed 8 percent, and that of householders aged 65 or older increased 15 percent.

■ The devastating decline in the incomes of 45-to-54-year-olds—who were once the nation's peak earners—will be a drag on the economy for years to come.

Householders aged 45 to 54 have seen their median income fall 14 percent since 2000

(percent change in median household income by age of householder, 2000 to 2010; in 2010 dollars)

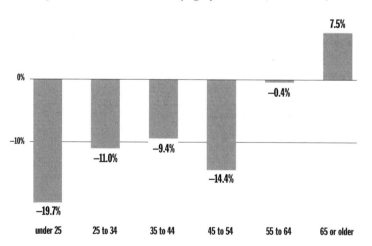

Table 1.3 Median Income of Households by Age of Householder, 1990 to 2010

(median household income by age of householder, 1990 to 2010; percent change for selected years; in 2010 dollars)

	total households	under 25	25 to 34	35 to 44	45 to 54	55 to 64	65 or older
2010	$49,445	$28,322	$50,059	$61,644	$62,485	$56,575	$31,408
2009	50,599	31,240	51,028	62,091	65,295	57,914	31,872
2008	50,939	32,678	52,050	63,750	65,163	57,989	30,120
2007	52,823	33,429	53,646	65,327	68,852	60,345	29,764
2006	52,124	33,455	53,166	65,321	70,154	59,035	30,061
2005	51,739	32,132	52,915	64,871	69,718	58,366	29,078
2004	51,174	31,830	52,480	65,427	70,443	58,167	28,299
2003	51,353	32,071	53,085	65,254	71,416	58,344	28,199
2002	51,398	33,726	54,938	64,865	71,531	57,208	28,059
2001	52,005	34,724	55,518	65,666	71,485	56,483	28,471
2000	53,164	35,257	56,233	68,069	72,981	56,789	29,226
1999	53,252	32,907	55,076	66,486	74,457	58,445	29,831
1998	51,944	31,478	53,526	64,723	72,333	57,664	29,026
1997	50,123	30,588	51,706	62,793	70,264	56,016	28,120
1996	49,112	29,665	49,660	61,466	69,841	55,094	26,911
1995	48,408	29,802	49,296	61,746	68,271	54,092	27,128
1994	46,937	28,136	48,228	60,617	68,755	51,255	26,324
1993	46,419	28,726	46,479	60,715	68,657	49,737	26,375
1992	46,646	26,893	47,564	60,680	67,658	51,757	26,090
1991	47,032	28,590	48,150	61,431	68,304	51,994	26,501
1990	48,423	29,112	49,096	62,360	67,795	52,340	27,257
Percent change							
2000 to 2010	−7.0%	−19.7%	−11.0%	−9.4%	−14.4%	−0.4%	7.5%
1990 to 2010	2.1	−2.7	2.0	−1.1	−7.8	8.1	15.2

Source: Bureau of the Census, Current Population Surveys, Annual Social and Economic Supplement, Internet site http://www .census.gov/hhes/www/income/data/historical/household/index.html; calculations by New Strategist

Every Household Type Has Seen Its Income Decline

Even married couples lost ground between 2000 and 2010.

The median income of American households fell 7 percent between 2000 and 2010, from $53,164 to $49,445 after adjusting for inflation. No household type escaped the economic decline. Among married couples, median income fell by 3 percent during those years. Women who live alone experienced a slightly smaller 2 percent loss. Median income fell 7 to 10 percent among male- and female-headed families. Men who live alone saw the biggest loss, their median income falling by 12 percent.

Despite declining incomes between 2000 and 2010, the median income of most household types was greater in 2010 than in 1990. Married couples and women who live alone were the biggest gainers during those years, with a 12 percent rise in their median household incomes, after adjusting for inflation. In contrast, the median income of male-headed families fell 3 percent, and the median income of men who live alone fell 6 percent.

■ A growing share of dual-earner couples is behind the rising incomes of married couples since 1990—until the Great Recession intervened. As boomers begin to retire, the median income of married couples may continue to decline.

Men who live alone lost the most between 2000 and 2010

(percent change in median household income by household type, 2000 to 2010; in 2010 dollars)

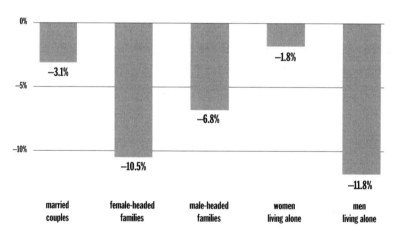

Table 1.4 Median Income of Households by Type of Household, 1990 to 2010

(median household income by type of household, 1990 to 2010; percent change for selected years; in 2010 dollars)

	total households	family households			nonfamily households	
		married couples	female hh, no spouse present	male hh, no spouse present	women living alone	men living alone
2010	$49,445	$72,751	$32,031	$49,718	$25,456	$30,333
2009	50,599	73,016	33,135	48,878	25,686	32,117
2008	50,939	73,934	33,491	49,808	25,330	31,115
2007	52,823	76,538	35,091	52,409	25,547	33,236
2006	52,124	75,390	34,408	50,910	25,819	33,813
2005	51,739	73,787	34,231	52,219	25,339	33,528
2004	51,174	73,658	34,428	51,966	25,236	31,643
2003	51,353	73,980	34,743	49,742	25,266	32,527
2002	51,398	74,237	35,148	50,552	25,346	32,490
2001	52,005	74,472	34,658	50,142	24,956	34,832
2000	53,164	75,045	35,785	53,373	25,930	34,378
1999	53,252	74,133	34,276	54,658	25,872	35,035
1998	51,944	72,504	32,585	52,651	24,867	34,760
1997	50,123	70,001	31,207	49,620	23,857	32,333
1996	49,112	68,991	29,839	49,342	22,691	33,279
1995	48,408	66,951	30,327	47,638	22,576	32,085
1994	46,937	65,525	28,910	44,330	21,746	30,865
1993	46,419	64,083	27,555	44,351	22,114	31,756
1992	46,646	63,897	27,964	46,150	21,983	30,420
1991	47,032	64,126	28,047	48,412	22,367	31,628
1990	48,423	64,680	29,221	51,025	22,801	32,285
Percent change						
2000 to 2010	–7.0%	–3.1%	–10.5%	–6.8%	–1.8%	–11.8%
1990 to 2010	2.1	12.5	9.6	–2.6	11.6	–6.0

Note: "hh" stands for householder.
Source: Bureau of the Census, Current Population Surveys, Annual Social and Economic Supplement, Internet site http://www
.census.gov/hhes/www/income/data/historical/household/index.html; calculations by New Strategist

Non-Hispanic Whites Have Lost the Least

Blacks have seen their incomes fall the most since 2000.

Between 2000 and 2010, the median income of the average household fell 7 percent, after adjusting for inflation. The median income of Asian and Hispanic households fell 10 percent during those years. Households headed by blacks saw their median income fall by an even larger 15 percent. For households headed by non-Hispanic whites, median income fell only 5 percent.

Among racial and ethnic groups, blacks have the lowest median household income, just $32,106 in 2010. The median income of Hispanics is slightly higher, at $37,759. Asian households have the highest incomes by far, with a median of $63,726—well above the $54,620 median of non-Hispanic whites. Demographics are behind the income differences: Black households are less likely to be headed by married couples, the most affluent household type. Asians are the best educated, which boosts their incomes.

Although household incomes fell between 2000 and 2010, they are still above their 1990 levels regardless of race or Hispanic origin. Between 1990 and 2010, black households made the greatest gain—a 6 percent increase in median income, after adjusting for inflation. The median income of Hispanic and non-Hispanic white households climbed 5 percent during those years, while Asian households saw a 2 percent rise.

■ Although blacks made great progress in closing the income gap with non-Hispanic whites during the past few decades, the Great Recession has reversed the trend.

Every racial and ethnic group lost ground between 2000 and 2010

(percent change in median household income by race and Hispanic origin of householder, 2000 to 2010; in 2010 dollars)

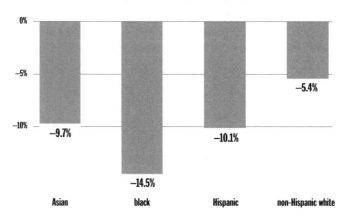

Table 1.5 Median Income of Households by Race and Hispanic Origin of Householder, 1990 to 2010

(median household income by race and Hispanic origin of householder, 1990 to 2010; percent change in median for selected years; in 2010 dollars)

	total households	Asian	black	Hispanic	non-Hispanic white
2010	$49,445	$63,726	$32,106	$37,759	$54,620
2009	50,599	66,147	33,291	38,667	55,360
2008	50,939	66,396	34,779	38,393	56,232
2007	52,823	69,273	35,849	40,673	57,752
2006	52,124	69,101	34,747	40,856	56,690
2005	51,739	68,181	34,571	40,170	56,718
2004	51,174	66,313	34,900	39,559	56,456
2003	51,353	65,512	35,196	39,118	56,639
2002	51,398	63,367	35,361	40,120	56,841
2001	52,005	66,054	36,293	41,337	57,026
2000	53,164	70,595	37,562	41,994	57,764
1999	53,252	66,683	36,521	40,232	57,781
1998	51,944	62,299	33,865	37,844	56,692
1997	50,123	61,289	33,930	36,067	54,961
1996	49,112	59,883	32,493	34,464	53,672
1995	48,408	57,696	31,811	32,475	52,815
1994	46,937	58,893	30,590	34,073	51,101
1993	46,419	56,978	29,023	34,005	50,776
1992	46,646	57,555	28,556	34,406	50,687
1991	47,032	56,904	29,361	35,425	50,462
1990	48,423	62,180	30,202	36,111	51,661

Percent change

2000 to 2010	−7.0%	−9.7%	−14.5%	−10.1%	−5.4%
1990 to 2010	2.1	2.5	6.3	4.6	5.7

Note: Beginning in 2002, data for Asians and blacks are for those who identify themselves as being of the race alone and those who identify themselves as being of the race in combination with one or more other races. Hispanics may be of any race. Beginning in 2002, data for non-Hispanic whites are for those who identify themselves as being white alone and not Hispanic.
Source: Bureau of the Census, Current Population Surveys, Annual Social and Economic Supplement, Internet site http://www.census.gov/hhes/www/income/data/historical/household/index.html; calculations by New Strategist

Even the College Educated Have Lost Ground

Every educational group has seen its median income decline since 2000.

Some may argue that colleges are pricing themselves out of business, and if current trends continue they will be right. The median household income of college graduates is declining even as college tuition rises faster than inflation. Between 2000 and 2010, the median income of households headed by people with a bachelor's degree fell 10 percent, after adjusting for inflation—a loss of $8,775 per household.

Some less educated householders saw their incomes decline even more. The biggest losers were households headed by people with a high school diploma. Their median income fell 16 percent between 2000 and 2010, after adjusting for inflation. Because the incomes of high school graduates are falling faster than those of college graduates, the income gap between the two groups is still growing. In 2000, householders with only a high school diploma had a median income 55 percent as high as that of householders with a bachelor's degree. By 2010, the median income of high school graduates was only 52 percent as high as that of college graduates.

■ Because an investment in education still provides monetary rewards, most young adults will continue to pursue a college degree—but the economic downturn will drive more to community colleges and less-expensive public universities.

Income has declined across the board

(percent change in median household income by educational attainment of householder, 2000 to 2010; in 2010 dollars)

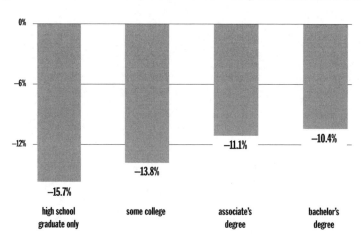

Table 1.6 Median Income of Households by Education of Householder, 1991 to 2010

(median income of households by educational attainment of householders aged 25 or older, 1991 to 2010; percent change for selected years; in 2010 dollars)

	total households	less than 9th grade	9th to 12th grade	high school graduate	some college	associate's degree	bachelor's degree or more				
							total	bachelor's degree	master's degree	professional degree	doctoral degree
2010	$49,445	$21,254	$24,787	$38,976	$48,722	$56,811	$82,109	$75,568	$90,802	$119,825	$118,714
2009	50,599	21,992	26,027	40,301	49,212	57,726	84,088	76,765	93,173	125,827	122,868
2008	50,939	21,511	25,641	40,468	50,960	59,911	86,204	79,280	93,814	101,265	101,265
2007	52,823	21,878	25,755	42,542	53,019	63,232	88,865	81,606	95,334	105,156	105,156
2006	52,124	22,602	28,021	42,635	53,735	60,576	88,375	82,035	95,619	108,139	108,139
2005	51,739	22,587	27,558	42,653	53,926	61,102	86,197	80,887	90,490	111,685	111,685
2004	51,174	22,516	25,959	43,090	54,656	62,228	85,767	78,973	92,496	115,429	115,429
2003	51,353	22,272	26,932	43,667	54,359	61,610	87,069	81,476	93,109	118,549	114,791
2002	51,398	22,276	28,199	43,202	54,942	61,880	89,200	83,814	92,679	121,196	119,538
2001	52,005	22,315	28,635	44,403	56,417	63,008	89,021	82,716	97,171	123,154	114,294
2000	53,164	22,163	28,705	46,246	56,498	63,940	90,960	84,343	99,175	126,611	120,380
1999	53,252	22,533	28,424	46,614	57,599	64,349	91,230	84,078	97,323	130,854	127,101
1998	51,944	21,579	27,684	45,917	55,648	64,927	88,798	83,073	94,959	127,317	112,344
1997	50,123	21,050	26,888	45,753	54,200	61,301	85,728	79,980	92,261	124,921	118,154
1996	49,112	21,277	27,193	44,688	53,133	61,589	82,995	76,296	88,404	125,014	112,304
1995	48,408	21,370	25,994	44,572	52,783	59,832	82,468	75,088	92,281	116,502	113,654
1994	46,937	20,767	25,521	43,747	52,197	58,567	83,563	76,188	88,808	113,477	113,702
1993	46,419	20,683	26,695	42,644	52,332	58,814	83,380	76,491	89,657	130,258	111,072
1992	46,646	20,433	26,374	44,035	53,650	58,279	82,099	75,187	87,925	128,987	106,608
1991	47,032	20,640	27,375	44,474	54,876	61,979	81,603	76,038	86,136	121,693	109,777

Percent change

	total households	less than 9th grade	9th to 12th grade	high school graduate	some college	associate's degree	total	bachelor's degree	master's degree	professional degree	doctoral degree
2000 to 2010	−7.0%	−4.1%	−13.7%	−15.7%	−13.8%	−11.1%	−9.7%	−10.4%	−8.4%	−5.4%	−1.4%
1991 to 2010	5.1	3.0	−9.5	−12.4	−11.2	−8.3	0.6	−0.6	5.4	−1.5	8.1

Source: Bureau of the Census, Current Population Surveys, Annual Social and Economic Supplement, Internet site http://www .census.gov/hhes/www/income/data/historical/household/index.html; calculations by New Strategist

Incomes Fell in Households Large and Small

The largest households experienced the biggest declines.

Between 2000 and 2010, the median income of households large and small declined after adjusting for inflation. The losses by household size ranged from 3 to 12 percent. Despite the declines, households of every size had higher incomes in 2010 than they did in 1990.

Older widows head many single-person households. The median income of single-person households fell 6 percent between 2000 and 2010, after adjusting for inflation. Two-person households fared better, with a smaller 3 percent decline during those years. Many two-person households are empty-nest couples, some postponing retirement because of the Great Recession. Three- and four-person households saw their median income decline 6 to 7 percent between 2000 and 2010. Many of these households consist of married couples with one or two children at home, who are now being forced to stretch their budgets as the costs of childrearing continue to rise. Households with five or more people—some of them extended immigrant families sharing living quarters—experienced both the largest and smallest declines in median income between 2000 and 2010.

■ Households of every size saw their incomes decline because of rising unemployment.

Seven-person households experienced the biggest income decline

(median income of households by household size, 2000 to 2010; in 2010 dollars)

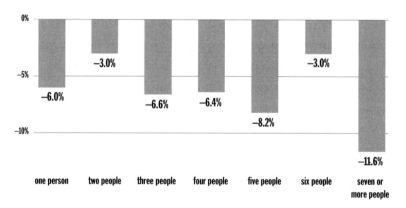

Table 1.7 Median Income of Households by Size, 1990 to 2010

(median income of households by size of household, 1990 to 2010; percent change in income for selected years; in 2010 dollars)

	total households	one person	two people	three people	four people	five people	six people	seven people or more
2010	$49,445	$25,538	$54,617	$62,791	$73,884	$69,368	$66,060	$60,572
2009	50,599	26,511	54,562	63,503	74,277	70,830	63,781	65,735
2008	50,939	25,966	56,119	64,637	76,704	70,147	68,008	68,144
2007	52,823	27,028	57,669	67,724	79,144	74,637	68,169	67,114
2006	52,124	27,580	55,731	66,436	78,801	72,262	66,894	65,818
2005	51,739	26,509	55,054	65,801	77,738	74,256	68,510	63,432
2004	51,174	26,042	54,436	66,853	75,936	71,958	65,955	67,322
2003	51,353	25,998	55,628	66,062	76,315	71,281	68,887	71,747
2002	51,398	26,085	55,212	66,395	75,708	74,685	67,987	68,296
2001	52,005	26,800	55,721	67,095	77,088	73,767	70,873	67,193
2000	53,164	27,170	56,290	67,227	78,941	75,573	68,086	68,538
1999	53,252	27,441	56,670	67,016	77,931	70,854	67,724	68,053
1998	51,944	26,922	55,453	65,548	74,655	71,742	65,563	62,311
1997	50,123	25,413	53,289	63,817	72,011	68,275	62,936	57,353
1996	49,112	24,765	51,590	62,010	71,132	66,200	58,724	55,816
1995	48,408	24,239	50,715	60,011	70,363	64,935	62,879	55,421
1994	46,937	23,600	49,398	59,709	68,022	64,207	62,095	53,277
1993	46,419	23,870	48,192	58,563	66,992	62,764	61,059	49,211
1992	46,646	23,478	48,443	58,778	67,020	64,171	56,482	50,487
1991	47,032	24,106	48,742	59,706	67,215	63,684	57,599	53,293
1990	48,423	24,814	50,711	59,455	67,069	63,514	61,710	58,393
Percent change								
2000 to 2010	−7.0%	−6.0%	−3.0%	−6.6%	−6.4%	−8.2%	−3.0%	−11.6%
1990 to 2010	2.1	2.9	7.7	5.6	10.2	9.2	7.0	3.7

Source: Bureau of the Census, Current Population Surveys, Annual Social and Economic Supplement, Internet site http://www .census.gov/hhes/www/income/data/historical/household/index.html; calculations by New Strategist

More Earners Help Stabilize Incomes

Households with no earners or only one earner are falling behind.

Although the median income of the average household fell 7 percent between 2000 and 2010, the income declines were limited to households with no earners or only one earner. Households with no earners saw their median income fall 4 percent between 2000 and 2010, after adjusting for inflation. Those with only one earner experienced a 2 percent decline. The median income of households with two earners rose by 3 percent, while the medians of those with three or more earners held steady.

Regardless of the number of earners in the household, median incomes were still higher in 2010 than in 1990. Households with no or only one earner experienced the smallest increases in median income during the two decades (up 2 and 5 percent, respectively, after adjusting for inflation). Two-earner households experienced the biggest gain, their median income rising 20 percent between 1990 and 2010 after adjusting for inflation.

■ By definition, two-earner households include two employed members, a fact that will stabilize their income through the economic downturn.

Income of households with two earners is still rising

(percent change in median income of households by number of earners, 2000 to 2010; in 2010 dollars)

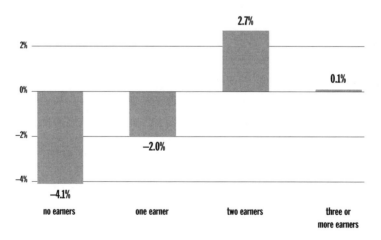

Table 1.8 Median Income of Households by Number of Earners, 1990 to 2010

(median income of households by number of earners, 1990 to 2010; percent change for selected years; in 2010 dollars)

	total households	no earners	one earner	two earners	three earners	four or more earners
2010	$49,445	$18,484	$41,711	$80,884	$96,120	$117,034
2009	50,599	19,836	41,812	79,768	95,384	118,599
2008	50,939	18,864	41,288	79,446	95,726	101,265
2007	52,823	18,394	42,809	81,767	99,926	105,156
2006	52,124	19,319	42,508	80,578	98,947	108,139
2005	51,739	18,867	41,928	79,243	98,176	111,685
2004	51,174	18,616	41,741	79,553	96,757	115,429
2003	51,353	18,566	42,650	79,840	97,760	118,549
2002	51,398	18,665	42,175	79,437	97,210	119,796
2001	52,005	19,030	42,000	79,498	95,143	116,490
2000	53,164	19,284	42,565	78,780	96,040	116,882
1999	53,252	20,227	41,820	78,111	96,934	117,100
1998	51,944	19,292	41,627	76,661	93,525	115,785
1997	50,123	19,155	40,337	73,402	90,997	114,882
1996	49,112	18,432	38,600	72,531	86,385	108,630
1995	48,408	18,613	39,161	71,029	89,768	105,469
1994	46,937	17,712	38,130	69,443	87,900	108,056
1993	46,419	17,543	37,978	69,034	85,097	107,341
1992	46,646	17,450	38,451	67,895	85,402	105,369
1991	47,032	17,969	38,771	67,184	86,504	107,983
1990	48,423	18,046	39,742	67,365	86,129	108,351
Percent change						
2000 to 2010	−7.0%	−4.1%	−2.0%	2.7%	0.1%	0.1%
1990 to 2010	2.1	2.4	5.0	20.1	11.6	8.0

Source: Bureau of the Census, Current Population Surveys, Annual Social and Economic Supplement, Internet site http://www .census.gov/hhes/www/income/data/historical/household/index.html; calculations by New Strategist

Families with Children Are Losing Ground

Families without children at home experienced a smaller decline in median income.

Between 2000 and 2010, the median income of families with children under age 18 at home fell by a substantial 11 percent, after adjusting for inflation. The median income of families without children at home fell by a smaller 3 percent. Married couples with children saw their median income fall 3 percent during those years, while the median income of those without children held steady.

Despite the declines in median household income over the past decade, for married couples and female-headed families with children median income in 2010 was still 15 to 16 percent above the level of 1990. All male-headed families lost ground between 1990 and 2010 regardless of the presence of children in the home.

■ The Great Recession has hurt many families, but especially single-parent families.

Families with children have experienced a sharp decline in median income

(percent change in median income of family households by presence of children under age 18 at home, 2000 to 2010; in 2010 dollars)

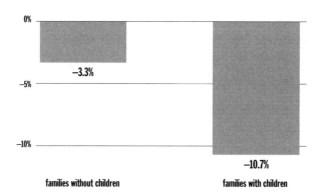

–3.3%	
families without children	families with children
	–10.7%

Table 1.9 Median Income of Families by Type and Presence of Children, 1990 to 2010

(median income of family households by type and presence of related children under age 18 at home, 1990 to 2010; percent change in income for selected years; in 2010 dollars)

	total families		married-couple families		female hh, no spouse present		male hh, no spouse present	
	no children	with children	no children	with children	no children	with children	no children	with children
2010	$62,179	$57,313	$68,650	$77,749	$39,162	$24,487	$51,731	$36,290
2009	62,923	58,233	68,488	77,914	40,025	25,588	49,755	36,681
2008	63,981	60,815	69,406	78,698	41,843	25,885	50,286	38,753
2007	66,774	62,238	72,512	80,666	46,697	26,235	54,110	40,047
2006	64,855	61,410	69,601	80,076	44,896	26,379	52,485	40,431
2005	63,948	61,623	68,694	79,132	43,706	25,834	54,081	40,841
2004	63,763	60,979	68,710	78,280	42,764	27,020	52,279	42,015
2003	64,685	60,865	69,368	78,739	43,184	26,822	53,291	37,832
2002	63,713	61,629	68,955	79,261	43,540	27,435	53,735	38,969
2001	63,892	62,796	68,253	80,300	43,431	27,090	54,025	39,325
2000	64,281	64,189	68,702	79,925	43,581	27,747	56,421	41,127
1999	65,304	62,551	69,426	78,531	44,466	26,075	57,688	42,374
1998	64,423	60,703	68,559	76,172	43,093	24,591	55,897	41,236
1997	61,797	58,981	65,812	73,677	42,040	23,373	56,188	38,830
1996	60,938	56,713	64,948	71,634	42,267	22,678	55,109	36,671
1995	58,599	56,846	62,955	70,985	40,470	23,063	49,309	38,342
1994	57,687	55,173	61,373	68,730	41,086	21,679	46,662	35,049
1993	56,238	53,788	59,869	67,677	40,391	20,017	46,865	33,206
1992	57,383	54,102	60,352	67,286	41,763	20,202	51,931	33,827
1991	57,675	54,626	61,016	66,372	40,764	20,314	50,462	37,736
1990	59,090	55,356	61,863	66,725	43,696	21,172	54,727	40,771
Percent change								
2000 to 2010	–3.3%	–10.7%	–0.1%	–2.7%	–10.1%	–11.7%	–8.3%	–11.8%
1990 to 2010	5.2	3.5	11.0	16.5	–10.4	15.7	–5.5	–11.0

Note: "–" means data are not available. "hh" stands for householder.
Source: Bureau of the Census, Current Population Surveys, Annual Social and Economic Supplement, Internet site http://www
.census.gov/hhes/www/income/data/historical/families/index.html; calculations by New Strategist

Working Wives Are Keeping Families Afloat

Incomes have fallen only among married couples with a nonworking wife.

Between 2000 and 2010, the median income of the average household fell 7 percent, after adjusting for inflation. Among married couples, median household income fell by a smaller 3 percent during those years. But some couples lost ground while others made gains. Among married couples in which both husband and wife work full-time, median household income grew 5 percent between 2000 and 2010. Among couples in which the husband works full-time and the wife does not work, median household income fell 1 percent during those years.

In 1990, the median income of couples in which the husband worked full-time and the wife did not work was 71 percent as high as that of the couples in which both husband and wife worked full-time. By 2010, it was 65 percent as high.

■ Working wives may not be able to insulate their families from the economic downturn much longer. Between 2009 and 2010, median income declined among married couples in which both husband and wife work full-time.

Dual-earner couples are faring better than single-earner couples

(percent change in median household income of married couples by work status, 2000 to 2010; in 2010 dollars)

Table 1.10 Median Income of Married Couples by Work Experience, 1990 to 2010

(median income of married couples by work experience of husband and wife, 1990 to 2010; percent change for selected years; in 2010 dollars)

	total married couples	husband worked				husband worked full-time, year-round				husband did not work		
			wife worked		wife did not work		wife worked		wife did not work		wife worked	wife did not work
	total	total	total	full-time		total	total	full-time		total	total	full-time
2010	$72,426	$84,834	$92,829	$99,498	$60,351	$91,513	$99,499	$103,704	$67,108	$39,700	$54,573	$61,928	$33,990
2009	72,809	84,642	92,828	100,657	60,671	91,952	99,097	105,236	66,484	39,202	51,693	58,619	34,209
2008	73,663	83,971	91,738	97,968	60,796	89,577	96,730	101,265	65,254	38,341	51,507	58,610	33,310
2007	76,332	87,146	94,955	101,115	63,146	91,122	98,400	104,252	65,783	38,411	53,959	60,207	33,480
2006	75,053	86,285	93,836	99,994	61,439	89,580	97,599	102,752	65,555	38,629	51,740	56,289	33,658
2005	73,607	84,177	91,460	98,266	61,906	88,383	95,563	101,208	66,612	37,703	52,223	57,338	33,102
2004	73,443	84,325	92,378	98,783	60,082	88,581	95,464	101,359	64,651	36,783	51,364	57,702	32,191
2003	73,833	84,982	92,348	98,534	60,819	89,675	96,327	101,379	65,932	36,800	52,080	58,583	32,162
2002	74,087	85,157	91,669	98,589	62,096	89,898	95,511	101,587	67,516	36,754	50,323	57,812	32,807
2001	74,305	84,293	90,404	96,710	62,717	88,702	94,165	99,922	66,455	37,259	48,727	56,689	33,499
2000	74,826	84,475	90,485	96,759	63,675	89,100	94,189	99,099	67,783	37,759	51,602	56,746	34,062
1999	73,934	83,363	89,536	96,713	60,867	87,573	93,265	99,702	65,964	38,916	49,443	55,298	35,154
1998	72,376	81,308	87,378	94,735	60,835	85,160	90,937	97,423	64,807	38,055	51,854	57,548	34,274
1997	69,879	78,281	83,757	90,822	58,896	83,294	87,909	94,146	65,706	37,437	50,440	60,340	33,843
1996	68,782	76,974	82,794	88,945	56,732	81,792	86,116	91,503	62,244	36,192	47,222	55,722	33,415
1995	66,856	75,062	80,973	88,368	56,397	79,916	85,062	91,320	61,267	36,555	49,235	57,514	32,965
1994	65,406	74,304	79,817	87,846	55,653	79,340	84,203	90,724	61,202	34,562	45,791	54,934	31,493
1993	63,899	73,475	77,998	86,017	55,693	78,555	83,233	90,207	62,073	34,365	44,770	51,501	31,183
1992	63,781	72,183	77,723	85,446	55,902	78,334	82,949	89,967	62,682	35,012	45,509	53,228	32,063
1991	64,001	71,807	76,776	84,915	56,578	78,203	82,286	89,131	63,256	36,039	44,581	53,514	33,747
1990	64,517	71,715	76,547	85,131	57,445	76,939	81,328	89,054	63,204	36,100	44,909	52,784	33,648
Percent change												
2000 to 2010	-3.2%	0.4%	2.6%	2.8%	-5.2%	2.7%	5.6%	4.6%	-1.0%	5.1%	5.8%	9.1%	-0.2%
1990 to 2010	12.3	18.3	21.3	16.9	5.1	18.9	22.3	16.5	6.2	10.0	21.5	17.3	1.0

Source: Bureau of the Census, Current Population Surveys, Annual Social and Economic Supplement, Internet site http://www.census.gov/hhes/www/income/data/historical/families/index.html; calculations by New Strategist

Northeast Has Fared Better than Other Regions

Households in the Midwest experienced the steepest decline in median income between 2000 and 2010.

Median household income fell 4 percent in the Northeast between 2000 and 2010, after adjusting for inflation. This compares with a larger 6 percent decline in the South, a 7 percent decline in the West, and an enormous 14 percent decline in the Midwest. In 2010, households in the Northeast had the highest median household income—$53,283, which surpassed the $53,142 median income of Western households by just $141.

During the past two decades, median household income grew more slowly in the Midwest than in any other region. Between 1990 and 2010, median household income climbed only 0.2 percent in the Midwest after adjusting for inflation. The increase in the Northeast was only slightly larger at 0.8 percent. The South and West saw their median household incomes grow by a larger 3 to 4 percent over those two decades. Despite the income stagnation in the Midwest, in 2010 the region's $48,445 median household income still surpassed the $45,492 median in the South.

■ The Great Recession hit the Midwest hard because of the loss of manufacturing jobs.

The Northeast experienced the smallest decline in median household income

(percent change in median household income by region, 2000 to 2010; in 2010 dollars)

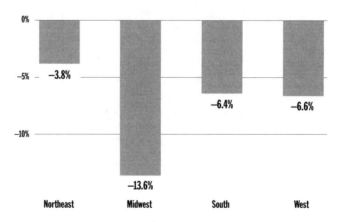

Table 1.11 Median Income of Households by Region, 1990 to 2010

(median income of households by region, 1990 to 2010; percent change in income for selected years; in 2010 dollars)

	total households	Northeast	Midwest	South	West
2010	$49,445	$53,283	$48,445	$45,492	$53,142
2009	50,599	53,949	49,684	46,368	54,722
2008	50,939	55,033	50,746	46,167	55,782
2007	52,823	54,969	52,869	48,567	56,929
2006	52,124	56,294	51,729	47,456	56,502
2005	51,739	56,827	51,319	47,062	55,845
2004	51,174	55,245	51,529	47,032	55,003
2003	51,353	55,412	53,029	47,210	55,504
2002	51,398	55,583	52,868	47,899	54,712
2001	52,005	56,301	53,983	47,912	55,526
2000	53,164	55,392	56,039	48,605	56,867
1999	53,252	54,804	55,629	48,867	55,698
1998	51,944	54,280	54,247	47,819	54,747
1997	50,123	52,729	51,898	46,520	53,044
1996	49,112	51,761	50,616	44,864	51,372
1995	48,408	51,299	50,912	43,956	51,111
1994	46,937	50,810	47,288	43,674	50,121
1993	46,419	50,143	46,656	42,259	50,131
1992	46,646	50,244	46,902	42,037	50,739
1991	47,032	52,248	46,722	42,430	50,353
1990	48,423	52,843	48,349	43,570	51,363
Percent change					
2000 to 2010	−7.0%	−3.8%	−13.6%	−6.4%	−6.6%
1990 to 2010	2.1	0.8	0.2	4.4	3.5

Source: Bureau of the Census, Current Population Surveys, Annual Social and Economic Supplement, Internet site http://www.census.gov/hhes/www/income/data/historical/household/index.html; calculations by New Strategist

Many States Have Seen Double-Digit Declines in Median Household Income

Between 1999–2000 and 2009–10, median household income fell in 35 states.

The economic wellbeing of households by state is closely tied to local economies. The Great Recession has had a devastating impact on households in most states, but some have suffered more than others. Michigan experienced the steepest decline in median household income between 1999–2000 and 2009–10, a 21 percent drop after adjusting for inflation. Minnesota was second with a 16 percent decline. In all, 14 states experienced double-digit declines in median household income during the decade. In contrast, two states saw double-digit increases in median household income: North Dakota and West Virginia.

Despite the decline in median household incomes by state during the past decade, incomes in 2009–10 were higher than in 1989–90 in all but 12 states after adjusting for inflation. The biggest loser over the two decades was Michigan with a 7 percent loss. In Colorado, median household income was 23 percent greater in 2009–10 than in 1989–90, after adjusting for inflation.

■ As the United States struggles to recover from the Great Recession, the income losses in Michigan may be a harbinger of what is to come in many other states.

North Dakota was the biggest gainer, Michigan the biggest loser

(percent change in median household income for the states with the biggest gain and loss, two-year averages 1999–2000 to 2009–10; in 2009–10 dollars)

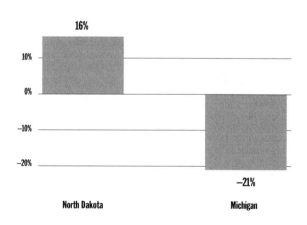

Table 1.12 Median Income of Households by State 1989–90 to 2009–10

(median income of households by state, two-year averages for 1989–90, 1999–2000, and 2009–10; percent change in income for selected years; in 2009–10 dollars)

	2009–10	1999–2000	1989–90	percent change 1999–2000 to 2009–10	percent change 1989–90 to 2009–10
United States	**$50,022**	**$53,208**	**$48,749**	**−6.0%**	**2.6%**
Alabama	40,808	46,143	36,954	−11.6	10.4
Alaska	60,410	67,082	62,341	−9.9	−3.1
Arizona	46,887	49,390	47,868	−5.1	−2.0
Arkansas	37,856	38,220	36,619	−1.0	3.4
California	55,760	58,182	54,939	−4.2	1.5
Colorado	58,648	62,059	47,606	−5.5	23.2
Connecticut	66,187	64,863	67,355	2.0	−1.7
Delaware	54,122	62,391	52,130	−13.3	3.8
District of Columbia	54,773	51,396	44,858	6.6	22.1
Florida	45,314	48,041	43,720	−5.7	3.6
Georgia	44,082	52,320	45,665	−15.7	−3.5
Hawaii	57,538	61,749	61,212	−6.8	−6.0
Idaho	47,282	47,233	41,390	0.1	14.2
Illinois	52,252	59,473	52,883	−12.1	−1.2
Indiana	45,679	52,589	43,758	−13.1	4.4
Iowa	50,368	52,839	44,361	−4.7	13.5
Kansas	45,842	50,428	46,993	−9.1	−2.4
Kentucky	42,302	45,032	39,801	−6.1	6.3
Louisiana	42,813	40,811	37,523	4.9	14.1
Maine	48,210	49,018	46,163	−1.6	4.4
Maryland	64,636	68,680	61,993	−5.9	4.3
Massachusetts	60,843	58,388	59,942	4.2	1.5
Michigan	46,597	58,966	50,331	−21.0	−7.4
Minnesota	54,785	65,120	51,066	−15.9	7.3
Mississippi	36,821	42,963	33,223	−14.3	10.8
Missouri	47,879	55,625	44,593	−13.9	7.4
Montana	41,286	41,057	39,013	0.6	5.8
Nebraska	51,571	51,702	44,563	−0.3	15.7
Nevada	51,904	56,094	50,800	−7.5	2.2
New Hampshire	65,949	62,371	64,855	5.7	1.7
New Jersey	64,693	64,449	64,528	0.4	0.3
New Mexico	44,680	43,528	39,433	2.6	13.3
New York	50,436	51,957	52,281	−2.9	−3.5
North Carolina	43,176	48,631	43,705	−11.2	−1.2
North Dakota	51,141	44,158	41,845	15.8	22.2
Ohio	46,365	53,034	48,904	−12.6	−5.2
Oklahoma	45,018	41,915	39,807	7.4	13.1
Oregon	50,218	53,480	47,894	−6.1	4.9
Pennsylvania	48,714	51,404	47,808	−5.2	1.9

	2009–10	1999–2000	1989–90	percent change	
				1999–2000 to 2009–10	1989–90 to 2009–10
Rhode Island	$52,200	$54,663	$51,421	–4.5%	1.5%
South Carolina	41,744	47,640	43,437	–12.4	–3.9
South Dakota	46,126	46,532	40,333	–0.9	14.4
Tennessee	39,936	45,480	37,462	–12.2	6.6
Texas	47,862	49,754	44,799	–3.8	6.8
Utah	58,122	60,231	50,448	–3.5	15.2
Vermont	54,562	52,272	51,711	4.4	5.5
Virginia	60,932	59,752	57,322	2.0	6.3
Washington	58,821	56,672	53,097	3.8	10.8
West Virginia	41,999	37,787	36,301	11.1	15.7
Wisconsin	51,303	58,422	49,555	–12.2	3.5
Wyoming	52,848	49,458	48,881	6.9	8.1

Note: Two-year averages are used to compare state median incomes over time.
Source: Bureau of the Census, Current Population Surveys, Annual Social and Economic Supplement, Internet site http://www
.census.gov/hhes/www/income/data/historical/household/index.html; calculations by New Strategist

Household Income, 2010

Dual-Earner Couples Dominate the Affluent

Householders aged 45 to 54 account for nearly one-third of those with incomes in the top 5 percent.

By examining the characteristics of households within income quintiles, or fifths, the requirements of affluence become apparent. Among households in the top fifth of the income distribution—those with household incomes of $100,065 or greater in 2010—three out of four are headed by married couples. Those in the peak earning age group of 35 to 54 head the 52 percent majority. And 75 percent have at least two earners. Households in the top 5 percent of the income distribution are even more likely to be headed by married couples (82 percent) and 35-to-54-year-olds (54 percent).

Looking at the distribution of households by income quintile confirms these findings. Among married couples, 32 percent are in the top fifth of the income distribution compared with only 7 percent of female-headed families. Well more than one-third of households with at least two earners are in the top income quintile versus just 12 percent of households with one earner.

■ Differences in household composition lead to unequal incomes, with dual-income married couples making more money than other household types.

The more earners in a household, the higher the income

(percent of households with two or more earners, by household income quintile, 2010)

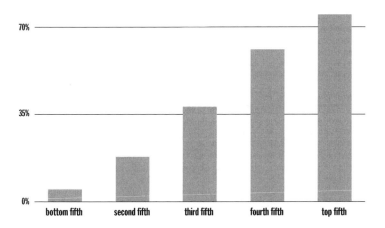

Table 1.13 Number of Households by Income Quintile and Household Characteristic, 2010

(total number of households, lower income limit of each income quintile and top 5 percent, and number of households by quintile and selected characteristics, 2010; households in thousands)

	total	bottom fifth	second fifth	third fifth	fourth fifth	top fifth	top 5 percent
Total households	**118,682**	**23,736**	**23,736**	**23,736**	**23,736**	**23,736**	**5,933**
Lower limit of income quintile	–	–	$20,000	$38,040	$61,720	$100,065	$180,812
AGE OF HOUSEHOLDER							
Total households	**118,682**	**23,736**	**23,736**	**23,736**	**23,736**	**23,736**	**5,933**
Under age 25	6,140	2,214	1,633	1,196	719	378	84
Aged 25 to 34	19,572	3,327	4,062	4,620	4,471	3,093	554
Aged 35 to 44	21,250	2,807	3,591	4,293	5,104	5,455	1,383
Aged 45 to 54	24,530	3,667	3,880	4,588	5,560	6,835	1,838
Aged 55 to 64	21,828	3,901	3,614	4,274	4,609	5,430	1,471
Aged 65 or older	25,362	7,816	6,958	4,766	3,275	2,548	603
Aged 65 to 74	13,348	3,142	3,291	2,818	2,224	1,872	492
Aged 75 or older	12,015	4,674	3,667	1,948	1,051	675	111
TYPE OF HOUSEHOLD							
Total households	**118,682**	**23,736**	**23,736**	**23,736**	**23,736**	**23,736**	**5,933**
Family households	78,613	9,411	13,969	16,162	18,543	20,528	5,231
Married couples	58,036	4,037	8,521	11,587	15,270	18,621	4,888
Female householder, no spouse present	15,019	4,549	4,182	3,162	2,048	1,078	172
Male householder, no spouse present	5,559	824	1,267	1,414	1,225	829	171
Nonfamily households	40,069	14,320	9,768	7,575	5,195	3,211	702
Female householder	21,234	8,797	5,267	3,676	2,216	1,278	241
Living alone	18,184	8,355	4,661	2,967	1,525	676	118
Male householder	18,835	5,523	4,501	3,899	2,979	1,933	460
Living alone	14,539	5,022	3,761	2,910	1,850	996	253
RACE AND HISPANIC ORIGIN OF HOUSEHOLDER							
Total households	**118,682**	**23,731**	**23,737**	**23,737**	**23,738**	**23,739**	**5,933**
Asian	5,040	773	757	914	1,052	1,543	445
Black	15,613	5,177	3,695	2,958	2,303	1,481	248
Hispanic	13,665	3,363	3,552	2,916	2,306	1,527	271
Non-Hispanic white	83,471	14,199	15,559	16,770	17,894	19,050	4,949
NUMBER OF EARNERS							
Total households	**118,682**	**23,731**	**23,737**	**23,737**	**23,738**	**23,739**	**5,933**
No earners	27,388	14,805	7,037	3,327	1,496	722	91
One earner	44,922	7,845	12,474	11,488	7,853	5,263	1,394
Two earners or more	46,373	1,080	4,226	8,923	14,389	17,754	4,447
Two earners	37,470	1,020	3,790	7,702	11,700	13,258	3,245
Three earners	6,705	55	379	1,040	2,112	3,119	776
Four earners	2,197	5	58	180	577	1,377	427

	total	bottom fifth	second fifth	third fifth	fourth fifth	top fifth	top 5 percent
WORK EXPERIENCE OF HOUSEHOLDER							
Total households	**118,682**	**23,731**	**23,737**	**23,737**	**23,738**	**23,739**	**5,933**
Householder worked	78,542	7,533	13,754	17,137	19,544	20,574	5,228
Worked at full-time job	64,763	4,142	10,599	14,493	17,213	18,316	4,642
Worked 50 or more weeks	54,312	2,232	8,253	12,108	15,148	16,571	4,270
Worked 27 to 29 weeks	6,215	766	1,347	1,444	1,412	1,246	269
Worked 26 or fewer weeks	4,235	1,143	1,000	941	653	499	102
Worked at part-time job	13,779	3,392	3,154	2,644	2,331	2,258	586
Worked 50 or more weeks	7,408	1,446	1,693	1,483	1,355	1,431	359
Worked 27 to 29 weeks	2,909	732	685	572	484	437	122
Worked 26 or fewer weeks	3,461	1,214	777	588	492	389	106
Householder did not work	40,141	16,197	9,984	6,601	4,194	3,165	705
HOMEOWNERSHIP STATUS							
Total households	**118,682**	**23,731**	**23,737**	**23,737**	**23,738**	**23,739**	**5,933**
Owner occupied	78,573	10,340	13,270	15,858	18,367	20,738	5,366
Renter occupied	38,472	12,644	10,107	7,604	5,199	2,917	545
Occupier paid no cash rent	1,637	746	361	275	172	84	21

Note: Data for Asians and blacks are for those who identify themselves as being of the race alone and those who identify themselves as being of the race in combination with one or more other races. Data for non-Hispanic whites are for those who identify themselves as being white alone and not Hispanic. Hispanics may be of any race. "–" means not applicable.
Source: Bureau of the Census, 2011 Current Population Survey, Internet site http://www.census.gov/hhes/www/income/data/incpovhlth/2010/dtables.html; calculations by New Strategist

Table 1.14 Distribution of Households within Income Quintile by Household Characteristic, 2010

(total number of households, lower income limit of each income quintile and top 5 percent, and percent distribution of households within quintile by selected characteristics, 2010; households in thousands)

	total	bottom fifth	second fifth	third fifth	fourth fifth	top fifth	top 5 percent
Total households	**118,682**	**23,736**	**23,736**	**23,736**	**23,736**	**23,736**	**5,933**
Lower limit of income quintile	–	–	$20,000	$38,040	$61,720	$100,065	$180,812
AGE OF HOUSEHOLDER							
Total households	**100.0%**	**100.0%**	**100.0%**	**100.0%**	**100.0%**	**100.0%**	**100.0%**
Under age 25	5.2	9.3	6.9	5.0	3.0	1.6	1.4
Aged 25 to 34	16.5	14.0	17.1	19.5	18.8	13.0	9.3
Aged 35 to 44	17.9	11.8	15.1	18.1	21.5	23.0	23.3
Aged 45 to 54	20.7	15.4	16.3	19.3	23.4	28.8	31.0
Aged 55 to 64	18.4	16.4	15.2	18.0	19.4	22.9	24.8
Aged 65 or older	21.4	32.9	29.3	20.1	13.8	10.7	10.2
Aged 65 to 74	11.2	13.2	13.9	11.9	9.4	7.9	8.3
Aged 75 or older	10.1	19.7	15.4	8.2	4.4	2.8	1.9
TYPE OF HOUSEHOLD							
Total households	**100.0**	**100.0**	**100.0**	**100.0**	**100.0**	**100.0**	**100.0**
Family households	66.2	39.6	58.9	68.1	78.1	86.5	88.2
Married couples	48.9	17.0	35.9	48.8	64.3	78.5	82.4
Female householder, no spouse present	12.7	19.2	17.6	13.3	8.6	4.5	2.9
Male householder, no spouse present	4.7	3.5	5.3	6.0	5.2	3.5	2.9
Nonfamily households	33.8	60.3	41.2	31.9	21.9	13.5	11.8
Female householder	17.9	37.1	22.2	15.5	9.3	5.4	4.1
Living alone	15.3	35.2	19.6	12.5	6.4	2.8	2.0
Male householder	15.9	23.3	19.0	16.4	12.6	8.1	7.8
Living alone	12.3	21.2	15.8	12.3	7.8	4.2	4.3
RACE AND HISPANIC ORIGIN OF HOUSEHOLDER							
Total households	**100.0**	**100.0**	**100.0**	**100.0**	**100.0**	**100.0**	**100.0**
Asian	4.2	3.3	3.2	3.9	4.4	6.5	7.5
Black	13.2	21.8	15.6	12.5	9.7	6.2	4.2
Hispanic	11.5	14.2	15.0	12.3	9.7	6.4	4.6
Non-Hispanic white	70.3	59.8	65.5	70.6	75.4	80.2	83.4
NUMBER OF EARNERS							
Total households	**100.0**	**100.0**	**100.0**	**100.0**	**100.0**	**100.0**	**100.0**
No earners	23.1	62.4	29.6	14.0	6.3	3.0	1.5
One earner	37.9	33.1	52.6	48.4	33.1	22.2	23.5
Two earners or more	39.1	4.6	17.8	37.6	60.6	74.8	75.0
Two earners	31.6	4.3	16.0	32.4	49.3	55.8	54.7
Three earners	5.6	0.2	1.6	4.4	8.9	13.1	13.1
Four earners	1.9	0.0	0.2	0.8	2.4	5.8	7.2

	total	bottom fifth	second fifth	third fifth	fourth fifth	top fifth	top 5 percent
WORK EXPERIENCE OF HOUSEHOLDER							
Total households	100.0%	100.0%	100.0%	100.0%	100.0%	100.0%	100.0%
Householder worked	66.2	31.7	57.9	72.2	82.3	86.7	88.1
Worked at full-time job	54.6	17.5	44.7	61.1	72.5	77.2	78.2
Worked 50 or more weeks	45.8	9.4	34.8	51.0	63.8	69.8	72.0
Worked 27 to 29 weeks	5.2	3.2	5.7	6.1	5.9	5.2	4.5
Worked 26 or fewer weeks	3.6	4.8	4.2	4.0	2.8	2.1	1.7
Worked at part-time job	11.6	14.3	13.3	11.1	9.8	9.5	9.9
Worked 50 or more weeks	6.2	6.1	7.1	6.2	5.7	6.0	6.1
Worked 27 to 29 weeks	2.5	3.1	2.9	2.4	2.0	1.8	2.1
Worked 26 or fewer weeks	2.9	5.1	3.3	2.5	2.1	1.6	1.8
Householder did not work	33.8	68.3	42.1	27.8	17.7	13.3	11.9
HOMEOWNERSHIP STATUS							
Total households	100.0	100.0	100.0	100.0	100.0	100.0	100.0
Owner occupied	66.2	43.6	55.9	66.8	77.4	87.4	90.4
Renter occupied	32.4	53.3	42.6	32.0	21.9	12.3	9.2
Occupier paid no cash rent	1.4	3.1	1.5	1.2	0.7	0.4	0.4

Note: Data for Asians and blacks are for those who identify themselves as being of the race alone and those who identify themselves as being of the race in combination with one or more other races. Data for non-Hispanic whites are for those who identify themselves as being white alone and not Hispanic. Hispanics may be of any race. "–" means not applicable.
Source: Bureau of the Census, 2011 Current Population Survey, Internet site http://www.census.gov/hhes/www/income/data/incpovhlth/2010/dtables.html; calculations by New Strategist

Table 1.15 Distribution of Household Characteristics by Income Quintile, 2010

(total number of households, lower income limit of each income quintile and top 5 percent, and percent distribution of selected household characteristics by quintile, 2010; households in thousands)

	total	bottom fifth	second fifth	third fifth	fourth fifth	top fifth	top 5 percent
Total households	118,682	23,736	23,736	23,736	23,736	23,736	5,933
Lower limit of income quintile	–	–	$20,000	$38,040	$61,720	$100,065	$180,812
AGE OF HOUSEHOLDER							
Total households	100.0%	20.0%	20.0%	20.0%	20.0%	20.0%	5.0%
Under age 25	100.0	36.1	26.6	19.5	11.7	6.2	1.4
Aged 25 to 34	100.0	17.0	20.8	23.6	22.8	15.8	2.8
Aged 35 to 44	100.0	13.2	16.9	20.2	24.0	25.7	6.5
Aged 45 to 54	100.0	14.9	15.8	18.7	22.7	27.9	7.5
Aged 55 to 64	100.0	17.9	16.6	19.6	21.1	24.9	6.7
Aged 65 or older	100.0	30.8	27.4	18.8	12.9	10.0	2.4
Aged 65 to 74	100.0	23.5	24.7	21.1	16.7	14.0	3.7
Aged 75 or older	100.0	38.9	30.5	16.2	8.7	5.6	0.9
TYPE OF HOUSEHOLD							
Total households	100.0	20.0	20.0	20.0	20.0	20.0	5.0
Family households	100.0	12.0	17.8	20.6	23.6	26.1	6.7
Married couples	100.0	7.0	14.7	20.0	26.3	32.1	8.4
Female householder, no spouse present	100.0	30.3	27.8	21.1	13.6	7.2	1.1
Male householder, no spouse present	100.0	14.8	22.8	25.4	22.0	14.9	3.1
Nonfamily households	100.0	35.7	24.4	18.9	13.0	8.0	1.8
Female householder	100.0	41.4	24.8	17.3	10.4	6.0	1.1
Living alone	100.0	45.9	25.6	16.3	8.4	3.7	0.6
Male householder	100.0	29.3	23.9	20.7	15.8	10.3	2.4
Living alone	100.0	34.5	25.9	20.0	12.7	6.9	1.7
RACE AND HISPANIC ORIGIN OF HOUSEHOLDER							
Total households	100.0	20.0	20.0	20.0	20.0	20.0	5.0
Asian	100.0	15.3	15.0	18.1	20.9	30.6	8.8
Black	100.0	33.2	23.7	18.9	14.8	9.5	1.6
Hispanic	100.0	24.6	26.0	21.3	16.9	11.2	2.0
Non-Hispanic white	100.0	17.0	18.6	20.1	21.4	22.8	5.9
NUMBER OF EARNERS							
Total households, percent	100.0	20.0	20.0	20.0	20.0	20.0	5.0
No earners	100.0	54.1	25.7	12.1	5.5	2.6	0.3
One earner	100.0	17.5	27.8	25.6	17.5	11.7	3.1
Two earners or more	100.0	2.3	9.1	19.2	31.0	38.3	9.6
Two earners	100.0	2.7	10.1	20.6	31.2	35.4	8.7
Three earners	100.0	0.8	5.7	15.5	31.5	46.5	11.6
Four earners	100.0	0.2	2.6	8.2	26.3	62.7	19.4

	total	bottom fifth	second fifth	third fifth	fourth fifth	top fifth	top 5 percent
WORK EXPERIENCE OF HOUSEHOLDER							
Total households	**100.0%**	**20.0%**	**20.0%**	**20.0%**	**20.0%**	**20.0%**	**5.0%**
Householder worked	100.0	9.6	17.5	21.8	24.9	26.2	6.7
Worked at full-time job	100.0	6.4	16.4	22.4	26.6	28.3	7.2
Worked 50 or more weeks	100.0	4.1	15.2	22.3	27.9	30.5	7.9
Worked 27 to 29 weeks	100.0	12.3	21.7	23.2	22.7	20.0	4.3
Worked 26 or fewer weeks	100.0	27.0	23.6	22.2	15.4	11.8	2.4
Worked at part-time job	100.0	24.6	22.9	19.2	16.9	16.4	4.3
Worked 50 or more weeks	100.0	19.5	22.9	20.0	18.3	19.3	4.8
Worked 27 to 29 weeks	100.0	25.2	23.5	19.7	16.6	15.0	4.2
Worked 26 or fewer weeks	100.0	35.1	22.5	17.0	14.2	11.2	3.1
Householder did not work	100.0	40.4	24.9	16.4	10.4	7.9	1.8
HOMEOWNERSHIP STATUS							
Total households	**100.0**	**20.0**	**20.0**	**20.0**	**20.0**	**20.0**	**5.0**
Owner occupied	100.0	13.2	16.9	20.2	23.4	26.4	6.8
Renter occupied	100.0	32.9	26.3	19.8	13.5	7.6	1.4
Occupier paid no cash rent	100.0	45.6	22.1	16.8	10.5	5.1	1.3

Note: Data for Asians and blacks are for those who identify themselves as being of the race alone and those who identify themselves as being of the race in combination with one or more other races. Data for non-Hispanic whites are for those who identify themselves as being white alone and not Hispanic. Hispanics may be of any race. "–" means not applicable.
Source: Bureau of the Census, 2011 Current Population Survey, Internet site http://www.census.gov/hhes/www/income/data/incpovhlth/2010/dtables.html; calculations by New Strategist

Married Couples Have the Highest Incomes

Among the nation's married couples, nearly one in three had an income of $100,000 or more in 2010.

With a median income of $72,751 in 2010, married couples are by far the most-affluent household type. Behind the higher incomes of married couples is the fact that most are dual earners. Male-headed families rank second in income among household types, with a median of $49,718. Female-headed families have a much lower median of $32,031. Women who live alone have the lowest incomes, a median of $22,196 in 2010.

By race and Hispanic origin, Asian households have the highest incomes—a median of $63,726 in 2010. Asian married couples have a median income of $85,565, significantly higher than the $77,661 median of non-Hispanic white married couples. The median income of black households is only 59 percent as high as that of non-Hispanic whites, $32,106 versus $54,620 in 2010. Differences in household composition explain most of the gap. Married couples head the 52 percent majority of non-Hispanic white households. In contrast, couples head only 28 percent of black households. Female-headed families—one of the poorest household types—account for a larger 29 percent of black households.

The median household income of Hispanics is higher than that of blacks for one reason only— married couples head a larger share of Hispanic households (49 percent), which boosts their overall median to $37,759. In fact, however, Hispanic married couples have much lower incomes than black couples ($50,410 for Hispanics versus $61,161 for blacks). Hispanic couples have low incomes because they are less likely to be dual-earners than either whites or blacks and because many Hispanics are recent immigrants with little earning power.

■ The gap between the incomes of married couples and other household types may shrink in the years ahead as dual-income baby-boom couples retire and their incomes drop.

Women who live alone have the lowest incomes

(median household income by household type, 2010)

Table 1.16 Households by Income and Household Type, 2010: Total Households

(number and percent distribution of households by household income and household type, 2010; households in thousands as of 2011)

| | family households | | | | nonfamily households | | | |
| | total | married couples | female hh, no spouse present | male hh, no spouse present | female householder | | male householder | |
					total	living alone	total	living alone
Total households	**118,682**	**58,036**	**15,019**	**5,559**	**21,234**	**18,184**	**18,835**	**14,539**
Under $5,000	4,176	697	1,003	125	1,243	1,143	1,108	1,016
$5,000 to $9,999	5,055	520	1,115	172	2,026	1,950	1,221	1,137
$10,000 to $14,999	7,061	1,142	1,184	227	2,858	2,754	1,650	1,493
$15,000 to $19,999	7,260	1,646	1,204	283	2,641	2,481	1,487	1,327
$20,000 to $24,999	6,937	2,093	1,321	370	1,692	1,544	1,461	1,220
$25,000 to $29,999	6,730	2,429	1,180	343	1,603	1,437	1,175	994
$30,000 to $34,999	6,148	2,368	1,046	332	1,248	1,084	1,154	973
$35,000 to $39,999	5,907	2,446	984	323	1,084	894	1,070	839
$40,000 to $44,999	5,624	2,499	818	366	999	841	942	758
$45,000 to $49,999	4,933	2,356	724	253	756	620	845	615
$50,000 to $54,999	5,088	2,579	606	310	717	583	877	682
$55,000 to $59,999	4,203	2,308	495	244	566	414	591	392
$60,000 to $64,999	4,412	2,367	466	307	567	413	704	475
$65,000 to $69,999	3,579	2,154	331	181	407	302	507	332
$70,000 to $74,999	3,769	2,245	382	219	458	349	465	280
$75,000 to $79,999	3,118	2,006	277	143	256	171	436	295
$80,000 to $84,999	3,143	2,092	240	170	237	144	405	262
$85,000 to $89,999	2,680	1,873	199	133	205	132	269	133
$90,000 to $94,999	2,516	1,758	205	100	205	133	249	147
$95,000 to $99,999	2,110	1,517	150	105	144	75	195	100
$100,000 to $124,999	9,008	6,664	549	378	581	346	835	458
$125,000 to $149,999	5,294	4,177	223	183	288	146	419	198
$150,000 to $174,999	3,386	2,719	119	101	186	97	263	131
$175,000 to $199,999	1,919	1,552	57	57	82	35	171	70
$200,000 or more	4,627	3,828	143	133	187	99	336	212
Median income	$49,445	$72,751	$32,031	$49,718	$25,456	$22,196	$35,627	$30,333

PERCENT DISTRIBUTION

Total households	**100.0%**	**100.0%**	**100.0%**	**100.0%**	**100.0%**	**100.0%**	**100.0%**	**100.0%**
Under $25,000	25.7	10.5	38.8	21.2	49.3	54.3	36.8	42.6
$25,000 to $49,999	24.7	20.8	31.6	29.1	26.8	26.8	27.5	28.7
$50,000 to $74,999	17.7	20.1	15.2	22.7	12.8	11.3	16.7	14.9
$75,000 to $99,999	11.4	15.9	7.1	11.7	4.9	3.6	8.3	6.4
$100,000 or more	20.4	32.6	7.3	15.3	6.2	4.0	10.7	7.4

Note: "hh" stands for householder.
Source: Bureau of the Census, 2011 Current Population Survey, Internet site http://www.census.gov/hhes/www/cpstables/ 032011/hhinc/toc.htm; calculations by New Strategist

Table 1.17 Households by Income and Household Type, 2010: Asian Households

(number and percent distribution of Asian households by household income and household type, 2010; households in thousands as of 2011)

| | family households | | | | nonfamily households | | | |
| | | | | | female householder | | male householder | |
	total	married couples	female hh, no spouse present	male hh, no spouse present	total	living alone	total	living alone
Asian households	**5,040**	**2,939**	**492**	**291**	**702**	**558**	**616**	**437**
Under $5,000	232	67	29	7	70	59	58	40
$5,000 to $9,999	121	19	15	12	52	52	23	22
$10,000 to $14,999	180	53	15	5	66	66	40	38
$15,000 to $19,999	226	91	35	10	59	57	31	26
$20,000 to $24,999	261	98	47	19	49	37	48	41
$25,000 to $29,999	199	92	26	9	43	39	29	23
$30,000 to $34,999	183	93	33	8	35	27	15	15
$35,000 to $39,999	175	97	22	6	24	17	27	17
$40,000 to $44,999	196	94	27	14	36	25	25	19
$45,000 to $49,999	186	91	20	19	20	14	36	21
$50,000 to $54,999	232	107	30	15	42	28	39	35
$55,000 to $59,999	144	78	11	16	17	14	22	11
$60,000 to $64,999	227	139	14	15	30	24	29	23
$65,000 to $69,999	160	92	14	17	26	16	11	6
$70,000 to $74,999	146	92	17	9	16	6	11	3
$75,000 to $79,999	119	76	17	6	12	12	8	8
$80,000 to $84,999	126	80	15	9	9	6	14	10
$85,000 to $89,999	117	86	6	6	5	4	14	9
$90,000 to $94,999	122	88	7	9	13	9	4	4
$95,000 to $99,999	91	64	6	6	4	2	11	2
$100,000 to $124,999	508	376	34	26	34	28	39	20
$125,000 to $149,999	335	247	18	14	14	7	43	20
$150,000 to $174,999	258	222	11	10	11	6	6	5
$175,000 to $199,999	135	105	4	5	4	0	18	10
$200,000 or more	358	293	20	21	10	4	15	11
Median income	$63,726	$85,565	$43,529	$63,056	$31,078	$25,523	$46,544	$38,904

PERCENT DISTRIBUTION

Asian households	**100.0%**	**100.0%**	**100.0%**	**100.0%**	**100.0%**	**100.0%**	**100.0%**	**100.0%**
Under $25,000	20.2	11.2	28.7	18.2	42.2	48.6	32.5	38.2
$25,000 to $49,999	18.6	15.9	26.0	19.2	22.5	21.9	21.4	21.7
$50,000 to $74,999	18.0	17.3	17.5	24.7	18.7	15.8	18.2	17.8
$75,000 to $99,999	11.4	13.4	10.4	12.4	6.1	5.9	8.3	7.6
$100,000 or more	31.6	42.3	17.7	26.1	10.4	8.1	19.6	15.1

Note: Asians are those who identify themselves as being of the race alone and those who identify themselves as being of the race in combination with other races. "hh" stands for householder.
Source: Bureau of the Census, 2011 Current Population Survey, Internet site http://www.census.gov/hhes/www/cpstables/032011/hhinc/toc.htm; calculations by New Strategist

Table 1.18 Households by Income and Household Type, 2010: Black Households

(number and percent distribution of black households by household income and household type, 2010; households in thousands as of 2011)

| | family households | | | | nonfamily households | | | |
| | | | female hh, no spouse present | male hh, no spouse present | female householder | | male householder | |
	total	married couples			total	living alone	total	living alone
Black households	**15,613**	**4,353**	**4,459**	**954**	**3,238**	**2,933**	**2,609**	**2,189**
Under $5,000	1,174	87	439	37	332	320	279	256
$5,000 to $9,999	1,390	58	447	55	486	458	343	318
$10,000 to $14,999	1,432	105	443	62	503	479	318	299
$15,000 to $19,999	1,141	137	397	56	343	315	208	186
$20,000 to $24,999	1,163	208	445	82	239	224	188	168
$25,000 to $29,999	1,045	229	337	83	213	190	183	156
$30,000 to $34,999	957	240	322	68	164	155	163	145
$35,000 to $39,999	813	181	264	54	159	142	156	121
$40,000 to $44,999	799	240	229	58	159	138	112	89
$45,000 to $49,999	655	211	189	44	107	93	103	80
$50,000 to $54,999	606	227	158	44	87	74	90	60
$55,000 to $59,999	457	191	100	26	73	62	67	40
$60,000 to $64,999	462	192	110	27	85	65	48	38
$65,000 to $69,999	374	171	84	29	36	30	55	42
$70,000 to $74,999	442	172	108	40	60	54	62	48
$75,000 to $79,999	335	180	60	20	35	30	39	29
$80,000 to $84,999	285	162	46	23	23	19	30	19
$85,000 to $89,999	222	144	27	19	11	5	22	10
$90,000 to $94,999	202	119	43	11	21	14	8	4
$95,000 to $99,999	152	87	26	9	11	9	18	11
$100,000 to $124,999	675	412	118	52	44	27	51	32
$125,000 to $149,999	345	251	31	27	11	5	23	9
$150,000 to $174,999	213	154	17	16	7	7	20	13
$175,000 to $199,999	84	57	5	5	11	5	5	3
$200,000 or more	192	137	14	10	16	15	15	13
Median income	$32,106	$61,161	$25,724	$38,398	$19,201	$17,923	$23,818	$20,819

PERCENT DISTRIBUTION

Black households	**100.0%**	**100.0%**	**100.0%**	**100.0%**	**100.0%**	**100.0%**	**100.0%**	**100.0%**
Under $25,000	40.4	13.7	48.7	30.6	58.8	61.2	51.2	56.1
$25,000 to $49,999	27.3	25.3	30.1	32.2	24.8	24.5	27.5	27.0
$50,000 to $74,999	15.0	21.9	12.6	17.4	10.5	9.7	12.3	10.4
$75,000 to $99,999	7.7	15.9	4.5	8.6	3.1	2.6	4.5	3.3
$100,000 or more	9.7	23.2	4.1	11.5	2.7	2.0	4.4	3.2

Note: Blacks are those who identify themselves as being of the race alone and those who identify themselves as being of the race in combination with other races. "hh" stands for householder.
Source: Bureau of the Census, 2011 Current Population Survey, Internet site http://www.census.gov/hhes/www/cpstables/032011/hhinc/toc.htm; calculations by New Strategist

Table 1.19 Households by Income and Household Type, 2010: Hispanic Households

(number and percent distribution of Hispanic households by household income and household type, 2010; households in thousands as of 2011)

| | family households | | | | nonfamily households | | | |
| | total | married couples | female hh, no spouse present | male hh, no spouse present | female householder | | male householder | |
					total	living alone	total	living alone
Hispanic households	**13,665**	**6,725**	**2,754**	**1,180**	**1,371**	**1,098**	**1,635**	**1,100**
Under $5,000	594	155	229	22	101	92	87	78
$5,000 to $9,999	769	140	240	39	230	220	121	111
$10,000 to $14,999	1,018	285	264	57	230	219	182	158
$15,000 to $19,999	949	349	279	57	125	109	139	117
$20,000 to $24,999	1,067	459	247	103	99	85	160	110
$25,000 to $29,999	1,033	486	252	80	99	79	115	86
$30,000 to $34,999	856	383	204	97	68	53	104	80
$35,000 to $39,999	822	416	171	73	66	47	96	57
$40,000 to $44,999	707	339	147	74	53	30	94	57
$45,000 to $49,999	622	315	136	61	45	26	65	41
$50,000 to $54,999	644	361	95	80	43	28	65	37
$55,000 to $59,999	488	311	80	39	19	10	38	14
$60,000 to $64,999	508	302	65	59	35	17	47	27
$65,000 to $69,999	387	255	46	36	22	13	29	16
$70,000 to $74,999	329	208	36	32	14	9	40	15
$75,000 to $79,999	350	213	37	39	19	9	42	25
$80,000 to $84,999	328	211	29	43	22	13	24	5
$85,000 to $89,999	236	137	24	24	13	5	38	13
$90,000 to $94,999	226	158	23	21	5	1	20	2
$95,000 to $99,999	165	94	27	20	6	1	19	11
$100,000 to $124,999	665	465	54	64	31	20	50	18
$125,000 to $149,999	390	289	36	33	9	2	25	12
$150,000 to $174,999	211	162	19	13	4	2	12	2
$175,000 to $199,999	97	77	6	4	3	1	6	0
$200,000 or more	200	153	9	11	11	6	16	5
Median income	$37,759	$50,410	$27,172	$44,224	$20,005	$15,593	$30,428	$23,552

PERCENT DISTRIBUTION

Hispanic households	**100.0%**	**100.0%**	**100.0%**	**100.0%**	**100.0%**	**100.0%**	**100.0%**	**100.0%**
Under $25,000	32.2	20.6	45.7	23.6	57.3	66.0	42.1	52.2
$25,000 to $49,999	29.6	28.8	33.0	32.6	24.1	21.4	29.0	29.2
$50,000 to $74,999	17.2	21.4	11.7	20.8	9.7	7.0	13.4	9.9
$75,000 to $99,999	9.5	12.1	5.1	12.5	4.7	2.6	8.7	5.1
$100,000 or more	11.4	17.0	4.5	10.6	4.2	2.8	6.7	3.4

Note: "hh" stands for householder.
Source: Bureau of the Census, 2011 Current Population Survey, Internet site http://www.census.gov/hhes/www/cpstables/032011/hhinc/toc.htm; calculations by New Strategist

Table 1.20 Households by Income and Household Type, 2010: Non-Hispanic White Households

(number and percent distribution of non-Hispanic white households by household income and household type, 2010; households in thousands as of 2011)

| | family households | | | | nonfamily households | | | |
| | total | married couples | female hh, no spouse present | male hh, no spouse present | female householder | | male householder | |
					total	living alone	total	living alone
Non-Hispanic white households	**83,471**	**43,554**	**7,277**	**3,078**	**15,749**	**13,456**	**13,813**	**10,675**
Under $5,000	2,138	378	313	50	720	657	676	633
$5,000 to $9,999	2,721	301	409	62	1,238	1,202	711	664
$10,000 to $14,999	4,365	681	460	102	2,042	1,975	1,081	972
$15,000 to $19,999	4,882	1,056	493	156	2,096	1,983	1,082	975
$20,000 to $24,999	4,399	1,308	586	162	1,288	1,182	1,054	892
$25,000 to $29,999	4,397	1,608	554	172	1,233	1,119	831	722
$30,000 to $34,999	4,108	1,647	485	155	966	836	855	721
$35,000 to $39,999	4,049	1,728	525	182	825	676	790	640
$40,000 to $44,999	3,882	1,804	418	216	742	641	702	582
$45,000 to $49,999	3,430	1,716	373	122	581	485	638	471
$50,000 to $54,999	3,575	1,861	320	174	543	454	677	549
$55,000 to $59,999	3,075	1,711	297	158	448	324	461	323
$60,000 to $64,999	3,186	1,720	275	197	416	308	577	387
$65,000 to $69,999	2,627	1,619	182	104	315	237	407	264
$70,000 to $74,999	2,827	1,750	219	141	362	279	355	213
$75,000 to $79,999	2,289	1,510	157	78	191	122	352	236
$80,000 to $84,999	2,370	1,611	153	94	184	108	329	223
$85,000 to $89,999	2,085	1,483	139	84	178	117	202	101
$90,000 to $94,999	1,953	1,383	130	59	165	108	216	137
$95,000 to $99,999	1,688	1,257	92	70	122	62	147	76
$100,000 to $124,999	7,093	5,357	340	237	467	268	689	385
$125,000 to $149,999	4,187	3,366	144	106	250	129	323	158
$150,000 to $174,999	2,686	2,160	72	64	164	83	227	110
$175,000 to $199,999	1,596	1,306	44	42	62	27	140	58
$200,000 or more	3,863	3,233	100	89	151	73	290	184
Median income	$54,620	$77,661	$38,131	$54,452	$26,875	$23,681	$38,649	$32,829

PERCENT DISTRIBUTION

Non-Hispanic white households	**100.0%**	**100.0%**	**100.0%**	**100.0%**	**100.0%**	**100.0%**	**100.0%**	**100.0%**
Under $25,000	22.2	8.6	31.1	17.3	46.9	52.0	33.3	38.7
$25,000 to $49,999	23.8	19.5	32.4	27.5	27.6	27.9	27.6	29.4
$50,000 to $74,999	18.3	19.9	17.8	25.1	13.2	11.9	17.9	16.3
$75,000 to $99,999	12.4	16.6	9.2	12.5	5.3	3.8	9.0	7.2
$100,000 or more	23.3	35.4	9.6	17.5	6.9	4.3	12.1	8.4

Note: Non-Hispanic whites are those who identify themselves as being white alone and not Hispanic. "hh" stands for householder.
Source: Bureau of the Census, 2011 Current Population Survey, Internet site http://www.census.gov/hhes/www/cpstables/032011/hhinc/toc.htm; calculations by New Strategist

Household Income Peaks in the 45-to-54 Age Group

But for Asians, blacks, and non-Hispanic whites, it peaks in the 35 to 44 age group.

Median household income stood at $49,445 in 2010. For householders aged 45 to 54, however, median income was a higher $62,485. Not far behind are householders aged 35 to 44, with a median income of $61,644. Household incomes are highest in middle age because people in their thirties, forties, and fifties are usually at the height of their career. More than one in four households headed by people ranging in age from 35 to 64 had an income of $100,000 or more in 2010.

Median household income is lowest among the oldest and the youngest householders. Householders under age 25 had a median income of $28,322 in 2010, while those aged 75 or older had a median income of $25,318. Income rises with age as people develop job skills, then falls after retirement.

By race and Hispanic origin, Hispanics are the only ones for whom household income peaks at ages 45 to 54 (at $45,703). Median household income peaks in the 35-to-44 age group among Asians ($79,596), blacks ($40,353), and non-Hispanic whites ($71,708). Black and Hispanic incomes peak at a much lower level because of the unique household characteristics of each group. Black households are much less likely than Asian or non-Hispanic white households to be headed by married couples, and married couples are by far the most affluent household type. Hispanic couples are less likely to be dual-earners and many are recent immigrants with little education and few job skills.

■ The incomes of householders aged 55 to 64 should grow in the years ahead as two-income baby-boom couples fill the age group and fewer opt for early retirement.

Incomes are lowest for the oldest householders

(median income of households by age of householder, 2010)

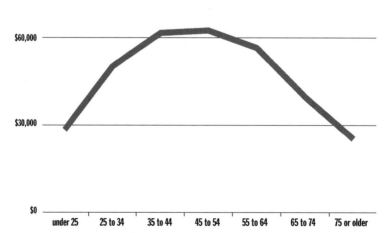

Table 1.21 Households by Income and Age of Householder, 2010: Total Households

(number and percent distribution of households by household income and age of householder, 2010; households in thousands as of 2011)

	total	15 to 24	25 to 34	35 to 44	45 to 54	55 to 64	65 or older total	65 to 74	75 or older
Total households	**118,682**	**6,140**	**19,572**	**21,250**	**24,530**	**21,828**	**25,362**	**13,348**	**12,015**
Under $5,000	4,176	608	765	670	806	754	573	276	297
$5,000 to $9,999	5,055	530	706	548	887	927	1,456	634	822
$10,000 to $14,999	7,061	529	840	753	965	1,128	2,845	1,077	1,768
$15,000 to $19,999	7,260	533	970	795	972	1,068	2,922	1,139	1,783
$20,000 to $24,999	6,937	529	1,169	969	1,084	973	2,213	953	1,260
$25,000 to $29,999	6,730	469	1,106	935	1,051	1,007	2,161	992	1,169
$30,000 to $34,999	6,148	372	1,003	1,026	1,064	1,001	1,682	846	836
$35,000 to $39,999	5,907	384	1,131	980	980	990	1,440	797	644
$40,000 to $44,999	5,624	322	1,147	924	1,033	998	1,200	655	545
$45,000 to $49,999	4,933	249	933	920	881	892	1,059	626	433
$50,000 to $54,999	5,088	207	1,037	964	1,057	896	927	553	374
$55,000 to $59,999	4,203	203	779	791	880	801	749	483	265
$60,000 to $64,999	4,412	210	831	851	936	792	791	522	270
$65,000 to $69,999	3,579	151	690	739	800	647	553	388	165
$70,000 to $74,999	3,769	124	769	782	882	721	492	348	143
$75,000 to $79,999	3,118	78	556	686	748	657	393	241	152
$80,000 to $84,999	3,143	103	641	728	701	587	383	270	114
$85,000 to $89,999	2,680	65	513	519	691	547	344	261	84
$90,000 to $94,999	2,516	38	458	592	577	526	325	188	138
$95,000 to $99,999	2,110	41	355	462	600	382	270	197	73
$100,000 to $124,999	9,008	178	1,452	2,163	2,420	1,828	969	667	303
$125,000 to $149,999	5,294	86	765	1,202	1,449	1,211	580	403	177
$150,000 to $174,999	3,386	40	337	722	1,073	847	368	295	75
$175,000 to $199,999	1,919	30	216	442	522	499	213	169	44
$200,000 or more	4,627	62	404	1,089	1,469	1,150	453	368	85
Median income	$49,445	$28,322	$50,059	$61,644	$62,485	$56,575	$31,408	$39,747	$25,318

PERCENT DISTRIBUTION

	total	15 to 24	25 to 34	35 to 44	45 to 54	55 to 64	65 or older total	65 to 74	75 or older
Total households	**100.0%**	**100.0%**	**100.0%**	**100.0%**	**100.0%**	**100.0%**	**100.0%**	**100.0%**	**100.0%**
Under $25,000	25.7	44.4	22.7	17.6	19.2	22.2	39.5	30.6	49.4
$25,000 to $49,999	24.7	29.3	27.2	22.5	20.4	22.4	29.7	29.3	30.2
$50,000 to $74,999	17.7	14.6	21.0	19.4	18.6	17.7	13.8	17.2	10.1
$75,000 to $99,999	11.4	5.3	12.9	14.1	13.5	12.4	6.8	8.7	4.7
$100,000 or more	20.4	6.4	16.2	26.4	28.3	25.4	10.2	14.2	5.7

Source: Bureau of the Census, 2011 Current Population Survey, Internet site http://www.census.gov/hhes/www/cpstables/ 032011/hhinc/toc.htm; calculations by New Strategist

Table 1.22 Households by Income and Age of Householder, 2010: Asian Households

(number and percent distribution of Asian households by household income and age of householder, 2010; households in thousands as of 2011)

	total	15 to 24	25 to 34	35 to 44	45 to 54	55 to 64	65 or older total	65 to 74	75 or older
Asian households	**5,040**	**295**	**1,070**	**1,163**	**1,050**	**763**	**698**	**428**	**270**
Under $5,000	232	38	34	42	33	27	58	27	31
$5,000 to $9,999	121	18	10	16	13	17	47	29	18
$10,000 to $14,999	180	8	26	27	16	33	69	40	28
$15,000 to $19,999	226	16	49	31	43	17	71	35	36
$20,000 to $24,999	261	27	65	40	40	39	50	27	23
$25,000 to $29,999	199	14	42	28	35	32	49	14	35
$30,000 to $34,999	183	19	32	38	31	33	32	17	15
$35,000 to $39,999	175	14	48	25	35	26	29	17	12
$40,000 to $44,999	196	16	50	44	37	21	27	17	11
$45,000 to $49,999	186	20	52	43	31	29	11	8	3
$50,000 to $54,999	232	13	53	52	63	21	30	20	11
$55,000 to $59,999	144	5	38	45	20	23	12	11	1
$60,000 to $64,999	227	13	50	48	52	33	30	24	7
$65,000 to $69,999	160	6	41	37	30	28	19	14	5
$70,000 to $74,999	146	15	40	35	34	14	8	6	2
$75,000 to $79,999	119	3	20	32	28	22	13	13	1
$80,000 to $84,999	126	6	30	33	32	18	7	4	3
$85,000 to $89,999	117	3	37	21	24	26	6	3	3
$90,000 to $94,999	122	1	26	24	24	33	13	9	4
$95,000 to $99,999	91	5	21	16	30	9	10	4	6
$100,000 to $124,999	508	13	122	144	117	77	35	26	8
$125,000 to $149,999	335	8	68	88	85	65	19	19	1
$150,000 to $174,999	258	6	41	77	69	46	19	19	0
$175,000 to $199,999	135	5	27	57	20	19	7	7	0
$200,000 or more	358	6	47	121	105	54	26	21	5
Median income	$63,726	$37,306	$62,432	$79,596	$76,784	$70,340	$30,811	$42,166	$24,498

PERCENT DISTRIBUTION

	total	15 to 24	25 to 34	35 to 44	45 to 54	55 to 64	65 or older total	65 to 74	75 or older
Asian households	**100.0%**	**100.0%**	**100.0%**	**100.0%**	**100.0%**	**100.0%**	**100.0%**	**100.0%**	**100.0%**
Under $25,000	20.2	36.3	17.2	13.4	13.8	17.4	42.3	36.9	50.4
$25,000 to $49,999	18.6	28.1	20.9	15.3	16.1	18.5	21.2	17.1	28.1
$50,000 to $74,999	18.0	17.6	20.7	18.7	19.0	15.6	14.2	17.5	9.6
$75,000 to $99,999	11.4	6.1	12.5	10.8	13.1	14.2	7.0	7.7	6.3
$100,000 or more	31.6	12.9	28.5	41.9	37.7	34.2	15.2	21.5	5.2

Note: Asians are those who identify themselves as being of the race alone and those who identify themselves as being of the race in combination with other races.
Source: Bureau of the Census, 2011 Current Population Survey, Internet site http://www.census.gov/hhes/www/cpstables/ 032011/hhinc/toc.htm; calculations by New Strategist

Table 1.23 Households by Income and Age of Householder, 2010: Black Households

(number and percent distribution of black households by household income and age of householder, 2010; households in thousands as of 2011)

	total	15 to 24	25 to 34	35 to 44	45 to 54	55 to 64	65 or older total	65 to 74	75 or older
Black households	**15,613**	**1,201**	**2,997**	**3,008**	**3,311**	**2,682**	**2,413**	**1,423**	**990**
Under $5,000	1,174	189	274	193	239	164	114	62	52
$5,000 to $9,999	1,390	170	249	158	232	292	288	136	151
$10,000 to $14,999	1,432	156	239	168	226	229	412	223	189
$15,000 to $19,999	1,141	94	226	177	207	193	244	123	121
$20,000 to $24,999	1,163	87	273	234	236	144	189	110	79
$25,000 to $29,999	1,045	113	208	171	193	189	172	106	66
$30,000 to $34,999	957	60	156	232	184	154	171	91	80
$35,000 to $39,999	813	52	187	155	177	136	107	75	32
$40,000 to $44,999	799	68	198	151	171	123	88	49	39
$45,000 to $49,999	655	36	129	158	132	124	78	55	23
$50,000 to $54,999	606	31	128	122	151	91	84	53	30
$55,000 to $59,999	457	22	85	100	117	83	50	42	8
$60,000 to $64,999	462	20	98	121	100	74	49	19	31
$65,000 to $69,999	374	23	63	79	107	70	33	25	8
$70,000 to $74,999	442	10	91	107	105	79	51	40	11
$75,000 to $79,999	335	20	57	80	66	74	38	25	14
$80,000 to $84,999	285	4	53	79	79	48	23	21	2
$85,000 to $89,999	222	6	35	52	60	39	30	27	3
$90,000 to $94,999	202	9	33	50	53	33	24	15	9
$95,000 to $99,999	152	2	16	34	50	31	18	13	4
$100,000 to $124,999	675	8	81	205	168	136	77	50	26
$125,000 to $149,999	345	6	46	96	97	70	28	25	5
$150,000 to $174,999	213	6	34	20	84	42	25	22	4
$175,000 to $199,999	84	1	15	20	18	26	5	5	0
$200,000 or more	192	8	21	46	62	39	15	14	2
Median income	$32,106	$19,531	$30,811	$40,353	$38,709	$34,101	$23,798	$27,364	$18,778

PERCENT DISTRIBUTION

Black households	**100.0%**	**100.0%**	**100.0%**	**100.0%**	**100.0%**	**100.0%**	**100.0%**	**100.0%**	**100.0%**
Under $25,000	40.4	58.0	42.1	30.9	34.4	38.1	51.7	46.0	59.8
$25,000 to $49,999	27.3	27.4	29.3	28.8	25.9	27.1	25.5	26.4	24.2
$50,000 to $74,999	15.0	8.8	15.5	17.6	17.5	14.8	11.1	12.6	8.9
$75,000 to $99,999	7.7	3.4	6.5	9.8	9.3	8.4	5.5	7.1	3.2
$100,000 or more	9.7	2.4	6.6	12.9	13.0	11.7	6.2	8.2	3.7

Note: Blacks are those who identify themselves as being of the race alone and those who identify themselves as being of the race in combination with other races.
Source: Bureau of the Census, 2011 Current Population Survey, Internet site http://www.census.gov/hhes/www/cpstables/ 032011/hhinc/toc.htm; calculations by New Strategist

Table 1.24 Households by Income and Age of Householder, 2010: Hispanic Households

(number and percent distribution of Hispanic households by household income and age of householder, 2010; households in thousands as of 2011)

	total	15 to 24	25 to 34	35 to 44	45 to 54	55 to 64	65 or older total	65 to 74	75 or older
Hispanic households	**13,665**	**1,135**	**3,212**	**3,367**	**2,730**	**1,729**	**1,492**	**917**	**574**
Under $5,000	594	93	152	138	96	66	50	33	17
$5,000 to $9,999	769	90	143	121	109	114	192	93	99
$10,000 to $14,999	1,018	94	210	180	186	127	219	101	118
$15,000 to $19,999	949	103	231	212	147	96	161	96	65
$20,000 to $24,999	1,067	117	269	233	190	117	141	74	67
$25,000 to $29,999	1,033	102	261	247	174	111	139	95	44
$30,000 to $34,999	856	66	204	230	183	93	80	60	20
$35,000 to $39,999	822	68	223	213	149	104	65	44	21
$40,000 to $44,999	707	70	186	189	109	100	53	35	19
$45,000 to $49,999	622	50	138	180	131	72	52	31	21
$50,000 to $54,999	644	40	153	169	135	88	58	47	11
$55,000 to $59,999	488	41	115	112	125	57	37	29	9
$60,000 to $64,999	508	39	117	151	94	70	36	24	13
$65,000 to $69,999	387	21	111	103	79	49	24	20	4
$70,000 to $74,999	329	14	75	110	72	35	23	14	8
$75,000 to $79,999	350	19	89	97	80	48	17	14	3
$80,000 to $84,999	328	18	82	99	63	36	29	25	4
$85,000 to $89,999	236	12	60	61	64	30	10	6	4
$90,000 to $94,999	226	7	67	51	52	39	11	4	7
$95,000 to $99,999	165	10	39	40	50	21	6	3	3
$100,000 to $124,999	665	35	151	173	173	97	37	31	5
$125,000 to $149,999	390	11	88	99	113	57	22	16	5
$150,000 to $174,999	211	4	33	63	60	41	11	8	3
$175,000 to $199,999	97	2	11	29	34	16	6	4	2
$200,000 or more	200	10	6	67	63	43	12	11	1
Median income	$37,759	$28,246	$37,658	$42,370	$45,703	$41,444	$24,242	$28,305	$18,465

PERCENT DISTRIBUTION

	total	15 to 24	25 to 34	35 to 44	45 to 54	55 to 64	65 or older total	65 to 74	75 or older
Hispanic households	**100.0%**	**100.0%**	**100.0%**	**100.0%**	**100.0%**	**100.0%**	**100.0%**	**100.0%**	**100.0%**
Under $25,000	32.2	43.8	31.3	26.3	26.7	30.1	51.1	43.3	63.8
$25,000 to $49,999	29.6	31.4	31.5	31.5	27.3	27.8	26.1	28.9	21.8
$50,000 to $74,999	17.2	13.7	17.8	19.2	18.5	17.3	11.9	14.6	7.8
$75,000 to $99,999	9.5	5.8	10.5	10.3	11.3	10.1	4.9	5.7	3.7
$100,000 or more	11.4	5.5	9.0	12.8	16.2	14.7	5.9	7.6	2.8

Source: Bureau of the Census, 2011 Current Population Survey, Internet site http://www.census.gov/hhes/www/cpstables/032011/hhinc/toc.htm; calculations by New Strategist

Table 1.25 Households by Income and Age of Householder, 2010: Non-Hispanic White Households

(number and percent distribution of non-Hispanic white households by household income and age of householder, 2010; households in thousands as of 2011)

	total	15 to 24	25 to 34	35 to 44	45 to 54	55 to 64	65 or older total	65 to 74	75 or older
Non-Hispanic white households	**83,471**	**3,481**	**12,188**	**13,560**	**17,237**	**16,439**	**20,566**	**10,473**	**10,093**
Under $5,000	2,138	281	297	290	434	485	350	155	196
$5,000 to $9,999	2,721	246	306	245	519	495	909	370	540
$10,000 to $14,999	4,365	263	359	373	526	718	2,125	702	1,423
$15,000 to $19,999	4,882	306	450	389	562	737	2,438	884	1,554
$20,000 to $24,999	4,399	302	563	452	603	664	1,814	731	1,083
$25,000 to $29,999	4,397	240	590	480	644	669	1,774	768	1,006
$30,000 to $34,999	4,108	228	604	513	657	713	1,393	680	713
$35,000 to $39,999	4,049	252	661	574	616	711	1,236	657	579
$40,000 to $44,999	3,882	174	697	539	706	742	1,023	549	474
$45,000 to $49,999	3,430	144	611	532	584	649	910	528	382
$50,000 to $54,999	3,575	120	699	622	701	687	746	425	321
$55,000 to $59,999	3,075	130	542	516	609	633	644	399	245
$60,000 to $64,999	3,186	135	564	523	680	610	673	455	218
$65,000 to $69,999	2,627	99	475	514	579	494	467	323	144
$70,000 to $74,999	2,827	86	558	527	659	591	405	284	121
$75,000 to $79,999	2,289	41	385	473	572	505	314	181	134
$80,000 to $84,999	2,370	73	469	513	516	476	323	220	103
$85,000 to $89,999	2,085	46	379	384	536	446	294	221	73
$90,000 to $94,999	1,953	21	333	464	445	418	272	155	117
$95,000 to $99,999	1,688	26	281	363	463	319	235	176	59
$100,000 to $124,999	7,093	122	1,094	1,609	1,942	1,515	809	552	257
$125,000 to $149,999	4,187	59	554	921	1,143	1,002	507	344	165
$150,000 to $174,999	2,686	27	227	558	855	712	309	240	69
$175,000 to $199,999	1,596	22	164	330	447	436	194	154	41
$200,000 or more	3,863	37	326	855	1,236	1,009	400	323	77
Median income	$54,620	$32,093	$57,051	$71,708	$71,304	$62,008	$32,963	$42,461	$26,218

PERCENT DISTRIBUTION

Non-Hispanic white households	100.0%	100.0%	100.0%	100.0%	100.0%	100.0%	100.0%	100.0%	100.0%
Under $25,000	22.2	40.2	16.2	12.9	15.3	18.9	37.1	27.1	47.5
$25,000 to $49,999	23.8	29.8	26.0	19.5	18.6	21.2	30.8	30.4	31.2
$50,000 to $74,999	18.3	16.4	23.3	19.9	18.7	18.3	14.3	18.0	10.4
$75,000 to $99,999	12.4	5.9	15.2	16.2	14.7	13.2	7.0	9.1	4.8
$200,000 or more	23.3	7.7	19.4	31.5	32.6	28.4	10.8	15.4	6.0

Note: Non-Hispanic whites are those who identify themselves as being white alone and not Hispanic.
Source: Bureau of the Census, 2011 Current Population Survey, Internet site http://www.census.gov/hhes/www/cpstables/ 032011/hhinc/toc.htm; calculations by New Strategist

Among Couples, the Middle Aged Have the Highest Incomes

Married couples aged 45 to 54 had a median income of $88,442 in 2010.

The incomes of married couples peak in the 45-to-54 age group. While most couples ranging in age from 35 to 64 have an income of $80,000 or more, those aged 45 to 54 have the highest income by a hefty margin. More than 40 percent of couples in the 45-to-54 age group had an income of $100,000 or more in 2010, as did more than one-third of couples aged 35 to 44 and 55 to 64.

The youngest and the oldest married couples have the lowest incomes. Married couples aged 75 or older had a median income of $38,957 in 2010, a figure that surpassed the $38,301 median of couples under age 25. Incomes are relatively low for young couples because many have preschoolers, and wives are less likely to be in the labor force. Among older couples, incomes are low because husband and wife are no longer in the labor force.

By race and Hispanic origin, the incomes of married couples peak in the 45-to-54 age group among Hispanics (with a median income of $57,651) and non-Hispanic whites ($95,262). The income peak is in the 35-to-44 age group for Asians ($101,029) and blacks ($71,853).

■ Hispanic incomes will continue to lag behind the incomes of other racial and ethnic groups until immigrants become a smaller share of the Hispanic population.

Asian married couples have the highest median income

(median income of married couples by race and Hispanic origin, 2010)

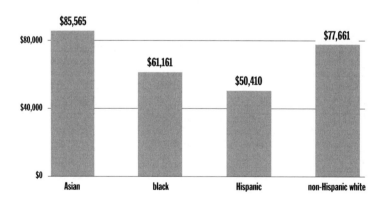

Table 1.26 Married Couples by Household Income and Age of Householder, 2010: Total Married Couples

(number and percent distribution of married couples by household income and age of householder, 2010; married couples in thousands as of 2011)

	total	15 to 24	25 to 34	35 to 44	45 to 54	55 to 64	65 or older total	65 to 74	75 or older
Total married couples	**58,036**	**1,077**	**8,551**	**12,087**	**13,506**	**11,851**	**10,963**	**6,871**	**4,092**
Under $5,000	697	52	83	125	142	154	141	72	69
$5,000 to $9,999	520	45	115	71	108	87	94	44	50
$10,000 to $14,999	1,142	58	188	194	217	223	262	144	118
$15,000 to $19,999	1,646	90	260	217	237	235	607	302	305
$20,000 to $24,999	2,093	74	307	323	293	304	790	357	433
$25,000 to $29,999	2,429	80	341	370	355	336	947	504	443
$30,000 to $34,999	2,368	77	315	370	408	387	810	447	363
$35,000 to $39,999	2,446	88	402	371	383	441	759	443	317
$40,000 to $44,999	2,499	83	443	406	412	481	674	365	310
$45,000 to $49,999	2,356	55	367	436	413	468	618	363	255
$50,000 to $54,999	2,579	47	486	513	523	465	545	345	199
$55,000 to $59,999	2,308	60	413	445	415	476	500	327	172
$60,000 to $64,999	2,367	42	417	471	498	475	464	314	150
$65,000 to $69,999	2,154	51	375	459	499	423	348	256	92
$70,000 to $74,999	2,245	33	416	491	546	454	305	228	78
$75,000 to $79,999	2,006	19	328	444	491	452	272	180	92
$80,000 to $84,999	2,092	32	366	518	461	429	286	211	75
$85,000 to $89,999	1,873	13	336	395	499	393	239	194	45
$90,000 to $94,999	1,758	10	306	471	429	349	193	126	67
$95,000 to $99,999	1,517	9	218	363	448	302	178	143	35
$100,000 to $124,999	6,664	43	965	1,687	1,895	1,396	676	513	164
$125,000 to $149,999	4,177	5	487	996	1,248	995	447	328	118
$150,000 to $174,999	2,719	3	218	615	900	697	284	228	58
$175,000 to $199,999	1,552	1	141	386	459	412	156	124	30
$200,000 or more	3,828	8	257	950	1,227	1,018	369	314	56
Median income	$72,751	$38,301	$66,584	$82,537	$88,442	$80,570	$48,115	$55,735	$38,957

PERCENT DISTRIBUTION

	total	15 to 24	25 to 34	35 to 44	45 to 54	55 to 64	65 or older total	65 to 74	75 or older
Total married couples	**100.0%**	**100.0%**	**100.0%**	**100.0%**	**100.0%**	**100.0%**	**100.0%**	**100.0%**	**100.0%**
Under $25,000	10.5	29.6	11.1	7.7	7.4	8.5	17.3	13.4	23.8
$25,000 to $49,999	20.8	35.6	21.8	16.2	14.6	17.8	34.7	30.9	41.3
$50,000 to $74,999	20.1	21.6	24.6	19.7	18.4	19.3	19.7	21.4	16.9
$75,000 to $99,999	15.9	7.7	18.2	18.1	17.2	16.2	10.7	12.4	7.7
$100,000 or more	32.6	5.6	24.2	38.3	42.4	38.1	17.6	21.9	10.4

Source: Bureau of the Census, 2011 Current Population Survey, Internet site http://www.census.gov/hhes/www/cpstables/ 032011/hhinc/toc.htm; calculations by New Strategist

Table 1.27 Married Couples by Household Income and Age of Householder, 2010: Asian Married Couples

(number and percent distribution of Asian married couples by household income and age of householder, 2010; married couples in thousands as of 2011)

	total	15 to 24	25 to 34	35 to 44	45 to 54	55 to 64	65 or older total	65 to 74	75 or older
Asian married couples	**2,939**	**27**	**505**	**795**	**739**	**502**	**370**	**256**	**115**
Under $5,000	67	2	6	13	18	4	25	13	13
$5,000 to $9,999	19	0	0	9	2	3	6	5	1
$10,000 to $14,999	53	0	8	13	7	10	15	9	6
$15,000 to $19,999	91	3	20	7	20	6	35	22	13
$20,000 to $24,999	98	0	23	15	17	12	31	17	14
$25,000 to $29,999	92	2	17	15	25	15	18	8	10
$30,000 to $34,999	93	2	16	22	16	19	19	12	7
$35,000 to $39,999	97	3	12	16	25	19	22	13	9
$40,000 to $44,999	94	3	18	21	23	15	13	5	8
$45,000 to $49,999	91	0	21	22	18	21	9	6	3
$50,000 to $54,999	107	0	20	31	32	11	12	10	3
$55,000 to $59,999	78	0	16	27	8	17	9	9	1
$60,000 to $64,999	139	2	23	34	39	19	22	16	6
$65,000 to $69,999	92	0	22	16	20	18	16	12	5
$70,000 to $74,999	92	3	18	28	24	13	6	4	2
$75,000 to $79,999	76	0	15	20	19	16	8	7	0
$80,000 to $84,999	80	3	13	27	22	13	3	2	1
$85,000 to $89,999	86	0	29	13	22	16	5	3	3
$90,000 to $94,999	88	0	17	19	18	28	6	6	0
$95,000 to $99,999	64	0	8	16	25	9	6	4	2
$100,000 to $124,999	376	4	66	123	94	59	27	20	7
$125,000 to $149,999	247	0	42	62	75	55	15	15	1
$150,000 to $174,999	222	0	32	68	62	43	17	17	0
$175,000 to $199,999	105	0	17	50	17	17	4	4	0
$200,000 or more	293	0	26	108	92	45	22	21	0
Median income	$85,565	–	$78,461	$101,029	$93,389	$90,751	$45,440	$60,046	$30,236

PERCENT DISTRIBUTION

	total	15 to 24	25 to 34	35 to 44	45 to 54	55 to 64	65 or older total	65 to 74	75 or older
Asian married couples	**100.0%**	**100.0%**	**100.0%**	**100.0%**	**100.0%**	**100.0%**	**100.0%**	**100.0%**	**100.0%**
Under $25,000	11.2	18.5	11.3	7.2	8.7	7.0	30.3	25.8	40.9
$25,000 to $49,999	15.9	37.0	16.6	12.1	14.5	17.7	21.9	17.2	32.2
$50,000 to $74,999	17.3	18.5	19.6	17.1	16.6	15.5	17.6	19.9	14.8
$75,000 to $99,999	13.4	11.1	16.2	11.9	14.3	16.3	7.6	8.6	5.2
$100,000 or more	42.3	14.8	36.2	51.7	46.0	43.6	23.0	30.1	7.0

Note: Asians are those who identify themselves as being of the race alone and those who identify themselves as being of the race in combination with other races. "–" means sample is too small to make a reliable estimate.
Source: Bureau of the Census, 2011 Current Population Survey, Internet site http://www.census.gov/hhes/www/cpstables/ 032011/hhinc/toc.htm; calculations by New Strategist

Table 1.28 Married Couples by Household Income and Age of Householder, 2010: Black Married Couples

(number and percent distribution of black married couples by household income and age of householder, 2010; married couples in thousands as of 2011)

	total	15 to 24	25 to 34	35 to 44	45 to 54	55 to 64	65 or older total	65 to 74	75 or older
Black married couples	**4,353**	**83**	**642**	**988**	**1,088**	**892**	**662**	**462**	**200**
Under $5,000	87	7	6	16	24	17	17	12	5
$5,000 to $9,999	58	9	17	10	7	9	6	2	4
$10,000 to $14,999	105	6	13	13	19	27	28	20	8
$15,000 to $19,999	137	4	21	23	26	21	43	29	14
$20,000 to $24,999	208	4	31	57	29	35	52	27	25
$25,000 to $29,999	229	8	27	42	41	43	68	47	21
$30,000 to $34,999	240	3	35	52	42	50	58	33	26
$35,000 to $39,999	181	1	31	23	44	42	39	26	14
$40,000 to $44,999	240	15	57	50	41	44	32	20	12
$45,000 to $49,999	211	2	29	39	53	54	34	24	10
$50,000 to $54,999	227	5	35	41	65	46	35	22	13
$55,000 to $59,999	191	2	35	38	46	46	23	21	3
$60,000 to $64,999	192	0	46	39	46	40	21	9	13
$65,000 to $69,999	171	6	28	32	48	44	14	13	1
$70,000 to $74,999	172	0	34	45	47	35	13	11	1
$75,000 to $79,999	180	2	26	46	43	40	24	18	6
$80,000 to $84,999	162	0	28	48	40	33	14	14	0
$85,000 to $89,999	144	1	25	33	41	28	16	14	2
$90,000 to $94,999	119	5	21	36	30	14	15	9	6
$95,000 to $99,999	87	2	10	23	28	15	9	9	0
$100,000 to $124,999	412	1	32	141	115	78	45	33	10
$125,000 to $149,999	251	0	18	79	82	49	22	20	3
$150,000 to $174,999	154	0	17	12	75	30	19	16	4
$175,000 to $199,999	57	0	5	18	14	18	4	4	0
$200,000 or more	137	0	13	35	43	36	10	10	0
Median income	$61,161	$37,774	$56,767	$71,853	$70,944	$61,230	$42,829	$47,637	$34,709

PERCENT DISTRIBUTION

	total	15 to 24	25 to 34	35 to 44	45 to 54	55 to 64	65 or older total	65 to 74	75 or older
Black married couples	**100.0%**	**100.0%**	**100.0%**	**100.0%**	**100.0%**	**100.0%**	**100.0%**	**100.0%**	**100.0%**
Under $25,000	13.7	36.1	13.7	12.0	9.7	12.2	22.1	19.5	28.0
$25,000 to $49,999	25.3	34.9	27.9	20.9	20.3	26.1	34.9	32.5	41.5
$50,000 to $74,999	21.9	15.7	27.7	19.7	23.2	23.7	16.0	16.5	15.5
$75,000 to $99,999	15.9	12.0	17.1	18.8	16.7	14.6	11.8	13.9	7.0
$100,000 or more	23.2	1.2	13.2	28.8	30.2	23.7	15.1	18.0	8.5

Note: Blacks are those who identify themselves as being of the race alone and those who identify themselves as being of the race in combination with other races.
Source: Bureau of the Census, 2011 Current Population Survey, Internet site http://www.census.gov/hhes/www/cpstables/ 032011/hhinc/toc.htm; calculations by New Strategist

Table 1.29 Married Couples by Household Income and Age of Householder, 2010: Hispanic Married Couples

(number and percent distribution of Hispanic married couples by household income and age of householder, 2010; married couples in thousands as of 2011)

	total	15 to 24	25 to 34	35 to 44	45 to 54	55 to 64	65 or older total	65 to 74	75 or older
Hispanic married couples	**6,725**	**269**	**1,526**	**1,919**	**1,520**	**878**	**612**	**416**	**196**
Under $5,000	155	16	32	47	23	22	15	9	5
$5,000 to $9,999	140	11	43	25	29	15	17	13	3
$10,000 to $14,999	285	17	76	66	62	21	44	27	17
$15,000 to $19,999	349	22	105	80	48	32	62	33	29
$20,000 to $24,999	459	34	111	107	87	54	66	32	34
$25,000 to $29,999	486	28	119	127	87	56	68	53	15
$30,000 to $34,999	383	13	86	109	101	34	39	29	10
$35,000 to $39,999	416	25	116	114	74	58	30	23	7
$40,000 to $44,999	339	24	83	104	58	44	26	14	12
$45,000 to $49,999	315	7	59	114	68	40	27	15	13
$50,000 to $54,999	361	10	80	107	78	49	36	27	9
$55,000 to $59,999	311	15	72	82	76	39	27	20	7
$60,000 to $64,999	302	7	65	93	71	48	18	12	6
$65,000 to $69,999	255	6	62	78	62	32	15	12	3
$70,000 to $74,999	208	7	42	79	49	21	11	4	7
$75,000 to $79,999	213	4	51	70	55	21	12	10	1
$80,000 to $84,999	211	6	46	73	42	26	19	17	2
$85,000 to $89,999	137	3	31	40	39	14	10	6	4
$90,000 to $94,999	158	1	44	34	40	33	6	4	2
$95,000 to $99,999	94	2	23	25	29	16	0	0	0
$100,000 to $124,999	465	8	99	133	128	74	22	21	2
$125,000 to $149,999	289	1	53	74	94	47	19	15	4
$150,000 to $174,999	162	1	16	55	48	34	10	6	3
$175,000 to $199,999	77	0	8	28	23	15	2	2	0
$200,000 or more	153	1	3	55	50	33	11	10	1
Median income	$50,410	$32,027	$44,155	$52,284	$57,651	$56,192	$34,219	$36,384	$26,842

PERCENT DISTRIBUTION

Hispanic married couples	**100.0%**	**100.0%**	**100.0%**	**100.0%**	**100.0%**	**100.0%**	**100.0%**	**100.0%**	**100.0%**
Under $25,000	20.6	37.2	24.0	16.9	16.4	16.4	33.3	27.4	44.9
$25,000 to $49,999	28.8	36.1	30.3	29.6	25.5	26.4	31.0	32.2	29.1
$50,000 to $74,999	21.4	16.7	21.0	22.9	22.1	21.5	17.5	18.0	16.3
$75,000 to $99,999	12.1	5.9	12.8	12.6	13.5	12.5	7.7	8.9	4.6
$100,000 or more	17.0	4.1	11.7	18.0	22.6	23.1	10.5	13.0	5.1

Source: Bureau of the Census, 2011 Current Population Survey, Internet site http://www.census.gov/hhes/www/cpstables/ 032011/hhinc/toc.htm; calculations by New Strategist

Table 1.30 Married Couples by Household Income and Age of Householder, 2010: Non-Hispanic White Married Couples

(number and percent distribution of non-Hispanic white married couples by household income and age of householder, 2010; married couples in thousands as of 2011)

	total	15 to 24	25 to 34	35 to 44	45 to 54	55 to 64	65 or older total	65 to 74	75 or older
Non-Hispanic white married couples	43,554	694	5,847	8,269	10,049	9,467	9,229	5,672	3,557
Under $5,000	378	29	37	49	75	104	85	38	47
$5,000 to $9,999	301	25	59	25	71	58	64	22	41
$10,000 to $14,999	681	30	93	101	123	163	171	86	86
$15,000 to $19,999	1,056	58	112	106	141	174	464	219	246
$20,000 to $24,999	1,308	37	143	133	157	201	637	274	363
$25,000 to $29,999	1,608	42	182	185	198	218	782	393	389
$30,000 to $34,999	1,647	59	179	186	248	281	695	376	320
$35,000 to $39,999	1,728	60	236	210	240	318	664	378	286
$40,000 to $44,999	1,804	44	276	226	286	371	601	324	277
$45,000 to $49,999	1,716	45	257	255	271	345	543	315	228
$50,000 to $54,999	1,861	28	346	328	347	357	455	280	175
$55,000 to $59,999	1,711	42	296	287	279	371	436	275	161
$60,000 to $64,999	1,720	33	282	298	337	365	404	279	125
$65,000 to $69,999	1,619	39	266	327	366	329	291	213	78
$70,000 to $74,999	1,750	23	315	335	421	383	273	205	67
$75,000 to $79,999	1,510	14	231	304	372	370	220	137	83
$80,000 to $84,999	1,611	23	274	370	344	353	247	176	71
$85,000 to $89,999	1,483	8	249	304	390	327	204	168	36
$90,000 to $94,999	1,383	3	225	378	339	273	165	106	59
$95,000 to $99,999	1,257	7	179	291	360	258	162	130	33
$100,000 to $124,999	5,357	31	767	1,262	1,546	1,180	574	432	141
$125,000 to $149,999	3,366	4	369	789	986	828	388	277	110
$150,000 to $174,999	2,160	1	152	478	716	582	233	183	50
$175,000 to $199,999	1,306	1	110	289	401	362	145	115	30
$200,000 or more	3,233	6	211	753	1,037	899	327	272	55
Median income	$77,661	$40,683	$71,971	$91,037	$95,262	$84,415	$49,133	$57,287	$40,037

PERCENT DISTRIBUTION

	total	15 to 24	25 to 34	35 to 44	45 to 54	55 to 64	65 or older total	65 to 74	75 or older
Non-Hispanic white married couples	100.0%	100.0%	100.0%	100.0%	100.0%	100.0%	100.0%	100.0%	100.0%
Under $25,000	8.6	25.8	7.6	5.0	5.6	7.4	15.4	11.3	22.0
$25,000 to $49,999	19.5	36.0	19.3	12.8	12.4	16.2	35.6	31.5	42.2
$50,000 to $74,999	19.9	23.8	25.7	19.0	17.4	19.1	20.1	22.1	17.0
$75,000 to $99,999	16.6	7.9	19.8	19.9	18.0	16.7	10.8	12.6	7.9
$100,000 or more	35.4	6.2	27.5	43.2	46.6	40.7	18.1	22.5	10.9

Note: Non-Hispanic whites are those who identify themselves as being white alone and not Hispanic.
Source: Bureau of the Census, 2011 Current Population Survey, Internet site http://www.census.gov/hhes/www/cpstables/ 032011/hhinc/toc.htm; calculations by New Strategist

Incomes of Female-Headed Families Are below Average

The youngest are the poorest.

The median income of female-headed families was just $32,031 in 2010—meaning half had incomes below that level and half above.

Female family householders under age 25 have the lowest incomes, a median of just $21,627 in 2010. Female family householders 25 to 34 have a median income that is only slightly higher, at $25,305. Female family householders aged 35 or older have a larger median income that ranges from $33,000 to about $40,000. The majority of younger female-headed families include children. Many of these households have only one earner, or even none, which explains their low incomes. Many families headed by older women include other adults—such as grown children or siblings. These households often include two or more earners, which explains their higher incomes.

The poorest female-headed families are those headed by young black women. Black female family householders under age 25 had a median income of just $16,739 in 2010. Non-Hispanic white female family householders in the 45-to-54 age group have the highest incomes, a median of $48,373 and close to the all-household median of $49,445.

■ Female-headed families have low incomes because their households are likely to have just one earner, and many have no earners.

Incomes peak in middle age for female-headed families

(median household income of female-headed families by age of householder, 2010)

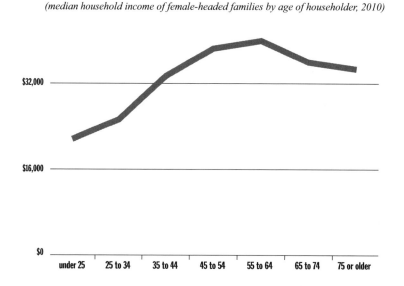

Table 1.31 Female-Headed Families by Household Income and Age of Householder, 2010: Total Female-Headed Families

(number and percent distribution of female-headed families by household income and age of householder, 2010; female-headed families in thousands as of 2011)

	total	15 to 24	25 to 34	35 to 44	45 to 54	55 to 64	65 or older total	65 to 74	75 or older
Total female-headed families	**15,019**	**1,414**	**3,281**	**3,480**	**3,134**	**1,745**	**1,964**	**976**	**988**
Under $5,000	1,003	160	340	200	177	84	42	20	22
$5,000 to $9,999	1,115	186	336	234	203	73	84	47	37
$10,000 to $14,999	1,184	160	311	246	190	117	160	84	75
$15,000 to $19,999	1,204	141	302	289	214	117	141	63	78
$20,000 to $24,999	1,321	136	331	301	233	128	193	98	95
$25,000 to $29,999	1,180	124	297	266	207	120	167	67	100
$30,000 to $34,999	1,046	90	192	272	197	107	189	97	92
$35,000 to $39,999	984	65	188	258	202	127	143	63	80
$40,000 to $44,999	818	58	185	193	149	115	118	59	59
$45,000 to $49,999	724	49	177	178	128	86	106	56	50
$50,000 to $54,999	606	50	119	153	130	68	86	33	52
$55,000 to $59,999	495	18	68	120	154	78	57	29	27
$60,000 to $64,999	466	24	69	120	122	61	71	39	32
$65,000 to $69,999	331	20	49	67	104	51	40	20	20
$70,000 to $74,999	382	14	46	103	103	56	58	41	17
$75,000 to $79,999	277	13	40	68	73	46	37	18	19
$80,000 to $84,999	240	10	29	66	66	30	40	31	9
$85,000 to $89,999	199	18	18	29	58	43	33	17	15
$90,000 to $94,999	205	6	33	35	43	60	29	14	15
$95,000 to $99,999	150	2	20	27	58	15	28	14	14
$100,000 to $124,999	549	24	68	128	148	91	89	32	55
$125,000 to $149,999	223	24	37	52	48	32	30	17	13
$150,000 to $174,999	119	5	10	26	42	13	18	11	7
$175,000 to $199,999	57	4	1	15	17	13	5	4	1
$200,000 or more	143	15	12	31	68	13	4	2	2
Median income	$32,031	$21,627	$25,305	$33,426	$38,563	$39,989	$35,277	$35,967	$34,696

PERCENT DISTRIBUTION

	total	15 to 24	25 to 34	35 to 44	45 to 54	55 to 64	65 or older total	65 to 74	75 or older
Total female-headed families	**100.0%**	**100.0%**	**100.0%**	**100.0%**	**100.0%**	**100.0%**	**100.0%**	**100.0%**	**100.0%**
Under $25,000	38.8	55.4	49.4	36.5	32.5	29.7	31.6	32.0	31.1
$25,000 to $49,999	31.6	27.3	31.7	33.5	28.2	31.8	36.8	35.0	38.6
$50,000 to $74,999	15.2	8.9	10.7	16.2	19.6	18.0	15.9	16.6	15.0
$75,000 to $99,999	7.1	3.5	4.3	6.5	9.5	11.1	8.5	9.6	7.3
$100,000 or more	7.3	5.1	3.9	7.2	10.3	9.3	7.4	6.8	7.9

Source: Bureau of the Census, 2011 Current Population Survey, Internet site http://www.census.gov/hhes/www/cpstables/032011/hhinc/toc.htm; calculations by New Strategist

Table 1.32 Female-Headed Families by Household Income and Age of Householder, 2010: Asian Female-Headed Families

(number and percent distribution of Asian female-headed families by household income and age of householder, 2010; female-headed families in thousands as of 2011)

	total	under 45	45 or older
Asian female-headed families	**492**	**263**	**229**
Under $5,000	29	17	11
$5,000 to $9,999	15	10	5
$10,000 to $14,999	15	10	6
$15,000 to $19,999	35	17	18
$20,000 to $24,999	47	26	21
$25,000 to $29,999	26	15	12
$30,000 to $34,999	33	20	13
$35,000 to $39,999	22	13	8
$40,000 to $44,999	27	13	14
$45,000 to $49,999	20	13	8
$50,000 to $54,999	30	21	9
$55,000 to $59,999	11	8	4
$60,000 to $64,999	14	5	9
$65,000 to $69,999	14	6	9
$70,000 to $74,999	17	12	6
$75,000 to $79,999	17	7	10
$80,000 to $84,999	15	5	10
$85,000 to $89,999	6	4	2
$90,000 to $94,999	7	2	5
$95,000 to $99,999	6	1	5
$100,000 to $124,999	34	17	17
$125,000 to $149,999	18	10	7
$150,000 to $174,999	11	1	9
$175,000 to $199,999	4	0	4
$200,000 or more	20	11	9
Median income	$43,529	$41,346	$49,062

PERCENT DISTRIBUTION

	total	under 45	45 or older
Asian female-headed families	**100.0%**	**100.0%**	**100.0%**
Under $25,000	28.7	30.4	26.6
$25,000 to $49,999	26.0	28.1	24.0
$50,000 to $74,999	17.5	19.8	16.2
$75,000 to $99,999	10.4	7.2	14.0
$100,000 or more	17.7	14.8	20.1

Note: Asians are those who identify themselves as being of the race alone and those who identify themselves as being of the race in combination with other races.
Source: Bureau of the Census, 2011 Current Population Survey, Internet site http://www.census.gov/hhes/www/cpstables/032011/hhinc/toc.htm; calculations by New Strategist

Table 1.33 Female-Headed Families by Household Income and Age of Householder, 2010: Black Female-Headed Families

(number and percent distribution of black female-headed families by household income and age of householder, 2010; female-headed families in thousands as of 2011)

	total	15 to 24	25 to 34	35 to 44	45 to 54	55 to 64	65 or older total	65 to 74	75 or older
Black female-headed families	**4,459**	**460**	**1,174**	**1,039**	**857**	**475**	**454**	**239**	**216**
Under $5,000	439	73	159	74	72	39	20	8	13
$5,000 to $9,999	447	71	159	85	84	27	22	11	10
$10,000 to $14,999	443	74	140	75	55	46	53	30	23
$15,000 to $19,999	397	32	111	102	72	42	40	16	24
$20,000 to $24,999	445	33	135	114	94	28	42	29	13
$25,000 to $29,999	337	40	93	68	58	44	33	14	19
$30,000 to $34,999	322	24	55	102	52	43	45	20	26
$35,000 to $39,999	264	23	52	74	56	34	25	18	7
$40,000 to $44,999	229	22	73	43	55	16	20	11	9
$45,000 to $49,999	189	10	54	58	23	19	24	14	10
$50,000 to $54,999	158	16	30	44	36	11	21	8	13
$55,000 to $59,999	100	4	12	36	27	12	9	4	5
$60,000 to $64,999	110	8	16	29	23	16	17	6	10
$65,000 to $69,999	84	5	10	15	34	11	9	4	5
$70,000 to $74,999	108	2	13	37	21	14	21	16	5
$75,000 to $79,999	60	7	10	18	10	10	5	2	3
$80,000 to $84,999	46	2	6	11	14	5	7	5	2
$85,000 to $89,999	27	2	4	4	7	4	6	5	1
$90,000 to $94,999	43	3	4	7	12	10	7	3	4
$95,000 to $99,999	26	0	0	5	10	8	3	2	1
$100,000 to $124,999	118	2	17	27	30	24	17	4	12
$125,000 to $149,999	31	1	12	3	1	8	4	2	2
$150,000 to $174,999	17	2	5	4	4	1	2	2	0
$175,000 to $199,999	5	1	0	0	2	1	1	1	0
$200,000 or more	14	3	3	3	4	0	0	0	0
Median income	$25,724	$16,739	$20,572	$30,084	$29,325	$31,532	$31,573	$32,235	$31,069

PERCENT DISTRIBUTION

Black female-headed families	**100.0%**	**100.0%**	**100.0%**	**100.0%**	**100.0%**	**100.0%**	**100.0%**	**100.0%**	**100.0%**
Under $25,000	48.7	61.5	60.0	43.3	44.0	38.3	39.0	39.3	38.4
$25,000 to $49,999	30.1	25.9	27.9	33.2	28.5	32.8	32.4	32.2	32.9
$50,000 to $74,999	12.6	7.6	6.9	15.5	16.5	13.5	17.0	15.9	17.6
$75,000 to $99,999	4.5	3.0	2.0	4.3	6.2	7.8	6.2	7.1	5.1
$100,000 or more	4.1	2.0	3.2	3.6	4.8	7.2	5.3	3.8	6.5

Note: Blacks are those who identify themselves as being of the race alone and those who identify themselves as being of the race in combination with other races.
Source: Bureau of the Census, 2011 Current Population Survey, Internet site http://www.census.gov/hhes/www/cpstables/ 032011/hhinc/toc.htm; calculations by New Strategist

Table 1.34 Female-Headed Families by Household Income and Age of Householder, 2010: Hispanic Female-Headed Families

(number and percent distribution of Hispanic female-headed families by household income and age of householder, 2010; female-headed families in thousands as of 2011)

	total	15 to 24	25 to 34	35 to 44	45 to 54	55 to 64	65 or older total	65 to 74	75 or older
Hispanic female-headed families	**2,754**	**336**	**720**	**710**	**515**	**266**	**208**	**135**	**73**
Under $5,000	229	42	87	54	33	9	6	5	1
$5,000 to $9,999	240	45	67	58	35	23	12	8	4
$10,000 to $14,999	264	33	63	66	48	24	29	20	9
$15,000 to $19,999	279	32	78	88	45	15	20	14	7
$20,000 to $24,999	247	31	83	52	43	17	21	12	9
$25,000 to $29,999	252	29	70	66	48	19	21	11	10
$30,000 to $34,999	204	21	44	60	45	21	13	10	4
$35,000 to $39,999	171	11	42	38	38	21	20	13	7
$40,000 to $44,999	147	14	34	47	19	21	13	8	5
$45,000 to $49,999	136	18	31	32	29	16	9	7	2
$50,000 to $54,999	95	12	21	29	17	12	4	4	0
$55,000 to $59,999	80	8	12	19	22	13	6	4	2
$60,000 to $64,999	65	7	13	21	9	6	8	6	2
$65,000 to $69,999	46	8	16	10	7	4	1	1	0
$70,000 to $74,999	36	4	4	13	6	4	4	4	0
$75,000 to $79,999	37	2	7	12	7	8	2	0	1
$80,000 to $84,999	29	2	5	3	10	5	5	3	1
$85,000 to $89,999	24	1	5	5	7	6	0	0	0
$90,000 to $94,999	23	1	6	4	3	5	3	0	3
$95,000 to $99,999	27	0	6	4	8	4	4	1	3
$100,000 to $124,999	54	5	9	18	10	7	3	1	2
$125,000 to $149,999	36	7	14	5	7	1	0	0	0
$150,000 to $174,999	19	0	3	4	7	3	0	0	0
$175,000 to $199,999	6	1	0	0	5	0	0	0	0
$200,000 or more	9	1	0	0	6	1	0	0	0
Median income	$27,172	$21,689	$23,398	$27,199	$30,538	$36,558	$28,787	$29,162	–

PERCENT DISTRIBUTION

Hispanic female-headed families	100.0%	100.0%	100.0%	100.0%	100.0%	100.0%	100.0%	100.0%	100.0%
Under $25,000	45.7	54.5	52.5	44.8	39.6	33.1	42.3	43.7	41.1
$25,000 to $49,999	33.0	27.7	30.7	34.2	34.8	36.8	36.5	36.3	38.4
$50,000 to $74,999	11.7	11.6	9.2	13.0	11.8	14.7	11.1	14.1	5.5
$75,000 to $99,999	5.1	1.8	4.0	3.9	6.8	10.5	6.7	3.0	11.0
$100,000 or more	4.5	4.2	3.6	3.8	6.8	4.5	1.4	0.7	2.7

Note: "–" means sample is too small to make a reliable estimate.
Source: Bureau of the Census, 2011 Current Population Survey, Internet site http://www.census.gov/hhes/www/cpstables/ 032011/hhinc/toc.htm; calculations by New Strategist

Table 1.35 Female-Headed Families by Household Income and Age of Householder, 2010: Non-Hispanic White Female-Headed Families

(number and percent distribution of non-Hispanic white female-headed families by household income and age of householder, 2010; female-headed families in thousands as of 2011)

	total	15 to 24	25 to 34	35 to 44	45 to 54	55 to 64	65 or older total	65 to 74	75 or older
Non-Hispanic white female-headed families	**7,277**	**575**	**1,270**	**1,642**	**1,653**	**917**	**1,221**	**556**	**665**
Under $5,000	313	50	82	62	72	35	13	7	6
$5,000 to $9,999	409	67	106	84	85	25	41	22	19
$10,000 to $14,999	460	49	96	108	87	43	76	34	42
$15,000 to $19,999	493	72	111	101	82	53	75	31	44
$20,000 to $24,999	586	65	109	129	87	72	123	55	68
$25,000 to $29,999	554	56	126	117	96	53	106	40	66
$30,000 to $34,999	485	39	88	97	94	40	126	64	62
$35,000 to $39,999	525	28	87	141	106	66	97	31	67
$40,000 to $44,999	418	24	74	101	70	75	74	30	44
$45,000 to $49,999	373	18	82	87	71	44	71	33	38
$50,000 to $54,999	320	18	57	80	69	38	59	19	40
$55,000 to $59,999	297	4	40	62	100	51	40	21	19
$60,000 to $64,999	275	7	37	72	83	31	45	25	19
$65,000 to $69,999	182	7	21	39	56	31	29	14	15
$70,000 to $74,999	219	5	23	50	74	37	30	19	11
$75,000 to $79,999	157	4	22	33	49	22	28	15	13
$80,000 to $84,999	153	6	14	50	40	16	28	22	5
$85,000 to $89,999	139	12	8	19	43	31	26	12	14
$90,000 to $94,999	130	2	20	24	27	42	15	7	9
$95,000 to $99,999	92	1	12	17	40	6	16	11	6
$100,000 to $124,999	340	12	34	77	103	54	60	21	40
$125,000 to $149,999	144	16	11	38	34	21	24	13	11
$150,000 to $174,999	72	3	2	18	26	7	15	8	7
$175,000 to $199,999	44	3	1	15	8	11	4	3	1
$200,000 or more	100	9	5	22	52	10	2	2	0
Median income	$38,131	$23,373	$30,241	$39,295	$48,373	$44,628	$37,560	$39,000	$36,995

PERCENT DISTRIBUTION

	total	15 to 24	25 to 34	35 to 44	45 to 54	55 to 64	65 or older total	65 to 74	75 or older
Non-Hispanic white female-headed families	**100.0%**	**100.0%**	**100.0%**	**100.0%**	**100.0%**	**100.0%**	**100.0%**	**100.0%**	**100.0%**
Under $25,000	31.1	52.7	39.7	29.5	25.0	24.9	26.9	26.8	26.9
$25,000 to $49,999	32.4	28.7	36.0	33.1	26.4	30.3	38.8	35.6	41.7
$50,000 to $74,999	17.8	7.1	14.0	18.5	23.1	20.5	16.6	17.6	15.6
$75,000 to $99,999	9.2	4.3	6.0	8.7	12.0	12.8	9.3	12.1	7.1
$100,000 or more	9.6	7.5	4.2	10.4	13.5	11.2	8.6	8.5	8.9

Note: Non-Hispanic whites are those who identify themselves as being white alone and not Hispanic.
Source: Bureau of the Census, 2011 Current Population Survey, Internet site http://www.census.gov/hhes/www/cpstables/032011/hhinc/toc.htm; calculations by New Strategist

Male-Headed Families Have Average Incomes

The median income of male-headed families is about the same as the national median.

Male-headed families are the least-common household type and account for only 5 percent of the nation's households. In 2010, there were 5.6 million male-headed families versus 15.0 million families headed by women. The median income of male-headed families stood at $49,718 in 2010, a substantial 55 percent higher than the median income of female-headed families and slightly above the $49,445 national median.

The incomes of male-headed families peak in the 55-to-64 age group—at $53,323 in 2010. Male family heads under age 25 have the lowest incomes, a median of $41,003 in 2010.

Black male-headed families had a median income of $38,398 in 2010, which was 71 percent as high as the $54,452 median of their non-Hispanic white counterparts. Hispanic male-headed families had a median income of $44,224. Asian male-headed families had the highest incomes—a median of $63,056.

■ Male-headed families are more likely than female-headed families to include two or more earners, which explains their higher incomes.

Among male-headed families, Asians have the highest incomes

(median income of male-headed families by race and Hispanic origin, 2010)

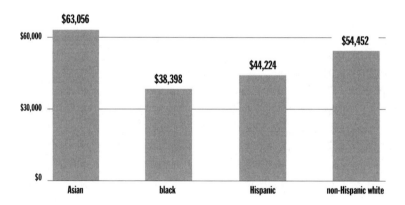

Table 1.36 Male-Headed Families by Household Income and Age of Householder, 2010: Total Male-Headed Families

(number and percent distribution of male-headed families by household income and age of householder, 2010; male-headed families in thousands as of 2011)

	total	15 to 24	25 to 34	35 to 44	45 to 54	55 to 64	65 or older total	65 to 74	75 or older
Total male-headed families	**5,559**	**825**	**1,234**	**1,141**	**1,150**	**672**	**537**	**300**	**237**
Under $5,000	125	22	22	23	38	14	5	0	5
$5,000 to $9,999	172	47	43	27	29	10	16	11	5
$10,000 to $14,999	227	46	54	42	43	22	19	13	5
$15,000 to $19,999	283	72	49	42	58	33	29	25	4
$20,000 to $24,999	370	63	91	70	73	31	42	25	17
$25,000 to $29,999	343	55	66	65	62	48	46	25	21
$30,000 to $34,999	332	45	81	77	58	47	25	17	7
$35,000 to $39,999	323	53	76	71	62	27	35	17	18
$40,000 to $44,999	366	45	89	77	81	39	35	13	22
$45,000 to $49,999	253	39	58	44	49	32	30	13	17
$50,000 to $54,999	310	23	61	75	72	49	31	10	21
$55,000 to $59,999	244	40	47	60	48	29	20	14	6
$60,000 to $64,999	307	48	69	57	62	33	38	23	15
$65,000 to $69,999	181	19	31	39	46	21	25	18	7
$70,000 to $74,999	219	18	48	65	37	36	15	4	11
$75,000 to $79,999	143	14	39	26	30	29	4	2	3
$80,000 to $84,999	170	20	35	46	46	19	4	1	3
$85,000 to $89,999	133	11	18	32	35	26	11	5	6
$90,000 to $94,999	100	13	24	20	21	17	5	3	2
$95,000 to $99,999	105	14	27	19	22	13	11	9	2
$100,000 to $124,999	378	47	86	79	81	40	45	22	24
$125,000 to $149,999	183	29	44	47	37	14	9	5	3
$150,000 to $174,999	101	11	13	19	22	24	11	8	3
$175,000 to $199,999	57	7	23	4	13	3	4	3	1
$200,000 or more	133	24	35	14	23	16	21	12	9
Median income	$49,718	$41,003	$48,900	$51,637	$51,091	$53,323	$48,405	$46,178	$49,402

PERCENT DISTRIBUTION

	total	15 to 24	25 to 34	35 to 44	45 to 54	55 to 64	65 or older total	65 to 74	75 or older
Total male-headed families	**100.0%**	**100.0%**	**100.0%**	**100.0%**	**100.0%**	**100.0%**	**100.0%**	**100.0%**	**100.0%**
Under $25,000	21.2	30.3	21.0	17.9	21.0	16.4	20.7	24.7	15.2
$25,000 to $49,999	29.1	28.7	30.0	29.3	27.1	28.7	31.8	28.3	35.9
$50,000 to $74,999	22.7	17.9	20.7	25.9	23.0	25.0	24.0	23.0	25.3
$75,000 to $99,999	11.7	8.7	11.6	12.5	13.4	15.5	6.5	6.7	6.8
$100,000 or more	15.3	14.3	16.3	14.3	15.3	14.4	16.8	16.7	16.9

Source: Bureau of the Census, 2011 Current Population Survey, Internet site http://www.census.gov/hhes/www/cpstables/ 032011/hhinc/toc.htm; calculations by New Strategist

Table 1.37 Male-Headed Families by Household Income and Age of Householder, 2010: Asian Male-Headed Families

(number and percent distribution of Asian male-headed families by household income and age of householder, 2010; male-headed families in thousands as of 2011)

	total	under 45	45 or older
Asian male-headed families	**291**	**204**	**87**
Under $5,000	7	0	8
$5,000 to $9,999	12	8	4
$10,000 to $14,999	5	4	2
$15,000 to $19,999	10	6	4
$20,000 to $24,999	19	10	9
$25,000 to $29,999	9	6	3
$30,000 to $34,999	8	7	1
$35,000 to $39,999	6	4	2
$40,000 to $44,999	14	10	4
$45,000 to $49,999	19	13	7
$50,000 to $54,999	15	6	10
$55,000 to $59,999	16	14	2
$60,000 to $64,999	15	9	5
$65,000 to $69,999	17	17	1
$70,000 to $74,999	9	6	3
$75,000 to $79,999	6	5	0
$80,000 to $84,999	9	8	1
$85,000 to $89,999	6	3	3
$90,000 to $94,999	9	5	3
$95,000 to $99,999	6	3	2
$100,000 to $124,999	26	22	4
$125,000 to $149,999	14	14	0
$150,000 to $174,999	10	9	0
$175,000 to $199,999	5	4	2
$200,000 or more	21	16	6
Median income	$63,056	$66,471	$49,643

PERCENT DISTRIBUTION

Asian male-headed families	**100.0%**	**100.0%**	**100.0%**
Under $25,000	18.2	13.7	31.0
$25,000 to $49,999	19.2	19.6	19.5
$50,000 to $74,999	24.7	25.5	24.1
$75,000 to $99,999	12.4	11.8	10.3
$100,000 or more	26.1	31.9	13.8

Note: Asians are those who identify themselves as being of the race alone and those who identify themselves as being of the race in combination with other races.
Source: Bureau of the Census, 2011 Current Population Survey, Internet site http://www.census.gov/hhes/www/cpstables/032011/hhinc/toc.htm; calculations by New Strategist

Table 1.38 Male-Headed Families by Household Income and Age of Householder, 2010: Black Male-Headed Families

(number and percent distribution of black male-headed families by household income and age of householder, 2010; male-headed families in thousands as of 2011)

	total	under 45	45 or older
Black male-headed families	**954**	**582**	**371**
Under $5,000	37	24	13
$5,000 to $9,999	55	31	24
$10,000 to $14,999	62	33	30
$15,000 to $19,999	56	34	22
$20,000 to $24,999	82	47	35
$25,000 to $29,999	83	44	40
$30,000 to $34,999	68	44	24
$35,000 to $39,999	54	38	16
$40,000 to $44,999	58	43	14
$45,000 to $49,999	44	28	17
$50,000 to $54,999	44	32	13
$55,000 to $59,999	26	16	10
$60,000 to $64,999	27	21	5
$65,000 to $69,999	29	17	12
$70,000 to $74,999	40	23	17
$75,000 to $79,999	20	10	11
$80,000 to $84,999	23	13	11
$85,000 to $89,999	19	9	10
$90,000 to $94,999	11	6	6
$95,000 to $99,999	9	4	5
$100,000 to $124,999	52	32	19
$125,000 to $149,999	27	16	9
$150,000 to $174,999	16	8	7
$175,000 to $199,999	5	4	1
$200,000 or more	10	7	4
Median income	$38,398	$39,474	$34,479

PERCENT DISTRIBUTION

	total	under 45	45 or older
Black male-headed families	**100.0%**	**100.0%**	**100.0%**
Under $25,000	30.6	29.0	33.4
$25,000 to $49,999	32.2	33.8	29.9
$50,000 to $74,999	17.4	18.7	15.4
$75,000 to $99,999	8.6	7.2	11.6
$100,000 or more	11.5	11.5	10.8

Note: Blacks are those who identify themselves as being of the race alone and those who identify themselves as being of the race in combination with other races.
Source: Bureau of the Census, 2011 Current Population Survey, Internet site http://www.census.gov/hhes/www/cpstables/ 032011/hhinc/toc.htm; calculations by New Strategist

Table 1.39 Male-Headed Families by Household Income and Age of Householder, 2010: Hispanic Male-Headed Families

(number and percent distribution of Hispanic male-headed families by household income and age of householder, 2010; male-headed families in thousands as of 2011)

	total	under 45	45 or older
Hispanic male-headed families	**1,180**	**852**	**327**
Under $5,000	22	21	1
$5,000 to $9,999	39	34	4
$10,000 to $14,999	57	45	12
$15,000 to $19,999	57	44	13
$20,000 to $24,999	103	78	26
$25,000 to $29,999	80	59	22
$30,000 to $34,999	97	69	27
$35,000 to $39,999	73	55	18
$40,000 to $44,999	74	52	22
$45,000 to $49,999	61	48	14
$50,000 to $54,999	80	45	35
$55,000 to $59,999	39	30	9
$60,000 to $64,999	59	46	13
$65,000 to $69,999	36	23	13
$70,000 to $74,999	32	19	13
$75,000 to $79,999	39	28	11
$80,000 to $84,999	43	36	6
$85,000 to $89,999	24	13	11
$90,000 to $94,999	21	15	6
$95,000 to $99,999	20	14	6
$100,000 to $124,999	64	43	20
$125,000 to $149,999	33	21	13
$150,000 to $174,999	13	6	6
$175,000 to $199,999	4	2	2
$200,000 or more	11	8	3
Median income	$44,224	$42,019	$50,643

PERCENT DISTRIBUTION

	total	under 45	45 or older
Hispanic male-headed families	**100.0%**	**100.0%**	**100.0%**
Under $25,000	23.6	26.1	17.1
$25,000 to $49,999	32.6	33.2	31.5
$50,000 to $74,999	20.8	19.1	25.4
$75,000 to $99,999	12.5	12.4	12.2
$100,000 or more	10.6	9.4	13.5

Source: Bureau of the Census, 2011 Current Population Survey, Internet site http://www.census.gov/hhes/www/cpstables/032011/hhinc/toc.htm; calculations by New Strategist

Table 1.40 Male-Headed Families by Household Income and Age of Householder, 2010: Non-Hispanic White Male-Headed Families

(number and percent distribution of non-Hispanic white male-headed families by household income and age of householder, 2010; male-headed families in thousands as of 2011)

	total	15 to 24	25 to 34	35 to 44	45 to 54	55 to 64	65 or older total	65 to 74	75 or older
Non-Hispanic white male-headed families	**3,078**	**339**	**586**	**606**	**734**	**435**	**378**	**206**	**172**
Under $5,000	50	1	8	10	23	7	0	0	0
$5,000 to $9,999	62	11	13	15	18	1	3	3	0
$10,000 to $14,999	102	23	20	14	22	13	10	10	1
$15,000 to $19,999	156	28	27	25	35	21	20	16	4
$20,000 to $24,999	162	23	44	23	32	12	28	19	10
$25,000 to $29,999	172	11	35	32	38	27	29	15	14
$30,000 to $34,999	155	14	30	38	34	28	11	10	0
$35,000 to $39,999	182	28	32	36	38	19	29	13	16
$40,000 to $44,999	216	18	38	48	52	32	29	11	18
$45,000 to $49,999	122	9	23	20	30	16	25	10	15
$50,000 to $54,999	174	10	25	45	40	33	20	5	15
$55,000 to $59,999	158	23	21	41	33	23	17	11	6
$60,000 to $64,999	197	19	45	27	51	26	30	21	9
$65,000 to $69,999	104	8	13	16	37	13	18	11	7
$70,000 to $74,999	141	11	32	43	21	24	11	0	11
$75,000 to $79,999	78	4	16	19	21	16	3	0	3
$80,000 to $84,999	94	11	15	19	35	13	2	0	2
$85,000 to $89,999	84	8	9	19	26	16	6	0	6
$90,000 to $94,999	59	9	14	11	12	12	1	1	0
$95,000 to $99,999	70	7	19	12	14	9	8	6	2
$100,000 to $124,999	237	26	43	45	57	27	39	18	22
$125,000 to $149,999	106	16	24	24	23	10	8	5	2
$150,000 to $174,999	64	5	1	12	16	19	11	8	3
$175,000 to $199,999	42	4	18	3	12	2	3	2	1
$200,000 or more	89	14	20	7	15	16	17	10	7
Median income	$54,452	$50,958	$54,363	$54,587	$55,561	$56,361	$51,217	$48,359	$52,310

PERCENT DISTRIBUTION

	total	15 to 24	25 to 34	35 to 44	45 to 54	55 to 64	65 or older total	65 to 74	75 or older
Non-Hispanic white male-headed families	**100.0%**	**100.0%**	**100.0%**	**100.0%**	**100.0%**	**100.0%**	**100.0%**	**100.0%**	**100.0%**
Under $25,000	17.3	25.4	19.1	14.4	17.7	12.4	16.1	23.3	8.7
$25,000 to $49,999	27.5	23.6	27.0	28.7	26.2	28.0	32.5	28.6	36.6
$50,000 to $74,999	25.1	20.9	23.2	28.4	24.8	27.4	25.4	23.3	27.9
$75,000 to $99,999	12.5	11.5	12.5	13.2	14.7	15.2	5.3	3.4	7.6
$100,000 or more	17.5	19.2	18.1	15.0	16.8	17.0	20.6	20.9	20.3

Note: Non-Hispanic whites are those who identify themselves as being white alone and not Hispanic.
Source: Bureau of the Census, 2011 Current Population Survey, Internet site http://www.census.gov/hhes/www/cpstables/032011/hhinc/toc.htm; calculations by New Strategist

Women Who Live Alone Have the Lowest Incomes

Most women who live alone are older, which accounts for their low incomes.

Households headed by people who live alone are the second-most-common household type in the United States. They outnumber married couples with children under age 18 at home and are second only to married couples without children at home. Among single-person households, those headed by women are more numerous than those headed by men—18 million versus 15 million.

Women who live alone have much lower incomes than their male counterparts. The median income of women who live alone stood at $22,196 in 2010—the lowest median of any household type and only 73 percent as high as the median income of men who live alone. But there is great variation in the incomes of women who live alone by age.

Sixty-four percent of women who live alone are aged 55 or older, and 45 percent are aged 65 or older. Many older women who live alone are widows and not in the workforce, which explains their low incomes. The median income of women aged 65 or older who live alone was just $17,759 in 2010. In contrast, younger women who live alone have much higher incomes. Those aged 25 to 44 had a median income of more than $30,000 in 2010. Women aged 25 to 34 who live alone had a median income almost as high as their male counterparts—$35,097 for women versus $35,628 for men.

Older black and Hispanic women who live alone have the lowest incomes of any householders in the nation. The median income of black women aged 75 or older who live alone stood at $12,139 in 2010. For Hispanics, the figure was an even lower $11,238.

■ The incomes of older women who live alone should rise as more of the working women of the baby-boom generation—with their own pensions, retirement savings, and Social Security benefits—enter the 55-or-older age group.

Among women who live alone, those aged 25 to 44 have the highest incomes

(median household income of women who live alone, by age, 2010)

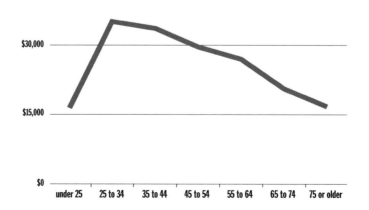

Table 1.41 Women Who Live Alone by Household Income and Age of Householder, 2010: Total Women Who Live Alone

(number and percent distribution of women who live alone by household income and age of householder, 2010; women who live alone in thousands as of 2011)

	total	15 to 24	25 to 34	35 to 44	45 to 54	55 to 64	65 or older total	65 to 74	75 or older
Total women who live alone	18,184	711	1,839	1,390	2,538	3,613	8,094	3,207	4,887
Under $5,000	1,143	164	120	156	208	241	255	116	139
$5,000 to $9,999	1,950	86	91	92	279	434	969	362	607
$10,000 to $14,999	2,754	86	95	100	204	423	1,846	576	1,270
$15,000 to $19,999	2,481	68	135	107	192	371	1,608	510	1,098
$20,000 to $24,999	1,544	70	158	73	214	233	796	269	526
$25,000 to $29,999	1,437	46	160	83	184	266	698	273	425
$30,000 to $34,999	1,084	27	156	103	164	231	404	160	243
$35,000 to $39,999	894	42	164	76	131	186	294	160	134
$40,000 to $44,999	841	23	151	71	175	197	223	133	90
$45,000 to $49,999	620	29	101	67	120	128	175	102	74
$50,000 to $54,999	583	18	117	75	91	147	134	86	47
$55,000 to $59,999	414	17	59	48	99	97	94	58	36
$60,000 to $64,999	413	7	43	62	75	121	107	83	24
$65,000 to $69,999	302	8	56	44	46	69	79	47	32
$70,000 to $74,999	349	4	65	28	70	111	70	48	22
$75,000 to $79,999	171	2	19	37	29	48	36	16	20
$80,000 to $84,999	144	4	33	19	32	28	28	17	11
$85,000 to $89,999	132	0	12	23	36	33	27	23	3
$90,000 to $94,999	133	0	15	8	25	34	50	28	22
$95,000 to $99,999	75	0	7	10	20	14	24	17	7
$100,000 to $124,999	346	6	36	48	84	95	75	51	24
$125,000 to $149,999	146	0	17	18	17	48	45	25	19
$150,000 to $174,999	97	0	15	12	17	24	28	25	3
$175,000 to $199,999	35	0	5	8	0	7	15	12	3
$200,000 or more	99	5	8	23	24	24	14	7	7
Median income	$22,196	$16,415	$35,097	$33,602	$29,592	$26,980	$17,759	$20,601	$16,727

PERCENT DISTRIBUTION

	total	15 to 24	25 to 34	35 to 44	45 to 54	55 to 64	65 or older total	65 to 74	75 or older
Total women who live alone	100.0%	100.0%	100.0%	100.0%	100.0%	100.0%	100.0%	100.0%	100.0%
Under $25,000	54.3	66.7	32.6	38.0	43.2	47.1	67.6	57.2	74.5
$25,000 to $49,999	26.8	23.5	39.8	28.8	30.5	27.9	22.2	25.8	19.8
$50,000 to $74,999	11.3	7.6	18.5	18.5	15.0	15.1	6.0	10.0	3.3
$75,000 to $99,999	3.6	0.8	4.7	7.0	5.6	4.3	2.0	3.1	1.3
$100,000 or more	4.0	1.5	4.4	7.8	5.6	5.5	2.2	3.7	1.1

Source: Bureau of the Census, 2011 Current Population Survey, Internet site http://www.census.gov/hhes/www/cpstables/ 032011/hhinc/toc.htm; calculations by New Strategist

Table 1.42 Women Who Live Alone by Household Income and Age of Householder, 2010: Asian Women Who Live Alone

(number and percent distribution of Asian women who live alone by household income and age of householder, 2010; women who live alone in thousands as of 2011)

	total	under 45	45 or older
Asian women who live alone	**558**	**214**	**345**
Under $5,000	59	22	37
$5,000 to $9,999	52	11	41
$10,000 to $14,999	66	8	59
$15,000 to $19,999	57	16	41
$20,000 to $24,999	37	18	20
$25,000 to $29,999	39	12	26
$30,000 to $34,999	27	8	19
$35,000 to $39,999	17	12	5
$40,000 to $44,999	25	19	5
$45,000 to $49,999	14	11	2
$50,000 to $54,999	28	12	16
$55,000 to $59,999	14	7	7
$60,000 to $64,999	24	9	15
$65,000 to $69,999	16	10	6
$70,000 to $74,999	6	4	2
$75,000 to $79,999	12	2	11
$80,000 to $84,999	6	4	2
$85,000 to $89,999	4	2	2
$90,000 to $94,999	9	3	6
$95,000 to $99,999	2	0	1
$100,000 to $124,999	28	15	14
$125,000 to $149,999	7	4	3
$150,000 to $174,999	6	5	1
$175,000 to $199,999	0	0	0
$200,000 or more	4	1	3
Median income	$25,523	$40,000	$19,329

PERCENT DISTRIBUTION

	total	under 45	45 or older
Asian women who live alone	**100.0%**	**100.0%**	**100.0%**
Under $25,000	48.6	35.0	57.4
$25,000 to $49,999	21.9	29.0	16.5
$50,000 to $74,999	15.8	19.6	13.3
$75,000 to $99,999	5.9	5.1	6.4
$100,000 or more	8.1	11.7	6.1

Note: Asians are those who identify themselves as being of the race alone and those who identify themselves as being of the race in combination with other races.
Source: Bureau of the Census, 2011 Current Population Survey, Internet site http://www.census.gov/hhes/www/cpstables/032011/hhinc/toc.htm; calculations by New Strategist

Table 1.43 Women Who Live Alone by Household Income and Age of Householder, 2010: Black Women Who Live Alone

(number and percent distribution of black women who live alone by household income and age of householder, 2010; women who live alone in thousands as of 2011)

	total	15 to 24	25 to 34	35 to 44	45 to 54	55 to 64	65 or older total	65 to 74	75 or older
Black women who live alone	2,933	212	394	354	557	607	808	433	375
Under $5,000	320	52	49	52	73	49	46	18	27
$5,000 to $9,999	458	24	23	31	67	129	183	82	102
$10,000 to $14,999	479	34	28	36	66	77	237	118	119
$15,000 to $19,999	315	21	39	30	55	66	106	46	60
$20,000 to $24,999	224	19	44	20	52	40	50	31	19
$25,000 to $29,999	190	19	24	19	38	53	38	31	8
$30,000 to $34,999	155	12	23	27	31	27	35	20	15
$35,000 to $39,999	142	4	45	18	19	32	24	18	6
$40,000 to $44,999	138	7	31	14	36	39	12	7	4
$45,000 to $49,999	93	4	15	19	27	18	9	9	0
$50,000 to $54,999	74	2	19	15	11	15	12	12	1
$55,000 to $59,999	62	5	17	8	13	9	11	10	0
$60,000 to $64,999	65	3	4	27	20	5	6	3	3
$65,000 to $69,999	30	2	2	10	6	6	4	2	2
$70,000 to $74,999	54	0	13	0	15	12	14	10	4
$75,000 to $79,999	30	0	4	10	2	6	7	3	5
$80,000 to $84,999	19	0	3	4	9	3	0	0	0
$85,000 to $89,999	5	0	0	0	2	2	1	1	0
$90,000 to $94,999	14	0	6	0	5	2	2	2	0
$95,000 to $99,999	9	0	2	2	1	3	0	0	0
$100,000 to $124,999	27	0	3	7	5	6	6	6	0
$125,000 to $149,999	5	0	0	0	0	2	2	2	0
$150,000 to $174,999	7	0	0	2	0	3	1	1	0
$175,000 to $199,999	5	0	0	2	0	3	0	0	0
$200,000 or more	15	5	1	3	4	0	2	0	2
Median income	$17,923	$14,115	$27,171	$27,834	$21,740	$18,160	$13,369	$14,894	$12,139

PERCENT DISTRIBUTION

	total	15 to 24	25 to 34	35 to 44	45 to 54	55 to 64	65 or older total	65 to 74	75 or older
Black women who live alone	100.0%	100.0%	100.0%	100.0%	100.0%	100.0%	100.0%	100.0%	100.0%
Under $25,000	61.2	70.8	46.4	47.7	56.2	59.5	77.0	68.1	87.2
$25,000 to $49,999	24.5	21.7	35.0	27.4	27.1	27.8	14.6	19.6	8.8
$50,000 to $74,999	9.7	5.7	14.0	16.9	11.7	7.7	5.8	8.5	2.7
$75,000 to $99,999	2.6	0.0	3.8	4.5	3.4	2.6	1.2	1.4	1.3
$100,000 or more	2.0	2.4	1.0	4.0	1.6	2.3	1.4	2.1	0.5

Note: Blacks are those who identify themselves as being of the race alone and those who identify themselves as being of the race in combination with other races.
Source: Bureau of the Census, 2011 Current Population Survey, Internet site http://www.census.gov/hhes/www/cpstables/ 032011/hhinc/toc.htm; calculations by New Strategist

Table 1.44 Women Who Live Alone by Household Income and Age of Householder, 2010: Hispanic Women Who Live Alone

(number and percent distribution of Hispanic women who live alone by household income and age of householder, 2010; women who live alone in thousands as of 2011)

	total	15 to 24	25 to 34	35 to 44	45 to 54	55 to 64	65 or older total	65 to 74	75 or older
Hispanic women who live alone	**1,098**	**64**	**151**	**89**	**171**	**225**	**398**	**203**	**195**
Under $5,000	92	17	11	7	16	17	23	17	6
$5,000 to $9,999	220	9	7	10	21	45	127	53	74
$10,000 to $14,999	219	14	18	11	26	49	102	39	63
$15,000 to $19,999	109	14	6	6	19	21	43	25	18
$20,000 to $24,999	85	4	11	11	16	18	24	15	9
$25,000 to $29,999	79	0	24	6	13	14	22	11	11
$30,000 to $34,999	53	0	16	12	11	5	9	7	2
$35,000 to $39,999	47	0	11	7	9	13	7	2	5
$40,000 to $44,999	30	3	8	4	8	4	4	4	0
$45,000 to $49,999	26	0	8	2	4	5	8	6	1
$50,000 to $54,999	28	1	8	2	4	9	4	4	0
$55,000 to $59,999	10	0	3	0	6	0	1	1	0
$60,000 to $64,999	17	0	4	3	1	4	5	4	1
$65,000 to $69,999	13	0	7	0	0	2	5	4	1
$70,000 to $74,999	9	0	0	0	2	2	4	3	2
$75,000 to $79,999	9	0	2	0	3	4	0	0	0
$80,000 to $84,999	13	0	2	1	1	3	5	3	2
$85,000 to $89,999	5	0	2	0	1	2	0	0	0
$90,000 to $94,999	1	0	1	0	0	0	0	0	0
$95,000 to $99,999	1	0	0	0	1	0	0	0	0
$100,000 to $124,999	20	2	0	2	5	7	3	3	0
$125,000 to $149,999	2	0	0	0	0	0	2	2	0
$150,000 to $174,999	2	0	0	0	2	0	0	0	0
$175,000 to $199,999	1	0	1	0	0	0	0	0	0
$200,000 or more	6	0	0	4	0	2	0	0	0
Median income	$15,593	–	$29,425	$24,649	$21,011	$15,164	$12,096	$13,789	$11,238

PERCENT DISTRIBUTION

	total	15 to 24	25 to 34	35 to 44	45 to 54	55 to 64	65 or older total	65 to 74	75 or older
Hispanic women who live alone	**100.0%**	**100.0%**	**100.0%**	**100.0%**	**100.0%**	**100.0%**	**100.0%**	**100.0%**	**100.0%**
Under $25,000	66.0	90.6	35.1	50.6	57.3	66.7	80.2	73.4	87.2
$25,000 to $49,999	21.4	4.7	44.4	34.8	26.3	18.2	12.6	14.8	9.7
$50,000 to $74,999	7.0	1.6	14.6	5.6	7.6	7.6	4.8	7.9	2.1
$75,000 to $99,999	2.6	0.0	4.6	1.1	3.5	4.0	1.3	1.5	1.0
$100,000 or more	2.8	3.1	0.7	6.7	4.1	4.0	1.3	2.5	0.0

Note: "–" means sample is too small to make a reliable estimate.
Source: Bureau of the Census, 2011 Current Population Survey, Internet site http://www.census.gov/hhes/www/cpstables/ 032011/hhinc/toc.htm; calculations by New Strategist

Table 1.45 **Women Who Live Alone by Household Income and Age of Householder, 2010: Non-Hispanic White Women Who Live Alone**

(number and percent distribution of non-Hispanic white women who live alone by household income and age of house-holder, 2010; women who live alone in thousands as of 2011)

	total	15 to 24	25 to 34	35 to 44	45 to 54	55 to 64	65 or older total	65 to 74	75 or older
Non-Hispanic white women who live alone	13,456	397	1,154	877	1,707	2,669	6,653	2,461	4,192
Under $5,000	657	77	56	87	113	157	167	73	94
$5,000 to $9,999	1,202	46	57	47	180	248	624	216	409
$10,000 to $14,999	1,975	41	45	46	112	276	1,455	392	1,063
$15,000 to $19,999	1,983	33	72	68	111	268	1,431	428	1,003
$20,000 to $24,999	1,182	46	85	39	140	171	702	215	486
$25,000 to $29,999	1,119	23	105	55	127	200	609	222	387
$30,000 to $34,999	836	15	109	61	112	193	347	131	216
$35,000 to $39,999	676	36	97	48	99	138	258	138	121
$40,000 to $44,999	641	13	98	47	128	152	203	118	85
$45,000 to $49,999	485	25	73	41	89	102	155	84	71
$50,000 to $54,999	454	10	85	58	69	122	110	64	46
$55,000 to $59,999	324	12	37	36	77	82	80	44	36
$60,000 to $64,999	308	4	28	29	49	108	90	70	20
$65,000 to $69,999	237	4	42	29	35	57	70	41	30
$70,000 to $74,999	279	4	49	28	49	97	52	35	17
$75,000 to $79,999	122	2	10	27	22	36	24	9	15
$80,000 to $84,999	108	4	26	13	21	22	24	14	10
$85,000 to $89,999	117	0	11	21	31	29	25	22	3
$90,000 to $94,999	108	0	5	8	15	31	48	26	22
$95,000 to $99,999	62	0	5	8	15	10	23	17	7
$100,000 to $124,999	268	4	21	36	61	84	64	39	23
$125,000 to $149,999	129	0	16	16	15	45	38	18	19
$150,000 to $174,999	83	0	14	6	15	21	27	24	3
$175,000 to $199,999	27	0	3	6	0	3	15	12	3
$200,000 or more	73	0	6	16	20	19	12	7	5
Median income	$23,681	$20,212	$36,938	$38,105	$32,229	$30,319	$18,620	$22,245	$17,401

PERCENT DISTRIBUTION

Non-Hispanic white women who live alone	100.0%	100.0%	100.0%	100.0%	100.0%	100.0%	100.0%	100.0%	100.0%
Under $25,000	52.0	61.2	27.3	32.7	38.4	42.0	65.8	53.8	72.9
$25,000 to $49,999	27.9	28.2	41.8	28.7	32.5	29.4	23.6	28.2	21.0
$50,000 to $74,999	11.9	8.6	20.9	20.5	16.3	17.5	6.0	10.3	3.6
$75,000 to $99,999	3.8	1.5	4.9	8.8	6.1	4.8	2.2	3.6	1.4
$100,000 or more	4.3	1.0	5.2	9.1	6.5	6.4	2.3	4.1	1.3

Note: Non-Hispanic whites are those who identify themselves as being white alone and not Hispanic.
Source: Bureau of the Census, 2011 Current Population Survey, Internet site http://www.census.gov/hhes/www/cpstables/032011/hhinc/toc.htm; calculations by New Strategist

Incomes Are Low for Men Who Live Alone

The median income of men who live alone was well below the national average in 2010.

Both men and women who live alone have below-average incomes, but the median income of men who live alone is considerably higher than that of women who live alone—$30,333 versus $22,196 in 2010. The income gap by age is much smaller, however, and almost disappears in some age groups. The median income of men aged 25 to 34 who live alone is only about $500 higher than that of their female counterparts—$35,628 versus $35,097. The incomes of men who live alone peak in the 35-to-44 age group. Men under age 25 or older who live alone have a median income of just $17,118.

Most of the income gap between men and women who live alone is explained by their differing ages. While nearly two-thirds (64 percent) of women who live alone are aged 55 or older, most men who live alone (57 percent) are under age 55. Many women who live alone are not in the labor force—they are widows who either never worked or are now retired. Most men who live alone have jobs, which is why their overall median is substantially higher.

Black and Hispanic men who live alone have incomes well below those of their non-Hispanic white counterparts. The median income of black men who live alone was just $20,819 in 2010, while the figure was slightly higher for Hispanic men at $23,552. The median income of non-Hispanic white men who live alone stood at $32,829, while their Asian counterparts had a higher median of $38,904.

■ The incomes of older men who live alone will rise in the years ahead as fewer opt for early retirement and remain in the labor force well into their sixties.

Among men who live alone, incomes peak in the 35-to-44 age group

(median household income of men who live alone, by age, 2010)

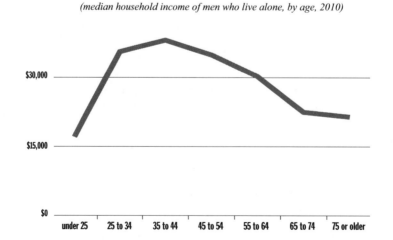

Table 1.46 Men Who Live Alone by Household Income and Age of Householder, 2010: Total Men Who Live Alone

(number and percent distribution of men who live alone by household income and age of householder, 2010; men who live alone in thousands as of 2011)

	total	15 to 24	25 to 34	35 to 44	45 to 54	55 to 64	65 or older total	65 to 74	75 or older
Total men who live alone	14,539	734	2,318	2,162	3,034	3,081	3,210	1,598	1,612
Under $5,000	1,016	125	167	149	217	242	115	60	55
$5,000 to $9,999	1,137	108	103	106	240	299	280	161	119
$10,000 to $14,999	1,493	91	152	147	269	300	534	245	289
$15,000 to $19,999	1,327	75	164	111	204	267	507	226	281
$20,000 to $24,999	1,220	80	206	156	203	231	344	173	171
$25,000 to $29,999	994	60	164	130	194	190	257	96	160
$30,000 to $34,999	973	44	174	163	190	183	218	100	118
$35,000 to $39,999	839	35	185	161	139	161	158	85	73
$40,000 to $44,999	758	27	185	143	182	107	113	63	51
$45,000 to $49,999	615	9	102	141	117	146	100	65	35
$50,000 to $54,999	682	18	141	111	163	148	101	54	47
$55,000 to $59,999	392	13	74	63	112	79	52	38	13
$60,000 to $64,999	475	13	82	97	133	69	82	41	40
$65,000 to $69,999	332	4	70	84	72	60	41	32	10
$70,000 to $74,999	280	7	71	50	80	38	34	18	16
$75,000 to $79,999	295	2	51	54	84	69	35	15	20
$80,000 to $84,999	262	4	69	43	69	55	22	7	15
$85,000 to $89,999	133	4	19	21	37	27	24	14	10
$90,000 to $94,999	147	4	10	24	37	38	34	9	26
$95,000 to $99,999	100	0	17	11	29	24	19	10	9
$100,000 to $124,999	458	4	62	99	104	148	43	19	23
$125,000 to $149,999	198	6	19	36	42	71	26	12	14
$150,000 to $174,999	131	2	9	27	30	46	17	15	1
$175,000 to $199,999	70	0	0	11	16	30	14	11	3
$200,000 or more	212	0	24	24	73	52	39	28	11
Median income	$30,333	$17,118	$35,628	$38,154	$34,978	$30,269	$21,976	$22,482	$21,457

PERCENT DISTRIBUTION

	total	15 to 24	25 to 34	35 to 44	45 to 54	55 to 64	65 or older total	65 to 74	75 or older
Total men who live alone	100.0%	100.0%	100.0%	100.0%	100.0%	100.0%	100.0%	100.0%	100.0%
Under $25,000	42.6	65.3	34.2	30.9	37.3	43.5	55.5	54.1	56.8
$25,000 to $49,999	28.7	23.8	34.9	34.1	27.1	25.5	26.4	25.6	27.1
$50,000 to $74,999	14.9	7.5	18.9	18.7	18.5	12.8	9.7	11.5	7.8
$75,000 to $99,999	6.4	1.9	7.2	7.1	8.4	6.9	4.2	3.4	5.0
$100,000 or more	7.4	1.6	4.9	9.1	8.7	11.3	4.3	5.3	3.2

Source: Bureau of the Census, 2011 Current Population Survey, Internet site http://www.census.gov/hhes/www/cpstables/ 032011/hhinc/toc.htm; calculations by New Strategist

Table 1.47 Men Who Live Alone by Household Income and Age of Householder, 2010: Asian Men Who Live Alone

(number and percent distribution of Asian men who live alone by household income and age of householder, 2010; men who live alone in thousands as of 2011)

	total	under 45	45 or older
Asian men who live alone	**437**	**258**	**177**
Under $5,000	40	25	15
$5,000 to $9,999	22	6	16
$10,000 to $14,999	38	16	21
$15,000 to $19,999	26	20	7
$20,000 to $24,999	41	22	19
$25,000 to $29,999	23	12	10
$30,000 to $34,999	15	10	5
$35,000 to $39,999	17	10	6
$40,000 to $44,999	19	13	5
$45,000 to $49,999	21	15	7
$50,000 to $54,999	35	13	21
$55,000 to $59,999	11	10	0
$60,000 to $64,999	23	16	6
$65,000 to $69,999	6	6	0
$70,000 to $74,999	3	3	0
$75,000 to $79,999	8	9	0
$80,000 to $84,999	10	5	5
$85,000 to $89,999	9	6	2
$90,000 to $94,999	4	0	4
$95,000 to $99,999	2	2	0
$100,000 to $124,999	20	14	7
$125,000 to $149,999	20	12	7
$150,000 to $174,999	5	4	2
$175,000 to $199,999	10	6	4
$200,000 or more	11	5	5
Median income	$38,904	$43,077	$30,500

PERCENT DISTRIBUTION

	total	under 45	45 or older
Asian men who live alone	**100.0%**	**100.0%**	**100.0%**
Under $25,000	38.2	34.5	44.1
$25,000 to $49,999	21.7	23.3	18.6
$50,000 to $74,999	17.8	18.6	15.3
$75,000 to $99,999	7.6	8.5	6.2
$100,000 or more	15.1	15.9	14.1

Note: Asians are those who identify themselves as being of the race alone and those who identify themselves as being of the race in combination with other races.
Source: Bureau of the Census, 2011 Current Population Survey, Internet site http://www.census.gov/hhes/www/cpstables/032011/hhinc/toc.htm; calculations by New Strategist

Table 1.48 Men Who Live Alone by Household Income and Age of Householder, 2010: Black Men Who Live Alone

(number and percent distribution of black men who live alone by household income and age of householder, 2010; men who live alone in thousands as of 2011)

	total	15 to 24	25 to 34	35 to 44	45 to 54	55 to 64	65 or older total	65 to 74	75 or older
Black men who live alone	**2,189**	**149**	**360**	**335**	**505**	**499**	**341**	**199**	**142**
Under $5,000	256	37	40	42	58	53	26	22	4
$5,000 to $9,999	318	31	30	27	59	110	60	32	28
$10,000 to $14,999	299	26	42	22	63	66	80	45	35
$15,000 to $19,999	186	6	38	18	35	49	41	22	19
$20,000 to $24,999	168	13	36	27	30	28	34	17	17
$25,000 to $29,999	156	12	30	30	37	32	16	4	12
$30,000 to $34,999	145	6	17	28	45	19	29	16	13
$35,000 to $39,999	121	6	23	28	27	26	10	8	2
$40,000 to $44,999	89	5	12	27	21	12	12	8	3
$45,000 to $49,999	80	4	10	23	19	18	5	2	3
$50,000 to $54,999	60	0	15	6	15	15	9	8	2
$55,000 to $59,999	40	0	3	10	17	6	4	4	0
$60,000 to $64,999	38	0	10	11	7	9	2	0	2
$65,000 to $69,999	42	0	11	11	13	6	0	0	0
$70,000 to $74,999	48	0	20	7	11	9	1	1	0
$75,000 to $79,999	29	2	3	5	8	9	2	2	0
$80,000 to $84,999	19	0	7	3	6	2	2	2	0
$85,000 to $89,999	10	0	0	4	6	0	0	0	0
$90,000 to $94,999	4	0	0	1	2	1	0	0	0
$95,000 to $99,999	11	0	2	2	5	1	2	0	2
$100,000 to $124,999	32	0	10	1	10	12	1	0	1
$125,000 to $149,999	9	2	0	0	2	4	1	1	0
$150,000 to $174,999	13	0	2	0	3	5	2	2	0
$175,000 to $199,999	3	0	0	0	0	3	0	0	0
$200,000 or more	13	0	0	0	9	3	2	2	0
Median income	$20,819	$11,226	$24,104	$30,213	$25,588	$16,967	$15,409	$15,029	$15,768

PERCENT DISTRIBUTION

	total	15 to 24	25 to 34	35 to 44	45 to 54	55 to 64	65 or older total	65 to 74	75 or older
Black men who live alone	**100.0%**	**100.0%**	**100.0%**	**100.0%**	**100.0%**	**100.0%**	**100.0%**	**100.0%**	**100.0%**
Under $25,000	56.1	75.8	51.7	40.6	48.5	61.3	70.7	69.3	72.5
$25,000 to $49,999	27.0	22.1	25.6	40.6	29.5	21.4	21.1	19.1	23.2
$50,000 to $74,999	10.4	0.0	16.4	13.4	12.5	9.0	4.7	6.5	2.8
$75,000 to $99,999	3.3	1.3	3.3	4.5	5.3	2.6	1.8	2.0	1.4
$100,000 or more	3.2	1.3	3.3	0.3	4.8	5.4	1.8	2.5	0.7

Note: Blacks are those who identify themselves as being of the race alone and those who identify themselves as being of the race in combination with other races.
Source: Bureau of the Census, 2011 Current Population Survey, Internet site http://www.census.gov/hhes/www/cpstables/032011/hhinc/toc.htm; calculations by New Strategist

Table 1.49 Men Who Live Alone by Household Income and Age of Householder, 2010: Hispanic Men Who Live Alone

(number and percent distribution of Hispanic men who live alone by household income and age of householder, 2010; men who live alone in thousands as of 2011)

	total	15 to 24	25 to 34	35 to 44	45 to 54	55 to 64	65 or older total	65 to 74	75 or older
Hispanic men who live alone	**1,100**	**62**	**211**	**246**	**202**	**198**	**180**	**105**	**75**
Under $5,000	78	6	12	20	19	16	5	1	4
$5,000 to $9,999	111	9	10	16	18	27	32	16	16
$10,000 to $14,999	158	12	16	27	35	27	41	14	27
$15,000 to $19,999	117	5	25	18	17	21	31	20	11
$20,000 to $24,999	110	9	22	29	20	12	19	15	4
$25,000 to $29,999	86	9	23	17	9	15	13	10	3
$30,000 to $34,999	80	3	16	25	5	23	9	7	2
$35,000 to $39,999	57	3	20	18	12	0	5	3	1
$40,000 to $44,999	57	2	17	17	5	11	6	5	1
$45,000 to $49,999	41	1	6	15	9	5	5	2	3
$50,000 to $54,999	37	0	13	8	5	7	4	4	0
$55,000 to $59,999	14	0	3	1	6	2	2	2	0
$60,000 to $64,999	27	3	6	9	2	6	1	0	1
$65,000 to $69,999	16	0	5	4	4	3	0	0	0
$70,000 to $74,999	15	0	2	3	7	2	2	2	0
$75,000 to $79,999	25	0	3	3	6	12	2	2	0
$80,000 to $84,999	5	0	0	2	4	0	0	0	0
$85,000 to $89,999	13	0	3	2	7	1	0	0	0
$90,000 to $94,999	2	0	0	0	0	0	1	0	1
$95,000 to $99,999	11	0	3	5	3	0	0	0	0
$100,000 to $124,999	18	0	4	1	7	3	2	2	0
$125,000 to $149,999	12	0	0	7	1	4	0	0	0
$150,000 to $174,999	2	0	1	0	0	0	1	1	0
$175,000 to $199,999	0	0	0	0	0	0	0	0	0
$200,000 or more	5	0	1	1	1	1	0	0	0
Median income	$23,552	–	$28,776	$28,812	$22,390	$23,800	$16,763	$20,429	$13,056

PERCENT DISTRIBUTION

Hispanic men who live alone	100.0%	100.0%	100.0%	100.0%	100.0%	100.0%	100.0%	100.0%	100.0%
Under $25,000	52.2	66.1	40.3	44.7	54.0	52.0	71.1	62.9	82.7
$25,000 to $49,999	29.2	29.0	38.9	37.4	19.8	27.3	21.1	25.7	13.3
$50,000 to $74,999	9.9	4.8	13.7	10.2	11.9	10.1	5.0	7.6	1.3
$75,000 to $99,999	5.1	0.0	4.3	4.9	9.9	6.6	1.7	1.9	1.3
$100,000 or more	3.4	0.0	2.8	3.7	4.5	4.0	1.7	2.9	0.0

Note: "–" means sample is too small to make a reliable estimate.
Source: Bureau of the Census, 2011 Current Population Survey, Internet site http://www.census.gov/hhes/www/cpstables/ 032011/hhinc/toc.htm; calculations by New Strategist

Table 1.50 Men Who Live Alone by Household Income and Age of Householder, 2010: Non-Hispanic White Men Who Live Alone

(number and percent distribution of non-Hispanic white men who live alone by household income and age of householder, 2010; men who live alone in thousands as of 2011)

	total	15 to 24	25 to 34	35 to 44	45 to 54	55 to 64	65 or older total	65 to 74	75 or older
Non-Hispanic white men who live alone	**10,675**	**485**	**1,600**	**1,464**	**2,223**	**2,298**	**2,605**	**1,254**	**1,352**
Under $5,000	633	74	102	77	138	169	74	30	44
$5,000 to $9,999	664	65	61	61	150	152	174	104	71
$10,000 to $14,999	972	52	85	89	154	195	397	175	222
$15,000 to $19,999	975	56	83	71	145	191	429	182	246
$20,000 to $24,999	892	54	139	92	143	178	287	140	147
$25,000 to $29,999	722	36	102	82	146	137	219	82	137
$30,000 to $34,999	721	31	137	103	136	135	179	77	102
$35,000 to $39,999	640	26	131	112	98	131	143	72	70
$40,000 to $44,999	582	19	145	94	153	78	94	48	46
$45,000 to $49,999	471	2	79	96	86	118	89	61	29
$50,000 to $54,999	549	17	107	90	132	125	78	39	39
$55,000 to $59,999	323	13	60	45	88	71	46	33	13
$60,000 to $64,999	387	9	59	70	120	53	76	39	37
$65,000 to $69,999	264	3	48	67	54	51	41	32	10
$70,000 to $74,999	213	7	46	40	61	27	31	16	16
$75,000 to $79,999	236	0	44	40	71	50	31	11	20
$80,000 to $84,999	223	4	59	37	54	50	21	5	15
$85,000 to $89,999	101	4	12	13	23	24	24	14	10
$90,000 to $94,999	137	4	9	22	35	37	29	9	21
$95,000 to $99,999	76	0	11	4	21	23	17	10	8
$100,000 to $124,999	385	4	42	89	82	130	38	18	19
$125,000 to $149,999	158	4	16	20	34	60	24	10	14
$150,000 to $174,999	110	0	4	27	25	42	13	12	1
$175,000 to $199,999	58	0	0	5	14	27	12	9	3
$200,000 or more	184	0	21	19	61	46	37	26	10
Median income	$32,829	$19,223	$38,149	$41,600	$40,061	$34,653	$23,671	$24,813	$22,625

PERCENT DISTRIBUTION

Non-Hispanic white men who live alone	100.0%	100.0%	100.0%	100.0%	100.0%	100.0%	100.0%	100.0%	100.0%
Under $25,000	38.7	62.1	29.4	26.6	32.8	38.5	52.2	50.3	54.0
$25,000 to $49,999	29.4	23.5	37.1	33.3	27.8	26.1	27.8	27.1	28.4
$50,000 to $74,999	16.3	10.1	20.0	21.3	20.5	14.2	10.4	12.7	8.5
$75,000 to $99,999	7.2	2.5	8.4	7.9	9.2	8.0	4.7	3.9	5.5
$100,000 or more	8.4	1.6	5.2	10.9	9.7	13.3	4.8	6.0	3.5

Note: Non-Hispanic whites are those who identify themselves as being white alone and not Hispanic.
Source: Bureau of the Census, 2011 Current Population Survey, Internet site http://www.census.gov/hhes/www/cpstables/032011/hhinc/toc.htm; calculations by New Strategist

Two-Earner Households Have Above-Average Incomes

Households with only one earner have incomes well below average.

The country's 46 million households with two or more earners account for 39 percent of the nation's 119 million households. Those with only one earner constitute another 38 percent, while households with no earners—many of them headed by retirees—account for the remaining 23 percent.

The median income of households with one earner stood at $41,711 in 2010, 16 percent below the national median of $49,445. In contrast, the median income of two-earner households was $80,884—64 percent higher than average. Only 12 percent of one-earner households have incomes of $100,000 or more versus 36 percent of households with two earners. Households with no earners had a median income of just $18,484 in 2010.

Not surprisingly, households with four or more earners have the highest incomes, a median of $117,034. More than 60 percent of households with four or more earners have incomes of $100,000 or more. Only 2 percent of households have four or more earners, however.

The median income of black households is just 59 percent as high as that of non-Hispanic white households, but among households with two earners the black median is 76 percent of the non-Hispanic white median. The overall black household median is much lower than the non-Hispanic white median because only 28 percent of black households have two or more earners versus 40 percent of non-Hispanic white households. Asian households are even more likely to have two or more earners, at 48 percent. Among two-earner households, blacks have higher incomes than Hispanics ($66,024 versus $56,229), while Asians and non-Hispanic whites have the highest incomes of all ($93,087 and $86,571, respectively).

■ The number of households with no earners should grow as the oldest boomers begin to retire.

Households with four or more earners have the highest incomes

(median income of households by number of earners, 2010)

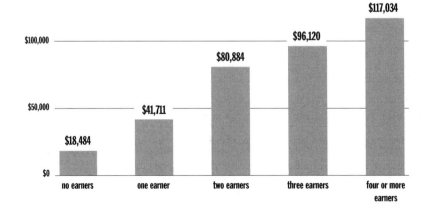

Table 1.51 Households by Income and Number of Earners, 2010: Total Households

(number and percent distribution of total households by household income and number of earners, 2010; households in thousands as of 2011)

				two or more earners			
	total	no earners	one earner	total	two earners	three earners	four or more earners
Total households	**118,682**	**27,388**	**44,922**	**46,373**	**37,470**	**6,705**	**2,197**
Under $5,000	4,176	3,216	900	60	60	0	0
$5,000 to $9,999	5,055	3,431	1,478	146	140	5	1
$10,000 to $14,999	7,061	4,293	2,427	341	321	18	2
$15,000 to $19,999	7,260	3,844	2,891	525	490	33	2
$20,000 to $24,999	6,937	2,581	3,532	825	753	67	5
$25,000 to $29,999	6,730	2,166	3,442	1,122	1,016	92	13
$30,000 to $34,999	6,148	1,524	3,354	1,270	1,129	122	19
$35,000 to $39,999	5,907	1,242	3,122	1,543	1,363	154	26
$40,000 to $44,999	5,624	930	2,986	1,707	1,504	183	20
$45,000 to $49,999	4,933	788	2,320	1,825	1,604	184	37
$50,000 to $54,999	5,088	561	2,561	1,967	1,695	223	48
$55,000 to $59,999	4,203	430	1,777	1,995	1,669	280	47
$60,000 to $64,999	4,412	443	1,877	2,092	1,777	253	62
$65,000 to $69,999	3,579	280	1,336	1,963	1,628	278	57
$70,000 to $74,999	3,769	235	1,401	2,133	1,712	344	77
$75,000 to $79,999	3,118	205	1,058	1,855	1,528	251	76
$80,000 to $84,999	3,143	159	1,013	1,971	1,590	300	81
$85,000 to $89,999	2,680	126	759	1,794	1,458	255	82
$90,000 to $94,999	2,516	125	706	1,686	1,348	252	86
$95,000 to $99,999	2,110	84	461	1,565	1,219	267	79
$100,000 to $124,999	9,008	348	2,294	6,365	4,934	1,051	380
$125,000 to $149,999	5,294	211	968	4,114	3,068	731	315
$150,000 to $174,999	3,386	64	729	2,595	1,885	498	210
$175,000 to $199,999	1,919	37	357	1,524	1,122	262	140
$200,000 or more	4,627	67	1,170	3,390	2,457	601	332
Median income	$49,445	$18,484	$41,711	$84,525	$80,884	$96,120	$117,034

PERCENT DISTRIBUTION

Total households	**100.0%**	**100.0%**	**100.0%**	**100.0%**	**100.0%**	**100.0%**	**100.0%**
Under $25,000	25.7	63.4	25.0	4.1	4.7	1.8	0.5
$25,000 to $49,999	24.7	24.3	33.9	16.1	17.7	11.0	5.2
$50,000 to $74,999	17.7	7.1	19.9	21.9	22.6	20.6	13.2
$75,000 to $99,999	11.4	2.6	8.9	19.1	19.1	19.8	18.4
$100,000 or more	20.4	2.7	12.3	38.8	35.9	46.9	62.7

Source: Bureau of the Census, 2011 Current Population Survey, Internet site http://www.census.gov/hhes/www/cpstables/ 032011/hhinc/toc.htm; calculations by New Strategist

Table 1.52 Households by Income and Number of Earners, 2010: Asian Households

(number and percent distribution of Asian households by household income and number of earners, 2010; households in thousands as of 2011)

	total	no earners	one earner	two or more earners			
				total	two earners	three earners	four or more earners
Asian households	**5,040**	**759**	**1,884**	**2,397**	**1,842**	**389**	**166**
Under $5,000	232	191	39	2	2	0	0
$5,000 to $9,999	121	80	32	9	9	0	0
$10,000 to $14,999	180	96	76	7	6	2	0
$15,000 to $19,999	226	82	125	19	19	0	0
$20,000 to $24,999	261	77	141	44	41	1	2
$25,000 to $29,999	199	44	109	46	44	1	0
$30,000 to $34,999	183	31	106	46	41	6	0
$35,000 to $39,999	175	30	84	61	56	4	2
$40,000 to $44,999	196	23	91	83	75	6	1
$45,000 to $49,999	186	13	90	83	68	15	0
$50,000 to $54,999	232	22	123	87	70	15	3
$55,000 to $59,999	144	8	62	74	65	7	2
$60,000 to $64,999	227	18	101	108	86	17	6
$65,000 to $69,999	160	9	58	93	76	17	0
$70,000 to $74,999	146	4	55	87	58	25	4
$75,000 to $79,999	119	4	47	69	51	14	4
$80,000 to $84,999	126	2	48	77	52	13	12
$85,000 to $89,999	117	1	46	71	57	5	8
$90,000 to $94,999	122	6	42	74	57	10	6
$95,000 to $99,999	91	5	19	67	47	14	5
$100,000 to $124,999	508	10	169	328	219	79	32
$125,000 to $149,999	335	1	72	260	201	44	17
$150,000 to $174,999	258	2	56	201	155	30	17
$175,000 to $199,999	135	0	17	118	86	18	14
$200,000 or more	358	0	76	282	203	46	34
Median income	$63,726	$15,777	$51,596	$99,269	$93,087	$105,123	$122,216

PERCENT DISTRIBUTION

	total	no earners	one earner	two or more earners			
				total	two earners	three earners	four or more earners
Asian households	**100.0%**	**100.0%**	**100.0%**	**100.0%**	**100.0%**	**100.0%**	**100.0%**
Under $25,000	20.2	69.3	21.9	3.4	4.2	0.8	1.2
$25,000 to $49,999	18.6	18.6	25.5	13.3	15.4	8.2	1.8
$50,000 to $74,999	18.0	8.0	21.2	18.7	19.3	20.8	9.0
$75,000 to $99,999	11.4	2.4	10.7	14.9	14.3	14.4	21.1
$100,000 or more	31.6	1.7	20.7	49.6	46.9	55.8	68.7

Note: Asians are those who identify themselves as being of the race alone and those who identify themselves as being of the race in combination with other races.
Source: Bureau of the Census, 2011 Current Population Survey, Internet site http://www.census.gov/hhes/www/cpstables/032011/hhinc/toc.htm; calculations by New Strategist

Table 1.53 Households by Income and Number of Earners, 2010: Black Households

(number and percent distribution of black households by household income and number of earners, 2010; households in thousands as of 2011)

| | total | no earners | one earner | two or more earners | | | |
				total	two earners	three earners	four or more earners
Black households	**15,613**	**4,187**	**7,098**	**4,327**	**3,515**	**646**	**166**
Under $5,000	1,174	884	275	14	14	0	0
$5,000 to $9,999	1,390	960	410	19	19	0	0
$10,000 to $14,999	1,432	806	583	43	42	1	0
$15,000 to $19,999	1,141	482	587	72	66	6	0
$20,000 to $24,999	1,163	278	764	121	111	10	0
$25,000 to $29,999	1,045	202	683	161	146	14	2
$30,000 to $34,999	957	143	632	182	155	23	4
$35,000 to $39,999	813	93	544	176	161	15	0
$40,000 to $44,999	799	75	482	242	219	21	2
$45,000 to $49,999	655	39	372	244	217	23	4
$50,000 to $54,999	606	64	306	236	220	10	5
$55,000 to $59,999	457	24	230	203	165	33	5
$60,000 to $64,999	462	13	227	222	183	30	9
$65,000 to $69,999	374	16	150	207	160	45	3
$70,000 to $74,999	442	22	176	245	190	48	6
$75,000 to $79,999	335	21	122	191	156	32	4
$80,000 to $84,999	285	11	100	174	149	22	4
$85,000 to $89,999	222	13	50	159	126	27	6
$90,000 to $94,999	202	6	47	148	103	37	8
$95,000 to $99,999	152	7	37	108	91	12	4
$100,000 to $124,999	675	18	161	496	383	78	34
$125,000 to $149,999	345	9	43	294	190	76	28
$150,000 to $174,999	213	0	49	163	101	42	18
$175,000 to $199,999	84	0	14	70	48	18	4
$200,000 or more	192	0	55	137	99	21	17
Median income	$32,106	$11,317	$31,573	$70,403	$66,024	$83,227	$109,190

PERCENT DISTRIBUTION

	total	no earners	one earner	total	two earners	three earners	four or more earners
Black households	**100.0%**	**100.0%**	**100.0%**	**100.0%**	**100.0%**	**100.0%**	**100.0%**
Under $25,000	40.4	81.4	36.9	6.2	7.2	2.6	0.0
$25,000 to $49,999	27.3	13.2	38.2	23.2	25.5	14.9	7.2
$50,000 to $74,999	15.0	3.3	15.3	25.7	26.1	25.7	16.9
$75,000 to $99,999	7.7	1.4	5.0	18.0	17.8	20.1	15.7
$100,000 or more	9.7	0.6	4.5	26.8	23.4	36.4	60.8

Note: Blacks are those who identify themselves as being of the race alone and those who identify themselves as being of the race in combination with other races.
Source: Bureau of the Census, 2011 Current Population Survey, Internet site http://www.census.gov/hhes/www/cpstables/ 032011/hhinc/toc.htm; calculations by New Strategist

Table 1.54 Households by Income and Number of Earners, 2010: Hispanic Households

(number and percent distribution of Hispanic households by household income and number of earners, 2010; households in thousands as of 2011)

	total	no earners	one earner	two or more earners total	two earners	three earners	four or more earners
Hispanic households	**13,665**	**2,030**	**5,469**	**6,165**	**4,514**	**1,125**	**526**
Under $5,000	594	444	140	10	10	0	0
$5,000 to $9,999	769	444	292	33	29	3	1
$10,000 to $14,999	1,018	396	536	86	81	4	1
$15,000 to $19,999	949	231	599	119	110	9	0
$20,000 to $24,999	1,067	159	646	262	226	33	3
$25,000 to $29,999	1,033	123	593	317	271	43	3
$30,000 to $34,999	856	57	447	352	293	50	8
$35,000 to $39,999	822	40	412	370	311	52	7
$40,000 to $44,999	707	30	303	374	297	66	11
$45,000 to $49,999	622	26	236	360	287	58	15
$50,000 to $54,999	644	25	248	370	276	68	26
$55,000 to $59,999	488	8	145	335	232	86	17
$60,000 to $64,999	508	14	160	334	245	66	23
$65,000 to $69,999	387	3	90	294	215	49	29
$70,000 to $74,999	329	8	83	239	171	48	20
$75,000 to $79,999	350	2	95	253	169	50	34
$80,000 to $84,999	328	6	75	247	162	55	31
$85,000 to $89,999	236	1	55	180	116	41	23
$90,000 to $94,999	226	2	44	179	121	31	27
$95,000 to $99,999	165	0	29	136	85	32	19
$100,000 to $124,999	665	7	109	547	343	113	92
$125,000 to $149,999	390	3	52	336	190	79	68
$150,000 to $174,999	211	0	28	183	110	41	34
$175,000 to $199,999	97	0	7	90	57	15	20
$200,000 or more	200	0	44	156	106	34	17
Median income	$37,759	$11,402	$29,207	$61,123	$56,229	$67,190	$92,518

PERCENT DISTRIBUTION

	total	no earners	one earner	two or more earners total	two earners	three earners	four or more earners
Hispanic households	**100.0%**	**100.0%**	**100.0%**	**100.0%**	**100.0%**	**100.0%**	**100.0%**
Under $25,000	32.2	82.5	40.5	8.3	10.1	4.4	1.0
$25,000 to $49,999	29.6	13.6	36.4	28.8	32.3	23.9	8.4
$50,000 to $74,999	17.2	2.9	13.3	25.5	25.2	28.2	21.9
$75,000 to $99,999	9.5	0.5	5.4	16.1	14.5	18.6	25.5
$100,000 or more	11.4	0.5	4.4	21.3	17.9	25.1	43.9

Source: Bureau of the Census, 2011 Current Population Survey, Internet site http://www.census.gov/hhes/www/cpstables/ 032011/hhinc/toc.htm; calculations by New Strategist

Table 1.55 Households by Income and Number of Earners, 2010: Non-Hispanic White Households

(number and percent distribution of non-Hispanic white households by household income and number of earners, 2010; households in thousands as of 2011)

	total	no earners	one earner	two or more earners total	two earners	three earners	four or more earners
Non-Hispanic white households	**83,471**	**20,160**	**30,139**	**33,171**	**27,329**	**4,503**	**1,339**
Under $5,000	2,138	1,663	444	31	31	0	0
$5,000 to $9,999	2,721	1,896	742	83	82	2	0
$10,000 to $14,999	4,365	2,955	1,215	196	184	11	1
$15,000 to $19,999	4,882	3,033	1,538	312	293	17	2
$20,000 to $24,999	4,399	2,046	1,952	401	376	25	0
$25,000 to $29,999	4,397	1,773	2,029	594	552	33	9
$30,000 to $34,999	4,108	1,270	2,152	686	638	41	7
$35,000 to $39,999	4,049	1,071	2,068	910	807	85	17
$40,000 to $44,999	3,882	796	2,084	1,003	905	92	6
$45,000 to $49,999	3,430	697	1,613	1,120	1,016	85	18
$50,000 to $54,999	3,575	448	1,863	1,264	1,125	121	18
$55,000 to $59,999	3,075	388	1,320	1,366	1,190	150	25
$60,000 to $64,999	3,186	398	1,378	1,410	1,251	136	22
$65,000 to $69,999	2,627	247	1,016	1,365	1,168	170	27
$70,000 to $74,999	2,827	202	1,078	1,547	1,285	215	47
$75,000 to $79,999	2,289	177	790	1,321	1,132	154	34
$80,000 to $84,999	2,370	139	776	1,455	1,216	202	36
$85,000 to $89,999	2,085	110	603	1,372	1,144	183	44
$90,000 to $94,999	1,953	110	566	1,277	1,059	172	46
$95,000 to $99,999	1,688	73	371	1,244	985	209	51
$100,000 to $124,999	7,093	310	1,840	4,940	3,953	766	221
$125,000 to $149,999	4,187	195	796	3,197	2,458	538	202
$150,000 to $174,999	2,686	60	592	2,035	1,507	385	145
$175,000 to $199,999	1,596	37	320	1,238	923	212	103
$200,000 or more	3,863	67	992	2,804	2,045	499	260
Median income	$54,620	$21,190	$47,285	$90,484	$86,571	$104,088	$129,230

PERCENT DISTRIBUTION

Non-Hispanic white households	100.0%	100.0%	100.0%	100.0%	100.0%	100.0%	100.0%
Under $25,000	22.2	57.5	19.5	3.1	3.5	1.2	0.2
$25,000 to $49,999	23.8	27.8	33.0	13.0	14.3	7.5	4.3
$50,000 to $74,999	18.3	8.3	22.1	21.0	22.0	17.6	10.4
$75,000 to $99,999	12.4	3.0	10.3	20.1	20.3	20.4	15.8
$100,000 or more	23.3	3.3	15.1	42.9	39.8	53.3	69.5

Note: Non-Hispanic whites are those who identify themselves as being white alone and not Hispanic.
Source: Bureau of the Census, 2011 Current Population Survey, Internet site http://www.census.gov/hhes/www/cpstables/032011/hhinc/toc.htm; calculations by New Strategist

Married Couples with School-Aged Children Have the Highest Incomes

Empty-nesters have lower incomes than couples with children.

Married couples with children aged 6 to 17 and none younger had a median income of $83,097 in 2010, much higher than the median income of couples with younger or no children at home. Behind these income differences are the differing ages of the couples. Those with only school-aged children at home are generally older and more likely to be in their peak earning years than those with younger children. Many couples without children at home are empty-nesters and retired, which accounts for their lower incomes.

The income pattern is the same for Asians, blacks, Hispanics, and non-Hispanic whites, although there are substantial income differences among them. Non-Hispanic white couples with children aged 6 to 17 and none younger had a median income of $92,484 in 2010. The median income of black couples with children aged 6 to 17 and none younger stood at $69,686, while their Hispanic counterparts had a much lower median of $51,503. Among Asian couples, the median income of couples with school-aged children was $95,406 in 2010.

■ Many of the nation's affluent couples have seen their incomes decline because of the economic downturn.

Couples with school-aged children are the most affluent

(median income of married couples by presence and age of children under age 18 at home, 2010)

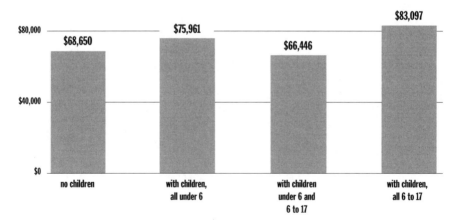

Table 1.56 Married Couples by Family Income and Presence of Children, 2010: Total Married Couples

(number and percent distribution of married couples by family income and presence and age of related children under age 18 at home, 2010; married couples in thousands as of 2011)

	total	no children	total	all under 6	some < 6, some 6 to 17	all 6 to 17
				one or more children under age 18		
Total married couples	**58,047**	**32,562**	**25,485**	**6,334**	**5,519**	**13,632**
Under $5,000	701	435	266	69	71	126
$5,000 to $9,999	523	281	241	81	71	89
$10,000 to $14,999	1,157	700	457	132	126	198
$15,000 to $19,999	1,661	1,051	610	192	196	222
$20,000 to $24,999	2,108	1,303	805	182	270	353
$25,000 to $29,999	2,432	1,549	883	222	262	398
$30,000 to $34,999	2,376	1,518	857	217	208	432
$35,000 to $39,999	2,476	1,530	946	239	268	438
$40,000 to $44,999	2,510	1,512	997	287	244	466
$45,000 to $49,999	2,362	1,408	954	224	233	498
$50,000 to $54,999	2,591	1,448	1,143	317	276	550
$55,000 to $59,999	2,298	1,323	975	240	236	500
$60,000 to $64,999	2,388	1,338	1,050	257	224	569
$65,000 to $69,999	2,158	1,190	968	209	214	545
$70,000 to $74,999	2,232	1,240	992	245	187	560
$75,000 to $79,999	1,988	1,083	904	231	157	516
$80,000 to $84,999	2,091	1,100	992	269	200	523
$85,000 to $89,999	1,884	1,056	827	202	167	459
$90,000 to $94,999	1,747	892	855	224	162	469
$95,000 to $99,999	1,520	839	681	143	135	403
$100,000 to $124,999	6,653	3,405	3,246	840	620	1,786
$125,000 to $149,999	4,143	2,215	1,929	458	341	1,131
$150,000 to $174,999	2,713	1,414	1,299	281	193	824
$175,000 to $199,999	1,537	826	711	175	123	414
$200,000 or more	3,800	1,907	1,893	397	333	1,162
Median income	$72,426	$68,650	$77,749	$75,961	$66,446	$83,097

PERCENT DISTRIBUTION

Total married couples	**100.0%**	**100.0%**	**100.0%**	**100.0%**	**100.0%**	**100.0%**
Under $25,000	10.6	11.6	9.3	10.4	13.3	7.2
$25,000 to $49,999	20.9	23.1	18.2	18.8	22.0	16.4
$50,000 to $74,999	20.1	20.1	20.1	20.0	20.6	20.0
$75,000 to $99,999	15.9	15.3	16.7	16.9	14.9	17.4
$100,000 or more	32.5	30.0	35.6	34.0	29.2	39.0

Note: The median income of married couples in this table is slightly different from the figure shown in the household income tables because this figure includes the incomes only of family members and not any unrelated members of the household.
Source: Bureau of the Census, 2011 Current Population Survey, Internet site http://www.census.gov/hhes/www/cpstables/032011/hhinc/toc.htm; calculations by New Strategist

Table 1.57 Married Couples by Family Income and Presence of Children, 2010: Asian Married Couples

(number and percent distribution of Asian married couples by family income and presence and age of related children under age 18 at home, 2010; married couples in thousands as of 2011)

			one or more children under age 18			
Asian married couples	total **2,939**	no children **1,351**	total **1,587**	all under 6 **431**	some < 6, some 6 to 17 **340**	all 6 to 17 **816**
Under $5,000	69	50	18	7	6	5
$5,000 to $9,999	19	11	8	3	3	1
$10,000 to $14,999	52	29	23	7	4	13
$15,000 to $19,999	93	54	39	19	7	13
$20,000 to $24,999	96	50	46	3	18	25
$25,000 to $29,999	92	35	58	18	8	31
$30,000 to $34,999	93	53	40	14	9	17
$35,000 to $39,999	100	54	45	16	12	18
$40,000 to $44,999	94	46	48	11	11	27
$45,000 to $49,999	94	38	56	16	12	28
$50,000 to $54,999	107	44	62	18	9	35
$55,000 to $59,999	76	46	30	6	11	13
$60,000 to $64,999	139	63	76	19	12	44
$65,000 to $69,999	93	51	42	5	13	24
$70,000 to $74,999	92	28	64	24	11	29
$75,000 to $79,999	73	35	38	12	4	22
$80,000 to $84,999	82	34	48	15	11	22
$85,000 to $89,999	85	48	37	7	17	13
$90,000 to $94,999	87	47	39	11	3	25
$95,000 to $99,999	64	28	36	8	4	24
$100,000 to $124,999	379	149	230	61	62	106
$125,000 to $149,999	242	111	131	37	25	69
$150,000 to $174,999	224	92	134	34	13	87
$175,000 to $199,999	104	44	60	24	16	24
$200,000 or more	288	110	178	37	41	100
Median income	$85,237	$78,148	$91,600	$86,215	$86,735	$95,406

PERCENT DISTRIBUTION

Asian married couples	100.0%	100.0%	100.0%	100.0%	100.0%	100.0%
Under $25,000	11.2	14.4	8.4	9.0	11.2	7.0
$25,000 to $49,999	16.1	16.7	15.6	17.4	15.3	14.8
$50,000 to $74,999	17.3	17.2	17.3	16.7	16.5	17.8
$75,000 to $99,999	13.3	14.2	12.5	12.3	11.5	13.0
$100,000 or more	42.1	37.5	46.2	44.8	46.2	47.3

Note: Asians are those who identify themselves as being of the race alone and those who identify themselves as being of the race in combination with other races. The median income of married couples in this table is slightly different from the figure shown in the household income tables because this figure includes the incomes only of family members and not any unrelated members of the household.
Source: Bureau of the Census, 2011 Current Population Survey, Internet site http://www.census.gov/hhes/www/cpstables/ 032011/hhinc/toc.htm; calculations by New Strategist

Table 1.58 Married Couples by Family Income and Presence of Children, 2010: Black Married Couples

(number and percent distribution of black married couples by family income and presence and age of related children under age 18 at home, 2010; married couples in thousands as of 2011)

Black married couples	total	no children	one or more children under age 18			
			total	all under 6	some < 6, some 6 to 17	all 6 to 17
Black married couples	**4,354**	**2,219**	**2,135**	**487**	**491**	**1,158**
Under $5,000	87	51	35	6	13	16
$5,000 to $9,999	58	14	44	22	9	14
$10,000 to $14,999	107	67	40	16	7	17
$15,000 to $19,999	139	81	58	17	19	21
$20,000 to $24,999	206	99	108	26	38	44
$25,000 to $29,999	230	129	101	25	24	53
$30,000 to $34,999	240	138	102	29	30	43
$35,000 to $39,999	180	101	78	11	22	46
$40,000 to $44,999	241	118	122	38	25	60
$45,000 to $49,999	213	123	89	13	22	54
$50,000 to $54,999	229	122	107	24	21	62
$55,000 to $59,999	189	95	94	14	22	58
$60,000 to $64,999	194	91	104	28	31	44
$65,000 to $69,999	169	81	88	18	20	50
$70,000 to $74,999	172	93	80	16	19	44
$75,000 to $79,999	180	91	89	12	20	57
$80,000 to $84,999	160	80	80	25	11	45
$85,000 to $89,999	144	66	78	9	29	40
$90,000 to $94,999	118	47	70	26	6	39
$95,000 to $99,999	88	39	49	9	13	27
$100,000 to $124,999	412	197	216	41	36	139
$125,000 to $149,999	251	123	129	19	26	85
$150,000 to $174,999	152	81	72	21	9	45
$175,000 to $199,999	55	27	28	5	4	20
$200,000 or more	137	66	71	19	13	38
Median income	$61,081	$58,111	$63,400	$60,434	$57,876	$69,686

PERCENT DISTRIBUTION

Black married couples						
Black married couples	**100.0%**	**100.0%**	**100.0%**	**100.0%**	**100.0%**	**100.0%**
Under $25,000	13.7	14.1	13.3	17.9	17.5	9.7
$25,000 to $49,999	25.4	27.4	23.0	23.8	25.1	22.1
$50,000 to $74,999	21.9	21.7	22.2	20.5	23.0	22.3
$75,000 to $99,999	15.8	14.6	17.1	16.6	16.1	18.0
$100,000 or more	23.1	22.3	24.2	21.6	17.9	28.2

Note: Blacks are those who identify themselves as being of the race alone and those who identify themselves as being of the race in combination with other races. The median income of married couples in this table is slightly different from the figure shown in the household income tables because this figure includes the incomes only of family members and not any unrelated members of the household.
Source: Bureau of the Census, 2011 Current Population Survey, Internet site http://www.census.gov/hhes/www/cpstables/ 032011/hhinc/toc.htm; calculations by New Strategist

Table 1.59 Married Couples by Family Income and Presence of Children, 2010: Hispanic Married Couples

(number and percent distribution of Hispanic married couples by family income and presence and age of related children under age 18 at home, 2010; married couples in thousands as of 2011)

			one or more children under age 18			
Hispanic married couples	total	no children	total	all under 6	some < 6, some 6 to 17	all 6 to 17
Hispanic married couples	**6,726**	**2,296**	**4,430**	**935**	**1,397**	**2,098**
Under $5,000	158	62	96	20	29	47
$5,000 to $9,999	141	43	98	17	41	41
$10,000 to $14,999	297	93	203	49	77	77
$15,000 to $19,999	360	118	242	62	93	88
$20,000 to $24,999	467	156	311	66	117	128
$25,000 to $29,999	487	171	316	69	128	119
$30,000 to $34,999	383	116	268	40	87	140
$35,000 to $39,999	419	132	287	54	94	139
$40,000 to $44,999	341	107	234	50	76	108
$45,000 to $49,999	315	96	219	28	73	119
$50,000 to $54,999	361	122	240	51	80	109
$55,000 to $59,999	306	94	212	43	63	106
$60,000 to $64,999	304	99	205	41	49	115
$65,000 to $69,999	255	76	179	37	51	91
$70,000 to $74,999	204	62	143	24	40	79
$75,000 to $79,999	204	71	133	29	28	76
$80,000 to $84,999	206	70	136	25	40	71
$85,000 to $89,999	144	55	89	13	22	53
$90,000 to $94,999	156	64	91	31	29	31
$95,000 to $99,999	93	37	56	8	13	35
$100,000 to $124,999	464	170	293	94	66	134
$125,000 to $149,999	280	111	169	35	46	90
$150,000 to $174,999	157	77	80	23	21	38
$175,000 to $199,999	73	32	41	8	13	21
$200,000 or more	153	67	86	20	22	44
Median income	$49,914	$52,040	$48,307	$51,257	$41,700	$51,503

PERCENT DISTRIBUTION

Hispanic married couples	**100.0%**	**100.0%**	**100.0%**	**100.0%**	**100.0%**	**100.0%**
Under $25,000	21.2	20.6	21.4	22.9	25.6	18.2
$25,000 to $49,999	28.9	27.1	29.9	25.8	32.8	29.8
$50,000 to $74,999	21.3	19.7	22.1	21.0	20.3	23.8
$75,000 to $99,999	11.9	12.9	11.4	11.3	9.4	12.7
$100,000 or more	16.8	19.9	15.1	19.3	12.0	15.6

Note: The median income of married couples in this table is slightly different from the figure shown in the household income tables because this figure includes the incomes only of family members and not any unrelated members of the household.
Source: Bureau of the Census, 2011 Current Population Survey, Internet site http://www.census.gov/hhes/www/cpstables/ 032011/hhinc/toc.htm; calculations by New Strategist

Table 1.60 Married Couples by Family Income and Presence of Children, 2010: Non-Hispanic White Married Couples

(number and percent distribution of non-Hispanic white married couples by family income and presence and age of related children under age 18 at home, 2010; married couples in thousands as of 2011)

	total	no children	one or more children under age 18			
			total	all under 6	some < 6, some 6 to 17	all 6 to 17
Non-Hispanic white married couples	**43,562**	**26,419**	**17,143**	**4,464**	**3,244**	**9,435**
Under $5,000	378	270	108	35	24	50
$5,000 to $9,999	302	207	96	42	21	32
$10,000 to $14,999	684	494	190	62	37	91
$15,000 to $19,999	1,057	792	266	92	76	98
$20,000 to $24,999	1,317	983	334	84	96	154
$25,000 to $29,999	1,608	1,196	411	112	103	195
$30,000 to $34,999	1,656	1,207	449	131	86	233
$35,000 to $39,999	1,750	1,223	527	158	138	231
$40,000 to $44,999	1,811	1,235	576	186	125	265
$45,000 to $49,999	1,718	1,137	582	166	122	293
$50,000 to $54,999	1,874	1,146	728	224	163	342
$55,000 to $59,999	1,709	1,078	631	178	137	316
$60,000 to $64,999	1,739	1,081	658	167	131	360
$65,000 to $69,999	1,621	965	656	152	128	376
$70,000 to $74,999	1,739	1,048	690	177	112	402
$75,000 to $79,999	1,504	874	630	173	104	353
$80,000 to $84,999	1,618	900	718	203	137	377
$85,000 to $89,999	1,485	874	611	171	97	342
$90,000 to $94,999	1,377	729	648	158	121	368
$95,000 to $99,999	1,260	726	534	116	104	314
$100,000 to $124,999	5,343	2,864	2,478	646	446	1,388
$125,000 to $149,999	3,345	1,854	1,491	371	240	879
$150,000 to $174,999	2,157	1,157	1,000	202	150	650
$175,000 to $199,999	1,299	723	576	137	90	349
$200,000 or more	3,210	1,657	1,552	319	257	977
Median income	$77,416	$70,827	$87,166	$82,065	$80,530	$92,484

PERCENT DISTRIBUTION

Non-Hispanic white married couples	**100.0%**	**100.0%**	**100.0%**	**100.0%**	**100.0%**	**100.0%**
Under $25,000	8.6	10.4	5.8	7.1	7.8	4.5
$25,000 to $49,999	19.6	22.7	14.8	16.9	17.7	12.9
$50,000 to $74,999	19.9	20.1	19.6	20.1	20.7	19.0
$75,000 to $99,999	16.6	15.5	18.3	18.4	17.4	18.6
$100,000 or more	35.2	31.2	41.4	37.5	36.5	45.0

Note: Non-Hispanic whites are those who identify themselves as being white alone and not Hispanic. The median income of married couples in this table is slightly different from the figure shown in the household income tables because this figure includes the incomes only of family members and not any unrelated members of the household.
Source: Bureau of the Census, 2011 Current Population Survey, Internet site http://www.census.gov/hhes/www/cpstables/032011/hhinc/toc.htm; calculations by New Strategist

Dual Earners Are the Majority of Married Couples

Single-earner couples account for a small share of total couples.

Of the nation's 58 million married couples, 31 million—or 54 percent—are dual earners, meaning both husband and wife are in the labor force. The 16 million dual-earner couples with full-time jobs account for 28 percent of all married couples. The median income of these dual-earners was $103,704 in 2010, more than $35,000 greater than the median income of single-earner couples in which only the husband works full-time. Those single-earner couples had a median income of $67,108 in 2010.

Among dual-earner couples with full-time jobs, incomes are similar regardless of the age of their children with one exception. Those with both preschoolers and school-aged children had a slightly lower income than the others. Among single-earner couples in which the husband works full-time, incomes are more varied by age of children. Those without children at home had the highest median income—$73,087 in 2010. Those with both preschoolers and school-aged children had the lowest income—$54,634.

■ The number of dual-earner couples in which both husband and wife work full-time fell by more than 2 million between 2007 and 2010 because of the Great Recession.

Single-earner couples have much lower incomes

(median income of married couples by work status of husband and wife, 2010)

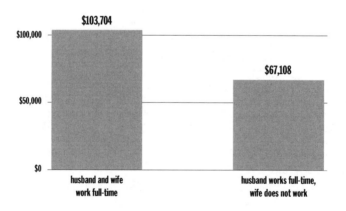

Table 1.61 Dual-Income Married Couples by Household Income and Presence of Children, 2010: Husband and Wife Work

(number and percent distribution of married couples in which both husband and wife work by household income and presence and age of related children under age 18 at home, 2010; married couples in thousands as of 2011)

Husband and wife work	total	no children	one or more children under age 18			
			total	all under 6	some < 6, some 6 to 17	all 6 to 17
Husband and wife work	**31,427**	**15,047**	**16,380**	**4,044**	**3,068**	**9,268**
Under $5,000	25	16	9	3	1	4
$5,000 to $9,999	47	27	20	7	1	12
$10,000 to $14,999	124	49	75	14	17	44
$15,000 to $19,999	205	84	121	50	21	51
$20,000 to $24,999	335	131	204	45	62	97
$25,000 to $29,999	481	182	298	87	72	139
$30,000 to $34,999	605	245	360	104	75	181
$35,000 to $39,999	777	371	406	110	107	189
$40,000 to $44,999	907	395	512	150	119	243
$45,000 to $49,999	1,040	478	562	132	126	305
$50,000 to $54,999	1,212	573	639	160	145	334
$55,000 to $59,999	1,169	536	633	156	149	328
$60,000 to $64,999	1,284	604	680	162	138	380
$65,000 to $69,999	1,266	578	688	140	147	401
$70,000 to $74,999	1,415	681	734	185	136	413
$75,000 to $79,999	1,275	599	677	172	112	393
$80,000 to $84,999	1,407	670	736	201	122	413
$85,000 to $89,999	1,305	677	628	151	112	364
$90,000 to $94,999	1,248	572	676	164	126	386
$95,000 to $99,999	1,166	591	574	123	97	355
$100,000 to $124,999	4,886	2,338	2,550	659	435	1,454
$125,000 to $149,999	3,202	1,598	1,603	381	268	953
$150,000 to $174,999	2,080	1,059	1,020	220	157	643
$175,000 to $199,999	1,198	595	602	161	104	339
$200,000 or more	2,769	1,396	1,372	306	220	847
Median income	$92,829	$95,395	$91,221	$89,651	$84,234	$94,341

PERCENT DISTRIBUTION

Husband and wife work						
Husband and wife work	**100.0%**	**100.0%**	**100.0%**	**100.0%**	**100.0%**	**100.0%**
Under $25,000	2.3	2.0	2.6	2.9	3.3	2.2
$25,000 to $49,999	12.1	11.1	13.1	14.4	16.3	11.4
$50,000 to $74,999	20.2	19.8	20.6	19.9	23.3	20.0
$75,000 to $99,999	20.4	20.7	20.1	20.1	18.5	20.6
$100,000 or more	45.0	46.4	43.6	42.7	38.6	45.7

Source: Bureau of the Census, 2011 Current Population Survey, Internet site http://www.census.gov/hhes/www/cpstables/ 032011/hhinc/toc.htm; calculations by New Strategist

Table 1.62 Dual-Income Married Couples by Household Income and Presence of Children, 2010: Husband and Wife Work Full-Time

(number and percent distribution of married couples in which both husband and wife work full-time, year-round by household income and presence and age of related children under age 18 at home, 2010; married couples in thousands as of 2011)

			one or more children under age 18			
	total	no children	total	all under 6	some < 6, some 6 to 17	all 6 to 17
Husband and wife work full-time	**16,345**	**8,245**	**8,100**	**1,910**	**1,389**	**4,800**
Under $5,000	6	5	0	0	0	0
$5,000 to $9,999	3	3	0	0	0	0
$10,000 to $14,999	7	4	3	0	2	1
$15,000 to $19,999	22	11	11	2	2	7
$20,000 to $24,999	28	16	12	0	3	9
$25,000 to $29,999	55	23	32	7	6	20
$30,000 to $34,999	112	55	56	11	12	33
$35,000 to $39,999	185	73	112	19	25	69
$40,000 to $44,999	271	143	128	31	28	68
$45,000 to $49,999	383	186	197	32	51	114
$50,000 to $54,999	512	263	249	56	55	138
$55,000 to $59,999	456	232	224	54	47	123
$60,000 to $64,999	587	278	309	77	65	167
$65,000 to $69,999	649	302	347	81	70	195
$70,000 to $74,999	732	387	346	74	56	216
$75,000 to $79,999	674	343	331	85	49	196
$80,000 to $84,999	785	357	428	106	78	244
$85,000 to $89,999	725	392	334	81	56	196
$90,000 to $94,999	704	348	356	82	74	200
$95,000 to $99,999	687	369	318	58	48	212
$100,000 to $124,999	2,934	1,458	1,476	384	227	865
$125,000 to $149,999	2,035	1,051	983	226	166	592
$150,000 to $174,999	1,274	677	597	142	84	371
$175,000 to $199,999	735	362	373	99	56	217
$200,000 or more	1,785	905	880	200	131	549
Median income	$103,704	$104,675	$102,817	$105,352	$96,227	$103,730

PERCENT DISTRIBUTION

Husband and wife work full-time	**100.0%**	**100.0%**	**100.0%**	**100.0%**	**100.0%**	**100.0%**
Under $25,000	0.4	0.5	0.3	0.1	0.5	0.4
$25,000 to $49,999	6.2	5.8	6.5	5.2	8.8	6.3
$50,000 to $74,999	18.0	17.7	18.2	17.9	21.1	17.5
$75,000 to $99,999	21.9	21.9	21.8	21.6	22.0	21.8
$100,000 or more	53.6	54.0	53.2	55.0	47.8	54.0

Source: Bureau of the Census, 2011 Current Population Survey, Internet site http://www.census.gov/hhes/www/cpstables/ 032011/hhinc/toc.htm; calculations by New Strategist

Table 1.63 Married Couples by Work Status, Household Income, and Presence of Children, 2010: Husband Works Full-Time, Wife Does Not Work

(number and percent distribution of married couples in which the husband works full-time and the wife does not work, by household income and presence and age of related children under age 18 at home, 2010; married couples in thousands as of 2011)

	total	no children	one or more children under age 18			
			total	all under 6	some < 6, some 6 to 17	all 6 to 17
Husband works full-time, wife does not work	**9,386**	**3,803**	**5,584**	**1,474**	**1,612**	**2,498**
Under $5,000	21	14	8	3	2	3
$5,000 to $9,999	32	10	22	13	5	4
$10,000 to $14,999	144	51	93	30	42	20
$15,000 to $19,999	236	54	182	58	78	46
$20,000 to $24,999	377	100	277	64	115	98
$25,000 to $29,999	421	129	292	89	107	96
$30,000 to $34,999	504	205	300	60	85	154
$35,000 to $39,999	459	148	311	89	102	120
$40,000 to $44,999	494	192	302	98	88	116
$45,000 to $49,999	378	120	258	63	87	107
$50,000 to $54,999	569	222	348	115	98	135
$55,000 to $59,999	407	173	234	67	68	99
$60,000 to $64,999	464	195	268	76	66	126
$65,000 to $69,999	359	155	204	47	50	107
$70,000 to $74,999	345	170	176	43	37	96
$75,000 to $79,999	300	131	169	46	37	86
$80,000 to $84,999	342	163	179	45	64	70
$85,000 to $89,999	273	134	139	39	40	60
$90,000 to $94,999	259	115	144	53	30	61
$95,000 to $99,999	156	80	76	12	33	31
$100,000 to $124,999	981	429	554	152	154	246
$125,000 to $149,999	471	216	255	59	66	130
$150,000 to $174,999	416	178	238	51	33	152
$175,000 to $199,999	187	102	84	15	18	52
$200,000 or more	790	318	472	87	103	282
Median income	$67,108	$73,087	$62,151	$58,119	$54,634	$70,634

PERCENT DISTRIBUTION

Husband works full-time, wife does not work	**100.0%**	**100.0%**	**100.0%**	**100.0%**	**100.0%**	**100.0%**
Under $25,000	8.6	6.0	10.4	11.4	15.0	6.8
$25,000 to $49,999	24.0	20.9	26.2	27.1	29.1	23.7
$50,000 to $74,999	22.8	24.1	22.0	23.6	19.8	22.5
$75,000 to $99,999	14.2	16.4	12.7	13.2	12.7	12.3
$100,000 or more	30.3	32.7	28.7	24.7	23.2	34.5

Source: Bureau of the Census, 2011 Current Population Survey, Internet site http://www.census.gov/hhes/www/cpstables/ 032011/hhinc/toc.htm; calculations by New Strategist

Female-Headed Families without Children Have Higher Incomes

Those with preschoolers have the lowest incomes.

The median income of all female-headed families stood at $29,220 in 2010. Women who head families that include children under age 18 have lower incomes (a median of $24,487) than those who head families without children ($39,162). Behind this income difference is the fact that female-headed families without children include adult relatives and are more likely to have an additional earner in the home.

Black and Hispanic female-headed families with children have the lowest incomes—a median of $21,195 for blacks and $20,344 for Hispanics. The median income of non-Hispanic white female-headed families with children is a higher $29,570. Their Asian counterparts have the highest median income, $32,449 in 2010.

■ Until the Great Recession, female-headed families were making gains in income. High rates of unemployment have erased those gains.

Female-headed families with children have lower incomes

(median income of female-headed families by presence and age of children under age 18 at home, 2010)

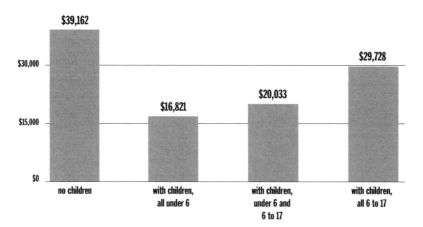

Table 1.64 Female-Headed Families by Family Income and Presence of Children, 2010: Total Female-Headed Families

(number and percent distribution of total female-headed families by family income and presence and age of related children under age 18 at home, 2010; female-headed families in thousands as of 2011)

	total	no children	total	all under 6	some < 6, some 6 to 17	all 6 to 17
			one or more children under age 18			
Total female-headed families	**15,026**	**4,990**	**10,036**	**2,245**	**1,957**	**5,835**
Under $5,000	1,343	164	1,179	415	276	488
$5,000 to $9,999	1,235	194	1,040	331	250	460
$10,000 to $14,999	1,318	305	1,014	282	213	519
$15,000 to $19,999	1,295	340	955	217	238	500
$20,000 to $24,999	1,328	419	908	202	193	513
$25,000 to $29,999	1,154	377	777	155	163	459
$30,000 to $34,999	1,039	381	658	137	103	418
$35,000 to $39,999	962	374	588	84	96	408
$40,000 to $44,999	798	336	461	74	84	303
$45,000 to $49,999	659	282	377	60	55	261
$50,000 to $54,999	555	236	319	32	48	239
$55,000 to $59,999	456	184	272	36	33	203
$60,000 to $64,999	432	197	235	33	27	175
$65,000 to $69,999	293	139	155	30	17	108
$70,000 to $74,999	351	184	166	23	24	120
$75,000 to $79,999	241	90	151	20	24	107
$80,000 to $84,999	212	98	114	20	12	81
$85,000 to $89,999	179	96	82	11	11	60
$90,000 to $94,999	178	98	80	7	14	59
$95,000 to $99,999	118	56	62	7	14	41
$100,000 to $124,999	465	242	223	28	32	164
$125,000 to $149,999	175	82	92	23	11	59
$150,000 to $174,999	97	42	54	5	8	41
$175,000 to $199,999	32	16	16	4	4	8
$200,000 or more	111	51	60	10	6	44
Median income	$29,220	$39,162	$24,487	$16,821	$20,033	$29,728

PERCENT DISTRIBUTION

Total female-headed families	**100.0%**	**100.0%**	**100.0%**	**100.0%**	**100.0%**	**100.0%**
Under $25,000	43.4	28.5	50.8	64.5	59.8	42.5
$25,000 to $49,999	30.7	35.1	28.5	22.7	25.6	31.7
$50,000 to $74,999	13.9	18.8	11.4	6.9	7.6	14.5
$75,000 to $99,999	6.2	8.8	4.9	2.9	3.8	6.0
$100,000 or more	5.9	8.7	4.4	3.1	3.1	5.4

Note: The median income of female-headed families in this table is slightly different from the figure shown in the household income tables because this figure includes the incomes only of family members and not any unrelated members of the household. Source: Bureau of the Census, 2011 Current Population Survey, Internet site http://www.census.gov/hhes/www/cpstables/032011/hhinc/toc.htm; calculations by New Strategist

Table 1.65 Female-Headed Families by Family Income and Presence of Children, 2010: Asian Female-Headed Families

(number and percent distribution of Asian female-headed families by family income and presence of related children under age 18 at home, 2010; female-headed families in thousands as of 2011)

	total	no children	with one or more children
Asian female-headed families	**492**	**215**	**277**
Under $5,000	32	9	23
$5,000 to $9,999	24	5	20
$10,000 to $14,999	16	6	10
$15,000 to $19,999	38	14	25
$20,000 to $24,999	43	11	31
$25,000 to $29,999	27	9	18
$30,000 to $34,999	33	9	24
$35,000 to $39,999	22	7	15
$40,000 to $44,999	31	15	15
$45,000 to $49,999	23	13	10
$50,000 to $54,999	25	17	8
$55,000 to $59,999	9	5	4
$60,000 to $64,999	14	7	7
$65,000 to $69,999	12	6	6
$70,000 to $74,999	19	12	7
$75,000 to $79,999	15	5	10
$80,000 to $84,999	17	13	5
$85,000 to $89,999	4	3	1
$90,000 to $94,999	8	5	3
$95,000 to $99,999	6	4	2
$100,000 to $124,999	31	25	6
$125,000 to $149,999	18	6	12
$150,000 to $174,999	10	3	6
$175,000 to $199,999	2	0	2
$200,000 or more	15	7	9
Median income	$41,236	$52,184	$32,449

PERCENT DISTRIBUTION

	total	no children	with one or more children
Asian female-headed families	**100.0%**	**100.0%**	**100.0%**
Under $25,000	31.1	20.9	39.4
$25,000 to $49,999	27.6	24.7	29.6
$50,000 to $74,999	16.1	21.9	11.6
$75,000 to $99,999	10.2	14.0	7.6
$100,000 or more	15.4	19.1	12.6

Note: Asians are those who identify themselves as being of the race alone and those who identify themselves as being of the race in combination with other races. The median income of female-headed families in this table is slightly different from the figure shown in the household income tables because this figure includes the incomes only of family members and not any unrelated members of the household.
Source: Bureau of the Census, 2011 Current Population Survey, Internet site http://www.census.gov/hhes/www/cpstables/032011/hhinc/toc.htm; calculations by New Strategist

Table 1.66 Female-Headed Families by Family Income and Presence of Children, 2010: Black Female-Headed Families

(number and percent distribution of black female-headed families by family income and presence and age of related children under age 18 at home, 2010; female-headed families in thousands as of 2011)

			one or more children under age 18			
	total	no children	total	all under 6	some < 6, some 6 to 17	all 6 to 17
Black female-headed families	**4,459**	**1,324**	**3,135**	**677**	**741**	**1,718**
Under $5,000	480	74	406	135	93	179
$5,000 to $9,999	466	64	402	121	106	175
$10,000 to $14,999	464	101	363	82	105	176
$15,000 to $19,999	409	99	310	53	96	160
$20,000 to $24,999	449	119	330	64	90	176
$25,000 to $29,999	345	114	230	54	61	114
$30,000 to $34,999	323	112	212	39	33	140
$35,000 to $39,999	260	95	165	30	32	103
$40,000 to $44,999	223	82	141	17	32	92
$45,000 to $49,999	185	67	118	18	20	81
$50,000 to $54,999	149	52	97	7	17	73
$55,000 to $59,999	102	34	68	8	9	51
$60,000 to $64,999	101	44	58	16	5	37
$65,000 to $69,999	76	31	46	8	9	29
$70,000 to $74,999	92	64	28	4	5	19
$75,000 to $79,999	52	25	28	4	6	18
$80,000 to $84,999	43	18	26	5	2	19
$85,000 to $89,999	26	16	10	1	4	5
$90,000 to $94,999	40	25	15	0	4	11
$95,000 to $99,999	21	15	5	0	0	5
$100,000 to $124,999	97	44	52	5	11	36
$125,000 to $149,999	25	17	9	4	1	3
$150,000 to $174,999	14	6	9	1	0	8
$175,000 to $199,999	5	4	1	0	1	0
$200,000 or more	9	2	7	0	1	6
Median income	$24,521	$34,031	$21,195	$15,082	$18,422	$24,823

PERCENT DISTRIBUTION

Black female-headed families	**100.0%**	**100.0%**	**100.0%**	**100.0%**	**100.0%**	**100.0%**
Under $25,000	50.9	34.5	57.8	67.2	66.1	50.4
$25,000 to $49,999	30.0	35.5	27.6	23.3	24.0	30.8
$50,000 to $74,999	11.7	17.0	9.5	6.4	6.1	12.2
$75,000 to $99,999	4.1	7.5	2.7	1.5	2.2	3.4
$100,000 or more	3.4	5.5	2.5	1.5	1.9	3.1

Note: Blacks are those who identify themselves as being of the race alone and those who identify themselves as being of the race in combination with other races. The median income of female-headed families in this table is slightly different from the figure shown in the household income tables because this figure includes the incomes only of family members and not any unrelated members of the household.
Source: Bureau of the Census, 2011 Current Population Survey, Internet site http://www.census.gov/hhes/www/cpstables/ 032011/hhinc/toc.htm; calculations by New Strategist

Table 1.67 Female-Headed Families by Family Income and Presence of Children, 2010: Hispanic Female-Headed Families

(number and percent distribution of Hispanic female-headed families by family income and presence and age of related children under age 18 at home, 2010; female-headed families in thousands as of 2011)

	total	no children	one or more children under age 18 total	all under 6	some < 6, some 6 to 17	all 6 to 17
Hispanic female-headed families	**2,760**	**650**	**2,111**	**416**	**553**	**1,142**
Under $5,000	340	15	324	108	109	107
$5,000 to $9,999	269	38	231	49	78	104
$10,000 to $14,999	294	55	239	51	52	136
$15,000 to $19,999	292	48	244	28	74	142
$20,000 to $24,999	245	52	193	42	51	100
$25,000 to $29,999	249	45	203	38	52	113
$30,000 to $34,999	191	51	140	23	28	89
$35,000 to $39,999	168	59	109	10	28	71
$40,000 to $44,999	129	48	80	13	20	48
$45,000 to $49,999	119	44	74	15	11	49
$50,000 to $54,999	79	27	52	4	12	36
$55,000 to $59,999	58	18	40	6	9	25
$60,000 to $64,999	57	26	31	3	5	23
$65,000 to $69,999	38	18	21	7	1	12
$70,000 to $74,999	30	10	20	0	2	18
$75,000 to $79,999	34	9	25	5	3	17
$80,000 to $84,999	27	11	16	0	2	13
$85,000 to $89,999	22	9	13	0	3	10
$90,000 to $94,999	18	10	8	5	0	3
$95,000 to $99,999	22	9	13	0	8	5
$100,000 to $124,999	31	19	12	2	3	7
$125,000 to $149,999	20	11	7	2	0	5
$150,000 to $174,999	16	8	8	2	2	3
$175,000 to $199,999	5	2	3	2	1	0
$200,000 or more	8	4	4	1	0	3
Median income	$23,451	$36,561	$20,344	$14,982	$17,313	$23,900

PERCENT DISTRIBUTION

Hispanic female-headed families	**100.0%**	**100.0%**	**100.0%**	**100.0%**	**100.0%**	**100.0%**
Under $25,000	52.2	32.0	58.3	66.8	65.8	51.6
$25,000 to $49,999	31.0	38.0	28.7	23.8	25.1	32.4
$50,000 to $74,999	9.5	15.2	7.8	4.8	5.2	10.0
$75,000 to $99,999	4.5	7.4	3.6	2.4	2.9	4.2
$100,000 or more	2.9	6.8	1.6	2.2	1.1	1.6

Note: The median income of female-headed families in this table is slightly different from the figure shown in the household income tables because this figure includes the incomes only of family members and not any unrelated members of the household. Source: Bureau of the Census, 2011 Current Population Survey, Internet site http://www.census.gov/hhes/www/cpstables/032011/hhinc/toc.htm; calculations by New Strategist

Table 1.68 Female-Headed Families by Family Income and Presence of Children, 2010: Non-Hispanic White Female-Headed Families

(number and percent distribution of non-Hispanic white female-headed families by family income and presence and age of related children under age 18 at home, 2010; female-headed families in thousands as of 2011)

	total	no children	one or more children under age 18			
			total	all under 6	some < 6, some 6 to 17	all 6 to 17
Non-Hispanic white female-headed families	**7,279**	**2,771**	**4,508**	**1,095**	**619**	**2,794**
Under $5,000	491	67	424	168	63	192
$5,000 to $9,999	467	85	383	144	64	174
$10,000 to $14,999	551	144	407	139	56	211
$15,000 to $19,999	563	173	390	130	73	188
$20,000 to $24,999	594	229	365	97	52	215
$25,000 to $29,999	516	204	312	63	44	205
$30,000 to $34,999	490	211	278	64	38	177
$35,000 to $39,999	511	209	302	44	34	223
$40,000 to $44,999	418	188	231	43	29	159
$45,000 to $49,999	332	156	176	27	24	124
$50,000 to $54,999	297	133	164	21	19	124
$55,000 to $59,999	285	127	158	23	13	122
$60,000 to $64,999	256	120	136	14	17	104
$65,000 to $69,999	162	84	78	15	7	56
$70,000 to $74,999	207	96	112	17	16	79
$75,000 to $79,999	133	46	87	10	15	62
$80,000 to $84,999	127	60	67	13	7	47
$85,000 to $89,999	124	67	57	9	4	44
$90,000 to $94,999	111	59	53	1	8	43
$95,000 to $99,999	71	29	41	6	6	29
$100,000 to $124,999	304	157	147	22	13	113
$125,000 to $149,999	112	51	62	14	7	41
$150,000 to $174,999	57	25	31	0	2	28
$175,000 to $199,999	22	10	11	2	1	8
$200,000 or more	78	39	39	8	4	27
Median income	$34,558	$41,435	$29,570	$18,583	$25,034	$35,658

PERCENT DISTRIBUTION

	total	no children	total	all under 6	some < 6, some 6 to 17	all 6 to 17
Non-Hispanic white female-headed families	**100.0%**	**100.0%**	**100.0%**	**100.0%**	**100.0%**	**100.0%**
Under $25,000	36.6	25.2	43.7	61.9	49.8	35.1
$25,000 to $49,999	31.1	34.9	28.8	22.0	27.3	31.8
$50,000 to $74,999	16.6	20.2	14.4	8.2	11.6	17.4
$75,000 to $99,999	7.8	9.4	6.8	3.6	6.5	8.1
$100,000 or more	7.9	10.2	6.4	4.2	4.4	7.8

Note: Non-Hispanic whites are those who identify themselves as being of the race alone and not Hispanic. The median income of female-headed families in this table is slightly different from the figure shown in the household income tables because this figure includes the incomes only of family members and not any unrelated members of the household.
Source: Bureau of the Census, 2011 Current Population Survey, Internet site http://www.census.gov/hhes/www/cpstables/032011/hhinc/toc.htm; calculations by New Strategist

Male-Headed Families with Children Have Below-Average Incomes

Those with preschoolers have the lowest incomes.

The median income of male-headed families stood at $43,058 in 2010, far above the $29,220 median of their female counterparts. Male-headed families that do not include children under age 18 have above-average incomes, with a median of $51,731 in 2010. These men live with relatives such as adult children, siblings, or parents, and many of the families have more than one wage earner. Of the nation's 5.6 million male-headed families, only half include children under age 18. A much larger 67 percent of female-headed families have children under age 18 at home.

The incomes of black and Hispanic male-headed families are well below those of non-Hispanic whites or Asians. Black male-headed families had a median income of $32,127 in 2010, while the Hispanic median was $36,880. The non-Hispanic white median is a higher $48,355. Asian male-headed families are least likely to include children under age 18 (31 percent), and their median income was the highest at $57,290.

■ Male-headed families are the least-common household type and account for only 5 percent of households, a status that is unlikely to change in the years ahead.

Incomes vary for male-headed families

(median income of male-headed families by presence and age of children under age 18 at home, 2010)

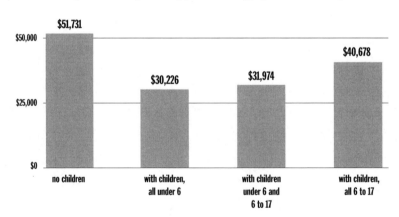

Table 1.69 **Male-Headed Families by Family Income and Presence of Children, 2010:**
        Total Male-Headed Families

(number and percent distribution of total male-headed families by family income and presence and age of related children under age 18 at home, 2010; male-headed families in thousands as of 2011)

			one or more children under age 18			
	total	no children	total	all under 6	some < 6, some 6 to 17	all 6 to 17
Total male-headed families	**5,560**	**2,808**	**2,753**	**863**	**360**	**1,529**
Under $5,000	221	62	160	42	33	85
$5,000 to $9,999	219	72	147	56	24	66
$10,000 to $14,999	268	82	185	58	27	101
$15,000 to $19,999	316	128	188	79	29	79
$20,000 to $24,999	425	180	245	101	24	120
$25,000 to $29,999	373	184	189	92	24	73
$30,000 to $34,999	356	157	199	52	29	118
$35,000 to $39,999	347	148	198	69	26	103
$40,000 to $44,999	370	193	177	53	16	108
$45,000 to $49,999	269	127	143	48	24	70
$50,000 to $54,999	310	172	138	32	17	89
$55,000 to $59,999	204	115	89	15	7	67
$60,000 to $64,999	279	154	125	24	12	89
$65,000 to $69,999	150	89	60	15	6	40
$70,000 to $74,999	190	111	79	23	10	46
$75,000 to $79,999	132	69	62	10	7	45
$80,000 to $84,999	147	95	51	16	10	25
$85,000 to $89,999	111	70	41	5	4	33
$90,000 to $94,999	83	52	32	8	0	23
$95,000 to $99,999	86	47	40	12	2	26
$100,000 to $124,999	337	238	99	26	20	55
$125,000 to $149,999	133	93	40	9	4	29
$150,000 to $174,999	75	57	18	5	2	12
$175,000 to $199,999	41	30	12	5	0	7
$200,000 or more	119	85	34	10	2	22
Median income	$43,058	$51,731	$36,290	$30,226	$31,974	$40,678

PERCENT DISTRIBUTION

Total male-headed families	**100.0%**	**100.0%**	**100.0%**	**100.0%**	**100.0%**	**100.0%**
Under $25,000	26.1	18.7	33.6	38.9	38.1	29.5
$25,000 to $49,999	30.8	28.8	32.9	36.4	33.1	30.9
$50,000 to $74,999	20.4	22.8	17.8	12.6	14.4	21.6
$75,000 to $99,999	10.1	11.9	8.2	5.9	6.4	9.9
$100,000 or more	12.7	17.9	7.4	6.4	7.8	8.2

Note: The median income of male-headed families in this table is slightly different from the figure shown in the household income tables because this figure includes the incomes only of family members and not any unrelated members of the household. Source: Bureau of the Census, 2011 Current Population Survey, Internet site http://www.census.gov/hhes/www/cpstables/ 032011/hhinc/toc.htm; calculations by New Strategist

Table 1.70 Male-Headed Families by Family Income and Presence of Children, 2010: Asian Male-Headed Families

(number and percent distribution of Asian male-headed families by family income and presence of related children under age 18 at home, 2010; male-headed families in thousands as of 2011)

	total	no children	with one or more children
Asian male-headed families	**291**	**202**	**89**
Under $5,000	9	5	4
$5,000 to $9,999	13	11	2
$10,000 to $14,999	5	3	2
$15,000 to $19,999	9	9	0
$20,000 to $24,999	18	12	6
$25,000 to $29,999	10	7	3
$30,000 to $34,999	11	9	2
$35,000 to $39,999	6	5	1
$40,000 to $44,999	21	14	7
$45,000 to $49,999	19	7	12
$50,000 to $54,999	14	14	0
$55,000 to $59,999	16	10	7
$60,000 to $64,999	17	7	10
$65,000 to $69,999	5	5	0
$70,000 to $74,999	8	4	4
$75,000 to $79,999	5	5	0
$80,000 to $84,999	9	7	2
$85,000 to $89,999	6	3	3
$90,000 to $94,999	9	6	3
$95,000 to $99,999	7	3	4
$100,000 to $124,999	27	19	9
$125,000 to $149,999	14	13	1
$150,000 to $174,999	12	9	3
$175,000 to $199,999	4	2	2
$200,000 or more	18	16	2
Median income	$57,290	$57,819	$56,894

PERCENT DISTRIBUTION

Asian male-headed families	**100.0%**	**100.0%**	**100.0%**
Under $25,000	18.6	19.8	15.7
$25,000 to $49,999	23.0	20.8	28.1
$50,000 to $74,999	20.6	19.8	23.6
$75,000 to $99,999	12.4	11.9	13.5
$100,000 or more	25.8	29.2	19.1

Note: Asians are those who identify themselves as being of the race alone and those who identify themselves as being of the race in combination with other races. The median income of male-headed families in this table is slightly different from the figure shown in the household income tables because this figure includes the incomes only of family members and not any unrelated members of the household.
Source: Bureau of the Census, 2011 Current Population Survey, Internet site http://www.census.gov/hhes/www/cpstables/032011/hhinc/toc.htm; calculations by New Strategist

Table 1.71 Male-Headed Families by Family Income and Presence of Children, 2010: Black Male-Headed Families

(number and percent distribution of black male-headed families by family income and presence and age of related children under age 18 at home, 2010; male-headed families in thousands as of 2011)

Black male-headed families	total	no children	one or more children under age 18			
			total	all under 6	some < 6, some 6 to 17	all 6 to 17
Black male-headed families	**954**	**472**	**482**	**146**	**84**	**252**
Under $5,000	75	14	61	17	15	30
$5,000 to $9,999	64	20	43	12	13	18
$10,000 to $14,999	77	25	51	10	3	38
$15,000 to $19,999	56	32	25	13	7	5
$20,000 to $24,999	90	40	50	15	7	28
$25,000 to $29,999	77	44	33	14	9	11
$30,000 to $34,999	73	32	41	5	4	32
$35,000 to $39,999	62	22	39	18	7	15
$40,000 to $44,999	49	28	21	11	1	9
$45,000 to $49,999	44	26	17	11	2	4
$50,000 to $54,999	37	21	16	4	2	10
$55,000 to $59,999	16	12	4	0	0	4
$60,000 to $64,999	22	8	14	2	1	11
$65,000 to $69,999	24	14	11	3	2	7
$70,000 to $74,999	41	27	13	3	3	7
$75,000 to $79,999	21	17	4	0	2	1
$80,000 to $84,999	14	10	3	0	0	3
$85,000 to $89,999	15	10	5	2	0	3
$90,000 to $94,999	8	6	2	0	0	2
$95,000 to $99,999	7	5	2	0	0	2
$100,000 to $124,999	45	32	13	3	3	8
$125,000 to $149,999	17	13	3	1	0	2
$150,000 to $174,999	9	6	3	0	2	1
$175,000 to $199,999	1	1	0	0	0	0
$200,000 or more	10	5	5	2	2	2
Median income	$32,127	$41,186	$26,098	$26,296	$21,924	$26,938

PERCENT DISTRIBUTION

Black male-headed families	100.0%	100.0%	100.0%	100.0%	100.0%	100.0%
Under $25,000	37.9	27.8	47.7	45.9	53.6	47.2
$25,000 to $49,999	32.0	32.2	31.3	40.4	27.4	28.2
$50,000 to $74,999	14.7	17.4	12.0	8.2	9.5	15.5
$75,000 to $99,999	6.8	10.2	3.3	1.4	2.4	4.4
$100,000 or more	8.6	12.1	5.0	4.1	8.3	5.2

Note: Blacks are those who identify themselves as being of the race alone and those who identify themselves as being of the race in combination with other races. The median income of male-headed families in this table is slightly different from the figure shown in the household income tables because this figure includes the incomes only of family members and not any unrelated members of the household.
Source: Bureau of the Census, 2011 Current Population Survey, Internet site http://www.census.gov/hhes/www/cpstables/032011/hhinc/toc.htm; calculations by New Strategist

Table 1.72 Male-Headed Families by Family Income and Presence of Children, 2010: Hispanic Male-Headed Families

(number and percent distribution of Hispanic male-headed families by family income and presence and age of related children under age 18 at home, 2010; male-headed families in thousands as of 2011)

			one or more children under age 18			
	total	no children	total	all under 6	some < 6, some 6 to 17	all 6 to 17
Hispanic male-headed families	**1,181**	**525**	**656**	**208**	**128**	**321**
Under $5,000	42	10	32	10	8	14
$5,000 to $9,999	52	19	32	11	7	14
$10,000 to $14,999	72	18	55	19	16	20
$15,000 to $19,999	75	19	56	21	9	26
$20,000 to $24,999	115	45	70	27	11	32
$25,000 to $29,999	93	37	56	31	7	18
$30,000 to $34,999	104	46	58	16	15	26
$35,000 to $39,999	69	34	35	13	8	14
$40,000 to $44,999	61	35	26	5	4	17
$45,000 to $49,999	64	35	29	13	4	11
$50,000 to $54,999	79	38	41	12	4	25
$55,000 to $59,999	42	26	16	0	2	13
$60,000 to $64,999	53	25	28	3	7	18
$65,000 to $69,999	26	8	18	5	4	9
$70,000 to $74,999	27	13	14	5	2	7
$75,000 to $79,999	31	14	16	1	1	14
$80,000 to $84,999	40	27	13	6	4	3
$85,000 to $89,999	16	6	11	3	2	6
$90,000 to $94,999	18	8	10	2	0	8
$95,000 to $99,999	10	7	3	0	0	3
$100,000 to $124,999	49	29	19	0	7	12
$125,000 to $149,999	25	11	13	1	3	8
$150,000 to $174,999	5	4	1	0	0	1
$175,000 to $199,999	3	3	0	0	0	0
$200,000 or more	11	8	3	3	0	0
Median income	$36,880	$44,982	$31,650	$27,060	$30,866	$37,325

PERCENT DISTRIBUTION

Hispanic male-headed families	**100.0%**	**100.0%**	**100.0%**	**100.0%**	**100.0%**	**100.0%**
Under $25,000	30.1	21.1	37.3	42.3	39.8	33.0
$25,000 to $49,999	33.1	35.6	31.1	37.5	29.7	26.8
$50,000 to $74,999	19.2	21.0	17.8	12.0	14.8	22.4
$75,000 to $99,999	9.7	11.8	8.1	5.8	5.5	10.6
$100,000 or more	7.9	10.5	5.5	1.9	7.8	6.5

Note: The median income of male-headed families in this table is slightly different from the figure shown in the household income tables because this figure includes the incomes only of family members and not any unrelated members of the household. Source: Bureau of the Census, 2011 Current Population Survey, Internet site http://www.census.gov/hhes/www/cpstables/032011/hhinc/toc.htm; calculations by New Strategist

Table 1.73 **Male-Headed Families by Family Income and Presence of Children, 2010: Non-Hispanic White Male-Headed Families**

(number and percent distribution of non-Hispanic white male-headed families by family income and presence and age of related children under age 18 at home, 2010; male-headed families in thousands as of 2011)

| | total | no children | one or more children under age 18 | | | |
			total	all under 6	some < 6, some 6 to 17	all 6 to 17
Non-Hispanic white male-headed families	**3,078**	**1,587**	**1,491**	**470**	**143**	**878**
Under $5,000	81	28	53	13	8	32
$5,000 to $9,999	86	22	64	30	3	31
$10,000 to $14,999	113	39	75	29	9	37
$15,000 to $19,999	172	68	105	45	13	47
$20,000 to $24,999	200	81	119	54	6	58
$25,000 to $29,999	192	95	97	44	8	45
$30,000 to $34,999	164	67	97	28	10	59
$35,000 to $39,999	205	88	117	35	11	71
$40,000 to $44,999	236	113	124	38	9	77
$45,000 to $49,999	137	56	81	23	17	41
$50,000 to $54,999	177	100	77	14	11	51
$55,000 to $59,999	128	67	61	13	5	43
$60,000 to $64,999	181	111	70	16	5	48
$65,000 to $69,999	93	62	31	7	0	24
$70,000 to $74,999	118	69	49	15	6	28
$75,000 to $79,999	73	33	40	8	3	29
$80,000 to $84,999	84	51	33	10	6	17
$85,000 to $89,999	75	50	25	0	2	23
$90,000 to $94,999	48	32	17	6	0	10
$95,000 to $99,999	61	32	29	8	2	20
$100,000 to $124,999	212	149	62	21	9	33
$125,000 to $149,999	78	56	23	5	0	19
$150,000 to $174,999	49	39	11	2	0	9
$175,000 to $199,999	34	24	10	3	0	7
$200,000 or more	78	57	21	3	0	18
Median income	$48,355	$58,063	$40,537	$32,364	$41,513	$42,614

PERCENT DISTRIBUTION

Non-Hispanic white male-headed families	**100.0%**	**100.0%**	**100.0%**	**100.0%**	**100.0%**	**100.0%**
Under $25,000	21.2	15.0	27.9	36.4	27.3	23.3
$25,000 to $49,999	30.3	26.4	34.6	35.7	38.5	33.4
$50,000 to $74,999	22.6	25.8	19.3	13.8	18.9	22.1
$75,000 to $99,999	11.1	12.5	9.7	6.8	9.1	11.3
$100,000 or more	14.7	20.5	8.5	7.2	6.3	9.8

Note: Non-Hispanic whites are those who identify themselves as being of the race alone and not Hispanic. The median income of male-headed families in this table is slightly different from the figure shown in the household income tables because this figure includes the incomes only of family members and not any unrelated members of the household.
Source: Bureau of the Census, 2011 Current Population Survey, Internet site http://www.census.gov/hhes/www/cpstables/032011/hhinc/toc.htm; calculations by New Strategist

Household Incomes Rise with Education

Householders with at least a bachelor's degree had a median income of $82,109 in 2010.

Household income rises with education. Householders with an associate's degree or more education have above-average incomes, while those with only some college or less education have average or below-average incomes. Household income peaks among those with a doctoral or professional degree, a category that includes physicians and lawyers. The 59 to 60 percent majority of this group has an income of $100,000 or more. Thirty-six percent of householders with a bachelor's degree have an income of $100,000 or more.

Median household income is lowest among the least educated. Householders with a high school diploma had a median income of $38,976—23 percent below the all-household average. Those who dropped out of high school had a median income of just $24,787.

The pattern is the same regardless of race and Hispanic origin, with better-educated householders commanding higher incomes. Black householders with a bachelor's degree had a median income of $55,230 in 2010, while Hispanic householders with a bachelor's degree had a median income of $65,441. Among Asians with a bachelor's degree, median household income is a higher $78,339, and for non-Hispanic whites the figure is $79,386. Few Hispanic householders are highly educated, a factor that accounts in part for their lower household incomes. Among Asian householders aged 25 or older, the 55 percent majority has at least a bachelor's degree. Among non-Hispanic whites, the figure is a smaller 35 percent. Among black householders, 21 percent have at least a bachelor's degree. For Hispanics, the figure is just 15 percent.

■ The financial rewards of a college degree appear to be worth the cost, but many blacks and Hispanics cannot afford the cost regardless of the benefits.

Education boosts income

(median household income by educational attainment of householders aged 25 or older, 2010)

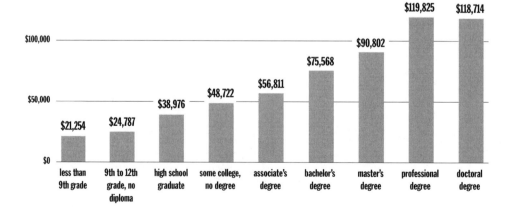

Table 1.74 Households by Income and Educational Attainment of Householder, 2010: Total Households

(number and percent distribution of total households headed by people aged 25 or older by household income and educational attainment of householder, 2010; households in thousands as of 2011)

	total households	less than 9th grade	9th to 12th grade	high school graduate	some college	associate's degree	bachelor's degree or more total	bachelor's degree	master's degree	professional degree	doctoral degree
Total households	**112,542**	**5,092**	**8,059**	**32,720**	**20,223**	**10,953**	**35,496**	**22,458**	**9,436**	**1,761**	**1,841**
Under $5,000	3,568	303	563	1,210	601	276	615	425	133	30	28
$5,000 to $9,999	4,525	654	892	1,564	756	275	383	270	105	4	4
$10,000 to $14,999	6,531	801	921	2,496	1,115	480	718	537	141	19	22
$15,000 to $19,999	6,727	626	939	2,613	1,189	491	869	664	163	27	15
$20,000 to $24,999	6,408	537	740	2,461	1,142	480	1,047	747	234	37	30
$25,000 to $29,999	6,261	407	660	2,319	1,233	570	1,072	743	248	46	34
$30,000 to $34,999	5,776	345	572	2,059	1,160	577	1,063	746	232	41	44
$35,000 to $39,999	5,523	274	440	1,994	1,120	553	1,142	819	278	30	15
$40,000 to $44,999	5,302	176	393	1,761	1,079	532	1,361	925	343	48	45
$45,000 to $49,999	4,684	141	286	1,575	950	529	1,204	828	303	44	28
$50,000 to $54,999	4,881	141	286	1,573	984	534	1,363	966	312	35	50
$55,000 to $59,999	4,000	99	226	1,193	857	441	1,183	811	302	36	34
$60,000 to $64,999	4,202	116	177	1,220	817	450	1,422	944	386	35	57
$65,000 to $69,999	3,428	75	149	891	704	399	1,210	792	319	54	44
$70,000 to $74,999	3,645	58	121	1,025	692	417	1,331	904	301	57	70
$75,000 to $79,999	3,040	55	93	830	533	344	1,185	764	334	38	49
$80,000 to $84,999	3,040	46	98	747	640	406	1,104	770	250	35	48
$85,000 to $89,999	2,615	27	73	659	474	396	987	624	280	42	41
$90,000 to $94,999	2,478	23	56	577	479	295	1,049	666	293	56	34
$95,000 to $99,999	2,069	13	32	480	424	297	823	537	221	16	49
$100,000 to $124,999	8,832	74	194	1,699	1,492	994	4,377	2,726	1,217	187	247
$125,000 to $149,999	5,208	52	70	827	777	540	2,942	1,707	892	172	170
$150,000 to $174,999	3,346	21	38	388	433	276	2,193	1,209	660	149	176
$175,000 to $199,999	1,888	9	14	199	207	160	1,303	688	395	105	114
$200,000 or more	4,565	18	27	362	365	243	3,550	1,644	1,093	418	395
Median income	$50,813	$21,254	$24,787	$38,976	$48,722	$56,811	$82,109	$75,568	$90,802	$119,825	$118,714

PERCENT DISTRIBUTION

Total households	**100.0%**	**100.0%**	**100.0%**	**100.0%**	**100.0%**	**100.0%**	**100.0%**	**100.0%**	**100.0%**	**100.0%**	**100.0%**
Under $25,000	24.7	57.4	50.3	31.6	23.8	18.3	10.2	11.8	8.2	6.6	5.4
$25,000 to $49,999	24.5	26.4	29.2	29.7	27.4	25.2	16.5	18.1	14.9	11.9	9.0
$50,000 to $74,999	17.9	9.6	11.9	18.0	20.0	20.5	18.3	19.7	17.2	12.3	13.9
$75,000 to $99,999	11.8	3.2	4.4	10.1	12.6	15.9	14.5	15.0	14.6	10.6	12.0
$100,000 or more	21.2	3.4	4.3	10.6	16.2	20.2	40.5	35.5	45.1	58.5	59.9

Source: Bureau of the Census, 2011 Current Population Survey, Internet site http://www.census.gov/hhes/www/cpstables/ 032011/hhinc/toc.htm; calculations by New Strategist

Table 1.75 Households by Income and Educational Attainment of Householder, 2010: Asian Households

(number and percent distribution of Asian households headed by people aged 25 or older by household income and educational attainment of householder, 2010; households in thousands as of 2011)

	total households	less than 9th grade	9th to 12th grade	high school graduate	some college	associate's degree	bachelor's degree or more				
							total	bachelor's degree	master's degree	professional degree	doctoral degree
Asian households	4,745	213	197	884	516	310	2,625	1,529	744	136	217
Under $5,000	193	22	26	45	19	10	73	53	14	3	3
$5,000 to $9,999	103	24	10	32	17	0	20	15	4	0	1
$10,000 to $14,999	172	22	13	53	20	10	53	36	16	0	2
$15,000 to $19,999	211	29	19	65	22	8	67	49	14	3	1
$20,000 to $24,999	234	29	8	69	30	16	82	51	25	0	5
$25,000 to $29,999	185	13	15	65	18	14	60	40	13	5	2
$30,000 to $34,999	165	11	12	50	21	19	53	37	8	7	1
$35,000 to $39,999	162	6	19	34	26	19	59	43	15	0	1
$40,000 to $44,999	180	4	10	37	30	8	90	48	30	6	7
$45,000 to $49,999	167	4	9	55	14	13	71	50	16	3	1
$50,000 to $54,999	219	4	9	52	33	12	110	86	18	3	2
$55,000 to $59,999	139	3	0	28	34	6	68	37	25	3	3
$60,000 to $64,999	214	7	5	40	24	14	125	93	22	2	8
$65,000 to $69,999	154	5	8	27	15	11	88	48	30	4	7
$70,000 to $74,999	131	7	0	26	8	13	76	47	23	2	3
$75,000 to $79,999	116	6	5	16	8	19	63	39	19	4	2
$80,000 to $84,999	120	1	7	17	20	8	67	36	21	4	6
$85,000 to $89,999	114	0	1	23	12	6	71	46	16	4	6
$90,000 to $94,999	121	1	5	20	14	10	70	34	22	7	8
$95,000 to $99,999	86	1	2	16	14	5	49	31	13	1	3
$100,000 to $124,999	495	8	5	47	51	34	349	202	104	7	35
$125,000 to $149,999	327	4	3	27	22	25	245	130	73	19	23
$150,000 to $174,999	254	2	3	16	21	5	207	108	69	10	21
$175,000 to $199,999	131	1	2	8	4	13	103	45	35	9	14
$200,000 or more	353	0	0	14	17	14	307	124	99	33	51
Median income	$65,870	$21,362	$32,427	$43,786	$56,097	$67,459	$90,930	$78,339	$100,670	$125,139	$128,869

PERCENT DISTRIBUTION

Asian households	100.0%	100.0%	100.0%	100.0%	100.0%	100.0%	100.0%	100.0%	100.0%	100.0%	100.0%
Under $25,000	19.2	59.2	38.6	29.9	20.9	14.2	11.2	13.3	9.8	4.4	5.5
$25,000 to $49,999	18.1	17.8	33.0	27.3	21.1	23.5	12.7	14.3	11.0	15.4	5.5
$50,000 to $74,999	18.1	12.2	11.2	19.6	22.1	18.1	17.8	20.3	15.9	10.3	10.6
$75,000 to $99,999	11.7	4.2	10.2	10.4	13.2	15.5	12.2	12.2	12.2	14.7	11.5
$100,000 or more	32.9	7.0	6.6	12.7	22.3	29.4	46.1	39.8	51.1	57.4	66.4

Note: Asians are those who identify themselves as being of the race alone and those who identify themselves as being of the race in combination with other races.
Source: Bureau of the Census, 2011 Current Population Survey, Internet site http://www.census.gov/hhes/www/cpstables/032011/hhinc/toc.htm; calculations by New Strategist

Table 1.76 Households by Income and Educational Attainment of Householder, 2010: Black Households

(number and percent distribution of black households headed by people aged 25 or older by household income and educational attainment of householder, 2010; households in thousands as of 2011)

	total households	less than 9th grade	9th to 12th grade	high school graduate	some college	associate's degree	bachelor's degree or more				
							total	bachelor's degree	master's degree	professional degree	doctoral degree
Black households	**14,411**	**574**	**1,681**	**4,613**	**3,019**	**1,526**	**2,997**	**1,949**	**823**	**116**	**109**
Under $5,000	984	58	223	385	157	70	92	59	28	2	3
$5,000 to $9,999	1,220	140	300	469	195	75	41	35	4	0	2
$10,000 to $14,999	1,275	109	213	512	246	96	99	75	19	4	2
$15,000 to $19,999	1,047	67	190	415	217	91	68	57	11	0	0
$20,000 to $24,999	1,075	44	141	404	254	107	127	99	20	7	1
$25,000 to $29,999	932	40	138	325	220	124	86	65	17	3	1
$30,000 to $34,999	897	31	83	312	204	108	160	116	31	5	8
$35,000 to $39,999	762	19	84	257	161	78	163	117	42	5	0
$40,000 to $44,999	731	9	68	204	150	97	203	136	62	2	4
$45,000 to $49,999	619	6	40	201	121	91	161	126	31	2	3
$50,000 to $54,999	575	9	44	190	131	72	130	85	40	2	3
$55,000 to $59,999	435	10	27	113	119	51	115	74	35	2	4
$60,000 to $64,999	442	5	24	127	97	46	142	94	36	5	7
$65,000 to $69,999	351	7	11	95	67	37	134	93	33	2	6
$70,000 to $74,999	432	3	15	111	111	53	140	97	38	2	3
$75,000 to $79,999	315	5	15	70	59	51	115	73	33	3	7
$80,000 to $84,999	281	0	13	49	87	55	77	54	20	4	0
$85,000 to $89,999	216	0	10	63	45	33	65	46	16	0	2
$90,000 to $94,999	193	2	4	50	45	23	70	39	27	3	0
$95,000 to $99,999	149	1	2	31	29	24	61	42	14	0	4
$100,000 to $124,999	667	6	25	119	152	72	295	175	100	10	11
$125,000 to $149,999	338	4	5	71	68	37	152	85	56	7	2
$150,000 to $174,999	207	1	2	21	40	18	127	46	51	19	10
$175,000 to $199,999	83	0	4	1	19	9	49	20	13	8	8
$200,000 or more	184	0	2	18	25	11	128	39	46	20	23
Median income	$33,509	$14,006	$17,323	$26,589	$35,468	$40,642	$61,432	$55,230	$70,390	$111,162	$96,230

PERCENT DISTRIBUTION

Black households	**100.0%**	**100.0%**	**100.0%**	**100.0%**	**100.0%**	**100.0%**	**100.0%**	**100.0%**	**100.0%**	**100.0%**	**100.0%**
Under $25,000	38.9	72.8	63.5	47.4	35.4	28.8	14.2	16.7	10.0	11.2	7.3
$25,000 to $49,999	27.3	18.3	24.6	28.2	28.4	32.6	25.8	28.7	22.2	14.7	14.7
$50,000 to $74,999	15.5	5.9	7.2	13.8	17.4	17.0	22.1	22.7	22.1	11.2	21.1
$75,000 to $99,999	8.0	1.4	2.6	5.7	8.8	12.2	12.9	13.0	13.4	8.6	11.9
$100,000 or more	10.3	1.9	2.3	5.0	10.1	9.6	25.1	18.7	32.3	55.2	49.5

Note: Blacks are those who identify themselves as being of the race alone and those who identify themselves as being of the race in combination with other races.
Source: Bureau of the Census, 2011 Current Population Survey, Internet site http://www.census.gov/hhes/www/cpstables/032011/hhinc/toc.htm; calculations by New Strategist

Table 1.77 Households by Income and Educational Attainment of Householder, 2010: Hispanic Households

(number and percent distribution of Hispanic households headed by people aged 25 or older by household income and educational attainment of householder, 2010; households in thousands as of 2011)

	total households	less than 9th grade	9th to 12th grade	high school graduate	some college	associate's degree	bachelor's degree or more total	bachelor's degree	master's degree	professional degree	doctoral degree
Hispanic households	12,530	2,387	1,852	3,517	1,902	939	1,933	1,326	417	82	109
Under $5,000	501	140	96	157	54	21	33	21	10	1	1
$5,000 to $9,999	679	242	149	156	76	23	32	21	9	3	0
$10,000 to $14,999	923	284	206	247	89	40	58	46	5	3	4
$15,000 to $19,999	847	265	176	237	79	37	54	38	15	1	0
$20,000 to $24,999	950	239	189	312	98	53	59	47	5	3	4
$25,000 to $29,999	931	234	159	262	145	67	64	54	4	1	4
$30,000 to $34,999	790	166	141	259	98	50	77	55	15	2	4
$35,000 to $39,999	754	165	123	214	115	50	88	68	15	6	0
$40,000 to $44,999	637	99	94	177	138	54	75	55	15	2	4
$45,000 to $49,999	572	93	74	190	90	47	79	67	6	2	4
$50,000 to $54,999	604	86	74	198	124	33	89	62	20	2	6
$55,000 to $59,999	447	58	57	135	83	42	72	59	11	3	0
$60,000 to $64,999	468	63	50	143	81	48	84	63	17	3	2
$65,000 to $69,999	367	40	44	107	79	36	60	49	11	0	1
$70,000 to $74,999	315	38	31	97	65	24	60	43	15	0	2
$75,000 to $79,999	331	35	32	95	46	35	87	62	19	2	5
$80,000 to $84,999	309	27	35	83	59	29	76	51	20	1	4
$85,000 to $89,999	225	17	14	42	47	44	60	39	12	3	5
$90,000 to $94,999	219	9	16	62	41	30	61	35	23	1	1
$95,000 to $99,999	155	6	8	37	29	33	41	22	17	1	0
$100,000 to $124,999	630	37	39	147	140	69	196	146	41	3	6
$125,000 to $149,999	380	21	27	83	61	40	149	92	44	4	9
$150,000 to $174,999	208	9	9	42	26	20	101	57	27	5	11
$175,000 to $199,999	95	3	4	15	8	5	61	25	15	11	11
$200,000 or more	190	8	6	21	28	10	118	47	29	19	22
Median income	$39,047	$25,424	$27,800	$37,273	$48,101	$53,936	$73,210	$65,441	$84,757	$108,532	$109,364

PERCENT DISTRIBUTION

	total households	less than 9th grade	9th to 12th grade	high school graduate	some college	associate's degree	bachelor's degree or more total	bachelor's degree	master's degree	professional degree	doctoral degree
Hispanic households	100.0%	100.0%	100.0%	100.0%	100.0%	100.0%	100.0%	100.0%	100.0%	100.0%	100.0%
Under $25,000	31.1	49.0	44.1	31.5	20.8	18.5	12.2	13.0	10.6	13.4	8.3
$25,000 to $49,999	29.4	31.7	31.9	31.3	30.8	28.5	19.8	22.5	13.2	15.9	14.7
$50,000 to $74,999	17.6	11.9	13.8	19.3	22.7	19.5	18.9	20.8	17.7	9.8	10.1
$75,000 to $99,999	9.9	3.9	5.7	9.1	11.7	18.2	16.8	15.8	21.8	9.8	13.8
$100,000 or more	12.0	3.3	4.6	8.8	13.8	15.3	32.3	27.7	37.4	51.2	54.1

Source: Bureau of the Census, 2011 Current Population Survey, Internet site http://www.census.gov/hhes/www/cpstables/032011/hhinc/toc.htm; calculations by New Strategist

Table 1.78 Households by Income and Educational Attainment of Householder, 2010: Non-Hispanic White Households

(number and percent distribution of non-Hispanic white households headed by people aged 25 or older by household income and educational attainment of householder, 2010; households in thousands as of 2011)

| | total households | less than 9th grade | 9th to 12th grade | high school graduate | some college | associate's degree | bachelor's degree or more | | | | |
							total	bachelor's degree	master's degree	professional degree	doctoral degree
Non-Hispanic white households	**79,990**	**1,938**	**4,239**	**23,450**	**14,570**	**8,053**	**27,739**	**17,522**	**7,403**	**1,425**	**1,389**
Under $5,000	1,857	85	206	615	362	175	414	284	84	24	22
$5,000 to $9,999	2,475	256	423	893	449	170	283	193	88	2	2
$10,000 to $14,999	4,102	392	476	1,663	742	328	502	374	102	12	14
$15,000 to $19,999	4,576	272	553	1,871	857	350	674	514	123	23	14
$20,000 to $24,999	4,096	217	392	1,666	743	301	778	546	184	28	21
$25,000 to $29,999	4,157	114	339	1,653	841	361	849	577	209	37	26
$30,000 to $34,999	3,880	138	332	1,416	827	399	769	535	177	26	30
$35,000 to $39,999	3,797	87	210	1,478	803	396	823	582	208	19	14
$40,000 to $44,999	3,709	63	214	1,328	756	362	985	679	236	39	31
$45,000 to $49,999	3,286	39	161	1,120	711	369	886	580	249	38	19
$50,000 to $54,999	3,455	46	157	1,126	691	410	1,025	725	233	29	38
$55,000 to $59,999	2,944	32	140	898	616	341	918	638	225	27	27
$60,000 to $64,999	3,050	44	94	900	607	337	1,068	690	313	25	40
$65,000 to $69,999	2,528	23	85	653	533	310	924	602	243	48	31
$70,000 to $74,999	2,740	9	72	786	505	323	1,046	711	222	53	60
$75,000 to $79,999	2,248	10	39	642	410	236	912	590	259	30	33
$80,000 to $84,999	2,297	18	45	589	461	311	873	621	188	26	38
$85,000 to $89,999	2,039	10	46	519	367	313	785	487	235	35	28
$90,000 to $94,999	1,932	11	31	441	374	233	843	555	220	44	25
$95,000 to $99,999	1,661	4	20	393	345	235	665	438	172	13	41
$100,000 to $124,999	6,971	25	120	1,369	1,136	798	3,521	2,198	965	168	193
$125,000 to $149,999	4,127	25	41	641	619	428	2,374	1,381	715	142	134
$150,000 to $174,999	2,661	7	22	305	348	230	1,749	994	509	115	132
$175,000 to $199,999	1,574	3	5	175	173	132	1,085	599	329	78	78
$200,000 or more	3,825	10	19	308	294	206	2,988	1,428	917	345	299
Median income	$55,908	$19,222	$25,930	$41,474	$51,223	$60,757	$85,741	$79,386	$92,360	$119,779	$119,352

PERCENT DISTRIBUTION

Non-Hispanic white households	100.0%	100.0%	100.0%	100.0%	100.0%	100.0%	100.0%	100.0%	100.0%	100.0%	100.0%
Under $25,000	21.4	63.1	48.4	28.6	21.6	16.4	9.6	10.9	7.8	6.2	5.3
$25,000 to $49,999	23.5	22.8	29.6	29.8	27.0	23.4	15.5	16.9	14.6	11.2	8.6
$50,000 to $74,999	18.4	7.9	12.9	18.6	20.3	21.4	18.0	19.2	16.7	12.8	14.1
$75,000 to $99,999	12.7	2.7	4.3	11.0	13.4	16.5	14.7	15.4	14.5	10.4	11.9
$100,000 or more	24.0	3.6	4.9	11.9	17.6	22.3	42.2	37.7	46.4	59.5	60.2

Note: Non-Hispanic whites are those who identify themselves as white alone and not Hispanic.
Source: Bureau of the Census, 2011 Current Population Survey, Internet site http://www.census.gov/hhes/www/cpstables/032011/hhinc/toc.htm; calculations by New Strategist

Household Incomes Are Highest in New England

Incomes are lowest in the East South Central states.

Among the country's four geographical regions, only the South—which is home to 37 percent of the nation's households—has a median household income significantly below the national average, $45,492 in the South versus $49,445 nationally. Median household income is about average in the Midwest ($48,445) and well above average in the Northeast ($53,283) and West ($53,142).

Median household income is far above average in the New England states, at $60,363 in 2010—22 percent above the national median. The Pacific division ranks second, with a much lower median income of $54,490. The lowest household incomes are found in the East South Central states of Alabama, Kentucky, Mississippi, and Tennessee. Median household income in the division was just $39,911 in 2010, 19 percent below the national figure. The West South Central division (Arkansas, Louisiana, Oklahoma, and Texas) had a higher median household income of $45,355.

■ The recession is reducing incomes in every region, the biggest losses occurring in the Midwest.

Incomes are lowest in the South

(median household income by region, 2010)

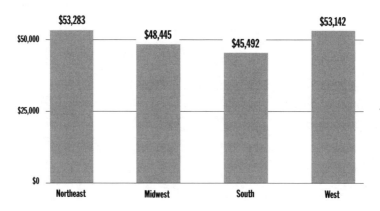

Table 1.79 Households by Income and Region, 2010

(number and percent distribution of households by household income and region of residence, 2010; households in thousands as of 2011)

	total	Northeast	Midwest	South	West
Total households	**118,682**	**21,597**	**26,669**	**44,161**	**26,254**
Under $5,000	4,176	723	896	1,740	816
$5,000 to $9,999	5,055	875	1,153	2,151	876
$10,000 to $14,999	7,061	1,263	1,438	2,892	1,467
$15,000 to $19,999	7,260	1,274	1,710	2,883	1,393
$20,000 to $24,999	6,937	1,085	1,612	2,768	1,471
$25,000 to $29,999	6,730	1,139	1,525	2,683	1,383
$30,000 to $34,999	6,148	1,067	1,475	2,254	1,353
$35,000 to $39,999	5,907	896	1,478	2,285	1,247
$40,000 to $44,999	5,624	944	1,239	2,217	1,224
$45,000 to $49,999	4,933	876	1,160	1,819	1,079
$50,000 to $54,999	5,088	860	1,219	1,864	1,145
$55,000 to $59,999	4,203	795	1,012	1,463	933
$60,000 to $64,999	4,412	839	965	1,582	1,026
$65,000 to $69,999	3,579	601	862	1,290	826
$70,000 to $74,999	3,769	685	893	1,313	878
$75,000 to $79,999	3,118	510	731	1,141	735
$80,000 to $84,999	3,143	556	742	1,156	689
$85,000 to $89,999	2,680	516	611	981	571
$90,000 to $94,999	2,516	464	556	916	580
$95,000 to $99,999	2,110	360	506	725	519
$100,000 to $124,999	9,008	1,799	1,998	3,043	2,169
$125,000 to $149,999	5,294	1,094	1,072	1,783	1,342
$150,000 to $174,999	3,386	807	637	1,114	830
$175,000 to $199,999	1,919	411	423	612	471
$200,000 or more	4,627	1,156	756	1,483	1,232
Median income	$49,445	$53,283	$48,445	$45,492	$53,142

PERCENT DISTRIBUTION

Total households	**100.0%**	**100.0%**	**100.0%**	**100.0%**	**100.0%**
Under $25,000	25.7	24.2	25.5	28.2	22.9
$25,000 to $49,999	24.7	22.8	25.8	25.5	23.9
$50,000 to $74,999	17.7	17.5	18.6	17.0	18.3
$75,000 to $99,999	11.4	11.1	11.8	11.1	11.8
$100,000 or more	20.4	24.4	18.3	18.2	23.0

Source: Bureau of the Census, 2011 Current Population Survey, Internet site http://www.census.gov/hhes/www/cpstables/ 032011/hhinc/toc.htm; calculations by New Strategist

Table 1.80 Households by Income, Region, and Division, 2010: Northeast

(number and percent distribution of total households and households in the Northeast region and divisions by household income, 2010; households in thousands as of 2011)

	total	Northeast total	New England	Middle Atlantic
Total households	**118,682**	**21,597**	**5,717**	**15,881**
Under $5,000	4,176	723	135	588
$5,000 to $9,999	5,055	875	194	681
$10,000 to $14,999	7,061	1,263	319	944
$15,000 to $19,999	7,260	1,274	324	950
$20,000 to $24,999	6,937	1,085	247	838
$25,000 to $29,999	6,730	1,139	248	891
$30,000 to $34,999	6,148	1,067	267	800
$35,000 to $39,999	5,907	896	208	688
$40,000 to $44,999	5,624	944	248	696
$45,000 to $49,999	4,933	876	233	643
$50,000 to $54,999	5,088	860	228	632
$55,000 to $59,999	4,203	795	188	607
$60,000 to $64,999	4,412	839	224	615
$65,000 to $69,999	3,579	601	151	450
$70,000 to $74,999	3,769	685	182	503
$75,000 to $79,999	3,118	510	137	374
$80,000 to $84,999	3,143	556	159	396
$85,000 to $89,999	2,680	516	142	375
$90,000 to $94,999	2,516	464	140	324
$95,000 to $99,999	2,110	360	100	260
$100,000 to $124,999	9,008	1,799	547	1,253
$125,000 to $149,999	5,294	1,094	320	774
$150,000 to $174,999	3,386	807	265	542
$175,000 to $199,999	1,919	411	141	269
$200,000 or more	4,627	1,156	369	787
Median income	$49,445	$53,283	$60,363	$51,323

PERCENT DISTRIBUTION

	total	Northeast total	New England	Middle Atlantic
Total households	**100.0%**	**100.0%**	**100.0%**	**100.0%**
Under $25,000	25.7	24.2	21.3	25.2
$25,000 to $49,999	24.7	22.8	21.1	23.4
$50,000 to $74,999	17.7	17.5	17.0	17.7
$75,000 to $99,999	11.4	11.1	11.9	10.9
$100,000 or more	20.4	24.4	28.7	22.8

Source: Bureau of the Census, 2011 Current Population Survey, Internet site http://www.census.gov/hhes/www/cpstables/ 032011/hhinc/toc.htm; calculations by New Strategist

Table 1.81 Households by Income, Region, and Division, 2010: Midwest

(number and percent distribution of total households and households in the Midwest region and divisions by household income, 2010; households in thousands as of 2011)

		Midwest		
	total	total	East North Central	West North Central
Total households	**118,682**	**26,669**	**18,336**	**8,334**
Under $5,000	4,176	896	660	237
$5,000 to $9,999	5,055	1,153	804	349
$10,000 to $14,999	7,061	1,438	962	476
$15,000 to $19,999	7,260	1,710	1,204	506
$20,000 to $24,999	6,937	1,612	1,128	484
$25,000 to $29,999	6,730	1,525	1,031	494
$30,000 to $34,999	6,148	1,475	983	491
$35,000 to $39,999	5,907	1,478	1,046	433
$40,000 to $44,999	5,624	1,239	856	383
$45,000 to $49,999	4,933	1,160	814	346
$50,000 to $54,999	5,088	1,219	834	385
$55,000 to $59,999	4,203	1,012	713	299
$60,000 to $64,999	4,412	965	674	291
$65,000 to $69,999	3,579	862	595	268
$70,000 to $74,999	3,769	893	624	269
$75,000 to $79,999	3,118	731	492	239
$80,000 to $84,999	3,143	742	501	241
$85,000 to $89,999	2,680	611	415	195
$90,000 to $94,999	2,516	556	385	171
$95,000 to $99,999	2,110	506	333	173
$100,000 to $124,999	9,008	1,998	1,324	674
$125,000 to $149,999	5,294	1,072	696	377
$150,000 to $174,999	3,386	637	442	194
$175,000 to $199,999	1,919	423	299	124
$200,000 or more	4,627	756	521	235
Median income	$49,445	$48,445	$48,032	$49,500

PERCENT DISTRIBUTION

Total households	**100.0%**	**100.0%**	**100.0%**	**100.0%**
Under $25,000	25.7	25.5	25.9	24.6
$25,000 to $49,999	24.7	25.8	25.8	25.8
$50,000 to $74,999	17.7	18.6	18.8	18.1
$75,000 to $99,999	11.4	11.8	11.6	12.2
$100,000 or more	20.4	18.3	17.9	19.2

Source: Bureau of the Census, 2011 Current Population Survey, Internet site http://www.census.gov/hhes/www/cpstables/ 032011/hhinc/toc.htm; calculations by New Strategist

Table 1.82 Households by Income, Region, and Division, 2010: South

(number and percent distribution of total households and households in the South region and divisions by household income, 2010; households in thousands as of 2011)

		South			
	total	total	South Atlantic	East South Central	West South Central
Total households	**118,682**	**44,161**	**23,479**	**7,321**	**13,361**
Under $5,000	4,176	1,740	902	314	525
$5,000 to $9,999	5,055	2,151	1,056	427	667
$10,000 to $14,999	7,061	2,892	1,508	525	859
$15,000 to $19,999	7,260	2,883	1,445	594	845
$20,000 to $24,999	6,937	2,768	1,412	543	812
$25,000 to $29,999	6,730	2,683	1,351	451	881
$30,000 to $34,999	6,148	2,254	1,166	425	663
$35,000 to $39,999	5,907	2,285	1,216	389	680
$40,000 to $44,999	5,624	2,217	1,143	369	705
$45,000 to $49,999	4,933	1,819	1,017	260	542
$50,000 to $54,999	5,088	1,864	1,025	272	567
$55,000 to $59,999	4,203	1,463	762	242	459
$60,000 to $64,999	4,412	1,582	846	238	498
$65,000 to $69,999	3,579	1,290	637	213	440
$70,000 to $74,999	3,769	1,313	718	215	380
$75,000 to $79,999	3,118	1,141	630	187	325
$80,000 to $84,999	3,143	1,156	650	168	339
$85,000 to $89,999	2,680	981	523	156	302
$90,000 to $94,999	2,516	916	511	138	267
$95,000 to $99,999	2,110	725	415	135	175
$100,000 to $124,999	9,008	3,043	1,599	466	976
$125,000 to $149,999	5,294	1,783	1,002	228	554
$150,000 to $174,999	3,386	1,114	664	112	338
$175,000 to $199,999	1,919	612	348	87	179
$200,000 or more	4,627	1,483	935	166	383
Median income	$49,445	$45,492	$47,316	$39,911	$45,355

PERCENT DISTRIBUTION

Total households	**100.0%**	**100.0%**	**100.0%**	**100.0%**	**100.0%**
Under $25,000	25.7	28.2	26.9	32.8	27.8
$25,000 to $49,999	24.7	25.5	25.1	25.9	26.0
$50,000 to $74,999	17.7	17.0	17.0	16.1	17.5
$75,000 to $99,999	11.4	11.1	11.6	10.7	10.5
$100,000 or more	20.4	18.2	19.4	14.5	18.2

Source: Bureau of the Census, 2011 Current Population Survey, Internet site http://www.census.gov/hhes/www/cpstables/ 032011/hhinc/toc.htm; calculations by New Strategist

Table 1.83 Households by Income, Region, and Division, 2010: West

(number and percent distribution of total households and households in the West region and divisions by household income, 2010; households in thousands as of 2011)

	total	West total	Mountain	Pacific
Total households	**118,682**	**26,254**	**8,404**	**17,850**
Under $5,000	4,176	816	287	529
$5,000 to $9,999	5,055	876	336	540
$10,000 to $14,999	7,061	1,467	466	1,001
$15,000 to $19,999	7,260	1,393	451	942
$20,000 to $24,999	6,937	1,471	499	972
$25,000 to $29,999	6,730	1,383	431	952
$30,000 to $34,999	6,148	1,353	435	917
$35,000 to $39,999	5,907	1,247	415	833
$40,000 to $44,999	5,624	1,224	424	800
$45,000 to $49,999	4,933	1,079	354	725
$50,000 to $54,999	5,088	1,145	371	775
$55,000 to $59,999	4,203	933	323	609
$60,000 to $64,999	4,412	1,026	340	686
$65,000 to $69,999	3,579	826	282	544
$70,000 to $74,999	3,769	878	269	609
$75,000 to $79,999	3,118	735	267	469
$80,000 to $84,999	3,143	689	234	456
$85,000 to $89,999	2,680	571	219	352
$90,000 to $94,999	2,516	580	192	388
$95,000 to $99,999	2,110	519	122	397
$100,000 to $124,999	9,008	2,169	644	1,522
$125,000 to $149,999	5,294	1,342	345	997
$150,000 to $174,999	3,386	830	256	574
$175,000 to $199,999	1,919	471	131	340
$200,000 or more	4,627	1,232	311	921
Median income	$49,445	$53,142	$51,131	$54,490

PERCENT DISTRIBUTION

	total	West total	Mountain	Pacific
Total households	**100.0%**	**100.0%**	**100.0%**	**100.0%**
Under $25,000	25.7	22.9	24.3	22.3
$25,000 to $49,999	24.7	23.9	24.5	23.7
$50,000 to $74,999	17.7	18.3	18.9	18.1
$75,000 to $99,999	11.4	11.8	12.3	11.6
$100,000 or more	20.4	23.0	20.1	24.4

Source: Bureau of the Census, 2011 Current Population Survey, Internet site http://www.census.gov/hhes/www/cpstables/032011/hhinc/toc.htm; calculations by New Strategist

Among Blacks, Household Incomes Are Highest in the West

Hispanic household income also peaks in the West.

In every region, the incomes of Asian and non-Hispanic white households surpass those of blacks and Hispanics. The median income of Asian households surpasses that of non-Hispanic whites in every region except the Northeast. Asian household income is highest in the South, at $70,209 in 2010. Non-Hispanic white median household income is highest in the West, at $60,075.

For black households, median income is higher in the West than in the other regions, at $35,279 in 2010. This compares with a median household income of more than $60,000 for Asian and non-Hispanic white households in the region. In the South, which is home to the majority of black households, the median income of blacks is only $32,127 versus more than $70,000 for Asian households in the region and more than $50,000 for non-Hispanic whites. One reason for the lower incomes of blacks is their household composition. Black households are much less likely than average to be headed by married couples, the most-affluent household type.

Hispanic household median incomes range from a low of $35,888 in the Midwest to a high of $40,109 in the West. Hispanic incomes are relatively low because many Hispanics are poorly educated immigrants with little earning power.

■ Income disparities by race and Hispanic origin will continue as long as differences in household composition persist and until immigrants make up a much smaller share of the Hispanic population.

Among households in the South, blacks have the lowest incomes

(median income of households in the South by race and Hispanic origin of householder, 2010)

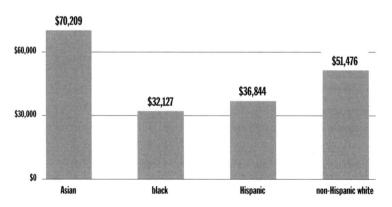

Table 1.84 Households by Income, Region, Race, and Hispanic Origin, 2010: Northeast

(number and percent distribution of households in the Northeast by household income, race, and Hispanic origin, 2010; households in thousands as of 2011)

	total	Asian	black	Hispanic	non-Hispanic white
Households in the Northeast	**21,597**	**1,075**	**2,693**	**2,016**	**15,960**
Under $5,000	723	84	198	94	363
$5,000 to $9,999	875	32	263	175	433
$10,000 to $14,999	1,263	31	239	159	849
$15,000 to $19,999	1,274	51	166	148	917
$20,000 to $24,999	1,085	61	164	133	734
$25,000 to $29,999	1,139	61	149	119	813
$30,000 to $34,999	1,067	43	176	140	716
$35,000 to $39,999	896	39	115	105	636
$40,000 to $44,999	944	45	132	90	688
$45,000 to $49,999	876	37	103	77	660
$50,000 to $54,999	860	62	91	93	628
$55,000 to $59,999	795	20	106	80	596
$60,000 to $64,999	839	38	99	73	633
$65,000 to $69,999	601	21	66	52	462
$70,000 to $74,999	685	26	91	51	519
$75,000 to $79,999	510	22	55	37	398
$80,000 to $84,999	556	16	52	47	441
$85,000 to $89,999	516	13	46	32	428
$90,000 to $94,999	464	30	30	26	381
$95,000 to $99,999	360	6	23	21	314
$100,000 to $124,999	1,799	90	152	120	1,447
$125,000 to $149,999	1,094	73	62	74	890
$150,000 to $174,999	807	52	66	34	654
$175,000 to $199,999	411	39	15	16	343
$200,000 or more	1,156	83	36	21	1,016
Median income	$53,283	$54,011	$34,726	$36,410	$59,497

PERCENT DISTRIBUTION

	total	Asian	black	Hispanic	non-Hispanic white
Households in the Northeast	**100.0%**	**100.0%**	**100.0%**	**100.0%**	**100.0%**
Under $25,000	24.2	24.1	38.2	35.2	20.7
$25,000 to $49,999	22.8	20.9	25.1	26.3	22.0
$50,000 to $74,999	17.5	15.5	16.8	17.3	17.8
$75,000 to $99,999	11.1	8.1	7.6	8.1	12.3
$100,000 or more	24.4	31.3	12.3	13.1	27.3

Note: Asians and blacks are those who identify themselves as being of the race alone and those who identify themselves as being of the race in combination with other races. Non-Hispanic whites are those who identify themselves as being white alone and not Hispanic. Numbers do not add to total because some people identify themselves as being of more than one race, not all races are shown, and Hispanics may be of any race.
Source: Bureau of the Census, 2011 Current Population Survey, Internet site http://www.census.gov/hhes/www/cpstables/032011/hhinc/toc.htm; calculations by New Strategist

Table 1.85 Households by Income, Region, Race, and Hispanic Origin, 2010: Midwest

(number and percent distribution of households in the Midwest by household income, race, and Hispanic origin, 2010; households in thousands as of 2011)

	total	Asian	black	Hispanic	non-Hispanic white
Households in the Midwest	**26,669**	**573**	**2,783**	**1,130**	**21,989**
Under $5,000	896	22	272	48	540
$5,000 to $9,999	1,153	22	295	57	767
$10,000 to $14,999	1,438	21	254	71	1,075
$15,000 to $19,999	1,710	37	220	90	1,351
$20,000 to $24,999	1,612	36	214	96	1,260
$25,000 to $29,999	1,525	16	191	104	1,193
$30,000 to $34,999	1,475	21	163	83	1,189
$35,000 to $39,999	1,478	25	165	73	1,203
$40,000 to $44,999	1,239	9	129	58	1,041
$45,000 to $49,999	1,160	22	107	61	952
$50,000 to $54,999	1,219	28	122	57	1,007
$55,000 to $59,999	1,012	23	67	40	874
$60,000 to $64,999	965	32	75	33	824
$65,000 to $69,999	862	22	56	31	751
$70,000 to $74,999	893	24	84	29	759
$75,000 to $79,999	731	11	49	23	648
$80,000 to $84,999	742	16	34	25	664
$85,000 to $89,999	611	13	34	19	539
$90,000 to $94,999	556	12	19	19	505
$95,000 to $99,999	506	10	26	5	459
$100,000 to $124,999	1,998	52	99	43	1,794
$125,000 to $149,999	1,072	40	40	22	961
$150,000 to $174,999	637	21	27	22	558
$175,000 to $199,999	423	14	18	13	377
$200,000 or more	756	23	25	8	696
Median income	$48,445	$60,626	$28,116	$35,888	$51,798

PERCENT DISTRIBUTION

	total	Asian	black	Hispanic	non-Hispanic white
Households in the Midwest	**100.0%**	**100.0%**	**100.0%**	**100.0%**	**100.0%**
Under $25,000	25.5	24.1	45.1	32.0	22.7
$25,000 to $49,999	25.8	16.2	27.1	33.5	25.4
$50,000 to $74,999	18.6	22.5	14.5	16.8	19.2
$75,000 to $99,999	11.8	10.8	5.8	8.1	12.8
$100,000 or more	18.3	26.2	7.5	9.6	19.9

Note: Asians and blacks are those who identify themselves as being of the race alone and those who identify themselves as being of the race in combination with other races. Non-Hispanic whites are those who identify themselves as being white alone and not Hispanic. Numbers do not add to total because some people identify themselves as being of more than one race, not all races are shown, and Hispanics may be of any race.
Source: Bureau of the Census, 2011 Current Population Survey, Internet site http://www.census.gov/hhes/www/cpstables/032011/hhinc/toc.htm; calculations by New Strategist

Table 1.86 Households by Income, Region, Race, and Hispanic Origin, 2010: South

(number and percent distribution of households in the South by household income, race, and Hispanic origin, 2010; households in thousands as of 2011)

	total	Asian	black	Hispanic	non-Hispanic white
Households in the South	**44,161**	**1,097**	**8,627**	**5,143**	**28,924**
Under $5,000	1,740	36	608	245	843
$5,000 to $9,999	2,151	22	715	285	1,096
$10,000 to $14,999	2,892	32	794	397	1,649
$15,000 to $19,999	2,883	41	662	373	1,782
$20,000 to $24,999	2,768	44	687	442	1,584
$25,000 to $29,999	2,683	39	592	413	1,616
$30,000 to $34,999	2,254	44	530	278	1,395
$35,000 to $39,999	2,285	41	455	301	1,472
$40,000 to $44,999	2,217	35	457	285	1,406
$45,000 to $49,999	1,819	28	373	228	1,173
$50,000 to $54,999	1,864	45	327	239	1,234
$55,000 to $59,999	1,463	44	235	164	1,000
$60,000 to $64,999	1,582	62	251	175	1,079
$65,000 to $69,999	1,290	34	212	141	892
$70,000 to $74,999	1,313	30	227	116	927
$75,000 to $79,999	1,141	22	200	146	759
$80,000 to $84,999	1,156	42	167	117	810
$85,000 to $89,999	981	42	123	100	715
$90,000 to $94,999	916	23	127	101	663
$95,000 to $99,999	725	19	85	66	554
$100,000 to $124,999	3,043	126	353	216	2,311
$125,000 to $149,999	1,783	69	194	129	1,379
$150,000 to $174,999	1,114	74	106	84	849
$175,000 to $199,999	612	25	48	27	511
$200,000 or more	1,483	81	101	80	1,223
Median income	$45,492	$70,209	$32,127	$36,844	$51,476

PERCENT DISTRIBUTION

	total	Asian	black	Hispanic	non-Hispanic white
Households in the South	**100.0%**	**100.0%**	**100.0%**	**100.0%**	**100.0%**
Under $25,000	28.2	16.0	40.2	33.9	24.0
$25,000 to $49,999	25.5	17.0	27.9	29.3	24.4
$50,000 to $74,999	17.0	19.6	14.5	16.2	17.7
$75,000 to $99,999	11.1	13.5	8.1	10.3	12.1
$100,000 or more	18.2	34.2	9.3	10.4	21.7

Note: Asians and blacks are those who identify themselves as being of the race alone and those who identify themselves as being of the race in combination with other races. Non-Hispanic whites are those who identify themselves as being white alone and not Hispanic. Numbers do not add to total because some people identify themselves as being of more than one race, not all races are shown, and Hispanics may be of any race.
Source: Bureau of the Census, 2011 Current Population Survey, Internet site http://www.census.gov/hhes/www/cpstables/032011/hhinc/toc.htm; calculations by New Strategist

Table 1.87 Households by Income, Region, Race, and Hispanic Origin, 2010: West

(number and percent distribution of households in the West by household income, race, and Hispanic origin, 2010; households in thousands as of 2011)

	total	Asian	black	Hispanic	non-Hispanic white
Households in the West	**26,254**	**2,295**	**1,509**	**5,375**	**16,598**
Under $5,000	816	90	95	206	391
$5,000 to $9,999	876	45	117	252	425
$10,000 to $14,999	1,467	97	145	391	792
$15,000 to $19,999	1,393	97	93	338	832
$20,000 to $24,999	1,471	120	98	396	821
$25,000 to $29,999	1,383	83	113	398	775
$30,000 to $34,999	1,353	76	88	355	808
$35,000 to $39,999	1,247	71	78	343	737
$40,000 to $44,999	1,224	107	81	274	748
$45,000 to $49,999	1,079	99	72	256	646
$50,000 to $54,999	1,145	98	67	255	705
$55,000 to $59,999	933	58	49	203	605
$60,000 to $64,999	1,026	95	37	226	649
$65,000 to $69,999	826	83	40	163	522
$70,000 to $74,999	878	65	40	133	622
$75,000 to $79,999	735	64	32	144	484
$80,000 to $84,999	689	52	33	139	455
$85,000 to $89,999	571	50	19	86	403
$90,000 to $94,999	580	57	25	80	404
$95,000 to $99,999	519	56	17	74	360
$100,000 to $124,999	2,169	240	70	287	1,538
$125,000 to $149,999	1,342	154	48	167	957
$150,000 to $174,999	830	111	15	72	626
$175,000 to $199,999	471	58	5	41	365
$200,000 or more	1,232	171	31	92	927
Median income	$53,142	$65,637	$35,279	$40,109	$60,075

PERCENT DISTRIBUTION

Households in the West	**100.0%**	**100.0%**	**100.0%**	**100.0%**	**100.0%**
Under $25,000	22.9	19.6	36.3	29.5	19.6
$25,000 to $49,999	23.9	19.0	28.6	30.3	22.4
$50,000 to $74,999	18.3	17.4	15.4	18.2	18.7
$75,000 to $99,999	11.8	12.2	8.3	9.7	12.7
$100,000 or more	23.0	32.0	11.2	12.3	26.6

Note: Asians and blacks are those who identify themselves as being of the race alone and those who identify themselves as being of the race in combination with other races. Non-Hispanic whites are those who identify themselves as being white alone and not Hispanic. Numbers do not add to total because some people identify themselves as being of more than one race, not all races are shown, and Hispanics may be of any race.
Source: Bureau of the Census, 2011 Current Population Survey, Internet site http://www.census.gov/hhes/www/cpstables/032011/hhinc/toc.htm; calculations by New Strategist

Household Incomes Are Highest in Maryland

Incomes are lowest in Mississippi.

When the 50 states and the District of Columbia are ranked by median household income, Maryland comes out on top with a median income of $68,854 in 2010. Mississippi is at the bottom of the heap, with a median income of just $36,851—more than $32,000 less than in Maryland. Some of the difference between the median household incomes of Maryland and Mississippi results from the higher cost of living in Maryland—particularly in the areas surrounding the District of Columbia, but other factors such as education, household composition, and the health of each state's economy are also at play.

Other states at the bottom of the household income ranking include West Virginia, Arkansas, Kentucky, and Alabama. States at the top include New Jersey, Alaska, Connecticut, and Hawaii.

■ Most states have experienced a decline in median household income in the past few years because of the economic downturn.

The median income gap between the top and bottom states is enormous

(median household income in the states with the highest and the lowest median household income, 2010)

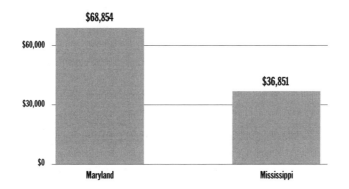

Table 1.88 Median Household Income by State, 2010

(median income of households by state, state rank, and index to national median, 2010)

	median household income	rank among 50 states	index to national median
United States	**$50,046**	–	**100**
Alabama	40,474	47	81
Alaska	64,576	3	129
Arizona	46,789	29	93
Arkansas	38,307	49	77
California	57,708	10	115
Colorado	54,046	16	108
Connecticut	64,032	4	128
Delaware	55,847	11	112
District of Columbia	60,903	8	122
Florida	44,409	37	89
Georgia	46,430	31	93
Hawaii	63,030	5	126
Idaho	43,490	39	87
Illinois	52,972	18	106
Indiana	44,613	36	89
Iowa	47,961	28	96
Kansas	48,257	27	96
Kentucky	40,062	48	80
Louisiana	42,505	42	85
Maine	45,815	33	92
Maryland	68,854	1	138
Massachusetts	62,072	6	124
Michigan	45,413	34	91
Minnesota	55,459	13	111
Mississippi	36,851	51	74
Missouri	44,301	38	89
Montana	42,666	41	85
Nebraska	48,408	26	97
Nevada	51,001	20	102
New Hampshire	61,042	7	122
New Jersey	67,681	2	135
New Mexico	42,090	43	84
New York	54,148	15	108
North Carolina	43,326	40	87
North Dakota	48,670	24	97
Ohio	45,090	35	90
Oklahoma	42,072	44	84
Oregon	46,560	30	93
Pennsylvania	49,288	22	98
Rhode Island	52,254	19	104

	median household income	rank among 50 states	index to national median
South Carolina	$42,018	45	84
South Dakota	45,904	32	92
Tennessee	41,461	46	83
Texas	48,615	25	97
Utah	54,744	14	109
Vermont	49,406	21	99
Virginia	60,674	9	121
Washington	55,631	12	111
West Virginia	38,218	50	76
Wisconsin	49,001	23	98
Wyoming	53,512	17	107

*Note: The index is calculated by dividing the median income of each state by the national median and multiplying by 100. "–"
means not applicable.*
*Source: Bureau of the Census, 2010 American Community Survey, Internet site http://factfinder2.census.gov/faces/nav/jsf/pages/
index.xhtml; calculations by New Strategist*

Suburban Households Have the Highest Incomes

Households in principal cities have below-average incomes.

Fifty percent of the nation's households are located in the suburbs of metropolitan areas—defined as the portion of a metropolitan area outside the principal cities. Suburban households have the highest incomes—a median of $56,140 in 2010, according to the Census Bureau's Current Population Survey. Twenty-four percent have incomes of $100,000 or more.

Thirty-three percent of households are in the principal cities of metropolitan areas. Their median income is below the national average, at $44,049 in 2010. Only 16 percent of households are not in metropolitan areas. They have the lowest incomes—a median of just $40,287 in 2010.

Among the 50 largest metropolitan areas, Washington, D.C., has the highest median household income, according to the Census Bureau's 2010 American Community Survey. The $84,523 median income of households in Washington, D.C., was 69 percent above the national median. Also ranking at the top among the largest metropolitan areas are San Jose, San Francisco, and Boston.

The median household income of Tampa—$43,547—was at the bottom of the list in 2010. Other metros with relatively low median incomes are Birmingham, Louisville, and Miami.

■ More than 80 percent of Americans now live in metropolitan areas.

Nonmetropolitan households have the lowest incomes

(median household income by metropolitan residence, 2010)

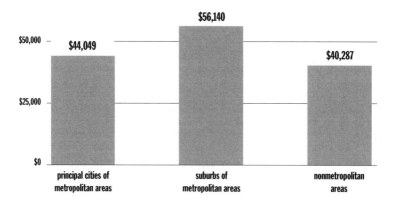

Table 1.89 Households by Income and Metropolitan Residence, 2010

(number and percent distribution of households by household income and metropolitan residence, 2010; households in thousands as of 2011)

		in metropolitan area			not in metropolitan area
	total	total	inside principal cities	outside principal cities	
Total households	**118,682**	**99,266**	**39,472**	**59,793**	**19,417**
Under $5,000	4,176	3,554	1,931	1,622	622
$5,000 to $9,999	5,055	3,931	2,102	1,828	1,124
$10,000 to $14,999	7,061	5,609	2,643	2,966	1,451
$15,000 to $19,999	7,260	5,675	2,484	3,190	1,585
$20,000 to $24,999	6,937	5,611	2,552	3,059	1,326
$25,000 to $29,999	6,730	5,419	2,338	3,080	1,311
$30,000 to $34,999	6,148	5,020	2,083	2,937	1,128
$35,000 to $39,999	5,907	4,812	1,979	2,833	1,095
$40,000 to $44,999	5,624	4,653	1,872	2,781	971
$45,000 to $49,999	4,933	4,069	1,556	2,513	864
$50,000 to $54,999	5,088	4,215	1,704	2,511	873
$55,000 to $59,999	4,203	3,487	1,262	2,225	715
$60,000 to $64,999	4,412	3,686	1,446	2,240	726
$65,000 to $69,999	3,579	2,945	1,056	1,889	635
$70,000 to $74,999	3,769	3,171	1,206	1,966	597
$75,000 to $79,999	3,118	2,636	962	1,673	482
$80,000 to $84,999	3,143	2,666	889	1,777	477
$85,000 to $89,999	2,680	2,296	793	1,504	384
$90,000 to $94,999	2,516	2,179	724	1,455	337
$95,000 to $99,999	2,110	1,759	548	1,212	351
$100,000 to $124,999	9,008	7,869	2,637	5,231	1,139
$125,000 to $149,999	5,294	4,716	1,593	3,124	575
$150,000 to $174,999	3,386	3,151	989	2,162	236
$175,000 to $199,999	1,919	1,778	587	1,191	142
$200,000 or more	4,627	4,358	1,535	2,823	269
Median income	$49,445	$51,244	$44,049	$56,140	$40,287

PERCENT DISTRIBUTION

Total households	**100.0%**	**100.0%**	**100.0%**	**100.0%**	**100.0%**
Under $25,000	25.7	24.6	29.7	21.2	31.5
$25,000 to $49,999	24.7	24.2	24.9	23.7	27.7
$50,000 to $74,999	17.7	17.6	16.9	18.1	18.3
$75,000 to $99,999	11.4	11.6	9.9	12.7	10.5
$100,000 or more	20.4	22.0	18.6	24.3	12.2

Source: Bureau of the Census, 2011 Current Population Survey, Internet site http://www.census.gov/hhes/www/cpstables/ 032011/hhinc/toc.htm; calculations by New Strategist

Table 1.90 Median Household Income in the 50 Largest Metropolitan Areas, 2010

(median household income in the 50 largest metropolitan areas, rank among 50 largest metropolitan areas, and index to national median, 2010)

	median household income	rank among 50 metro areas	index to national median
United States	**$50,046**	–	**100**
Atlanta–Sandy Springs–Marietta, GA	53,182	25	106
Austin–Round Rock–San Marcos, TX	55,744	19	111
Baltimore–Towson, MD	64,812	5	130
Birmingham–Hoover, AL	44,216	49	88
Boston–Cambridge–Quincy, MA–NH	68,020	4	136
Buffalo–Niagara Falls, NY	46,420	42	93
Charlotte–Gastonia–Rock Hill, NC–SC	50,449	32	101
Chicago–Joliet–Naperville, IL–IN–WI	57,104	16	114
Cincinnati–Middletown, OH–KY–IN	51,572	28	103
Cleveland–Elyria–Mentor, OH	46,231	44	92
Columbus, OH	51,039	30	102
Dallas–Fort Worth–Arlington, TX	54,449	21	109
Denver–Aurora–Broomfield, CO	58,732	11	117
Detroit–Warren–Livonia, MI	48,198	38	96
Hartford–West Hartford–East Hartford, CT	63,104	6	126
Houston–Sugar Land–Baytown, TX	53,942	22	108
Indianapolis–Carmel, IN	48,867	37	98
Jacksonville, FL	50,324	34	101
Kansas City, MO–KS	53,919	23	108
Las Vegas–Paradise, NV	51,437	29	103
Los Angeles–Long Beach–Santa Ana, CA	56,691	17	113
Louisville/Jefferson County, KY–IN	44,678	48	89
Memphis, TN–MS–AR	45,377	46	91
Miami–Fort Lauderdale–Pompano Beach, FL	45,352	47	91
Milwaukee–Waukesha–West Allis, WI	49,774	36	99
Minneapolis–St. Paul–Bloomington, MN–WI	62,352	8	125
Nashville–Davidson–Murfreesboro–Franklin, TN	47,975	39	96
New Orleans–Metairie–Kenner, LA	46,134	45	92
New York–Northern New Jersey–Long Island, NY–NJ–PA	61,927	9	124
Oklahoma City, OK	46,238	43	92
Orlando–Kissimmee–Sanford, FL	46,478	41	93
Philadelphia–Camden–Wilmington, PA–NJ–DE–MD	58,095	12	116
Phoenix–Mesa–Glendale, AZ	50,385	33	101
Pittsburgh, PA	46,700	40	93
Portland–Vancouver–Hillsboro, OR–WA	53,078	26	106
Providence–New Bedford–Fall River, RI–MA	51,935	27	104
Raleigh–Cary, NC	57,840	13	116
Richmond, VA	55,325	20	111
Riverside–San Bernardino–Ontario, CA	53,548	24	107
Sacramento–Arden-Arcade–Roseville, CA	56,233	18	112

	median household income	rank among 50 metro areas	index to national median
Salt Lake City, UT	$57,419	14	115
San Antonio–New Braunfels, TX	50,225	35	100
San Diego–Carlsbad–San Marcos, CA	59,923	10	120
San Francisco–Oakland–Fremont, CA	73,027	3	146
San Jose–Sunnyvale–Santa Clara, CA	83,944	2	168
Seattle–Tacoma–Bellevue, WA	63,088	7	126
St. Louis, MO–IL	50,912	31	102
Tampa–St. Petersburg–Clearwater, FL	43,547	50	87
Virginia Beach–Norfolk–Newport News, VA–NC	57,315	15	115
Washington–Arlington–Alexandria, DC–VA–MD–WV	84,523	1	169

Note: The index is calculated by dividing the median income of each metropolitan area by the national median and multiplying by 100. "–" means not applicable.
Source: Bureau of the Census, 2010 American Community Survey, Internet site http://factfinder2.census.gov/faces/nav/jsf/pages/index.xhtml; calculations by New Strategist

2

Men's Income

Men under age 55 have seen their incomes fall for decades. The overall median income of men fell 2 percent between 1990 and 2010, to $32,137 after adjusting for inflation. Among men ranging in age from 25 to 54, median income fell by a larger 8 to 12 percent during those years. The earnings of working women are the only thing that has kept household incomes afloat over the past few decades, but the Great Recession has finally put an end to that.

In contrast to their younger counterparts, men aged 55 or older have gained ground since 1990. Behind their growing incomes is greater labor force participation.

The median incomes of men fell in every racial and ethnic group between 2000 and 2010, after adjusting for inflation. The losses ranged from a low of 7 percent (non-Hispanic whites) to a high of 15 percent (blacks). Between 2000 and 2010, median earnings fell even among college graduates with full-time jobs. Most men with full-time jobs experienced a decline in earnings regardless of occupation.

■ Men's incomes are likely to decline further in the years ahead because of the ongoing economic downturn and high unemployment rates.

Men's Income Trends

Men's Incomes Have Shrunk in Almost Every Age Group

Since 2000, men under age 65 have fared the worst.

The median income of men fell 10 percent between 2000 and 2010, to $32,137 after adjusting for inflation. Men aged 65 or older were the only ones to see income gains during those years—a 5 percent rise—as fewer men in the age group opted for early retirement. The median income of men under age 35 fell by 17 to 18 percent between 2000 and 2010. Men aged 35 to 54 saw their incomes decline by 12 to 13 percent.

Some men have fared better than others during the past 20 years. Those aged 65 or older experienced the biggest gain in income—up 12 percent between 1990 and 2010. In contrast, the incomes of men aged 25 to 54 were 8 to 12 percent lower in 2010 than in 1990, after adjusting for inflation.

■ The disappearance of relatively high-paying manufacturing jobs has reduced the earning power of men.

The median income of men aged 65 or older grew between 2000 and 2010

(percent change in median income of men by age, 2000 to 2010; in 2010 dollars)

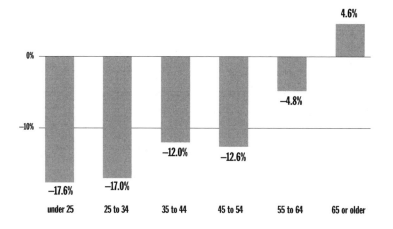

Table 2.1 Median Income of Men by Age, 1990 to 2010

(median income of men aged 15 or older with income by age, 1990 to 2010; percent change in income for selected years; in 2010 dollars)

	total men	15 to 24	25 to 34	35 to 44	45 to 54	55 to 64	aged 65 or older total	65 to 74	75 or older
2010	$32,137	$9,959	$31,793	$42,252	$45,420	$41,197	$25,704	$29,286	$21,987
2009	32,715	10,202	32,441	42,921	45,469	41,978	26,304	29,430	23,138
2008	33,580	10,914	33,838	44,748	46,116	42,285	25,826	29,360	22,188
2007	34,908	11,787	34,570	47,339	48,213	44,301	25,577	29,219	21,871
2006	34,891	11,856	34,746	46,107	49,412	44,853	25,413	28,411	22,319
2005	34,929	11,692	34,802	45,751	48,725	45,404	24,329	27,163	21,714
2004	35,224	11,638	35,774	46,788	48,324	45,350	24,391	27,949	21,615
2003	35,483	11,809	36,231	46,465	49,884	46,133	24,140	27,457	21,078
2002	35,435	11,686	37,179	45,924	49,653	43,966	23,556	25,804	21,219
2001	35,839	11,455	37,574	47,217	50,621	43,888	24,247	26,718	21,578
2000	35,885	12,086	38,305	48,014	51,960	43,287	24,577	27,178	21,770
1999	35,714	10,926	38,441	47,627	53,394	43,816	25,255	28,081	22,215
1998	35,389	10,941	37,560	46,991	51,993	43,783	24,267	26,361	22,013
1997	34,149	10,115	35,211	44,496	50,961	42,202	24,066	26,617	20,869
1996	32,980	9,631	34,841	44,511	50,136	40,857	23,087	25,745	20,056
1995	32,051	9,821	33,539	44,635	50,553	41,169	23,417	26,063	20,115
1994	31,598	10,253	32,887	44,672	50,820	39,389	22,186	24,148	19,871
1993	31,354	9,553	32,580	45,084	49,262	37,353	22,262	24,199	19,943
1992	31,145	9,588	32,731	44,903	48,998	39,001	22,225	24,072	19,620
1991	31,956	9,806	33,714	45,744	49,613	39,748	22,414	23,941	20,353
1990	32,817	10,219	34,596	48,148	50,144	40,112	22,936	25,823	18,890
Percent change									
2000 to 2010	−10.4%	−17.6%	−17.0%	−12.0%	−12.6%	−4.8%	4.6%	7.8%	1.0%
1990 to 2010	−2.1	−2.5	−8.1	−12.2	−9.4	2.7	12.1	13.4	16.4

Source: Bureau of the Census, Current Population Surveys, Annual Social and Economic Supplement, Internet site http://www .census.gov/hhes/www/income/data/historical/people/index.html; calculations by New Strategist

Men in Every Racial and Ethnic Group Lost Ground between 2000 and 2010

Median incomes are still higher than in 1990, however.

Between 2000 and 2010, men in every racial and ethnic group saw their median income decline. The loss ranged from a low of 7 percent for non-Hispanic whites to a high of 15 percent for blacks. Non-Hispanic white men have the highest median income, $37,037 in 2010. Asian men are in second place with a median income of $35,622. Black men had a median income of $23,061. Hispanic men have the lowest median income—just $22,233 in 2010.

Despite these declines, the median income of men in every racial and ethnic group was higher in 2010 than in 1990. The median income of Asian men rose 14 percent during those years, after adjusting for inflation. The median income of black men climbed 11 percent, while non-Hispanic white men experienced a smaller 4 percent increase and Hispanics just 2 percent.

■ These median income figures include both the employed and the unemployed, workers and retirees. As more men struggle with unemployment, their median income falls.

Non-Hispanic white men lost the least between 2000 and 2010

(percent change in median income of men by race and Hispanic origin, 2000 to 2010; in 2010 dollars)

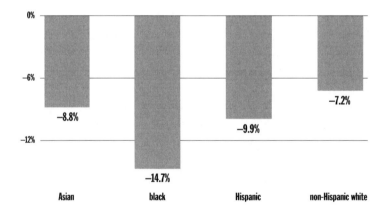

Table 2.2 Median Income of Men by Race and Hispanic Origin, 1990 to 2010

(median income of men aged 15 or older with income by race and Hispanic origin, 1990 to 2010; percent change in income for selected years; in 2010 dollars)

	total men	Asian	black	Hispanic	non-Hispanic white
2010	$32,137	$35,622	$23,061	$22,233	$37,037
2009	32,715	37,495	24,065	22,623	37,392
2008	33,580	36,662	25,436	24,307	37,882
2007	34,908	38,623	27,122	25,712	39,300
2006	34,891	40,125	27,116	25,361	39,540
2005	34,929	36,896	25,251	24,670	39,475
2004	35,224	37,475	26,217	24,882	38,874
2003	35,483	37,624	26,004	24,958	38,328
2002	35,435	37,376	26,068	25,090	38,824
2001	35,839	38,296	26,436	24,864	39,152
2000	35,885	39,038	27,023	24,687	39,893
1999	35,714	36,480	26,748	23,380	40,393
1998	35,389	33,562	25,810	23,053	39,891
1997	34,149	33,924	24,511	21,964	37,328
1996	32,980	32,344	22,819	21,361	36,379
1995	32,051	31,483	22,738	21,081	36,198
1994	31,598	33,300	21,796	21,095	35,093
1993	31,354	32,155	21,701	20,340	34,429
1992	31,145	30,284	19,891	20,415	34,104
1991	31,956	30,643	20,236	21,573	34,618
1990	32,817	31,363	20,810	21,783	35,510
Percent change					
2000 to 2010	−10.4%	−8.8%	−14.7%	−9.9%	−7.2%
1990 to 2010	−2.1	13.6	10.8	2.1	4.3

Note: Beginning in 2002, data for Asians and blacks are for those who identify themselves as being of the race alone and those who identify themselves as being of the race in combination with one or more other races. Hispanics may be of any race. Beginning in 2002, data for non-Hispanic whites are for those who identify themselves as white alone and not Hispanic.
Source: Bureau of the Census, Current Population Surveys, Annual Social and Economic Supplement, Internet site http://www .census.gov/hhes/www/income/data/historical/people/index.html; calculations by New Strategist

Table 2.3 Median Income of Asian Men by Age, 2002 to 2010

(median income of Asian men aged 15 or older with income by age, 2002 to 2010; percent change in income, 2002–10; in 2010 dollars)

	total Asian men	15 to 24	25 to 34	35 to 44	45 to 54	55 to 64	aged 65 or older total	65 to 74	75 or older
2010	$35,622	$10,946	$36,232	$55,262	$46,199	$41,385	$20,834	$23,576	$17,320
2009	37,495	7,870	37,999	58,422	45,046	37,547	22,009	26,403	17,701
2008	36,662	10,052	41,875	52,315	49,569	41,253	18,718	21,090	14,225
2007	38,623	11,201	43,771	54,863	50,366	41,843	19,932	20,560	18,347
2006	40,125	7,905	44,944	55,095	49,947	45,889	20,156	24,124	17,291
2005	36,896	10,137	41,505	54,007	45,821	43,576	21,297	21,459	20,885
2004	37,475	11,159	39,192	55,204	47,569	42,394	18,731	19,987	16,611
2003	37,624	8,131	43,442	52,256	49,550	47,344	16,775	17,066	16,183
2002	37,376	11,857	42,594	50,487	49,929	38,194	18,573	19,915	15,915

Percent change

	total Asian men	15 to 24	25 to 34	35 to 44	45 to 54	55 to 64	aged 65 or older total	65 to 74	75 or older
2002 to 2010	−4.7%	−7.7%	−14.9%	9.5%	−7.5%	8.4%	12.2%	18.4%	8.8%

Note: Asians are those who identify themselves as being of the race alone and those who identify themselves as being of the race in combination with other races.
Source: Bureau of the Census, Current Population Surveys, Annual Social and Economic Supplement, Internet site http://www .census.gov/hhes/www/income/data/historical/people/index.html; calculations by New Strategist

Table 2.4 Median Income of Black Men by Age, 1990 to 2010

(median income of black men aged 15 or older with income by age, 1990 to 2010; percent change in income for selected years; in 2010 dollars)

	total black men	15 to 24	25 to 34	35 to 44	45 to 54	55 to 64	aged 65 or older total	65 to 74	75 or older
2010	$23,061	$9,068	$23,462	$31,722	$30,915	$27,548	$18,553	$20,329	$16,781
2009	24,065	8,744	24,853	34,729	31,247	29,960	18,383	20,446	15,066
2008	25,436	9,573	26,661	32,513	32,266	29,181	19,287	20,895	16,216
2007	27,122	10,511	28,289	34,132	37,249	31,797	16,879	17,699	15,691
2006	27,116	10,699	28,863	34,954	34,022	31,324	16,967	17,085	16,795
2005	25,251	10,377	26,525	35,257	34,221	30,051	15,195	16,473	13,967
2004	26,217	8,913	29,315	35,266	35,025	30,107	17,309	18,591	15,590
2003	26,004	9,555	29,219	35,746	35,651	30,859	17,040	19,451	14,935
2002	26,068	9,190	29,998	34,960	32,653	31,031	17,164	18,362	15,594
2001	26,436	9,228	31,520	36,215	34,266	29,365	16,966	18,015	15,325
2000	27,023	9,626	29,723	34,464	34,403	30,583	17,602	20,045	15,055
1999	26,748	8,800	29,726	35,350	35,431	30,110	15,867	16,549	15,175
1998	25,810	7,905	30,126	34,246	36,383	23,242	15,136	15,629	14,334
1997	24,511	8,703	28,758	31,997	36,839	28,097	16,766	18,241	13,974
1996	22,819	7,972	27,101	31,681	34,240	23,753	16,090	16,831	13,572
1995	22,738	7,903	25,652	29,666	30,881	26,556	16,436	18,860	13,545
1994	21,796	8,465	25,289	29,735	35,845	26,981	14,824	15,249	14,117
1993	21,701	7,438	24,643	29,660	32,020	25,053	14,236	14,766	13,187
1992	19,891	7,100	23,676	28,865	31,792	24,355	12,470	13,070	11,422
1991	20,236	7,473	23,805	30,662	31,102	23,663	13,131	13,756	11,968
1990	20,810	7,811	24,657	32,502	32,774	24,345	12,048	14,144	10,170
Percent change									
2000 to 2010	−14.7%	−5.8%	−21.1%	−8.0%	−10.1%	−9.9%	5.4%	1.4%	11.5%
1990 to 2010	10.8	16.1	−4.8	−2.4	−5.7	13.2	54.0	43.7	65.0

Note: Beginning in 2002, blacks are those who identify themselves as being of the race alone and those who identify themselves as being of the race in combination with other races.
Source: Bureau of the Census, Current Population Surveys, Annual Social and Economic Supplement, Internet site http://www.census.gov/hhes/www/income/data/historical/people/index.html; calculations by New Strategist

Table 2.5 Median Income of Hispanic Men by Age, 1990 to 2010

(median income of Hispanic men aged 15 or older with income by age, 1990 to 2010; percent change in income for selected years; in 2010 dollars)

	total Hispanic men	15 to 24	25 to 34	35 to 44	45 to 54	55 to 64	aged 65 or older total	65 to 74	75 or older
2010	$22,233	$11,912	$22,499	$27,913	$28,302	$26,070	$15,707	$18,739	$13,331
2009	22,623	11,969	23,052	28,553	29,519	27,266	16,165	18,287	13,772
2008	24,307	12,990	25,670	30,776	30,627	28,239	15,562	16,777	14,266
2007	25,712	15,654	26,597	32,003	31,800	30,760	16,252	17,237	14,727
2006	25,361	16,226	26,465	32,527	33,114	27,438	15,640	17,703	13,992
2005	24,670	15,650	25,494	30,212	32,036	28,898	15,500	16,691	14,043
2004	24,882	14,149	25,716	31,087	31,623	30,450	15,650	17,006	14,064
2003	24,958	14,660	26,279	31,080	31,278	30,201	15,066	15,896	13,868
2002	25,090	15,094	26,684	31,016	31,439	27,141	14,093	16,182	11,866
2001	24,864	15,107	26,582	31,199	30,598	26,540	15,195	17,068	12,397
2000	24,687	15,486	26,701	31,465	32,225	25,291	14,194	16,090	12,050
1999	23,380	14,505	25,473	30,077	32,444	26,371	15,661	16,739	14,389
1998	23,053	13,374	26,611	30,385	30,812	24,935	15,374	16,256	13,292
1997	21,964	12,811	25,437	29,166	28,550	23,330	13,603	14,974	10,667
1996	21,361	11,520	23,929	28,453	28,253	22,136	14,297	15,263	12,890
1995	21,081	11,194	23,151	28,017	28,510	23,035	13,913	14,807	12,792
1994	21,095	12,149	23,201	29,361	28,726	23,939	14,301	14,852	13,393
1993	20,340	11,481	22,717	27,574	28,051	23,546	13,610	13,306	14,228
1992	20,415	10,698	22,726	28,329	28,028	23,961	14,005	15,465	12,095
1991	21,573	12,401	23,432	28,877	30,365	26,019	14,074	15,178	12,174
1990	21,783	12,179	24,452	29,761	28,941	26,235	15,438	16,670	13,668
Percent change									
2000 to 2010	−9.9%	−23.1%	−15.7%	−11.3%	−12.2%	3.1%	10.7%	16.5%	10.6%
1990 to 2010	2.1	−2.2	−8.0	−6.2	−2.2	−0.6	1.7	12.4	−2.5

Source: Bureau of the Census, Current Population Surveys, Annual Social and Economic Supplement, Internet site http://www.census.gov/hhes/www/income/data/historical/people/index.html; calculations by New Strategist

Table 2.6 Median Income of Non-Hispanic White Men by Age, 1990 to 2010

(median income of non-Hispanic white men aged 15 or older with income by age, 1990 to 2010; percent change in income for selected years; in 2010 dollars)

	total non-Hispanic white men	15 to 24	25 to 34	35 to 44	45 to 54	55 to 64	aged 65 or older total	65 to 74	75 or older
2010	$37,037	$9,531	$36,946	$50,175	$51,126	$45,784	$27,500	$31,688	$23,758
2009	37,392	10,161	38,795	50,254	51,068	46,446	28,086	31,610	24,658
2008	37,882	10,751	38,773	51,716	51,384	46,798	27,572	32,036	23,270
2007	39,300	11,234	39,525	53,494	53,373	48,892	27,581	32,194	23,079
2006	39,540	11,359	39,645	54,190	55,064	49,067	27,299	30,798	23,680
2005	39,475	11,020	39,612	51,697	55,200	48,707	26,057	29,745	22,903
2004	38,874	10,974	41,264	52,383	54,241	48,694	25,884	30,516	22,546
2003	38,328	11,172	40,040	51,100	55,540	48,950	25,916	29,763	22,348
2002	38,824	10,734	41,514	51,350	54,954	48,003	25,191	27,953	22,612
2001	39,152	10,666	41,037	51,688	55,295	47,152	25,685	28,515	22,792
2000	39,893	11,265	41,746	52,937	57,122	46,747	26,163	28,817	23,491
1999	40,393	10,463	42,291	53,385	58,231	47,753	26,922	29,959	23,623
1998	39,891	11,261	41,861	51,557	55,922	48,381	26,015	28,733	23,504
1997	37,328	9,989	38,948	49,504	55,553	46,067	25,699	28,576	22,403
1996	36,379	9,740	37,504	49,762	54,835	44,394	24,487	27,503	20,949
1995	36,198	10,031	37,261	50,069	55,319	44,582	24,511	27,548	20,833
1994	35,093	10,265	36,614	48,440	54,275	42,620	23,723	25,914	20,840
1993	34,429	9,587	36,174	48,520	54,220	39,743	23,831	25,805	21,038
1992	34,104	9,738	36,708	48,549	53,688	41,675	23,705	25,761	20,835
1991	34,618	9,932	37,039	48,848	54,048	42,329	23,897	25,742	21,541
1990	35,510	10,368	37,717	50,850	53,208	42,878	24,356	27,734	20,038

Percent change

2000 to 2010	−7.2%	−15.4%	−11.5%	−5.2%	−10.5%	−2.1%	5.1%	10.0%	1.1%
1990 to 2010	4.3	−8.1	−2.0	−1.3	−3.9	6.8	12.9	14.3	18.6

Note: Beginning in 2002, data are for those who identify themselves as being white alone and not Hispanic.
Source: Bureau of the Census, Current Population Surveys, Annual Social and Economic Supplement, Internet site http://www.census.gov/hhes/www/income/data/historical/people/index.html; calculations by New Strategist

In Every Region, Men Have Lost Ground since 2000

Only in the South have men made gains since 1990.

In every region, men saw their median income decline between 2000 and 2010. The greatest loss occurred among men in the Midwest (down 15 percent, after adjusting for inflation). The smallest declines were in the South and Northeast, down 7 and 8 percent, respectively. Men in the West saw their median income decline by 10 percent.

Men in the South were the only ones whose median income rose between 1990 and 2010—up 5 percent, after adjusting for inflation. This compares with stability (a loss of just 0.2 percent) in the Northeast, a decline of 3 percent in the Midwest and 5 percent in the West.

■ Men in the South had the lowest median income in 2010 ($31,173), and men in the Northeast had the highest ($35,363).

Since 2000, men's incomes fell the most in the Midwest

(percent change in median income of men by region, 2000 to 2010; in 2010 dollars)

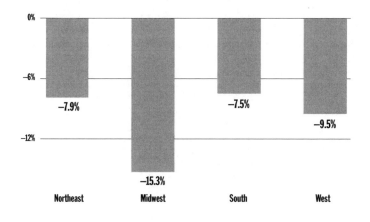

Table 2.7 Median Income of Men by Region, 1990 to 2010

(median income of men aged 15 or older with income by region, 1990 to 2010; percent change in income for selected years; in 2010 dollars)

	total men	Northeast	Midwest	South	West
2010	$32,137	$35,363	$32,275	$31,173	$32,361
2009	32,715	35,999	32,589	31,560	33,739
2008	33,580	36,220	33,684	32,076	35,500
2007	34,908	36,722	36,094	33,531	36,393
2006	34,891	38,087	35,538	33,685	35,454
2005	34,929	36,435	35,726	33,488	35,277
2004	35,224	36,876	35,947	33,222	35,389
2003	35,483	37,239	35,907	32,735	36,070
2002	35,435	37,145	36,647	33,358	35,261
2001	35,839	37,729	37,293	33,676	35,324
2000	35,885	38,411	38,121	33,686	35,768
1999	35,714	37,823	38,612	33,915	35,400
1998	35,389	36,764	36,960	33,793	35,210
1997	34,149	35,729	35,603	32,367	33,635
1996	32,980	34,984	35,156	30,766	32,373
1995	32,051	34,961	34,517	30,062	31,699
1994	31,598	34,492	32,406	29,595	32,048
1993	31,354	33,109	32,237	29,292	31,999
1992	31,145	33,634	31,930	28,305	31,973
1991	31,956	34,891	32,115	28,841	33,678
1990	32,817	35,427	33,432	29,803	33,943
Percent change					
2000 to 2010	−10.4%	−7.9%	−15.3%	−7.5%	−9.5%
1990 to 2010	−2.1	−0.2	−3.5	4.6	−4.7

Source: Bureau of the Census, Current Population Surveys, Annual Social and Economic Supplement, Internet site http://www .census.gov/hhes/www/income/data/historical/people/index.html; calculations by New Strategist

Men's Earnings Fell between 2000 and 2010

Men working full-time, year-round saw their earnings rise during those years, after adjusting for inflation.

Between 2000 and 2010, the median earnings of men fell 6 percent, to $36,676 after adjusting for inflation. But men who managed to hold on to a full-time job saw their median earnings rise by 1 percent during the decade to $47,715 in 2010. Men working part-time saw their earnings grow 20 percent during those years as more men were forced to work part-time in the Great Recession.

Since 1990, the median earnings of men have grown by 5 percent, after adjusting for inflation. Among men working full-time, year-round, median earnings rose by a slightly greater 7 percent.

■ It looks like men with full-time, year-round jobs are gaining ground, but only because more men have been forced into part-time or part-year work, lowering overall median earnings.

Men who work full-time, year-round are struggling to stay even

(median income of men who work full-time, year-round for selected years, 1990 to 2010; in 2010 dollars)

Year	Median income
1990	$44,760
2000	$47,165
2010	$47,715

Table 2.8 Median Earnings of Men by Employment Status, 1990 to 2010

(median earnings of men aged 15 or older with earnings by employment status, 1990 to 2010; percent change in earnings for selected years; in 2010 dollars)

	total men with earnings	worked full-time		worked part-time	
		total	year-round	total	year-round
2010	$36,676	$41,954	$47,715	$8,713	$12,660
2009	36,931	42,249	47,905	9,024	13,328
2008	37,031	41,894	46,954	8,078	12,435
2007	38,524	43,104	47,439	7,878	12,918
2006	38,799	43,573	45,701	7,765	12,813
2005	38,363	42,589	46,222	7,726	13,117
2004	37,495	42,750	47,090	7,579	12,777
2003	37,992	43,499	48,211	7,721	13,061
2002	38,355	43,438	47,786	7,656	12,983
2001	38,626	43,493	47,137	7,004	12,822
2000	39,187	43,762	47,165	7,289	13,095
1999	39,360	42,753	47,619	6,832	12,256
1998	38,412	42,413	47,215	6,918	11,985
1997	36,358	41,699	45,611	6,687	12,158
1996	35,680	40,965	44,479	6,065	11,850
1995	35,540	40,065	44,743	6,334	11,548
1994	34,415	39,345	44,886	6,277	11,352
1993	33,347	38,980	45,180	5,798	10,753
1992	33,349	39,298	45,978	6,036	10,751
1991	34,123	39,852	45,932	6,212	10,816
1990	34,805	40,172	44,760	6,373	11,107
Percent change					
2000 to 2010	−6.4%	−4.1%	1.2%	19.5%	−3.3%
1990 to 2010	5.4	4.4	6.6	36.7	14.0

Note: Earnings include wages and salaries only.
Source: Bureau of the Census, Current Population Surveys, Annual Social and Economic Supplement, Internet site http://www
.census.gov/hhes/www/income/data/historical/people/index.html; calculations by New Strategist

Black Men Earn More than Hispanic Men

Hispanic men have seen their earnings grow since 2000, however.

Between 2000 and 2010, Hispanic men with full-time jobs gained the most ground. Their median earnings climbed 4 percent, after adjusting for inflation. In contrast, the median earnings of Asian men rose only 0.5 percent. The median earnings of non-Hispanic white men with full-time jobs fell 0.7 percent during those years, and black men saw their median earnings decline by 3 percent.

Between 1990 and 2010, the median earnings of black men rose 8 percent, after adjusting for inflation. The median earnings of their Hispanic counterparts climbed by just 1 percent during those years. In 2010, the median earnings of black men who work full-time stood at $36,859, substantially higher than the $31,408 median of their Hispanic counterparts. Asian and non-Hispanic white men had the highest earnings in 2010, a median of more than $51,000.

■ Black men earn more than Hispanic men because they are better educated.

Among men with full-time jobs, Hispanics earn the least

(median earnings of men who work full-time, year-round, by race and Hispanic origin, 2010)

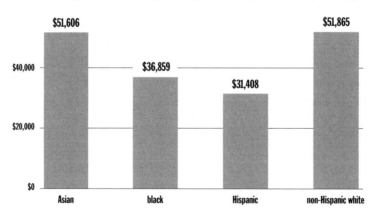

Table 2.9 Median Earnings of Men Who Work Full-Time, by Race and Hispanic Origin, 1990 to 2010

(median earnings of men aged 15 or older who work full-time, year-round, by race and Hispanic origin, 1990 to 2010; percent change in earnings for selected years; in 2010 dollars)

	total men working full-time	Asian	black	Hispanic	non-Hispanic white
2010	$47,715	$51,606	$36,859	$31,408	$51,865
2009	47,905	52,492	38,116	31,911	52,254
2008	46,954	51,811	37,724	31,350	51,892
2007	47,439	53,134	37,972	31,755	52,925
2006	45,701	55,288	37,752	31,426	52,361
2005	46,222	52,606	36,829	29,897	51,863
2004	47,090	52,794	36,104	30,769	52,568
2003	48,211	53,461	38,239	30,921	53,059
2002	47,786	50,588	38,113	31,476	51,482
2001	47,137	51,544	38,610	30,891	51,332
2000	47,165	51,348	38,111	30,106	52,225
1999	47,619	48,275	38,915	29,335	52,925
1998	47,215	46,525	36,134	29,769	50,408
1997	45,611	46,976	35,802	29,277	49,570
1996	44,479	47,673	36,537	29,136	49,043
1995	44,743	44,854	34,702	28,950	48,871
1994	44,886	46,642	34,540	29,553	47,483
1993	45,180	45,917	34,203	29,938	47,504
1992	45,978	46,472	34,101	29,753	48,298
1991	45,932	47,084	34,463	30,866	48,470
1990	44,760	43,284	34,145	30,946	48,730
Percent change					
2000 to 2010	1.2%	0.5%	−3.3%	4.3%	−0.7%
1990 to 2010	6.6	19.2	7.9	1.5	6.4

Note: Beginning in 2002, data for Asians and blacks are for those who identify themselves as being of the race alone and those who identify themselves as being of the race in combination with other races. Hispanics may be of any race. Beginning in 2002, data for non-Hispanic whites are for those who identify themselves as white alone and not Hispanic.
Source: Bureau of the Census, Current Population Surveys, Annual Social and Economic Supplement, Internet site http://www.census.gov/hhes/www/income/data/historical/people/index.html; calculations by New Strategist

College Graduates Lost Ground between 2000 and 2010

Since 2000, men with doctoral degrees are the only ones who have made gains.

Between 2000 and 2010, the median earnings of men aged 25 or older who work full-time, year-round, fell 0.8 percent, after adjusting for inflation. College graduates saw their median income fall more than those with less education. Among men with at least a bachelor's degree, median earnings fell 6.1 percent. This decline was larger than the 2.5 percent drop experienced by men who went no further than high school.

Since 1991, the median earnings of men with a college degree have grown, while less-educated men have lost ground. The biggest losers during those years were high school dropouts, who experienced a decline in median earnings of 7 to 10 percent after adjusting for inflation. Men whose highest educational achievement is a high school diploma saw their earnings fall 2 percent. In contrast, the median earnings of men with an associate's degree held steady. Those with a bachelor's degree or more education saw their median earnings rise by 8.5 percent.

■ The labor market pays a premium to highly educated workers, but the premium may be beginning to shrink.

Between 2000 and 2010, college graduates lost the most ground

(percent change in median earnings of men aged 25 or older who work full-time, year-round, by educational attainment, 2000 to 2010; in 2010 dollars)

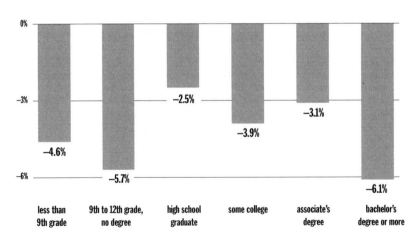

Table 2.10 Median Earnings of Men Who Work Full-Time by Education, 1991 to 2010

(median earnings of men aged 25 or older who work full-time, year-round, by educational attainment, 1991 to 2010; percent change in earnings for selected years; in 2010 dollars)

	total men	less than 9th grade	9th to 12th grade	high school graduate	some college	associate's degree	bachelor's degree or more				
							total	bachelor's degree	master's degree	professional degree	doctoral degree
2010	$50,361	$24,453	$29,435	$40,055	$46,434	$50,282	$71,778	$63,737	$80,958	$115,298	$101,222
2009	50,819	24,340	28,486	40,130	47,874	51,133	72,646	63,475	80,652	125,277	102,403
2008	49,620	24,562	30,053	39,502	46,401	50,781	73,129	66,632	81,986	–	–
2007	49,428	24,580	30,829	39,807	47,214	51,571	74,031	65,288	80,217	–	96,837
2006	49,483	24,556	29,904	40,045	47,402	50,903	72,381	65,863	81,572	–	–
2005	48,378	24,939	30,366	40,544	47,374	52,693	73,897	67,033	83,791	–	95,897
2004	48,577	24,986	30,335	41,238	48,372	51,245	72,353	66,024	82,456	–	95,110
2003	49,718	25,152	31,377	41,980	49,018	50,823	73,589	66,982	83,743	–	103,293
2002	49,875	25,353	31,393	40,244	49,510	51,940	74,778	67,963	81,542	–	100,962
2001	50,131	26,033	31,844	40,686	49,457	51,303	74,573	65,405	82,432	–	99,849
2000	50,756	25,639	31,205	41,063	48,334	51,889	76,411	66,471	82,652	118,098	95,422
1999	49,973	25,558	31,334	41,910	48,633	52,894	73,842	66,728	80,889	125,649	100,394
1998	48,997	24,784	31,309	41,235	48,022	51,407	69,882	66,768	80,375	121,098	92,424
1997	48,375	25,127	32,834	41,522	47,525	49,678	69,347	62,652	77,955	106,043	95,770
1996	47,688	23,864	30,728	41,637	46,069	49,915	69,373	60,581	77,595	108,132	91,548
1995	46,678	24,849	31,092	40,546	45,974	47,544	68,278	60,520	73,606	106,946	87,650
1994	46,744	24,951	31,639	39,624	45,599	51,094	68,340	61,173	74,709	104,876	87,680
1993	46,953	24,338	31,800	39,850	46,474	48,462	68,330	61,533	74,034	114,685	91,152
1992	47,686	25,660	32,061	40,652	47,719	49,240	66,612	61,427	71,907	112,065	85,792
1991	48,200	26,353	32,776	40,931	48,450	50,303	66,143	62,282	73,379	109,727	85,282

Percent change

	total men	less than 9th grade	9th to 12th grade	high school graduate	some college	associate's degree	total	bachelor's degree	master's degree	professional degree	doctoral degree
2000 to 2010	–0.8%	–4.6%	–5.7%	–2.5%	–3.9%	–3.1%	–6.1%	–4.1%	–2.0%	–2.4%	6.1%
1991 to 2010	4.5	–7.2	–10.2	–2.1	–4.2	0.0	8.5	2.3	10.3	5.1	18.7

Note: Earnings include wages and salaries only. "–" means data are not available.
Source: Bureau of the Census, Current Population Surveys, Annual Social and Economic Supplement, Internet site http://www
.census.gov/hhes/www/income/data/historical/people/index.html; calculations by New Strategist

Most Occupations Saw Earnings Decline between 2002 and 2010

Some men have gained ground, however.

Among all men who work full-time, year-round, median earnings fell 0.1 percent between 2002 and 2010, after adjusting for inflation. Only four occupational groups saw earnings grow during that time period. Men in health care support experienced the biggest gain—up 11 percent. Men in the armed forces saw their median earnings grow 6 percent. Men in construction (the few that are left) experienced a 5 percent growth in median earnings, and those in protective service occupations saw their median earnings climb 3 percent.

The biggest earnings decline occurred among men working in personal care and service occupations, with a loss of 17 percent in median earnings between 2002 and 2010 after adjusting for inflation. Men in farming, forestry, and fishing occupations saw their median earnings drop by 12 percent. Managers were not immune to economic turmoil. Men working in management occupations saw their median earnings fall by 0.5 percent between 2002 and 2010, and professional experienced a 1.6 percent decline.

■ The Great Recession has hurt men in most occupations.

The recession hurt some more than others

(percent change in median earnings of men who work full-time, year-round, by selected occupations, 2002 to 2010; in 2010 dollars)

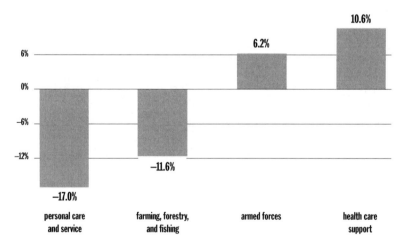

Table 2.11 Median Earnings of Men Who Work Full-Time by Occupation, 2002 to 2010

(median earnings of men aged 15 or older who work full-time, year-round, by occupation of longest job held, 2002 to 2010; in 2010 dollars)

	2010	2009	2008	2007	2006	2005	2004	2003	2002	percent change 2002–10
Total men who work full-time	**$47,715**	**$47,905**	**$46,954**	**$47,439**	**$45,701**	**$46,222**	**$47,090**	**$48,211**	**$47,786**	**−0.1%**
Management, business, and financial	72,013	71,342	71,821	73,618	71,131	73,452	71,499	71,659	72,373	−0.5
Professional and related	67,339	67,465	67,954	65,645	66,992	68,156	66,630	69,786	68,401	−1.6
Health care support	33,747	31,255	29,023	27,597	28,991	26,569	24,690	26,608	30,520	10.6
Protective service	51,251	50,608	50,448	52,403	50,912	51,082	51,682	53,662	49,543	3.4
Food preparation	23,368	22,233	22,269	22,918	22,862	23,092	22,166	22,371	24,354	−4.0
Building and grounds	28,682	27,680	27,656	27,438	27,885	26,736	27,207	26,641	29,306	−2.1
Personal care and service	31,253	31,450	31,505	32,921	33,731	30,469	31,536	36,276	37,646	−17.0
Sales and related	47,183	48,093	47,941	48,598	49,465	47,096	48,762	49,423	50,268	−6.1
Office, administrative support	37,298	38,066	36,699	38,681	38,382	38,963	40,277	38,487	39,106	−4.6
Farming, fishing, and forestry	24,074	27,028	24,271	24,804	23,193	24,861	25,836	26,154	27,228	−11.6
Construction and extraction	40,109	40,330	38,081	37,358	38,121	35,828	37,140	37,829	38,190	5.0
Installation, maintenance, repair	42,533	44,254	42,746	43,319	43,698	44,685	43,738	44,303	43,948	−3.2
Production occupations	37,184	37,379	37,207	38,437	38,055	39,374	38,573	38,202	38,099	−2.4
Transportation, material moving	35,808	37,170	36,484	37,275	34,935	36,963	37,311	37,427	37,302	−4.0
Armed forces	46,953	48,375	47,158	44,233	44,009	45,878	47,108	43,064	44,197	6.2

Source: Bureau of the Census, Current Population Surveys, Annual Social and Economic Supplement, Internet site http://www .census.gov/hhes/www/income/data/historical/people/index.html; calculations by New Strategist

Men's Incomes, 2010

Income Peaks among Men Aged 45 to 54

Among full-time workers, however, income continues to rise into old age.

The median income of men stood at $32,137 in 2010, meaning half of men had incomes above that amount and half below. Men's median incomes rise with age to a peak of $45,420 in the 45-to-54 age group. Sixty-seven percent of men aged 45 to 54 work full-time, year-round, and those who do have a median income of $56,122.

Among full-time workers, median income surpasses $66,000 in the 65-to 74 age group. Only 18 percent of men aged 65 to 74 or older work full-time, however.

Among full-time workers, the $54,192 median income of non-Hispanic white men is higher than that of their Asian, black, or Hispanic counterparts. The median income of Asian men who work full-time was slightly lower, at $52,444. The median income of black men was $37,805. Hispanic men had the lowest median income, at $31,671 in 2010. Asians are the only ones in which a majority of men aged 15 or older are full-time workers. Fifty-three percent of Asian men work full-time versus 49 percent of non-Hispanic whites, 46 percent of Hispanics, and 38 percent of blacks.

■ When the economy begins to recover, men's median income may rise as growing numbers of highly paid older men postpone retirement.

Among men who work full-time, incomes are high well into old age

(median income of men aged 15 or older who work full-time, year-round, by age, 2010)

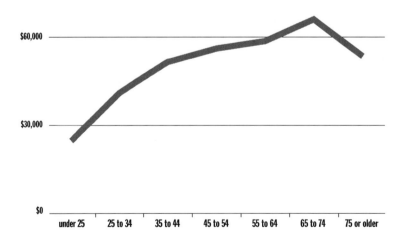

Table 2.12 Men by Income and Age, 2010: Total Men

(number and percent distribution of men aged 15 or older by income and age, 2010; median income of men with income and of men working full-time, year-round; percent working full-time, year-round; men in thousands as of 2011)

	total	15 to 24	25 to 34	35 to 44	45 to 54	55 to 64	65 or older total	65 to 74	75 or older
Total men	**118,871**	**21,651**	**20,985**	**19,714**	**21,495**	**17,946**	**17,081**	**9,842**	**7,239**
Without income	13,520	8,613	1,550	1,043	1,096	806	414	243	171
With income	105,351	13,038	19,435	18,671	20,399	17,140	16,667	9,599	7,068
Under $5,000	7,350	3,986	951	633	720	607	452	255	198
$5,000 to $9,999	7,741	2,551	1,339	816	962	869	1,205	669	536
$10,000 to $14,999	8,933	1,667	1,515	1,027	1,307	1,162	2,254	1,084	1,170
$15,000 to $19,999	8,914	1,419	1,683	986	1,180	1,203	2,443	1,164	1,280
$20,000 to $24,999	8,525	1,015	1,870	1,384	1,316	1,179	1,760	961	800
$25,000 to $29,999	7,133	687	1,510	1,177	1,157	1,119	1,485	769	716
$30,000 to $34,999	6,846	491	1,620	1,283	1,217	1,129	1,106	604	503
$35,000 to $39,999	5,840	300	1,412	1,184	1,047	968	929	575	355
$40,000 to $44,999	5,714	259	1,357	1,206	1,193	975	725	448	277
$45,000 to $49,999	4,325	154	974	999	943	690	566	381	185
$50,000 to $54,999	4,978	111	1,082	1,108	1,225	929	525	324	201
$55,000 to $59,999	3,091	63	561	637	815	615	401	309	92
$60,000 to $64,999	3,416	73	666	841	868	621	347	241	107
$65,000 to $69,999	2,335	51	459	547	530	460	289	214	74
$70,000 to $74,999	2,371	45	424	603	596	452	252	167	84
$75,000 to $79,999	2,040	15	355	498	584	399	188	132	56
$80,000 to $84,999	1,979	17	289	475	564	431	205	143	61
$85,000 to $89,999	1,211	18	187	279	336	251	139	91	48
$90,000 to $94,999	1,362	20	145	343	398	300	157	99	58
$95,000 to $99,999	860	14	90	186	234	235	101	74	26
$100,000 or more	10,386	84	948	2,461	3,207	2,546	1,140	897	243
Median income									
Men with income	$32,137	$9,959	$31,793	$42,252	$45,420	$41,197	$25,704	$29,286	$21,987
Working full-time	50,063	24,695	40,989	51,549	56,122	58,650	63,661	66,037	53,504
Percent full-time	**47.5%**	**16.3%**	**61.7%**	**69.9%**	**67.3%**	**53.2%**	**12.6%**	**18.4%**	**4.6%**
PERCENT DISTRIBUTION									
Total men	**100.0%**	**100.0%**	**100.0%**	**100.0%**	**100.0%**	**100.0%**	**100.0%**	**100.0%**	**100.0%**
Without income	11.4	39.8	7.4	5.3	5.1	4.5	2.4	2.5	2.4
With income	88.6	60.2	92.6	94.7	94.9	95.5	97.6	97.5	97.6
Under $15,000	20.2	37.9	18.1	12.6	13.9	14.7	22.9	20.4	26.3
$15,000 to $24,999	14.7	11.2	16.9	12.0	11.6	13.3	24.6	21.6	28.7
$25,000 to $34,999	11.8	5.4	14.9	12.5	11.0	12.5	15.2	14.0	16.8
$35,000 to $49,999	13.4	3.3	17.8	17.2	14.8	14.7	13.0	14.3	11.3
$50,000 to $74,999	13.6	1.6	15.2	19.0	18.8	17.1	10.6	12.8	7.7
$75,000 or more	15.0	0.8	9.6	21.5	24.8	23.2	11.3	14.6	6.8

Source: Bureau of the Census, 2011 Current Population Survey Annual Social and Economic Supplement, Internet site http://www.census.gov/hhes/www/cpstables/032011/perinc/toc.htm; calculations by New Strategist

Table 2.13 Men by Income and Age, 2010: Asian Men

(number and percent distribution of Asian men aged 15 or older by income and age, 2010; median income of men with income and of men working full-time, year-round; percent working full-time, year-round; men in thousands as of 2011)

	total	15 to 24	25 to 34	35 to 44	45 to 54	55 to 64	65 or older total	65 to 74	75 or older
Total Asian men	**5,787**	**1,059**	**1,209**	**1,191**	**987**	**708**	**633**	**391**	**242**
Without income	865	490	100	62	69	56	88	46	42
With income	4,922	569	1,109	1,129	918	652	545	345	200
Under $5,000	356	173	72	29	26	20	34	26	9
$5,000 to $9,999	304	86	37	32	26	30	93	61	31
$10,000 to $14,999	401	90	75	57	54	50	77	32	45
$15,000 to $19,999	334	57	98	39	57	28	56	30	26
$20,000 to $24,999	395	57	86	88	64	50	49	28	21
$25,000 to $29,999	318	31	73	55	56	57	45	27	18
$30,000 to $34,999	314	21	87	72	65	50	19	12	7
$35,000 to $39,999	227	15	67	43	52	31	19	15	5
$40,000 to $44,999	210	4	58	59	41	32	14	7	6
$45,000 to $49,999	186	10	53	41	42	26	16	14	2
$50,000 to $54,999	202	4	44	48	48	37	21	10	11
$55,000 to $59,999	111	2	28	29	27	18	8	8	0
$60,000 to $64,999	195	4	63	56	35	19	18	15	3
$65,000 to $69,999	100	0	38	23	12	15	14	13	1
$70,000 to $74,999	135	3	38	34	34	17	7	3	4
$75,000 to $79,999	108	4	29	38	21	12	3	2	1
$80,000 to $84,999	100	2	14	37	17	26	4	4	0
$85,000 to $89,999	91	0	25	36	10	18	3	0	3
$90,000 to $94,999	78	0	16	27	12	14	10	5	5
$95,000 to $99,999	40	0	3	17	8	11	0	0	0
$100,000 or more	716	5	101	271	211	92	35	32	3
Median income									
Men with income	$35,622	$10,946	$36,232	$55,262	$46,199	$41,385	$20,834	$23,576	$17,320
Working full-time	52,444	25,349	48,457	66,818	52,895	52,332	54,775	56,047	–
Percent full-time	**53.0%**	**12.4%**	**63.2%**	**75.9%**	**74.2%**	**60.9%**	**16.3%**	**23.5%**	**4.5%**
PERCENT DISTRIBUTION									
Total Asian men	**100.0%**	**100.0%**	**100.0%**	**100.0%**	**100.0%**	**100.0%**	**100.0%**	**100.0%**	**100.0%**
Without income	14.9	46.3	8.3	5.2	7.0	7.9	13.9	11.8	17.4
With income	85.1	53.7	91.7	94.8	93.0	92.1	86.1	88.2	82.6
Under $15,000	18.3	33.0	15.2	9.9	10.7	14.1	32.2	30.4	35.1
$15,000 to $24,999	12.6	10.8	15.2	10.7	12.3	11.0	16.6	14.8	19.4
$25,000 to $34,999	10.9	4.9	13.2	10.7	12.3	15.1	10.1	10.0	10.3
$35,000 to $49,999	10.8	2.7	14.7	12.0	13.7	12.6	7.7	9.2	5.4
$50,000 to $74,999	12.8	1.2	17.5	16.0	15.8	15.0	10.7	12.5	7.9
$75,000 or more	19.6	1.0	15.6	35.8	28.3	24.4	8.7	11.0	5.0

Note: Asians are those who identify themselves as being of the race alone and those who identify themselves as being of the race in combination with other races. "–" means sample is too small to make a reliable estimate.
Source: Bureau of the Census, 2011 Current Population Survey Annual Social and Economic Supplement, Internet site http://www.census.gov/hhes/www/cpstables/032011/perinc/toc.htm; calculations by New Strategist

Table 2.14 Men by Income and Age, 2010: Black Men

(number and percent distribution of black men aged 15 or older by income and age, 2010; median income of men with income and of men working full-time, year-round; percent working full-time, year-round; men in thousands as of 2011)

	total	15 to 24	25 to 34	35 to 44	45 to 54	55 to 64	65 or older total	65 to 74	75 or older
Total black men	**14,101**	**3,341**	**2,779**	**2,336**	**2,461**	**1,813**	**1,369**	**857**	**512**
Without income	2,843	1,648	445	268	255	173	52	38	15
With income	11,258	1,693	2,334	2,068	2,206	1,640	1,317	819	497
Under $5,000	1,052	493	202	111	117	66	63	44	19
$5,000 to $9,999	1,471	433	261	166	197	212	202	117	85
$10,000 to $14,999	1,270	242	232	165	222	158	253	138	115
$15,000 to $19,999	1,035	183	213	105	177	158	198	105	93
$20,000 to $24,999	1,067	108	306	225	156	151	121	72	50
$25,000 to $29,999	831	83	196	150	191	123	89	47	42
$30,000 to $34,999	795	54	178	216	157	123	66	38	28
$35,000 to $39,999	617	36	152	121	151	109	49	41	8
$40,000 to $44,999	568	28	143	142	137	67	51	38	12
$45,000 to $49,999	432	7	96	136	94	64	37	28	9
$50,000 to $54,999	367	4	89	83	96	52	41	31	10
$55,000 to $59,999	252	2	31	57	80	58	26	21	5
$60,000 to $64,999	244	5	53	76	60	34	17	8	9
$65,000 to $69,999	195	8	36	47	44	45	16	14	2
$70,000 to $74,999	217	0	36	70	63	37	13	11	2
$75,000 to $79,999	122	2	23	34	32	23	7	6	1
$80,000 to $84,999	132	0	22	25	47	26	12	12	0
$85,000 to $89,999	55	0	0	16	19	10	9	9	0
$90,000 to $94,999	66	0	7	20	20	16	3	3	0
$95,000 to $99,999	51	0	3	10	19	10	9	7	2
$100,000 or more	418	7	56	92	127	98	39	31	8
Median income									
Men with income	$23,061	$9,068	$23,462	$31,722	$30,915	$27,548	$18,553	$20,329	$16,781
Working full-time	37,805	22,969	33,400	41,044	42,219	44,279	57,992	58,524	–
Percent full-time	**38.0%**	**11.9%**	**49.4%**	**59.2%**	**53.9%**	**40.7%**	**10.2%**	**14.0%**	**3.7%**
PERCENT DISTRIBUTION									
Total black men	**100.0%**	**100.0%**	**100.0%**	**100.0%**	**100.0%**	**100.0%**	**100.0%**	**100.0%**	**100.0%**
Without income	20.2	49.3	16.0	11.5	10.4	9.5	3.8	4.4	2.9
With income	79.8	50.7	84.0	88.5	89.6	90.5	96.2	95.6	97.1
Under $15,000	26.9	35.0	25.0	18.9	21.8	24.0	37.8	34.9	42.8
$15,000 to $24,999	14.9	8.7	18.7	14.1	13.5	17.0	23.3	20.7	27.9
$25,000 to $34,999	11.5	4.1	13.5	15.7	14.1	13.6	11.3	9.9	13.7
$35,000 to $49,999	11.5	2.1	14.1	17.1	15.5	13.2	10.0	12.5	5.7
$50,000 to $74,999	9.0	0.6	8.8	14.3	13.9	12.5	8.3	9.9	5.5
$75,000 or more	6.0	0.3	4.0	8.4	10.7	10.1	5.8	7.9	2.1

Note: Blacks are those who identify themselves as being of the race alone and those who identify themselves as being of the race in combination with other races. "–" means sample is too small to make a reliable estimate.
Source: Bureau of the Census, 2011 Current Population Survey Annual Social and Economic Supplement, Internet site http:// www.census.gov/hhes/www/cpstables/032011/perinc/toc.htm; calculations by New Strategist

Table 2.15 Men by Income and Age, 2010: Hispanic Men

(number and percent distribution of Hispanic men aged 15 or older by income and age, 2010; median income of men with income and of men working full-time, year-round; percent working full-time, year-round; men in thousands as of 2011)

	total	15 to 24	25 to 34	35 to 44	45 to 54	55 to 64	65 or older total	65 to 74	75 or older
Total Hispanic men	**18,105**	**4,506**	**4,414**	**3,687**	**2,693**	**1,573**	**1,232**	**739**	**493**
Without income	3,140	2,106	358	256	197	133	90	52	37
With income	14,965	2,400	4,056	3,431	2,496	1,440	1,142	687	456
Under $5,000	1,094	561	186	135	102	67	42	20	22
$5,000 to $9,999	1,573	464	337	236	165	135	236	118	118
$10,000 to $14,999	1,918	335	536	321	280	179	267	133	133
$15,000 to $19,999	1,902	335	602	374	256	170	164	94	70
$20,000 to $24,999	1,669	245	522	395	280	136	91	65	27
$25,000 to $29,999	1,305	167	352	363	220	117	85	63	22
$30,000 to $34,999	1,041	92	341	235	218	123	32	24	9
$35,000 to $39,999	780	48	245	252	137	53	44	27	18
$40,000 to $44,999	711	42	226	185	133	97	29	25	4
$45,000 to $49,999	503	33	152	157	98	40	24	15	9
$50,000 to $54,999	516	16	150	153	113	58	26	19	6
$55,000 to $59,999	275	8	69	66	79	32	22	20	2
$60,000 to $64,999	328	18	70	112	69	48	11	9	2
$65,000 to $69,999	171	5	41	66	27	23	9	7	3
$70,000 to $74,999	168	12	38	46	40	21	10	8	2
$75,000 to $79,999	149	0	32	52	37	18	9	8	1
$80,000 to $84,999	147	1	46	47	30	18	5	4	2
$85,000 to $89,999	91	4	19	28	27	13	1	1	0
$90,000 to $94,999	71	2	12	20	27	6	4	2	2
$95,000 to $99,999	42	2	10	11	15	4	0	0	0
$100,000 or more	511	10	67	177	144	84	30	28	2
Median income									
Men with income	$22,233	$11,912	$22,499	$27,913	$28,302	$26,070	$15,707	$18,739	$13,331
Working full-time	31,671	21,974	30,606	35,797	36,474	36,513	40,555	42,342	–
Percent full-time	**46.3%**	**19.4%**	**58.5%**	**63.3%**	**60.9%**	**49.3%**	**14.2%**	**19.4%**	**6.5%**
PERCENT DISTRIBUTION									
Total Hispanic men	**100.0%**	**100.0%**	**100.0%**	**100.0%**	**100.0%**	**100.0%**	**100.0%**	**100.0%**	**100.0%**
Without income	17.3	46.7	8.1	6.9	7.3	8.5	7.3	7.0	7.5
With income	82.7	53.3	91.9	93.1	92.7	91.5	92.7	93.0	92.5
Under $15,000	25.3	30.2	24.0	18.8	20.3	24.2	44.2	36.7	55.4
$15,000 to $24,999	19.7	12.9	25.5	20.9	19.9	19.5	20.7	21.5	19.7
$25,000 to $34,999	13.0	5.7	15.7	16.2	16.3	15.3	9.5	11.8	6.3
$35,000 to $49,999	11.0	2.7	14.1	16.1	13.7	12.1	7.9	9.1	6.3
$50,000 to $74,999	8.1	1.3	8.3	12.0	12.2	11.6	6.3	8.5	3.0
$75,000 or more	5.6	0.4	4.2	9.1	10.4	9.1	4.0	5.8	1.4

Note: "–" means sample is too small to make a reliable estimate.
Source: Bureau of the Census, 2011 Current Population Survey Annual Social and Economic Supplement, Internet site http://www.census.gov/hhes/www/cpstables/032011/perinc/toc.htm; calculations by New Strategist

Table 2.16 Men by Income and Age, 2010: Non-Hispanic White Men

(number and percent distribution of non-Hispanic white men aged 15 or older by income and age, 2010; median income of men with income and of men working full-time, year-round; percent working full-time, year-round; men in thousands as of 2011)

	total	15 to 24	25 to 34	35 to 44	45 to 54	55 to 64	65 or older total	65 to 74	75 or older
Total non-Hispanic white men	**80,108**	**12,688**	**12,524**	**12,354**	**15,165**	**13,666**	**13,711**	**7,768**	**5,944**
Without income	6,617	4,360	646	438	562	431	179	106	74
With income	73,491	8,328	11,878	11,916	14,603	13,235	13,532	7,662	5,870
Under $5,000	4,754	2,705	485	348	465	443	307	161	147
$5,000 to $9,999	4,356	1,580	706	378	548	480	664	368	295
$10,000 to $14,999	5,318	1,013	676	475	740	766	1,646	772	874
$15,000 to $19,999	5,542	837	730	462	672	833	2,008	924	1,084
$20,000 to $24,999	5,388	613	988	674	806	825	1,484	791	692
$25,000 to $29,999	4,633	399	879	602	686	816	1,249	623	627
$30,000 to $34,999	4,634	316	994	764	766	815	980	520	459
$35,000 to $39,999	4,169	198	945	748	699	771	808	487	320
$40,000 to $44,999	4,193	184	931	801	878	772	625	375	251
$45,000 to $49,999	3,165	102	673	664	697	546	483	319	163
$50,000 to $54,999	3,860	83	796	807	964	773	435	264	172
$55,000 to $59,999	2,412	51	432	478	612	499	341	256	86
$60,000 to $64,999	2,615	46	475	589	695	510	300	208	92
$65,000 to $69,999	1,868	41	341	418	444	377	247	179	68
$70,000 to $74,999	1,840	29	308	451	459	373	220	145	76
$75,000 to $79,999	1,650	10	268	368	492	343	168	116	52
$80,000 to $84,999	1,586	14	206	363	468	353	183	123	59
$85,000 to $89,999	968	14	141	198	278	210	127	81	46
$90,000 to $94,999	1,133	18	109	270	334	263	139	88	52
$95,000 to $99,999	718	11	73	144	193	208	88	64	25
$100,000 or more	8,691	62	722	1,913	2,707	2,260	1,027	798	230
Median income									
Men with income	$37,037	$9,531	$36,946	$50,175	$51,126	$45,784	$27,500	$31,688	$23,758
Working full-time	54,192	25,849	45,405	57,288	61,212	62,165	68,736	70,051	58,997
Percent full-time	**49.1%**	**16.7%**	**65.6%**	**73.4%**	**70.5%**	**55.1%**	**12.5%**	**18.6%**	**4.5%**
PERCENT DISTRIBUTION									
Total non-Hispanic white men	**100.0%**	**100.0%**	**100.0%**	**100.0%**	**100.0%**	**100.0%**	**100.0%**	**100.0%**	**100.0%**
Without income	8.3	34.4	5.2	3.5	3.7	3.2	1.3	1.4	1.2
With income	91.7	65.6	94.8	96.5	96.3	96.8	98.7	98.6	98.8
Under $15,000	18.0	41.8	14.9	9.7	11.6	12.4	19.1	16.7	22.1
$15,000 to $24,999	13.6	11.4	13.7	9.2	9.7	12.1	25.5	22.1	29.9
$25,000 to $34,999	11.6	5.6	15.0	11.1	9.6	11.9	16.3	14.7	18.3
$35,000 to $49,999	14.4	3.8	20.4	17.9	15.0	15.3	14.0	15.2	12.3
$50,000 to $74,999	15.7	2.0	18.8	22.2	20.9	18.5	11.3	13.5	8.3
$75,000 or more	18.4	1.0	12.1	26.4	29.5	26.6	12.6	16.3	7.8

Note: Non-Hispanic whites are those who identify themselves as being white alone and not Hispanic.
Source: Bureau of the Census, 2011 Current Population Survey Annual Social and Economic Supplement, Internet site http://www.census.gov/hhes/www/cpstables/032011/perinc/toc.htm; calculations by New Strategist

Table 2.17 Men by Income, Race, and Hispanic Origin, 2010

(number and percent distribution of men aged 15 or older by income, race, and Hispanic origin, 2010; median income of men with income and of men working full-time, year-round; percent working full-time, year-round; men in thousands as of 2011)

	total	Asian	black	Hispanic	non-Hispanic white
Total men	**118,871**	**5,787**	**14,101**	**18,105**	**80,108**
Without income	13,520	865	2,843	3,140	6,617
With income	105,351	4,922	11,258	14,965	73,491
Under $5,000	7,350	356	1,052	1,094	4,754
$5,000 to $9,999	7,741	304	1,471	1,573	4,356
$10,000 to $14,999	8,933	401	1,270	1,918	5,318
$15,000 to $19,999	8,914	334	1,035	1,902	5,542
$20,000 to $24,999	8,525	395	1,067	1,669	5,388
$25,000 to $29,999	7,133	318	831	1,305	4,633
$30,000 to $34,999	6,846	314	795	1,041	4,634
$35,000 to $39,999	5,840	227	617	780	4,169
$40,000 to $44,999	5,714	210	568	711	4,193
$45,000 to $49,999	4,325	186	432	503	3,165
$50,000 to $54,999	4,978	202	367	516	3,860
$55,000 to $59,999	3,091	111	252	275	2,412
$60,000 to $64,999	3,416	195	244	328	2,615
$65,000 to $69,999	2,335	100	195	171	1,868
$70,000 to $74,999	2,371	135	217	168	1,840
$75,000 to $79,999	2,040	108	122	149	1,650
$80,000 to $84,999	1,979	100	132	147	1,586
$85,000 to $89,999	1,211	91	55	91	968
$90,000 to $94,999	1,362	78	66	71	1,133
$95,000 to $99,999	860	40	51	42	718
$100,000 or more	10,386	716	418	511	8,691
Median income					
Men with income	$32,137	$35,622	$23,061	$22,233	$37,037
Working full-time	50,063	52,444	37,805	31,671	54,192
Percent full-time	**47.5%**	**53.0%**	**38.0%**	**46.3%**	**49.1%**
PERCENT DISTRIBUTION					
Total men	**100.0%**	**100.0%**	**100.0%**	**100.0%**	**100.0%**
Without income	11.4	14.9	20.2	17.3	8.3
With income	88.6	85.1	79.8	82.7	91.7
Under $15,000	20.2	18.3	26.9	25.3	18.0
$15,000 to $24,999	14.7	12.6	14.9	19.7	13.6
$25,000 to $34,999	11.8	10.9	11.5	13.0	11.6
$35,000 to $49,999	13.4	10.8	11.5	11.0	14.4
$50,000 to $74,999	13.6	12.8	9.0	8.1	15.7
$75,000 or more	15.0	19.6	6.0	5.6	18.4

Note: Asians and blacks are those who identify themselves as being of the race alone and those who identify themselves as being of the race in combination with other races. Non-Hispanic whites are those who identify themselves as white alone and not Hispanic. Numbers do not add to total because some people identify themselves as being of more than one race, not all races are shown, and Hispanics may be of any race.
Source: Bureau of the Census, 2011 Current Population Survey Annual Social and Economic Supplement, Internet site http://www.census.gov/hhes/www/cpstables/032011/perinc/toc.htm; calculations by New Strategist

Men in the South Have the Lowest Incomes

Among full-time workers, incomes are highest in the Northeast.

The median income of men in the South was $31,173 in 2010, less than the median income of their counterparts in the other three regions. In the Midwest, men's median income was a higher $32,275. In the West, the median income of men stood at an almost identical $32,361. Men's median income was highest in the Northeast, at $35,363 in 2010. Among full-time workers, men in the Northeast are ahead of those in the other regions, with a median income of $52,614. Among men who work full-time in the South, median income was just $46,515.

Among Asian men who work full-time, incomes are highest in the South, at $56,480 in 2010. Among their non-Hispanic white counterparts, median income is highest in the West, at $60,488. The median income of black men who work full-time is also highest in the West, at $41,972. Hispanic men who work full-time have a lower income than Asians, blacks, and non-Hispanic whites. Their median income peaks at $32,236 in the West.

■ Hispanic men have low incomes because many are poorly educated immigrants with little earning power.

Men's income is highest in the Northeast

(median income of men aged 15 or older who work full-time, year-round, by region, 2010)

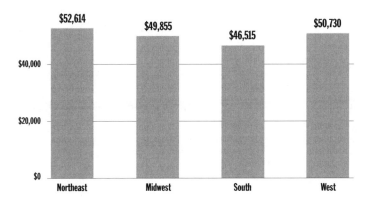

Table 2.18 Men by Income and Region, 2010: Total Men

(number and percent distribution of men aged 15 or older by income and region, 2010; median income of men with income and of men working full-time, year-round; percent working full-time, year-round; men in thousands as of 2011)

	total	Northeast	Midwest	South	West
Total men	**118,871**	**21,578**	**25,756**	**43,374**	**28,162**
Without income	13,520	2,336	2,396	5,334	3,454
With income	105,351	19,242	23,360	38,040	24,708
Under $5,000	7,350	1,428	1,718	2,447	1,758
$5,000 to $9,999	7,741	1,355	1,700	3,090	1,595
$10,000 to $14,999	8,933	1,492	1,783	3,445	2,214
$15,000 to $19,999	8,914	1,492	2,037	3,385	2,000
$20,000 to $24,999	8,525	1,391	1,851	3,213	2,072
$25,000 to $29,999	7,133	1,219	1,635	2,605	1,675
$30,000 to $34,999	6,846	1,147	1,639	2,479	1,580
$35,000 to $39,999	5,840	1,034	1,343	2,150	1,312
$40,000 to $44,999	5,714	1,018	1,309	2,127	1,259
$45,000 to $49,999	4,325	764	1,037	1,577	946
$50,000 to $54,999	4,978	931	1,165	1,737	1,146
$55,000 to $59,999	3,091	560	755	1,055	721
$60,000 to $64,999	3,416	655	788	1,117	856
$65,000 to $69,999	2,335	465	523	809	539
$70,000 to $74,999	2,371	453	582	763	571
$75,000 to $79,999	2,040	441	444	665	489
$80,000 to $84,999	1,979	372	414	725	468
$85,000 to $89,999	1,211	249	258	352	351
$90,000 to $94,999	1,362	306	247	497	311
$95,000 to $99,999	860	166	171	304	219
$100,000 or more	10,386	2,304	1,958	3,497	2,626
Median income					
Men with income	$32,137	$35,363	$32,275	$31,173	$32,361
Working full-time	50,063	52,614	49,855	46,515	50,730
Percent full-time	**47.5%**	**48.2%**	**47.6%**	**48.0%**	**45.9%**
PERCENT DISTRIBUTION					
Total men	**100.0%**	**100.0%**	**100.0%**	**100.0%**	**100.0%**
Without income	11.4	10.8	9.3	12.3	12.3
With income	88.6	89.2	90.7	87.7	87.7
Under $15,000	20.2	19.8	20.2	20.7	19.8
$15,000 to $24,999	14.7	13.4	15.1	15.2	14.5
$25,000 to $34,999	11.8	11.0	12.7	11.7	11.6
$35,000 to $49,999	13.4	13.1	14.3	13.5	12.5
$50,000 to $74,999	13.6	14.2	14.8	12.6	13.6
$75,000 or more	15.0	17.8	13.6	13.9	15.9

Source: Bureau of the Census, 2011 Current Population Survey Annual Social and Economic Supplement, Internet site http://www.census.gov/hhes/www/cpstables/032011/perinc/toc.htm; calculations by New Strategist

Table 2.19 Men by Income and Region, 2010: Asian Men

(number and percent distribution of Asian men aged 15 or older by income and region, 2010; median income of men with income and of men working full-time, year-round; percent working full-time, year-round; men in thousands as of 2011)

	total	Northeast	Midwest	South	West
Total Asian men	**5,787**	**1,188**	**630**	**1,290**	**2,679**
Without income	865	184	85	205	391
With income	4,922	1,004	545	1,085	2,288
Under $5,000	356	81	26	92	157
$5,000 to $9,999	304	56	40	51	158
$10,000 to $14,999	401	73	36	82	210
$15,000 to $19,999	334	82	56	70	126
$20,000 to $24,999	395	70	42	70	214
$25,000 to $29,999	318	69	25	78	146
$30,000 to $34,999	314	53	45	58	157
$35,000 to $39,999	227	44	25	41	115
$40,000 to $44,999	210	43	9	44	115
$45,000 to $49,999	186	49	21	51	66
$50,000 to $54,999	202	32	26	48	95
$55,000 to $59,999	111	16	16	21	58
$60,000 to $64,999	195	31	34	41	87
$65,000 to $69,999	100	15	14	24	48
$70,000 to $74,999	135	22	21	40	52
$75,000 to $79,999	108	26	11	24	46
$80,000 to $84,999	100	21	4	39	36
$85,000 to $89,999	91	19	13	19	41
$90,000 to $94,999	78	22	8	16	33
$95,000 to $99,999	40	7	6	5	23
$100,000 or more	716	173	67	170	306
Median income					
Men with income	$35,622	$36,491	$35,387	$40,027	$33,648
Working full-time	52,444	51,965	53,557	56,480	51,982
Percent full-time	**53.0%**	**55.1%**	**54.9%**	**56.6%**	**49.8%**
PERCENT DISTRIBUTION					
Total Asian men	**100.0%**	**100.0%**	**100.0%**	**100.0%**	**100.0%**
Without income	14.9	15.5	13.5	15.9	14.6
With income	85.1	84.5	86.5	84.1	85.4
Under $15,000	18.3	17.7	16.2	17.4	19.6
$15,000 to $24,999	12.6	12.8	15.6	10.9	12.7
$25,000 to $34,999	10.9	10.3	11.1	10.5	11.3
$35,000 to $49,999	10.8	11.4	8.7	10.5	11.0
$50,000 to $74,999	12.8	9.8	17.6	13.5	12.7
$75,000 or more	19.6	22.6	17.3	21.2	18.1

Note: Asians are those who identify themselves as being of the race alone and those who identify themselves as being of the race in combination with other races.
Source: Bureau of the Census, 2011 Current Population Survey Annual Social and Economic Supplement, Internet site http:// www.census.gov/hhes/www/cpstables/032011/perinc/toc.htm; calculations by New Strategist

Table 2.20 Men by Income and Region, 2010: Black Men

(number and percent distribution of black men aged 15 or older by income and region, 2010; median income of men with income and of men working full-time, year-round; percent working full-time, year-round; men in thousands as of 2011)

	total	Northeast	Midwest	South	West
Total black men	**14,101**	**2,499**	**2,402**	**7,719**	**1,480**
Without income	2,843	484	503	1,560	295
With income	11,258	2,015	1,899	6,159	1,185
Under $5,000	1,052	198	200	537	116
$5,000 to $9,999	1,471	281	300	774	116
$10,000 to $14,999	1,270	201	175	750	143
$15,000 to $19,999	1,035	160	205	588	82
$20,000 to $24,999	1,067	213	187	552	116
$25,000 to $29,999	831	139	156	460	76
$30,000 to $34,999	795	126	121	466	81
$35,000 to $39,999	617	105	71	365	76
$40,000 to $44,999	568	118	82	306	61
$45,000 to $49,999	432	56	80	240	56
$50,000 to $54,999	367	60	61	199	47
$55,000 to $59,999	252	41	39	138	35
$60,000 to $64,999	244	52	33	121	38
$65,000 to $69,999	195	47	27	98	23
$70,000 to $74,999	217	64	43	84	27
$75,000 to $79,999	122	12	24	69	16
$80,000 to $84,999	132	25	10	82	15
$85,000 to $89,999	55	18	7	24	6
$90,000 to $94,999	66	12	10	42	4
$95,000 to $99,999	51	11	2	35	3
$100,000 or more	418	76	67	229	47
Median income					
Men with income	$23,061	$23,327	$21,519	$23,197	$26,062
Working full-time	37,805	40,421	36,489	36,827	41,972
Percent full-time	**38.0%**	**37.1%**	**33.1%**	**39.7%**	**38.5%**
PERCENT DISTRIBUTION					
Total black men	**100.0%**	**100.0%**	**100.0%**	**100.0%**	**100.0%**
Without income	20.2	19.4	20.9	20.2	19.9
With income	79.8	80.6	79.1	79.8	80.1
Under $15,000	26.9	27.2	28.1	26.7	25.3
$15,000 to $24,999	14.9	14.9	16.3	14.8	13.4
$25,000 to $34,999	11.5	10.6	11.5	12.0	10.6
$35,000 to $49,999	11.5	11.2	9.7	11.8	13.0
$50,000 to $74,999	9.0	10.6	8.5	8.3	11.5
$75,000 or more	6.0	6.2	5.0	6.2	6.1

Note: Blacks are those who identify themselves as being of the race alone and those who identify themselves as being of the race in combination with other races.
Source: Bureau of the Census, 2011 Current Population Survey Annual Social and Economic Supplement, Internet site http:// www.census.gov/hhes/www/cpstables/032011/perinc/toc.htm; calculations by New Strategist

Table 2.21 Men by Income and Region, 2010: Hispanic Men

(number and percent distribution of Hispanic men aged 15 or older by income and region, 2010; median income of men with income and of men working full-time, year-round; percent working full-time, year-round; men in thousands as of 2011)

	total	Northeast	Midwest	South	West
Total Hispanic men	**18,105**	**2,539**	**1,529**	**6,508**	**7,530**
Without income	3,140	430	237	1,109	1,364
With income	14,965	2,109	1,292	5,399	6,166
Under $5,000	1,094	172	102	342	479
$5,000 to $9,999	1,573	241	142	606	584
$10,000 to $14,999	1,918	269	152	699	799
$15,000 to $19,999	1,902	295	176	657	775
$20,000 to $24,999	1,669	219	162	633	653
$25,000 to $29,999	1,305	202	113	447	544
$30,000 to $34,999	1,041	126	115	339	461
$35,000 to $39,999	780	98	58	284	342
$40,000 to $44,999	711	106	44	285	277
$45,000 to $49,999	503	53	41	187	221
$50,000 to $54,999	516	63	50	201	204
$55,000 to $59,999	275	35	19	103	119
$60,000 to $64,999	328	43	24	113	148
$65,000 to $69,999	171	29	8	72	62
$70,000 to $74,999	168	23	11	59	76
$75,000 to $79,999	149	23	12	43	72
$80,000 to $84,999	147	18	16	50	62
$85,000 to $89,999	91	22	2	27	39
$90,000 to $94,999	71	7	4	31	29
$95,000 to $99,999	42	3	3	20	16
$100,000 or more	511	63	38	205	206
Median income					
Men with income	$22,233	$21,408	$21,613	$22,217	$22,843
Working full-time	31,671	30,868	30,313	31,700	32,236
Percent full-time	**46.3%**	**44.3%**	**47.4%**	**49.2%**	**44.2%**
PERCENT DISTRIBUTION					
Total Hispanic men	**100.0%**	**100.0%**	**100.0%**	**100.0%**	**100.0%**
Without income	17.3	16.9	15.5	17.0	18.1
With income	82.7	83.1	84.5	83.0	81.9
Under $15,000	25.3	26.9	25.9	25.3	24.7
$15,000 to $24,999	19.7	20.2	22.1	19.8	19.0
$25,000 to $34,999	13.0	12.9	14.9	12.1	13.3
$35,000 to $49,999	11.0	10.1	9.4	11.6	11.2
$50,000 to $74,999	8.1	7.6	7.3	8.4	8.1
$75,000 or more	5.6	5.4	4.9	5.8	5.6

Source: Bureau of the Census, 2011 Current Population Survey Annual Social and Economic Supplement, Internet site http:// www.census.gov/hhes/www/cpstables/032011/perinc/toc.htm; calculations by New Strategist

Table 2.22 Men by Income and Region, 2010: Non-Hispanic White Men

(number and percent distribution of non-Hispanic white men aged 15 or older by income and region, 2010; median income of men with income and of men working full-time, year-round; percent working full-time, year-round; men in thousands as of 2011)

	total	Northeast	Midwest	South	West
Total non-Hispanic white men	**80,108**	**15,515**	**21,017**	**27,570**	**16,006**
Without income	6,617	1,290	1,552	2,441	1,334
With income	73,491	14,225	19,465	25,129	14,672
Under $5,000	4,754	982	1,367	1,448	957
$5,000 to $9,999	4,356	801	1,211	1,646	699
$10,000 to $14,999	5,318	983	1,394	1,908	1,031
$15,000 to $19,999	5,542	955	1,588	2,031	967
$20,000 to $24,999	5,388	913	1,452	1,955	1,068
$25,000 to $29,999	4,633	827	1,322	1,598	886
$30,000 to $34,999	4,634	845	1,346	1,588	856
$35,000 to $39,999	4,169	788	1,184	1,443	755
$40,000 to $44,999	4,193	763	1,173	1,469	786
$45,000 to $49,999	3,165	603	892	1,083	586
$50,000 to $54,999	3,860	773	1,023	1,279	784
$55,000 to $59,999	2,412	466	677	778	492
$60,000 to $64,999	2,615	523	694	836	564
$65,000 to $69,999	1,868	382	471	612	402
$70,000 to $74,999	1,840	343	509	574	414
$75,000 to $79,999	1,650	379	397	526	349
$80,000 to $84,999	1,586	309	382	550	345
$85,000 to $89,999	968	195	233	282	258
$90,000 to $94,999	1,133	266	223	407	237
$95,000 to $99,999	718	144	158	241	174
$100,000 or more	8,691	1,986	1,771	2,871	2,064
Median income					
Men with income	$37,037	$40,089	$35,179	$36,109	$40,533
Working full-time	54,192	58,985	51,175	51,827	60,488
Percent full-time	**49.1%**	**50.0%**	**49.2%**	**49.7%**	**47.1%**
PERCENT DISTRIBUTION					
Total non-Hispanic white men	**100.0%**	**100.0%**	**100.0%**	**100.0%**	**100.0%**
Without income	8.3	8.3	7.4	8.9	8.3
With income	91.7	91.7	92.6	91.1	91.7
Under $15,000	18.0	17.8	18.9	18.1	16.8
$15,000 to $24,999	13.6	12.0	14.5	14.5	12.7
$25,000 to $34,999	11.6	10.8	12.7	11.6	10.9
$35,000 to $49,999	14.4	13.9	15.5	14.5	13.3
$50,000 to $74,999	15.7	16.0	16.1	14.8	16.6
$75,000 or more	18.4	21.1	15.1	17.7	21.4

Note: Non-Hispanic whites are those who identify themselves as being white alone and not Hispanic.
Source: Bureau of the Census, 2011 Current Population Survey Annual Social and Economic Supplement, Internet site http://www.census.gov/hhes/www/cpstables/032011/perinc/toc.htm; calculations by New Strategist

Men in the Suburbs Have the Highest Incomes

They are also most likely to work full-time.

Not surprisingly, men who live outside the principal cities of the nation's metropolitan areas (in other words, in the suburbs) have the highest incomes. Their median income stood at $35,973 in 2010. Nearly half—49 percent—have full-time jobs, and their median income was $52,158.

At the other extreme, men living in nonmetropolitan areas had the lowest incomes, a median of just $28,896 in 2010. The 44 percent who worked full-time had a median income of $41,748—only 80 percent as much as their suburban counterparts. The cost of living is often lower in nonmetropolitan areas than in the suburbs, making the gap in spending power smaller than the gap in income.

■ The Great Recession has lowered men's incomes regardless of where they live.

Men in nonmetropolitan areas have the lowest incomes

(median income of men aged 15 or older who work full-time, year-round, by metropolitan status, 2010)

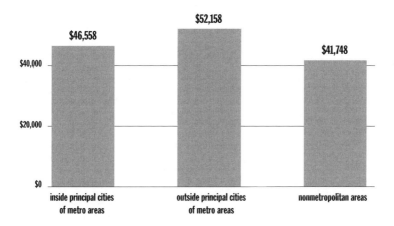

Table 2.23 Men by Income and Metropolitan Residence, 2010

(number and percent distribution of men aged 15 or older by income and metropolitan residence, 2010; median income of men with income and of men working full-time, year-round; percent working full-time, year-round; men in thousands as of 2011)

| | total | in metropolitan area | | | not in metropolitan area |
		total	inside principal cities	outside principal cities	
Total men	**118,871**	**100,236**	**37,961**	**62,276**	**18,634**
Without income	13,520	11,725	4,789	6,937	1,794
With income	105,351	88,511	33,172	55,339	16,840
Under $5,000	7,350	6,139	2,287	3,851	1,212
$5,000 to $9,999	7,741	6,308	2,840	3,468	1,432
$10,000 to $14,999	8,933	7,353	3,109	4,244	1,580
$15,000 to $19,999	8,914	7,268	2,938	4,329	1,646
$20,000 to $24,999	8,525	7,074	2,951	4,123	1,451
$25,000 to $29,999	7,133	5,800	2,362	3,439	1,333
$30,000 to $34,999	6,846	5,578	2,123	3,455	1,268
$35,000 to $39,999	5,840	4,713	1,671	3,041	1,127
$40,000 to $44,999	5,714	4,841	1,682	3,159	874
$45,000 to $49,999	4,325	3,584	1,235	2,351	740
$50,000 to $54,999	4,978	4,080	1,428	2,651	899
$55,000 to $59,999	3,091	2,650	856	1,794	442
$60,000 to $64,999	3,416	2,947	997	1,950	470
$65,000 to $69,999	2,335	1,973	656	1,317	362
$70,000 to $74,999	2,371	2,014	672	1,342	357
$75,000 to $79,999	2,040	1,805	575	1,230	234
$80,000 to $84,999	1,979	1,718	539	1,178	262
$85,000 to $89,999	1,211	1,071	368	703	138
$90,000 to $94,999	1,362	1,216	405	811	145
$95,000 to $99,999	860	763	271	492	96
$100,000 or more	10,386	9,617	3,206	6,411	769
Median income					
Men with income	$32,137	$33,110	$30,169	$35,973	$28,896
Working full-time	50,063	50,869	46,558	52,158	41,748
Percent full-time	**47.5%**	**48.0%**	**46.8%**	**48.8%**	**44.4%**
PERCENT DISTRIBUTION					
Total men	**100.0%**	**100.0%**	**100.0%**	**100.0%**	**100.0%**
Without income	11.4	11.7	12.6	11.1	9.6
With income	88.6	88.3	87.4	88.9	90.4
Under $15,000	20.2	19.8	21.7	18.6	22.7
$15,000 to $24,999	14.7	14.3	15.5	13.6	16.6
$25,000 to $34,999	11.8	11.4	11.8	11.1	14.0
$35,000 to $49,999	13.4	13.1	12.1	13.7	14.7
$50,000 to $74,999	13.6	13.6	12.1	14.5	13.6
$75,000 or more	15.0	16.2	14.1	17.4	8.8

Source: Bureau of the Census, 2011 Current Population Survey Annual Social and Economic Supplement, Internet site http:// www.census.gov/hhes/www/cpstables/032011/perinc/toc.htm; calculations by New Strategist

Most Men Have Modest Earnings

Only 25 percent of men who work full-time, year-round earn $75,000 or more.

Among the nation's 81 million men with earnings in 2010, about 56 million work full-time, year-round. Fewer than 13 million men work part-time. Among men with full-time, year-round jobs, median earnings stood at $47,715 in 2010. Only 25 percent earn $75,000 or more.

Non-Hispanic white men who work full-time, year-round earned a median of $51,865 in 2010. This amount is slightly higher than the $51,606 median earnings of Asian men who work full-time, year-round.

The median earnings of black men who work full-time, year-round are below the earnings of Asians or non-Hispanic whites, at $36,859 in 2010. The median earnings of Hispanic men who work full-time, year-round are even lower, at $31,408. The Hispanic median is just 61 percent as high as that of non-Hispanic whites.

■ The earnings of black men should rise in the years ahead if they can boost their educational attainment. The earnings of Hispanic men are unlikely to rise until immigrants become a smaller share of the Hispanic population.

Most men earn less than $50,000 per year

(percent distribution of men aged 15 or older who work full-time, year-round, by earnings, 2010)

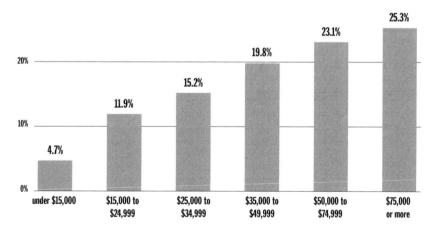

Table 2.24 Men by Earnings and Employment Status, 2010: Total Men

(number and percent distribution of men aged 15 or older with earnings by employment status and median earnings, 2010; men in thousands as of 2011)

	total	worked full-time		worked part-time	
		total	year-round	total	year-round
Total men with earnings	**81,180**	**68,411**	**56,412**	**12,769**	**5,893**
Under $5,000	6,316	2,076	373	4,240	743
$5,000 to $9,999	4,908	2,239	571	2,669	1,218
$10,000 to $14,999	5,329	3,262	1,697	2,067	1,318
$15,000 to $19,999	5,277	4,130	2,731	1,147	787
$20,000 to $24,999	5,897	5,118	3,979	778	509
$25,000 to $29,999	5,131	4,717	3,972	413	272
$30,000 to $34,999	5,484	5,178	4,586	306	217
$35,000 to $39,999	4,648	4,464	3,844	184	119
$40,000 to $44,999	4,940	4,744	4,220	197	130
$45,000 to $49,999	3,549	3,450	3,131	99	68
$50,000 to $54,999	4,631	4,521	4,167	109	88
$55,000 to $59,999	2,537	2,484	2,336	52	41
$60,000 to $64,999	3,156	3,100	2,872	54	40
$65,000 to $69,999	1,929	1,886	1,747	43	36
$70,000 to $74,999	2,078	2,035	1,909	43	34
$75,000 to $79,999	1,824	1,790	1,695	34	27
$80,000 to $84,999	1,802	1,779	1,666	23	19
$85,000 to $89,999	1,017	1,004	955	14	14
$90,000 to $94,999	1,181	1,165	1,125	16	13
$95,000 to $99,999	635	622	579	14	14
$100,000 or more	8,913	8,647	8,255	266	188
Median earnings	$36,676	$41,954	$47,715	$8,713	$12,660
PERCENT DISTRIBUTION					
Total men with earnings	**100.0%**	**100.0%**	**100.0%**	**100.0%**	**100.0%**
Under $15,000	20.4	11.1	4.7	70.3	55.6
$15,000 to $24,999	13.8	13.5	11.9	15.1	22.0
$25,000 to $34,999	13.1	14.5	15.2	5.6	8.3
$35,000 to $49,999	16.2	18.5	19.8	3.8	5.4
$50,000 to $74,999	17.7	20.5	23.1	2.4	4.1
$75,000 or more	18.9	21.9	25.3	2.9	4.7

Note: Earnings include wages and salary only.
Source: Bureau of the Census, 2011 Current Population Survey Annual Social and Economic Supplement, Internet site http://www.census.gov/hhes/www/cpstables/032011/perinc/toc.htm; calculations by New Strategist

Table 2.25 Men by Earnings and Employment Status, 2010: Asian Men

(number and percent distribution of Asian men aged 15 or older with earnings by employment status and median earnings, 2010; men in thousands as of 2011)

	total	worked full-time total	worked full-time year-round	worked part-time total	worked part-time year-round
Asian men with earnings	**4,068**	**3,516**	**3,066**	**553**	**271**
Under $5,000	239	90	24	148	14
$5,000 to $9,999	194	93	21	101	48
$10,000 to $14,999	264	146	99	118	79
$15,000 to $19,999	245	180	144	64	41
$20,000 to $24,999	322	283	230	41	30
$25,000 to $29,999	241	220	197	21	13
$30,000 to $34,999	254	244	229	9	8
$35,000 to $39,999	205	200	168	4	2
$40,000 to $44,999	201	196	179	6	5
$45,000 to $49,999	162	158	145	4	2
$50,000 to $54,999	189	184	175	5	1
$55,000 to $59,999	101	98	95	2	2
$60,000 to $64,999	183	180	165	4	2
$65,000 to $69,999	87	87	80	0	0
$70,000 to $74,999	131	130	123	1	1
$75,000 to $79,999	101	95	92	6	6
$80,000 to $84,999	93	91	87	2	2
$85,000 to $89,999	77	76	72	1	0
$90,000 to $94,999	72	71	71	2	2
$95,000 to $99,999	38	38	37	0	0
$100,000 or more	669	653	633	15	12
Median earnings	$41,024	$47,154	$51,606	$10,691	$13,891

PERCENT DISTRIBUTION

Asian men with earnings	**100.0%**	**100.0%**	**100.0%**	**100.0%**	**100.0%**
Under $15,000	17.1	9.4	4.7	66.4	52.0
$15,000 to $24,999	13.9	13.2	12.2	19.0	26.2
$25,000 to $34,999	12.2	13.2	13.9	5.4	7.7
$35,000 to $49,999	14.0	15.8	16.0	2.5	3.3
$50,000 to $74,999	17.0	19.3	20.8	2.2	2.2
$75,000 or more	25.8	29.1	32.4	4.7	8.1

Note: Asians are those who identify themselves as being of the race alone and those who identify themselves as being of the race in combination with other races. Earnings include wages and salary only.
Source: Bureau of the Census, 2011 Current Population Survey Annual Social and Economic Supplement, Internet site http://www.census.gov/hhes/www/cpstables/032011/perinc/toc.htm; calculations by New Strategist

Table 2.26 Men by Earnings and Employment Status, 2010: Black Men

(number and percent distribution of black men aged 15 or older with earnings by employment status and median earnings, 2010; men in thousands as of 2011)

	total	worked full-time		worked part-time	
		total	year-round	total	year-round
Black men with earnings	**8,152**	**6,650**	**5,349**	**1,501**	**609**
Under $5,000	837	253	30	583	69
$5,000 to $9,999	614	270	64	344	159
$10,000 to $14,999	670	433	241	237	148
$15,000 to $19,999	615	502	332	113	90
$20,000 to $24,999	846	756	604	91	52
$25,000 to $29,999	644	605	555	39	22
$30,000 to $34,999	719	681	613	37	24
$35,000 to $39,999	496	483	434	14	10
$40,000 to $44,999	508	490	439	17	14
$45,000 to $49,999	357	354	330	4	2
$50,000 to $54,999	330	325	303	4	4
$55,000 to $59,999	219	219	204	0	0
$60,000 to $64,999	233	230	208	3	0
$65,000 to $69,999	165	164	154	1	0
$70,000 to $74,999	180	175	164	5	5
$75,000 to $79,999	96	96	92	0	0
$80,000 to $84,999	124	124	118	0	0
$85,000 to $89,999	57	55	50	2	2
$90,000 to $94,999	74	74	69	0	0
$95,000 to $99,999	32	32	32	0	0
$100,000 or more	334	327	312	7	7
Median earnings	$28,137	$32,269	$36,859	$7,290	$11,827
PERCENT DISTRIBUTION					
Black men with earnings	**100.0%**	**100.0%**	**100.0%**	**100.0%**	**100.0%**
Under $15,000	26.0	14.4	6.3	77.5	61.7
$15,000 to $24,999	17.9	18.9	17.5	13.6	23.3
$25,000 to $34,999	16.7	19.3	21.8	5.1	7.6
$35,000 to $49,999	16.7	20.0	22.5	2.3	4.3
$50,000 to $74,999	13.8	16.7	19.3	0.9	1.5
$75,000 or more	8.8	10.6	12.6	0.6	1.5

Note: Blacks are those who identify themselves as being of the race alone and those who identify themselves as being of the race in combination with other races. Earnings include wages and salary only.
Source: Bureau of the Census, 2011 Current Population Survey Annual Social and Economic Supplement, Internet site http:// www.census.gov/hhes/www/cpstables/032011/perinc/toc.htm; calculations by New Strategist

Table 2.27 Men by Earnings and Employment Status, 2010: Hispanic Men

(number and percent distribution of Hispanic men aged 15 or older with earnings by employment status and median earnings, 2010; men in thousands as of 2011)

	total	worked full-time		worked part-time	
		total	year-round	total	year-round
Hispanic men with earnings	**12,743**	**10,709**	**8,381**	**2,034**	**1,018**
Under $5,000	888	366	32	523	86
$5,000 to $9,999	1,025	547	174	479	226
$10,000 to $14,999	1,468	1,032	569	437	267
$15,000 to $19,999	1,600	1,342	975	258	196
$20,000 to $24,999	1,455	1,330	1,107	125	79
$25,000 to $29,999	1,184	1,112	961	72	53
$30,000 to $34,999	971	917	818	54	45
$35,000 to $39,999	714	693	612	22	16
$40,000 to $44,999	685	671	606	15	8
$45,000 to $49,999	462	444	410	16	14
$50,000 to $54,999	504	490	458	14	14
$55,000 to $59,999	244	242	220	2	2
$60,000 to $64,999	312	308	276	4	2
$65,000 to $69,999	143	143	133	0	0
$70,000 to $74,999	160	158	150	2	2
$75,000 to $79,999	132	131	129	1	1
$80,000 to $84,999	147	147	135	0	0
$85,000 to $89,999	77	75	71	2	2
$90,000 to $94,999	75	75	74	0	0
$95,000 to $99,999	37	35	34	2	2
$100,000 or more	460	453	436	7	4
Median earnings	$24,615	$27,370	$31,408	$10,124	$12,834

PERCENT DISTRIBUTION

Hispanic men with earnings	**100.0%**	**100.0%**	**100.0%**	**100.0%**	**100.0%**
Under $15,000	26.5	18.2	9.2	70.7	56.9
$15,000 to $24,999	24.0	25.0	24.8	18.8	27.0
$25,000 to $34,999	16.9	18.9	21.2	6.2	9.6
$35,000 to $49,999	14.6	16.9	19.4	2.6	3.7
$50,000 to $74,999	10.7	12.5	14.8	1.1	2.0
$75,000 or more	7.3	8.6	10.5	0.6	0.9

Note: Earnings include wages and salary only.
Source: Bureau of the Census, 2011 Current Population Survey Annual Social and Economic Supplement, Internet site http://www.census.gov/hhes/www/cpstables/032011/perinc/toc.htm; calculations by New Strategist

Table 2.28 Men by Earnings and Employment Status, 2010: Non-Hispanic White Men

(number and percent distribution of non-Hispanic white men aged 15 or older with earnings by employment status and median earnings, 2010; men in thousands as of 2011)

	total	worked full-time		worked part-time	
		total	year-round	total	year-round
Non-Hispanic white men with earnings	**55,780**	**47,151**	**39,334**	**8,629**	**3,957**
Under $5,000	4,284	1,333	279	2,951	561
$5,000 to $9,999	3,078	1,326	318	1,752	786
$10,000 to $14,999	2,935	1,659	806	1,276	821
$15,000 to $19,999	2,756	2,067	1,255	689	439
$20,000 to $24,999	3,292	2,768	2,054	524	348
$25,000 to $29,999	3,045	2,759	2,241	286	189
$30,000 to $34,999	3,493	3,290	2,893	202	138
$35,000 to $39,999	3,199	3,054	2,603	145	90
$40,000 to $44,999	3,523	3,366	2,982	157	101
$45,000 to $49,999	2,538	2,465	2,223	74	49
$50,000 to $54,999	3,564	3,477	3,192	86	69
$55,000 to $59,999	1,949	1,903	1,798	46	34
$60,000 to $64,999	2,395	2,351	2,187	44	35
$65,000 to $69,999	1,531	1,490	1,379	41	36
$70,000 to $74,999	1,608	1,573	1,473	35	27
$75,000 to $79,999	1,481	1,454	1,370	27	21
$80,000 to $84,999	1,424	1,402	1,311	21	17
$85,000 to $89,999	804	794	759	10	10
$90,000 to $94,999	942	928	894	14	11
$95,000 to $99,999	525	514	474	12	12
$100,000 or more	7,414	7,177	6,841	237	165
Median earnings	$41,594	$48,372	$51,865	$8,496	$12,759

PERCENT DISTRIBUTION

	total	total	year-round	total	year-round
Non-Hispanic white men with earnings	**100.0%**	**100.0%**	**100.0%**	**100.0%**	**100.0%**
Under $15,000	18.5	9.2	3.6	69.3	54.8
$15,000 to $24,999	10.8	10.3	8.4	14.1	19.9
$25,000 to $34,999	11.7	12.8	13.1	5.7	8.3
$35,000 to $49,999	16.6	18.8	19.9	4.4	6.1
$50,000 to $74,999	19.8	22.9	25.5	2.9	5.1
$75,000 or more	22.6	26.0	29.6	3.7	6.0

Note: Non-Hispanic whites are those who identify themselves as being white alone and not Hispanic. Earnings include wages and salary only.
Source: Bureau of the Census, 2011 Current Population Survey Annual Social and Economic Supplement, Internet site http://www.census.gov/hhes/www/cpstables/032011/perinc/toc.htm; calculations by New Strategist

Men's Earnings Rise with Education

Those with a professional degree earn the most.

Earnings rise in lockstep with education. Among full-time workers, the least-educated men earned a median of just $24,453 in 2010, well below the $50,361 median of all men aged 25 or older. Median earnings are a larger $40,055 among high school graduates, and rise to $71,778 for men with a bachelor's degree or more education.

Men holding a professional degree have the highest earnings. Their median earnings exceed $115,298 and fully 61 percent earn above that level. Men with a doctoral degree also have median earnings above $100,000, but a smaller 53 percent earn more than that.

Education pays off almost immediately. Among men aged 25 to 34 who work full-time, the median earnings of those with a bachelor's degree are 54 percent higher than the median earnings of men with no more than a high school diploma—$51,141 versus $33,262 in 2010.

■ The economic downturn has affected men at every level of education, but men with college degrees still have higher earnings than those with less education.

A college diploma adds to earning power

(median earnings of men aged 25 or older who work full-time, year-round, by educational attainment, 2010)

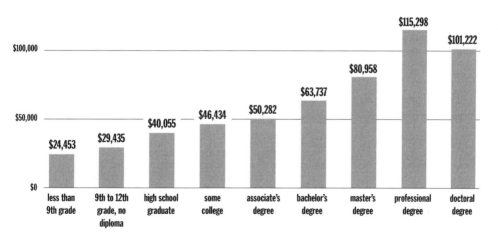

Table 2.29 Men Who Work Full-Time by Earnings and Education, 2010: Total Men

(number and percent distribution of men aged 25 or older who work full-time, year-round, by earnings and educational attainment, 2010; median earnings of men with earnings; men in thousands as of 2011)

	total men	less than 9th grade	9th to 12th grade	high school graduate	some college	associate's degree	bachelor's degree or more				
							total	bachelor's degree	master's degree	professional degree	doctoral degree
Total men who work full-time	52,890	1,600	2,615	15,104	8,541	5,042	19,990	12,836	4,670	1,237	1,246
Under $5,000	354	22	22	102	72	30	104	83	17	2	2
$5,000 to $9,999	436	36	91	151	70	20	69	46	12	8	4
$10,000 to $14,999	1,280	188	196	438	190	83	184	142	24	7	10
$15,000 to $19,999	2,103	292	329	809	302	115	255	193	33	23	7
$20,000 to $24,999	3,340	282	382	1,465	546	231	435	339	89	6	2
$25,000 to $29,999	3,488	192	310	1,490	570	346	580	463	97	1	18
$30,000 to $34,999	4,221	158	313	1,682	775	412	882	696	145	16	25
$35,000 to $39,999	3,666	133	195	1,391	716	403	828	670	121	22	15
$40,000 to $44,999	4,044	79	184	1,445	816	506	1,013	758	186	37	33
$45,000 to $49,999	3,018	55	123	1,020	604	328	887	645	203	25	13
$50,000 to $54,999	4,069	30	146	1,265	724	486	1,417	1,043	248	58	69
$55,000 to $59,999	2,289	25	65	632	443	258	865	599	200	14	52
$60,000 to $64,999	2,813	38	75	724	488	332	1,156	813	271	23	49
$65,000 to $69,999	1,708	17	26	378	280	214	793	553	177	24	39
$70,000 to $74,999	1,880	5	34	425	353	213	853	560	210	43	39
$75,000 to $79,999	1,684	10	21	350	244	219	839	512	223	25	79
$80,000 to $84,999	1,648	11	25	281	296	148	887	586	234	39	28
$85,000 to $89,999	943	0	5	117	154	116	551	342	134	38	35
$90,000 to $94,999	1,114	2	14	173	151	125	650	405	166	47	33
$95,000 to $99,999	579	5	3	60	53	37	419	245	119	21	34
$100,000 or more	8,216	19	56	704	694	420	6,323	3,143	1,762	758	660
Median earnings	$50,361	$24,453	$29,435	$40,055	$46,434	$50,282	$71,778	$63,737	$80,958	$115,298	$101,222

PERCENT DISTRIBUTION

Total men who work full-time	100.0%	100.0%	100.0%	100.0%	100.0%	100.0%	100.0%	100.0%	100.0%	100.0%	100.0%
Under $15,000	3.9	15.4	11.8	4.6	3.9	2.6	1.8	2.1	1.1	1.4	1.3
$15,000 to $24,999	10.3	35.9	27.2	15.1	9.9	6.9	3.5	4.1	2.6	2.3	0.7
$25,000 to $34,999	14.6	21.9	23.8	21.0	15.7	15.0	7.3	9.0	5.2	1.4	3.5
$35,000 to $49,999	20.3	16.7	19.2	25.5	25.0	24.5	13.6	16.1	10.9	6.8	4.9
$50,000 to $74,999	24.1	7.2	13.2	22.7	26.8	29.8	25.4	27.8	23.7	13.1	19.9
$75,000 to $99,999	11.3	1.8	2.6	6.5	10.5	12.8	16.7	16.3	18.8	13.7	16.8
$100,000 or more	15.5	1.2	2.1	4.7	8.1	8.3	31.6	24.5	37.7	61.3	53.0

Note: Earnings include wages and salary only.
Source: Bureau of the Census, 2011 Current Population Survey Annual Social and Economic Supplement, Internet site http://www.census.gov/hhes/www/cpstables/032011/perinc/toc.htm; calculations by New Strategist

Table 2.30 Men Who Work Full-Time by Earnings and Education, 2010: Men Aged 25 to 34

(number and percent distribution of men aged 25 to 34 who work full-time, year-round, by earnings and educational attainment, 2010; median earnings of men with earnings; men in thousands as of 2011)

	total men	less than 9th grade	9th to 12th grade	high school graduate	some college	associate's degree	bachelor's degree or more total	bachelor's degree	master's degree	professional degree	doctoral degree
Men aged 25 to 34 who work full-time	**12,951**	**378**	**728**	**3,689**	**2,253**	**1,282**	**4,620**	**3,517**	**766**	**182**	**155**
Under $5,000	49	2	3	22	12	0	11	11	0	0	0
$5,000 to $9,999	133	10	18	58	23	9	15	10	6	0	0
$10,000 to $14,999	422	47	66	137	91	32	48	46	2	0	0
$15,000 to $19,999	783	98	115	303	137	50	78	66	8	3	3
$20,000 to $24,999	1,148	72	151	466	209	91	159	136	19	4	0
$25,000 to $29,999	1,133	44	113	451	209	115	201	183	13	0	5
$30,000 to $34,999	1,379	32	75	482	272	156	360	301	45	5	9
$35,000 to $39,999	1,161	27	47	349	256	125	356	298	45	11	1
$40,000 to $44,999	1,176	13	34	390	230	138	372	312	37	17	4
$45,000 to $49,999	874	16	26	218	188	104	322	255	51	10	6
$50,000 to $54,999	996	4	33	255	137	122	445	360	37	26	22
$55,000 to $59,999	514	4	10	128	70	50	252	175	58	7	12
$60,000 to $64,999	616	0	10	105	101	67	332	263	62	1	5
$65,000 to $69,999	404	4	2	53	56	54	236	173	42	8	12
$70,000 to $74,999	382	0	3	62	81	37	198	138	50	8	2
$75,000 to $79,999	310	3	2	53	37	28	186	129	46	4	7
$80,000 to $84,999	267	0	3	31	28	21	184	127	50	4	4
$85,000 to $89,999	157	0	2	22	8	16	110	83	13	7	8
$90,000 to $94,999	128	0	5	19	9	14	82	55	25	1	0
$95,000 to $99,999	80	0	0	6	6	4	63	30	25	8	0
$100,000 or more	844	2	9	79	95	50	610	366	131	58	55
Median earnings	$40,716	$21,741	$25,307	$33,262	$37,766	$41,331	$52,596	$51,141	$64,852	$67,652	$66,971

PERCENT DISTRIBUTION

Men aged 25 to 34 who work full-time	**100.0%**	**100.0%**	**100.0%**	**100.0%**	**100.0%**	**100.0%**	**100.0%**	**100.0%**	**100.0%**	**100.0%**	**100.0%**
Under $15,000	4.7	15.6	12.0	5.9	5.6	3.2	1.6	1.9	1.0	0.0	0.0
$15,000 to $24,999	14.9	45.0	36.5	20.8	15.4	11.0	5.1	5.7	3.5	3.8	1.9
$25,000 to $34,999	19.4	20.1	25.8	25.3	21.3	21.1	12.1	13.8	7.6	2.7	9.0
$35,000 to $49,999	24.8	14.8	14.7	25.9	29.9	28.6	22.7	24.6	17.4	20.9	7.1
$50,000 to $74,999	22.5	3.2	8.0	16.3	19.8	25.7	31.7	31.5	32.5	27.5	34.2
$75,000 to $99,999	7.3	0.8	1.6	3.6	3.9	6.5	13.5	12.1	20.8	13.2	12.3
$100,000 or more	6.5	0.5	1.2	2.1	4.2	3.9	13.2	10.4	17.1	31.9	35.5

Note: Earnings include wages and salary only.
Source: Bureau of the Census, 2011 Current Population Survey Annual Social and Economic Supplement, Internet site http://www.census.gov/hhes/www/cpstables/032011/perinc/toc.htm; calculations by New Strategist

Table 2.31 Men Who Work Full-Time by Earnings and Education, 2010: Men Aged 35 to 44

(number and percent distribution of men aged 35 to 44 who work full-time, year-round, by earnings and educational attainment, 2010; median earnings of men with earnings; men in thousands as of 2011)

	total men	less than 9th grade	9th to 12th grade	high school graduate	some college	associate's degree	bachelor's degree or more				
							total	bachelor's degree	master's degree	professional degree	doctoral degree
Men aged 35 to 44 who work full-time	**13,773**	**451**	**693**	**3,804**	**2,162**	**1,357**	**5,305**	**3,432**	**1,296**	**250**	**328**
Under $5,000	75	5	7	25	14	5	19	15	2	2	0
$5,000 to $9,999	102	12	29	37	9	3	10	9	1	0	0
$10,000 to $14,999	301	68	42	79	39	21	50	34	10	0	7
$15,000 to $19,999	470	78	82	208	44	27	30	24	5	0	1
$20,000 to $24,999	830	65	98	400	134	60	74	54	17	1	1
$25,000 to $29,999	870	54	99	376	124	92	126	104	19	0	3
$30,000 to $34,999	1,019	40	68	436	195	77	202	165	32	1	5
$35,000 to $39,999	979	52	63	369	186	128	182	138	33	4	9
$40,000 to $44,999	1,061	19	49	372	239	146	236	182	45	4	4
$45,000 to $49,999	826	10	41	295	164	96	220	157	58	2	2
$50,000 to $54,999	1,009	9	36	274	200	115	375	272	78	8	16
$55,000 to $59,999	565	7	15	139	130	82	193	128	51	2	12
$60,000 to $64,999	771	13	23	200	107	85	342	263	61	8	11
$65,000 to $69,999	496	6	10	111	97	56	217	161	44	3	10
$70,000 to $74,999	537	1	10	100	106	65	256	184	46	9	16
$75,000 to $79,999	455	4	1	85	59	67	239	146	63	4	27
$80,000 to $84,999	442	2	8	67	83	47	237	153	74	3	8
$85,000 to $89,999	259	0	0	23	35	25	175	100	56	12	7
$90,000 to $94,999	329	0	3	33	59	36	199	128	52	10	9
$95,000 to $99,999	158	0	0	14	11	7	125	72	34	6	14
$100,000 or more	2,220	8	9	161	130	115	1,798	942	517	171	168
Median earnings	$51,052	$24,746	$29,112	$39,284	$47,588	$50,633	$76,523	$70,142	$85,561	$131,313	$100,449

PERCENT DISTRIBUTION

Men aged 35 to 44 who work full-time	**100.0%**	**100.0%**	**100.0%**	**100.0%**	**100.0%**	**100.0%**	**100.0%**	**100.0%**	**100.0%**	**100.0%**	**100.0%**
Under $15,000	3.5	18.8	11.3	3.7	2.9	2.1	1.5	1.7	1.0	0.8	2.1
$15,000 to $24,999	9.4	31.7	26.0	16.0	8.2	6.4	2.0	2.3	1.7	0.4	0.6
$25,000 to $34,999	13.7	20.8	24.1	21.3	14.8	12.5	6.2	7.8	3.9	0.4	2.4
$35,000 to $49,999	20.8	18.0	22.1	27.2	27.2	27.3	12.0	13.9	10.5	4.0	4.6
$50,000 to $74,999	24.5	8.0	13.6	21.7	29.6	29.7	26.1	29.4	21.6	12.0	19.8
$75,000 to $99,999	11.9	1.3	1.7	5.8	11.4	13.4	18.4	17.5	21.5	14.0	19.8
$100,000 or more	16.1	1.8	1.3	4.2	6.0	8.5	33.9	27.4	39.9	68.4	51.2

Note: Earnings include wages and salary only.
Source: Bureau of the Census, 2011 Current Population Survey Annual Social and Economic Supplement, Internet site http://www.census.gov/hhes/www/cpstables/032011/perinc/toc.htm; calculations by New Strategist

Table 2.32 Men Who Work Full-Time by Earnings and Education, 2010: Men Aged 45 to 54

(number and percent distribution of men aged 45 to 54 who work full-time, year-round, by earnings and educational attainment, 2010; median earnings of men with earnings; men in thousands as of 2011)

	total men	less than 9th grade	9th to 12th grade	high school graduate	some college	associate's degree	bachelor's degree or more total	bachelor's degree	master's degree	professional degree	doctoral degree
Men aged 45 to 54 who work full-time	**14,471**	**411**	**685**	**4,507**	**2,207**	**1,470**	**5,191**	**3,264**	**1,271**	**363**	**293**
Under $5,000	91	5	4	26	20	12	23	18	6	0	0
$5,000 to $9,999	95	10	29	31	12	5	8	3	2	0	3
$10,000 to $14,999	294	32	59	118	30	16	40	25	6	7	1
$15,000 to $19,999	463	62	88	176	68	20	50	37	9	4	0
$20,000 to $24,999	770	85	67	374	103	48	91	80	10	0	1
$25,000 to $29,999	814	52	63	406	120	75	98	70	22	1	5
$30,000 to $34,999	993	44	97	459	161	94	138	106	24	4	4
$35,000 to $39,999	847	31	53	385	142	95	142	109	26	4	3
$40,000 to $44,999	998	24	47	393	196	124	214	152	47	10	4
$45,000 to $49,999	791	21	26	347	133	73	190	142	41	6	2
$50,000 to $54,999	1,141	12	47	419	203	170	290	224	43	9	14
$55,000 to $59,999	684	7	16	225	122	69	244	184	41	3	16
$60,000 to $64,999	819	11	27	247	150	115	271	179	69	8	15
$65,000 to $69,999	462	1	3	134	69	81	176	125	38	6	6
$70,000 to $74,999	538	2	8	137	102	72	217	153	43	13	8
$75,000 to $79,999	548	2	13	121	96	85	230	135	73	10	13
$80,000 to $84,999	514	0	5	104	107	46	251	169	66	13	3
$85,000 to $89,999	296	0	2	35	72	49	136	88	33	11	4
$90,000 to $94,999	362	2	5	71	41	50	194	143	34	10	7
$95,000 to $99,999	159	1	3	25	18	13	100	63	23	5	8
$100,000 or more	2,792	7	22	272	242	159	2,089	1,056	617	238	179
Median earnings	$54,084	$25,820	$30,979	$42,254	$51,695	$55,162	$81,900	$75,464	$95,578	$125,971	$110,119

PERCENT DISTRIBUTION

	total men	less than 9th grade	9th to 12th grade	high school graduate	some college	associate's degree	bachelor's degree or more total	bachelor's degree	master's degree	professional degree	doctoral degree
Men aged 45 to 54 who work full-time	**100.0%**	**100.0%**	**100.0%**	**100.0%**	**100.0%**	**100.0%**	**100.0%**	**100.0%**	**100.0%**	**100.0%**	**100.0%**
Under $15,000	3.3	11.4	13.4	3.9	2.8	2.2	1.4	1.4	1.1	1.9	1.4
$15,000 to $24,999	8.5	35.8	22.6	12.2	7.7	4.6	2.7	3.6	1.5	1.1	0.3
$25,000 to $34,999	12.5	23.4	23.4	19.2	12.7	11.5	4.5	5.4	3.6	1.4	3.1
$35,000 to $49,999	18.2	18.5	18.4	25.0	21.3	19.9	10.5	12.3	9.0	5.5	3.1
$50,000 to $74,999	25.2	8.0	14.7	25.8	29.3	34.5	23.1	26.5	18.4	10.7	20.1
$75,000 to $99,999	13.0	1.2	4.1	7.9	15.1	16.5	17.5	18.3	18.0	13.5	11.9
$100,000 or more	19.3	1.7	3.2	6.0	11.0	10.8	40.2	32.4	48.5	65.6	61.1

Note: Earnings include wages and salary only.
Source: Bureau of the Census, 2011 Current Population Survey Annual Social and Economic Supplement, Internet site http://www.census.gov/hhes/www/cpstables/032011/perinc/toc.htm; calculations by New Strategist

Table 2.33 Men Who Work Full-Time by Earnings and Education, 2010: Men Aged 55 to 64

(number and percent distribution of men aged 55 to 64 who work full-time, year-round, by earnings and educational attainment, 2010; median earnings of men with earnings; men in thousands as of 2011)

	total men	less than 9th grade	9th to 12th grade	high school graduate	some college	associate's degree	bachelor's degree or more total	bachelor's degree	master's degree	professional degree	doctoral degree
Men aged 55 to 64 who work full-time	**9,555**	**250**	**402**	**2,514**	**1,633**	**821**	**3,935**	**2,221**	**1,091**	**305**	**317**
Under $5,000	80	0	6	16	20	9	29	23	7	0	0
$5,000 to $9,999	66	3	10	18	11	3	20	14	4	2	1
$10,000 to $14,999	181	29	22	63	30	11	24	20	4	0	0
$15,000 to $19,999	265	36	34	85	41	14	55	42	4	5	3
$20,000 to $24,999	430	42	52	171	80	22	65	41	23	0	0
$25,000 to $29,999	539	33	31	210	90	57	118	86	29	0	4
$30,000 to $34,999	710	35	54	263	125	78	154	107	38	5	4
$35,000 to $39,999	560	14	23	226	121	48	128	109	15	3	1
$40,000 to $44,999	678	12	45	253	132	90	144	90	40	3	12
$45,000 to $49,999	448	9	19	145	95	48	132	79	47	5	1
$50,000 to $54,999	793	6	25	279	149	69	265	164	79	9	12
$55,000 to $59,999	443	3	20	100	111	49	161	103	46	4	9
$60,000 to $64,999	508	11	10	137	119	57	174	96	58	6	13
$65,000 to $69,999	298	6	11	77	57	19	128	79	44	0	5
$70,000 to $74,999	355	2	7	96	58	36	155	73	57	12	13
$75,000 to $79,999	306	1	5	74	53	33	141	87	37	3	15
$80,000 to $84,999	343	4	9	64	66	30	170	115	35	10	10
$85,000 to $89,999	206	0	2	30	37	27	110	62	30	2	17
$90,000 to $94,999	243	0	0	50	38	25	130	60	45	16	10
$95,000 to $99,999	155	3	0	12	17	11	112	78	24	0	9
$100,000 or more	1,951	1	16	144	186	81	1,521	695	428	222	176
Median earnings	$55,221	$26,610	$32,288	$42,407	$51,404	$51,157	$81,316	$72,229	$81,276	$150,317	$101,845

PERCENT DISTRIBUTION

Men aged 55 to 64 who work full-time	100.0%	100.0%	100.0%	100.0%	100.0%	100.0%	100.0%	100.0%	100.0%	100.0%	100.0%
Under $15,000	3.4	12.8	9.5	3.9	3.7	2.8	1.9	2.6	1.4	0.7	0.3
$15,000 to $24,999	7.3	31.2	21.4	10.2	7.4	4.4	3.0	3.7	2.5	1.6	0.9
$25,000 to $34,999	13.1	27.2	21.1	18.8	13.2	16.4	6.9	8.7	6.1	1.6	2.5
$35,000 to $49,999	17.6	14.0	21.6	24.8	21.3	22.7	10.3	12.5	9.3	3.6	4.4
$50,000 to $74,999	25.1	11.2	18.2	27.4	30.3	28.0	22.4	23.2	26.0	10.2	16.4
$75,000 to $99,999	13.1	3.2	4.0	9.1	12.9	15.3	16.8	18.1	15.7	10.2	19.2
$100,000 or more	20.4	0.4	4.0	5.7	11.4	9.9	38.7	31.3	39.2	72.8	55.5

Note: Earnings include wages and salary only.
Source: Bureau of the Census, 2011 Current Population Survey Annual Social and Economic Supplement, Internet site http://www.census.gov/hhes/www/cpstables/032011/perinc/toc.htm; calculations by New Strategist

Table 2.34 Men Who Work Full-Time by Earnings and Education, 2010: Men Aged 65 or Older

(number and percent distribution of men aged 65 or older who work full-time, year-round, by earnings and educational attainment, 2010; median earnings of men with earnings; men in thousands as of 2011)

	total men	less than 9th grade	9th to 12th grade	high school graduate	some college	associate's degree	bachelor's degree or more				
							total	bachelor's degree	master's degree	professional degree	doctoral degree
Men aged 65 or older who work full-time	**2,141**	**110**	**107**	**589**	**285**	**111**	**938**	**402**	**246**	**137**	**153**
Under $5,000	59	12	1	13	7	4	22	18	2	0	2
$5,000 to $9,999	42	1	5	6	15	0	16	11	0	5	0
$10,000 to $14,999	84	11	6	40	0	4	22	18	2	0	2
$15,000 to $19,999	121	18	8	37	12	4	42	24	6	12	0
$20,000 to $24,999	161	17	15	54	19	9	46	27	19	0	0
$25,000 to $29,999	133	10	4	46	28	8	35	19	14	0	2
$30,000 to $34,999	120	8	18	42	20	4	27	16	7	2	2
$35,000 to $39,999	119	9	9	61	12	8	20	18	1	0	2
$40,000 to $44,999	131	12	9	36	19	7	47	20	16	3	8
$45,000 to $49,999	80	0	10	16	24	7	23	13	7	3	1
$50,000 to $54,999	131	0	6	37	35	9	45	22	12	5	5
$55,000 to $59,999	84	4	5	40	10	8	17	9	5	0	4
$60,000 to $64,999	98	2	4	36	12	7	37	12	20	1	4
$65,000 to $69,999	48	0	0	4	3	4	36	14	9	7	7
$70,000 to $74,999	68	0	4	29	7	1	26	12	14	0	0
$75,000 to $79,999	65	0	0	18	0	4	43	15	5	6	17
$80,000 to $84,999	83	5	0	15	12	5	45	22	10	9	5
$85,000 to $89,999	27	0	0	7	1	0	18	9	4	4	1
$90,000 to $94,999	51	0	0	1	5	0	45	18	11	9	6
$95,000 to $99,999	27	0	0	3	2	3	20	1	13	2	3
$100,000 or more	410	1	0	48	41	16	304	84	70	68	82
Median earnings	$50,454	$22,165	$31,786	$39,150	$46,217	$50,251	$75,442	$53,637	$70,920	$100,005	$115,026

PERCENT DISTRIBUTION

Men aged 65 or older who work full-time	**100.0%**	**100.0%**	**100.0%**	**100.0%**	**100.0%**	**100.0%**	**100.0%**	**100.0%**	**100.0%**	**100.0%**	**100.0%**
Under $15,000	8.6	21.8	11.2	10.0	7.7	7.2	6.4	11.7	1.6	3.6	2.6
$15,000 to $24,999	13.2	31.8	21.5	15.4	10.9	11.7	9.4	12.7	10.2	8.8	0.0
$25,000 to $34,999	11.8	16.4	20.6	14.9	16.8	10.8	6.6	8.7	8.5	1.5	2.6
$35,000 to $49,999	15.4	19.1	26.2	19.2	19.3	19.8	9.6	12.7	9.8	4.4	7.2
$50,000 to $74,999	20.0	5.5	17.8	24.8	23.5	26.1	17.2	17.2	24.4	9.5	13.1
$75,000 to $99,999	11.8	4.5	0.0	7.5	7.0	10.8	18.2	16.2	17.5	21.9	20.9
$100,000 or more	19.1	0.9	0.0	8.1	14.4	14.4	32.4	20.9	28.5	49.6	53.6

Note: Earnings include wages and salary only.
Source: Bureau of the Census, 2011 Current Population Survey Annual Social and Economic Supplement, Internet site http://www.census.gov/hhes/www/cpstables/032011/perinc/toc.htm; calculations by New Strategist

Education Boosts Earnings of Asian, Black, and Hispanic Men

Asians are the best-educated men, which accounts for their relatively high earnings.

Education lifts earnings in every racial and ethnic group. Among full-time workers, Asian men with at least a college degree earned a median of $72,468 in 2010, more than double the $30,897 median of Asian men with only a high school diploma. Fully 60 percent of Asian men with earnings who work full-time have a bachelor's degree.

Among men who work full-time, non-Hispanic white men are less likely than Asians to have a bachelor's degree (42 percent), but among those who do earnings exceed those of their Asian counterparts. Non-Hispanic white men with at least a bachelor's degree earned a median of $66,810 in 2010.

Twenty-five percent of black men with full-time jobs have a bachelor's degree. Their median earnings of $55,734 in 2010 were 76 percent greater than the $31,596 median earnings of black men with no more than a high school diploma. Hispanic men who work full-time are least likely to have a bachelor's degree, but the 16 percent who do have median earnings about equal to their black counterparts, at $58,652 in 2010. The lower earnings of college-educated blacks and Hispanics relative to Asians and non-Hispanic whites are due in part to different occupational choices. Discrimination also plays a role in the earnings gap.

■ The earnings of educated blacks and Hispanics should rise in the years ahead as they gain job experience—but only when the economy recovers from the Great Recession.

Among the college educated, non-Hispanic white men earn the most

(median earnings of men aged 25 or older with at least a bachelor's degree who work full-time, year-round, by race and Hispanic origin, 2010)

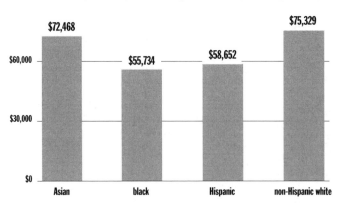

Table 2.35 Men Who Work Full-Time by Earnings and Education, 2010: Asian Men

(number and percent distribution of Asian men aged 25 or older who work full-time, year-round, by earnings and educational attainment, 2010; median earnings of men with earnings; men in thousands as of 2011)

	total men	less than 9th grade	9th to 12th grade	high school graduate	some college	associate's degree	bachelor's degree or more				
							total	bachelor's degree	master's degree	professional degree	doctoral degree
Asian men who work full-time	2,935	68	102	535	284	181	1,765	982	507	107	169
Under $5,000	24	0	1	10	0	1	12	10	2	0	0
$5,000 to $9,999	16	0	1	9	2	0	4	2	3	0	0
$10,000 to $14,999	86	5	12	34	7	6	21	16	4	0	2
$15,000 to $19,999	131	16	15	51	10	7	31	23	7	2	0
$20,000 to $24,999	192	10	21	70	25	15	51	35	16	0	0
$25,000 to $29,999	182	15	14	75	10	22	47	36	11	0	0
$30,000 to $34,999	213	5	16	58	30	11	95	75	12	2	4
$35,000 to $39,999	161	2	7	42	34	12	64	49	12	2	2
$40,000 to $44,999	174	0	4	45	33	11	80	50	21	6	4
$45,000 to $49,999	139	4	0	31	13	16	76	59	11	5	2
$50,000 to $54,999	172	2	2	24	35	11	97	52	24	11	10
$55,000 to $59,999	95	0	1	12	12	7	62	38	14	4	7
$60,000 to $64,999	164	0	0	24	13	11	115	79	24	1	12
$65,000 to $69,999	80	0	2	3	9	7	60	40	16	2	3
$70,000 to $74,999	119	3	3	11	17	8	77	40	27	4	6
$75,000 to $79,999	89	2	0	8	3	8	68	39	16	4	9
$80,000 to $84,999	86	2	2	5	3	2	71	42	20	2	8
$85,000 to $89,999	72	0	0	2	7	7	57	29	19	3	7
$90,000 to $94,999	71	0	0	5	5	4	56	30	18	1	6
$95,000 to $99,999	37	0	0	0	4	0	33	15	16	0	2
$100,000 or more	631	3	1	15	13	14	585	223	217	59	86
Median earnings	$52,488	–	$25,401	$30,897	$42,148	$45,978	$72,468	$61,666	$87,375	$102,187	$100,190

PERCENT DISTRIBUTION

Asian men who work full-time	100.0%	100.0%	100.0%	100.0%	100.0%	100.0%	100.0%	100.0%	100.0%	100.0%	100.0%
Under $15,000	4.3	7.4	13.7	9.9	3.2	3.9	2.1	2.9	1.8	0.0	1.2
$15,000 to $24,999	11.0	38.2	35.3	22.6	12.3	12.2	4.6	5.9	4.5	1.9	0.0
$25,000 to $34,999	13.5	29.4	29.4	24.9	14.1	18.2	8.0	11.3	4.5	1.9	2.4
$35,000 to $49,999	16.1	8.8	10.8	22.1	28.2	21.5	12.5	16.1	8.7	12.1	4.7
$50,000 to $74,999	21.5	7.4	7.8	13.8	30.3	24.3	23.3	25.4	20.7	20.6	22.5
$75,000 to $99,999	12.1	5.9	2.0	3.7	7.7	11.6	16.1	15.8	17.6	9.3	18.9
$100,000 or more	21.5	4.4	1.0	2.8	4.6	7.7	33.1	22.7	42.8	55.1	50.9

Note: Asians are those who identify themselves as being of the race alone and those who identify themselves as being of the race in combination with other races. Earnings include wages and salary only. "–" means sample is too small to make a reliable estimate.
Source: Bureau of the Census, 2011 Current Population Survey Annual Social and Economic Supplement, Internet site http:// www.census.gov/hhes/www/cpstables/032011/perinc/toc.htm; calculations by New Strategist

Table 2.36 Men Who Work Full-Time by Earnings and Education, 2010: Black Men

(number and percent distribution of black men aged 25 or older who work full-time, year-round, by earnings and educational attainment, 2010; median earnings of men with earnings; men in thousands as of 2011)

	total men	less than 9th grade	9th to 12th grade	high school graduate	some college	associate's degree	bachelor's degree or more				
							total	bachelor's degree	master's degree	professional degree	doctoral degree
Black men who work full-time	**4,953**	**88**	**308**	**1,765**	**1,008**	**535**	**1,249**	**842**	**282**	**56**	**68**
Under $5,000	27	4	8	8	9	0	0	0	0	0	0
$5,000 to $9,999	56	7	21	20	5	2	1	0	0	0	1
$10,000 to $14,999	171	10	40	55	20	28	18	18	0	0	0
$15,000 to $19,999	255	6	37	130	43	21	19	15	4	0	0
$20,000 to $24,999	530	5	43	294	99	44	46	40	6	0	0
$25,000 to $29,999	494	16	30	248	87	50	62	47	11	0	5
$30,000 to $34,999	571	10	40	245	126	64	85	69	13	2	2
$35,000 to $39,999	415	11	29	149	93	40	94	79	12	0	2
$40,000 to $44,999	419	6	21	142	94	67	89	74	10	2	2
$45,000 to $49,999	329	4	7	86	98	39	95	67	26	2	0
$50,000 to $54,999	302	0	5	97	66	35	98	81	13	2	3
$55,000 to $59,999	203	1	7	70	49	14	61	43	13	2	3
$60,000 to $64,999	202	0	11	50	35	24	82	55	20	2	5
$65,000 to $69,999	149	6	0	33	27	29	55	43	10	0	2
$70,000 to $74,999	164	0	5	30	50	25	55	38	15	0	0
$75,000 to $79,999	92	0	1	21	17	11	42	21	17	3	2
$80,000 to $84,999	116	0	2	18	25	10	60	38	21	0	1
$85,000 to $89,999	50	0	0	9	14	4	23	9	13	0	2
$90,000 to $94,999	69	0	0	17	5	12	35	23	6	5	2
$95,000 to $99,999	32	0	0	4	0	0	28	21	5	0	2
$100,000 or more	308	2	3	40	47	17	199	61	67	36	36
Median earnings	$39,067	$27,110	$25,684	$31,596	$40,669	$41,052	$55,734	$50,405	$70,455	–	–

PERCENT DISTRIBUTION

Black men who work full-time	**100.0%**	**100.0%**	**100.0%**	**100.0%**	**100.0%**	**100.0%**	**100.0%**	**100.0%**	**100.0%**	**100.0%**	**100.0%**
Under $15,000	5.1	23.9	22.4	4.7	3.4	5.6	1.5	2.1	0.0	0.0	1.5
$15,000 to $24,999	15.8	12.5	26.0	24.0	14.1	12.1	5.2	6.5	3.5	0.0	0.0
$25,000 to $34,999	21.5	29.5	22.7	27.9	21.1	21.3	11.8	13.8	8.5	3.6	10.3
$35,000 to $49,999	23.5	23.9	18.5	21.4	28.3	27.3	22.3	26.1	17.0	7.1	5.9
$50,000 to $74,999	20.6	8.0	9.1	15.9	22.5	23.7	28.1	30.9	25.2	10.7	19.1
$75,000 to $99,999	7.2	0.0	1.0	3.9	6.1	6.9	15.1	13.3	22.0	14.3	13.2
$100,000 or more	6.2	2.3	1.0	2.3	4.7	3.2	15.9	7.2	23.8	64.3	52.9

Note: Blacks are those who identify themselves as being of the race alone and those who identify themselves as being of the race in combination with other races. Earnings include wages and salary only. "–" means sample is too small to make a reliable estimate.
Source: Bureau of the Census, 2011 Current Population Survey Annual Social and Economic Supplement, Internet site http://www.census.gov/hhes/www/cpstables/032011/perinc/toc.htm; calculations by New Strategist

Table 2.37 Men Who Work Full-Time by Earnings and Education, 2010: Hispanic Men

(number and percent distribution of Hispanic men aged 25 or older who work full-time, year-round, by earnings and educational attainment, 2010; median earnings of men with earnings; men in thousands as of 2011)

	total men	less than 9th grade	9th to 12th grade	high school graduate	some college	associate's degree	bachelor's degree or more total	bachelor's degree	master's degree	professional degree	doctoral degree
Hispanic men who work full-time	7,508	1,219	1,050	2,447	1,077	519	1,195	860	213	63	60
Under $5,000	32	7	2	11	4	2	7	6	1	0	0
$5,000 to $9,999	133	32	35	37	17	8	4	2	2	0	0
$10,000 to $14,999	452	158	92	126	44	11	22	17	0	1	3
$15,000 to $19,999	785	249	171	227	75	24	39	31	5	3	0
$20,000 to $24,999	934	220	190	338	103	24	58	50	8	0	0
$25,000 to $29,999	834	147	139	334	100	46	68	57	8	1	3
$30,000 to $34,999	751	114	96	293	103	56	89	73	10	4	2
$35,000 to $39,999	576	105	78	211	78	41	63	40	14	7	1
$40,000 to $44,999	570	58	66	203	118	64	61	47	7	5	2
$45,000 to $49,999	381	40	52	133	75	26	56	47	6	0	2
$50,000 to $54,999	445	16	37	153	88	50	100	79	16	1	4
$55,000 to $59,999	213	14	21	83	40	16	38	29	8	0	1
$60,000 to $64,999	263	26	19	82	46	22	67	50	18	0	1
$65,000 to $69,999	131	11	5	33	27	16	38	28	9	1	0
$70,000 to $74,999	138	1	9	31	29	19	49	39	5	4	1
$75,000 to $79,999	129	3	7	39	20	20	41	27	7	2	5
$80,000 to $84,999	135	2	12	35	26	12	48	34	11	3	0
$85,000 to $89,999	69	0	2	10	6	17	34	28	5	0	1
$90,000 to $94,999	72	2	5	8	10	5	43	23	19	0	1
$95,000 to $99,999	34	1	3	3	5	5	15	11	0	1	3
$100,000 or more	432	13	10	56	62	35	256	145	53	27	30
Median earnings	$32,462	$23,108	$25,948	$31,626	$40,353	$42,286	$58,652	$52,261	$65,771	–	–

PERCENT DISTRIBUTION

Hispanic men who work full-time	100.0%	100.0%	100.0%	100.0%	100.0%	100.0%	100.0%	100.0%	100.0%	100.0%	100.0%
Under $15,000	8.2	16.2	12.3	7.1	6.0	4.0	2.8	2.9	1.4	1.6	5.0
$15,000 to $24,999	22.9	38.5	34.4	23.1	16.5	9.2	8.1	9.4	6.1	4.8	0.0
$25,000 to $34,999	21.1	21.4	22.4	25.6	18.8	19.7	13.1	15.1	8.5	7.9	8.3
$35,000 to $49,999	20.3	16.7	18.7	22.4	25.2	25.2	15.1	15.6	12.7	19.0	8.3
$50,000 to $74,999	15.8	5.6	8.7	15.6	21.4	23.7	24.4	26.2	26.3	9.5	11.7
$75,000 to $99,999	5.8	0.7	2.8	3.9	6.2	11.4	15.1	14.3	19.7	9.5	16.7
$100,000 or more	5.8	1.1	1.0	2.3	5.8	6.7	21.4	16.9	24.9	42.9	50.0

Note: Earnings include wages and salary only. "–" means sample is too small to make a reliable estimate.
Source: Bureau of the Census, 2011 Current Population Survey Annual Social and Economic Supplement, Internet site http://www.census.gov/hhes/www/cpstables/032011/perinc/toc.htm; calculations by New Strategist

Table 2.38 Men Who Work Full-Time by Earnings and Education, 2010: Non-Hispanic White Men

(number and percent distribution of non-Hispanic white men aged 25 or older who work full-time, year-round, by earnings and educational attainment, 2010; median earnings of men with earnings; men in thousands as of 2011)

	total men	less than 9th grade	9th to 12th grade	high school graduate	some college	associate's degree	bachelor's degree or more				
							total	bachelor's degree	master's degree	professional degree	doctoral degree
Non-Hispanic white men who work full-time	**37,216**	**252**	**1,135**	**10,238**	**6,135**	**3,756**	**15,700**	**10,107**	**3,648**	**1,007**	**937**
Under $5,000	262	12	10	74	59	22	84	68	13	2	2
$5,000 to $9,999	236	0	36	83	48	9	60	42	8	8	3
$10,000 to $14,999	581	17	56	226	121	39	122	91	20	6	5
$15,000 to $19,999	907	23	104	379	163	67	170	126	20	18	7
$20,000 to $24,999	1,696	46	128	763	326	148	285	219	58	6	1
$25,000 to $29,999	1,971	21	123	818	374	228	406	328	67	0	11
$30,000 to $34,999	2,655	29	153	1,072	519	275	607	474	107	8	17
$35,000 to $39,999	2,488	20	81	976	500	307	605	499	84	13	9
$40,000 to $44,999	2,865	21	93	1,047	572	358	773	577	148	24	25
$45,000 to $49,999	2,147	8	61	766	413	246	653	469	159	18	8
$50,000 to $54,999	3,114	12	101	974	534	381	1,112	825	193	44	51
$55,000 to $59,999	1,761	10	33	458	341	217	700	484	165	9	42
$60,000 to $64,999	2,148	12	45	555	381	269	885	626	208	20	30
$65,000 to $69,999	1,348	4	18	308	216	163	639	440	143	22	34
$70,000 to $74,999	1,459	0	15	351	261	161	671	443	163	34	31
$75,000 to $79,999	1,361	5	14	279	202	179	682	423	179	17	64
$80,000 to $84,999	1,298	7	10	222	234	122	703	470	179	34	20
$85,000 to $89,999	748	0	4	95	125	87	438	280	99	34	26
$90,000 to $94,999	885	0	9	144	124	101	507	324	121	39	24
$95,000 to $99,999	474	3	0	53	46	31	340	195	99	20	27
$100,000 or more	6,812	2	42	594	573	346	5,256	2,704	1,417	634	500
Median earnings	$53,380	$30,740	$32,130	$42,194	$49,581	$51,430	$75,329	$66,810	$81,386	$120,176	$101,606

PERCENT DISTRIBUTION

Non-Hispanic white men who work full-time	**100.0%**	**100.0%**	**100.0%**	**100.0%**	**100.0%**	**100.0%**	**100.0%**	**100.0%**	**100.0%**	**100.0%**	**100.0%**
Under $15,000	2.9	11.5	9.0	3.7	3.7	1.9	1.7	2.0	1.1	1.6	1.1
$15,000 to $24,999	7.0	27.4	20.4	11.2	8.0	5.7	2.9	3.4	2.1	2.4	0.9
$25,000 to $34,999	12.4	19.8	24.3	18.5	14.6	13.4	6.5	7.9	4.8	0.8	3.0
$35,000 to $49,999	20.2	19.4	20.7	27.2	24.2	24.3	12.9	15.3	10.7	5.5	4.5
$50,000 to $74,999	26.4	15.1	18.7	25.8	28.2	31.7	25.5	27.9	23.9	12.8	20.1
$75,000 to $99,999	12.8	6.0	3.3	7.7	11.9	13.8	17.0	16.7	18.6	14.3	17.2
$100,000 or more	18.3	0.8	3.7	5.8	9.3	9.2	33.5	26.8	38.8	63.0	53.4

Note: Non-Hispanic whites are those who identify themselves as being of the race alone and not Hispanic. Earnings include wages and salary only.
Source: Bureau of the Census, 2011 Current Population Survey Annual Social and Economic Supplement, Internet site http://www.census.gov/hhes/www/cpstables/032011/perinc/toc.htm; calculations by New Strategist

Men's Earnings Vary Widely by Occupation

Men in several occupations have median earnings exceeding $100,000.

The median earnings of all men aged 15 or older who work full-time stood at $47,715 in 2010. By occupation, men's earnings vary widely. The highest-paid men are, not surprisingly, chief executives, lawyers, and doctors, with median earnings of more than $100,000 in 2010. Doctors had the highest median earnings of all ($158,575). Other highly paid men are aircraft pilots ($96,531), mathematicians ($85,746), and engineers ($83,110).

The occupation with the lowest earnings for men is food preparation ($22,402). Other low-paying occupations include farming, fishing, and forestry ($23,055); and cashier ($24,173).

■ Many men in low-paying occupations are young adults working their way up the career ladder. As they gain experience, they should get jobs with higher pay.

Career choice affects earnings

(median earnings of men aged 15 or older who work full-time, year-round, by selected occupation, 2010)

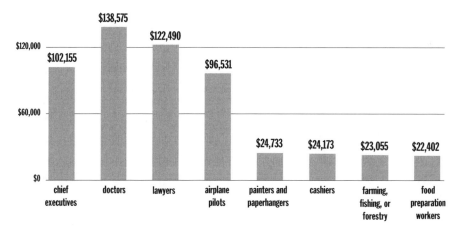

Table 2.39 Median Earnings of Men by Occupation, 2010

(number and median earnings of men aged 15 or older who work full-time, year-round, by occupation of longest job held, 2010; men in thousands as of 2011)

	number with earnings	median earnings
TOTAL MEN WORKING FULL-TIME, YEAR-ROUND	**56,412**	**$47,715**
Management, science, and arts occupations	**21,389**	**70,346**
Management, business, and financial operations occupations	10,708	72,013
Management occupations	8,244	75,375
Chief executives, general and operations managers	1,671	102,155
All other managers	6,570	67,290
Business and financial operations occupations	2,464	67,033
Business operations specialists	1,163	62,328
Financial specialists	1,301	70,662
Professional and related occupations	10,681	67,339
Computer and mathematical occupations	2,287	75,516
Computer scientists, analysts, programmers, engineers, and administrators	2,206	75,327
Mathematicians, statisticians, operations research and other math occupations	76	85,746
Architecture and engineering occupations	2,165	77,071
Architects, except naval	123	75,874
Engineers	1,581	83,110
Drafters, engineering technicians, and surveying and mapping technicians	450	60,662
Life, physical, and social science occupations	578	65,202
All other scientists	422	66,384
Science technicians	101	51,277
Community and social services occupations	707	42,993
Legal occupations	706	115,828
Lawyers, judges, and magistrates	633	122,490
Education, training, and library occupations	1,626	52,705
Postsecondary teachers	498	72,222
All other teachers	1,030	50,578
Archivists, curators, museum technicians, librarians, and other technicians and assistants	97	45,516
Arts, design, entertainment, sports, and media occupations	1,044	50,284
Health care practitioner and technical occupations	1,569	76,573
Doctors	606	158,575
Nurses	287	66,177
All other health and technical occupations	675	53,362
Service occupations	**6,695**	**31,433**
Health care support occupations	245	33,747
Protective service occupations	2,085	51,251
Supervisors	234	61,297
Fire fighters and police	947	65,030
All other protective service occupations	904	35,671
Food preparation and serving related occupations	1,762	23,368
Supervisors	155	36,053
Chefs and cooks	909	22,483
All other food preparation occupations	698	22,402
Building and grounds cleaning and maintenance occupations	2,020	28,682
Supervisors	346	41,889
All other maintenance occupations	1,674	26,236
Personal care and service occupations	583	31,253
All other personal care and service occupations	519	30,717

	number with earnings	median earnings
Sales and office occupations	**9,442**	**$42,165**
Sales and related occupations	5,891	47,183
Supervisors	2,410	46,419
Cashiers	331	24,173
Insurance sales agents	231	71,285
Real estate brokers and sales agents	285	52,089
All other sales and related occupations	2,635	48,887
Office and administrative support occupations	3,551	37,298
Supervisors	425	47,400
Postal workers	307	54,813
All other office and administrative support occupations	2,819	34,863
Natural resources, construction, and maintenance occupations	**8,709**	**40,884**
Farming, fishing, and forestry occupations	452	24,074
Farming, fishing, and forestry occupations, except supervisors	417	23,055
Construction and extraction occupations	4,456	40,109
Construction	4,270	39,285
Supervisors	497	58,476
Carpenters	779	32,095
Electricians	479	51,013
Painters and paperhangers	256	24,733
Sheet metal workers	114	45,815
All other construction trades	2,025	36,289
Extraction workers	185	53,611
Installation, maintenance, and repair occupations	3,801	42,533
Supervisors	280	47,238
Aircraft mechanics and service	110	55,548
Auto, bus, truck, heavy equipment, mechanics	1,114	40,912
Heating, air conditioning, and refrigeration mechanics and installers	271	45,100
Electrical power-line and telecommunications-line installers and repairers	239	54,839
All other occupations	1,786	41,893
Production, transportation, and material-moving occupations	**9,527**	**36,620**
Production occupations	4,713	37,184
Supervisors	545	50,838
All other occupations	4,167	36,015
Transportation and material-moving occupations	4,814	35,808
Supervisors	136	41,183
Aircraft pilots and flight engineers	80	96,531
Auto, bus, truck, ambulance, taxi drivers	2,516	40,578
Rail and subway workers	88	60,010
All other transportation occupations	1,936	29,319
Armed forces	**649**	**46,953**

Note: Number of workers does not add to total because only occupations with data on median earnings are shown. Earnings include wages and salary only.
Source: Bureau of the Census, 2011 Current Population Survey Annual Social and Economic Supplement, Internet site http:// www.census.gov/hhes/www/cpstables/032011/perinc/toc.htm; calculations by New Strategist

Fewer Men Are Receiving Wage or Salary Income

Nearly one in five receives Social Security income.

Seventy-one percent of men received income from wages or salaries in 2010, down from the 75 percent of 2007 and 3 million fewer than in that pre-recession year. As usual, interest income ranks second as a source of income, with 41 percent of men receiving it. Eleven percent of men receive retirement income, and 19 percent Social Security. The median amount of Social Security income received stood at $14,781. For those who receive retirement income, the median amount was $16,511. Interest income amounted to a median of just $1,454.

Asian and Hispanic men are more likely to receive wage and salary income, but less likely to receive Social Security or interest income than non-Hispanic white men and black men. Eighty percent of Hispanics and 77 percent of Asians receive wage or salary income versus 70 percent of non-Hispanic whites and 69 percent of blacks. But 21 percent of non-Hispanic white men receive Social Security income compared with 18 percent of blacks, 10 percent of Asians, and 9 percent of Hispanics. Interest income accrues to 48 percent of non-Hispanic whites versus 41 percent of Asians, 21 percent of blacks, and 18 percent of Hispanics.

■ Non-Hispanic white men are more likely to receive Social Security and interest income because they are older, on average, than Asian, black, or Hispanic men.

Wage and salary income is most common

(percent of men aged 15 or older who receive income, by source, 2010)

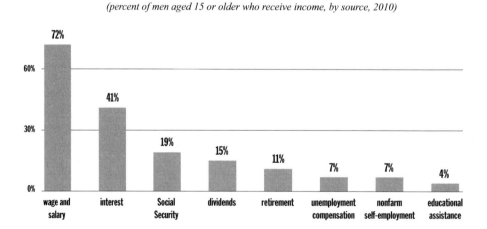

Table 2.40 Median Income of Men by Source of Income, 2010: Total Men

(number and percent of men aged 15 or older with income, and median income of those with income, 2010; men in thousands as of 2011)

	number	percent receiving	median income
Men with income	**105,351**	**100.0%**	**$32,137**
Earnings	81,180	77.1	36,676
Wages and salary	75,435	71.6	37,102
Nonfarm self-employment	7,236	6.9	18,979
Farm self-employment	1,359	1.3	4,150
Social Security	19,745	18.7	14,781
SSI (Supplemental Security)	2,360	2.2	7,835
Public Assistance	453	0.4	1,919
Veteran's benefits	2,381	2.3	7,754
Survivor's benefits	661	0.6	7,484
Disability benefits	817	0.8	11,974
Unemployment compensation	7,501	7.1	5,983
Worker's compensation	841	0.8	4,539
Property income	45,927	43.6	1,644
Interest	42,757	40.6	1,454
Dividends	15,974	15.2	1,695
Rents, royalties, estates, trusts	5,580	5.3	2,274
Retirement income	11,088	10.5	16,511
Company or union retirement	6,200	5.9	11,742
Federal government retirement	1,102	1.0	27,657
Military retirement	980	0.9	18,908
State or local government retirement	2,050	1.9	23,221
Railroad retirement	167	0.2	29,401
Annuities	206	0.2	7,494
IRA or Keogh, or 401(k)	412	0.4	13,569
Pension income	9,780	9.3	16,978
Company or union retirement	5,826	5.5	11,797
Federal government retirement	997	0.9	29,658
Military retirement	892	0.8	19,706
State or local government retirement	1,857	1.8	24,590
Railroad retirement	143	0.1	31,069
Annuities	96	0.1	13,679
Alimony	12	0.0	–
Child support	336	0.3	2,684
Educational assistance	3,973	3.8	4,584
Financial assistance from outside the household	941	0.9	4,484
Other income	513	0.5	1,562

Note: "–" means sample is too small to make a reliable estimate.
Source: Bureau of the Census, 2011 Current Population Survey Annual Social and Economic Supplement, Internet site http://www.census.gov/hhes/www/cpstables/032011/perinc/toc.htm; calculations by New Strategist

Table 2.41 Median Income of Men by Source of Income, 2010: Asian Men

(number and percent of Asian men aged 15 or older with income, and median income of those with income, 2010; men in thousands as of 2011)

	number	percent receiving	median income
Asian men with income	**4,922**	**100.0%**	**$35,622**
Earnings	4,068	82.6	41,024
Wages and salary	3,794	77.1	41,656
Nonfarm self-employment	354	7.2	21,447
Farm self-employment	32	0.7	–
Social Security	502	10.2	12,809
SSI (Supplemental Security)	83	1.7	7,210
Public Assistance	17	0.3	–
Veteran's benefits	65	1.3	–
Survivor's benefits	10	0.2	–
Disability benefits	23	0.5	–
Unemployment compensation	253	5.1	6,777
Worker's compensation	38	0.8	–
Property income	2,166	44.0	1,557
Interest	2,027	41.2	1,406
Dividends	711	14.4	1,604
Rents, royalties, estates, trusts	235	4.8	2,305
Retirement income	267	5.4	19,926
Company or union retirement	136	2.8	12,875
Federal government retirement	38	0.8	–
Military retirement	25	0.5	–
State or local government retirement	55	1.1	–
Railroad retirement	0	0.0	–
Annuities	5	0.1	–
IRA or Keogh, or 401(k)	9	0.2	–
Pension income	238	4.8	21,046
Company or union retirement	131	2.7	13,116
Federal government retirement	35	0.7	–
Military retirement	25	0.5	–
State or local government retirement	46	0.9	–
Railroad retirement	0	0.0	–
Annuities	3	0.1	–
Alimony	0	0.0	–
Child support	7	0.1	–
Educational assistance	257	5.2	5,862
Financial assistance from outside the household	95	1.9	7,132
Other income	18	0.4	–

Note: Asians are those who identify themselves as being of the race alone and those who identify themselves as being of the race in combination with other races. "–" means sample is too small to make a reliable estimate.
Source: Bureau of the Census, 2011 Current Population Survey Annual Social and Economic Supplement, Internet site http:// www.census.gov/hhes/www/cpstables/032011/perinc/toc.htm; calculations by New Strategist

Table 2.42 Median Income of Men by Source of Income, 2010: Black Men

(number and percent of black men aged 15 or older with income, and median income of those with income, 2010; men in thousands as of 2011)

	number	percent receiving	median income
Black men with income	**11,258**	**100.0%**	**$23,061**
Earnings	8,152	72.4	28,137
Wages and salary	7,786	69.2	28,718
Nonfarm self-employment	518	4.6	13,131
Farm self-employment	77	0.7	1,607
Social Security	1,994	17.7	12,034
SSI (Supplemental Security)	576	5.1	8,049
Public Assistance	108	1.0	1,930
Veteran's benefits	316	2.8	9,417
Survivor's benefits	48	0.4	–
Disability benefits	111	1.0	11,148
Unemployment compensation	956	8.5	5,502
Worker's compensation	86	0.8	2,508
Property income	2,556	22.7	1,485
Interest	2,340	20.8	1,377
Dividends	560	5.0	1,546
Rents, royalties, estates, trusts	273	2.4	2,089
Retirement income	896	8.0	16,295
Company or union retirement	455	4.0	13,059
Federal government retirement	96	0.9	33,216
Military retirement	143	1.3	18,289
State or local government retirement	151	1.3	18,657
Railroad retirement	10	0.1	–
Annuities	13	0.1	–
IRA or Keogh, or 401(k)	13	0.1	–
Pension income	780	6.9	17,883
Company or union retirement	427	3.8	13,633
Federal government retirement	80	0.7	35,018
Military retirement	125	1.1	19,170
State or local government retirement	134	1.2	19,530
Railroad retirement	10	0.1	–
Annuities	8	0.1	–
Alimony	1	0.0	–
Child support	47	0.4	–
Educational assistance	686	6.1	4,724
Financial assistance from outside the household	109	1.0	2,096
Other income	30	0.3	–

Note: Blacks are those who identify themselves as being of the race alone and those who identify themselves as being of the race in combination with other races. "–" means sample is too small to make a reliable estimate.
Source: Bureau of the Census, 2011 Current Population Survey Annual Social and Economic Supplement, Internet site http:// www.census.gov/hhes/www/cpstables/032011/perinc/toc.htm; calculations by New Strategist

Table 2.43 Median Income of Men by Source of Income, 2010: Hispanic Men

(number and percent of Hispanic men aged 15 or older with income, and median income of those with income, 2010; men in thousands as of 2011)

	number	percent receiving	median income
Hispanic men with income	**14,965**	**100.0%**	**$22,233**
Earnings	12,743	85.2	24,615
Wages and salary	11,996	80.2	25,088
Nonfarm self-employment	893	6.0	15,683
Farm self-employment	72	0.5	–
Social Security	1,368	9.1	11,439
SSI (Supplemental Security)	366	2.4	7,872
Public Assistance	97	0.6	2,094
Veteran's benefits	130	0.9	9,308
Survivor's benefits	31	0.2	–
Disability benefits	106	0.7	10,107
Unemployment compensation	1,010	6.7	5,544
Worker's compensation	114	0.8	5,135
Property income	2,920	19.5	1,476
Interest	2,689	18.0	1,368
Dividends	526	3.5	1,547
Rents, royalties, estates, trusts	363	2.4	2,126
Retirement income	530	3.5	12,035
Company or union retirement	277	1.9	10,572
Federal government retirement	54	0.4	–
Military retirement	29	0.2	–
State or local government retirement	109	0.7	14,196
Railroad retirement	9	0.1	–
Annuities	7	0.0	–
IRA or Keogh, or 401(k)	14	0.1	–
Pension income	413	2.8	12,866
Company or union retirement	247	1.7	10,454
Federal government retirement	46	0.3	–
Military retirement	26	0.2	–
State or local government retirement	72	0.5	–
Railroad retirement	7	0.0	–
Annuities	3	0.0	–
Alimony	0	0.0	–
Child support	40	0.3	–
Educational assistance	509	3.4	3,930
Financial assistance from outside the household	105	0.7	2,292
Other income	27	0.2	–

Note: "–" means sample is too small to make a reliable estimate.
Source: Bureau of the Census, 2011 Current Population Survey Annual Social and Economic Supplement, Internet site http://www.census.gov/hhes/www/cpstables/032011/perinc/toc.htm; calculations by New Strategist

Table 2.44 Median Income of Men by Source of Income, 2010: Non-Hispanic White Men

(number and percent of non-Hispanic white men aged 15 or older with income, and median income of those with income, 2010; men in thousands as of 2011)

	number	percent receiving	median income
Non-Hispanic white men with income	**73,491**	**100.0**	**$37,037**
Earnings	55,780	75.9	41,594
Wages and salary	51,451	70.0	42,019
Nonfarm self-employment	5,442	7.4	20,309
Farm self-employment	1,168	1.6	5,307
Social Security	15,693	21.4	15,379
SSI (Supplemental Security)	1,293	1.8	7,711
Public Assistance	225	0.3	1,894
Veteran's benefits	1,814	2.5	7,125
Survivor's benefits	561	0.8	8,045
Disability benefits	559	0.8	13,457
Unemployment compensation	5,199	7.1	6,089
Worker's compensation	592	0.8	4,374
Property income	37,928	51.6	1,677
Interest	35,395	48.2	1,469
Dividends	14,051	19.1	1,713
Rents, royalties, estates, trusts	4,647	6.3	2,306
Retirement income	9,275	12.6	16,750
Company or union retirement	5,273	7.2	11,742
Federal government retirement	902	1.2	26,789
Military retirement	771	1.0	19,186
State or local government retirement	1,711	2.3	24,601
Railroad retirement	143	0.2	29,839
Annuities	181	0.2	7,215
IRA or Keogh, or 401(k)	371	0.5	14,208
Pension income	8,249	11.2	16,976
Company or union retirement	4,967	6.8	11,789
Federal government retirement	825	1.1	28,485
Military retirement	705	1.0	19,980
State or local government retirement	1,584	2.2	25,463
Railroad retirement	122	0.2	31,426
Annuities	82	0.1	13,452
Alimony	10	0.0	–
Child support	239	0.3	2,519
Educational assistance	2,488	3.4	4,597
Financial assistance from outside the household	631	0.9	4,819
Other income	418	0.6	1,553

Note: Non-Hispanic whites are those who identify themselves as white alone and not Hispanic. "–" means sample is too small to make a reliable estimate.
Source: Bureau of the Census, 2011 Current Population Survey Annual Social and Economic Supplement, Internet site http://www.census.gov/hhes/www/cpstables/032011/perinc/toc.htm; calculations by New Strategist

3

Women's Income

Women's incomes have grown substantially since 1990. The median income of all women rose 28 percent between 1990 and 2010, from $16,285 to $20,831 after adjusting for inflation. Women of all ages made income gains, the largest increases occurring among women aged 55 to 64. Between 2000 and 2010, however, most women under age 55 saw their incomes decline.

Women's rising labor force participation is behind their income growth over the past few decades. An ever-larger percentage of women work full-time, and the educational attainment and career aspirations of those who work full-time have been increasing. This can be seen in the 19 percent increase in the median income of women aged 55 to 64 between 2000 and 2010, despite the recession. Behind the increase was the entry of the career-oriented baby-boom generation into the age group, along with the postponement of retirement by older Americans.

Women's incomes still lag men's for many reasons. The average female worker is younger and less educated than the average male worker, which lowers her earnings. Women make different career choices from men and more often choose less-demanding jobs with greater flexibility—jobs that typically pay less. Finally, many women choose to drop out of the labor force for a few years while their children are young, which diminishes their earning power.

■ Among young adults, women are more educated than men. As they age, the gap between the incomes of men and women should continue to narrow.

Women's Income Trends

Older Women Made Gains between 2000 and 2010

Most younger women lost ground.

The median income of women has grown substantially in every age group during the past 20 years. Between 1990 and 2010, women's income gains ranged from a low of 11 percent for those under age 25 to a 68 percent increase among women aged 55 to 64. Women's growing labor force participation is behind the increase.

Between 2000 and 2010, the rise in women's incomes reversed in most age groups. Among all women, median income rose 2 percent during those years—to $20,831. But median income declined in most age groups under age 55. The biggest loss occurred among women aged 45 to 54, whose median income fell by 8 percent between 2000 and 2010. In contrast, women aged 55 to 64 saw their median income climb by 19 percent, from $21,423 in 2000 to $25,502 in 2010. Behind this growth was the career-oriented baby-boom generation filling the age group, as well as the postponement of retirement by many older Americans as the recession took hold.

■ The incomes of women aged 55 to 64 may continue to climb as the recession forces more boomers to postpone retirement.

Women's median income declined in most age groups between 2000 and 2010

(percent change in median income of women by age, 2000 to 2010; in 2010 dollars)

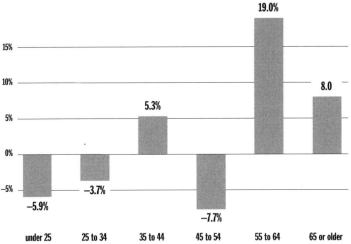

Table 3.1 Median Income of Women by Age, 1990 to 2010

(median income of women aged 15 or older with income by age, 1990 to 2010; percent change in income for selected years; in 2010 dollars)

	total women	15 to 24	25 to 34	35 to 44	45 to 54	55 to 64	aged 65 or older total	65 to 74	75 or older
2010	$20,831	$8,765	$25,655	$29,447	$27,748	$25,502	$15,072	$16,090	$14,386
2009	21,303	9,098	25,653	28,354	29,089	25,527	15,534	16,374	14,956
2008	21,131	9,014	25,876	27,717	28,593	25,838	14,743	15,019	14,560
2007	22,001	9,421	27,219	29,130	30,972	26,565	14,744	15,187	14,403
2006	21,643	9,357	26,147	28,514	30,110	26,155	14,710	15,225	14,385
2005	20,747	9,180	25,481	28,407	29,570	24,707	13,955	14,340	13,727
2004	20,393	8,891	25,472	28,167	30,279	24,012	13,945	14,183	13,785
2003	20,460	8,814	26,071	27,826	30,664	24,146	14,042	14,395	13,792
2002	20,375	9,189	26,238	27,053	30,499	23,227	13,824	13,670	13,941
2001	20,461	9,196	26,445	27,674	29,723	21,950	13,932	13,794	14,035
2000	20,338	9,319	26,650	27,952	30,047	21,423	13,956	13,811	14,067
1999	20,026	8,738	25,265	27,034	29,531	20,861	14,339	14,365	14,319
1998	19,276	8,728	24,388	27,097	28,838	19,603	14,032	13,963	14,086
1997	18,560	8,590	23,903	25,337	27,813	19,472	13,629	13,736	13,539
1996	17,733	8,138	22,671	25,526	26,355	18,426	13,320	13,362	13,281
1995	17,232	7,543	22,100	24,714	25,177	17,588	13,290	13,179	13,392
1994	16,681	8,013	21,653	23,552	24,806	15,809	13,020	12,840	13,183
1993	16,413	7,951	20,784	23,542	24,255	16,090	12,628	12,848	12,429
1992	16,313	7,872	20,754	23,474	24,136	15,428	12,459	12,508	12,411
1991	16,355	8,114	20,239	23,613	22,987	15,459	12,785	12,700	12,866
1990	16,285	7,927	20,359	23,455	23,012	15,201	13,009	13,245	12,761
Percent change									
2000 to 2010	2.4%	−5.9%	−3.7%	5.3%	−7.7%	19.0%	8.0%	16.5%	2.3%
1990 to 2010	27.9	10.6	26.0	25.5	20.6	67.8	15.9	21.5	12.7

Source: Bureau of the Census, Current Population Surveys, Annual Social and Economic Supplement, Internet site http://www .census.gov/hhes/www/income/data/historical/people/index.html; calculations by New Strategist

Incomes of Asian, Hispanic, and Non-Hispanic White Women Are Growing

Black women saw a decline between 2000 and 2010.

Between 1990 and 2010, the median income of black women grew by a stunning 46 percent, rising to $20,831 after adjusting for inflation. The median income of Hispanic women grew by 34 percent during those years, to $16,269, and Asian women experienced a 32 percent increase (to $23,664). Non-Hispanic white women saw the smallest gain, up 27 percent over the two decades to $21,754. Growing labor force participation is behind women's income gains during the past 20 years.

Between 2000 and 2010, the median income of black women fell 2 percent, after adjusting for inflation. The median income of Asian, Hispanic, and non-Hispanic white women climbed 3 to 8 percent during those years.

■ The median income of black women is significantly higher than the median income of Hispanic women.

Asian women experienced the biggest income gain between 2000 and 2010

(percent change in median income of women by race and Hispanic origin, 2000 to 2010; in 2010 dollars)

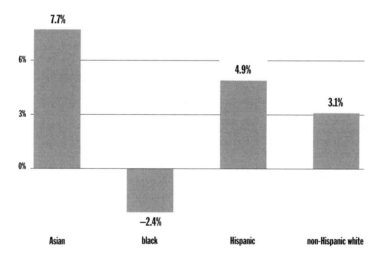

Table 3.2 Median Income of Women by Race and Hispanic Origin, 1990 to 2010

(median income of women aged 15 or older with income by race and Hispanic origin, 1990 to 2010; percent change in income for selected years; in 2010 dollars)

	total women	Asian	black	Hispanic	non-Hispanic white
2010	$20,831	$23,664	$19,634	$16,269	$21,754
2009	21,303	24,569	19,733	16,478	22,301
2008	21,131	23,306	20,459	16,625	22,024
2007	22,001	25,337	20,728	17,612	22,805
2006	21,643	23,879	20,617	17,041	22,414
2005	20,747	24,150	19,651	16,793	21,724
2004	20,393	23,797	20,023	16,682	21,279
2003	20,460	21,195	19,608	16,172	21,696
2002	20,375	21,692	20,205	16,197	21,075
2001	20,461	22,814	20,052	15,496	21,218
2000	20,338	21,975	20,107	15,507	21,100
1999	20,026	21,980	19,335	14,886	20,820
1998	19,276	20,342	17,549	14,510	20,327
1997	18,560	19,385	17,673	13,897	19,490
1996	17,733	20,250	16,290	13,123	18,700
1995	17,232	18,272	15,571	12,683	18,193
1994	16,681	17,984	15,339	12,530	17,378
1993	16,413	18,372	14,127	12,035	17,234
1992	16,313	18,075	13,531	12,650	17,132
1991	16,355	17,214	13,763	12,510	17,173
1990	16,285	17,928	13,468	12,181	17,111
Percent change					
2000 to 2010	2.4%	7.7%	–2.4%	4.9%	3.1%
1990 to 2010	27.9	32.0	45.8	33.6	27.1

Note: Beginning in 2002, data for Asians and blacks are for those who identify themselves as being of the race alone and those who identify themselves as being of the race in combination with one or more other races. Hispanics may be of any race. Beginning in 2002, data for non-Hispanic whites are for those who identify themselves as white alone and not Hispanic.
Source: Bureau of the Census, Current Population Surveys, Annual Social and Economic Supplement, Internet site http://www.census.gov/hhes/www/income/data/historical/people/index.html; calculations by New Strategist

Table 3.3 Median Income of Asian Women by Age, 2002 to 2010

(median income of Asian women aged 15 or older with income by age, 2002 to 2010; percent change in income, 2002–10; in 2010 dollars)

	total Asian women	15 to 24	25 to 34	35 to 44	45 to 54	55 to 64	aged 65 or older total	65 to 74	75 or older
2010	$23,664	$7,491	$31,461	$32,013	$29,922	$26,625	$11,977	$12,514	$11,363
2009	24,569	7,490	31,176	32,649	31,269	26,039	11,951	12,325	11,563
2008	23,306	10,436	32,867	32,042	29,698	23,857	11,742	12,247	11,160
2007	25,337	9,309	33,928	31,144	36,183	25,104	12,873	13,487	12,034
2006	23,879	10,015	32,046	34,065	29,403	24,145	12,090	12,619	11,326
2005	24,150	9,839	30,816	33,346	28,893	26,077	13,630	15,597	12,198
2004	23,797	8,942	30,261	33,320	30,300	25,200	11,050	11,770	10,447
2003	21,195	11,555	30,322	27,865	26,922	23,914	10,825	10,544	11,209
2002	21,692	9,406	27,072	27,556	30,226	24,947	11,201	11,795	10,305

Percent change

2002 to 2010	9.1%	−20.4%	16.2%	16.2%	−1.0%	6.7%	6.9%	6.1%	10.3%

Note: Asians are those who identify themselves as being of the race alone and those who identify themselves as being of the race in combination with other races.
Source: Bureau of the Census, Current Population Surveys, Annual Social and Economic Supplement, Internet site http://www .census.gov/hhes/www/income/data/historical/people/index.html; calculations by New Strategist

Table 3.4 Median Income of Black Women by Age, 1990 to 2010

(median income of black women aged 15 or older with income by age, 1990 to 2010; percent change in income for selected years; in 2010 dollars)

	total black women	15 to 24	25 to 34	35 to 44	45 to 54	55 to 64	aged 65 or older total	65 to 74	75 or older
2010	$19,634	$8,602	$21,718	$28,958	$25,036	$21,439	$13,145	$14,487	$11,854
2009	19,733	9,061	22,541	27,570	27,043	20,532	13,086	14,388	11,925
2008	20,459	8,682	22,621	27,608	26,509	21,358	12,685	13,821	11,894
2007	20,728	8,496	23,359	30,099	27,250	22,301	12,170	12,934	11,256
2006	20,617	8,448	23,286	28,636	27,982	22,304	11,983	12,618	11,377
2005	19,651	9,003	22,774	28,869	26,941	22,212	11,945	12,984	11,011
2004	20,023	8,013	24,523	27,630	27,639	21,267	11,452	12,619	10,610
2003	19,608	8,175	24,144	27,359	27,373	21,782	11,626	12,583	10,916
2002	20,205	8,623	24,892	26,836	27,876	21,990	11,488	11,884	11,175
2001	20,052	9,357	25,096	28,362	27,144	19,735	11,147	11,637	10,601
2000	20,107	9,149	25,643	27,920	27,601	18,688	11,167	11,777	10,473
1999	19,335	8,513	24,048	26,917	28,449	19,281	11,370	12,237	10,196
1998	17,549	8,199	21,377	25,115	26,993	15,950	10,417	10,493	10,327
1997	17,673	8,471	22,214	23,949	27,176	16,859	10,665	11,422	9,977
1996	16,290	8,063	19,053	24,362	25,519	17,071	10,006	10,076	9,923
1995	15,571	7,306	18,367	23,408	23,217	15,143	10,082	10,397	9,738
1994	15,339	7,172	19,033	22,529	23,386	14,977	10,163	10,493	9,815
1993	14,127	6,444	15,484	22,659	21,395	14,799	9,780	10,257	9,220
1992	13,531	6,763	16,164	22,035	21,873	12,432	9,466	9,866	9,017
1991	13,763	7,241	16,862	23,199	21,037	12,346	9,658	9,586	9,751
1990	13,468	7,227	16,401	23,991	21,820	12,193	9,084	9,700	8,139
Percent change									
2000 to 2010	−2.4%	−6.0%	−15.3%	3.7%	−9.3%	14.7%	17.7%	23.0%	13.2%
1990 to 2010	45.8	19.0	32.4	20.7	14.7	75.8	44.7	49.4	45.6

Note: Beginning in 2002, blacks are those who identify themselves as being of the race alone and those who identify themselves as being of the race in combination with other races.
Source: Bureau of the Census, Current Population Surveys, Annual Social and Economic Supplement, Internet site http://www .census.gov/hhes/www/income/data/historical/people/index.html; calculations by New Strategist

Table 3.5 Median Income of Hispanic Women by Age, 1990 to 2010

(median income of Hispanic women aged 15 or older with income by age, 1990 to 2010; percent change in income for selected years; in 2010 dollars)

	total Hispanic women	15 to 24	25 to 34	35 to 44	45 to 54	55 to 64	aged 65 or older total	65 to 74	75 or older
2010	$16,269	$9,071	$20,140	$21,035	$20,744	$16,319	$10,438	$10,905	$10,008
2009	16,478	9,736	19,891	20,483	20,460	18,397	10,272	10,542	10,069
2008	16,625	9,678	20,261	20,604	20,894	17,796	10,066	9,915	10,320
2007	17,612	10,229	21,934	22,408	22,316	17,654	10,291	10,121	10,528
2006	17,041	10,578	20,776	21,018	22,294	17,149	10,331	10,514	10,159
2005	16,793	10,172	19,353	20,302	21,046	18,166	9,762	9,669	9,865
2004	16,682	10,070	19,700	20,819	21,059	16,400	10,376	10,241	10,524
2003	16,172	10,289	18,815	20,688	20,467	14,830	9,873	10,211	9,426
2002	16,197	10,400	19,928	20,432	20,471	14,398	9,262	9,265	9,258
2001	15,496	10,360	19,642	20,495	20,160	14,266	9,341	9,080	9,744
2000	15,507	9,786	19,365	20,325	20,388	14,916	9,420	9,412	9,433
1999	14,886	9,529	17,727	19,858	19,310	13,064	9,227	9,123	9,384
1998	14,510	9,082	17,199	19,241	18,246	11,771	9,187	9,168	9,217
1997	13,897	8,019	16,745	16,878	17,504	12,813	9,290	9,277	9,309
1996	13,123	7,804	15,851	16,406	16,836	12,508	9,587	9,523	9,667
1995	12,683	7,663	15,351	16,739	16,386	10,349	9,450	9,151	9,967
1994	12,530	7,998	15,377	16,956	16,260	10,751	9,324	9,113	9,670
1993	12,035	7,504	15,248	16,429	15,884	10,552	9,059	8,972	9,199
1992	12,650	7,942	16,066	17,227	16,455	10,393	9,081	9,178	8,941
1991	12,510	8,035	14,797	16,088	16,254	11,323	9,227	9,294	9,138
1990	12,181	7,609	14,640	17,506	16,047	11,699	8,689	8,049	9,528
Percent change									
2000 to 2010	4.9%	−7.3%	4.0%	3.5%	1.7%	9.4%	10.8%	15.9%	6.1%
1990 to 2010	33.6	19.2	37.6	20.2	29.3	39.5	20.1	35.5	5.0

Source: Bureau of the Census, Current Population Surveys, Annual Social and Economic Supplement, Internet site http://www .census.gov/hhes/www/income/data/historical/people/index.html; calculations by New Strategist

Table 3.6 Median Income of Non-Hispanic White Women by Age, 1990 to 2010

(median income of non-Hispanic white women aged 15 or older with income by age, 1990 to 2010; percent change in income for selected years; in 2010 dollars)

	total non-Hispanic white women	15 to 24	25 to 34	35 to 44	45 to 54	55 to 64	aged 65 or older total	65 to 74	75 or older
2010	$21,754	$8,794	$28,377	$31,274	$30,450	$27,067	$15,895	$16,947	$15,085
2009	22,301	9,064	27,529	31,161	31,281	27,122	16,496	17,527	15,783
2008	22,024	8,906	27,654	30,309	30,853	27,287	15,572	16,135	15,197
2007	22,805	9,528	28,907	31,256	32,510	28,175	15,485	16,144	15,090
2006	22,414	9,217	28,362	29,913	32,800	27,844	15,536	16,298	15,094
2005	21,724	8,973	27,936	29,558	32,153	26,216	14,675	15,061	14,405
2004	21,279	8,941	27,803	29,573	31,860	25,038	14,636	15,031	14,403
2003	21,696	8,758	28,714	29,788	32,380	25,442	14,784	15,480	14,411
2002	21,075	9,198	28,355	28,705	31,979	24,251	14,514	14,409	14,587
2001	21,218	9,025	28,785	29,201	31,598	23,159	14,691	14,687	14,692
2000	21,100	9,262	28,438	29,402	32,042	22,619	14,724	14,653	14,774
1999	20,820	8,665	27,146	28,119	31,299	21,877	15,163	15,433	14,995
1998	20,327	8,750	26,872	28,509	30,469	21,070	14,981	15,131	14,868
1997	19,490	8,815	25,681	27,156	28,940	20,516	14,455	14,620	14,322
1996	18,700	8,243	25,050	27,332	27,488	19,568	14,041	14,261	13,846
1995	18,193	7,636	23,566	26,289	26,794	18,622	13,981	13,922	14,035
1994	17,378	8,221	23,179	24,723	26,131	16,403	13,688	13,524	13,832
1993	17,234	8,377	23,001	24,622	25,502	16,934	13,294	13,575	13,052
1992	17,132	8,220	22,991	24,495	25,152	16,465	13,301	13,373	13,233
1991	17,173	8,426	22,170	24,572	23,992	16,372	13,618	13,681	13,920
1990	17,111	8,149	22,585	24,167	23,687	16,020	13,961	14,293	13,625
Percent change									
2000 to 2010	3.1%	−5.0%	−0.2%	6.4%	−5.0%	19.7%	8.0%	15.7%	2.1%
1990 to 2010	27.1	7.9	25.6	29.4	28.6	69.0	13.9	18.6	10.7

Note: Beginning in 2002, data are only for those who identify themselves as being white alone and not Hispanic.
Source: Bureau of the Census, Current Population Surveys, Annual Social and Economic Supplement, Internet site http://www
.census.gov/hhes/www/income/data/historical/people/index.html; calculations by New Strategist

Women in the Midwest Lost Ground between 2000 and 2010

In every region, women's incomes have grown substantially since 1990.

Between 2000 and 2010, women's median income grew in all but the Midwest, despite the lingering aftereffects of the Great Recession. The biggest increase was in the South and Northeast, where women's median income climbed 4 to 5 percent, respectively, after adjusting for inflation. In the West, women's median income grew by a scant 0.4 percent, and in the Midwest it declined by the same percentage.

Between 1990 and 2010, women's median income rose by 23 percent in the West, 24 percent in the Northeast, 27 percent in the Midwest, and 35 percent in the South, after adjusting for inflation. Behind these gains is the growing labor force participation of women.

■ Women in the Northeast had the highest median income in 2010 ($21,498), while women in the South had the lowest ($20,547).

Between 2000 and 2010, women's median income grew the most in the South

(percent change in median income of women by region, 2000 to 2010; in 2010 dollars)

Table 3.7 **Median Income of Women by Region, 1990 to 2010**

(median income of women aged 15 or older with income by region, 1990 to 2010; percent change in income for selected years; in 2010 dollars)

	total women	Northeast	Midwest	South	West
2010	$20,831	$21,498	$20,777	$20,547	$20,835
2009	21,303	22,431	21,333	20,595	21,480
2008	21,131	22,207	21,080	20,381	21,679
2007	22,001	22,809	21,617	21,386	22,790
2006	21,643	21,935	21,785	20,854	22,250
2005	20,747	21,742	21,060	20,116	20,739
2004	20,393	21,120	20,654	19,817	20,728
2003	20,460	21,281	20,744	19,754	20,745
2002	20,375	20,898	20,508	19,662	20,946
2001	20,461	21,020	20,796	19,615	20,912
2000	20,338	20,639	20,869	19,660	20,743
1999	20,026	20,624	20,293	19,267	20,345
1998	19,276	19,785	19,400	18,671	19,599
1997	18,560	19,414	18,826	17,657	18,965
1996	17,733	18,613	18,059	17,099	17,755
1995	17,232	17,732	17,587	16,463	17,696
1994	16,681	17,404	16,835	15,914	17,162
1993	16,413	16,902	16,390	15,686	17,188
1992	16,313	17,205	16,043	15,448	17,274
1991	16,355	17,246	15,923	15,695	17,136
1990	16,285	17,355	16,364	15,229	16,927
Percent change					
2000 to 2010	2.4%	4.2%	–0.4%	4.5%	0.4%
1990 to 2010	27.9	23.9	27.0	34.9	23.1

Source: Bureau of the Census, Current Population Surveys, Annual Social and Economic Supplement, Internet site http://www .census.gov/hhes/www/income/data/historical/people/index.html; calculations by New Strategist

Earnings of Working Women Have Increased

Between 2000 and 2010, women's earnings rose 3 percent, after adjusting for inflation.

Women who work full-time, year-round, saw their median earnings rise 6 percent between 2000 and 2010, after adjusting for inflation. While not a large increase, it dwarfed the 1 percent rise in the earnings of men with full-time jobs. Women who work part-time experienced an even bigger earnings gain of 17 percent between 2000 and 2010. Many part-time workers would prefer full-time work and are putting in as many hours as possible.

Between 1990 and 2010, women who work full-time, year-round saw their median earnings rise 15 percent, after adjusting for inflation. While this gain is substantial—particularly in comparison with men—the rise is much smaller than the 34 percent gain for all women with earnings. Behind the much larger earnings gain for all women over the past couple of decades is the growing percentage of women with full-time jobs.

■ The median earnings of women who work full-time, year-round have been treading water since 2007, after adjusting for inflation.

Among women with full-time jobs, earnings grew between 2000 and 2010

(median earnings of women who work full-time, year-round, 2000 to 2010; in 2010 dollars)

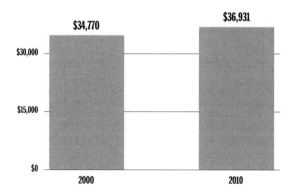

Table 3.8 Median Earnings of Women by Employment Status, 1990 to 2010

(median earnings of women aged 15 or older with earnings by employment status, 1990 to 2010; percent change in earnings for selected years; in 2010 dollars)

	total women with earnings	worked full-time		worked part-time	
		total	year-round	total	year-round
2010	$26,552	$34,379	$36,931	$9,813	$13,817
2009	26,460	33,163	36,877	9,682	13,001
2008	25,974	32,472	36,197	9,204	12,875
2007	27,212	33,491	36,912	9,429	13,199
2006	26,457	33,299	35,161	9,538	13,477
2005	25,770	33,540	35,581	8,897	13,705
2004	25,690	33,186	36,060	8,639	13,487
2003	26,085	32,904	36,423	8,961	13,769
2002	25,971	32,758	36,605	8,851	13,883
2001	25,679	32,435	35,979	8,696	13,625
2000	25,660	32,257	34,770	8,394	13,450
1999	24,129	31,066	34,436	8,169	13,402
1998	23,666	30,787	34,547	8,155	13,352
1997	22,642	29,640	33,826	7,787	12,766
1996	22,179	29,315	32,809	7,634	12,196
1995	21,766	28,927	31,959	7,178	12,440
1994	20,837	28,767	32,304	7,166	12,542
1993	20,647	28,733	32,313	7,044	12,006
1992	20,596	28,535	32,545	7,100	11,718
1991	20,114	27,948	32,087	6,988	11,459
1990	19,810	27,325	32,056	6,860	11,600
Percent change					
2000 to 2010	3.5%	6.6%	6.2%	16.9%	2.7%
1990 to 2010	34.0	25.8	15.2	43.0	19.1

Note: Earnings include wages and salaries only.
Source: Bureau of the Census, Current Population Surveys, Annual Social and Economic Supplement, Internet site http://www
.census.gov/hhes/www/income/data/historical/people/index.html; calculations by New Strategist

Non-Hispanic White Women Have Seen the Biggest Gains

Since 1990, their median earnings have grown 22 percent.

The median earnings of non-Hispanic white women with full-time jobs rose 22 percent between 1990 and 2010, after adjusting for inflation. Asian women experienced a 19 percent increase, while black and Hispanic women who work full-time saw their median earnings grow 10 to 11 percent during the two decades.

Between 2000 and 2010, women in every racial and ethnic group saw their earnings grow, after adjusting for inflation. The median earnings of black women climbed 2 percent, to $32,273. Hispanic women experienced a bigger increase, but their median earnings are still well below those of black women, at $27,992 in 2010. Asian and non-Hispanic white women saw their median earnings grow 7 percent between 2000 and 2010. Asian women had the highest median earnings in 2010, at $41,172, and non-Hispanic white women were not far behind with a median of $40,270.

■ The earnings of Asian women who work full-time are above average because most are college graduates. The earnings of Hispanic women are far below average because many are poorly educated immigrants.

Among women with full-time jobs, earnings are growing in every racial and ethnic group

(percent change in median earnings of women who work full-time, year-round, by race and Hispanic origin, 2000 to 2010; in 2010 dollars)

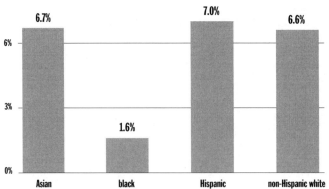

Table 3.9 Median Earnings of Women Who Work Full-Time, by Race and Hispanic Origin, 1990 to 2010

(median earnings of women aged 15 or older who work full-time, year-round, by race and Hispanic origin, 1990 to 2010; percent change in earnings for selected years; in 2010 dollars)

	total women working full-time	Asian	black	Hispanic	non-Hispanic white
2010	$36,931	$41,172	$32,273	$27,992	$40,270
2009	36,877	43,071	32,424	27,630	39,169
2008	36,197	42,721	31,908	27,186	37,862
2007	36,912	42,351	32,671	27,984	38,640
2006	35,161	42,744	32,876	27,249	38,642
2005	35,581	40,184	33,148	27,043	38,100
2004	36,060	41,439	32,067	27,097	37,544
2003	36,423	38,464	31,995	26,511	38,002
2002	36,605	38,128	32,616	26,554	38,058
2001	35,979	37,790	32,753	26,469	37,933
2000	34,770	38,585	31,766	26,157	37,777
1999	34,436	37,386	31,701	25,366	35,897
1998	34,547	36,160	30,254	25,676	35,906
1997	33,826	37,629	29,846	25,699	35,101
1996	32,809	35,362	29,713	25,828	34,442
1995	31,959	35,340	29,356	24,403	33,614
1994	32,304	35,573	28,965	25,559	33,745
1993	32,313	36,173	29,444	24,900	33,258
1992	32,545	34,717	30,092	26,015	33,336
1991	32,087	33,057	29,225	25,360	32,932
1990	32,056	34,485	29,174	25,344	32,921

Percent change

2000 to 2010	6.2%	6.7%	1.6%	7.0%	6.6%
1990 to 2010	15.2	19.4	10.6	10.4	22.3

Note: Beginning in 2002, data for Asians and blacks are for those who identify themselves as being of the race alone and those who identify themselves as being of the race in combination with other races. Hispanics may be of any race. Beginning in 2002, data for non-Hispanic whites are for those who identify themselves as white alone and not Hispanic.
Source: Bureau of the Census, Current Population Surveys, Annual Social and Economic Supplement, Internet site http://www .census.gov/hhes/www/income/data/historical/people/index.html; calculations by New Strategist

Education Does Not Guarantee Earnings Growth

The recession has hurt even highly educated workers.

Between 2000 and 2010, earnings growth came to a halt for many women. Those with more education were not immune from the recession. Among women who work full-time, year-round, only those with a doctoral degree gained substantial ground between 2000 and 2010. Their median earnings rose 7 percent during those years, after adjusting for inflation. In every other educational group, earnings were flat or fell. The biggest losses were experienced by women who did not graduate from high school, with declines of 4 to 8 percent.

The longer-term earnings trend has rewarded the highly educated more than those with less education. Between 1991 and 2010, the median earnings of women aged 25 or older who worked full-time grew 15 percent, to $38,294, after adjusting for inflation. Women with no more than a high school diploma saw their median earnings increase 6 percent during those years, while those with at least a bachelor's degree experienced a 9 percent increase in earnings.

■ Although the labor market still pays a premium to highly educated workers, the premium may be shrinking—especially when the cost of college is taken into consideration.

Earnings have fallen for most women, regardless of their educational level

(percent change in median earnings of women who work full-time, year-round, by educational attainment, 2000 to 2010; in 2010 dollars)

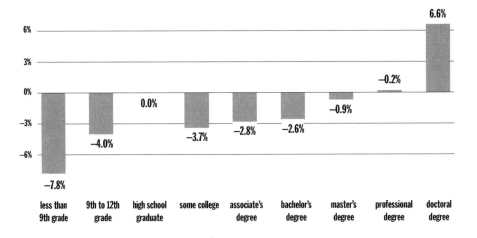

Table 3.10 Median Earnings of Women Who Work Full-Time by Education, 1991 to 2010

(median earnings of women aged 25 or older who work full-time, year-round, by educational attainment, 1991 to 2010; percent change in earnings for selected years; in 2010 dollars)

	total women	less than 9th grade	9th to 12th grade	high school graduate	some college	associate's degree	bachelor's degree or more				
							total	bachelor's degree	master's degree	professional degree	doctoral degree
2010	$38,294	$18,239	$20,883	$29,857	$33,401	$37,773	$51,942	$47,435	$59,099	$76,737	$77,392
2009	37,879	18,785	21,576	29,631	34,650	37,882	52,734	47,605	62,076	85,290	77,845
2008	37,161	18,870	20,663	28,741	33,039	37,225	52,059	47,621	58,240	72,199	74,961
2007	37,947	19,203	21,450	28,644	34,530	38,206	52,997	48,133	58,284	74,764	72,546
2006	37,951	19,609	21,768	28,913	34,555	38,021	53,606	49,104	56,706	82,447	76,259
2005	36,940	18,028	22,477	29,361	35,068	37,905	52,434	47,100	57,419	89,859	74,663
2004	36,947	19,640	22,124	30,063	35,578	38,656	53,025	48,137	59,237	86,687	78,938
2003	37,420	20,043	22,451	30,910	35,733	38,236	53,484	48,993	59,468	78,824	79,681
2002	37,583	20,009	23,399	30,520	35,632	38,328	52,411	49,512	59,253	69,104	79,644
2001	37,495	19,914	22,090	29,824	35,516	38,417	51,781	49,037	59,454	74,007	74,416
2000	36,934	19,779	21,759	29,844	34,570	38,871	52,404	48,690	59,491	76,576	72,613
1999	35,477	18,869	21,366	28,730	34,570	39,398	52,490	47,533	59,355	74,175	73,700
1998	35,682	18,878	21,169	29,339	34,764	37,907	49,983	47,299	56,108	74,085	69,687
1997	34,977	18,214	21,546	28,838	33,910	36,850	49,230	45,283	56,693	73,857	68,751
1996	34,321	18,780	22,323	28,368	32,978	37,047	48,610	44,155	55,924	78,086	71,940
1995	33,553	18,149	21,455	27,913	31,980	37,334	47,446	43,751	54,825	68,346	59,551
1994	33,700	17,500	21,057	28,411	32,254	36,681	48,453	44,720	54,622	70,243	67,617
1993	33,316	17,646	21,842	28,481	32,684	37,246	47,979	45,087	54,863	71,924	68,973
1992	33,712	18,504	20,867	28,343	33,422	37,786	47,713	44,469	53,292	67,470	66,656
1991	33,210	18,168	21,135	28,167	33,297	37,253	47,449	43,173	51,710	66,513	62,716
Percent change											
2000 to 2010	3.7%	−7.8%	−4.0%	0.0%	−3.4%	−2.8%	−0.9%	−2.6%	−0.7%	0.2%	6.6%
1991 to 2010	15.3	0.4	−1.2	6.0	0.3	1.4	9.5	9.9	14.3	15.4	23.4

Note: Earnings include wages and salaries only.
Source: Bureau of the Census, Current Population Surveys, Annual Social and Economic Supplement, Internet site http://www .census.gov/hhes/www/income/data/historical/people/index.html; calculations by New Strategist

Women in Many Occupations Have Lost Ground

In some occupations, earnings were higher in 2010 than in 2002, however.

Among women who work full-time, year-round, median earnings increased just 0.9 percent between 2002 and 2010, after adjusting for inflation. Earnings grew in some occupations during those years, however. The median earnings of women in management and business rose 4.4 percent, for example. In contrast, women in health care support occupations saw their earnings decline 3.4 percent between 2002 and 2010.

Women in male-dominated occupations experienced some of the biggest increases in earnings between 2002 and 2010. Women in installation, maintenance, and repair occupations saw their median earnings rise 5 percent, for example. Those in construction gained 4 percent, after adjusting for inflation. Few women work in those occupations, however. Women in office and administrative support occupations experienced a 1 percent decline in earnings during those years.

■ In many occupations, women's median earnings have been treading water since 2007.

Women's fortunes vary by occupation

(percent change in median earnings of women who work full-time, by selected occupation, 2002 to 2010; in 2010 dollars)

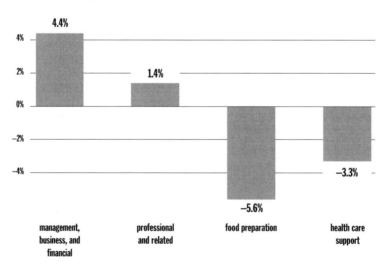

Table 3.11 Median Earnings of Women Who Work Full-Time by Occupation, 2002 to 2010

(median earnings of women aged 15 or older who work full-time, year-round, by occupation of longest job held, 2002 to 2010; in 2010 dollars)

	2010	2009	2008	2007	2006	2005	2004	2003	2002	percent change, 2002–10
Total women who work full-time	**$36,931**	**$36,877**	**$36,197**	**$36,912**	**$35,161**	**$35,581**	**$36,060**	**$36,423**	**$36,605**	**0.9%**
Management, business, and financial	52,236	51,856	51,719	52,897	54,370	52,263	48,905	49,866	50,025	4.4
Professional and related	49,244	49,663	47,353	48,206	46,505	46,921	47,778	47,773	48,575	1.4
Health care support	26,277	26,820	26,612	26,162	24,658	24,551	25,583	26,227	27,176	−3.3
Protective service	39,107	39,265	36,699	36,816	40,584	38,852	37,243	37,574	37,881	3.2
Food preparation	19,371	19,697	20,785	20,494	19,371	20,635	18,964	20,676	20,525	−5.6
Building and grounds	20,721	21,246	20,621	20,734	20,690	19,564	19,581	20,004	20,103	3.1
Personal care and service	22,155	23,489	22,994	23,439	22,430	22,915	24,039	23,106	23,758	−6.7
Sales and related	30,982	30,315	29,141	30,161	29,433	29,770	31,020	30,983	30,963	0.1
Office, administrative support	32,679	33,003	32,396	33,028	33,322	33,537	33,088	33,712	33,151	−1.4
Farming, fishing, and forestry	20,859	21,483	22,765	25,339	20,951	20,871	19,378	19,825	20,160	3.5
Construction and extraction	31,864	31,342	34,087	42,351	27,133	34,296	33,871	33,124	30,493	4.5
Installation, maintenance, repair	41,395	40,664	34,766	44,032	44,550	41,165	39,312	44,372	39,384	5.1
Production occupations	25,705	25,661	26,313	27,071	24,976	26,255	27,028	26,512	26,375	−2.5
Transportation, material moving	25,115	25,968	24,328	28,533	25,833	24,261	25,960	26,978	27,257	−7.9
Armed forces	50,597	–	–	–	–	–	–	38,170	–	–

Note: "–" means data are not available.
Source: Bureau of the Census, Current Population Surveys, Annual Social and Economic Supplement, Internet site http://www .census.gov/hhes/www/income/data/historical/people/index.html; calculations by New Strategist

Women Are Closing the Gap

Women's earnings have grown much faster than men's over the past 20 years.

Between 1990 and 2010, the median earnings of women with full-time jobs rose 15 percent, after adjusting for inflation. The median earnings of men who work full-time grew by less than half that rate, at 7 percent. Consequently, the earnings gap between women and men has narrowed considerably. In 1990, women earned 72 percent of what men earned. By 2010, they earned 77 percent as much as men.

The median earnings of women who work full-time stood at $36,931 in 2010, compared with a median of $47,715 for men. Men earned $12,704 more than women in 1990, a gap that shrank by nearly $2,000 to $10,784 in 2010.

■ The average male worker is older than the average female worker, which accounts for a portion of the gap in earnings between men and women.

Men's and women's earnings have become more alike

(median earnings of men and women who work full-time, year-round, 1990 and 2010; in 2010 dollars)

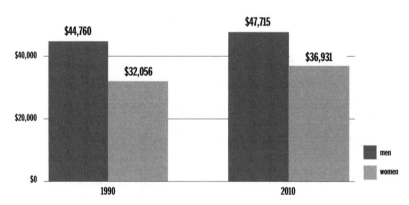

Table 3.12 Women's Earnings as a Percentage of Men's Earnings, 1990 to 2010

(median earnings of people aged 15 or older who work full-time, year-round, by sex, and women's earnings as a percentage of men's earnings, 1990 to 2010; in 2010 dollars)

	men	women	women's earnings as a percentage of men's earnings
2010	$47,715	$36,931	77.4%
2009	47,905	36,877	77.0
2008	46,954	36,197	77.1
2007	47,439	36,912	77.8
2006	45,701	35,161	76.9
2005	46,222	35,581	77.0
2004	47,090	36,060	76.6
2003	48,211	36,423	75.5
2002	47,786	36,605	76.6
2001	47,137	35,979	76.3
2000	47,165	34,770	73.7
1999	47,619	34,436	72.3
1998	47,215	34,547	73.2
1997	45,611	33,826	74.2
1996	44,479	32,809	73.8
1995	44,743	31,959	71.4
1994	44,886	32,304	72.0
1993	45,180	32,313	71.5
1992	45,978	32,545	70.8
1991	45,932	32,087	69.9
1990	44,760	32,056	71.6

	percent change		percentage point change
2000 to 2010	1.2%	6.2%	3.7
1990 to 2010	6.6	15.2	5.8

Note: Earnings include wages and salaries only.
Source: Bureau of the Census, Current Population Surveys, Annual Social and Economic Supplement, Internet site http://www
.census.gov/hhes/www/income/data/historical/people/index.html; calculations by New Strategist

Nine Million Wives Earn More than Their Husbands

More than one in four wives is the primary breadwinner.

Among the nation's 31 million dual-earner couples, 9 million wives earn more than their husbands—accounting for a substantial 29 percent of all dual-earner couples. The number and proportion of couples in which the wife earns more than the husband surged during the past few years, in part because of the Great Recession.

In 2010, only 54 percent of married couples were dual earners, down from 56 percent in 1990 and 60 percent in 2000 as unemployment climbed during the Great Recession and turned dual earners into single earners or even no earners. Between 1990 and 2000, the percentage of dual-earner couples in which the wife earns more than the husband climbed by 5 percentage points. Between 2000 and 2010, it grew by a larger 6 percentage points.

■ The incomes of working wives are increasingly important to family well-being, especially when husbands are unemployed.

A growing percentage of wives are earning more than their husbands

(percent of dual-earner couples in which the wife earns more than the husband, for selected years, 1990 to 2010)

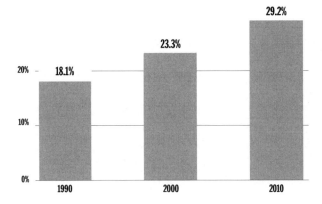

Table 3.13 Wives Who Earn More than Their Husbands, 1990 to 2010

(number of married couples, dual-earner couples, and wives who earn more than their husbands; wives who earn more than their husbands as a percent of all dual-earner couples, 1990 to 2010; couples in thousands as of the following year)

	total married couples	dual-earner couples	wives who earn more than their husbands	percent of dual-earner couples with wives who earn more
2010	58,047	31,373	9,146	29.2%
2009	58,428	32,285	9,291	28.8
2008	59,137	33,905	9,002	26.6
2007	58,395	33,678	8,700	25.8
2006	58,964	33,838	8,688	25.7
2005	58,189	33,364	8,521	25.5
2004	57,983	33,110	8,387	25.3
2003	57,725	33,189	8,355	25.2
2002	57,327	33,531	8,394	25.0
2001	56,755	33,666	8,109	24.1
2000	56,598	33,876	7,906	23.3
1999	55,315	33,344	7,420	22.3
1998	54,778	32,783	7,435	22.7
1997	54,321	32,745	7,446	22.7
1996	53,604	32,390	7,327	22.6
1995	53,570	32,030	7,028	21.9
1994	53,865	32,093	7,218	22.5
1993	53,181	31,267	6,960	22.3
1992	53,090	31,224	6,979	22.4
1991	52,457	31,003	6,499	21.0
1990	51,675	29,079	5,266	18.1

Note: Earnings include wages and salaries only.
Source: Bureau of the Census, Current Population Surveys, Annual Social and Economic Supplement, Internet site http://www
.census.gov/hhes/www/income/data/historical/families/index.html; calculations by New Strategist

Women's Incomes, 2010

Women's Incomes Peak in the 35-to-44 Age Group

Among full-time workers, however, income peaks among older women.

The incomes of women peak in the 35-to-44 age group, in part because women in that age group are most likely to be college graduates. The median income of women aged 35 to 44 stood at $29,447—41 percent greater than the $20,831 median of all women aged 15 or older. Among full-time workers aged 35 to 44, median income stood at $41,108, and it was a higher $47,311 among women aged 65 to 74 who work full-time. Only 11 percent of women aged 65 to 74 are full-time workers, however.

Asian and black women are more likely than average to work full-time, with 36 to 37 percent holding full-time jobs. This compares with 35 percent of non-Hispanic white women and 30 percent of Hispanic women. The median income of black women who work full-time stood at $33,918 in 2010. This is less than the $41,821 and $41,307 medians of their Asian and non-Hispanic white counterparts, respectively. But it is greater than the $28,944 median income of Hispanic women with full-time jobs.

■ Because education boosts earnings, better-educated Asian and non-Hispanic white women have higher incomes than less-educated black women and poorly educated Hispanic women.

Among women who work full time, income peaks in the middle and older age groups

(median income of women aged 15 or older who work full-time, year-round, by age, 2010)

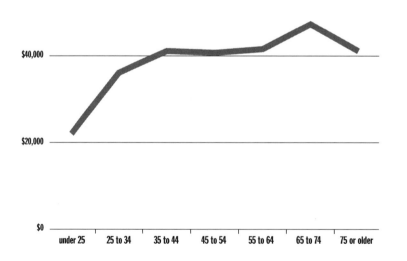

Table 3.14 Women by Income and Age, 2010: Total Women

(number and percent distribution of women aged 15 or older by income and age, 2010; median income of women with income and of women working full-time, year-round; percent working full-time, year-round; women in thousands as of 2011)

	total	15 to 24	25 to 34	35 to 44	45 to 54	55 to 64	65 or older total	65 to 74	75 or older
Total women	**125,084**	**20,761**	**20,599**	**20,128**	**22,459**	**19,038**	**22,098**	**11,573**	**10,525**
Without income	18,942	8,385	2,954	2,576	2,359	1,775	894	523	371
With income	106,142	12,376	17,645	17,552	20,100	17,263	21,204	11,050	10,154
Under $5,000	12,538	4,089	1,916	1,832	1,969	1,717	1,014	588	426
$5,000 to $9,999	14,061	2,685	1,695	1,406	1,649	1,887	4,738	2,393	2,346
$10,000 to $14,999	13,672	1,848	1,662	1,541	1,864	1,962	4,794	2,166	2,628
$15,000 to $19,999	10,971	1,268	1,681	1,426	1,766	1,612	3,219	1,451	1,768
$20,000 to $24,999	8,842	832	1,640	1,523	1,788	1,296	1,763	870	893
$25,000 to $29,999	7,228	489	1,398	1,146	1,513	1,285	1,398	722	678
$30,000 to $34,999	6,582	349	1,518	1,370	1,373	1,132	840	453	387
$35,000 to $39,999	5,443	276	1,267	1,124	1,196	924	656	421	235
$40,000 to $44,999	4,778	155	1,110	995	1,175	860	482	309	174
$45,000 to $49,999	3,701	116	792	825	872	698	397	267	130
$50,000 to $54,999	3,527	85	683	812	850	748	349	265	84
$55,000 to $59,999	2,239	47	392	554	581	447	219	156	62
$60,000 to $64,999	2,276	34	402	561	567	477	234	177	57
$65,000 to $69,999	1,464	20	305	339	374	274	155	101	54
$70,000 to $74,999	1,492	19	260	360	351	323	179	144	34
$75,000 to $79,999	1,060	7	182	239	291	249	91	60	31
$80,000 to $84,999	971	18	159	238	271	201	84	65	19
$85,000 to $89,999	669	3	100	150	197	175	45	38	7
$90,000 to $94,999	619	0	77	142	178	145	76	53	23
$95,000 to $99,999	425	0	38	74	141	114	57	45	12
$100,000 or more	3,584	38	369	894	1,134	737	411	304	107

Median income

	total	15 to 24	25 to 34	35 to 44	45 to 54	55 to 64	65 or older total	65 to 74	75 or older
Women with income	$20,831	$8,765	$25,655	$29,447	$27,748	$25,502	$15,072	$16,090	$14,386
Working full-time	38,531	22,024	36,138	41,108	40,726	41,578	46,577	47,311	41,117
Percent full-time	**34.2%**	**12.7%**	**46.6%**	**49.2%**	**51.3%**	**40.3%**	**6.7%**	**10.9%**	**2.2%**

PERCENT DISTRIBUTION

	total	15 to 24	25 to 34	35 to 44	45 to 54	55 to 64	65 or older total	65 to 74	75 or older
Total women	**100.0%**	**100.0%**	**100.0%**	**100.0%**	**100.0%**	**100.0%**	**100.0%**	**100.0%**	**100.0%**
Without income	15.1	40.4	14.3	12.8	10.5	9.3	4.0	4.5	3.5
With income	84.9	59.6	85.7	87.2	89.5	90.7	96.0	95.5	96.5
Under $15,000	32.2	41.5	25.6	23.7	24.4	29.2	47.7	44.5	51.3
$15,000 to $24,999	15.8	10.1	16.1	14.7	15.8	15.3	22.5	20.1	25.3
$25,000 to $34,999	11.0	4.0	14.2	12.5	12.9	12.7	10.1	10.2	10.1
$35,000 to $49,999	11.1	2.6	15.4	14.6	14.4	13.0	6.9	8.6	5.1
$50,000 to $74,999	8.8	1.0	9.9	13.0	12.1	11.9	5.1	7.3	2.8
$75,000 or more	5.9	0.3	4.5	8.6	9.8	8.5	3.5	4.9	1.9

Source: Bureau of the Census, 2011 Current Population Survey Annual Social and Economic Supplement, Internet site http://www.census.gov/hhes/www/cpstables/032011/perinc/toc.htm; calculations by New Strategist

Table 3.15 Women by Income and Age, 2010: Asian Women

(number and percent distribution of Asian women aged 15 or older by income and age, 2010; median income of women with income and of women working full-time, year-round; percent working full-time, year-round; women in thousands as of 2011)

	total	15 to 24	25 to 34	35 to 44	45 to 54	55 to 64	65 or older total	65 to 74	75 or older
Total Asian women	**6,460**	**1,011**	**1,300**	**1,336**	**1,099**	**862**	**850**	**507**	**343**
Without income	1,413	483	296	199	138	147	150	85	64
With income	5,047	528	1,004	1,137	961	715	700	422	279
Under $5,000	694	184	111	157	92	75	75	50	26
$5,000 to $9,999	617	118	92	79	67	63	199	109	90
$10,000 to $14,999	518	68	69	79	89	76	137	80	57
$15,000 to $19,999	397	35	59	80	92	66	67	35	31
$20,000 to $24,999	380	33	82	86	81	53	45	18	26
$25,000 to $29,999	293	27	62	47	61	55	41	19	23
$30,000 to $34,999	333	21	84	66	78	53	31	15	14
$35,000 to $39,999	229	16	62	63	44	34	12	9	2
$40,000 to $44,999	250	7	65	81	53	33	11	6	5
$45,000 to $49,999	144	3	50	35	27	22	9	7	0
$50,000 to $54,999	188	10	43	46	33	40	17	16	0
$55,000 to $59,999	113	6	19	30	25	23	10	10	0
$60,000 to $64,999	146	1	47	32	33	22	12	10	2
$65,000 to $69,999	89	0	17	37	15	13	8	8	0
$70,000 to $74,999	92	0	24	31	23	9	4	4	0
$75,000 to $79,999	68	0	18	17	14	9	9	9	0
$80,000 to $84,999	76	0	19	23	23	8	4	4	0
$85,000 to $89,999	42	0	10	17	11	4	0	0	0
$90,000 to $94,999	58	0	18	18	15	7	1	1	0
$95,000 to $99,999	20	0	6	7	5	4	0	0	0
$100,000 or more	297	1	48	110	82	46	10	10	0
Median income									
Women with income	$23,664	$7,491	$31,461	$32,013	$29,922	$26,625	$11,977	$12,514	$11,363
Working full-time	41,821	25,676	42,555	45,662	41,557	40,115	–	–	–
Percent full-time	**36.6%**	**9.2%**	**44.9%**	**49.5%**	**53.5%**	**43.7%**	**6.7%**	**10.3%**	**1.5%**
PERCENT DISTRIBUTION									
Total Asian women	**100.0%**	**100.0%**	**100.0%**	**100.0%**	**100.0%**	**100.0%**	**100.0%**	**100.0%**	**100.0%**
Without income	21.9	47.8	22.8	14.9	12.6	17.1	17.6	16.8	18.7
With income	78.1	52.2	77.2	85.1	87.4	82.9	82.4	83.2	81.3
Under $15,000	28.3	36.6	20.9	23.6	22.6	24.8	48.4	47.1	50.4
$15,000 to $24,999	12.0	6.7	10.8	12.4	15.7	13.8	13.2	10.5	16.6
$25,000 to $34,999	9.7	4.7	11.2	8.5	12.6	12.5	8.5	6.7	10.8
$35,000 to $49,999	9.6	2.6	13.6	13.4	11.3	10.3	3.8	4.3	2.0
$50,000 to $74,999	9.7	1.7	11.5	13.2	11.7	12.4	6.0	9.5	0.6
$75,000 or more	8.7	0.1	9.2	14.4	13.6	9.0	2.8	4.7	0.0

Note: Asians are those who identify themselves as being of the race alone and those who identify themselves as being of the race in combination with other races. "–" means sample is too small to make a reliable estimate.
Source: Bureau of the Census, 2011 Current Population Survey Annual Social and Economic Supplement, Internet site http://www.census.gov/hhes/www/cpstables/032011/perinc/toc.htm; calculations by New Strategist

Table 3.16 Women by Income and Age, 2010: Black Women

(number and percent distribution of black women aged 15 or older by income and age, 2010; median income of women with income and of women working full-time, year-round; percent working full-time, year-round; women in thousands as of 2011)

	total	15 to 24	25 to 34	35 to 44	45 to 54	55 to 64	65 or older total	65 to 74	75 or older
Total black women	**16,879**	**3,511**	**3,134**	**2,883**	**3,001**	**2,219**	**2,131**	**1,201**	**930**
Without income	2,948	1,641	336	326	307	235	103	65	38
With income	13,931	1,870	2,798	2,557	2,694	1,984	2,028	1,136	892
Under $5,000	1,507	610	287	151	210	137	112	43	69
$5,000 to $9,999	2,173	448	346	240	302	321	516	254	262
$10,000 to $14,999	1,965	276	314	255	295	257	568	297	271
$15,000 to $19,999	1,402	155	305	226	258	217	241	121	118
$20,000 to $24,999	1,274	108	343	250	280	157	135	85	50
$25,000 to $29,999	1,086	110	243	187	243	196	107	76	31
$30,000 to $34,999	925	49	199	280	174	130	92	63	30
$35,000 to $39,999	730	30	206	174	165	98	59	44	15
$40,000 to $44,999	612	21	169	134	158	97	33	23	10
$45,000 to $49,999	452	20	89	132	120	67	25	16	9
$50,000 to $54,999	416	12	87	109	115	66	28	24	4
$55,000 to $59,999	242	12	43	85	60	29	14	12	2
$60,000 to $64,999	248	3	19	104	67	37	17	11	5
$65,000 to $69,999	128	4	19	42	40	17	7	4	2
$70,000 to $74,999	144	3	26	15	46	23	31	26	5
$75,000 to $79,999	108	0	24	38	15	23	8	3	6
$80,000 to $84,999	111	0	16	33	40	17	4	4	0
$85,000 to $89,999	60	2	11	17	15	13	2	1	1
$90,000 to $94,999	65	0	16	10	18	13	8	8	0
$95,000 to $99,999	36	0	9	4	11	10	2	2	0
$100,000 or more	247	5	27	71	63	60	21	17	3
Median income									
Women with income	$19,634	$8,602	$21,718	$28,958	$25,036	$21,439	$13,145	$14,487	$11,854
Working full-time	33,918	22,278	31,813	36,862	36,490	35,216	35,368	36,046	–
Percent full-time	**35.7%**	**12.8%**	**45.4%**	**53.1%**	**51.8%**	**40.6%**	**8.1%**	**12.2%**	**2.8%**
PERCENT DISTRIBUTION									
Total black women	**100.0%**	**100.0%**	**100.0%**	**100.0%**	**100.0%**	**100.0%**	**100.0%**	**100.0%**	**100.0%**
Without income	17.5	46.7	10.7	11.3	10.2	10.6	4.8	5.4	4.1
With income	82.5	53.3	89.3	88.7	89.8	89.4	95.2	94.6	95.9
Under $15,000	33.4	38.0	30.2	22.4	26.9	32.2	56.1	49.5	64.7
$15,000 to $24,999	15.9	7.5	20.7	16.5	17.9	16.9	17.6	17.2	18.1
$25,000 to $34,999	11.9	4.5	14.1	16.2	13.9	14.7	9.3	11.6	6.6
$35,000 to $49,999	10.6	2.0	14.8	15.3	14.8	11.8	5.5	6.9	3.7
$50,000 to $74,999	7.0	1.0	6.2	12.3	10.9	7.8	4.6	6.4	1.9
$75,000 or more	3.7	0.2	3.3	6.0	5.4	6.1	2.1	2.9	1.1

Note: Blacks are those who identify themselves as being of the race alone and those who identify themselves as being of the race in combination with other races. "–" means sample is too small to make a reliable estimate.
Source: Bureau of the Census, 2011 Current Population Survey Annual Social and Economic Supplement, Internet site http:// www.census.gov/hhes/www/cpstables/032011/perinc/toc.htm; calculations by New Strategist

Table 3.17 Women by Income and Age, 2010: Hispanic Women

(number and percent distribution of Hispanic women aged 15 or older by income and age, 2010; median income of women with income and of women working full-time, year-round; percent working full-time, year-round; women in thousands as of 2011)

	total	15 to 24	25 to 34	35 to 44	45 to 54	55 to 64	65 or older total	65 to 74	75 or older
Total Hispanic women	**16,964**	**3,892**	**3,716**	**3,382**	**2,668**	**1,681**	**1,625**	**971**	**655**
Without income	4,842	1,968	977	814	523	349	212	125	87
With income	12,122	1,924	2,739	2,568	2,145	1,332	1,413	846	568
Under $5,000	1,654	600	322	249	190	155	138	105	32
$5,000 to $9,999	2,058	433	309	290	249	239	537	286	250
$10,000 to $14,999	1,901	328	375	344	314	221	318	153	165
$15,000 to $19,999	1,442	204	351	332	273	152	131	96	35
$20,000 to $24,999	1,165	154	315	258	246	118	74	42	32
$25,000 to $29,999	829	62	228	207	178	93	61	40	21
$30,000 to $34,999	713	52	221	200	148	63	29	20	9
$35,000 to $39,999	570	41	177	154	104	69	25	18	7
$40,000 to $44,999	410	23	112	137	81	41	16	16	1
$45,000 to $49,999	257	8	89	63	57	29	12	11	1
$50,000 to $54,999	270	10	68	79	71	29	14	12	2
$55,000 to $59,999	133	3	28	44	35	17	6	4	2
$60,000 to $64,999	154	0	36	46	45	18	9	8	1
$65,000 to $69,999	100	1	35	23	28	6	7	5	2
$70,000 to $74,999	68	0	10	20	13	16	8	6	2
$75,000 to $79,999	56	0	12	14	17	13	0	0	0
$80,000 to $84,999	59	0	12	18	12	10	8	6	2
$85,000 to $89,999	45	2	10	7	12	11	3	3	0
$90,000 to $94,999	33	0	6	12	10	3	1	0	1
$95,000 to $99,999	16	0	2	6	6	3	0	0	0
$100,000 or more	187	2	22	67	57	27	14	12	2
Median income									
Women with income	$16,269	$9,071	$20,140	$21,035	$20,744	$16,319	$10,438	$10,905	$10,008
Working full-time	28,944	20,922	29,401	30,860	29,769	29,298	31,557	32,016	–
Percent full-time	**30.5%**	**11.0%**	**38.3%**	**42.0%**	**45.5%**	**32.7%**	**8.1%**	**10.9%**	**4.1%**
PERCENT DISTRIBUTION									
Total Hispanic women	**100.0%**	**100.0%**	**100.0%**	**100.0%**	**100.0%**	**100.0%**	**100.0%**	**100.0%**	**100.0%**
Without income	28.5	50.6	26.3	24.1	19.6	20.8	13.0	12.9	13.3
With income	71.5	49.4	73.7	75.9	80.4	79.2	87.0	87.1	86.7
Under $15,000	33.1	35.0	27.1	26.1	28.2	36.6	61.1	56.0	68.2
$15,000 to $24,999	15.4	9.2	17.9	17.4	19.5	16.1	12.6	14.2	10.2
$25,000 to $34,999	9.1	2.9	12.1	12.0	12.2	9.3	5.5	6.2	4.6
$35,000 to $49,999	7.3	1.8	10.2	10.5	9.1	8.3	3.3	4.6	1.4
$50,000 to $74,999	4.3	0.4	4.8	6.3	7.2	5.1	2.7	3.6	1.4
$75,000 or more	2.3	0.1	1.7	3.7	4.3	4.0	1.6	2.2	0.8

Note: "–" means sample is too small to make a reliable estimate.
Source: Bureau of the Census, 2011 Current Population Survey Annual Social and Economic Supplement, Internet site http://www.census.gov/hhes/www/cpstables/032011/perinc/toc.htm; calculations by New Strategist

Table 3.18 Women by Income and Age, 2010: Non-Hispanic White Women

(number and percent distribution of non-Hispanic white women aged 15 or older by income and age, 2010; median income of women with income and of women working full-time, year-round; percent working full-time, year-round; women in thousands as of 2011)

	total	15 to 24	25 to 34	35 to 44	45 to 54	55 to 64	65 or older total	65 to 74	75 or older
Total non-Hispanic white women	**84,028**	**12,302**	**12,336**	**12,433**	**15,529**	**14,088**	**17,341**	**8,819**	**8,522**
Without income	9,663	4,263	1,337	1,238	1,387	1,018	421	244	178
With income	74,365	8,039	10,999	11,195	14,142	13,070	16,920	8,575	8,344
Under $5,000	8,605	2,693	1,186	1,255	1,454	1,336	680	387	294
$5,000 to $9,999	9,108	1,681	945	783	1,008	1,242	3,448	1,723	1,726
$10,000 to $14,999	9,217	1,163	903	859	1,158	1,386	3,749	1,627	2,121
$15,000 to $19,999	7,665	881	954	790	1,128	1,154	2,756	1,184	1,572
$20,000 to $24,999	5,946	531	885	912	1,174	953	1,490	716	774
$25,000 to $29,999	4,964	292	853	691	1,029	926	1,172	576	596
$30,000 to $34,999	4,551	221	1,002	817	956	873	683	351	332
$35,000 to $39,999	3,868	191	806	721	875	712	562	351	211
$40,000 to $44,999	3,505	106	759	660	874	685	422	265	157
$45,000 to $49,999	2,820	88	554	590	663	574	350	231	118
$50,000 to $54,999	2,638	51	483	575	631	607	290	212	77
$55,000 to $59,999	1,738	27	300	392	454	377	189	129	60
$60,000 to $64,999	1,728	30	306	378	418	401	195	147	48
$65,000 to $69,999	1,129	12	231	234	288	233	131	84	49
$70,000 to $74,999	1,172	16	199	287	264	270	135	108	28
$75,000 to $79,999	826	7	127	172	244	203	73	48	25
$80,000 to $84,999	717	18	111	162	194	161	71	53	17
$85,000 to $89,999	518	1	67	108	155	148	39	33	6
$90,000 to $94,999	462	0	35	103	134	123	66	44	22
$95,000 to $99,999	344	0	20	57	117	95	55	43	12
$100,000 or more	2,844	30	274	645	925	607	363	263	101
Median income									
Women with income	$21,754	$8,794	$28,377	$31,274	$30,450	$27,067	$15,895	$16,947	$15,085
Working full-time	41,307	22,263	38,255	44,890	42,334	44,968	49,176	50,248	43,998
Percent full-time	**34.6%**	**13.6%**	**49.6%**	**50.2%**	**52.2%**	**41.1%**	**6.5%**	**10.8%**	**2.1%**
PERCENT DISTRIBUTION									
Total non-Hispanic white women	**100.0%**	**100.0%**	**100.0%**	**100.0%**	**100.0%**	**100.0%**	**100.0%**	**100.0%**	**100.0%**
Without income	11.5	34.7	10.8	10.0	8.9	7.2	2.4	2.8	2.1
With income	88.5	65.3	89.2	90.0	91.1	92.8	97.6	97.2	97.9
Under $15,000	32.0	45.0	24.6	23.3	23.3	28.1	45.4	42.4	48.6
$15,000 to $24,999	16.2	11.5	14.9	13.7	14.8	15.0	24.5	21.5	27.5
$25,000 to $34,999	11.3	4.2	15.0	12.1	12.8	12.8	10.7	10.5	10.9
$35,000 to $49,999	12.1	3.1	17.2	15.9	15.5	14.0	7.7	9.6	5.7
$50,000 to $74,999	10.0	1.1	12.3	15.0	13.2	13.4	5.4	7.7	3.1
$75,000 or more	6.8	0.5	5.1	10.0	11.4	9.5	3.8	5.5	2.1

Note: Non-Hispanic whites are those who identify themselves as being white alone and not Hispanic.
Source: Bureau of the Census, 2011 Current Population Survey Annual Social and Economic Supplement, Internet site http://www.census.gov/hhes/www/cpstables/032011/perinc/toc.htm; calculations by New Strategist

Table 3.19 Women by Income, Race, and Hispanic Origin, 2010

(number and percent distribution of women aged 15 or older by income, race, and Hispanic origin, 2010; median income of women with income and of women working full-time, year-round; percent working full-time, year-round; women in thousands as of 2011)

	total	Asian	black	Hispanic	non-Hispanic white
Total women	**125,084**	**6,460**	**16,879**	**16,964**	**84,028**
Without income	18,942	1,413	2,948	4,842	9,663
With income	106,142	5,047	13,931	12,122	74,365
Under $5,000	12,538	694	1,507	1,654	8,605
$5,000 to $9,999	14,061	617	2,173	2,058	9,108
$10,000 to $14,999	13,672	518	1,965	1,901	9,217
$15,000 to $19,999	10,971	397	1,402	1,442	7,665
$20,000 to $24,999	8,842	380	1,274	1,165	5,946
$25,000 to $29,999	7,228	293	1,086	829	4,964
$30,000 to $34,999	6,582	333	925	713	4,551
$35,000 to $39,999	5,443	229	730	570	3,868
$40,000 to $44,999	4,778	250	612	410	3,505
$45,000 to $49,999	3,701	144	452	257	2,820
$50,000 to $54,999	3,527	188	416	270	2,638
$55,000 to $59,999	2,239	113	242	133	1,738
$60,000 to $64,999	2,276	146	248	154	1,728
$65,000 to $69,999	1,464	89	128	100	1,129
$70,000 to $74,999	1,492	92	144	68	1,172
$75,000 to $79,999	1,060	68	108	56	826
$80,000 to $84,999	971	76	111	59	717
$85,000 to $89,999	669	42	60	45	518
$90,000 to $94,999	619	58	65	33	462
$95,000 to $99,999	425	20	36	16	344
$100,000 or more	3,584	297	247	187	2,844
Median income					
Women with income	$20,831	$23,664	$19,634	$16,269	$21,754
Working full-time	38,531	41,821	33,918	28,944	41,307
Percent full-time	**34.2%**	**36.6%**	**35.7%**	**30.5%**	**34.6%**
PERCENT DISTRIBUTION					
Total women	**100.0%**	**100.0%**	**100.0%**	**100.0%**	**100.0%**
Without income	15.1	21.9	17.5	28.5	11.5
With income	84.9	78.1	82.5	71.5	88.5
Under $15,000	32.2	28.3	33.4	33.1	32.0
$15,000 to $24,999	15.8	12.0	15.9	15.4	16.2
$25,000 to $34,999	11.0	9.7	11.9	9.1	11.3
$35,000 to $49,999	11.1	9.6	10.6	7.3	12.1
$50,000 to $74,999	8.8	9.7	7.0	4.3	10.0
$75,000 or more	5.9	8.7	3.7	2.3	6.8

Note: Asians and blacks are those who identify themselves as being of the race alone and those who identify themselves as being of the race in combination with other races. Non-Hispanic whites are those who identify themselves as white alone and not Hispanic. Numbers do not add to total because some people identify themselves as being of more than one race, not all races are shown, and Hispanics may be of any race.
Source: Bureau of the Census, 2011 Current Population Survey Annual Social and Economic Supplement, Internet site http:// www.census.gov/hhes/www/cpstables/032011/perinc/toc.htm; calculations by New Strategist

Among Women Who Work Full-Time, Incomes Are Highest in the Northeast

Those in the South have the lowest incomes.

The median income of all women aged 15 or older does not vary much by geographical region, rounding to $21,000 in every region in 2010. Among full-time workers, median income ranges from a low of $36,400 in the South to a high of $42,277 in the Northeast. By region, the percentage of women who work full-time ranges from 32 to 36 percent.

Women's income patterns differ by race and Hispanic origin. Among Asian women who work full-time, median income is highest in the Northeast at $45,228. Among black women who work full-time, median income peaks in the West at $39,981. For Hispanic women with full-time jobs, median income is much lower, ranging from $27,384 in the Midwest to a peak of $31,112 in the Northeast. Non-Hispanic white women who work full-time in the Northeast and West have higher incomes than their Asian counterparts. Their median income peaks in the Northeast at $45,798. Non-Hispanic white women's median income is lowest in the Midwest, at $38,681.

■ The incomes of Hispanic women will not match those of Asian, non-Hispanic white, or black women until poorly educated immigrants become a smaller share of the Hispanic population.

Women's median income tops $40,000 in the Northeast and West

(median income of women aged 15 or older who work full-time, year-round, by region, 2010)

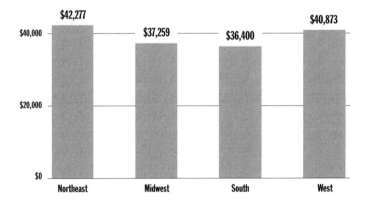

Table 3.20 Women by Income and Region, 2010: Total Women

(number and percent distribution of women aged 15 or older by income and region, 2010; median income of women with income and of women working full-time, year-round; percent working full-time, year-round; women in thousands as of 2011)

	total	Northest	Midwest	South	West
Total women	**125,084**	**23,170**	**27,168**	**46,229**	**28,517**
Without income	18,942	3,162	3,338	7,622	4,820
With income	106,142	20,008	23,830	38,607	23,697
Under $5,000	12,538	2,336	2,781	4,339	3,083
$5,000 to $9,999	14,061	2,612	2,998	5,408	3,044
$10,000 to $14,999	13,672	2,527	3,129	5,030	2,986
$15,000 to $19,999	10,971	1,937	2,609	4,071	2,356
$20,000 to $24,999	8,842	1,520	2,122	3,247	1,953
$25,000 to $29,999	7,228	1,228	1,712	2,818	1,471
$30,000 to $34,999	6,582	1,252	1,492	2,416	1,420
$35,000 to $39,999	5,443	970	1,348	2,048	1,077
$40,000 to $44,999	4,778	867	1,074	1,777	1,060
$45,000 to $49,999	3,701	655	840	1,417	787
$50,000 to $54,999	3,527	738	808	1,202	779
$55,000 to $59,999	2,239	453	510	782	494
$60,000 to $64,999	2,276	532	492	728	524
$65,000 to $69,999	1,464	366	281	446	371
$70,000 to $74,999	1,492	322	339	502	329
$75,000 to $79,999	1,060	250	205	352	252
$80,000 to $84,999	971	187	216	308	258
$85,000 to $89,999	669	158	105	214	192
$90,000 to $94,999	619	139	109	197	173
$95,000 to $99,999	425	109	84	130	102
$100,000 or more	3,584	849	577	1,171	987
Median income					
Women with income	$20,831	$21,498	$20,777	$20,547	$20,835
Working full-time	38,531	42,277	37,259	36,400	40,873
Percent full-time	**34.2%**	**34.1%**	**34.5%**	**35.7%**	**31.7%**
PERCENT DISTRIBUTION					
Total women	**100.0%**	**100.0%**	**100.0%**	**100.0%**	**100.0%**
Without income	15.1	13.6	12.3	16.5	16.9
With income	84.9	86.4	87.7	83.5	83.1
Under $15,000	32.2	32.3	32.8	32.0	32.0
$15,000 to $24,999	15.8	14.9	17.4	15.8	15.1
$25,000 to $34,999	11.0	10.7	11.8	11.3	10.1
$35,000 to $49,999	11.1	10.8	12.0	11.3	10.3
$50,000 to $74,999	8.8	10.4	8.9	7.9	8.8
$75,000 or more	5.9	7.3	4.8	5.1	6.9

Source: Bureau of the Census, 2011 Current Population Survey Annual Social and Economic Supplement, Internet site http://www.census.gov/hhes/www/cpstables/032011/perinc/toc.htm; calculations by New Strategist

Table 3.21 Women by Income and Region, 2010: Asian Women

(number and percent distribution of Asian women aged 15 or older by income and region, 2010; median income of women with income and of women working full-time, year-round; percent working full-time, year-round; women in thousands as of 2011)

	total	Northeast	Midwest	South	West
Total Asian women	**6,460**	**1,303**	**719**	**1,385**	**3,053**
Without income	1,413	366	148	353	547
With income	5,047	937	571	1,032	2,506
Under $5,000	694	127	86	152	329
$5,000 to $9,999	617	121	81	132	283
$10,000 to $14,999	518	85	58	82	292
$15,000 to $19,999	397	78	49	72	198
$20,000 to $24,999	380	73	51	68	188
$25,000 to $29,999	293	49	29	70	145
$30,000 to $34,999	333	65	23	82	163
$35,000 to $39,999	229	43	36	49	102
$40,000 to $44,999	250	40	21	49	141
$45,000 to $49,999	144	28	12	30	76
$50,000 to $54,999	188	33	18	38	100
$55,000 to $59,999	113	25	11	17	60
$60,000 to $64,999	146	32	24	23	67
$65,000 to $69,999	89	14	16	14	47
$70,000 to $74,999	92	10	17	20	45
$75,000 to $79,999	68	13	3	14	38
$80,000 to $84,999	76	17	13	10	36
$85,000 to $89,999	42	5	1	11	25
$90,000 to $94,999	58	10	7	21	20
$95,000 to $99,999	20	0	3	12	7
$100,000 or more	297	66	16	68	147
Median income					
Women with income	$23,664	$22,645	$21,030	$25,558	$23,918
Working full-time	41,821	45,228	40,188	40,545	42,090
Percent full-time	**36.6%**	**31.3%**	**36.7%**	**39.6%**	**37.4%**
PERCENT DISTRIBUTION					
Total Asian women	**100.0%**	**100.0%**	**100.0%**	**100.0%**	**100.0%**
Without income	21.9	28.1	20.6	25.5	17.9
With income	78.1	71.9	79.4	74.5	82.1
Under $15,000	28.3	25.6	31.3	26.4	29.6
$15,000 to $24,999	12.0	11.6	13.9	10.1	12.6
$25,000 to $34,999	9.7	8.7	7.2	11.0	10.1
$35,000 to $49,999	9.6	8.5	9.6	9.2	10.4
$50,000 to $74,999	9.7	8.7	12.0	8.1	10.4
$75,000 or more	8.7	8.5	6.0	9.8	8.9

Note: Asians are those who identify themselves as being of the race alone and those who identify themselves as being of the race in combination with other races.
Source: Bureau of the Census, 2011 Current Population Survey Annual Social and Economic Supplement, Internet site http://www.census.gov/hhes/www/cpstables/032011/perinc/toc.htm; calculations by New Strategist

Table 3.22 Women by Income and Region, 2010: Black Women

(number and percent distribution of black women aged 15 or older by income and region, 2010; median income of women with income and of women working full-time, year-round; percent working full-time, year-round; women in thousands as of 2011)

	total	Northeast	Midwest	South	West
Total black women	**16,879**	**3,015**	**2,898**	**9,406**	**1,560**
Without income	2,948	583	531	1,516	318
With income	13,931	2,432	2,367	7,890	1,242
Under $5,000	1,507	242	285	837	143
$5,000 to $9,999	2,173	404	369	1,233	165
$10,000 to $14,999	1,965	332	358	1,097	176
$15,000 to $19,999	1,402	196	233	840	134
$20,000 to $24,999	1,274	194	220	764	97
$25,000 to $29,999	1,086	164	198	626	98
$30,000 to $34,999	925	172	163	511	78
$35,000 to $39,999	730	133	133	407	58
$40,000 to $44,999	612	102	87	348	74
$45,000 to $49,999	452	93	54	260	44
$50,000 to $54,999	416	90	76	230	21
$55,000 to $59,999	242	55	41	124	23
$60,000 to $64,999	248	53	39	133	22
$65,000 to $69,999	128	36	19	59	15
$70,000 to $74,999	144	28	24	70	22
$75,000 to $79,999	108	24	13	67	3
$80,000 to $84,999	111	22	14	59	16
$85,000 to $89,999	60	14	3	43	0
$90,000 to $94,999	65	16	8	26	15
$95,000 to $99,999	36	7	7	16	6
$100,000 or more	247	53	24	137	32
Median income					
Women with income	$19,634	$20,863	$18,550	$19,499	$20,120
Working full-time	33,918	37,043	32,212	32,340	39,981
Percent full-time	**35.7%**	**35.4%**	**31.5%**	**37.9%**	**31.1%**
PERCENT DISTRIBUTION					
Total black women	**100.0%**	**100.0%**	**100.0%**	**100.0%**	**100.0%**
Without income	17.5	19.3	18.3	16.1	20.4
With income	82.5	80.7	81.7	83.9	79.6
Under $15,000	33.4	32.4	34.9	33.7	31.0
$15,000 to $24,999	15.9	12.9	15.6	17.1	14.8
$25,000 to $34,999	11.9	11.1	12.5	12.1	11.3
$35,000 to $49,999	10.6	10.9	9.5	10.8	11.3
$50,000 to $74,999	7.0	8.7	6.9	6.5	6.6
$75,000 or more	3.7	4.5	2.4	3.7	4.6

Note: Blacks are those who identify themselves as being of the race alone and those who identify themselves as being of the race in combination with other races.
Source: Bureau of the Census, 2011 Current Population Survey Annual Social and Economic Supplement, Internet site http:// www.census.gov/hhes/www/cpstables/032011/perinc/toc.htm; calculations by New Strategist

Table 3.23 Women by Income and Region, 2010: Hispanic Women

(number and percent distribution of Hispanic women aged 15 or older by income and region, 2010; median income of women with income and of women working full-time, year-round; percent working full-time, year-round; women in thousands as of 2011)

	total	Northeast	Midwest	South	West
Total Hispanic women	**16,964**	**2,530**	**1,285**	**6,177**	**6,972**
Without income	4,842	574	389	1,799	2,080
With income	12,122	1,956	896	4,378	4,892
Under $5,000	1,654	280	143	520	712
$5,000 to $9,999	2,058	355	139	771	794
$10,000 to $14,999	1,901	299	136	670	796
$15,000 to $19,999	1,442	205	119	528	590
$20,000 to $24,999	1,165	159	88	438	480
$25,000 to $29,999	829	102	67	343	318
$30,000 to $34,999	713	127	51	238	298
$35,000 to $39,999	570	90	42	244	194
$40,000 to $44,999	410	88	24	148	151
$45,000 to $49,999	257	37	14	101	105
$50,000 to $54,999	270	52	23	92	103
$55,000 to $59,999	133	27	10	43	54
$60,000 to $64,999	154	25	5	48	75
$65,000 to $69,999	100	15	6	34	44
$70,000 to $74,999	68	17	3	28	19
$75,000 to $79,999	56	3	2	19	32
$80,000 to $84,999	59	9	3	21	26
$85,000 to $89,999	45	14	4	17	11
$90,000 to $94,999	33	8	3	11	11
$95,000 to $99,999	16	0	2	4	11
$100,000 or more	187	44	13	60	70
Median income					
Women with income	$16,269	$15,899	$16,054	$16,653	$16,058
Working full-time	28,944	31,112	27,384	27,418	29,402
Percent full-time	**30.5%**	**33.4%**	**28.7%**	**32.7%**	**27.8%**
PERCENT DISTRIBUTION					
Total Hispanic women	**100.0%**	**100.0%**	**100.0%**	**100.0%**	**100.0%**
Without income	28.5	22.7	30.3	29.1	29.8
With income	71.5	77.3	69.7	70.9	70.2
Under $15,000	33.1	36.9	32.5	31.7	33.0
$15,000 to $24,999	15.4	14.4	16.1	15.6	15.3
$25,000 to $34,999	9.1	9.1	9.2	9.4	8.8
$35,000 to $49,999	7.3	8.5	6.2	8.0	6.5
$50,000 to $74,999	4.3	5.4	3.7	4.0	4.2
$75,000 or more	2.3	3.1	2.1	2.1	2.3

Source: Bureau of the Census, 2011 Current Population Survey Annual Social and Economic Supplement, Internet site http:// www.census.gov/hhes/www/cpstables/032011/perinc/toc.htm; calculations by New Strategist

Table 3.24 Women by Income and Region, 2010: Non-Hispanic White Women

(number and percent distribution of non-Hispanic white women aged 15 or older by income and region, 2010; median income of women with income and of women working full-time, year-round; percent working full-time, year-round; women in thousands as of 2011)

	total	Northeast	Midwest	South	West
Total non-Hispanic white women	**84,028**	**16,568**	**22,064**	**28,962**	**16,436**
Without income	9,663	1,716	2,248	3,904	1,797
With income	74,365	14,852	19,816	25,058	14,639
Under $5,000	8,605	1,704	2,242	2,812	1,847
$5,000 to $9,999	9,108	1,776	2,377	3,232	1,724
$10,000 to $14,999	9,217	1,842	2,555	3,166	1,655
$15,000 to $19,999	7,665	1,473	2,198	2,598	1,397
$20,000 to $24,999	5,946	1,099	1,746	1,950	1,152
$25,000 to $29,999	4,964	925	1,399	1,753	888
$30,000 to $34,999	4,551	889	1,246	1,563	854
$35,000 to $39,999	3,868	705	1,126	1,334	703
$40,000 to $44,999	3,505	659	939	1,226	682
$45,000 to $49,999	2,820	497	753	1,009	562
$50,000 to $54,999	2,638	570	685	839	544
$55,000 to $59,999	1,738	354	446	594	343
$60,000 to $64,999	1,728	423	422	524	357
$65,000 to $69,999	1,129	302	237	332	259
$70,000 to $74,999	1,172	265	291	380	237
$75,000 to $79,999	826	210	187	246	182
$80,000 to $84,999	717	138	186	220	174
$85,000 to $89,999	518	127	96	143	153
$90,000 to $94,999	462	105	91	140	126
$95,000 to $99,999	344	102	72	95	75
$100,000 or more	2,844	691	523	904	726
Median income					
Women with income	$21,754	$22,219	$21,241	$21,475	$22,633
Working full-time	41,307	45,798	38,681	40,094	45,608
Percent full-time	**34.6%**	**34.2%**	**35.2%**	**35.5%**	**32.5%**
PERCENT DISTRIBUTION					
Total non-Hispanic white women	**100.0%**	**100.0%**	**100.0%**	**100.0%**	**100.0%**
Without income	11.5	10.4	10.2	13.5	10.9
With income	88.5	89.6	89.8	86.5	89.1
Under $15,000	32.0	32.1	32.5	31.8	31.8
$15,000 to $24,999	16.2	15.5	17.9	15.7	15.5
$25,000 to $34,999	11.3	10.9	12.0	11.4	10.6
$35,000 to $49,999	12.1	11.2	12.8	12.3	11.8
$50,000 to $74,999	10.0	11.6	9.4	9.2	10.6
$75,000 or more	6.8	8.3	5.2	6.0	8.7

Note: Non-Hispanic whites are those who identify themselves as being white alone and not Hispanic.
Source: Bureau of the Census, 2011 Current Population Survey Annual Social and Economic Supplement, Internet site http://www.census.gov/hhes/www/cpstables/032011/perinc/toc.htm; calculations by New Strategist

Women in Nonmetropolitan Areas Have Lower Incomes

Those residing in metropolitan areas have higher incomes.

Women living in nonmetropolitan areas—the countryside and small towns of America—have the lowest incomes. The median income of women in nonmetropolitan areas who work full-time stood at $31,879 in 2010. The $40,466 median income of their counterparts living in the suburbs of the nation's metropolitan areas (outside principal cities) is 27 percent higher. Among women with full-time jobs who live in the principal cities of metropolitan areas, median income is only slightly lower at $40,044.

The proportion of women who work full-time varies somewhat by metropolitan status. Among women living in nonmetropolitan areas, only 32 percent have full-time jobs. Among women living in the principal cities or suburbs of metropolitan areas, 35 percent work full-time.

■ The nation's metropolitan areas attract the best-educated and most-career-oriented women, which is one reason why women residing there have higher incomes.

Women in the suburbs have the highest incomes

(median income of women aged 15 or older who work full-time, year-round, by metropolitan residence, 2010)

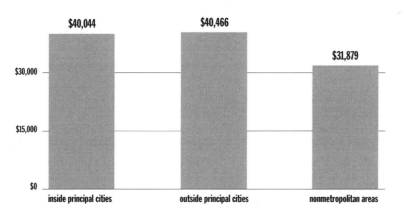

Table 3.25 Women by Income and Metropolitan Residence, 2010

(number and percent distribution of women aged 15 or older by income and metropolitan residence, 2010; median income of women with income and of women working full-time, year-round; percent working full-time, year-round; women in thousands as of 2011)

		in metropolitan area			
			inside principal cities	outside principal cities	not in metropolitan area
	total	total			
Total women	**125,084**	**105,255**	**40,421**	**64,834**	**19,829**
Without income	18,942	16,197	6,725	9,472	2,745
With income	106,142	89,058	33,696	55,362	17,084
Under $5,000	12,538	10,639	3,908	6,731	1,900
$5,000 to $9,999	14,061	11,268	4,448	6,819	2,794
$10,000 to $14,999	13,672	11,058	4,276	6,781	2,615
$15,000 to $19,999	10,971	8,896	3,269	5,627	2,076
$20,000 to $24,999	8,842	7,201	2,805	4,396	1,640
$25,000 to $29,999	7,228	5,967	2,264	3,703	1,261
$30,000 to $34,999	6,582	5,510	2,023	3,487	1,072
$35,000 to $39,999	5,443	4,610	1,730	2,880	833
$40,000 to $44,999	4,778	4,152	1,583	2,569	626
$45,000 to $49,999	3,701	3,190	1,148	2,042	511
$50,000 to $54,999	3,527	3,054	1,109	1,944	474
$55,000 to $59,999	2,239	1,970	721	1,247	270
$60,000 to $64,999	2,276	2,053	808	1,246	222
$65,000 to $69,999	1,464	1,320	514	806	144
$70,000 to $74,999	1,492	1,358	493	865	133
$75,000 to $79,999	1,060	965	351	614	95
$80,000 to $84,999	971	894	345	548	77
$85,000 to $89,999	669	620	227	392	50
$90,000 to $94,999	619	582	205	377	36
$95,000 to $99,999	425	394	136	259	31
$100,000 or more	3,584	3,359	1,331	2,027	225
Median income					
Women with income	$20,831	$21,494	$21,360	$21,580	$17,512
Working full-time	38,531	40,297	40,044	40,466	31,879
Percent full-time	**34.2%**	**34.7%**	**34.9%**	**34.6%**	**31.8%**
PERCENT DISTRIBUTION					
Total women	**100.0%**	**100.0%**	**100.0%**	**100.0%**	**100.0%**
Without income	15.1	15.4	16.6	14.6	13.8
With income	84.9	84.6	83.4	85.4	86.2
Under $15,000	32.2	31.3	31.3	31.4	36.9
$15,000 to $24,999	15.8	15.3	15.0	15.5	18.7
$25,000 to $34,999	11.0	10.9	10.6	11.1	11.8
$35,000 to $49,999	11.1	11.4	11.0	11.6	9.9
$50,000 to $74,999	8.8	9.3	9.0	9.4	6.3
$75,000 or more	5.9	6.5	6.4	6.5	2.6

Source: Bureau of the Census, 2011 Current Population Survey Annual Social and Economic Supplement, Internet site http://www.census.gov/hhes/www/cpstables/032011/perinc/toc.htm; calculations by New Strategist

Women Earn Little from Part-Time Work

Because women's earnings are increasingly important to their families, most women workers have full-time jobs.

Among the nation's nearly 72 million women with earnings in 2010, nearly 43 million worked full-time, year-round. The median earnings of full-time, year-round workers stood at $36,931—39 percent higher than the $26,552 median earnings of all women. The 21 million women with part-time jobs earned a median of just $9,813.

Among Asian women who work full-time, year-round, median earnings stood at $41,172 in 2010. Non-Hispanic white women who worked full-time, year-round had a lower median of $40,270. The median earnings of black women who work full-time, year-round were $32,273. The earnings of Hispanic women who work full-time, year-round were the lowest at $27,992. Among women with earnings, the proportion who work full time ranges from a low of 57 percent among Hispanics to a high of 64 percent among Asians.

■ Among working women, most have full-time jobs because part-time work pays little and offers few benefits.

Among women who work full-time, Asians have the highest median earnings

(median earnings of women aged 15 or older who work full-time, year-round, by race and Hispanic origin, 2010)

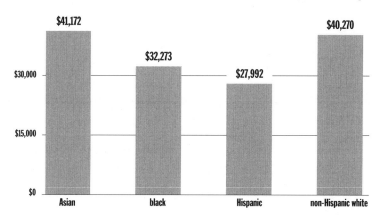

Table 3.26 Women by Earnings and Employment Status, 2010: Total Women

(number and percent distribution of women aged 15 or older with earnings by employment status and median earnings, 2010; women in thousands as of 2011)

	total	worked full-time		worked part-time	
		total	year-round	total	year-round
Total women with earnings	**72,118**	**51,546**	**42,834**	**20,572**	**11,215**
Under $5,000	7,909	1,897	284	6,010	1,130
$5,000 to $9,999	6,261	1,844	556	4,417	2,327
$10,000 to $14,999	6,783	3,172	2,059	3,611	2,497
$15,000 to $19,999	6,537	4,409	3,456	2,128	1,600
$20,000 to $24,999	6,291	5,084	4,369	1,207	1,003
$25,000 to $29,999	5,458	4,602	4,082	856	684
$30,000 to $34,999	5,689	5,071	4,525	618	484
$35,000 to $39,999	4,577	4,154	3,756	423	356
$40,000 to $44,999	4,075	3,835	3,520	240	205
$45,000 to $49,999	3,203	2,984	2,750	220	201
$50,000 to $54,999	3,180	2,971	2,742	210	191
$55,000 to $59,999	1,812	1,695	1,573	117	102
$60,000 to $64,999	1,897	1,791	1,622	105	83
$65,000 to $69,999	1,221	1,162	1,065	59	49
$70,000 to $74,999	1,269	1,211	1,130	58	54
$75,000 to $79,999	925	898	836	28	24
$80,000 to $84,999	880	820	773	60	51
$85,000 to $89,999	497	482	452	14	9
$90,000 to $94,999	534	506	475	28	24
$95,000 to $99,999	308	303	293	6	4
$100,000 or more	2,816	2,656	2,517	159	137
Median earnings	$26,552	$34,379	$36,931	$9,813	$13,817

PERCENT DISTRIBUTION

Total women with earnings	**100.0%**	**100.0%**	**100.0%**	**100.0%**	**100.0%**
Under $15,000	29.1	13.4	6.8	68.2	53.1
$15,000 to $24,999	17.8	18.4	18.3	16.2	23.2
$25,000 to $34,999	15.5	18.8	20.1	7.2	10.4
$35,000 to $49,999	16.4	21.3	23.4	4.3	6.8
$50,000 to $74,999	13.0	17.1	19.0	2.7	4.3
$75,000 or more	8.3	11.0	12.5	1.4	2.2

Note: Earnings include wages and salary only.
Source: Bureau of the Census, 2011 Current Population Survey Annual Social and Economic Supplement, Internet site http://www.census.gov/hhes/www/cpstables/032011/perinc/toc.htm; calculations by New Strategist

Table 3.27 Women by Earnings and Employment Status, 2010: Asian Women

(number and percent distribution of Asian women aged 15 or older with earnings by employment status and median earnings, 2010; women in thousands as of 2011)

	total	worked full-time		worked part-time	
		total	year-round	total	year-round
Asian women with earnings	**3,686**	**2,778**	**2,359**	**909**	**521**
Under $5,000	309	87	16	222	36
$5,000 to $9,999	303	80	26	223	127
$10,000 to $14,999	290	143	100	148	100
$15,000 to $19,999	289	194	139	95	78
$20,000 to $24,999	308	261	217	47	41
$25,000 to $29,999	245	213	191	31	25
$30,000 to $34,999	302	256	232	47	32
$35,000 to $39,999	212	200	179	12	11
$40,000 to $44,999	222	211	198	11	8
$45,000 to $49,999	138	126	114	13	13
$50,000 to $54,999	180	168	151	12	10
$55,000 to $59,999	85	78	74	7	7
$60,000 to $64,999	129	125	121	4	4
$65,000 to $69,999	81	74	66	6	5
$70,000 to $74,999	90	86	81	5	3
$75,000 to $79,999	56	56	54	0	0
$80,000 to $84,999	61	59	54	2	2
$85,000 to $89,999	33	33	32	0	0
$90,000 to $94,999	69	66	65	3	0
$95,000 to $99,999	19	18	17	1	1
$100,000 or more	270	250	236	20	20
Median earnings	$31,121	$37,988	$41,172	$10,202	$14,894

PERCENT DISTRIBUTION

	total	total	year-round	total	year-round
Asian women with earnings	**100.0%**	**100.0%**	**100.0%**	**100.0%**	**100.0%**
Under $15,000	24.5	11.2	6.0	65.2	50.5
$15,000 to $24,999	16.2	16.4	15.1	15.6	22.8
$25,000 to $34,999	14.8	16.9	17.9	8.6	10.9
$35,000 to $49,999	15.5	19.3	20.8	4.0	6.1
$50,000 to $74,999	15.3	19.1	20.9	3.7	5.6
$75,000 or more	13.8	17.4	19.4	2.9	4.4

Note: Asians are those who identify themselves as being of the race alone and those who identify themselves as being of the race in combination with other races. Earnings include wages and salary only.
Source: Bureau of the Census, 2011 Current Population Survey Annual Social and Economic Supplement, Internet site http:// www.census.gov/hhes/www/cpstables/032011/perinc/toc.htm; calculations by New Strategist

Table 3.28 Women by Earnings and Employment Status, 2010: Black Women

(number and percent distribution of black women aged 15 or older with earnings by employment status and median earnings, 2010; women in thousands as of 2011)

	total	worked full-time		worked part-time	
		total	year-round	total	year-round
Black women with earnings	**9,549**	**7,398**	**6,030**	**2,151**	**1,083**
Under $5,000	1,055	329	27	726	111
$5,000 to $9,999	806	296	91	510	275
$10,000 to $14,999	887	508	313	379	268
$15,000 to $19,999	987	768	611	219	180
$20,000 to $24,999	967	877	758	90	76
$25,000 to $29,999	886	817	727	69	54
$30,000 to $34,999	834	781	677	54	36
$35,000 to $39,999	622	598	549	25	15
$40,000 to $44,999	524	505	470	21	19
$45,000 to $49,999	434	418	407	17	17
$50,000 to $54,999	382	373	345	9	9
$55,000 to $59,999	194	191	178	3	3
$60,000 to $64,999	215	209	190	7	5
$65,000 to $69,999	99	98	93	1	1
$70,000 to $74,999	124	120	119	4	2
$75,000 to $79,999	100	98	86	2	0
$80,000 to $84,999	111	103	93	8	4
$85,000 to $89,999	42	42	37	0	0
$90,000 to $94,999	47	43	41	4	4
$95,000 to $99,999	31	31	31	0	0
$100,000 or more	199	196	186	3	3
Median earnings	$25,308	$30,431	$32,273	$8,357	$12,075

PERCENT DISTRIBUTION

	total	total	year-round	total	year-round
Black women with earnings	**100.0%**	**100.0%**	**100.0%**	**100.0%**	**100.0%**
Under $15,000	28.8	15.3	7.1	75.1	60.4
$15,000 to $24,999	20.5	22.2	22.7	14.4	23.6
$25,000 to $34,999	18.0	21.6	23.3	5.7	8.3
$35,000 to $49,999	16.5	20.6	23.6	2.9	4.7
$50,000 to $74,999	10.6	13.4	15.3	1.1	1.8
$75,000 or more	5.6	6.9	7.9	0.8	1.0

Note: Blacks are those who identify themselves as being of the race alone and those who identify themselves as being of the race in combination with other races. Earnings include wages and salary only.
Source: Bureau of the Census, 2011 Current Population Survey Annual Social and Economic Supplement, Internet site http:// www.census.gov/hhes/www/cpstables/032011/perinc/toc.htm; calculations by New Strategist

Table 3.29 Women by Earnings and Employment Status, 2010: Hispanic Women

(number and percent distribution of Hispanic women aged 15 or older with earnings by employment status and median earnings, 2010; women in thousands as of 2011)

	total	worked full-time		worked part-time	
		total	year-round	total	year-round
Hispanic women with earnings	**9,029**	**6,482**	**5,169**	**2,547**	**1,420**
Under $5,000	983	274	23	709	141
$5,000 to $9,999	1,028	366	96	662	366
$10,000 to $14,999	1,281	740	512	542	411
$15,000 to $19,999	1,179	894	744	284	214
$20,000 to $24,999	1,023	873	757	151	120
$25,000 to $29,999	745	666	603	79	69
$30,000 to $34,999	692	659	595	31	25
$35,000 to $39,999	521	489	451	33	25
$40,000 to $44,999	372	357	319	14	11
$45,000 to $49,999	218	207	181	11	11
$50,000 to $54,999	247	239	215	8	8
$55,000 to $59,999	119	118	113	0	0
$60,000 to $64,999	141	137	126	4	2
$65,000 to $69,999	77	73	67	4	2
$70,000 to $74,999	71	68	65	3	3
$75,000 to $79,999	50	49	47	1	1
$80,000 to $84,999	53	51	47	2	2
$85,000 to $89,999	34	32	29	1	1
$90,000 to $94,999	28	28	27	0	0
$95,000 to $99,999	20	18	18	1	0
$100,000 or more	149	142	131	7	7
Median earnings	$20,160	$25,518	$27,992	$9,172	$11,733

PERCENT DISTRIBUTION

	total	total	year-round	total	year-round
Hispanic women with earnings	**100.0%**	**100.0%**	**100.0%**	**100.0%**	**100.0%**
Under $15,000	36.5	21.3	12.2	75.1	64.6
$15,000 to $24,999	24.4	27.3	29.0	17.1	23.5
$25,000 to $34,999	15.9	20.4	23.2	4.3	6.6
$35,000 to $49,999	12.3	16.2	18.4	2.3	3.3
$50,000 to $74,999	7.3	9.8	11.3	0.7	1.1
$75,000 or more	3.7	4.9	5.8	0.5	0.8

Note: Earnings include wages and salary only.
Source: Bureau of the Census, 2011 Current Population Survey Annual Social and Economic Supplement, Internet site http://www.census.gov/hhes/www/cpstables/032011/perinc/toc.htm; calculations by New Strategist

Table 3.30 Women by Earnings and Employment Status, 2010: Non-Hispanic White Women

(number and percent distribution of non-Hispanic white women aged 15 or older with earnings by employment status, 2010; women in thousands as of 2011)

	total	worked full-time		worked part-time	
		total	year-round	total	year-round
Non-Hispanic white women with earnings	**49,420**	**34,599**	**29,048**	**14,820**	**8,124**
Under $5,000	5,501	1,183	217	4,318	844
$5,000 to $9,999	4,090	1,088	346	3,002	1,549
$10,000 to $14,999	4,286	1,776	1,130	2,512	1,702
$15,000 to $19,999	4,056	2,532	1,941	1,524	1,128
$20,000 to $24,999	3,926	3,020	2,595	906	755
$25,000 to $29,999	3,570	2,899	2,556	671	532
$30,000 to $34,999	3,817	3,343	2,993	474	380
$35,000 to $39,999	3,176	2,827	2,536	349	300
$40,000 to $44,999	2,962	2,769	2,545	193	167
$45,000 to $49,999	2,383	2,207	2,024	176	158
$50,000 to $54,999	2,360	2,182	2,018	179	162
$55,000 to $59,999	1,395	1,293	1,194	101	90
$60,000 to $64,999	1,410	1,319	1,185	90	73
$65,000 to $69,999	952	904	827	48	40
$70,000 to $74,999	971	925	855	46	46
$75,000 to $79,999	719	695	648	24	23
$80,000 to $84,999	647	601	570	46	41
$85,000 to $89,999	384	372	350	13	8
$90,000 to $94,999	388	367	339	21	20
$95,000 to $99,999	235	231	223	3	2
$100,000 or more	2,192	2,066	1,961	127	104
Median earnings	$28,464	$36,824	$40,270	$10,129	$14,837

PERCENT DISTRIBUTION

	total	worked full-time		worked part-time	
Non-Hispanic white women with earnings	**100.0%**	**100.0%**	**100.0%**	**100.0%**	**100.0%**
Under $15,000	28.1	11.7	5.8	66.3	50.4
$15,000 to $24,999	16.2	16.0	15.6	16.4	23.2
$25,000 to $34,999	14.9	18.0	19.1	7.7	11.2
$35,000 to $49,999	17.2	22.6	24.5	4.8	7.7
$50,000 to $74,999	14.3	19.1	20.9	3.1	5.1
$75,000 or more	9.2	12.5	14.1	1.6	2.4

Note: Non-Hispanic whites are those who identify themselves as being white alone and not Hispanic. Earnings include wages and salary only.
Source: Bureau of the Census, 2011 Current Population Survey Annual Social and Economic Supplement, Internet site http://www.census.gov/hhes/www/cpstables/032011/perinc/toc.htm; calculations by New Strategist

Women with Professional or Doctoral Degrees Earn the Most

Those who did not complete high school earn the least.

The more highly educated a woman, the more she earns. Among women with at least a bachelor's degree who work full-time, median earnings were $51,942 in 2010. More than one in four earned $75,000 or more. For full-time workers who went no further than high school, median earnings stood at a much lower $29,857. Women with doctoral degrees earned a median of $77,392, and women with professional degrees (such as doctors and lawyers) earned a median of $76,737.

By age and education, women aged 35 to 44 with a professional degree have the highest earnings, a median of $91,211 in 2010. Forty-four percent had incomes of $100,000 or more. Even the youngest women benefit from getting more education. Women aged 25 to 34 with at least a bachelor's degree earned $44,727. Their counterparts who went no further than high school earned just $25,433.

■ Among 25-to-34-year-olds, women are better educated than men. As well-educated, career-oriented women enter middle age, they should continue to close the income gap with men.

Women's earnings rise with education

(median earnings of women aged 25 or older who work full-time, year-round, by educational attainment, 2010)

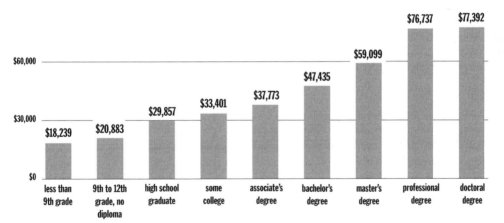

Table 3.31 Women Who Work Full-Time by Earnings and Education, 2010: Total Women

(number and percent distribution of women aged 25 or older who work full-time, year-round, by earnings and educational attainment, 2010; median earnings of women with earnings; women in thousands as of 2011)

	total women	less than 9th grade	9th to 12th grade	high school graduate	some college	associate's degree	bachelor's degree or more total	bachelor's degree	master's degree	professional degree	doctoral degree
Total women who work full-time	**40,196**	**732**	**1,371**	**10,117**	**7,150**	**4,999**	**15,826**	**9,903**	**4,576**	**622**	**725**
Under $5,000	257	11	16	59	53	28	91	62	19	9	1
$5,000 to $9,999	407	35	27	146	79	31	88	64	23	0	1
$10,000 to $14,999	1,623	174	232	599	271	145	200	175	16	3	8
$15,000 to $19,999	2,936	192	356	1,157	565	267	398	315	65	15	6
$20,000 to $24,999	3,949	151	241	1,752	838	468	500	400	84	11	6
$25,000 to $29,999	3,760	71	150	1,370	966	493	711	592	96	8	14
$30,000 to $34,999	4,283	38	132	1,344	987	658	1,123	850	246	14	12
$35,000 to $39,999	3,586	21	69	959	739	528	1,270	907	320	25	18
$40,000 to $44,999	3,413	4	49	829	644	471	1,414	1,015	343	29	28
$45,000 to $49,999	2,683	14	30	498	492	393	1,256	860	311	35	49
$50,000 to $54,999	2,683	5	10	452	463	394	1,358	791	486	36	45
$55,000 to $59,999	1,530	6	14	183	249	219	860	499	310	23	28
$60,000 to $64,999	1,608	5	18	235	160	198	992	596	311	40	46
$65,000 to $69,999	1,052	0	4	82	109	149	708	426	221	22	39
$70,000 to $74,999	1,112	3	3	111	115	188	692	388	244	25	34
$75,000 to $79,999	830	0	6	70	79	82	594	287	243	25	38
$80,000 to $84,999	765	1	2	79	94	75	515	260	199	20	36
$85,000 to $89,999	452	0	0	38	56	45	314	185	110	7	13
$90,000 to $94,999	475	0	5	29	29	32	380	184	148	20	28
$95,000 to $99,999	293	0	0	9	31	23	231	106	96	13	16
$100,000 or more	2,499	2	8	115	132	112	2,131	943	687	242	259
Median earnings	$38,294	$18,239	$20,883	$29,857	$33,401	$37,773	$51,942	$47,435	$59,099	$76,737	$77,392

PERCENT DISTRIBUTION

	total women	less than 9th grade	9th to 12th grade	high school graduate	some college	associate's degree	bachelor's degree or more total	bachelor's degree	master's degree	professional degree	doctoral degree
Total women who work full-time	**100.0%**	**100.0%**	**100.0%**	**100.0%**	**100.0%**	**100.0%**	**100.0%**	**100.0%**	**100.0%**	**100.0%**	**100.0%**
Under $15,000	5.7	30.1	20.1	7.9	5.6	4.1	2.4	3.0	1.3	1.9	1.4
$15,000 to $24,999	17.1	46.9	43.5	28.8	19.6	14.7	5.7	7.2	3.3	4.2	1.7
$25,000 to $34,999	20.0	14.9	20.6	26.8	27.3	23.0	11.6	14.6	7.5	3.5	3.6
$35,000 to $49,999	24.1	5.3	10.8	22.6	26.2	27.8	24.9	28.1	21.3	14.3	13.1
$50,000 to $74,999	19.9	2.6	3.6	10.5	15.3	23.0	29.1	27.3	34.4	23.5	26.5
$75,000 to $99,999	7.0	0.1	0.9	2.2	4.0	5.1	12.9	10.3	17.4	13.7	18.1
$100,000 or more	6.2	0.3	0.6	1.1	1.8	2.2	13.5	9.5	15.0	38.9	35.7

Note: Earnings include wages and salary only.
Source: Bureau of the Census, 2011 Current Population Survey Annual Social and Economic Supplement, Internet site http://www.census.gov/hhes/www/cpstables/032011/perinc/toc.htm; calculations by New Strategist

Table 3.32 Women Who Work Full-Time by Earnings and Education, 2010: Women Aged 25 to 34

(number and percent distribution of women aged 25 to 34 who work full-time, year-round, by earnings and educational attainment, 2010; median earnings of women with earnings; women in thousands as of 2011)

	total women	less than 9th grade	9th to 12th grade	high school graduate	some college	associate's degree	bachelor's degree or more				
							total	bachelor's degree	master's degree	professional degree	doctoral degree
Women aged 25 to 34 who work full-time	9,609	126	277	1,847	1,688	1,187	4,484	3,059	1,096	167	161
Under $5,000	34	2	6	12	6	3	5	3	2	0	0
$5,000 to $9,999	122	8	12	51	23	6	22	16	7	0	0
$10,000 to $14,999	431	28	59	155	95	35	58	54	5	0	0
$15,000 to $19,999	830	36	77	276	182	79	180	146	24	10	0
$20,000 to $24,999	1,064	25	60	402	278	116	183	158	22	3	0
$25,000 to $29,999	974	9	16	231	275	168	275	244	25	2	3
$30,000 to $34,999	1,190	10	21	256	258	184	461	361	97	4	0
$35,000 to $39,999	1,043	1	13	160	199	137	534	371	142	14	7
$40,000 to $44,999	867	0	1	111	105	111	538	356	161	8	13
$45,000 to $49,999	644	0	6	71	82	95	390	264	85	21	19
$50,000 to $54,999	561	1	0	30	83	73	373	224	125	15	10
$55,000 to $59,999	281	3	0	15	20	38	205	133	56	10	6
$60,000 to $64,999	321	0	0	25	14	34	248	170	58	6	13
$65,000 to $69,999	239	0	3	7	14	30	183	137	30	5	11
$70,000 to $74,999	227	0	0	14	18	44	152	97	37	14	3
$75,000 to $79,999	150	0	0	9	14	7	122	62	42	5	12
$80,000 to $84,999	148	1	0	15	7	12	113	57	41	6	9
$85,000 to $89,999	79	0	0	4	4	8	63	42	20	0	2
$90,000 to $94,999	60	0	0	3	0	1	56	29	18	3	7
$95,000 to $99,999	36	0	0	0	4	0	31	18	10	4	1
$100,000 or more	307	0	2	1	6	7	290	120	89	36	46
Median earnings	$35,504	$17,645	$18,304	$25,433	$29,644	$35,060	$44,727	$41,623	$48,078	$58,367	$69,013

PERCENT DISTRIBUTION

Women aged 25 to 34 who work full-time	100.0%	100.0%	100.0%	100.0%	100.0%	100.0%	100.0%	100.0%	100.0%	100.0%	100.0%
Under $15,000	6.1	30.2	27.8	11.8	7.3	3.7	1.9	2.4	1.3	0.0	0.0
$15,000 to $24,999	19.7	48.4	49.5	36.7	27.3	16.4	8.1	9.9	4.2	7.8	0.0
$25,000 to $34,999	22.5	15.1	13.4	26.4	31.6	29.7	16.4	19.8	11.1	3.6	1.9
$35,000 to $49,999	26.6	0.8	7.2	18.5	22.9	28.9	32.6	32.4	35.4	25.7	24.2
$50,000 to $74,999	17.0	3.2	1.1	4.9	8.8	18.4	25.9	24.9	27.9	29.9	26.7
$75,000 to $99,999	4.9	0.8	0.0	1.7	1.7	2.4	8.6	6.8	12.0	10.8	19.3
$100,000 or more	3.2	0.0	0.7	0.1	0.4	0.6	6.5	3.9	8.1	21.6	28.6

Note: Earnings include wages and salary only.
Source: Bureau of the Census, 2011 Current Population Survey Annual Social and Economic Supplement, Internet site http:// www.census.gov/hhes/www/cpstables/032011/perinc/toc.htm; calculations by New Strategist

Table 3.33 Women Who Work Full-Time by Earnings and Education, 2010: Women Aged 35 to 44

(number and percent distribution of women aged 35 to 44 who work full-time, year-round, by earnings and educational attainment, 2010; median earnings of women with earnings; women in thousands as of 2011)

	total women	less than 9th grade	9th to 12th grade	high school graduate	some college	associate's degree	total	bachelor's degree	master's degree	professional degree	doctoral degree
							bachelor's degree or more				
Women aged 35 to 44 who work full-time	**9,900**	**171**	**358**	**2,327**	**1,720**	**1,224**	**4,099**	**2,560**	**1,180**	**171**	**187**
Under $5,000	56	4	2	15	11	7	15	10	7	0	0
$5,000 to $9,999	71	5	7	28	12	8	11	3	8	0	0
$10,000 to $14,999	396	61	70	154	55	32	25	21	3	0	1
$15,000 to $19,999	648	41	97	270	131	52	59	47	11	0	1
$20,000 to $24,999	977	32	58	450	208	127	103	77	19	4	2
$25,000 to $29,999	774	10	51	282	204	93	135	105	27	1	3
$30,000 to $34,999	1,067	5	29	307	263	170	292	237	49	6	0
$35,000 to $39,999	859	6	6	231	193	151	270	197	66	0	6
$40,000 to $44,999	830	1	24	188	162	110	345	242	90	10	3
$45,000 to $49,999	730	2	4	135	133	77	380	277	88	7	8
$50,000 to $54,999	667	0	2	85	108	113	359	214	127	11	6
$55,000 to $59,999	433	2	2	29	68	73	258	144	94	10	12
$60,000 to $64,999	426	0	6	54	43	47	275	179	79	14	4
$65,000 to $69,999	278	0	0	13	20	43	202	116	69	6	10
$70,000 to $74,999	293	0	0	26	11	49	207	121	74	6	7
$75,000 to $79,999	206	0	0	16	22	14	154	81	45	5	22
$80,000 to $84,999	175	0	0	14	20	16	126	62	49	4	11
$85,000 to $89,999	126	0	0	7	14	12	93	59	28	0	7
$90,000 to $94,999	121	0	1	1	9	11	98	53	31	9	5
$95,000 to $99,999	63	0	0	0	2	3	57	27	20	4	6
$100,000 or more	705	1	0	26	32	13	633	290	195	75	72
Median earnings	$40,382	$16,317	$20,224	$29,272	$34,134	$37,856	$55,661	$50,890	$60,021	$91,211	$81,918

PERCENT DISTRIBUTION

Women aged 35 to 44 who work full-time	**100.0%**	**100.0%**	**100.0%**	**100.0%**	**100.0%**	**100.0%**	**100.0%**	**100.0%**	**100.0%**	**100.0%**	**100.0%**
Under $15,000	5.3	40.9	22.1	8.5	4.5	3.8	1.2	1.3	1.5	0.0	0.5
$15,000 to $24,999	16.4	42.7	43.3	30.9	19.7	14.6	4.0	4.8	2.5	2.3	1.6
$25,000 to $34,999	18.6	8.8	22.3	25.3	27.2	21.5	10.4	13.4	6.4	4.1	1.6
$35,000 to $49,999	24.4	5.3	9.5	23.8	28.4	27.6	24.3	28.0	20.7	9.9	9.1
$50,000 to $74,999	21.2	1.2	2.8	8.9	14.5	26.6	31.7	30.2	37.5	27.5	20.9
$75,000 to $99,999	7.0	0.0	0.3	1.6	3.9	4.6	12.9	11.0	14.7	12.9	27.3
$100,000 or more	7.1	0.6	0.0	1.1	1.9	1.1	15.4	11.3	16.5	43.9	38.5

Note: Earnings include wages and salary only.
Source: Bureau of the Census, 2011 Current Population Survey Annual Social and Economic Supplement, Internet site http://www.census.gov/hhes/www/cpstables/032011/perinc/toc.htm; calculations by New Strategist

Table 3.34 Women Who Work Full-Time by Earnings and Education, 2010: Women Aged 45 to 54

(number and percent distribution of women aged 45 to 54 who work full-time, year-round, by earnings and educational attainment, 2010; median earnings of women with earnings; women in thousands as of 2011)

	total women	less than 9th grade	9th to 12th grade	high school graduate	some college	associate's degree	bachelor's degree or more				
							total	bachelor's degree	master's degree	professional degree	doctoral degree
Women aged 45 to 54 who work full-time	**11,524**	**231**	**388**	**3,245**	**2,066**	**1,578**	**4,017**	**2,504**	**1,201**	**134**	**179**
Under $5,000	74	1	3	21	12	7	30	21	0	7	1
$5,000 to $9,999	108	15	5	33	20	8	28	19	9	0	0
$10,000 to $14,999	418	48	55	141	66	45	64	53	5	3	4
$15,000 to $19,999	845	60	111	356	162	74	81	65	13	1	2
$20,000 to $24,999	1,156	53	75	548	225	133	122	97	19	2	4
$25,000 to $29,999	1,087	29	40	455	251	143	168	140	18	4	6
$30,000 to $34,999	1,111	7	41	441	243	182	196	143	51	0	3
$35,000 to $39,999	956	8	23	289	206	138	293	213	72	5	3
$40,000 to $44,999	962	1	4	302	200	143	312	249	54	2	6
$45,000 to $49,999	754	3	14	167	143	148	279	174	93	7	5
$50,000 to $54,999	769	3	6	183	133	119	324	199	106	5	14
$55,000 to $59,999	459	0	2	48	90	69	251	165	82	2	2
$60,000 to $64,999	463	3	4	71	60	83	241	131	85	6	20
$65,000 to $69,999	288	0	0	35	35	43	174	88	68	6	13
$70,000 to $74,999	307	0	0	27	61	77	142	72	56	1	12
$75,000 to $79,999	272	0	3	17	25	38	189	101	81	5	2
$80,000 to $84,999	250	0	0	28	38	28	157	80	56	8	13
$85,000 to $89,999	143	0	0	14	25	15	89	48	34	5	1
$90,000 to $94,999	146	0	1	12	8	15	110	51	45	4	10
$95,000 to $99,999	110	0	0	1	10	11	87	33	43	5	6
$100,000 or more	845	0	1	54	50	59	680	360	211	55	53
Median earnings	$40,025	$18,797	$21,172	$30,473	$35,891	$41,285	$56,671	$51,172	$63,636	$86,484	$71,775

PERCENT DISTRIBUTION

	total women	less than 9th grade	9th to 12th grade	high school graduate	some college	associate's degree	total	bachelor's degree	master's degree	professional degree	doctoral degree
Women aged 45 to 54 who work full-time	**100.0%**	**100.0%**	**100.0%**	**100.0%**	**100.0%**	**100.0%**	**100.0%**	**100.0%**	**100.0%**	**100.0%**	**100.0%**
Under $15,000	5.2	27.7	16.2	6.0	4.7	3.8	3.0	3.7	1.2	7.5	2.8
$15,000 to $24,999	17.4	48.9	47.9	27.9	18.7	13.1	5.1	6.5	2.7	2.2	3.4
$25,000 to $34,999	19.1	15.6	20.9	27.6	23.9	20.6	9.1	11.3	5.7	3.0	5.0
$35,000 to $49,999	23.2	5.2	10.6	23.4	26.6	27.2	22.0	25.4	18.2	10.4	7.8
$50,000 to $74,999	19.8	2.6	3.1	11.2	18.3	24.8	28.2	26.2	33.1	14.9	34.1
$75,000 to $99,999	8.0	0.0	1.0	2.2	5.1	6.8	15.7	12.5	21.6	20.1	17.9
$100,000 or more	7.3	0.0	0.3	1.7	2.4	3.7	16.9	14.4	17.6	41.0	29.6

Note: Earnings include wages and salary only.
Source: Bureau of the Census, 2011 Current Population Survey Annual Social and Economic Supplement, Internet site http://www.census.gov/hhes/www/cpstables/032011/perinc/toc.htm; calculations by New Strategist

Table 3.35 Women Who Work Full-Time by Earnings and Education, 2010: Women Aged 55 to 64

(number and percent distribution of women aged 55 to 64 who work full-time, year-round, by earnings and educational attainment, 2010; median earnings of women with earnings; women in thousands as of 2011)

	total women	less than 9th grade	9th to 12th grade	high school graduate	some college	associate's degree	bachelor's degree or more				
							total	bachelor's degree	master's degree	professional degree	doctoral degree
Women aged 55 to 64 who work full-time	**7,673**	**144**	**276**	**2,218**	**1,409**	**873**	**2,752**	**1,549**	**933**	**116**	**153**
Under $5,000	69	2	3	6	18	10	29	22	8	0	0
$5,000 to $9,999	75	2	2	29	21	4	14	14	0	0	0
$10,000 to $14,999	269	23	30	103	46	27	41	37	1	0	3
$15,000 to $19,999	501	43	62	198	75	58	65	55	8	0	2
$20,000 to $24,999	657	29	41	305	112	81	89	66	21	1	0
$25,000 to $29,999	763	20	31	344	189	67	111	86	21	1	3
$30,000 to $34,999	777	12	30	287	200	108	138	98	33	0	8
$35,000 to $39,999	637	4	26	245	119	91	153	109	36	5	2
$40,000 to $44,999	651	2	19	190	152	91	197	150	36	7	4
$45,000 to $49,999	449	4	6	87	109	63	179	131	38	1	9
$50,000 to $54,999	576	1	0	121	105	86	264	136	109	4	13
$55,000 to $59,999	328	1	8	81	67	35	136	56	71	1	9
$60,000 to $64,999	341	2	5	69	35	32	198	98	80	10	9
$65,000 to $69,999	211	0	1	25	33	29	124	65	49	4	5
$70,000 to $74,999	227	0	0	30	20	16	162	89	65	4	5
$75,000 to $79,999	176	0	3	28	11	14	121	40	71	10	0
$80,000 to $84,999	162	0	2	18	28	15	99	47	47	2	3
$85,000 to $89,999	98	0	0	13	14	9	63	35	24	2	2
$90,000 to $94,999	117	0	0	13	9	5	90	41	38	5	6
$95,000 to $99,999	73	0	0	8	9	5	52	28	23	0	2
$100,000 or more	514	0	4	21	37	28	424	145	153	60	66
Median earnings	$40,425	$20,352	$24,744	$31,416	$36,171	$39,421	$57,845	$50,152	$65,221	$100,539	$84,923

PERCENT DISTRIBUTION

Women aged 55 to 64 who work full-time	**100.0%**	**100.0%**	**100.0%**	**100.0%**	**100.0%**	**100.0%**	**100.0%**	**100.0%**	**100.0%**	**100.0%**	**100.0%**
Under $15,000	5.4	18.8	12.7	6.2	6.0	4.7	3.1	4.7	1.0	0.0	2.0
$15,000 to $24,999	15.1	50.0	37.3	22.7	13.3	15.9	5.6	7.8	3.1	0.9	1.3
$25,000 to $34,999	20.1	22.2	22.1	28.4	27.6	20.0	9.0	11.9	5.8	0.9	7.2
$35,000 to $49,999	22.6	6.9	18.5	23.5	27.0	28.1	19.2	25.2	11.8	11.2	9.8
$50,000 to $74,999	21.9	2.8	5.1	14.7	18.5	22.7	32.1	28.7	40.1	19.8	26.8
$75,000 to $99,999	8.2	0.0	1.8	3.6	5.0	5.5	15.4	12.3	21.8	16.4	8.5
$100,000 or more	6.7	0.0	1.4	0.9	2.6	3.2	15.4	9.4	16.4	51.7	43.1

Note: Earnings include wages and salary only.
Source: Bureau of the Census, 2011 Current Population Survey Annual Social and Economic Supplement, Internet site http://www.census.gov/hhes/www/cpstables/032011/perinc/toc.htm; calculations by New Strategist

Table 3.36 Women Who Work Full-Time by Earnings and Education, 2010: Women Aged 65 or Older

(number and percent distribution of women aged 65 or older who work full-time, year-round, by earnings and educational attainment, 2010; median earnings of women with earnings; women in thousands as of 2011)

	total women	less than 9th grade	9th to 12th grade	high school graduate	some college	associate's degree	bachelor's degree or more				
							total	bachelor's degree	master's degree	professional degree	doctoral degree
Women aged 65 or older who work full-time	**1,490**	**60**	**72**	**479**	**267**	**137**	**475**	**231**	**166**	**33**	**45**
Under $5,000	25	2	0	5	5	1	13	7	3	2	0
$5,000 to $9,999	30	5	0	6	3	3	13	12	0	0	1
$10,000 to $14,999	108	15	18	48	10	7	11	9	2	0	0
$15,000 to $19,999	111	12	10	57	14	5	14	2	9	3	0
$20,000 to $24,999	94	10	6	49	15	12	3	1	2	0	0
$25,000 to $29,999	163	2	12	58	48	21	22	17	4	0	0
$30,000 to $34,999	138	3	12	53	22	14	35	12	17	4	1
$35,000 to $39,999	90	1	0	35	23	11	21	18	3	0	0
$40,000 to $44,999	102	0	1	39	24	16	22	17	3	2	0
$45,000 to $49,999	106	5	0	37	25	11	28	15	6	0	8
$50,000 to $54,999	111	0	2	32	35	4	38	20	18	0	0
$55,000 to $59,999	30	0	2	10	5	4	8	0	8	0	0
$60,000 to $64,999	57	0	3	18	6	1	29	17	8	4	0
$65,000 to $69,999	37	0	0	2	7	3	25	21	4	0	0
$70,000 to $74,999	57	3	3	13	6	1	29	10	12	1	7
$75,000 to $79,999	25	0	0	1	7	9	8	3	4	0	2
$80,000 to $84,999	30	0	0	4	1	4	20	14	6	0	0
$85,000 to $89,999	6	0	0	0	0	0	5	0	3	0	2
$90,000 to $94,999	30	0	4	0	2	0	24	9	15	0	0
$95,000 to $99,999	11	0	0	0	4	3	3	0	0	0	3
$100,000 or more	128	1	0	13	6	5	103	27	38	16	21
Median earnings	$38,946	–	–	$31,126	$39,124	$36,819	$60,873	$51,275	$62,081	–	–

PERCENT DISTRIBUTION

Women aged 65 or older who work full-time	100.0%	100.0%	100.0%	100.0%	100.0%	100.0%	100.0%	100.0%	100.0%	100.0%	100.0%
Under $15,000	10.9	36.7	25.0	12.3	6.7	8.0	7.8	12.1	3.0	6.1	2.2
$15,000 to $24,999	13.8	36.7	22.2	22.1	10.9	12.4	3.6	1.3	6.6	9.1	0.0
$25,000 to $34,999	20.2	8.3	33.3	23.2	26.2	25.5	12.0	12.6	12.7	12.1	2.2
$35,000 to $49,999	20.0	10.0	1.4	23.2	27.0	27.7	14.9	21.6	7.2	6.1	17.8
$50,000 to $74,999	19.6	5.0	13.9	15.7	22.1	9.5	27.2	29.4	30.1	15.2	15.6
$75,000 to $99,999	6.8	0.0	5.6	1.0	5.2	11.7	12.6	11.3	16.9	0.0	15.6
$100,000 or more	8.6	1.7	0.0	2.7	2.2	3.6	21.7	11.7	22.9	48.5	46.7

Note: Earnings include wages and salary only. "–" means sample is too small to make a reliable estimate.
Source: Bureau of the Census, 2011 Current Population Survey Annual Social and Economic Supplement, Internet site http://www.census.gov/hhes/www/cpstables/032011/perinc/toc.htm; calculations by New Strategist

Education Boosts the Earnings of Asian, Black, Hispanic, and Non-Hispanic White Women

Among women with college degrees, Asians earn the most.

The earnings of women vary much more by education than they do by race and Hispanic origin. Among full-time workers with at least a bachelor's degree, Asian women have the highest earnings. Their median earnings stood at $57,221 in 2010. Non-Hispanic white women rank second, with median earnings of $52,465. Black women with at least a bachelor's degree earned a median of $47,097 in 2010, while their Hispanic counterparts earned $46,710.

Regardless of race or Hispanic origin, earnings were lowest among women with the least education. Among women who have no more than a high school diploma, median earnings ranged from a low of $26,269 for Hispanics to a high of $30,840 for non-Hispanic whites.

■ If the educational attainment of black women continues to rise, their earnings will approach those of Asians and non-Hispanic whites in the years ahead. The educational attainment of Hispanics will not rise much until immigrants become a smaller share of the Hispanic population.

Among women with a bachelor's degree, Hispanics earn the least

(median earnings of women aged 25 or older with at least a bachelor's degree who work full-time, year-round, by race and Hispanic origin, 2010)

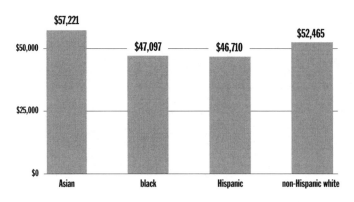

Table 3.37 Women Who Work Full-Time by Earnings and Education, 2010: Asian Women

(number and percent distribution of Asian women aged 25 or older who work full-time, year-round, by earnings and educational attainment, 2010; median earnings of women with earnings; women in thousands as of 2011)

| | total women | less than 9th grade | 9th to 12th grade | high school graduate | some college | associate's degree | bachelor's degree or more | | | | |
							total	bachelor's degree	master's degree	professional degree	doctoral degree
Asian women who work full-time	2,269	77	57	436	249	154	1,296	818	322	57	99
Under $5,000	15	2	1	2	2	0	7	6	2	0	0
$5,000 to $9,999	23	2	1	4	4	2	11	9	2	0	0
$10,000 to $14,999	82	11	6	28	10	4	23	19	2	0	1
$15,000 to $19,999	131	12	10	52	20	9	29	20	9	0	0
$20,000 to $24,999	203	25	9	70	31	19	49	42	1	2	3
$25,000 to $29,999	178	10	10	57	29	17	56	47	8	0	0
$30,000 to $34,999	228	3	4	64	43	21	94	66	26	2	1
$35,000 to $39,999	168	4	10	36	19	14	86	56	24	0	5
$40,000 to $44,999	194	1	3	51	22	20	99	68	24	3	3
$45,000 to $49,999	111	4	3	16	10	4	74	56	12	2	3
$50,000 to $54,999	147	2	0	19	29	6	90	60	22	4	5
$55,000 to $59,999	68	2	0	7	5	5	49	36	10	0	3
$60,000 to $64,999	121	0	1	9	10	11	90	62	20	4	3
$65,000 to $69,999	65	0	0	2	2	5	56	38	13	2	4
$70,000 to $74,999	81	0	0	1	2	9	68	39	20	4	5
$75,000 to $79,999	54	0	0	3	4	2	46	27	11	3	5
$80,000 to $84,999	54	0	0	8	4	0	41	20	15	2	4
$85,000 to $89,999	32	0	0	0	3	0	28	17	8	2	0
$90,000 to $94,999	65	0	0	0	0	2	63	38	16	0	9
$95,000 to $99,999	17	0	0	2	0	0	15	2	10	2	2
$100,000 or more	235	0	0	9	2	2	222	88	68	26	40
Median earnings	$41,600	$21,603	–	$30,279	$32,219	$35,799	$57,221	$51,040	$65,138	–	$90,311

PERCENT DISTRIBUTION

Asian women who work full-time	100.0%	100.0%	100.0%	100.0%	100.0%	100.0%	100.0%	100.0%	100.0%	100.0%	100.0%
Under $15,000	5.3	19.5	14.0	7.8	6.4	3.9	3.2	4.2	1.9	0.0	1.0
$15,000 to $24,999	14.7	48.1	33.3	28.0	20.5	18.2	6.0	7.6	3.1	3.5	3.0
$25,000 to $34,999	17.9	16.9	24.6	27.8	28.9	24.7	11.6	13.8	10.6	3.5	1.0
$35,000 to $49,999	20.8	11.7	28.1	23.6	20.5	24.7	20.0	22.0	18.6	8.8	11.1
$50,000 to $74,999	21.2	5.2	1.8	8.7	19.3	23.4	27.2	28.7	26.4	24.6	20.2
$75,000 to $99,999	9.8	0.0	0.0	3.0	4.4	2.6	14.9	12.7	18.6	15.8	20.2
$100,000 or more	10.4	0.0	0.0	2.1	0.8	1.3	17.1	10.8	21.1	45.6	40.4

Note: Asians are those who identify themselves as being of the race alone and those who identify themselves as being of the race in combination with other races. Earnings include wages and salary only. "–" means sample is too small to make a reliable estimate.

Source: Bureau of the Census, 2011 Current Population Survey Annual Social and Economic Supplement, Internet site http:// www.census.gov/hhes/www/cpstables/032011/perinc/toc.htm; calculations by New Strategist

Table 3.38 Women Who Work Full-Time by Earnings and Education, 2010: Black Women

(number and percent distribution of black women aged 25 or older who work full-time, year-round, by earnings and educational attainment, 2010; median earnings of women with earnings; women in thousands as of 2011)

	total women	less than 9th grade	9th to 12th grade	high school graduate	some college	associate's degree	bachelor's degree or more total	bachelor's degree	master's degree	professional degree	doctoral degree
Black women who work full-time	**5,583**	**45**	**263**	**1,518**	**1,304**	**727**	**1,725**	**1,124**	**468**	**78**	**55**
Under $5,000	23	0	4	5	8	3	4	3	0	0	1
$5,000 to $9,999	54	4	7	33	7	2	2	2	0	0	0
$10,000 to $14,999	243	8	47	87	44	29	28	28	0	0	0
$15,000 to $19,999	520	13	61	234	130	33	51	38	10	3	0
$20,000 to $24,999	704	10	58	290	196	83	68	53	11	4	0
$25,000 to $29,999	644	2	23	228	205	106	81	69	6	2	3
$30,000 to $34,999	645	2	21	230	149	96	148	121	22	2	4
$35,000 to $39,999	529	0	11	95	127	94	202	148	49	4	0
$40,000 to $44,999	458	0	7	100	113	75	162	110	47	3	3
$45,000 to $49,999	397	2	9	83	71	56	176	125	43	6	3
$50,000 to $54,999	336	1	1	63	93	51	127	78	43	2	3
$55,000 to $59,999	164	0	0	16	37	16	94	57	28	4	6
$60,000 to $64,999	187	0	9	23	42	14	99	69	29	2	0
$65,000 to $69,999	91	0	1	6	11	6	66	34	28	2	3
$70,000 to $74,999	116	3	0	4	27	19	64	42	17	4	2
$75,000 to $79,999	86	0	1	9	20	9	47	17	20	5	5
$80,000 to $84,999	93	0	0	6	6	20	60	20	35	4	2
$85,000 to $89,999	37	0	0	2	5	4	26	18	7	0	1
$90,000 to $94,999	41	0	0	0	6	3	33	19	11	1	1
$95,000 to $99,999	31	0	0	2	3	5	22	8	9	2	3
$100,000 or more	181	0	5	2	7	4	163	65	56	26	16
Median earnings	$34,200	–	$20,848	$26,785	$31,429	$35,442	$47,097	$44,171	$55,371	$72,449	–

PERCENT DISTRIBUTION

Black women who work full-time	**100.0%**	**100.0%**	**100.0%**	**100.0%**	**100.0%**	**100.0%**	**100.0%**	**100.0%**	**100.0%**	**100.0%**	**100.0%**
Under $15,000	5.7	26.7	22.1	8.2	4.5	4.7	2.0	2.9	0.0	0.0	1.8
$15,000 to $24,999	21.9	51.1	45.2	34.5	25.0	16.0	6.9	8.1	4.5	9.0	0.0
$25,000 to $34,999	23.1	8.9	16.7	30.2	27.1	27.8	13.3	16.9	6.0	5.1	12.7
$35,000 to $49,999	24.8	4.4	10.3	18.3	23.8	30.9	31.3	34.1	29.7	16.7	10.9
$50,000 to $74,999	16.0	8.9	4.2	7.4	16.1	14.6	26.1	24.9	31.0	17.9	25.5
$75,000 to $99,999	5.2	0.0	0.4	1.3	3.1	5.6	10.9	7.3	17.5	15.4	21.8
$100,000 or more	3.2	0.0	1.9	0.1	0.5	0.6	9.4	5.8	12.0	33.3	29.1

Note: Blacks are those who identify themselves as being of the race alone and those who identify themselves as being of the race in combination with other races. Earnings include wages and salary only. "–" means sample is too small to make a reliable estimate.
Source: Bureau of the Census, 2011 Current Population Survey Annual Social and Economic Supplement, Internet site http:// www.census.gov/hhes/www/cpstables/032011/perinc/toc.htm; calculations by New Strategist

Table 3.39 Women Who Work Full-Time by Earnings and Education, 2010: Hispanic Women

(number and percent distribution of Hispanic women aged 25 or older who work full-time, year-round, by earnings and educational attainment, 2010; median earnings of women with earnings; women in thousands as of 2011)

	total women	less than 9th grade	9th to 12th grade	high school graduate	some college	associate's degree	bachelor's degree or more				
							total	bachelor's degree	master's degree	professional degree	doctoral degree
Hispanic women who work full-time	**4,741**	**528**	**467**	**1,406**	**794**	**488**	**1,057**	**737**	**234**	**32**	**54**
Under $5,000	22	4	5	5	1	1	5	4	0	1	0
$5,000 to $9,999	75	23	13	22	9	3	4	3	2	0	0
$10,000 to $14,999	422	142	90	120	32	22	16	14	1	1	0
$15,000 to $19,999	655	148	128	205	74	41	59	48	7	2	3
$20,000 to $24,999	673	106	104	280	78	52	55	47	6	0	1
$25,000 to $29,999	558	50	41	201	124	70	70	59	7	2	3
$30,000 to $34,999	552	28	36	201	122	74	91	73	14	3	0
$35,000 to $39,999	426	15	24	150	84	48	105	85	17	2	2
$40,000 to $44,999	307	2	11	79	81	46	86	63	20	1	3
$45,000 to $49,999	175	4	7	31	40	25	69	47	18	0	3
$50,000 to $54,999	208	3	1	38	44	21	103	74	21	4	3
$55,000 to $59,999	110	0	1	11	24	19	56	39	16	0	2
$60,000 to $64,999	126	2	3	19	21	15	68	47	16	0	4
$65,000 to $69,999	66	0	0	10	11	11	34	23	8	0	2
$70,000 to $74,999	65	0	0	6	8	14	37	12	17	0	8
$75,000 to $79,999	47	0	0	7	7	6	27	13	10	0	2
$80,000 to $84,999	47	0	1	11	4	1	29	15	12	0	2
$85,000 to $89,999	29	0	0	4	5	4	17	11	4	0	2
$90,000 to $94,999	27	0	1	0	1	4	21	14	2	3	2
$95,000 to $99,999	18	0	0	0	3	0	15	6	7	1	0
$100,000 or more	130	1	1	7	19	9	92	38	31	9	14
Median earnings	$29,492	$17,367	$19,891	$26,269	$32,219	$32,365	$46,710	$41,684	$56,128	–	–

PERCENT DISTRIBUTION

Hispanic women who work full-time	**100.0%**	**100.0%**	**100.0%**	**100.0%**	**100.0%**	**100.0%**	**100.0%**	**100.0%**	**100.0%**	**100.0%**	**100.0%**
Under $15,000	10.9	32.0	23.1	10.5	5.3	5.3	2.4	2.8	1.3	6.3	0.0
$15,000 to $24,999	28.0	48.1	49.7	34.5	19.1	19.1	10.8	12.9	5.6	6.3	7.4
$25,000 to $34,999	23.4	14.8	16.5	28.6	31.0	29.5	15.2	17.9	9.0	15.6	5.6
$35,000 to $49,999	19.2	4.0	9.0	18.5	25.8	24.4	24.6	26.5	23.5	9.4	14.8
$50,000 to $74,999	12.1	0.9	1.1	6.0	13.6	16.4	28.2	26.5	33.3	12.5	35.2
$75,000 to $99,999	3.5	0.0	0.4	1.6	2.5	3.1	10.3	8.0	15.0	12.5	14.8
$100,000 or more	2.7	0.2	0.2	0.5	2.4	1.8	8.7	5.2	13.2	28.1	25.9

Note: Earnings include wages and salary only. "–" means sample is too small to make a reliable estimate.
Source: Bureau of the Census, 2011 Current Population Survey Annual Social and Economic Supplement, Internet site http://www.census.gov/hhes/www/cpstables/032011/perinc/toc.htm; calculations by New Strategist

Table 3.40 Women Who Work Full-Time by Earnings and Education, 2010: Non-Hispanic White Women

(number and percent distribution of non-Hispanic white women aged 25 or older who work full-time, year-round, by earnings and educational attainment, 2010; median earnings of women with earnings; women in thousands as of 2011)

	total women	less than 9th grade	9th to 12th grade	high school graduate	some college	associate's degree	bachelor's degree or more total	bachelor's degree	master's degree	professional degree	doctoral degree
Non-Hispanic white women who work full-time	**27,379**	**89**	**564**	**6,693**	**4,758**	**3,589**	**11,685**	**7,200**	**3,516**	**454**	**515**
Under $5,000	196	5	6	47	41	23	74	48	18	8	0
$5,000 to $9,999	255	7	6	90	59	23	70	49	19	0	1
$10,000 to $14,999	875	17	86	363	187	89	133	112	12	1	7
$15,000 to $19,999	1,609	23	151	649	344	180	261	209	40	10	2
$20,000 to $24,999	2,329	11	66	1,102	517	303	329	258	65	5	2
$25,000 to $29,999	2,375	6	73	878	613	295	510	427	72	4	7
$30,000 to $34,999	2,829	5	67	850	662	463	781	589	178	7	8
$35,000 to $39,999	2,418	3	24	661	490	366	874	615	232	18	9
$40,000 to $44,999	2,466	1	29	600	441	336	1,059	773	245	23	18
$45,000 to $49,999	1,974	4	12	365	360	305	928	631	233	25	38
$50,000 to $54,999	1,981	0	6	330	300	311	1,035	573	401	29	33
$55,000 to $59,999	1,174	3	13	147	179	182	650	362	253	19	17
$60,000 to $64,999	1,174	3	6	183	93	154	734	417	246	32	38
$65,000 to $69,999	820	0	3	65	82	120	550	331	171	18	30
$70,000 to $74,999	839	0	3	98	75	146	518	292	189	17	19
$75,000 to $79,999	641	0	5	51	47	65	472	228	200	18	27
$80,000 to $84,999	563	1	0	54	77	52	379	200	138	13	29
$85,000 to $89,999	350	0	0	32	41	36	241	138	88	5	10
$90,000 to $94,999	339	0	5	29	21	23	261	112	119	15	15
$95,000 to $99,999	223	0	0	5	22	19	177	88	69	8	13
$100,000 or more	1,950	1	1	96	105	96	1,651	751	527	182	191
Median earnings	$41,058	$17,857	$22,495	$30,840	$34,468	$40,485	$52,465	$48,762	$59,630	$76,832	$80,065

PERCENT DISTRIBUTION

Non-Hispanic white women who work full-time	100.0%	100.0%	100.0%	100.0%	100.0%	100.0%	100.0%	100.0%	100.0%	100.0%	100.0%
Under $15,000	4.8	32.6	17.4	7.5	6.0	3.8	2.4	2.9	1.4	2.0	1.6
$15,000 to $24,999	14.4	38.2	38.5	26.2	18.1	13.5	5.0	6.5	3.0	3.3	0.8
$25,000 to $34,999	19.0	12.4	24.8	25.8	26.8	21.1	11.0	14.1	7.1	2.4	2.9
$35,000 to $49,999	25.0	9.0	11.5	24.3	27.1	28.1	24.5	28.0	20.2	14.5	12.6
$50,000 to $74,999	21.9	6.7	5.5	12.3	15.3	25.4	29.8	27.4	35.8	25.3	26.6
$75,000 to $99,999	7.7	1.1	1.8	2.6	4.4	5.4	13.1	10.6	17.5	13.0	18.3
$100,000 or more	7.1	1.1	0.2	1.4	2.2	2.7	14.1	10.4	15.0	40.1	37.1

Note: Non-Hispanic whites are those who identify themselves as being of the race alone and not Hispanic. Earnings include wages and salary only.
Source: Bureau of the Census, 2011 Current Population Survey Annual Social and Economic Supplement, Internet site http://www.census.gov/hhes/www/cpstables/032011/perinc/toc.htm; calculations by New Strategist

Among Women, Lawyers and Doctors Earn the Most

Cashiers and cooks earn the least.

Among full-time workers, women earn 77 percent as much as men. While this figure has been rising, it is still far below parity with men. There are many reasons for the earnings gap between women and men. On average, working men are older and have more job experience than working women. In addition, the average male worker had been better educated (although this is changing), which boosts men's earnings. The different career choices of men and women also contribute to the gap.

Among women who work full-time, doctors earn the most, a median of $102,433 in 2010. Lawyers and judges earned a median of $87,336. Other high-paying occupations among women are chief executives and managers ($75,751), engineers ($73,666), psychologists ($67,762), and computer scientists ($65,964).

Women's earnings are lowest among occupations such as food preparation workers ($18,336), chefs and cooks ($19,899), cashiers ($20,423), and farm workers ($20,859). Among men, these are also low-paying jobs.

■ Women's earnings should continue to approach those of men during the years ahead as better-educated, career-oriented women replace older just-a-job women.

Women's earnings vary by occupation

(median earnings of women aged 15 or older who work full-time, year-round, by selected occupation, 2010)

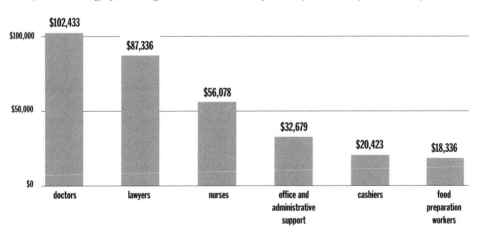

Table 3.41 Median Earnings of Women by Occupation, 2010

(number and median earnings of women aged 15 or older who work full-time, year-round, by occupation of longest job held, 2010; women in thousands as of 2011)

	number with earnings	median earnings
TOTAL WOMEN WORKING FULL-TIME, YEAR-ROUND	**42,834**	**$36,931**
Management, science, and arts occupations	**19,676**	**50,570**
Management, business, and financial operations occupations	7,607	52,236
Management occupations	4,804	54,761
Chief executives, general and operations managers	557	75,751
All other managers	4,247	52,511
Business and financial operations occupations	2,803	50,785
Business operations specialists	1,430	50,264
Financial specialists	1,373	51,219
Professional and related occupations	12,069	49,244
Computer and mathematical occupations	752	65,399
Computer scientists, analysts, programmers, engineers, and administrators	682	65,964
Architecture and engineering occupations	306	61,603
Engineers	206	73,666
Life, physical, and social science occupations	445	57,151
Psychologists	76	67,762
All other scientists	292	60,897
Community and social services occupations	1,216	39,374
Legal occupations	667	57,216
Lawyers, judges, and magistrates	284	87,336
Paralegals, legal assistants, and legal support workers	384	45,527
Education, training, and library occupations	3,929	42,457
Postsecondary teachers	407	53,597
All other teachers	2,927	44,636
Archivists, curators, museum technicians, librarians, and other technicians and assistants	595	26,309
Arts, design, entertainment, sports, and media occupations	642	41,311
Health care practitioner and technical occupations	4,112	53,603
Doctors	295	102,433
Nurses	2,248	56,078
All other health and technical occupations	1,569	47,904
Service occupations	**7,031**	**22,906**
Health care support occupations	1,796	26,277
Protective service occupations	519	39,107
Fire fighters and police	132	60,719
All other protective service occupations	335	34,461
Food preparation and serving related occupations	1,682	19,371
Supervisors	204	24,532
Chefs and cooks	470	19,899
All other food preparation occupations	1,007	18,336
Building and grounds cleaning and maintenance occupations	1,159	20,721
Supervisors	98	30,705
All other maintenance occupations	1,061	20,340
Personal care and service occupations	1,876	22,155
Supervisors	159	30,404
All other personal care and service occupations	1,717	21,886

	number with earnings	median earnings
Sales and office occupations	**13,318**	**$32,248**
Sales and related occupations	4,086	30,982
Supervisors	1,336	35,879
Cashiers	809	20,423
Insurance sales agents	223	38,627
Real estate brokers and sales agents	291	40,286
All other sales and related occupations	1,427	32,265
Office and administrative support occupations	9,232	32,679
Supervisors	888	42,688
Postal workers	193	53,093
All other office and administrative support occupations	8,150	31,852
Natural resources, construction, and maintenance occupations	**384**	**30,804**
Farming, fishing, and forestry occupations	102	20,859
Farming, fishing, and forestry occupations, except supervisors	102	20,859
Construction and extraction occupations	138	31,864
Construction	138	31,887
Installation, maintenance, and repair occupations	144	41,395
Production, transportation, and material moving occupations	**2,347**	**25,548**
Production occupations	1,654	25,705
Supervisors	125	40,875
All other occupations	1,528	25,109
Transportation and material-moving occupations	693	25,115
Auto, bus, truck, ambulance, taxi drivers	234	26,162
All other transportation occupations	413	23,628
Armed forces	**78**	**50,597**

Note: Number of workers does not add to total because only occupations with data on median earnings are shown. Earnings include wages and salary only.
Source: Bureau of the Census, 2011 Current Population Survey Annual Social and Economic Supplement, Internet site http:// www.census.gov/hhes/www/cpstables/032011/perinc/toc.htm; calculations by New Strategist

Two-Thirds of Women Receive Wage or Salary Income

Nearly one in four receives Social Security.

Wage or salary income is the only type of income the majority of women receive, with 65 percent earning wages or salaries in 2010. The second-most-common type of income is interest, which 42 percent of women receive. Social Security ranks third at 23 percent. Nine percent of women receive retirement income, and 4 percent receive child support. Among women with wage or salary income in 2010, the median amount received stood at $26,973. Among those getting Social Security checks, the median amount received was a much smaller $10,832. Those receiving interest income got a median of only $1,425 from this source.

Hispanic women are most likely to receive wage and salary income. Seventy-two percent of Hispanic women had wage or salary income in 2010 versus 69 percent of Asian women, 67 percent of black women, and 63 percent of non-Hispanic white women. Non-Hispanic white women are much more likely to receive Social Security income than other racial or ethnic groups. Twenty-six percent received Social Security checks in 2010 versus 19 percent of blacks, 14 percent of Hispanics, and 13 percent of Asians.

■ As the baby-boom generation begins to retire, the proportion of women with Social Security and retirement income will rise.

Few women receive retirement income

(percent of women aged 15 or older who receive income, by source of income, 2010)

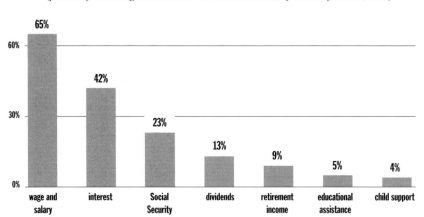

Table 3.42 Median Income of Women by Source of Income, 2010: Total Women

(number and percent of women aged 15 or older with income, and median income of those with income, 2010; women in thousands as of 2011)

	number	percent	median income
Women with income	**106,142**	**100.0%**	**$20,831**
Earnings	72,118	67.9	26,552
Wages and salary	68,865	64.9	26,973
Nonfarm self-employment	4,663	4.4	9,760
Farm self-employment	666	0.6	1,582
Social Security	24,770	23.3	10,832
SSI (Supplemental Security)	3,202	3.0	7,517
Public Assistance	1,771	1.7	2,606
Veteran's benefits	502	0.5	9,786
Survivor's benefits	2,281	2.1	7,337
Disability benefits	730	0.7	7,884
Unemployment compensation	4,947	4.7	5,351
Worker's compensation	628	0.6	3,523
Property income	46,961	44.2	1,577
Interest	44,130	41.6	1,425
Dividends	14,160	13.3	1,642
Rents, royalties, estates, trusts	5,127	4.8	2,246
Retirement income	9,734	9.2	9,494
Company or union retirement	4,882	4.6	6,237
Federal government retirement	756	0.7	12,854
Military retirement	339	0.3	11,454
State or local government retirement	2,790	2.6	15,383
Railroad retirement	148	0.1	14,801
Annuities	285	0.3	5,861
IRA or Keogh, or 401(k)	316	0.3	7,358
Pension income	7,196	6.8	9,796
Company or union retirement	3,756	3.5	5,910
Federal government retirement	530	0.5	13,737
Military retirement	123	0.1	13,596
State or local government retirement	2,405	2.3	16,451
Railroad retirement	113	0.1	14,890
Annuities	109	0.1	9,135
Alimony	380	0.4	8,559
Child support	4,412	4.2	3,912
Educational assistance	5,605	5.3	4,345
Financial assistance from outside the household	1,466	1.4	3,681
Other income	557	0.5	1,591

Source: Bureau of the Census, 2011 Current Population Survey Annual Social and Economic Supplement, Internet site http:// www.census.gov/hhes/www/cpstables/032011/perinc/toc.htm; calculations by New Strategist

Table 3.43 Median Income of Women by Source of Income, 2010: Asian Women

(number and percent of Asian women aged 15 or older with income, and median income of those with income, 2010; women in thousands as of 2011)

	number	percent	median income
Asian women with income	**5,047**	**100.0%**	**$23,664**
Earnings	3,686	73.0	31,121
Wages and salary	3,493	69.2	31,555
Nonfarm self-employment	235	4.7	15,874
Farm self-employment	23	0.5	–
Social Security	664	13.2	9,980
SSI (Supplemental Security)	143	2.8	7,194
Public Assistance	49	1.0	–
Veteran's benefits	8	0.2	–
Survivor's benefits	58	1.1	–
Disability benefits	18	0.4	–
Unemployment compensation	233	4.6	6,539
Worker's compensation	34	0.7	–
Property income	2,216	43.9	1,518
Interest	2,059	40.8	1,385
Dividends	630	12.5	1,578
Rents, royalties, estates, trusts	224	4.4	2,224
Retirement income	239	4.7	10,544
Company or union retirement	99	2.0	6,805
Federal government retirement	20	0.4	–
Military retirement	23	0.5	–
State or local government retirement	65	1.3	–
Railroad retirement	2	0.0	–
Annuities	2	0.0	–
IRA or Keogh, or 401(k)	9	0.2	–
Pension income	169	3.3	9,988
Company or union retirement	78	1.5	4,865
Federal government retirement	15	0.3	–
Military retirement	5	0.1	–
State or local government retirement	48	1.0	–
Railroad retirement	2	0.0	–
Annuities	2	0.0	–
Alimony	14	0.3	–
Child support	92	1.8	5,247
Educational assistance	261	5.2	4,199
Financial assistance from outside the household	121	2.4	9,282
Other income	23	0.5	–

Note: Asians are those who identify themselves as being of the race alone and those who identify themselves as being of the race in combination with other races. "–" means sample is too small to make a reliable estimate.
Source: Bureau of the Census, 2011 Current Population Survey Annual Social and Economic Supplement, Internet site http://www.census.gov/hhes/www/cpstables/032011/perinc/toc.htm; calculations by New Strategist

Table 3.44 Median Income of Women by Source of Income, 2010: Black Women

(number and percent of black women aged 15 or older with income, and median income of those with income, 2010; women in thousands as of 2011)

	number	percent	median income
Black women with income	**13,931**	**100.0%**	**$19,634**
Earnings	9,549	68.5	25,308
Wages and salary	9,349	67.1	25,419
Nonfarm self-employment	341	2.4	6,474
Farm self-employment	60	0.4	–
Social Security	2,696	19.4	10,128
SSI (Supplemental Security)	929	6.7	7,811
Public Assistance	604	4.3	2,845
Veteran's benefits	80	0.6	6,346
Survivor's benefits	161	1.2	8,012
Disability benefits	134	1.0	6,283
Unemployment compensation	927	6.7	5,305
Worker's compensation	96	0.7	2,899
Property income	3,130	22.5	1,449
Interest	2,904	20.8	1,368
Dividends	563	4.0	1,561
Rents, royalties, estates, trusts	247	1.8	2,207
Retirement income	982	7.0	11,335
Company or union retirement	515	3.7	7,714
Federal government retirement	104	0.7	23,575
Military retirement	35	0.3	–
State or local government retirement	244	1.8	15,898
Railroad retirement	6	0.0	–
Annuities	28	0.2	–
IRA or Keogh, or 401(k)	17	0.1	–
Pension income	755	5.4	13,380
Company or union retirement	429	3.1	9,658
Federal government retirement	82	0.6	25,409
Military retirement	22	0.2	–
State or local government retirement	204	1.5	17,661
Railroad retirement	2	0.0	–
Annuities	14	0.1	–
Alimony	19	0.1	–
Child support	896	6.4	2,807
Educational assistance	1,128	8.1	4,188
Financial assistance from outside the household	234	1.7	2,108
Other income	61	0.4	–

Note: Blacks are those who identify themselves as being of the race alone and those who identify themselves as being of the race in combination with other races. "–" means sample is too small to make a reliable estimate.
Source: Bureau of the Census, 2011 Current Population Survey Annual Social and Economic Supplement, Internet site http://www.census.gov/hhes/www/cpstables/032011/perinc/toc.htm; calculations by New Strategist

Table 3.45 Median Income of Women by Source of Income, 2010: Hispanic Women

(number and percent of Hispanic women aged 15 or older with income, and median income of those with income, 2010; women in thousands as of 2011)

	number	percent	median income
Hispanic women with income	**12,122**	**100.0%**	**$16,269**
Earnings	9,029	74.5	20,160
Wages and salary	8,691	71.7	20,339
Nonfarm self-employment	451	3.7	10,105
Farm self-employment	35	0.3	–
Social Security	1,720	14.2	8,887
SSI (Supplemental Security)	503	4.1	7,384
Public Assistance	466	3.8	3,271
Veteran's benefits	28	0.2	–
Survivor's benefits	106	0.9	6,364
Disability benefits	88	0.7	4,627
Unemployment compensation	675	5.6	5,132
Worker's compensation	94	0.8	2,828
Property income	2,789	23.0	1,438
Interest	2,603	21.5	1,350
Dividends	485	4.0	1,576
Rents, royalties, estates, trusts	308	2.5	1,916
Retirement income	438	3.6	7,970
Company or union retirement	213	1.8	5,350
Federal government retirement	23	0.2	–
Military retirement	11	0.1	–
State or local government retirement	130	1.1	11,947
Railroad retirement	8	0.1	–
Annuities	14	0.1	–
IRA or Keogh, or 401(k)	11	0.1	–
Pension income	271	2.2	9,667
Company or union retirement	149	1.2	6,188
Federal government retirement	10	0.1	–
Military retirement	9	0.1	–
State or local government retirement	86	0.7	18,963
Railroad retirement	4	0.0	–
Annuities	4	0.0	–
Alimony	32	0.3	–
Child support	602	5.0	3,671
Educational assistance	682	5.6	3,514
Financial assistance from outside the household	196	1.6	3,495
Other income	35	0.3	–

Note: "–" means sample is too small to make a reliable estimate.
Source: Bureau of the Census, 2011 Current Population Survey Annual Social and Economic Supplement, Internet site http://www.census.gov/hhes/www/cpstables/032011/perinc/toc.htm; calculations by New Strategist

Table 3.46 Median Income of Women by Source of Income, 2010: Non-Hispanic White Women

(number and percent of non-Hispanic white women aged 15 or older with income, and median income of those with income, 2010; women in thousands as of 2011)

	number	percent	median income
Non-Hispanic white women with income	**74,365**	**100.0%**	**$21,754**
Earnings	49,420	66.5	28,464
Wages and salary	46,932	63.1	29,553
Nonfarm self-employment	3,588	4.8	9,543
Farm self-employment	542	0.7	1,634
Social Security	19,490	26.2	11,197
SSI (Supplemental Security)	1,591	2.1	7,278
Public Assistance	648	0.9	2,268
Veteran's benefits	384	0.5	10,356
Survivor's benefits	1,947	2.6	7,291
Disability benefits	483	0.6	8,698
Unemployment compensation	3,077	4.1	5,291
Worker's compensation	385	0.5	3,773
Property income	38,495	51.8	1,603
Interest	36,275	48.8	1,438
Dividends	12,371	16.6	1,652
Rents, royalties, estates, trusts	4,287	5.8	2,283
Retirement income	8,005	10.8	9,399
Company or union retirement	4,034	5.4	6,099
Federal government retirement	595	0.8	12,242
Military retirement	265	0.4	11,376
State or local government retirement	2,323	3.1	15,634
Railroad retirement	132	0.2	14,655
Annuities	242	0.3	5,768
IRA or Keogh, or 401(k)	279	0.4	7,366
Pension income	5,943	8.0	9,456
Company or union retirement	3,081	4.1	5,655
Federal government retirement	414	0.6	12,705
Military retirement	86	0.1	14,006
State or local government retirement	2,045	2.7	16,197
Railroad retirement	104	0.1	14,557
Annuities	88	0.1	9,770
Alimony	316	0.4	9,321
Child support	2,797	3.8	4,321
Educational assistance	3,489	4.7	4,622
Financial assistance from outside the household	916	1.2	4,059
Other income	422	0.6	1,601

Note: Non-Hispanic whites are those who identify themselves as white alone and not Hispanic.
Source: Bureau of the Census, 2011 Current Population Survey Annual Social and Economic Supplement, Internet site http://www.census.gov/hhes/www/cpstables/032011/perinc/toc.htm; calculations by New Strategist

4

Discretionary Income

In 2009, the average American household had $13,179 in discretionary income. This is money house-holds could spend freely after paying their bills and buying necessities. In the aggregate, American households control $1.6 trillion in discretionary income.

Discretionary income is the money that remains for spending (or saving or paying down debt) after one has paid for all the necessary costs of living a middle-class lifestyle. Many businesses depend on discretionary dollars for sales and profits. This dependency makes discretionary income statistics important for marketers and other researchers. Despite this importance, however, discretion-ary income statistics can be hard to find because no government agency is charged with producing them. This chapter contains estimates of discretionary income for 2009 produced by New Strategist's researchers. New Strategist's previous discretionary income estimates were for 2007.

Between 2007 and 2009, the amount of discretionary income available to the average house-hold fell 2 percent, after adjusting for inflation (see table 4.1). This decline is not surprising. What is surprising is that the decline was not greater or more widespread. In fact, many households saw their discretionary income grow between 2007 and 2009. The households with growing discretionary income included those headed by people aged 25 to 44, households with incomes between $40,000 and $150,000, blacks and Hispanics, households in the Midwest, and householders with a high school degree but not a bachelor's degree. How could discretionary income increase for these typically strug-gling households in the midst of the Great Recession? For good reason, the trends in discretionary income during this difficult time are counterintuitive: the households with more discretionary income are those who cut their budgets the most.

To understand the increase in discretionary income for many struggling households, you need to be familiar with two terms: disposable income or take-home pay, and nondiscretionary—or nec-essary—spending. Disposable income is the income households bring home after taxes and manda-tory payroll deductions for retirement plans. Disposable income fell pretty much across the board between 2007 and 2009, after adjusting for inflation (see table 4.2). But—and this is the important point—many households cut their necessary spending even more than their incomes fell (see table 4.3). The households that succeeded in cutting their necessary spending the most were the ones who saw their discretionary income rise since discretionary income is what is left over after subtracting necessary spending from disposable income.

Let's look at some examples. Households headed by 35-to-44-year-olds cut their annual spend-ing on necessities by $2,696 between 2007 and 2009 (see table 4.3), after adjusting for inflation. This cut was far greater than the $1,657 decline in their disposable income during those years (see table 4.2). Consequently, their discretionary income grew (see table 4.1). Black households cut their spending on necessities by $1,708, while their disposable income fell by a smaller $1,004, so their discretionary income grew. Midwestern households cut their necessary spending by $2,151 while their disposable income fell by a smaller $1,175, so their discretionary income grew as well.

How did these households succeed in cutting their spending on necessities so severely? One of the most important factors was the decline in homeownership. The homeownership rate of 35-to-44-year-olds, for example, fell from 68 to 65 percent between 2007 and 2009. Consequently, the age group managed to cut its annual spending on housing by 4 percent during those years, after adjusting for inflation. Most households that experienced an increase in discretionary income between 2007 and 2009 saw their homeownership rate fall. By becoming or remaining renters rather than homeowners, they succeeded in cutting their spending on the single biggest item in the household budget—housing.

Just because many households had more discretionary *income* in 2009 than in 2007 does not mean they spent that money. In fact, they did not. Regardless of the demographics, most households cut their discretionary *spending* between 2007 and 2009, after adjusting for inflation (see table 4.4). Householders aged 35 to 44, for example, cut their discretionary spending by 8 percent between 2007 and 2009, after adjusting for inflation—a $982 cut. Households in the Midwest cut their discretionary spending by $978. Black households cut their discretionary spending by $299. It is likely that many households spent their extra discretionary income paying down debt.

Estimating discretionary income

New Strategist produced the estimates of discretionary income shown here in three steps. First we calculated disposable income—or take-home pay. We started with 2009 before-tax income data from the Bureau of Labor Statistics' Consumer Expenditure Survey (CEX). Disposable income is what remains after subtracting federal, state, and local income taxes; payroll taxes including Federal Insurance Contributions Act deductions; and mandatory deductions from paychecks for retirement plans.

In step two, we examined CEX expenditures item by item to determine necessary household expenses. The CEX is the only ongoing national survey of American household spending. It tracks the dollars Americans spend by detailed category of goods and services. By tagging necessities, we estimated nondiscretionary—or necessary—household spending.

In the third step, we subtracted necessary expenses from disposable income. The difference between necessary spending and disposable income is discretionary income. We calculated average and aggregate discretionary income for households by age of householder, household income, household type, race and Hispanic origin of householder, region of residence, and educational attainment of householder. Note that discretionary *income* is not the same as discretionary *spending*. Discretionary income is the money available to spend on discretionary items. Discretionary spending is the money households actually spend on discretionary items.

Most major expenditure categories have a mixture of discretionary and necessary spending. A brief description of how we define various items by category follows, along with the discretionary share of spending in each category.

• **Food at home, 19 percent discretionary.** Most food-at-home items (groceries) were defined as necessary expenses with the exception of sweets and snack foods. Items such as prepared desserts, colas, ice cream, candy, etc. were deemed discretionary. Spending on groceries purchased on trips was also defined as discretionary.

• **Food away from home, 59 percent discretionary.** Meals at fast-food restaurants and employer and school cafeterias were tagged as necessary expenses. Meals at full-service restaurants were deemed discretionary. All snacks were identified as discretionary, as were restaurant meals on trips and catered affairs.

• **Alcoholic beverages, 100 percent discretionary.**

• **Housing and household operations, 7 percent discretionary.** We tagged most housing expenses as necessary except for spending on other lodging, which includes hotel and motel expenses. Also identified as discretionary were expenditures on housekeeping services, gardening and lawn care services, and items such as outdoor equipment (grills), decorative items for the home, and luggage. Computers and cell phone service were considered necessary expenses. Note: the inclusion of computers as a necessary expense is new to this set of discretionary income estimates, making these discretionary income estimates incomparable with the 2007 estimates published in the previous edition of *American Incomes*. However, the 2007 discretionary income data shown in this chapter have been adjusted to include computers as a necessary rather than a discretionary expense.

• **Apparel, 11 percent discretionary.** Costumes, dry cleaning expenses, watches, and jewelry were the only apparel items identified as discretionary.

• **Transportation, 8 percent discretionary**. Spending on other vehicles such as motorcycles and airplanes was identified as discretionary. Vehicle audio and video equipment as well as global positioning services and automobile clubs were also classified as discretionary. Any spending on transportation related to travel, such as vehicle rentals, airline fares, ship fares, and so on, was considered discretionary.

• **Health care, 1 percent discretionary.** Vitamins were the only discretionary item in the health care category.

• **Entertainment, 100 percent discretionary.**

• **Personal care, 24 percent discretionary.** Cosmetics, perfume, and bath products were the only discretionary items in the personal care category.

• **Reading, 100 percent discretionary.**

• **Education, 16 percent discretionary.** The only discretionary items in the category were elementary and high school tuition and testing and tutoring services. We consider spending on college tuition a necessary expense in today's competitive economy.

• **Tobacco products and smoking supplies, 100 percent discretionary.**

• **Financial and miscellaneous products, 25 percent discretionary.** Discretionary expenses include lottery tickets, credit card memberships, and all cash gifts and charitable contributions. Also tagged as discretionary in this category were voluntary contributions to retirement plans.

Entertainment is the discretionary item on which the average household spends the most (see table 4.5). Not only is entertainment one of the biggest household expenses overall, but we tagged the entire category as discretionary. In 2009, the average household spent $2,693 on entertainment. Spending on the number-two discretionary item, cash contributions to religious organizations, is considerably smaller at $725. Interestingly, two of the top-10 discretionary expenses are contributions—religious contributions is number two and cash gifts to people in other households (mostly family members) is number seven. Eating at full-serve restaurants is an important part of discretionary spending, with dinner at full-service restaurants ranking third. Two travel categories also make the top-10 list—airline fares in ninth and lodging in tenth place. The vices place highly among discretionary expenses, with alcoholic beverages in fifth place and tobacco in sixth place.

What is discretionary?

No definition of necessary expenses can be exact. All are likely to include at least some discretionary items, and some necessary items are probably included in discretionary spending as well. One reason for the overlap is that categories of expenses in the Consumer Expenditure Survey can include both discretionary and necessary items.

Ultimately, defining basic expenses is subjective on the part of the consumer and a judgment call on the part of researchers. Some of the grocery spending we included as basic may be discretionary—for example buying an expensive steak in the grocery store. Others might argue that spending on fast food is discretionary, but many Americans would disagree. Fast-food meals have become a necessary expense for today's busy two-earner households.

Consumer Expenditure Survey data do not allow researchers to differentiate high-end homes, cars, or clothes from the bargain-basement variety. Consequently, some discretionary dollars are included in our calculations of necessary spending. For this reason, these estimates of discretionary income should be considered conservative.

Table 4.1 Discretionary Household Income Trends, 2007 and 2009

(average discretionary income per household by selected demographic characteristics of householder, 2007 and 2009; nominal and percent change, 2007–09; in 2009 dollars)

	2009	2007 (in 2009$)	change dollars	change percent
AGE OF HOUSEHOLDER				
Total households	**$13,179**	**$13,432**	**–$253**	**–1.9%**
Under age 25	0	2,775	–2,775	–100.0
Age 25 to 34	10,591	8,158	2,433	29.8
Age 35 to 44	16,811	15,772	1,038	6.6
Age 45 to 54	19,081	19,479	–398	–2.0
Age 55 to 64	17,174	18,161	–987	–5.4
Aged 65 or older	7,269	8,890	–1,621	–18.2
HOUSEHOLD INCOME				
Total households	**13,179**	**13,432**	**–253**	**–1.9**
Under $20,000	0	0	0	–
$20,000 to $39,999	0	0	0	–
$40,000 to $49,999	5,613	4,700	913	19.4
$50,000 to $69,999	9,896	8,417	1,479	17.6
$70,000 to $79,999	15,017	14,931	86	0.6
$80,000 to $99,999	20,667	18,801	1,866	9.9
$100,000 or more	60,100	64,750	–4,649	–7.2
$100,000 to $119,999	29,148	25,484	3,664	14.4
$120,000 to $149,999	40,324	36,672	3,652	10.0
$150,000 or more	100,414	115,806	–15,392	–13.3
HOUSEHOLD TYPE				
Total households	**13,179**	**13,432**	**–253**	**–1.9**
Married couples	20,018	24,996	–4,978	–19.9
Married couples without children at home	18,878	27,221	–8,343	–30.6
Married couples with children at home	21,167	23,668	–2,501	–10.6
Married couples with preschoolers	15,535	19,222	–3,688	–19.2
Married couples with children aged 6 to 17	21,255	22,864	–1,609	–7.0
Married couples with adult children at home	24,072	28,122	–4,050	–14.4
Single parents with children under age 18 at home	175	1,239	–1,064	–85.9
People living alone	4,397	5,996	–1,600	–26.7
RACE AND HISPANIC ORIGIN OF HOUSEHOLDER				
Total households	**13,179**	**13,432**	**–253**	**–1.9**
Asian	15,762	18,473	–2,711	–14.7
Black	7,726	7,022	705	10.0
Hispanic	6,292	5,852	441	7.5
Non-Hispanic white and other	14,517	15,592	–1,075	–6.9

	2009	2007 (in 2009$)	change	
			dollars	percent
REGION				
Total households	**$13,179**	**$13,432**	**−$253**	**−1.9%**
Northeast	17,119	18,498	−1,380	−7.5
Midwest	12,916	11,940	976	8.2
South	11,891	11,911	−21	−0.2
West	12,279	13,166	−887	−6.7
EDUCATION OF HOUSEHOLDER				
Total households	**13,179**	**13,432**	**−253**	**−1.9**
Not a high school graduate	3,594	4,065	−471	−11.6
High school graduate only	8,664	7,901	763	9.7
Some college	8,640	8,441	199	2.4
Associate's degree	11,315	10,398	917	8.8
College graduate	25,601	27,960	−2,360	−8.4
Bachelor's degree only	21,720	22,636	−916	−4.0
Graduate degree	33,075	37,799	−4,725	−12.5

Note: For the definition of discretionary income, see chapter introduction. "−" means denominator is 0.
Source: Calculations by New Strategist based on the Bureau of Labor Statistics' 2007 and 2009 Consumer Expenditure Surveys

Table 4.2 Disposable Household Income Trends, 2007 and 2009

(average disposable income per household by selected demographic characteristics of householder, 2007 and 2009; change in dollars and percent, 2007–09; in 2009 dollars)

	2009	2007 (in 2009$)	change dollars	change percent
AGE OF HOUSEHOLDER				
Total households	**$52,072**	**$53,823**	**–$1,751**	**–3.3%**
Under age 25	22,292	27,972	–5,680	–20.3
Age 25 to 34	48,863	48,747	115	0.2
Age 35 to 44	62,838	64,495	–1,657	–2.6
Age 45 to 54	65,775	66,979	–1,205	–1.8
Age 55 to 64	57,537	60,155	–2,618	–4.4
Aged 65 or older	35,701	37,135	–1,434	–3.9
HOUSEHOLD INCOME				
Total households	**52,072**	**53,823**	**–1,750**	**–3.3**
Under $20,000	9,059	9,756	–697	–7.1
$20,000 to $39,999	25,761	26,488	–727	–2.7
$40,000 to $49,999	37,899	38,882	–983	–2.5
$50,000 to $69,999	49,301	50,603	–1,302	–2.6
$70,000 to $79,999	61,014	62,913	–1,899	–3.0
$80,000 to $99,999	72,303	74,069	–1,765	–2.4
$100,000 or more	134,508	142,555	–8,047	–5.6
$100,000 to $119,999	88,503	88,023	480	0.5
$120,000 to $149,999	107,590	110,574	–2,984	–2.7
$150,000 or more	192,791	208,811	–16,020	–7.7
HOUSEHOLD TYPE				
Total households	**52,072**	**53,823**	**–1,751**	**–3.3**
Married couples	69,498	72,731	–3,233	–4.4
Married couples without children at home	61,991	66,698	–4,707	–7.1
Married couples with children at home	75,694	78,137	–2,443	–3.1
Marred couples with preschoolers	67,613	69,078	–1,465	–2.1
Married couples with children aged 6 to 17	76,357	78,245	–1,888	–2.4
Married couples with adult children at home	79,090	83,951	–4,862	–5.8
Single parents with children under age 18 at home	30,842	31,024	–182	–0.6
People living alone	27,637	27,358	279	1.0
RACE AND HISPANIC ORIGIN OF HOUSEHOLDER				
Total households	**52,072**	**53,823**	**–1,751**	**–3.3**
Asian	62,058	69,293	–7,234	–10.4
Black	37,868	38,872	–1,004	–2.6
Hispanic	42,027	42,275	–249	–0.6
Non-Hispanic white and other	55,885	57,935	–2,050	–3.5

	2009	2007 (in 2009$)	change dollars	percent
REGION				
Total households	**$52,072**	**$53,823**	**–$1,750**	**–3.3%**
Northeast	60,125	60,486	–362	–0.6
Midwest	49,728	50,904	–1,175	–2.3
South	48,422	49,385	–963	–2.0
West	53,696	58,332	–4,635	–7.9
EDUCATION OF HOUSEHOLDER				
Total households	**52,072**	**53,823**	**–1,750**	**–3.3**
Not a high school graduate	28,889	30,350	–1,461	–4.8
High school graduate only	40,117	40,820	–703	–1.7
Some college	44,406	46,715	–2,310	–4.9
Associate's degree	51,480	54,361	–2,881	–5.3
College graduate	79,069	82,639	–3,570	–4.3
Bachelor's degree only	73,143	74,682	–1,539	–2.1
Graduate degree	90,472	97,258	–6,786	–7.0

Note: Disposable income is what remains after subtracting federal, state, and local income taxes; payroll taxes including FICA; and mandatory deductions from paychecks for retirement plans from average household before-tax income.
Source: Calculations by New Strategist based on the Bureau of Labor Statistics' 2007 and 2009 Consumer Expenditure Surveys

Table 4.3 Non-Discretionary (Necessary) Household Spending Trends, 2007 and 2009

(average nondiscretionary (necessary) spending per household by selected demographic characteristics of house-holders, 2007 and 2009; nominal and percent change, 2007–09; in 2009 dollars)

	2009	2007 (in 2009$)	change dollars	change percent
AGE OF HOUSEHOLDER				
Total households	**$38,893**	**$40,391**	**–$1,498**	**–3.7%**
Under age 25	23,865	25,197	–1,331	–5.3
Age 25 to 34	38,272	40,589	–2,318	–5.7
Age 35 to 44	46,027	48,723	–2,696	–5.5
Age 45 to 54	46,694	47,500	–806	–1.7
Age 55 to 64	40,363	41,994	–1,631	–3.9
Aged 65 or older	28,433	28,245	187	0.7
HOUSEHOLD INCOME				
Total households	**38,893**	**40,391**	**–1,498**	**–3.7**
Under $20,000	17,962	17,698	264	1.5
$20,000 to $39,999	26,478	27,183	–705	–2.6
$40,000 to $49,999	32,286	34,182	–1,896	–5.5
$50,000 to $69,999	39,405	42,186	–2,781	–6.6
$70,000 to $79,999	45,997	47,982	–1,985	–4.1
$80,000 to $99,999	51,637	55,268	–3,631	–6.6
$100,000 or more	74,408	77,805	–3,397	–4.4
$100,000 to $119,999	59,355	62,539	–3,184	–5.1
$120,000 to $149,999	67,266	73,902	–6,636	–9.0
$150,000 or more	92,377	93,005	–628	–0.7
HOUSEHOLD TYPE				
Total households	**38,893**	**40,391**	**–1,498**	**–3.7**
Married couples	49,479	47,734	1,745	3.7
Married couples without children at home	43,113	39,478	3,636	9.2
Married couples with children at home	54,528	54,470	58	0.1
Marred couples with preschoolers	52,079	49,856	2,223	4.5
Married couples with children aged 6 to 17	55,102	55,380	–279	–0.5
Married couples with adult children at home	55,018	55,829	–812	–1.5
Single parents with children under age 18 at home	30,667	29,785	882	3.0
People living alone	23,241	21,362	1,879	8.8
RACE AND HISPANIC ORIGIN OF HOUSEHOLDER				
Total households	**38,893**	**40,391**	**–1,498**	**–3.7**
Asian	46,296	50,820	–4,523	–8.9
Black	30,142	31,851	–1,709	–5.4
Hispanic	35,734	36,424	–689	–1.9
Non-Hispanic white and other	41,368	42,343	–975	–2.3

	2009	2007 (in 2009$)	change	
			dollars	percent
REGION				
Total households	**$38,893**	**$40,391**	**−$1,498**	**−3.7%**
Northeast	43,006	41,988	1,018	2.4
Midwest	36,813	38,964	−2,151	−5.5
South	36,531	37,474	−942	−2.5
West	41,417	45,165	−3,748	−8.3
EDUCATION OF HOUSEHOLDER				
Total households	**38,893**	**40,391**	**−1,498**	**−3.7**
Not a high school graduate	25,295	26,285	−990	−3.8
High school graduate only	31,453	32,918	−1,466	−4.5
Some college	35,765	38,274	−2,509	−6.6
Associate's degree	40,165	43,963	−3,798	−8.6
College graduate	53,468	54,678	−1,210	−2.2
Bachelor's degree only	51,423	52,046	−623	−1.2
Graduate degree	57,397	59,459	−2,062	−3.5

Note: For the definition of nondiscretionary expenses, see chapter introduction.
Source: Calculations by New Strategist based on the Bureau of Labor Statistics' 2007 and 2009 Consumer Expenditure Surveys

Table 4.4 Discretionary Household Spending Trends, 2007 and 2009

(average discretionary spending per household by selected demographic characteristics of householder, 2007 and 2009; nominal and percent change, 2007–09; in 2009 dollars)

	2009	2007 (in 2009$)	change dollars	change percent
AGE OF HOUSEHOLDER				
Total households	**$10,174**	**$10,970**	**–$796**	**–7.3%**
Under age 25	4,253	5,282	–1,029	–19.5
Age 25 to 34	8,223	8,569	–347	–4.0
Age 35 to 44	11,274	12,256	–982	–8.0
Age 45 to 54	12,014	12,855	–841	–6.5
Age 55 to 64	12,100	13,659	–1,559	–11.4
Aged 65 or older	9,130	9,552	–423	–4.4
HOUSEHOLD INCOME				
Total households	**10,174**	**10,970**	**–796**	**–7.3**
Under $20,000	3,798	3,672	126	3.4
$20,000 to $39,999	5,956	6,016	–60	–1.0
$40,000 to $49,999	7,268	8,326	–1,059	–12.7
$50,000 to $69,999	9,495	9,992	–496	–5.0
$70,000 to $79,999	11,836	12,036	–200	–1.7
$80,000 to $99,999	13,391	14,720	–1,329	–9.0
$100,000 or more	23,168	26,742	–3,574	–13.4
$100,000 to $119,999	16,785	18,000	–1,215	–6.7
$120,000 to $149,999	18,541	21,150	–2,609	–12.3
$150,000 or more	31,930	37,826	–5,896	–15.6
HOUSEHOLD TYPE				
Total households	**10,174**	**10,970**	**–796**	**–7.3**
Married couples	13,625	14,763	–1,138	–7.7
Married couples without children at home	13,664	15,864	–2,200	–13.9
Married couples with children at home	13,953	14,277	–325	–2.3
Marred couples with preschoolers	10,059	10,714	–654	–6.1
Married couples with children aged 6 to 17	15,227	15,415	–188	–1.2
Married couples with adult children at home	14,072	14,748	–677	–4.6
Single parents with children under age 18 at home	6,096	6,807	–711	–10.4
People living alone	6,164	6,340	–176	–2.8
RACE AND HISPANIC ORIGIN OF HOUSEHOLDER				
Total households	**10,174**	**10,970**	**–796**	**–7.3**
Asian	10,012	11,678	–1,667	–14.3
Black	5,169	5,468	–299	–5.5
Hispanic	6,247	6,518	–271	–4.2
Non-Hispanic white and other	10,952	12,499	–1,548	–12.4

	2009	2007 (in 2009$)	change dollars	change percent
REGION				
Total households	**$10,174**	**$10,970**	**−$796**	**−7.3%**
Northeast	10,862	11,427	−565	−4.9
Midwest	9,738	10,717	−978	−9.1
South	9,218	9,568	−350	−3.7
West	11,588	13,079	−1,492	−11.4
EDUCATION OF HOUSEHOLDER				
Total households	**10,174**	**10,970**	**−796**	**−7.3**
Not a high school graduate	5,029	4,964	65	1.3
High school graduate only	7,240	7,605	−365	−4.8
Some college	8,932	9,194	−262	−2.9
Associate's degree	10,281	10,587	−306	−2.9
College graduate	15,921	18,377	−2,456	−13.4
Bachelor's degree only	14,485	15,941	−1,456	−9.1
Graduate degree	18,675	22,833	−4,158	−18.2

Note: For the definition of discretionary expenses, see chapter introduction.
Source: Calculations by New Strategist based on the Bureau of Labor Statistics' 2007 and 2009 Consumer Expenditure Surveys

Table 4.5 Top-10 Discretionary Expenditures, 2009

(amount spent by the average household on the 10 discretionary items on which the average household spends the most, 2009)

		average household spending
1.	Entertainment	$2,692.66
2.	Cash contributions to religious organizations	724.60
3.	Dinner at full service restaurants	699.59
4.	Nonpayroll deposit to retirement plans	461.03
5.	Alcoholic beverages	434.73
6.	Tobacco products and smoking supplies	379.69
7.	Cash gifts	369.31
8.	Owned vacation homes	303.02
9.	Airline fares	300.92
10.	Lodging on trips	300.46

Source: Calculations by New Strategist based on the Bureau of Labor Statistics' 2009 Consumer Expenditure Survey

Discretionary Income Peaks in Middle Age

Householders aged 55 to 64 have the most discretionary income.

The average household had $13,179 in discretionary income in 2009. That sounds like a lot of money, but it amounts to just $36 per day per household for all spending on entertainment, travel, charitable contributions, dinners at sit-down restaurants, and snack foods, among other items. Discretionary income was a higher $13,432 in 2007, after adjusting for inflation, but the 2 percent decline between 2007 and 2009 is a modest drop considering the severity of the economic downturn.

Discretionary income varies greatly by age, and young adults have the least. Householders under age 25, in fact, had no discretionary income in 2009 (down from $2,775 in 2007, after adjusting for inflation)—meaning their spending on necessities absorbs all their income. Discretionary income peaks in middle age, along with overall household income. Householders aged 45 to 54 have the most discretionary income—$19,081 in 2009.

Overall, American households controlled $1.6 trillion discretionary dollars in 2009. Householders aged 45 to 54 have the largest share—30 percent. Households headed by 35-to-44-year-olds control about the same amount of discretionary income as those headed by people aged 55 to 64 (23 and 22 percent, respectively).

■ Discretionary income increased for householders aged 25 to 44 between 2007 and 2009, but only because of sharp cutbacks in their spending on necessities (see chapter introduction for more about this).

Discretionary income fell in most age groups between 2007 and 2009

(percent change in discretionary income per household, by age of householder, 2007 to 2009; in 2009 dollars)

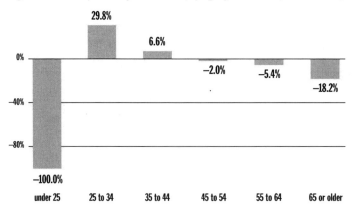

Table 4.6 Discretionary Income by Age of Householder, 2009

(number and percent distribution of total households, average before-tax household income, average discretionary income per household and per household member, aggregate discretionary income, and percent distribution of aggregate, by age of householder, 2009)

	total households		average before-tax household income	discretionary income			
	number (in 000s)	percent distribution		average per household	average per capita	aggregate (in millions)	percent distribution of aggregate
Total households	**120,847**	**100.0%**	**$62,857**	**$13,179**	**$5,272**	**$1,592,641**	**100.0%**
Under age 25	7,875	6.5	25,695	0	0	0	0.0
Age 25 to 34	20,044	16.6	58,946	10,591	3,782	212,283	13.3
Age 35 to 44	22,199	18.4	77,005	16,811	5,094	373,177	23.4
Age 45 to 54	25,440	21.1	80,976	19,081	6,815	485,417	30.5
Age 55 to 64	20,731	17.2	70,609	17,174	8,178	356,033	22.4
Aged 65 or older	24,557	20.3	39,862	7,269	4,276	178,494	11.2
Age 65 to 74	12,848	10.6	47,286	8,863	4,665	113,871	7.1
Age 75 or older	11,709	9.7	31,715	5,498	3,436	64,377	4.0

Note: For the definition of discretionary income, see chapter introduction.
Source: Calculations by New Strategist based on the Bureau of Labor Statistics' 2009 Consumer Expenditure Survey

More than 40 Percent of Households Have No Discretionary Income

The average household with an income of less than $40,000 has no discretionary dollars.

Discretionary income rises dramatically as household income increases. But 44 percent of households have no discretionary spending power. The average household with an income below $40,000 must spend all of its disposable income on necessities. Of course, many still find a few dollars for a movie, dinner at a full-service restaurant, cosmetics, or a six-pack of beer. That's because many lower income households spend more than they make. Family assistance, borrowing, and unreported income make up the difference.

Households with incomes between $40,000 and $49,999 had an average of $5,613 in discretionary income in 2009. The figure rises to a peak of $100,414 for households with incomes of $150,000 or more. Households with incomes of $150,000 or more control 53 percent of the nation's $1.6 billion discretionary dollars.

■ Discretionary income grew between 2007 and 2009 for households with incomes between $40,000 and $150,000, primarily because those households sharply cut their spending on necessities (see chapter introduction for more about this).

Discretionary income grew for middle-income households

(percent change in discretionary income per household, by household income, 2007 to 2009; in 2009 dollars)

Table 4.7 Discretionary Income by Household Income, 2009

(number and percent distribution of total households, average before-tax household income, average discretionary income per household and per household member, aggregate discretionary income, and percent distribution of aggregate, by household income, 2009)

	total households		average before-tax household income	discretionary income			
	number (in 000s)	percent distribution		average per household	average per capita	aggregate (in millions)	percent distribution of aggregate
Total households	**120,847**	**100.0%**	**$62,857**	**$13,179**	**$5,272**	**$1,592,641**	**100.0%**
Under $20,000	25,347	21.0	10,304	0	0	0	0.0
$20,000 to $39,999	28,075	23.2	29,460	0	0	0	0.0
$40,000 to $49,999	11,444	9.5	44,733	5,613	2,245	64,232	4.0
$50,000 to $69,999	17,799	14.7	59,009	9,896	3,665	176,138	11.1
$70,000 to $79,999	6,640	5.5	74,594	15,017	5,178	99,713	6.3
$80,000 to $99,999	9,951	8.2	89,096	20,667	6,889	205,655	12.9
$100,000 or more	21,589	17.9	165,062	60,100	19,387	1,297,509	81.5
$100,000 to $119,999	7,260	6.0	108,564	29,148	9,716	211,615	13.3
$120,000 to $149,999	5,882	4.9	132,565	40,324	12,601	237,186	14.9
$150,000 or more	8,447	7.0	236,246	100,414	31,379	848,198	53.3

Note: For the definition of discretionary income, see chapter introduction.
Source: Calculations by New Strategist based on the Bureau of Labor Statistics' 2009 Consumer Expenditure Survey

Couples with Adult Children at Home Have the Most Discretionary Income

Single-parent families have very little extra money.

Married couples with adult children at home have the most discretionary income per household—an average of $24,072 in 2009. At the other end of the scale, the average single-parent family had just $175 in discretionary dollars.

A look at discretionary income per household member finds a different pattern. Couples without children at home—many of them empty-nesters—have the most discretionary income, an average of $9,439 per household member. Married couples with children at home have a much smaller $5,292 in discretionary income per household member. People who live alone have $4,397 in discretionary income available to them.

■ Single parents saw their discretionary income fall the most between 2007 and 2009, after adjusting for inflation. Married couples with school-aged children experienced the smallest decline.

Every type of household saw its discretionary income fall

(percent change in discretionary income per household, by type of household, 2007 to 2009; in 2009 dollars)

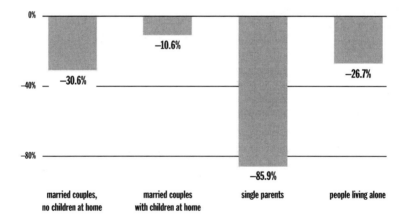

Table 4.8 Discretionary Income by Type of Household, 2009

(number and percent distribution of total households, average before-tax household income, average discretionary income per household and per household member, aggregate discretionary income, and percent distribution of aggregate, by type of household, 2009)

	total households		average before-tax household income	discretionary income			
	number (in 000s)	percent distribution		average per household	average per capita	aggregate (in millions)	percent distribution of aggregate
Total households	**120,847**	**100.0%**	**$62,857**	**$13,179**	**$5,272**	**$1,592,641**	**100.0%**
Married couple	61,271	50.7	84,785	20,018	6,256	1,226,548	77.0
Married couples, without children at home	26,852	22.2	75,876	18,878	9,439	506,912	31.8
Married couples with children at home	29,480	24.4	92,616	21,167	5,292	623,993	39.2
Oldest child under 6	5,154	4.3	81,821	15,535	4,438	80,065	5.0
Oldest child 6 to 17	14,983	12.4	94,302	21,255	5,184	318,461	20.0
Oldest child 18 or older	9,342	7.7	95,867	24,072	6,172	224,881	14.1
Single parent with children under age 18 at home	6,810	5.6	35,845	175	60	1,190	0.1
Single-person household	34,770	28.8	32,780	4,397	4,397	152,868	9.6

Note: For the definition of discretionary income, see chapter introduction.
Source: Calculations by New Strategist based on the Bureau of Labor Statistics' 2009 Consumer Expenditure Survey

Asian Households Have the Most Discretionary Income

Hispanic households have the least.

Asian households had the largest amount of discretionary income in 2009, an average of $15,762—20 percent more than the average household. Hispanic households had only $6,292 in discretionary dollars, 52 percent less than average. Non-Hispanic white households had slightly less discretionary income than Asians, at $14,517. Blacks had slightly more discretionary income than Hispanics, at $7,726.

After adjusting for household size, the pattern changes. Asian households have slightly less discretionary income per capita ($5,838) than non-Hispanic white households ($6,049). Hispanic households have the least amount of discretionary income per capita (just $1,907).

Because non-Hispanic whites head the great majority of households, they control 84 percent of the nation's discretionary income—$1.3 trillion in 2009. Black households control $113 billion in discretionary income, Hispanics $90 billion, and Asians $72 billion.

■ Discretionary income increased for blacks and Hispanics between 2007 and 2009, but only because of sharp cutbacks in their spending on necessities (see chapter introduction for more about this).

Asians and non-Hispanic whites saw their discretionary income fall

(percent change in discretionary income per household, by race and Hispanic origin of householder, 2007 to 2009; in 2009 dollars)

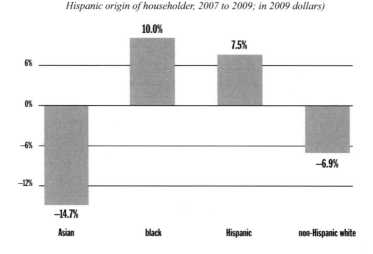

Table 4.9 Discretionary Income by Race and Hispanic Origin of Householder, 2009

(number and percent distribution of total households, average before-tax household income, average discretionary income per household and per household member, aggregate discretionary income, and percent distribution of aggregate, by race and Hispanic origin of householder, 2009)

	total households		average before-tax household income	discretionary income			
	number (in 000s)	percent distribution		average per household	average per capita	aggregate (in millions)	percent distribution of aggregate
Total households	**120,847**	**100.0%**	**$62,857**	**$13,179**	**$5,272**	**$1,592,615**	**100.0%**
Asian	4,584	3.8	76,633	15,762	5,838	72,254	4.5
Black	14,659	12.1	44,397	7,726	2,972	113,256	7.1
Hispanic	14,295	11.8	49,930	6,292	1,907	89,948	5.6
Non-Hispanic white and other	92,119	76.2	67,784	14,517	6,049	1,337,250	84.0

Note: Asians and blacks include Hispanics and non-Hispanics who identify themselves as being of the respective race alone. Hispanics includes people of any race who identify themselves as Hispanic. "Other" includes people who identify themselves as non-Hispanic and as Alaska Native, American Indian, Asian (who are also included in the Asian row), Native Hawaiian or other Pacific Islander, and non-Hispanics reporting more than one race. Race and Hispanic origin groups do not add to total because of overlapping categories. For the definition of discretionary income, see chapter introduction.
Source: Calculations by New Strategist based on the Bureau of Labor Statistics' 2009 Consumer Expenditure Survey

Discretionary Income Is Highest in the Northeast

Households in the South have the smallest amount of discretionary income.

Discretionary income varies considerably by region. Households in the Northeast have the largest amount of discretionary income, an average of $17,119 in 2009. Households in the South have the smallest amount of discretionary income—just $11,891.

On a per capita basis, households in the South and West lag in discretionary income, with $4,756 per household member in the South and $4,723 per household member in the West. Households in the Midwest are not far behind on a per capita basis, with $5,382 per household member. These figures compare with a much higher $7,133 per capita in the Northeast.

Despite the smaller average amount of discretionary income available to households in the South, the region controls the largest share of the nation's discretionary income—33 percent in 2009—because the region is home to the largest share of the population. The West controls the smallest share of discretionary income, just 21 percent in 2009.

■ Discretionary income increased for households in the Midwest between 2007 and 2009, but only because of sharp cutbacks in their spending on necessities (see chapter introduction for more about this).

Discretionary income fell the most in the Northeast and West

(percent change in discretionary income per household, by region, 2007 to 2009; in 2009 dollars)

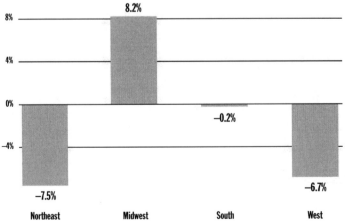

Table 4.10 Discretionary Income by Region of Residence, 2009

(number and percent distribution of total households, average before-tax household income, average discretionary income per household and per household member, aggregate discretionary income, and percent distribution of aggregate, by region, 2009)

	total households		average before-tax household income	discretionary income			
	number (in 000s)	percent distribution		average per household	average per capita	aggregate (in millions)	percent distribution of aggregate
Total households	**120,847**	**100.0%**	**$62,857**	**$13,179**	**$5,272**	**$1,592,666**	**100.0%**
Northeast	22,411	18.5	71,731	17,119	7,133	383,644	24.1
Midwest	27,536	22.8	59,908	12,916	5,382	355,648	22.3
South	43,819	36.3	58,641	11,891	4,756	521,032	32.7
West	27,080	22.4	65,332	12,279	4,723	332,517	20.9

Note: For the definition of discretionary income, see chapter introduction.
Source: Calculations by New Strategist based on the Bureau of Labor Statistics' 2009 Consumer Expenditure Survey

The College Educated Control Most Discretionary Income

Those who did not go to college control few of the nation's discretionary dollars.

Households headed by college graduates controlled 57 percent of the nation's $1.6 trillion in discretionary income in 2009. Households headed by people who went no further than high school controlled only 17 percent.

The most-educated householders have the most discretionary income. Households headed by people with a graduate degree had a substantial $33,075 in discretionary dollars available to them in 2009. Those headed by someone with a bachelor's degree had a smaller $21,720, but still far above the all-household average of $13,179. For households headed by high school graduates, discretionary income was just $8,664.

The discretionary income pattern is the same after adjusting for household size. Householders with a graduate degree averaged $13,781 in discretionary income per household member in 2009. Those who went no further than high school had just $3,466.

■ Discretionary income increased for householders with at least a high school diploma but not a bachelor's degree between 2007 and 2009, but only because of sharp cutbacks in their spending on necessities (see chapter introduction for more about this).

Discretionary income fell the most for households headed by people with a graduate degree

(percent change in discretionary income per household, by educational attainment of householder, 2007 to 2009; in 2009 dollars)

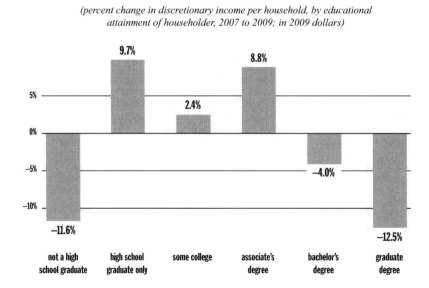

Table 4.11 Discretionary Income by Education of Householder, 2009

(number and percent distribution of total households, average before-tax household income, average discretionary income per household and per household member, aggregate discretionary income, and percent distribution of aggregate, by education of householder, 2009)

	total households		average before-tax household income	discretionary income			
	number (in 000s)	percent distribution		average per household	average per capita	aggregate (in millions)	percent distribution of aggregate
Total households	**120,847**	**100.0%**	**$62,857**	**$13,179**	**$5,272**	**$1,592,641**	**100.0%**
Not a high school graduate	16,692	13.8	33,262	3,594	1,284	59,993	3.8
High school graduate only	31,015	25.7	47,338	8,664	3,466	268,728	16.9
Some college	25,512	21.1	53,065	8,640	3,600	220,431	13.8
Associate's degree	12,051	10.0	62,570	11,315	4,526	136,359	8.6
College graduate	35,576	29.4	97,390	25,601	10,240	910,766	57.2
Bachelor's degree only	23,410	19.4	90,318	21,720	8,688	508,463	31.9
Graduate degree	12,166	10.1	110,998	33,075	13,781	402,387	25.3

Note: For the definition of discretionary income, see chapter introduction.
Source: Calculations by New Strategist based on the Bureau of Labor Statistics' 2009 Consumer Expenditure Survey

5

Wealth

Every three years the Federal Reserve Board fields the Survey of Consumer Finances, collecting information about household assets, debt, and net worth. The Survey of Consumer Finances is the only nationally representative source of historically comparable data on wealth at the household level. Shortly after the 2007 survey (the latest available) was taken, the Great Recession hit. To capture the effects of the Great Recession on household finances, the Federal Reserve Board authorized an unprecedented follow-up survey, re-interviewing in 2009 the households that took part in the 2007 survey to determine how the downturn had affected them. Those 2009 results are presented in this chapter.

Because most workers no longer have a defined-benefit pension plan, relying instead on shrunken defined-contribution plans, many are rethinking their retirement. The age at which workers expect to retire has climbed sharply in the past few years, according to the Retirement Confidence Survey, and retirement confidence has plunged.

■ The Great Recession greatly reduced household assets—in particular housing values and stock portfolios—lowering net worth by 23 percent between 2007 and 2009.

■ The percentage of workers who expect to retire at age 65 or older grew from 51 to 70 percent between 2000 and 2011.

Net Worth Fell Sharply during the Great Recession

Every demographic segment lost ground during the economic downturn.

Net worth is what remains when a household's debts are subtracted from its assets. During the Great Recession, which officially lasted from December 2007 until June 2009, the value of houses, stocks, and retirement accounts fell sharply. At the same time, debt increased. Consequently, net worth fell 23 percent between 2007 and 2009, after adjusting for inflation. These data come from a unique follow-up to the 2007 Survey of Consumer Finances. The survey is taken only every three years. Because of the severity of the Great Recession, however, the Federal Reserve Board arranged for the 2007 respondents to be re-interviewed in 2009 to determine the impact of the Great Recession on household assets, debt, and net worth.

The impact was severe. Net worth fell in every region and in all demographic segments. Net worth declined 32 percent in the West, where housing prices had increased the most, and fell a smaller 16 percent in the Northeast. It declined 37 percent among householders under age 35— many of them recent homebuyers who bought at the peak—and fell by a smaller 12 percent among householders aged 65 to 74, many of whom bought their house decades ago. It shrank by 29 percent among non-whites and Hispanics, and fell by a smaller 16 percent among non-Hispanic whites.

Net worth typically rises with age as people pay off their debts. That pattern has not changed. In 2009, net worth peaked in the 55-to-64 age group at $222,300.

■ Net worth will continue to decline until home values stabilize.

Net worth has fallen since reaching a peak in 2007

(median household net worth, 2007 and 2009; in 2009 dollars)

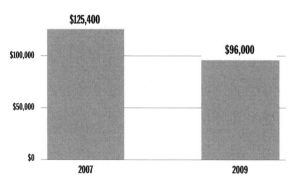

Table 5.1 Net Worth of Households, 2007 and 2009

(median net worth of households by selected characteristics, 2007 and 2009; percent change, 2007–09; in 2009 dollars)

	2009	2007	percent change
TOTAL HOUSEHOLDS	**$96,000**	**$125,400**	**–23.4%**
Household income percentile			
Below 20 percent	7,200	10,100	–28.7
20 to 39.9 percent	32,900	39,100	–15.9
40 to 59.9 percent	72,600	95,400	–23.9
60 to 79.9 percent	167,500	216,700	–22.7
80 to 89.9 percent	302,500	373,500	–19.0
90 percent or higher	894,500	1,205,100	–25.8
Age of householder			
Under age 35	9,000	14,200	–36.6
Aged 35 to 44	69,400	97,100	–28.5
Aged 45 to 54	150,400	203,000	–25.9
Aged 55 to 64	222,300	257,700	–13.7
Aged 65 to 74	205,500	232,700	–11.7
Aged 75 or older	191,000	228,900	–16.6
Education of householder			
No high school diploma	21,200	34,400	–38.4
High school diploma	64,200	80,900	–20.6
Some college	66,800	81,300	–17.8
College degree	244,000	294,600	–17.2
Race and Hispanic origin of householder			
Non-Hispanic white	149,900	178,800	–16.2
Nonwhite or Hispanic	23,300	32,800	–29.0
Region			
Northeast	141,400	168,900	–16.3
Midwest	92,200	121,000	–23.8
South	83,500	102,700	–18.7
West	103,200	151,000	–31.7
Housing status			
Owner	192,600	244,800	–21.3
Renter or other	3,600	5,500	–34.5

Source: Federal Reserve Board, Surveying the Aftermath of the Storm: Changes in Family Finances from 2007 to 2009, Jesse Bricker, Brian Bucks, Arthur Kennickell, Traci Mach, and Kevin Moore, Finance and Economics Discussion Series, 2011–17, Appendix tables, Internet site http://www.federalreserve.gov/pubs/oss/oss2/2009p/scf2009phome.html; calculations by New Strategist

Table 5.2 Distribution of Household Assets and Debts by Type, 2007 and 2009

(percent distribution of household assets and debts by type, 2007 and 2009; percentage point change, 2007–09)

	2009	2007	percentage point change
Financial assets	**100.0%**	**100.0%**	–
Transaction accounts	12.7	9.9	2.8
Certificates of deposit	5.0	3.6	1.4
Savings bonds	0.5	0.4	0.1
Bonds	6.1	4.0	2.1
Stocks	13.6	18.1	–4.5
Pooled investment funds	11.7	15.1	–3.4
Retirement accounts	38.2	37.7	0.5
Cash value of life insurance	3.1	3.1	0.0
Other managed assets	6.7	5.8	0.9
Other	2.4	2.2	0.2
Nonfinancial assets	**100.0%**	**100.0%**	–
Vehicles	4.6	4.4	0.2
Primary residence	48.5	47.6	0.9
Business equity	11.6	10.3	1.3
Other residential real estate	5.7	6.2	–0.5
Equity in nonresidential property	27.9	30.2	–2.3
Other	1.7	1.3	0.4
Debt	**100.0%**	**100.0%**	–
Secured by primary residence	72.9	75.0	–2.1
Secured by other residential property	10.0	9.5	0.5
Installment loans (education, vehicle, etc.)	11.7	10.3	1.4
Lines of credit, not secured by residential property	0.8	0.5	0.3
Credit card balances	3.5	3.5	0.0
Other	1.1	1.2	–0.1

Note: Pooled investment funds exclude money market funds and indirectly held mutual funds. They include open-end and closed-end mutual funds, real estate investment trusts, and hedge funds. "–" means not applicable.
Source: Federal Reserve Board, Surveying the Aftermath of the Storm: Changes in Family Finances from 2007 to 2009, Jesse Bricker, Brian Bucks, Arthur Kennickell, Traci Mach, and Kevin Moore, Finance and Economics Discussion Series, 2011-17, Appendix tables, Internet site http://www.federalreserve.gov/pubs/oss/oss2/2009p/scf2009phome.html; calculations by New Strategist

Financial Asset Values Fell between 2007 and 2009

Some demographic segments saw the median value of their financial assets increase, however.

Most households own financial assets, which range from transaction accounts (checking and saving) to stocks, mutual funds, retirement accounts, and life insurance. The median value of the financial assets owned by the average household stood at $29,600 in 2009, down 5 percent since 2007 after adjusting for inflation. The Great Recession greatly reduced the value of the stocks, bonds, and mutual funds.

Transaction accounts, the most commonly owned financial asset, are held by 92 percent of households. Their median value was just $4,000 in 2009—slightly lower than the $4,100 of 2007. Retirement accounts are the second most commonly owned financial asset, with 56 percent of households having one. Most retirement accounts are not large, however, with an overall median value of just $48,000 in 2009. This figure is 5 percent lower than the $50,600 of 2007, after adjusting for inflation.

Only 18.5 percent of households owned stock directly in 2009 (outside of a retirement account). The median value of stock owned by stockholding households was just $12,000 in 2009, 35 percent less than the value in 2007, after adjusting for inflation.

Retirement accounts were modest in 2009, and their value has declined since then

(median value of retirement accounts owned by households, by age of householder, 2009)

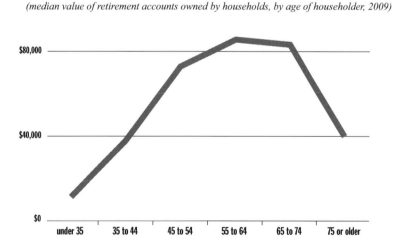

Table 5.3 Ownership and Value of Household Financial Assets, 2007 and 2009

(percentage of households owning any financial asset and median value of financial assets for owners, by selected characteristics, 2007 and 2009; percentage point change in ownership and percent change in value, 2007–09; in 2009 dollars)

	percent owning any financial asset			median value of financial assets		
	2009	**2007**	**percentage point change**	**2009**	**2007**	**percent change**
TOTAL HOUSEHOLDS	**94.6%**	**94.3%**	**0.3**	**$29,600**	**$31,300**	**−5.4%**
Household income percentile						
Below 20 percent	82.7	80.9	1.8	2,100	1,800	16.7
20 to 39.9 percent	94.3	93.7	0.6	8,800	8,500	3.5
40 to 59.9 percent	96.6	97.8	−1.2	21,600	19,000	13.7
60 to 79.9 percent	99.6	99.7	−0.1	63,900	68,600	−6.9
80 to 89.9 percent	100.0	100.0	0.0	134,100	149,000	−10.0
90 percent or higher	100.0	100.0	0.0	398,000	497,100	−19.9
Age of householder						
Under age 35	91.4	90.2	1.2	7,400	7,400	0.0
Aged 35 to 44	92.3	93.5	−1.2	27,500	25,500	7.8
Aged 45 to 54	96.0	94.1	1.9	58,500	64,300	−9.0
Aged 55 to 64	97.0	97.9	−0.9	72,500	78,200	−7.3
Aged 65 to 74	97.8	96.1	1.7	48,000	63,900	−24.9
Aged 75 or older	95.8	98.1	−2.3	39,000	41,400	−5.8
Education of householder						
No high school diploma	83.5	80.9	2.6	3,900	3,100	25.8
High school diploma	93.2	93.3	−0.1	15,800	15,300	3.3
Some college	96.4	96.0	0.4	16,700	20,100	−16.9
College degree	98.7	99.1	−0.4	101,100	107,500	−6.0
Race and Hispanic origin of householder						
Non-Hispanic white	96.9	97.3	−0.4	47,700	50,100	−4.8
Nonwhite or Hispanic	89.2	87.3	1.9	8,500	10,200	−16.7
Region						
Northeast	94.5	93.2	1.3	40,000	49,100	−18.5
Midwest	95.6	95.7	−0.1	34,000	34,200	−0.6
South	94.6	94.2	0.4	22,000	25,500	−13.7
West	93.6	94.2	−0.6	27,000	27,500	−1.8
Housing status						
Owner	97.9	98.5	−0.6	57,900	63,000	−8.1
Renter or other	87.3	85.2	2.1	4,000	4,200	−4.8

Source: Federal Reserve Board, Surveying the Aftermath of the Storm: Changes in Family Finances from 2007 to 2009, Jesse Bricker, Brian Bucks, Arthur Kennickell, Traci Mach, and Kevin Moore, Finance and Economics Discussion Series, 2011-17, Appendix tables, Internet site http://www.federalreserve.gov/pubs/oss/oss2/2009p/scf2009phome.html; calculations by New Strategist

Table 5.4 Percent of Households Owning Transaction Accounts, Life Insurance, and CDs, 2007 and 2009

(percent of households owning transaction accounts, cash value life insurance, and certificates of deposit by selected characteristics of households, 2007 and 2009; percentage point change, 2007–09)

	transaction accounts			cash value life insurance			certificates of deposit		
	2009	2007	percentage point change	2009	2007	percentage point change	2009	2007	percentage point change
TOTAL HOUSEHOLDS	**92.3%**	**92.6%**	**−0.3**	**24.3%**	**23.2%**	**1.1**	**15.9%**	**15.4%**	**0.5**
Household income percentile									
Below 20 percent	77.4	76.6	0.8	15.0	12.5	2.5	9.4	9.1	0.3
20 to 39.9 percent	91.2	90.5	0.7	22.1	18.2	3.9	13.7	12.9	0.8
40 to 59.9 percent	94.5	96.9	−2.4	21.8	21.3	0.5	13.8	13.3	0.5
60 to 79.9 percent	99.5	99.3	0.2	26.4	28.3	−1.9	18.8	19.0	−0.2
80 to 89.9 percent	98.8	100.0	−1.2	31.6	33.0	−1.4	20.8	19.3	1.5
90 percent or higher	100.0	100.0	0.0	40.9	39.3	1.6	26.4	26.8	−0.4
Age of householder									
Under age 35	88.5	88.0	0.5	13.1	12.4	0.7	7.9	6.5	1.4
Aged 35 to 44	89.8	91.8	−2.0	16.8	17.1	−0.3	9.4	8.9	0.5
Aged 45 to 54	94.1	92.8	1.3	25.3	22.0	3.3	13.9	14.5	−0.6
Aged 55 to 64	95.3	96.5	−1.2	33.4	35.7	−2.3	20.2	19.5	0.7
Aged 65 to 74	95.0	95.0	0.0	36.3	34.6	1.7	24.8	23.0	1.8
Aged 75 or older	94.2	95.1	−0.9	34.2	29.2	5.0	35.2	36.8	−1.6
Education of householder									
No high school diploma	79.3	76.8	2.5	14.3	12.7	1.6	11.8	8.3	3.5
High school diploma	90.5	90.7	−0.2	24.3	22.2	2.1	14.8	13.4	1.4
Some college	93.2	94.2	−1.0	23.3	23.9	−0.6	11.3	12.5	−1.2
College degree	98.0	98.9	−0.9	28.2	27.5	0.7	20.6	21.2	−0.6
Race and Hispanic origin of householder									
Non-Hispanic white	95.5	96.0	−0.5	25.8	25.4	0.4	19.4	18.7	0.7
Nonwhite or Hispanic	84.9	84.7	0.2	20.8	18.1	2.7	7.4	7.7	−0.3
Region									
Northeast	92.7	91.7	1.0	25.8	24.1	1.7	20.1	17.4	2.7
Midwest	93.0	93.7	−0.7	27.9	26.3	1.6	16.2	16.3	−0.1
South	91.7	91.9	−0.2	24.6	24.1	0.5	14.9	14.5	0.4
West	92.3	93.2	−0.9	18.7	17.9	0.8	13.5	14.4	−0.9
Housing status									
Owner	96.4	97.4	−1.0	30.2	29.0	1.2	20.0	19.1	0.9
Renter or other	83.4	82.0	1.4	11.1	10.4	0.7	6.7	7.3	−0.6

Source: Federal Reserve Board, Surveying the Aftermath of the Storm: Changes in Family Finances from 2007 to 2009, Jesse Bricker, Brian Bucks, Arthur Kennickell, Traci Mach, and Kevin Moore, Finance and Economics Discussion Series, 2011-17, Appendix tables, Internet site http://www.federalreserve.gov/pubs/oss/oss2/2009p/scf2009phome.html; calculations by New Strategist

Table 5.5 Percent of Households Owning Retirement Accounts and Stocks, 2007 and 2009

(percent of households owning retirement accounts and stocks by selected characteristics of households, 2007 and 2009; percentage point change, 2007–09)

	retirement accounts			stocks		
	2009	2007	percentage point change	2009	2007	percentage point change
TOTAL HOUSEHOLDS	**56.2%**	**55.6%**	**0.6**	**18.5%**	**18.4%**	**0.1**
Household income percentile						
Below 20 percent	14.7	12.7	2.0	4.8	5.6	–0.8
20 to 39.9 percent	41.5	39.5	2.0	9.8	8.9	0.9
40 to 59.9 percent	57.6	58.1	–0.5	14.0	13.4	0.6
60 to 79.9 percent	78.3	78.6	–0.3	24.2	25.1	–0.9
80 to 89.9 percent	87.9	89.3	–1.4	29.3	29.2	0.1
90 percent or higher	91.7	91.3	0.4	50.8	49.6	1.2
Age of householder						
Under age 35	48.4	44.9	3.5	12.6	14.6	–2.0
Aged 35 to 44	61.2	59.4	1.8	18.9	17.0	1.9
Aged 45 to 54	68.2	68.0	0.2	20.3	18.4	1.9
Aged 55 to 64	62.7	64.3	–1.6	21.3	21.2	0.1
Aged 65 to 74	51.8	53.3	–1.5	21.9	21.0	0.9
Aged 75 or older	29.5	31.3	–1.8	18.6	22.8	–4.2
Education of householder						
No high school diploma	23.3	23.2	0.1	3.5	3.8	–0.3
High school diploma	46.6	45.7	0.9	9.1	9.6	–0.5
Some college	56.7	56.2	0.5	17.8	17.8	0.0
College degree	75.6	75.2	0.4	32.4	31.6	0.8
Race and Hispanic origin of householder						
Non-Hispanic white	62.0	61.6	0.4	22.5	22.1	0.4
Nonwhite or Hispanic	42.3	41.5	0.8	9.1	9.7	–0.6
Region						
Northeast	59.3	56.9	2.4	20.2	22.2	–2.0
Midwest	59.9	60.1	–0.2	17.9	18.1	–0.2
South	52.0	52.3	–0.3	17.2	16.2	1.0
West	56.4	55.2	1.2	20.0	19.2	0.8
Housing status						
Owner	65.9	66.0	–0.1	23.1	23.0	0.1
Renter or other	34.6	32.5	2.1	8.4	8.3	0.1

Note: Stock ownership is direct ownership outside of a retirement account or mutual fund.
Source: Federal Reserve Board, Surveying the Aftermath of the Storm: Changes in Family Finances from 2007 to 2009, Jesse Bricker, Brian Bucks, Arthur Kennickell, Traci Mach, and Kevin Moore, Finance and Economics Discussion Series, 2011-17, Appendix tables, Internet site http://www.federalreserve.gov/pubs/oss/oss2/2009p/scf2009phome.html; calculations by New Strategist

Table 5.6 Percent of Households Owning Pooled Investment Funds and Bonds, 2007 and 2009

(percent of households owning pooled investment funds and bonds by selected characteristics of households, 2007 and 2009; percentage point change, 2007–09)

	pooled investment funds			bonds		
	2009	**2007**	**percentage point change**	**2009**	**2007**	**percentage point change**
TOTAL HOUSEHOLDS	**10.8%**	**11.5%**	**−0.7**	**2.6%**	**1.7%**	**0.9**
Household income percentile						
Below 20 percent	3.6	4.1	−0.5	0.7	0.4	0.3
20 to 39.9 percent	5.3	5.1	0.2	1.0	0.4	0.6
40 to 59.9 percent	6.8	6.6	0.2	1.8	0.6	1.2
60 to 79.9 percent	11.6	14.6	−3.0	2.0	1.4	0.6
80 to 89.9 percent	15.9	18.4	−2.5	3.8	1.6	2.2
90 percent or higher	38.0	36.6	1.4	11.4	9.5	1.9
Age of householder						
Under age 35	5.4	5.8	−0.4	0.5	0.2	0.3
Aged 35 to 44	10.0	11.7	−1.7	1.3	0.7	0.6
Aged 45 to 54	13.2	12.6	0.6	2.4	1.1	1.3
Aged 55 to 64	14.5	14.1	0.4	3.3	2.4	0.9
Aged 65 to 74	11.5	13.8	−2.3	6.2	4.5	1.7
Aged 75 or older	12.6	15.1	−2.5	5.5	3.9	1.6
Education of householder						
No high school diploma	2.0	1.9	0.1	0.6	0.2	0.4
High school diploma	4.7	5.6	−0.9	1.1	0.7	0.4
Some college	8.0	9.1	−1.1	2.2	1.1	1.1
College degree	20.7	21.4	−0.7	4.9	3.3	1.6
Race and Hispanic origin of householder						
Non-Hispanic white	13.1	14.0	−0.9	3.4	2.2	1.2
Nonwhite or Hispanic	5.4	5.8	−0.4	0.8	0.4	0.4
Region						
Northeast	13.1	16.0	−2.9	3.3	2.0	1.3
Midwest	10.3	10.6	−0.3	2.3	1.1	1.2
South	10.0	10.1	−0.1	2.8	1.9	0.9
West	10.9	11.3	−0.4	2.1	1.6	0.5
Housing status						
Owner	13.8	15.3	−1.5	3.5	2.2	1.3
Renter or other	4.3	3.3	1.0	0.8	0.4	0.4

Note: Pooled investment funds exclude money market funds and indirectly held mutual funds. They include open-end and closed-end mutual funds, real estate investment trusts, and hedge funds.
Source: Federal Reserve Board, Surveying the Aftermath of the Storm: Changes in Family Finances from 2007 to 2009, Jesse Bricker, Brian Bucks, Arthur Kennickell, Traci Mach, and Kevin Moore, Finance and Economics Discussion Series, 2011–17, Appendix tables, Internet site http://www.federalreserve.gov/pubs/oss/oss2/2009p/scf2009phome.html; calculations by New Strategist

Table 5.7 Median Value of Transaction Accounts, Life Insurance, and CDs, 2007 and 2009

(median value of transactions accounts, cash value life insurance, and certificates of deposit for households owning asset, by selected characteristics of households, 2007 and 2009; percent change, 2007–09; in 2009 dollars)

	transaction accounts			cash value life insurance			certificates of deposit		
	2009	2007	percent change	2009	2007	percent change	2009	2007	percent change
TOTAL HOUSEHOLDS	**$4,000**	**$4,100**	**–2.4%**	**$7,300**	**$8,300**	**–12.0%**	**$20,000**	**$20,700**	**–3.4%**
Household income percentile									
Below 20 percent	1,000	800	25.0	5,000	2,600	92.3	10,000	23,800	–58.0
20 to 39.9 percent	2,000	1,800	11.1	4,100	4,700	–12.8	20,000	18,600	7.5
40 to 59.9 percent	3,000	2,900	3.4	7,200	5,200	38.5	20,000	14,000	42.9
60 to 79.9 percent	5,700	6,200	–8.1	8,000	9,300	–14.0	20,000	13,000	53.8
80 to 89.9 percent	10,400	12,900	–19.4	8,000	9,300	–14.0	20,000	15,500	29.0
90 percent or higher	32,000	36,200	–11.6	20,000	29,100	–31.3	40,000	46,400	–13.8
Age of householder									
Under age 35	2,300	2,600	–11.5	2,500	3,600	–30.6	9,000	4,900	83.7
Aged 35 to 44	3,000	3,500	–14.3	7,000	8,300	–15.7	10,000	5,200	92.3
Aged 45 to 54	5,000	4,800	4.2	8,000	10,400	–23.1	18,000	18,600	–3.2
Aged 55 to 64	5,500	5,600	–1.8	10,000	10,400	–3.8	25,000	20,700	20.8
Aged 65 to 74	5,500	7,000	–21.4	10,000	10,600	–5.7	27,700	22,800	21.5
Aged 75 or older	7,000	6,200	12.9	8,000	5,200	53.8	31,400	31,100	1.0
Education of householder									
No high school diploma	1,200	1,300	–7.7	3,200	2,600	23.1	11,000	12,400	–11.3
High school diploma	2,500	2,600	–3.8	5,600	5,200	7.7	20,000	18,400	8.7
Some college	2,700	3,000	–10.0	8,700	8,100	7.4	14,000	15,500	–9.7
College degree	9,500	10,400	–8.7	10,000	14,500	–31.0	25,000	20,700	20.8
Race and Hispanic origin of householder									
Non-Hispanic white	5,300	5,200	1.9	8,000	9,300	–14.0	22,000	20,700	6.3
Nonwhite or Hispanic	1,800	2,100	–14.3	5,000	5,200	–3.8	11,300	10,400	8.7
Region									
Northeast	4,600	4,900	–6.1	7,500	9,300	–19.4	25,000	20,700	20.8
Midwest	3,800	3,900	–2.6	10,000	8,300	20.5	20,000	15,500	29.0
South	3,500	3,800	–7.9	6,800	8,300	–18.1	20,000	22,800	–12.3
West	5,000	4,200	19.0	7,500	7,800	–3.8	26,000	20,700	25.6
Housing status									
Owner	6,000	6,300	–4.8	8,400	10,100	–16.8	22,000	20,700	6.3
Renter or other	1,400	1,200	16.7	2,500	2,100	19.0	10,000	8,300	20.5

Source: Federal Reserve Board, Surveying the Aftermath of the Storm: Changes in Family Finances from 2007 to 2009, Jesse Bricker, Brian Bucks, Arthur Kennickell, Traci Mach, and Kevin Moore, Finance and Economics Discussion Series, 2011-17, Appendix tables, Internet site http://www.federalreserve.gov/pubs/oss/oss2/2009p/scf2009phome.html; calculations by New Strategist

Table 5.8 Median Value of Retirement Accounts and Stocks, 2007 and 2009

(median value of retirement accounts and stocks for households owning asset, by selected characteristics of households, 2007 and 2009; percent change, 2007–09; in 2009 dollars)

	retirement accounts			stocks		
	2009	2007	percent change	2009	2007	percent change
TOTAL HOUSEHOLDS	**$48,000**	**$50,600**	**–5.1%**	**$12,000**	**$18,500**	**–35.1%**
Household income percentile						
Below 20 percent	6,100	6,200	–1.6	6,000	4,100	46.3
20 to 39.9 percent	12,500	12,400	0.8	4,500	9,100	–50.5
40 to 59.9 percent	25,800	26,300	–1.9	4,400	6,900	–36.2
60 to 79.9 percent	50,000	51,800	–3.5	10,000	12,400	–19.4
80 to 89.9 percent	91,400	102,000	–10.4	10,000	16,100	–37.9
90 percent or higher	213,800	238,200	–10.2	55,300	72,500	–23.7
Age of householder						
Under age 35	11,400	10,400	9.6	3,000	3,100	–3.2
Aged 35 to 44	38,000	38,300	–0.8	12,000	15,500	–22.6
Aged 45 to 54	73,000	81,400	–10.3	11,700	19,700	–40.6
Aged 55 to 64	85,600	103,600	–17.4	16,000	24,900	–35.7
Aged 65 to 74	83,200	79,700	4.4	25,000	36,200	–30.9
Aged 75 or older	40,000	36,200	10.5	35,000	101,500	–65.5
Education of householder						
No high school diploma	17,000	17,600	–3.4	4,100	2,300	78.3
High school diploma	30,000	28,400	5.6	8,800	10,400	–15.4
Some college	28,600	33,100	–13.6	4,000	6,200	–35.5
College degree	80,000	88,000	–9.1	20,000	28,100	–28.8
Race and Hispanic origin of householder						
Non-Hispanic white	58,500	61,800	–5.3	14,000	20,700	–32.4
Nonwhite or Hispanic	26,000	29,500	–11.9	5,500	7,100	–22.5
Region						
Northeast	50,000	62,100	–19.5	26,000	18,200	42.9
Midwest	41,000	39,700	3.3	13,000	16,100	–19.3
South	50,000	49,100	1.8	9,400	18,500	–49.2
West	45,000	49,700	–9.5	9,000	18,600	–51.6
Housing status						
Owner	63,700	65,600	–2.9	15,000	20,700	–27.5
Renter or other	12,000	9,800	22.4	5,000	5,200	–3.8

Note: Stock ownership is direct ownership outside of a retirement account or mutual fund.
Source: Federal Reserve Board, Surveying the Aftermath of the Storm: Changes in Family Finances from 2007 to 2009, Jesse Bricker, Brian Bucks, Arthur Kennickell, Traci Mach, and Kevin Moore, Finance and Economics Discussion Series, 2011-17, Appendix tables, Internet site http://www.federalreserve.gov/pubs/oss/oss2/2009p/scf2009phome.html; calculations by New Strategist

Table 5.9 Median Value of Pooled Investment Funds and Bonds, 2007 and 2009

(median value of pooled investment funds and bonds for households owning asset, by selected characteristics of households, 2007 and 2009; percent change, 2007–09; in 2009 dollars)

	pooled investment funds			bonds		
	2009	2007	percent change	2009	2007	percent change
TOTAL HOUSEHOLDS	$47,000	$58,700	**–19.9%**	$50,000	$62,100	**–19.5%**
Household income percentile						
Below 20 percent	50,000	39,700	25.9	–	–	–
20 to 39.9 percent	30,000	31,100	–3.5	–	–	–
40 to 59.9 percent	35,000	44,700	–21.7	10,000	–	–
60 to 79.9 percent	19,000	35,400	–46.3	15,000	18,300	–18.0
80 to 89.9 percent	34,000	48,400	–29.8	25,000	–	–
90 percent or higher	104,000	207,100	–49.8	250,000	186,400	34.1
Age of householder						
Under age 35	10,000	15,000	–33.3	–	–	–
Aged 35 to 44	35,000	27,300	28.2	5,000	103,600	–95.2
Aged 45 to 54	35,000	51,800	–32.4	27,000	127,600	–78.8
Aged 55 to 64	70,400	115,000	–38.8	65,000	82,800	–21.5
Aged 65 to 74	100,000	155,300	–35.6	86,000	51,600	66.7
Aged 75 or older	70,000	77,700	–9.9	37,400	96,500	–61.2
Education of householder						
No high school diploma	–	22,300	–	–	–	–
High school diploma	30,000	31,100	–3.5	18,000	41,400	–56.5
Some college	25,100	28,400	–11.6	1,700	51,800	–96.7
College degree	60,000	80,800	–25.7	95,000	103,600	–8.3
Race and Hispanic origin of householder						
Non-Hispanic white	50,000	67,300	–25.7	50,000	70,400	–29.0
Nonwhite or Hispanic	20,000	30,800	–35.1	25,000	18,300	36.6
Region						
Northeast	39,400	51,800	–23.9	100,000	103,600	–3.5
Midwest	50,000	41,400	20.8	57,600	51,800	11.2
South	60,000	89,100	–32.7	30,000	82,800	–63.8
West	35,000	51,800	–32.4	25,000	51,800	–51.7
Housing status						
Owner	50,000	62,100	–19.5	58,700	72,500	–19.0
Renter or other	18,000	41,400	–56.5	10,000	–	–

Note: Pooled investment funds exclude money market funds and indirectly held mutual funds. They include open-end and closed-end mutual funds, real estate investment trusts, and hedge funds. "–" means sample is too small to make a reliable estimate.
Source: Federal Reserve Board, Surveying the Aftermath of the Storm: Changes in Family Finances from 2007 to 2009, Jesse Bricker, Brian Bucks, Arthur Kennickell, Traci Mach, and Kevin Moore, Finance and Economics Discussion Series, 2011-17, Appendix tables, Internet site http://www.federalreserve.gov/pubs/oss/oss2/2009p/scf2009phome.html; calculations by New Strategist

Nonfinancial Assets Are the Foundation of Household Wealth

The average household saw the value of its nonfinancial assets fall during the Great Recession.

The median value of the nonfinancial assets owned by the average American household stood at $204,000 in 2009, far surpassing the $29,600 median in financial assets. Between 2007 and 2009, the value of the nonfinancial assets owned by the average household fell 13 percent, after adjusting for inflation. Nearly every demographic segment saw its nonfinancial assets decline in value, primarily because of the decline in housing values.

Eighty-seven percent of households own a vehicle, the most commonly held nonfinancial asset. The value of the vehicles owned by the average household fell steeply (down 26 percent) between 2007 and 2009, after adjusting for inflation. Behind the decline was the reluctance of households to buy new vehicles during the Great Recession.

The second most commonly owned nonfinancial asset is a home, owned by 70 percent. Homes are by far the most valuable asset owned by Americans, and they account for the largest share of net worth. In 2009, the median value of the average owned home was $176,000, 15 percent below the 2007 median of $207,100 in 2007 (in 2009 dollars). Housing prices have continued to decline since 2009, driving median home values even lower than the numbers shown here.

■ The continuing decline in housing values has probably reduced average household net worth below the 2009 figure.

Median housing value peaks in the 45-to-54 age group

(median value of the primary residence among homeowners, by age of householder, 2009)

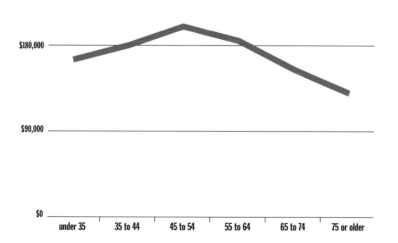

Table 5.10 Ownership and Value of Nonfinancial Assets, 2007 and 2009

(percentage of households owning any nonfinancial asset and median value of nonfinancial assets for owners, by selected characteristics, 2007 and 2009; percentage point change in ownership and percent change in value, 2007–09; in 2009 dollars)

	percent owning any nonfinancial asset			median value of nonfinancial assets		
	2009	2007	percentage point change	2009	2007	percent change
TOTAL HOUSEHOLDS	**92.6%**	**92.7%**	**–0.1**	**$204,000**	**$234,800**	**–13.1%**
Household income percentile						
Below 20 percent	77.7	76.2	1.5	20,400	26,400	–22.7
20 to 39.9 percent	92.0	91.8	0.2	85,200	89,600	–4.9
40 to 59.9 percent	95.5	97.5	–2.0	180,000	201,800	–10.8
60 to 79.9 percent	98.9	98.8	0.1	316,000	369,600	–14.5
80 to 89.9 percent	99.0	99.1	–0.1	503,000	608,700	–17.4
90 percent or higher	99.9	99.8	0.1	1,225,000	1,473,000	–16.8
Age of householder						
Under age 35	89.5	88.1	1.4	52,800	44,400	18.9
Aged 35 to 44	92.3	91.8	0.5	196,500	232,000	–15.3
Aged 45 to 54	95.0	95.2	–0.2	289,500	326,600	–11.4
Aged 55 to 64	95.5	96.1	–0.6	308,000	361,900	–14.9
Aged 65 to 74	96.0	95.3	0.7	253,000	306,200	–17.4
Aged 75 or older	86.2	90.4	–4.2	193,100	238,900	–19.2
Education of householder						
No high school diploma	82.9	82.8	0.1	60,100	71,500	–15.9
High school diploma	91.1	92.3	–1.2	152,900	167,800	–8.9
Some college	92.5	91.9	0.6	175,000	187,300	–6.6
College degree	97.3	96.7	0.6	397,800	455,800	–12.7
Race and Hispanic origin of householder						
Non-Hispanic white	95.4	95.1	0.3	259,800	287,700	–9.7
Nonwhite or Hispanic	86.0	86.9	–0.9	90,200	100,200	–10.0
Region						
Northeast	84.7	83.9	0.8	275,200	312,300	–11.9
Midwest	92.8	93.9	–1.1	192,300	226,000	–14.9
South	95.7	95.1	0.6	177,200	192,000	–7.7
West	93.9	94.5	–0.6	240,500	301,700	–20.3
Housing status						
Owner	99.6	100.0	–0.4	315,100	361,500	–12.8
Renter or other	77.2	76.4	0.8	14,100	15,200	–7.2

Source: Federal Reserve Board, Surveying the Aftermath of the Storm: Changes in Family Finances from 2007 to 2009, Jesse Bricker, Brian Bucks, Arthur Kennickell, Traci Mach, and Kevin Moore, Finance and Economics Discussion Series, 2011-17, Appendix tables, Internet site http://www.federalreserve.gov/pubs/oss/oss2/2009p/scf2009phome.html; calculations by New Strategist

Table 5.11 Percent of Households Owning Primary Residence, Other Residential Property, and Nonresidential Property, 2007 and 2009

(percent of households owning primary residence, other residential property, and nonresidential property by selected characteristics of households, 2007 and 2009; percentage point change, 2007–09)

	primary residence			other residential property			nonresidential property		
	2009	2007	percentage point change	2009	2007	percentage point change	2009	2007	percentage point change
TOTAL HOUSEHOLDS	70.3%	68.9%	1.4	13.0%	13.9%	−0.9	7.6%	8.3%	−0.7
Household income percentile									
Below 20 percent	42.6	42.0	0.6	3.3	5.7	−2.4	2.3	2.3	0.0
20 to 39.9 percent	57.5	55.3	2.2	7.9	8.0	−0.1	4.6	4.4	0.2
40 to 59.9 percent	72.4	70.3	2.1	10.4	9.5	0.9	5.9	7.6	−1.7
60 to 79.9 percent	86.6	84.7	1.9	13.7	16.0	−2.3	9.3	10.3	−1.0
80 to 89.9 percent	92.7	92.1	0.6	18.7	19.8	−1.1	12.3	12.3	0.0
90 percent or higher	94.3	94.2	0.1	40.5	40.6	−0.1	20.2	22.0	−1.8
Age of householder									
Under age 35	44.6	40.5	4.1	7.1	5.3	1.8	3.1	3.1	0.0
Aged 35 to 44	68.9	66.6	2.3	11.4	12.5	−1.1	7.0	7.9	−0.9
Aged 45 to 54	78.1	77.3	0.8	14.4	15.5	−1.1	9.5	10.0	−0.5
Aged 55 to 64	81.9	82.2	−0.3	18.6	21.0	−2.4	10.9	11.5	−0.6
Aged 65 to 74	86.8	85.5	1.3	17.9	19.2	−1.3	11.1	10.9	0.2
Aged 75 or older	77.2	79.2	−2.0	11.2	14.3	−3.1	5.7	9.0	−3.3
Education of householder									
No high school diploma	55.1	53.3	1.8	6.2	7.1	−0.9	3.0	3.8	−0.8
High school diploma	69.0	69.4	−0.4	8.5	9.5	−1.0	6.6	7.2	−0.6
Some college	63.8	61.9	1.9	12.2	13.6	−1.4	6.4	6.1	0.3
College degree	80.1	77.4	2.7	19.6	20.2	−0.6	10.8	12.0	−1.2
Race and Hispanic origin of householder									
Non-Hispanic white	77.3	75.8	1.5	15.0	15.6	−0.6	8.7	9.4	−0.7
Nonwhite or Hispanic	54.0	52.7	1.3	8.3	9.7	−1.4	5.2	5.7	−0.5
Region									
Northeast	66.5	65.1	1.4	12.3	12.5	−0.2	5.1	5.8	−0.7
Midwest	72.3	71.6	0.7	13.5	14.9	−1.4	8.0	8.4	−0.4
South	73.6	71.5	2.1	12.2	11.9	0.3	9.1	9.3	−0.2
West	66.0	65.0	1.0	14.3	17.3	−3.0	7.0	8.7	−1.7
Housing status									
Owner	96.4	100.0	−3.6	16.9	17.3	−0.4	10.0	11.1	−1.1
Renter or other	12.6	0.0	12.6	4.2	6.1	−1.9	2.3	2.1	0.2

Note: Renters were classified in the 2007 survey and when reinterviewed in 2009 some (12.6 percent) had bought a home.
Source: Federal Reserve Board, Surveying the Aftermath of the Storm: Changes in Family Finances from 2007 to 2009, Jesse Bricker, Brian Bucks, Arthur Kennickell, Traci Mach, and Kevin Moore, Finance and Economics Discussion Series, 2011-17, Appendix tables, Internet site http://www.federalreserve.gov/pubs/oss/oss2/2009p/scf2009phome.html; calculations by New Strategist

Table 5.12 Percent of Households Owning Vehicles and Business Equity, 2007 and 2009

(percent of households owning vehicles and business equity by selected characteristics of households, 2007 and 2009; percentage point change, 2007–09)

	vehicles			business equity		
	2009	2007	percentage point change	2009	2007	percentage point change
TOTAL HOUSEHOLDS	**86.8%**	**87.9%**	**–1.1**	**11.9%**	**12.4%**	**–0.5**
Household income percentile						
Below 20 percent	67.1	67.5	–0.4	2.5	3.1	–0.6
20 to 39.9 percent	86.0	87.2	–1.2	4.8	4.4	0.4
40 to 59.9 percent	91.7	94.9	–3.2	9.7	10.0	–0.3
60 to 79.9 percent	95.1	95.5	–0.4	14.9	16.2	–1.3
80 to 89.9 percent	94.5	95.0	–0.5	17.6	18.7	–1.1
90 percent or higher	95.0	95.1	–0.1	38.4	37.9	0.5
Age of householder						
Under age 35	87.2	85.8	1.4	7.7	7.1	0.6
Aged 35 to 44	87.6	87.9	–0.3	15.4	15.8	–0.4
Aged 45 to 54	90.6	91.1	–0.5	15.0	15.1	–0.1
Aged 55 to 64	90.5	92.5	–2.0	15.9	17.2	–1.3
Aged 65 to 74	88.3	90.8	–2.5	9.1	10.1	–1.0
Aged 75 or older	67.6	74.3	–6.7	3.8	5.4	–1.6
Education of householder						
No high school diploma	74.4	76.9	–2.5	5.9	6.0	–0.1
High school diploma	84.8	87.5	–2.7	8.4	8.7	–0.3
Some college	88.9	88.5	0.4	10.2	10.6	–0.4
College degree	91.8	91.8	0.0	18.1	18.8	–0.7
Race and Hispanic origin of householder						
Non-Hispanic white	90.0	90.3	–0.3	13.8	14.3	–0.5
Nonwhite or Hispanic	79.5	82.3	–2.8	7.5	7.8	–0.3
Region						
Northeast	76.4	76.3	0.1	8.3	8.5	–0.2
Midwest	87.8	90.4	–2.6	12.9	12.9	0.0
South	89.7	90.4	–0.7	11.5	12.1	–0.6
West	89.7	90.9	–1.2	14.7	15.6	–0.9
Housing status						
Owner	92.3	94.2	–1.9	15.3	15.9	–0.6
Renter or other	74.8	74.2	0.6	4.5	4.7	–0.2

Source: Federal Reserve Board, Surveying the Aftermath of the Storm: Changes in Family Finances from 2007 to 2009, Jesse Bricker, Brian Bucks, Arthur Kennickell, Traci Mach, and Kevin Moore, Finance and Economics Discussion Series, 2011-17, Appendix tables, Internet site http://www.federalreserve.gov/pubs/oss/oss2/2009p/scf2009phome.html; calculations by New Strategist

Table 5.13 Median Value of Primary Residence, Other Residential Property, and Nonresidential Property, 2007 and 2009

(median value of primary residence, other residential property, and nonresidential property for households owning asset, by selected characteristics of households, 2007 and 2009; percent change, 2007–09; in 2009 dollars)

	primary residence			other residential property			nonresidential property		
	2009	**2007**	**percent change**	**2009**	**2007**	**percent change**	**2009**	**2007**	**percent change**
TOTAL HOUSEHOLDS	$176,000	$207,100	−15.0%	$150,000	$141,700	5.9%	$69,000	$78,800	−12.4%
Household income percentile									
Below 20 percent	90,000	103,600	−13.1	75,800	62,100	22.1	30,000	39,400	−23.9
20 to 39.9 percent	103,300	124,300	−16.9	45,000	62,100	−27.5	40,000	77,700	−48.5
40 to 59.9 percent	145,000	165,700	−12.5	95,100	77,700	22.4	50,000	41,400	20.8
60 to 79.9 percent	190,000	220,000	−13.6	137,400	134,600	2.1	90,000	82,800	8.7
80 to 89.9 percent	262,000	310,700	−15.7	225,000	186,400	20.7	60,000	82,800	−27.5
90 percent or higher	450,000	517,800	−13.1	350,000	346,900	0.9	200,000	181,200	10.4
Age of householder									
Under age 35	165,000	186,400	−11.5	100,000	62,100	61.0	30,000	51,800	−42.1
Aged 35 to 44	180,000	212,300	−15.2	155,700	155,300	0.3	28,600	59,000	−51.5
Aged 45 to 54	200,000	238,200	−16.0	176,000	163,800	7.4	90,000	79,000	13.9
Aged 55 to 64	185,000	207,100	−10.7	150,000	155,300	−3.4	100,000	103,600	−3.5
Aged 65 to 74	155,000	191,600	−19.1	149,500	139,800	6.9	100,000	103,600	−3.5
Aged 75 or older	130,000	155,300	−16.3	160,000	103,600	54.4	60,000	103,600	−42.1
Education of householder									
No high school diploma	100,000	129,400	−22.7	60,000	63,700	−5.8	45,000	77,700	−42.1
High school diploma	135,000	155,300	−13.1	100,000	77,700	28.7	50,000	51,800	−3.5
Some college	160,000	196,800	−18.7	136,100	103,600	31.4	60,000	53,900	11.3
College degree	250,000	284,800	−12.2	200,000	207,100	−3.4	109,100	99,400	9.8
Race and Hispanic origin of householder									
Non-Hispanic white	180,000	207,100	−13.1	150,000	141,400	6.1	80,000	79,000	1.3
Nonwhite or Hispanic	150,000	186,400	−19.5	130,000	170,900	−23.9	45,000	67,300	−33.1
Region									
Northeast	250,000	290,000	−13.8	200,000	207,100	−3.4	100,000	103,800	−3.7
Midwest	145,000	160,500	−9.7	110,000	116,000	−5.2	60,000	61,000	−1.6
South	150,000	165,700	−9.5	150,000	133,600	12.3	61,000	77,700	−21.5
West	230,000	293,100	−21.5	175,000	196,800	−11.1	103,600	93,200	11.2
Housing status									
Owner	180,000	207,100	−13.1	160,000	155,300	3.0	80,000	82,800	−3.4
Renter or other	152,000	0	−	50,000	103,600	−51.7	20,000	51,800	−61.4

Note: Renters were classified in the 2007 survey and when reinterviewed in 2009 some had bought a home and had equity in a primary residence. "−" means not applicable.
Source: Federal Reserve Board, Surveying the Aftermath of the Storm: Changes in Family Finances from 2007 to 2009, Jesse Bricker, Brian Bucks, Arthur Kennickell, Traci Mach, and Kevin Moore, Finance and Economics Discussion Series, 2011-17, Appendix tables, Internet site http://www.federalreserve.gov/pubs/oss/oss2/2009p/scf2009phome.html; calculations by New Strategist

Table 5.14 Median Value of Vehicles and Business Equity, 2007 and 2009

(median value of vehicles and business equity for households owning asset, by selected characteristics of house-holds, 2007 and 2009; percent change, 2007–09; in 2009 dollars)

	vehicles			business equity		
	2009	2007	percent change	2009	2007	percent change
TOTAL HOUSEHOLDS	**$12,000**	**$16,200**	**−25.9%**	**$94,500**	**$103,600**	**−8.8%**
Household income percentile						
Below 20 percent	4,200	5,800	−27.6	35,000	93,200	−62.4
20 to 39.9 percent	8,000	10,500	−23.8	50,000	46,600	7.3
40 to 59.9 percent	12,000	15,100	−20.5	46,700	51,800	−9.8
60 to 79.9 percent	17,000	21,400	−20.6	60,000	82,600	−27.4
80 to 89.9 percent	25,000	26,700	−6.4	85,000	103,600	−18.0
90 percent or higher	30,000	34,900	−14.0	259,900	517,800	−49.8
Age of householder						
Under age 35	10,500	14,500	−27.6	41,300	46,600	−11.4
Aged 35 to 44	15,000	18,100	−17.1	70,000	98,700	−29.1
Aged 45 to 54	15,000	18,600	−19.4	80,000	103,600	−22.8
Aged 55 to 64	15,000	17,800	−15.7	150,000	152,500	−1.6
Aged 65 to 74	12,000	15,200	−21.1	500,000	517,800	−3.4
Aged 75 or older	7,900	9,700	−18.6	250,000	258,900	−3.4
Education of householder						
No high school diploma	6,000	10,500	−42.9	50,000	68,300	−26.8
High school diploma	11,000	13,700	−19.7	80,000	94,600	−15.4
Some college	11,000	15,100	−27.2	50,000	93,200	−46.4
College degree	17,000	20,600	−17.5	120,000	124,300	−3.5
Race and Hispanic origin of householder						
Non-Hispanic white	15,000	17,900	−16.2	100,000	108,700	−8.0
Nonwhite or Hispanic	9,000	12,400	−27.4	46,700	73,300	−36.3
Region						
Northeast	12,000	14,800	−18.9	125,000	120,800	3.5
Midwest	12,000	15,200	−21.1	100,000	103,600	−3.5
South	12,000	16,400	−26.8	75,000	103,600	−27.6
West	15,000	18,000	−16.7	87,200	103,600	−15.8
Housing status						
Owner	15,000	19,100	−21.5	100,000	109,300	−8.5
Renter or other	7,000	9,000	−22.2	50,000	61,100	−18.2

Source: Federal Reserve Board, Surveying the Aftermath of the Storm: Changes in Family Finances from 2007 to 2009, Jesse Bricker, Brian Bucks, Arthur Kennickell, Traci Mach, and Kevin Moore, Finance and Economics Discussion Series, 2011-17, Appendix tables, Internet site http://www.federalreserve.gov/pubs/oss/oss2/2009p/scf2009phome.html; calculations by New Strategist

Most Households Are in Debt

Among households with debt, the amount owed increased between 2007 and 2009.

Seventy-eight percent of households have debt, owing a median of $75,600 in 2009. The median amount of debt owed by the average debtor household increased by 7.5 percent between 2007 and 2009, after adjusting for inflation. The percentage of households in debt fell slightly, however.

Householders aged 35 to 54 are most likely to be in debt, with 87 to 88 percent owing money. Debt declines with age, and the share of households with debt falls to a low of 35 percent among householders aged 75 or older.

Four types of debt are most common—debt secured by the primary residence (mortgages), which is held by 47 percent of households; credit card debt (43 percent); vehicle loans (34 percent); and education loans (18 percent). Mortgages account for the largest share of debt. The median amount owed by the average homeowner for the primary residence stood at $113,500 in 2009. Education loans are second in size, the average household with this type of debt owing a median of $15,000—more than the $12,400 owed by (the more numerous) households with vehicle loans. Credit card debt is tiny by comparison, the average household with a credit card balance owing only $3,300.

■ Americans are attempting to pay down their debts because of the Great Recession, reducing consumer demand.

Home-secured debt accounts for the largest amount owed

(median amount of debt for debtors, for the four most common types of debt, 2009)

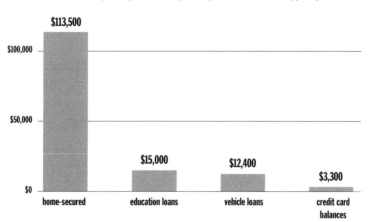

Table 5.15 Debt of Households, 2007 and 2009

(percentage of households with debts and median amount of debt for debtors, by selected characteristics of households, 2007 and 2009; percentage point change in households with debt and percent change in amount of debt, 2007–09; in 2009 dollars)

	percent with debt			median amount of debt		
	2009	**2007**	**percentage point change**	**2009**	**2007**	**percent change**
TOTAL HOUSEHOLDS	**77.5%**	**79.7%**	**–2.2**	**$75,600**	**$70,300**	**7.5%**
Household income percentile						
Below 20 percent	55.8	56.3	–0.5	10,000	9,000	11.1
20 to 39.9 percent	73.1	75.1	–2.0	23,000	19,200	19.8
40 to 59.9 percent	84.0	86.0	–2.0	69,300	63,900	8.5
60 to 79.9 percent	88.2	92.2	–4.0	130,000	122,200	6.4
80 to 89.9 percent	89.2	91.2	–2.0	192,500	188,700	2.0
90 percent or higher	84.4	87.5	–3.1	260,000	245,400	5.9
Age of householder						
Under age 35	84.6	85.4	–0.8	51,000	37,800	34.9
Aged 35 to 44	87.7	87.3	0.4	109,500	113,700	–3.7
Aged 45 to 54	86.6	88.1	–1.5	100,200	103,500	–3.2
Aged 55 to 64	77.7	83.4	–5.7	62,000	64,300	–3.6
Aged 65 to 74	62.1	68.5	–6.4	48,100	41,800	15.1
Aged 75 or older	35.0	36.2	–1.2	8,200	20,000	–59.0
Education of householder						
No high school diploma	59.9	60.4	–0.5	20,000	20,700	–3.4
High school diploma	75.8	77.7	–1.9	42,300	41,400	2.2
Some college	84.3	83.1	1.2	61,000	60,200	1.3
College degree	81.5	86.2	–4.7	141,300	131,500	7.5
Race and Hispanic origin of householder						
Non-Hispanic white	76.5	79.7	–3.2	89,000	82,800	7.5
Nonwhite or Hispanic	79.7	79.6	0.1	44,000	45,300	–2.9
Region						
Northeast	72.7	75.6	–2.9	76,800	64,500	19.1
Midwest	76.5	79.7	–3.2	65,000	65,300	–0.5
South	79.4	78.8	0.6	64,800	65,100	–0.5
West	79.2	84.5	–5.3	106,500	100,500	6.0
Housing status						
Owner	81.7	84.3	–2.6	111,000	117,000	–5.1
Renter or other	68.1	69.3	–1.2	13,000	9,400	38.3

Source: Federal Reserve Board, Surveying the Aftermath of the Storm: Changes in Family Finances from 2007 to 2009, Jesse Bricker, Brian Bucks, Arthur Kennickell, Traci Mach, and Kevin Moore, Finance and Economics Discussion Series, 2011-17, Appendix tables, Internet site http://www.federalreserve.gov/pubs/oss/oss2/2009p/scf2009phome.html; calculations by New Strategist

Table 5.16 Percent of Households with Residential Debt, 2007 and 2009

(percentage of households with residential debt by selected characteristics, 2007 and 2009; percentage point change, 2007–09)

| | secured by residential property | | | | | | | | |
| | secured by primary residence | | | home equity line of credit | | | other residential debt | | |
	2009	2007	percentage point change	2009	2007	percentage point change	2009	2007	percentage point change
TOTAL HOUSEHOLDS	**46.6%**	**47.8%**	**−1.2**	**10.5%**	**8.7%**	**1.8**	**5.1%**	**5.7%**	**−0.6**
Household income percentile									
Below 20 percent	12.6	14.3	−1.7	2.5	1.8	0.7	1.1	1.5	−0.4
20 to 39.9 percent	28.5	28.0	0.5	6.7	6.5	0.2	2.1	2.6	−0.5
40 to 59.9 percent	53.2	52.7	0.5	8.7	7.3	1.4	2.9	2.5	0.4
60 to 79.9 percent	67.4	69.9	−2.5	15.4	10.8	4.6	5.3	7.6	−2.3
80 to 89.9 percent	75.9	77.5	−1.6	16.2	16.1	0.1	7.7	7.3	0.4
90 percent or higher	68.9	73.1	−4.2	22.6	19.0	3.6	20.1	20.9	−0.8
Age of householder									
Under age 35	39.8	37.4	2.4	4.3	3.7	0.6	3.3	3.2	0.1
Aged 35 to 44	60.0	60.0	0.0	10.2	8.5	1.7	6.0	7.0	−1.0
Aged 45 to 54	62.2	64.3	−2.1	14.0	12.3	1.7	6.7	7.7	−1.0
Aged 55 to 64	46.8	51.9	−5.1	17.1	12.8	4.3	6.6	8.3	−1.7
Aged 65 to 74	34.9	37.4	−2.5	11.9	10.3	1.6	4.7	4.3	0.4
Aged 75 or older	11.5	13.4	−1.9	4.3	3.8	0.5	0.9	0.6	0.3
Education of householder									
No high school diploma	26.3	27.3	−1.0	4.2	3.5	0.7	1.4	2.5	−1.1
High school diploma	41.1	43.8	−2.7	8.8	7.8	1.0	3.1	3.2	−0.1
Some college	45.0	44.8	0.2	11.1	8.1	3.0	4.4	6.4	−2.0
College degree	59.3	60.0	−0.7	13.8	11.7	2.1	8.4	8.5	−0.1
Race and Hispanic origin of householder									
Non-Hispanic white	49.7	51.2	−1.5	12.2	10.2	2.0	5.5	6.0	−0.5
Nonwhite or Hispanic	39.3	39.9	−0.6	6.4	5.4	1.0	3.9	4.8	−0.9
Region									
Northeast	44.0	46.1	−2.1	12.6	10.8	1.8	3.5	5.0	−1.5
Midwest	47.9	48.9	−1.0	12.2	9.3	2.9	4.7	5.8	−1.1
South	46.4	47.4	−1.0	7.6	5.9	1.7	5.9	5.1	0.8
West	47.7	49.0	−1.3	11.7	11.2	0.5	5.4	7.0	−1.6
Housing status									
Owner	63.0	69.4	−6.4	15.1	12.7	2.4	6.7	6.8	−0.1
Renter or other	10.2	0.0	10.2	0.3	0.0	0.3	1.5	3.2	−1.7

Note: Renters were classified in the 2007 survey and when reinterviewed in 2009 some had bought a home and had residential debt.
Source: Federal Reserve Board, Surveying the Aftermath of the Storm: Changes in Family Finances from 2007 to 2009, Jesse Bricker, Brian Bucks, Arthur Kennickell, Traci Mach, and Kevin Moore, Finance and Economics Discussion Series, 2011-17, Internet site http://www.federalreserve.gov/pubs/oss/oss2/2009p/scf2009phome.html; calculations by New Strategist

Table 5.17 Percent of Households with Credit Card Debt, Vehicle Loans, and Education Loans, 2007 and 2009

(percentage of households with credit card, vehicle, and education debt by selected characteristics, 2007 and 2009; percentage point change, 2007–09)

	credit card balances			vehicle loans			education loans		
	2009	2007	percentage point change	2009	2007	percentage point change	2009	2007	percentage point change
TOTAL HOUSEHOLDS	**43.2%**	**47.8%**	**–4.6**	**33.9%**	**36.0%**	**–2.1**	**17.7%**	**16.3%**	**1.4**
Household income percentile									
Below 20 percent	28.4	28.3	0.1	14.1	14.5	–0.4	12.3	12.6	–0.3
20 to 39.9 percent	38.2	42.1	–3.9	32.0	30.9	1.1	16.2	13.7	2.5
40 to 59.9 percent	50.7	56.5	–5.8	40.2	41.2	–1.0	20.2	17.3	2.9
60 to 79.9 percent	56.9	63.3	–6.4	46.1	51.8	–5.7	22.2	20.1	2.1
80 to 89.9 percent	51.9	58.4	–6.5	43.4	48.7	–5.3	23.2	22.3	0.9
90 percent or higher	32.4	40.1	–7.7	31.9	36.6	–4.7	12.5	13.3	–0.8
Age of householder									
Under age 35	42.8	50.6	–7.8	43.1	46.0	–2.9	36.8	35.7	1.1
Aged 35 to 44	49.6	52.6	–3.0	44.7	44.1	0.6	19.7	15.7	4.0
Aged 45 to 54	50.5	54.1	–3.6	35.5	38.3	–2.8	18.0	14.8	3.2
Aged 55 to 64	44.6	50.4	–5.8	30.8	35.5	–4.7	9.9	11.3	–1.4
Aged 65 to 74	35.0	38.7	–3.7	21.3	21.9	–0.6	1.9	1.9	0.0
Aged 75 or older	20.2	21.8	–1.6	5.5	7.2	–1.7	0.0	0.5	–0.5
Education of householder									
No high school diploma	29.0	29.9	–0.9	19.1	25.1	–6.0	6.0	6.3	–0.3
High school diploma	45.4	47.9	–2.5	36.5	36.2	0.3	12.1	9.5	2.6
Some college	48.2	52.8	–4.6	38.6	39.7	–1.1	21.4	19.2	2.2
College degree	43.5	51.2	–7.7	34.3	37.8	–3.5	24.8	24.2	0.6
Race and Hispanic origin of householder									
Non-Hispanic white	42.2	46.7	–4.5	34.7	36.7	–2.0	15.9	15.2	0.7
Nonwhite or Hispanic	45.5	50.3	–4.8	32.1	34.6	–2.5	21.9	18.7	3.2
Region									
Northeast	36.1	45.7	–9.6	26.1	27.1	–1.0	18.6	18.7	–0.1
Midwest	41.1	46.2	–5.1	31.8	36.6	–4.8	19.6	15.5	4.1
South	43.3	45.8	–2.5	38.7	38.3	0.4	15.9	15.1	0.8
West	51.1	54.5	–3.4	34.6	39.2	–4.6	18.1	17.0	1.1
Housing status									
Owner	46.1	51.2	–5.1	36.2	38.5	–2.3	14.9	13.5	1.4
Renter or other	36.6	40.1	–3.5	28.9	30.7	–1.8	24.0	22.4	1.6

Source: Federal Reserve Board, Surveying the Aftermath of the Storm: Changes in Family Finances from 2007 to 2009, Jesse Bricker, Brian Bucks, Arthur Kennickell, Traci Mach, and Kevin Moore, Finance and Economics Discussion Series, 2011-17, Appendix tables, Internet site http://www.federalreserve.gov/pubs/oss/oss2/2009p/scf2009phome.html; calculations by New Strategist

Table 5.18 Median Value of Residential Debt Owed by Households, 2007 and 2009

(median value of residential debt owed by households with debt, by selected characteristics of households, 2007 and 2009; percent change, 2007–09; in 2009 dollars)

| | secured by residential property | | | | | | | | |
| | secured by primary residence | | | home equity line of credit | | | other residential debt | | |
	2009	2007	percent change	2009	2007	percent change	2009	2007	percent change
TOTAL HOUSEHOLDS	$113,500	$113,900	–0.4%	$21,500	$22,800	–5.7%	$130,000	$98,400	32.1%
Household income percentile									
Below 20 percent	47,900	35,300	35.7	22,000	–	–	–	63,700	–
20 to 39.9 percent	68,700	62,100	10.6	14,500	15,500	–6.5	43,000	60,800	–29.3
40 to 59.9 percent	91,500	92,700	–1.3	18,000	16,100	11.8	44,000	62,100	–29.1
60 to 79.9 percent	128,000	120,100	6.6	20,000	21,500	–7.0	70,000	87,000	–19.5
80 to 89.9 percent	169,200	169,800	–0.4	30,000	35,200	–14.8	150,000	129,200	16.1
90 percent or higher	215,000	207,100	3.8	51,000	49,700	2.6	190,000	152,800	24.3
Age of householder									
Under age 35	144,600	140,100	3.2	20,000	20,300	–1.5	118,000	80,800	46.0
Aged 35 to 44	127,800	128,300	–0.4	20,000	24,900	–19.7	150,000	110,600	35.6
Aged 45 to 54	111,600	113,900	–2.0	30,000	25,900	15.8	115,000	86,000	33.7
Aged 55 to 64	95,000	93,200	1.9	20,000	21,900	–8.7	155,000	110,900	39.8
Aged 65 to 74	80,000	81,800	–2.2	28,000	15,500	80.6	115,000	116,000	–0.9
Aged 75 or older	49,000	33,900	44.5	13,000	25,900	–49.8	23,000	51,800	–55.6
Education of householder									
No high school diploma	66,000	51,800	27.4	20,000	13,500	48.1	–	62,100	–
High school diploma	87,000	87,000	0.0	18,500	18,300	1.1	75,000	77,700	–3.5
Some college	113,100	103,700	9.1	25,000	20,700	20.8	118,000	82,800	42.5
College degree	140,500	145,000	–3.1	26,400	31,100	–15.1	150,000	116,000	29.3
Race and Hispanic origin of householder									
Non-Hispanic white	112,000	112,900	–0.8	20,000	20,700	–3.4	130,000	94,200	38.0
Nonwhite or Hispanic	120,000	119,100	0.8	30,000	25,900	15.8	150,000	103,600	44.8
Region									
Northeast	122,500	106,700	14.8	26,000	25,900	0.4	160,000	104,600	53.0
Midwest	96,000	100,500	–4.5	18,000	18,600	–3.2	100,000	86,000	16.3
South	100,100	104,400	–4.1	20,800	20,700	0.5	92,400	82,800	11.6
West	159,100	152,200	4.5	40,000	38,300	4.4	200,000	126,900	57.6
Housing status									
Owner	110,400	113,900	–3.1	21,000	22,800	–7.9	149,100	103,600	43.9
Renter or other	147,000	0	–	–	–	–	13,400	82,800	–83.8

Note: Renters were classified in the 2007 survey and when reinterviewed in 2009 some had bought a home and had debt secured by their primary residence. "–" means sample is too small to make a reliable estimate or not applicable.
Source: Federal Reserve Board, Surveying the Aftermath of the Storm: Changes in Family Finances from 2007 to 2009, Jesse Bricker, Brian Bucks, Arthur Kennickell, Traci Mach, and Kevin Moore, Finance and Economics Discussion Series, 2011-17, Internet site http://www.federalreserve.gov/pubs/oss/oss2/2009p/scf2009phome.html; calculations by New Strategist

Table 5.19 Median Amount of Credit Card Debt, Vehicle Loans, and Education Loans Owed by Households, 2007 and 2009

(median amount of credit card, vehicle, and education debt owed by households with debt, by selected characteristics of households, 2007 and 2009; percent change, 2007–09; in 2009 dollars)

	credit card balances			vehicle loans			education loans		
	2009	2007	percent change	2009	2007	percent change	2009	2007	percent change
TOTAL HOUSEHOLDS	**$3,300**	**$3,100**	**6.5%**	**$12,400**	**$11,200**	**10.7%**	**$15,000**	**$12,400**	**21.0%**
Household income percentile									
Below 20 percent	1,100	1,000	10.0	8,000	5,200	53.8	13,800	7,200	91.7
20 to 39.9 percent	2,100	1,800	16.7	9,000	9,500	–5.3	12,000	11,400	5.3
40 to 59.9 percent	3,000	2,600	15.4	12,000	11,500	4.3	12,100	11,100	9.0
60 to 79.9 percent	4,700	4,000	17.5	14,000	11,900	17.6	20,000	17,600	13.6
80 to 89.9 percent	7,500	6,200	21.0	17,000	14,500	17.2	19,000	11,200	69.6
90 percent or higher	9,300	7,200	29.2	18,000	17,700	1.7	17,200	16,700	3.0
Age of householder									
Under age 35	3,000	1,900	57.9	12,200	11,300	8.0	15,000	14,500	3.4
Aged 35 to 44	3,000	3,600	–16.7	13,000	12,300	5.7	16,000	12,400	29.0
Aged 45 to 54	4,000	3,700	8.1	13,000	10,900	19.3	15,000	10,700	40.2
Aged 55 to 64	4,500	4,100	9.8	12,000	9,600	25.0	12,000	7,300	64.4
Aged 65 to 74	2,900	3,200	–9.4	10,000	12,500	–20.0	–	–	–
Aged 75 or older	2,000	800	150.0	9,500	7,600	25.0	–	–	–
Education of householder									
No high school diploma	1,500	1,900	–21.1	11,000	11,400	–3.5	6,000	6,200	–3.2
High school diploma	3,000	2,400	25.0	11,000	10,600	3.8	10,000	6,700	49.3
Some college	3,000	2,900	3.4	12,000	10,500	14.3	13,000	9,900	31.3
College degree	5,500	4,100	34.1	14,300	12,100	18.2	20,300	19,200	5.7
Race and Hispanic origin of householder									
Non-Hispanic white	4,300	3,500	22.9	12,400	11,400	8.8	16,000	13,500	18.5
Nonwhite or Hispanic	2,000	2,100	–4.8	12,000	10,500	14.3	13,800	9,500	45.3
Region									
Northeast	2,700	2,600	3.8	12,000	9,700	23.7	15,000	13,100	14.5
Midwest	3,000	3,100	–3.2	10,000	9,700	3.1	16,000	13,500	18.5
South	4,000	3,100	29.0	13,000	11,500	13.0	16,000	11,400	40.4
West	3,600	3,100	16.1	13,000	12,300	5.7	15,000	13,500	11.1
Housing status									
Owner	4,000	3,800	5.3	13,000	11,800	10.2	17,300	15,300	13.1
Renter or other	1,900	1,300	46.2	9,500	9,300	2.2	12,000	10,400	15.4

Note: "–" means sample is too small to make a reliable estimate.
Source: Federal Reserve Board, Surveying the Aftermath of the Storm: Changes in Family Finances from 2007 to 2009, Jesse Bricker, Brian Bucks, Arthur Kennickell, Traci Mach, and Kevin Moore, Finance and Economics Discussion Series, 2011-17, Appendix tables, Internet site http://www.federalreserve.gov/pubs/oss/oss2/2009p/scf2009phome.html; calculations by New Strategist

Many Workers Do Not Have a Retirement Plan

Fewer than half of service workers have access to a retirement plan through work.

Retirement benefits have changed over the past few decades as the number of companies that offer defined-benefit pension plans has declined. Only 31 percent of workers had access to a defined-benefit pension plan in 2010. Fifty-four percent had access to a defined-contribution plan, according to the Bureau of Labor Statistics' Employee Benefits Survey.

The percentage of workers with access to a retirement plan varies widely from a low of 49 percent among service workers to a high of 86 percent among management and business workers. Only 31 percent of the lowest-paid workers have access to a retirement plan compared with 90 percent of the highest-paid workers. Unionized workers are more likely to have a retirement plan (92 percent) than those not in unions (65 percent). Most teachers, protective service workers, and union workers have defined-benefit retirement plans.

■ The Great Recession depleted savings in defined-contribution retirement plans and raises the question of whether these plans will be adequate to support the nation's retirees.

Highly paid workers are more likely to have access to a retirement plan at work

(percent of workers with access to a retirement plan, by average wage percentile, 2010)

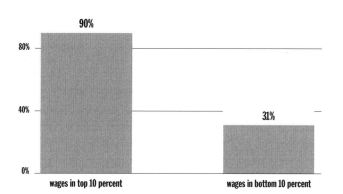

Table 5.20 Workers with Retirement Benefits, 2010

(percent of workers with access to and who participate in a retirement plan, and percent with access who participate (take-up rate), by selected characteristics, 2010)

	all retirement benefits			defined benefit			defined contribution		
	access	participation	take-up rate	access	participation	take-up rate	access	participation	take-up rate
TOTAL WORKERS	**69%**	**55%**	**80%**	**31%**	**28%**	**92%**	**54%**	**37%**	**69%**
Worker characteristics									
Management, business, and financial	86	78	90	43	40	93	74	59	81
Professional and related	82	73	88	47	44	93	56	42	74
Teachers	86	81	95	73	69	94	31	20	64
Registered nurses	82	69	85	38	35	94	66	48	72
Service	49	32	66	19	18	94	36	18	50
Protective service	75	63	84	55	51	94	38	20	53
Sales and office	71	56	78	25	22	86	62	44	71
Natural resources, construction, and maintenance	67	55	81	32	31	97	54	38	70
Production, transportation, and material moving	67	52	78	28	26	94	54	37	68
Full-time	78	65	84	36	34	94	61	45	72
Part-time	39	23	58	14	11	80	30	14	47
Union	92	87	94	82	78	96	41	29	71
Nonunion	65	49	77	21	19	90	57	39	69
Average wage within the following percentiles									
Lowest 10 percent	31	12	39	5	3	61	28	9	34
Lowest 25 percent	43	24	56	10	8	77	37	18	49
Second 25 percent	70	54	78	26	23	91	57	38	67
Third 25 percent	80	68	86	37	35	94	62	46	75
Highest 25 percent	88	81	92	54	51	95	64	51	79
Highest 10 percent	90	83	92	54	50	94	67	54	80

Note: Total workers includes all workers in the private, nonfarm economy except private household workers and includes all workers in the public sector except those working for the federal government.
Source: Bureau of Labor Statistics, Employee Benefits Survey, Internet site http://www.bls.gov/ncs/ebs/benefits/2010/ ownership_civilian.htm

Retirement Worries Are Growing

A record share of workers lack confidence in having enough money for a comfortable retirement.

Only 13 percent of workers are "very confident" in their ability to afford a comfortable retirement, according to the 2011 Retirement Confidence Survey. The 13 percent figure is just half of the 26 percent who felt very confident in 2000.

Reality may be dawning on many workers. Since 2000, the expected age of retirement has climbed sharply. The percentage of workers expecting to retire at age 65 or older increased from 51 to 70 percent between 2000 and 2011. At the same time, the percentage expecting to retire before age 65 fell from 44 to 23 percent.

■ Only 22 percent of workers are very confident that they are doing a good job of saving for retirement, down from 30 percent who felt that way in 2000.

Most workers are not planning on an early retirement

(percent of workers who expect to retire at age 65 or older, 2000 and 2011)

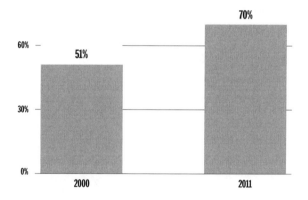

Table 5.21 Retirement Confidence, 2000 and 2011

(responses of workers aged 25 or older to selected questions about retirement, 2000 and 2011; percentage point change, 2000–11)

	2011	2000	percentage point change
Confidence in having enough money to live comfortably in retirement			
Very confident	13%	26%	–13
Somewhat confident	36	47	–11
Not too confident	23	18	5
Not at all confident	27	8	19
Confident that they are doing a good job of preparing financially for retirement			
Very confident	22	30	–8
Somewhat confident	41	49	–8
Not too confident	19	13	6
Not at all confident	17	8	9
Confidence that the Social Security system will continue to provide benefits of at least equal value to the benefits received by retirees today			
Very confident	5	7	–2
Somewhat confident	24	21	3
Not too confident	31	39	–8
Not at all confident	39	32	7
Confidence that the Medicare system will continue to provide benefits of at least equal value to the benefits received by retirees today			
Very confident	5	6	–1
Somewhat confident	25	29	–4
Not too confident	36	38	–2
Not at all confident	34	26	8

Source: Employee Benefit Research Institute, Retirement Confidence Surveys, Internet site http://www.ebri.org/surveys/rcs/

Table 5.22 Expected Age of Retirement, 2000 and 2011

(responses of workers aged 25 or older to question about expected age of retirement, 2000 and 2011; percentage point change, 2000–11)

	2011	2000	percentage point change
Expected age of retirement:			
Before age 60	7%	22%	–15
Aged 60 to 64	16	22	–6
Age 65	26	28	–2
Aged 66 or older	36	19	17
Never retire	8	4	4
Before age 65	23	44	–21
Aged 65 or older	70	51	19

Note: Figures may not sum to total because "don't know/refused" is not shown.
Source: Employee Benefit Research Institute, Retirement Confidence Surveys, Internet site http://www.ebri.org/surveys/rcs/

Table 5.23 Retirement Savings by Age, 2011

(percent distribution of workers aged 25 or older by savings and investments, not including value of primary residence, by age, 2011)

	total	25 to 34	35 to 44	45 to 54	55 or older
Total workers	**100%**	**100%**	**100%**	**100%**	**100%**
Less than $10,000	46	59	45	44	29
$10,000 to $24,999	10	12	10	8	7
$25,000 to $49,999	11	9	13	10	14
$50,000 to $99,999	9	9	8	10	10
$100,000 or more	25	12	24	27	41
$100,000 to $249,999	14	9	15	12	22
$250,000 or more	11	3	9	15	19

Source: Employee Benefit Research Institute, 2011 Retirement Confidence Survey, Internet site http://www.ebri.org/surveys/rcs/2009/

6

Poverty

Poverty rose sharply between 2000 and 2010 as the Great Recession destroyed businesses and jobs. In 2010, the poverty rate stood at 15.1 percent, up from the low of 11.3 percent reached in 2000 and matching the poverty rate of 1993 (also a recovery year following a recession).

The poverty population has changed over the years. The elderly were once most likely to be poor. Today, children have a much higher poverty rate (22.0 percent) than the elderly (9.0 percent). Among household types, married couples once accounted for half of poor families. Today, female-headed families are the majority of families in poverty. Non-Hispanic whites once accounted for most of the poor. Today, the majority is Hispanic or black. In 1990, blacks outnumbered Hispanics among the poor. Now poor Hispanics outnumber poor blacks.

■ Poverty rates may continue to rise because of high levels of unemployment in an economy that cannot seem to recover from the Great Recession.

Poverty Trends

Women Head More than Half of the Nation's Poor Families

The share of poor families headed by women has exceeded 50 percent for more than two decades.

In 2010, female-headed families accounted for the 51 percent majority of the nation's 9.2 million poor families. The proportion is little changed from the 53 percent of 1990. Married couples accounted for a smaller 39 percent of poor families in 2010.

Men head few poor families, although the proportion has doubled over the past few decades. Male-headed families accounted for about 10 percent of families in poverty in 2010, up from 5 percent in 1990.

■ The married-couple share of poor families has increased slightly since the low of 37 percent in 2007.

Married couples head a smaller share of poor families

(percent distribution of families in poverty by family type, 1990 and 2010)

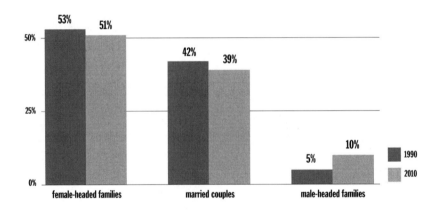

Table 6.1 Distribution of Families below Poverty Level by Family Type, 1990 to 2010

(total number of families below poverty level and percent distribution by family type, 1990 to 2010; families in thousands as of the following year)

	total families in poverty		married couples	female householder, no spouse present	male householder, no spouse present
	number	percent			
2010	9,221	100.0%	39.0%	51.5%	9.5%
2009	8,792	100.0	38.8	50.5	10.7
2008	8,147	100.0	40.0	51.1	8.9
2007	7,623	100.0	37.4	53.5	9.1
2006	7,668	100.0	37.9	53.3	8.8
2005	7,657	100.0	38.4	52.8	8.7
2004	7,835	100.0	41.0	50.6	8.4
2003	7,607	100.0	40.9	50.7	8.4
2002	7,229	100.0	42.2	50.0	7.8
2001	6,813	100.0	40.5	50.9	8.6
2000	6,400	100.0	41.2	51.2	7.6
1999	6,792	100.0	40.5	52.4	7.1
1998	7,186	100.0	40.1	53.3	6.6
1997	7,324	100.0	38.5	54.5	6.9
1996	7,708	100.0	39.1	54.1	6.9
1995	7,532	100.0	39.6	53.9	6.5
1994	8,053	100.0	40.6	52.6	6.8
1993	8,393	100.0	41.5	52.7	5.8
1992	8,144	100.0	41.6	52.5	5.9
1991	7,712	100.0	40.9	54.0	5.1
1990	7,098	100.0	42.0	53.1	4.9

Source: Bureau of the Census, Current Population Surveys, Annual Social and Economic Supplement, Internet site http://www .census.gov/hhes/www/poverty/data/historical/index.html

Poverty Rates Increased in 2010

Among blacks, poverty rates today are still below those of the early 1990s.

Family poverty was significantly higher in 2010 than the all-time low reached in 2000. In 2010, a substantial 11.7 percent of the nation's families were poor, up from 8.7 percent in 2000. The 2010 rate was still below the family poverty rate of the early 1990s, when it climbed to 12.3 percent. Poverty rates were higher in 2010 than in 2000 for every type of family.

Since the 1990s, poverty has fallen among black families—from 31.3 percent in 1993 to 24.1 percent in 2010. Among female-headed black families, the decline has been even more dramatic, their poverty rate falling from 51.2 percent in 1991 to 38.4 percent in 2010.

In contrast to blacks, the poverty rate of Hispanic families has not changed much over the decades. Hispanic married couples are twice as likely as black couples to be poor (17.1 percent of Hispanic couples were poor in 2010 versus only 9.0 percent of black couples). In 2010, 24.0 percent of all Hispanic families were poor, almost identical to the 24.1 percent poverty rate among black families.

Non-Hispanic white families are least likely to be poor, with a poverty rate of 7.3 percent. A larger 9.1 percent of Asian families were poor in 2010.

■ Because of Hispanic immigration, the number of Hispanic families in poverty has doubled since 1990.

Family poverty has grown among blacks, Hispanics, and non-Hispanic whites since 2000

(poverty rate of families by race and Hispanic origin of householder, 2000 and 2010)

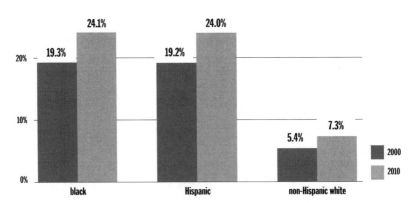

Table 6.2   **Number and Percent of Families below Poverty Level by Family Type, 1990 to 2010: Total Families**

(number and percent of families below poverty level by family type, 1990 to 2010; families in thousands as of the following year)

	total families in poverty		married couples		female householder, no spouse present		male householder, no spouse present	
	number	percent	number	percent	number	percent	number	percent
2010	9,221	11.7%	3,596	6.2%	4,745	31.6%	880	15.8%
2009	8,792	11.1	3,409	5.8	4,441	29.9	942	16.9
2008	8,147	10.3	3,261	5.5	4,163	28.7	723	13.8
2007	7,623	9.8	2,849	4.9	4,078	28.3	696	13.6
2006	7,668	9.8	2,910	4.9	4,087	28.3	671	13.2
2005	7,657	9.9	2,944	5.1	4,044	28.7	669	13.0
2004	7,835	10.2	3,216	5.5	3,962	28.3	657	13.4
2003	7,607	10.0	3,115	5.4	3,856	28.0	636	13.5
2002	7,229	9.6	3,052	5.3	3,613	26.5	564	12.1
2001	6,813	9.2	2,760	4.9	3,470	26.4	583	13.1
2000	6,400	8.7	2,637	4.7	3,278	25.4	485	11.3
1999	6,792	9.3	2,748	4.9	3,559	27.8	485	11.8
1998	7,186	10.0	2,879	5.3	3,831	29.9	476	12.0
1997	7,324	10.3	2,821	5.2	3,995	31.6	507	13.0
1996	7,708	11.0	3,010	5.6	4,167	32.6	531	13.8
1995	7,532	10.8	2,982	5.6	4,057	32.4	493	14.0
1994	8,053	11.6	3,272	6.1	4,232	34.6	549	17.0
1993	8,393	12.3	3,481	6.5	4,424	35.6	488	16.8
1992	8,144	11.9	3,385	6.4	4,275	35.4	484	15.8
1991	7,712	11.5	3,158	6.0	4,161	35.6	392	13.0
1990	7,098	10.7	2,981	5.7	3,768	33.4	349	12.0

Source: Bureau of the Census, Current Population Surveys, Annual Social and Economic Supplement, Internet site http://www .census.gov/hhes/www/poverty/data/historical/index.html

Table 6.3 Number and Percent of Families below Poverty Level by Family Type, 2002 to 2010: Asian Families

(number and percent of Asian families below poverty level by family type, 2002 to 2010; families in thousands as of the following year)

	total Asian families in poverty		married couples		female householder, no spouse present		male householder, no spouse present	
	number	percent	number	percent	number	percent	number	percent
2010	340	9.1%	211	7.2%	100	20.3%	29	10.0%
2009	359	9.6	239	8.0	87	18.0	34	12.3
2008	356	9.8	254	8.7	76	16.5	26	10.1
2007	281	8.1	187	6.8	77	17.0	17	7.0
2006	272	7.8	183	6.4	61	15.6	27	11.4
2005	306	9.1	201	7.5	83	20.0	22	8.8
2004	243	7.4	150	5.7	54	14.0	39	14.8
2003	320	10.0	203	7.9	89	23.5	28	11.8
2002	218	7.4	137	5.9	51	14.3	30	12.6

Note: Data are for those who identify themselves as being of the race alone and those who identify themselves as being of the race in combination with other races.

Source: Bureau of the Census, Current Population Surveys, Annual Social and Economic Supplement, Internet site http://www .census.gov/hhes/www/poverty/data/historical/index.html

Table 6.4 **Number and Percent of Families below Poverty Level by Family Type, 1990 to 2010: Black Families**

(number and percent of black families below poverty level by family type, 1990 to 2010; families in thousands as of the following year)

	total black families in poverty		married couples		female householder, no spouse present		male householder, no spouse present	
	number	percent	number	percent	number	percent	number	percent
2010	2,355	24.1%	390	9.0%	1,712	38.4%	253	26.5%
2009	2,193	22.7	383	8.6	1,569	36.8	241	24.9
2008	2,112	21.9	365	8.0	1,580	37.1	167	19.8
2007	2,091	22.0	313	7.0	1,570	37.2	208	25.1
2006	2,041	21.5	356	7.9	1,506	36.4	180	20.4
2005	2,050	22.0	348	8.2	1,524	36.2	178	21.3
2004	2,082	22.8	386	9.1	1,538	37.6	158	20.7
2003	2,021	22.1	331	7.8	1,496	36.8	194	24.1
2002	1,958	21.4	340	8.0	1,454	35.7	165	20.8
2001	1,829	20.7	328	7.8	1,351	35.2	150	19.4
2000	1,686	19.3	266	6.3	1,300	34.3	120	16.3
1999	1,887	21.8	295	7.1	1,487	39.2	105	14.8
1998	1,981	23.4	290	7.3	1,557	40.8	134	20.3
1997	1,985	23.6	312	8.0	1,563	39.8	111	19.7
1996	2,206	26.1	352	9.1	1,724	43.7	130	19.8
1995	2,127	26.4	314	8.5	1,701	45.1	112	19.5
1994	2,212	27.3	336	8.7	1,715	46.2	161	30.1
1993	2,499	31.3	458	12.3	1,908	49.9	133	29.6
1992	2,484	31.1	490	13.0	1,878	50.2	116	24.8
1991	2,343	30.4	399	11.0	1,834	51.2	110	21.9
1990	2,193	29.3	448	12.6	1,648	48.1	97	20.6

Note: Beginning in 2002, data are for those who identify themselves as being of the race alone and those who identify themselves as being of the race in combination with other races.
Source: Bureau of the Census, Current Population Surveys, Annual Social and Economic Supplement, Internet site http://www .census.gov/hhes/www/poverty/data/historical/index.html

Table 6.5 Number and Percent of Families below Poverty Level by Family Type, 1990 to 2010: Hispanic Families

(number and percent of Hispanic families below poverty level by family type, 1990 to 2010; families in thousands as of the following year)

	total Hispanic families in poverty		married couples		female householder, no spouse present		male householder, no spouse present	
	number	percent	number	percent	number	percent	number	percent
2010	2,557	24.0%	1,152	17.1%	1,167	42.3%	238	20.2%
2009	2,369	22.7	1,054	16.0	1,066	38.8	249	23.0
2008	2,239	21.3	1,078	15.6	1,007	39.2	154	15.1
2007	2,045	19.7	926	13.4	968	38.4	151	15.3
2006	1,922	18.9	903	13.3	881	36.0	139	14.7
2005	1,948	19.7	917	13.8	876	38.9	155	15.9
2004	1,953	20.5	934	14.7	872	38.9	147	15.9
2003	1,925	20.8	976	15.7	792	37.0	157	17.3
2002	1,792	19.7	927	15.0	717	35.3	148	17.0
2001	1,649	19.4	799	13.8	711	37.0	139	17.0
2000	1,540	19.2	772	14.2	664	36.4	104	13.6
1999	1,593	20.5	758	14.4	717	39.3	117	17.0
1998	1,648	22.7	775	15.7	756	43.7	117	19.6
1997	1,721	24.7	836	17.4	767	47.6	119	21.7
1996	1,748	26.4	815	18.0	823	50.9	110	22.3
1995	1,695	27.0	803	18.9	792	49.4	100	22.9
1994	1,724	27.8	827	19.5	773	52.1	124	25.8
1993	1,625	27.3	770	19.1	772	51.6	83	20.2
1992	1,529	26.7	743	18.8	664	49.3	122	27.4
1991	1,372	26.5	674	19.1	627	49.7	71	18.5
1990	1,244	25.0	605	17.5	573	48.3	66	19.4

Source: Bureau of the Census, Current Population Surveys, Annual Social and Economic Supplement, Internet site http://www .census.gov/hhes/www/poverty/data/historical/index.html

Table 6.6 **Number and Percent of Families below Poverty Level by Family Type, 1990 to 2010: Non-Hispanic White Families**

(number and percent of non-Hispanic white families below poverty level by family type, 1990 to 2010; families in thousands as of the following year)

	total non-Hispanic white families in poverty		married couples		female householder, no spouse present		male householder, no spouse present	
	number	percent	number	percent	number	percent	number	percent
2010	3,922	7.3%	1,812	4.2%	1,770	24.3%	339	11.0%
2009	3,797	7.0	1,697	3.9	1,701	23.3	399	12.5
2008	3,383	6.2	1,545	3.5	1,473	20.7	365	11.9
2007	3,184	5.9	1,388	3.2	1,489	20.7	308	10.3
2006	3,372	6.2	1,436	3.2	1,628	22.0	309	10.6
2005	3,285	6.1	1,450	3.3	1,537	21.5	298	9.9
2004	3,505	6.5	1,710	3.9	1,491	20.8	304	10.5
2003	3,270	6.1	1,575	3.6	1,455	20.4	241	8.9
2002	3,208	6.0	1,628	3.7	1,374	19.4	207	7.7
2001	3,051	5.7	1,477	3.3	1,305	19.0	270	10.3
2000	2,896	5.4	1,435	3.2	1,226	17.8	236	9.2
1999	2,953	5.5	1,474	3.3	1,248	18.4	231	9.3
1998	3,264	6.1	1,639	3.8	1,428	20.7	197	7.8
1997	3,357	6.3	1,501	3.5	1,598	23.4	258	9.8
1996	3,433	6.5	1,628	3.8	1,538	22.4	267	10.8
1995	3,384	6.4	1,664	3.8	1,463	21.5	257	11.2
1994	3,833	7.2	1,915	4.3	1,678	24.8	241	11.5
1993	3,988	7.6	2,042	4.7	1,699	25.0	248	12.9
1992	3,840	7.3	1,978	4.5	1,637	24.7	225	11.2
1991	3,719	7.1	1,918	4.4	1,610	24.6	190	9.4
1990	3,442	6.6	1,799	4.1	1,480	23.1	163	8.4

Note: Beginning in 2002, data are for those who identify themselves as being white alone and not Hispanic.
Source: Bureau of the Census, Current Population Surveys, Annual Social and Economic Supplement, Internet site http://www
.census.gov/hhes/www/poverty/data/historical/index.html

More Families with Children Are Slipping into Poverty

Since 2000, poverty rates have climbed sharply for male- and female-headed families with children.

More than 18 percent of families with children under age 18 were poor in 2010, a figure that has not topped 18 percent since the early 1990s. Between 2000 and 2010 the poverty rate for families with children climbed from 12.7 to 18.3 percent.

The poverty rate of female-headed families with children grew from 33.0 percent in 2000 to 40.7 percent in 2010. For their male counterparts, the percentage point increase in the poverty rate was even greater, the rate rising from 15.3 to 24.2 percent. Poverty also increased among married couples with children during the decade, but the increase was much smaller.

In 2010, Hispanic female-headed families with children had the highest poverty rate, at 50.3 percent. This figure was higher than the 42.9 percent of 2000 but still lower than their rate during most of the 1990s. Similarly, the 47.1 percent poverty rate of black female-headed families with children was much greater than the 41.0 of 2000 but still well below their rate during most of the 1990s. More than one in five Hispanic married couples with children were poor in 2010. Black married couples with children are much less likely to be poor, with a poverty rate of 12.4 percent.

Among families with children, the poverty rate is lowest for non-Hispanic white married couples (5.2 percent). Asian married couples with children had a poverty rate of 7.8 percent.

■ The poverty rate of female-headed families fell during the 1990s as welfare reform pushed many single parents into the labor force.

Poverty has grown among families with children

(poverty rate of families with children under age 18 by family type, 2000 and 2010)

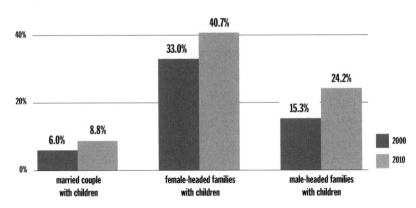

Table 6.7 Number and Percent of Families with Children below Poverty Level by Family Type, 1990 to 2010: Total Families with Children

(number and percent of families with related children under age 18 below poverty level by family type, 1990 to 2010; families in thousands as of the following year)

	total families with children in poverty		married couples		female householder, no spouse present		male householder, no spouse present	
	number	percent	number	percent	number	percent	number	percent
2010	6,997	18.3%	2,242	8.8%	4,089	40.7%	667	24.2%
2009	6,630	17.1	2,161	8.3	3,800	38.5	670	23.7
2008	6,104	15.7	1,989	7.5	3,645	37.2	471	17.6
2007	5,830	15.0	1,765	6.7	3,593	37.0	471	17.5
2006	5,822	14.6	1,746	6.4	3,615	36.5	461	17.9
2005	5,729	14.5	1,777	6.5	3,493	36.2	459	17.6
2004	5,819	14.8	1,903	7.0	3,477	35.9	439	17.1
2003	5,772	14.8	1,885	7.0	3,416	35.5	470	19.1
2002	5,397	13.9	1,831	6.8	3,171	33.7	395	16.6
2001	5,138	13.4	1,643	6.1	3,083	33.6	412	17.7
2000	4,866	12.7	1,615	6.0	2,906	33.0	345	15.3
1999	5,210	13.8	1,711	6.4	3,139	35.7	360	16.3
1998	5,628	15.1	1,822	6.9	3,456	38.7	350	16.6
1997	5,884	15.7	1,863	7.1	3,614	41.0	407	18.7
1996	6,131	16.5	1,964	7.5	3,755	41.9	412	20.0
1995	5,976	16.3	1,961	7.5	3,634	41.5	381	19.7
1994	6,408	17.4	2,197	8.3	3,816	44.0	395	22.6
1993	6,751	18.5	2,363	9.0	4,034	46.1	354	22.5
1992	6,457	18.0	2,237	8.6	3,867	46.2	353	22.5
1991	6,170	17.7	2,106	8.3	3,767	47.1	297	19.6
1990	5,676	16.4	1,990	7.8	3,426	44.5	260	18.8

Source: Bureau of the Census, Current Population Surveys, Annual Social and Economic Supplement, Internet site http://www.census.gov/hhes/www/poverty/data/historical/index.html

Table 6.8 **Number and Percent of Families with Children below Poverty Level by Family Type, 2002 to 2010: Asian Families with Children**

(number and percent of Asian families with related children under age 18 below poverty level by family type, 2002 to 2010; families in thousands as of the following year)

	total Asian families with children in poverty		married couples		female householder, no spouse present		male householder, no spouse present	
	number	percent	number	percent	number	percent	number	percent
2010	213	10.9%	124	7.8%	80	28.7%	10	11.1%
2009	238	11.5	153	9.0	64	23.4	21	20.7
2008	204	10.5	141	8.8	52	21.4	11	12.5
2007	178	9.6	109	7.1	65	27.8	4	5.1
2006	178	9.5	116	7.3	46	23.8	16	19.2
2005	189	10.4	121	8.1	54	24.3	14	15.5
2004	154	8.4	97	6.3	43	19.5	15	15.4
2003	199	10.9	121	8.0	66	28.2	12	15.2
2002	151	9.2	94	6.9	39	21.0	18	21.1

Note: Data are for those who identify themselves as being of the race alone and those who identify themselves as being of the race in combination with other races.
Source: Bureau of the Census, Current Population Surveys, Annual Social and Economic Supplement, Internet site http://www .census.gov/hhes/www/poverty/data/historical/index.html

Table 6.9 **Number and Percent of Families with Children below Poverty Level by Family Type, 1990 to 2010: Black Families with Children**

(number and percent of black families with related children under age 18 below poverty level by family type, 1990 to 2010; families in thousands as of the following year)

	total black families with children in poverty		married couples		female householder, no spouse present		male householder, no spouse present	
	number	percent	number	percent	number	percent	number	percent
2010	1,939	33.7%	264	12.4%	1,478	47.1%	197	40.8%
2009	1,787	30.4	259	11.4	1,365	44.3	163	30.5
2008	1,756	29.6	225	9.8	1,416	44.4	115	25.5
2007	1,706	29.0	194	8.5	1,385	43.7	128	29.5
2006	1,686	28.1	221	9.1	1,347	43.3	117	25.8
2005	1,679	28.3	213	9.2	1,335	42.0	131	29.6
2004	1,655	28.6	213	9.3	1,339	43.3	102	25.3
2003	1,698	28.6	210	9.1	1,341	42.7	146	30.7
2002	1,597	27.2	199	8.5	1,288	41.3	110	26.3
2001	1,524	26.6	205	8.7	1,220	40.8	99	24.6
2000	1,411	25.3	157	6.7	1,177	41.0	76	21.7
1999	1,603	28.9	199	8.7	1,320	46.0	84	21.7
1998	1,673	30.5	189	8.6	1,397	47.5	88	24.8
1997	1,721	30.5	205	9.0	1,436	46.9	81	25.8
1996	1,941	34.1	239	11.0	1,593	51.0	109	27.2
1995	1,821	34.1	209	9.9	1,533	53.2	79	23.4
1994	1,954	35.9	245	11.4	1,591	53.9	118	34.6
1993	2,171	39.3	298	13.9	1,780	57.7	93	31.6
1992	2,132	39.1	343	15.4	1,706	57.4	83	33.5
1991	2,016	39.2	263	12.4	1,676	60.5	77	31.7
1990	1,887	37.2	301	14.3	1,513	56.1	73	27.3

Note: Beginning in 2002, data are for those who identify themselves as being of the race alone and those who identify themselves as being of the race in combination with other races.
Source: Bureau of the Census, Current Population Surveys, Annual Social and Economic Supplement, Internet site http://www .census.gov/hhes/www/poverty/data/historical/index.html

Table 6.10 Number and Percent of Families with Children below Poverty Level by Family Type, 1990 to 2010: Hispanic Families with Children

(number and percent of Hispanic families with related children under age 18 below poverty level by family type, 1990 to 2010; families in thousands as of the following year)

	total Hispanic families with children in poverty		married couples		female householder, no spouse present		male householder, no spouse present	
	number	percent	number	percent	number	percent	number	percent
2010	2,204	30.6%	958	21.6%	1,061	50.3%	186	28.3%
2009	2,004	28.4	876	19.9	945	46.0	183	30.2
2008	1,905	26.8	874	18.9	912	46.6	119	22.0
2007	1,759	24.9	766	16.4	881	46.6	112	22.0
2006	1,636	23.4	718	15.6	811	42.5	106	22.8
2005	1,651	24.4	771	16.9	777	45.2	102	20.6
2004	1,685	25.5	778	17.8	806	46.0	102	20.4
2003	1,629	25.2	789	18.4	713	43.0	127	24.9
2002	1,527	24.1	752	17.7	657	41.4	118	23.6
2001	1,405	23.7	646	16.2	645	43.2	115	24.5
2000	1,323	23.3	649	16.8	597	42.9	77	18.4
1999	1,400	25.2	640	17.0	662	46.8	98	26.1
1998	1,454	28.6	656	19.3	707	52.2	91	28.0
1997	1,492	30.4	692	21.0	701	54.2	99	30.5
1996	1,549	33.0	687	22.0	760	59.7	102	35.1
1995	1,470	33.2	657	22.6	735	57.3	78	32.9
1994	1,497	34.2	698	23.9	700	59.2	99	36.4
1993	1,424	34.3	652	23.7	706	60.5	66	27.6
1992	1,302	32.9	615	22.9	598	57.7	89	38.2
1991	1,219	33.7	575	23.5	584	60.1	60	29.4
1990	1,085	31.0	501	20.8	536	58.2	48	28.1

Source: Bureau of the Census, Current Population Surveys, Annual Social and Economic Supplement, Internet site http://www .census.gov/hhes/www/poverty/data/historical/index.html

Table 6.11 Number and Percent of Families with Children below Poverty Level by Family Type, 1990 to 2010: Non-Hispanic White Families with Children

(number and percent of non-Hispanic white families with related children under age 18 below poverty level by family type, 1990 to 2010; families in thousands as of the following year)

	total non-Hispanic white families with children in poverty		married couples		female householder, no spouse present		male householder, no spouse present	
	number	percent	number	percent	number	percent	number	percent
2010	2,621	11.3%	888	5.2%	1,476	32.7%	256	17.2%
2009	2,553	10.8	854	4.9	1,412	31.7	286	18.5
2008	2,201	9.3	738	4.2	1,246	28.5	217	14.1
2007	2,176	9.2	678	3.8	1,283	29.2	215	13.2
2006	2,296	9.3	683	3.7	1,405	30.2	208	13.6
2005	2,171	8.8	661	3.6	1,308	29.2	201	13.1
2004	2,294	9.3	800	4.3	1,287	28.2	207	13.8
2003	2,185	8.9	746	4.0	1,269	28.1	170	12.5
2002	2,088	8.5	781	4.1	1,170	26.2	137	10.4
2001	2,014	8.1	696	3.6	1,135	25.7	184	13.4
2000	1,940	7.7	709	3.7	1,058	24.6	173	12.3
1999	1,973	8.0	743	3.9	1,069	25.3	161	12.0
1998	2,282	9.1	859	4.5	1,275	28.8	148	10.9
1997	2,478	9.8	842	4.3	1,420	32.9	215	14.7
1996	2,424	9.6	884	4.5	1,351	31.0	190	14.7
1995	2,445	9.6	948	4.8	1,294	29.7	202	15.9
1994	2,733	10.6	1,101	5.4	1,471	33.5	161	15.0
1993	2,946	11.6	1,263	6.3	1,506	34.8	177	18.0
1992	2,817	11.2	1,177	5.9	1,474	35.5	166	16.1
1991	2,722	10.9	1,152	5.8	1,429	35.1	141	14.1
1990	2,522	10.2	1,085	5.4	1,317	33.5	119	13.6

Note: Beginning in 2002, data are for those who identify themselves as being white alone and not Hispanic.
Source: Bureau of the Census, Current Population Surveys, Annual Social and Economic Supplement, Internet site http://www .census.gov/hhes/www/poverty/data/historical/index.html

Poverty Rate Has Increased since 2000

Poverty is higher among females than males.

The poverty rate climbed to 15.1 percent in 2010, up from the 11.3 percent low reached in 2000. Behind the rise in poverty is the Great Recession and lackluster recovery. The poverty rate is likely to continue to rise in the years ahead because of unemployment. The 2010 rate matches the rate of 1993, which was also a recovery period following a recession.

Among males, 14.0 percent were poor in 2010—the highest rate in all the years that the Census Bureau has been calculating these statistics (beginning in 1966). Among females, 16.2 percent were poor in 2010, up from 12.6 percent in 2000. The poverty rate among females is the highest since 1994.

■ Females have a higher poverty rate than males because they are more likely to be raising children alone, which limits their ability to work full-time.

The poverty rate among males is at an all-time high

(percent of males who are poor, 1990 to 2010)

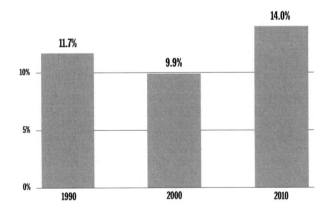

Table 6.12 Number and Percent of People below Poverty Level by Sex, 1990 to 2010

(number and percent of people below poverty level by sex, and female share of poor, 1990 to 2010; people in thousands as of the following year)

	total people in poverty		female		male		percent of poor who are female
	number	percent	number	percent	number	percent	
2010	46,180	15.1%	25,167	16.2%	21,012	14.0%	54%
2009	43,569	14.3	24,094	15.6	19,475	13.0	55
2008	39,829	13.2	22,131	14.4	17,698	12.0	56
2007	37,276	12.5	20,973	13.8	16,302	11.1	56
2006	36,460	12.3	20,460	13.6	16,000	11.0	56
2005	36,950	12.6	21,000	14.1	15,950	11.1	57
2004	37,040	12.7	20,641	13.9	16,399	11.5	56
2003	35,861	12.5	20,078	13.7	15,783	11.2	56
2002	34,570	12.1	19,408	13.3	15,162	10.9	56
2001	32,907	11.7	18,580	12.9	14,327	10.4	56
2000	31,581	11.3	18,045	12.6	13,536	9.9	57
1999	32,791	11.9	18,712	13.2	14,079	10.4	57
1998	34,476	12.7	19,764	14.3	14,712	11.1	57
1997	35,574	13.3	20,387	14.9	15,187	11.6	57
1996	36,529	13.7	20,918	15.4	15,611	12.0	57
1995	36,425	13.8	20,742	15.4	15,683	12.2	57
1994	38,059	14.5	21,744	16.3	16,316	12.8	57
1993	39,265	15.1	22,365	16.9	16,900	13.3	57
1992	38,014	14.8	21,792	16.6	16,222	12.9	57
1991	35,708	14.2	20,626	16.0	15,082	12.3	58
1990	33,585	13.5	19,373	15.2	14,211	11.7	58

Source: Bureau of the Census, Current Population Surveys, Annual Social and Economic Supplement, Internet site http://www.census.gov/hhes/www/poverty/data/historical/index.html

A Growing Share of Poor People Are Aged 18 to 64

The elderly make up a smaller share of the poor.

Most of the nation's 46 million poor are aged 18 to 64. In 2010, 57 percent of people in poverty were of working age, up from 49 percent in 1990 and 53 percent in 2000. Children under age 18 are a smaller percentage of the poor than they once were, their share falling from 40 percent in 1990 to 36 percent in 2010. The share of the poor who are aged 65 or older declined from 11 to 8 percent during those years.

The poverty rate of the elderly has fallen since 2000, while the rate for people under age 65 has climbed. Among children, the poverty rate was 16.2 percent in 2000 and a much larger 22.0 percent in 2010. The poverty rate of people aged 18 to 64 increased from 9.6 to 13.7 percent during those years. At the same time, the poverty rate of people aged 65 or older fell from 9.9 to 9.0 percent.

■ Poverty rates among the elderly have fallen because a more-educated and affluent generation has entered the age group.

The poverty rate has increased among people under age 65

(poverty rate of people by age, 2000 and 2010)

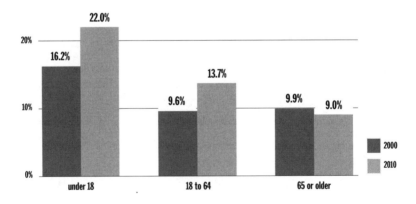

Table 6.13 Distribution of People below Poverty Level by Age, 1990 to 2010

(number of people below poverty level and percent distribution by age, 1990 to 2010; people in thousands as of the following year)

	total people in poverty		under 18	18 to 64	65 or older
	number	percent			
2010	46,180	100.0%	35.5%	56.9%	7.6%
2009	43,569	100.0	35.5	56.7	7.9
2008	39,829	100.0	35.3	55.5	9.2
2007	37,276	100.0	35.7	54.7	9.5
2006	36,460	100.0	35.2	55.5	9.3
2005	36,950	100.0	34.9	55.3	9.8
2004	37,040	100.0	35.2	55.5	9.3
2003	35,861	100.0	35.9	54.2	9.9
2002	34,570	100.0	35.1	54.6	10.3
2001	32,907	100.0	35.7	54.0	10.4
2000	31,581	100.0	36.7	52.8	10.5
1999	32,791	100.0	37.4	52.7	9.8
1998	34,476	100.0	39.1	51.1	9.8
1997	35,574	100.0	39.7	50.8	9.5
1996	36,529	100.0	39.6	51.0	9.4
1995	36,425	100.0	40.3	50.6	9.1
1994	38,059	100.0	40.2	50.2	9.6
1993	39,265	100.0	40.1	50.4	9.6
1992	38,014	100.0	40.2	49.4	10.3
1991	35,708	100.0	40.2	49.2	10.6
1990	33,585	100.0	40.0	49.1	10.9

Source: Bureau of the Census, Current Population Surveys, Annual Social and Economic Supplement, Internet site http://www.census.gov/hhes/www/poverty/data/historical/index.html

Table 6.14 Number and Percent of People below Poverty Level by Age, 1990 to 2010

(number and percent of people below poverty level by age, 1990 to 2010; people in thousands as of the following year)

	total people in poverty		under age 18		aged 18 to 64		aged 65 or older	
	number	percent	number	percent	number	percent	number	percent
2010	46,180	15.1%	16,401	22.0%	26,258	13.7%	3,520	9.0%
2009	43,569	14.3	15,451	20.7	24,684	12.9	3,433	8.9
2008	39,829	13.2	13,507	18.5	22,105	11.7	3,656	9.7
2007	37,276	12.5	12,802	17.6	20,396	10.9	3,556	9.7
2006	36,460	12.3	12,299	16.9	20,239	10.8	3,394	9.4
2005	36,950	12.6	12,896	17.6	20,450	11.1	3,603	10.1
2004	37,040	12.7	13,041	17.8	20,545	11.3	3,453	9.8
2003	35,861	12.5	12,866	17.6	19,443	10.8	3,552	10.2
2002	34,570	12.1	12,133	16.7	18,861	10.6	3,576	10.4
2001	32,907	11.7	11,733	16.3	17,760	10.1	3,414	10.1
2000	31,581	11.3	11,587	16.2	16,671	9.6	3,323	9.9
1999	32,791	11.9	12,280	17.1	17,289	10.1	3,222	9.7
1998	34,476	12.7	13,467	18.9	17,623	10.5	3,386	10.5
1997	35,574	13.3	14,113	19.9	18,085	10.9	3,376	10.5
1996	36,529	13.7	14,463	20.5	18,638	11.4	3,428	10.8
1995	36,425	13.8	14,665	20.8	18,442	11.4	3,318	10.5
1994	38,059	14.5	15,289	21.8	19,107	11.9	3,663	11.7
1993	39,265	15.1	15,727	22.7	19,781	12.4	3,755	12.2
1992	38,014	14.8	15,294	22.3	18,793	11.9	3,928	12.9
1991	35,708	14.2	14,341	21.8	17,586	11.4	3,781	12.4
1990	33,585	13.5	13,431	20.6	16,496	10.7	3,658	12.2

Source: Bureau of the Census, Current Population Surveys, Annual Social and Economic Supplement, Internet site http://www .census.gov/hhes/www/poverty/data/historical/index.html

Non-Hispanic Whites Are a Minority of the Poor

Hispanics and blacks account for the majority of the poor.

Non-Hispanic whites were only 42 percent of the poverty population in 2010, down from about 50 percent in 1990. The black share of the poor also fell during those years, from 29 to 25 percent. In contrast, the Hispanic share of the poor rose from 18 to 29 percent. Only 4 percent of poor Americans are Asian.

During the past decade, the poverty rate of Asians, blacks, Hispanics, and non-Hispanic whites has increased. The poverty rate of blacks and Hispanics grew by about 5 percentage points between 2000 and 2010, and that of Asians and non-Hispanic whites grew 2 percentage points. In 2010, the poverty rate of blacks and Hispanics was nearly identical, at 27.4 and 26.6 percent respectively. The poverty rate of Asians was much lower at 11.9 percent, and non-Hispanic whites had the lowest poverty rate at 9.9 percent.

■ Poverty will continue to grow until jobs become more plentiful.

The poverty rate has grown in every racial and ethnic group

(poverty rate of people by race and Hispanic origin, 2000 and 2010)

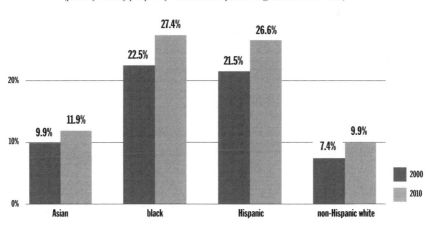

Table 6.15 Distribution of People below Poverty Level by Race and Hispanic Origin, 1990 to 2010

(number of people below poverty level and percent distribution by race and Hispanic origin, 1990 to 2010; people in thousands as of the following year)

	total people in poverty		Asian	black	Hispanic	non-Hispanic white
	number	percent				
2010	46,180	100.0%	4.0%	24.6%	28.7%	42.4%
2009	43,569	100.0	4.4	24.3	28.3	42.5
2008	39,829	100.0	4.2	24.8	27.6	42.7
2007	37,276	100.0	3.9	25.9	26.5	43.0
2006	36,460	100.0	4.0	25.9	25.4	43.9
2005	36,950	100.0	4.1	25.8	25.4	43.9
2004	37,040	100.0	3.5	25.4	24.6	45.6
2003	35,861	100.0	4.3	25.4	25.2	44.3
2002	34,570	100.0	3.6	25.7	24.7	45.0
2001	32,907	100.0	3.9	24.7	24.3	46.4
2000	31,581	100.0	4.0	25.3	24.5	45.5
1999	32,791	100.0	3.9	25.7	24.0	44.9
1998	34,476	100.0	3.9	26.4	23.4	45.8
1997	35,574	100.0	4.1	25.6	23.4	46.4
1996	36,529	100.0	4.0	26.5	23.8	45.1
1995	36,425	100.0	3.9	27.1	23.5	44.7
1994	38,059	100.0	2.6	26.8	22.1	47.6
1993	39,265	100.0	2.9	27.7	20.7	48.1
1992	38,014	100.0	2.6	28.5	20.0	47.9
1991	35,708	100.0	2.8	28.7	17.8	49.7
1990	33,585	100.0	2.6	29.3	17.9	49.5

Note: Beginning in 2002, data for Asians and blacks are for those who identify themselves as being of the race alone and those who identify themselves as being of the race in combination with other races. Data for non-Hispanic whites are for those who identify themselves as being white alone and not Hispanic.
Source: Bureau of the Census, Current Population Surveys, Annual Social and Economic Supplement, Internet site http://www .census.gov/hhes/www/poverty/data/historical/index.html

**Table 6.16 Number and Percent of People below Poverty Level by
Race and Hispanic Origin, 1990 to 2010**

*(number and percent of people below poverty level by race and Hispanic origin, 1990 to 2010; people in thousands
as of the following year)*

	total people in poverty		Asian		black		Hispanic		non-Hispanic white	
	number	percent	number	percent	number	percent	number	percent	number	percent
2010	46,180	15.1%	1,859	11.9%	11,361	27.4%	13,243	26.6%	19,599	9.9%
2009	43,569	14.3	1,901	12.4	10,575	25.9	12,350	25.3	18,530	9.4
2008	39,829	13.2	1,686	11.6	9,882	24.6	10,987	23.2	17,024	8.6
2007	37,276	12.5	1,467	10.2	9,668	24.4	9,890	21.5	16,032	8.2
2006	36,460	12.3	1,447	10.1	9,447	24.2	9,243	20.6	16,013	8.2
2005	36,950	12.6	1,501	10.9	9,517	24.7	9,368	21.8	16,227	8.3
2004	37,040	12.7	1,295	9.7	9,411	24.7	9,122	21.9	16,908	8.7
2003	35,861	12.5	1,527	11.8	9,108	24.3	9,051	22.5	15,902	8.2
2002	34,570	12.1	1,243	10.0	8,884	23.9	8,555	21.8	15,567	8.0
2001	32,907	11.7	1,275	10.2	8,136	22.7	7,997	21.4	15,271	7.8
2000	31,581	11.3	1,258	9.9	7,982	22.5	7,747	21.5	14,366	7.4
1999	32,791	11.9	1,285	10.7	8,441	23.6	7,876	22.7	14,735	7.7
1998	34,476	12.7	1,360	12.5	9,091	26.1	8,070	25.6	15,799	8.2
1997	35,574	13.3	1,468	14.0	9,116	26.5	8,308	27.1	16,491	8.6
1996	36,529	13.7	1,454	14.5	9,694	28.4	8,697	29.4	16,462	8.6
1995	36,425	13.8	1,411	14.6	9,872	29.3	8,574	30.3	16,267	8.5
1994	38,059	14.5	974	14.6	10,196	30.6	8,416	30.7	18,110	9.4
1993	39,265	15.1	1,134	15.3	10,877	33.1	8,126	30.6	18,882	9.9
1992	38,014	14.8	985	12.7	10,827	33.4	7,592	29.6	18,202	9.6
1991	35,708	14.2	996	13.8	10,242	32.7	6,339	28.7	17,741	9.4
1990	33,585	13.5	858	12.2	9,837	31.9	6,006	28.1	16,622	8.8

*Note: Beginning in 2002, data for Asians and blacks are for those who identify themselves as being of the race alone and those
who identify themselves as being of the race in combination with other races. Data for non-Hispanic whites are for those who
identify themselves as being white alone and not Hispanic.*
*Source: Bureau of the Census, Current Population Surveys, Annual Social and Economic Supplement, Internet site http://www
.census.gov/hhes/www/poverty/data/historical/index.html*

Poverty Has Grown in Every Region

The number of poor in the West is second only to the South.

The South and West are home to nearly two-thirds of the nation's poor. The 41 percent plurality of the poor lives in the South, a figure that has been fairly stable over the past two decades. Another 24 percent of the poor live in the West, up from 20 percent in 1990.

Poverty rates in the Midwest and South were higher in 2010 than at any time in the past two decades, at 13.9 and 16.9 percent, respectively. In the Northeast and West, poverty rates in 2010 are still lower than they had been during some years of the 1990s.

■ The Great Recession has hit the Midwest particularly hard, with many unemployed manufacturing workers joining the ranks of the nation's poor.

The poverty rate has grown the most in the Midwest

(poverty rate of people by region, 2000 and 2010)

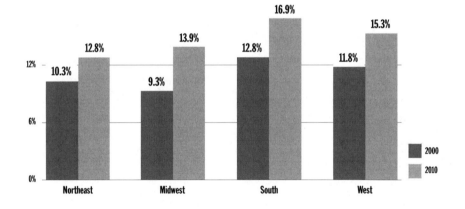

Table 6.17 Distribution of People below Poverty Level by Region, 1990 to 2010

(number of people below poverty level and percent distribution by region, 1990 to 2010; people in thousands as of the following year)

| | total people in poverty | | | | | |
	number	percent	Northeast	Midwest	South	West
2010	46,180	100.0%	15.1%	19.8%	41.3%	23.8%
2009	43,569	100.0	15.3	20.1	40.4	24.2
2008	39,829	100.0	15.8	20.4	39.8	24.0
2007	37,276	100.0	16.5	19.4	41.6	22.5
2006	36,460	100.0	17.1	20.1	40.8	22.0
2005	36,950	100.0	16.5	20.1	40.2	23.2
2004	37,040	100.0	16.9	20.4	40.0	22.7
2003	35,861	100.0	16.9	19.3	40.6	23.2
2002	34,570	100.0	17.0	19.1	40.6	23.3
2001	32,907	100.0	17.3	18.1	41.1	23.5
2000	31,581	100.0	17.3	18.7	40.2	23.7
1999	32,791	100.0	17.7	19.1	38.9	24.3
1998	34,476	100.0	18.4	18.9	37.7	25.0
1997	35,574	100.0	18.2	18.3	38.6	24.9
1996	36,529	100.0	18.0	18.2	38.6	25.2
1995	36,425	100.0	17.7	18.6	39.7	24.0
1994	38,059	100.0	17.3	20.9	38.7	23.0
1993	39,265	100.0	17.4	20.8	39.2	22.6
1992	38,014	100.0	16.9	21.2	40.0	21.9
1991	35,708	100.0	17.3	22.4	38.6	21.7
1990	33,585	100.0	17.3	22.2	40.1	20.5

Source: Bureau of the Census, Current Population Surveys, Annual Social and Economic Supplement, Internet site http://www .census.gov/hhes/www/poverty/data/historical/index.html

Table 6.18 Number and Percent of People below Poverty Level by Region, 1990 to 2010

(number and percent of people below poverty level by region, 1990 to 2010; people in thousands as of the following year)

	total people in poverty		Northeast		Midwest		South		West	
	number	percent	number	percent	number	percent	number	percent	number	percent
2010	46,180	15.1%	6,987	12.8%	9,148	13.9%	19,072	16.9%	10,973	15.3%
2009	43,569	14.3	6,650	12.2	8,768	13.3	17,609	15.7	10,542	14.8
2008	39,829	13.2	6,295	11.6	8,120	12.4	15,862	14.3	9,552	13.5
2007	37,276	12.5	6,166	11.4	7,237	11.1	15,501	14.2	8,372	12.0
2006	36,460	12.3	6,222	11.5	7,324	11.2	14,882	13.8	8,032	11.6
2005	36,950	12.6	6,103	11.3	7,419	11.4	14,854	14.0	8,573	12.6
2004	37,040	12.7	6,260	11.6	7,545	11.7	14,817	14.1	8,419	12.5
2003	35,861	12.5	6,052	11.3	6,932	10.7	14,548	14.1	8,329	12.6
2002	34,570	12.1	5,871	10.9	6,616	10.3	14,019	13.8	8,064	12.4
2001	32,907	11.7	5,687	10.7	5,966	9.4	13,515	13.5	7,739	12.1
2000	31,581	11.3	5,474	10.3	5,916	9.3	12,705	12.8	7,485	11.8
1999	32,791	11.9	5,814	11.0	6,250	9.8	12,744	13.2	7,982	12.7
1998	34,476	12.7	6,357	12.3	6,501	10.3	12,992	13.7	8,625	14.0
1997	35,574	13.3	6,474	12.6	6,493	10.4	13,748	14.6	8,858	14.6
1996	36,529	13.7	6,558	12.7	6,654	10.7	14,098	15.1	9,219	15.4
1995	36,425	13.8	6,445	12.5	6,785	11.0	14,458	15.7	8,736	14.9
1994	38,059	14.5	6,597	12.9	7,965	13.0	14,729	16.1	8,768	15.3
1993	39,265	15.1	6,839	13.3	8,172	13.4	15,375	17.1	8,879	15.6
1992	38,014	14.8	6,414	12.6	8,060	13.3	15,198	17.1	8,343	14.8
1991	35,708	14.2	6,177	12.2	7,989	13.2	13,783	16.0	7,759	14.3
1990	33,585	13.5	5,794	11.4	7,458	12.4	13,456	15.8	6,877	13.0

Source: Bureau of the Census, Current Population Surveys, Annual Social and Economic Supplement, Internet site http://www
.census.gov/hhes/www/poverty/data/historical/index.html

Naturalized Citizens Have the Lowest Poverty Rate

The poverty rate is highest among the foreign-born who are not citizens.

Native-born Americans had a poverty rate of 14.4 percent in 2010, slightly below the 15.1 percent rate among all U.S. residents. The poverty rate was a much higher 19.9 percent among the foreign-born population. But the poverty rate differs sharply among the foreign-born by citizenship status.

Naturalized citizens had a poverty rate of 11.3 percent in 2010, significantly lower than the rate among native-born Americans. The poverty rate of the foreign-born who are not citizens stood at 26.7 percent, more than double the rate among naturalized citizens. Since 2000, the poverty rate has increased for every citizenship category. The smallest increase has been among naturalized citizens, and the biggest increase has been among the foreign born who are not citizens.

■ The foreign-born account for only 16 percent of the nation's poor.

Only 11 percent of naturalized citizens are poor

(poverty rate of U.S. citizens by nativity and citizenship status, 2010)

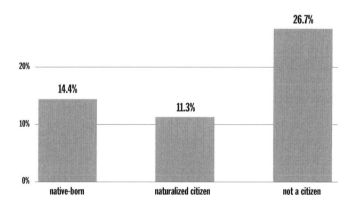

Table 6.19 Number and Percent of People below Poverty Level by Nativity Status, 1993 to 2010

(number and percent of people below poverty level by nativity status, 1993 to 2010; people in thousands as of the following year)

	total people in poverty		native-born		foreign-born total		naturalized citizen		not a citizen	
	number	percent	number	percent	number	percent	number	percent	number	percent
2010	46,180	15.1%	38,568	14.4%	7,611	19.9%	1,906	11.3%	5,706	26.7%
2009	43,569	14.3	36,407	13.7	7,162	19.0	1,736	10.8	5,425	25.1
2008	39,829	13.2	33,293	12.6	6,536	17.8	1,577	10.2	4,959	23.3
2007	37,276	12.5	31,126	11.9	6,150	16.5	1,426	9.5	4,724	21.3
2006	36,460	12.3	30,790	11.9	5,670	15.2	1,345	9.3	4,324	19.0
2005	36,950	12.6	31,080	12.1	5,870	16.5	1,441	10.4	4,429	20.4
2004	37,040	12.7	31,023	12.1	6,017	17.1	1,326	9.8	4,691	21.6
2003	35,861	12.5	29,965	11.8	5,897	17.2	1,309	10.0	4,588	21.7
2002	34,570	12.1	29,012	11.5	5,558	16.6	1,285	10.0	4,273	20.7
2001	32,907	11.7	27,698	11.1	5,209	16.1	1,186	9.9	4,023	19.7
2000	31,581	11.3	26,680	10.8	4,901	15.4	1,060	9.0	3,841	19.2
1999	32,791	11.9	27,757	11.3	5,034	16.8	996	9.0	4,039	21.4
1998	34,476	12.7	29,707	12.1	4,769	18.0	1,087	11.0	3,682	22.2
1997	35,574	13.3	30,336	12.5	5,238	19.9	1,111	11.4	4,127	25.0
1996	36,529	13.7	31,117	12.9	5,412	21.0	936	10.3	4,476	26.8
1995	36,425	13.8	30,972	12.9	5,452	22.2	833	10.5	4,619	27.8
1994	38,059	14.5	32,865	13.8	5,194	22.6	668	9.4	4,526	28.5
1993	39,265	15.1	34,086	14.4	5,179	23.0	707	10.1	4,472	28.7

Source: Bureau of the Census, Current Population Surveys, Annual Social and Economic Supplement, Internet site http://www .census.gov/hhes/www/poverty/data/historical/index.html

The Poverty Rate Has Increased in Most States since 2000

The number of poor also grew substantially in most states.

Among the 50 states, Mississippi had the highest poverty rate in 2010, 22.7 percent of its residents being poor. New Hampshire had the lowest poverty rate—just 6.6 percent of its population was poor. Between 2000 and 2010, the poverty rate climbed in 47 states, with Indiana, Mississippi, and Nevada seeing the biggest increases in rates. Wyoming, Arkansas, and Montana were the only states whose poverty rates declined between 2000 and 2010.

The number of poor increased by an enormous 46 percent nationally between 2000 and 2010, rising from 32 million to 46 million. The number of poor grew in all but one state (Wyoming) during those years. The poverty population doubled in size in Arizona, Indiana, and Nevada.

■ The economic downturn could drive poverty rates even higher in most states in the years ahead.

In 2010, Mississippi had the highest poverty rate and New Hampshire the lowest

(poverty rate in Mississippi and New Hampshire, 2010)

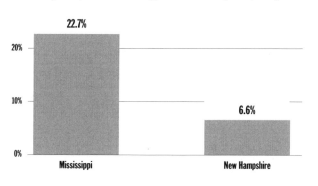

Table 6.20 Number of Poor by State, 1990 to 2010

(number of people below poverty level by state, selected years, 1990 to 2010; percent change for selected years; numbers in thousands)

	2010	2000	1990	percent change 2000–10	percent change 1990–2010
United States	**46,180**	**31,581**	**33,585**	**46.2%**	**37.5%**
Alabama	808	583	779	38.6	3.7
Alaska	86	47	57	83.0	50.9
Arizona	1,241	607	484	104.4	156.4
Arkansas	445	436	472	2.1	−5.7
California	6,077	4,294	4,128	41.5	47.2
Colorado	617	425	461	45.2	33.8
Connecticut	292	258	196	13.2	49.0
Delaware	106	65	48	63.1	120.8
District of Columbia	121	84	120	44.0	0.8
Florida	2,962	1,754	1,896	68.9	56.2
Georgia	1,836	982	1,001	87.0	83.4
Hawaii	152	106	121	43.4	25.6
Idaho	214	162	157	32.1	36.3
Illinois	1,817	1,307	1,606	39.0	13.1
Indiana	1,035	513	714	101.8	45.0
Iowa	305	237	289	28.7	5.5
Kansas	394	213	259	85.0	52.1
Kentucky	758	502	628	51.0	20.7
Louisiana	958	750	952	27.7	0.6
Maine	161	128	162	25.8	−0.6
Maryland	620	386	468	60.6	32.5
Massachusetts	702	618	626	13.6	12.1
Michigan	1,511	967	1,315	56.3	14.9
Minnesota	544	276	524	97.1	3.8
Mississippi	664	418	684	58.9	−2.9
Missouri	885	505	700	75.2	26.4
Montana	136	126	134	7.9	1.5
Nebraska	182	145	167	25.5	9.0
Nevada	432	180	119	140.0	263.0
New Hampshire	85	56	68	51.8	25.0
New Jersey	931	612	711	52.1	30.9
New Mexico	376	312	319	20.5	17.9
New York	3,086	2,604	2,571	18.5	20.0
North Carolina	1,609	1,000	829	60.9	94.1
North Dakota	77	65	87	18.5	−11.5
Ohio	1,739	1,117	1,256	55.7	38.5
Oklahoma	597	503	481	18.7	24.1
Oregon	535	371	267	44.2	100.4
Pennsylvania	1,521	1,033	1,328	47.2	14.5
Rhode Island	142	106	71	34.0	100.0

	2010	2000	1990	percent change 2000–10	percent change 1990–2010
South Carolina	767	441	548	73.9%	40.0%
South Dakota	106	79	93	34.2	14.0
Tennessee	1,050	759	833	38.3	26.1
Texas	4,635	3,204	2,684	44.7	72.7
Utah	283	170	143	66.5	97.9
Vermont	67	60	61	11.7	9.8
Virginia	832	577	705	44.2	18.0
Washington	774	634	434	22.1	78.3
West Virginia	304	261	328	16.5	−7.3
Wisconsin	553	493	448	12.2	23.4
Wyoming	51	52	51	−1.9	0.0

*Source: Bureau of the Census, Current Population Surveys, Annual Social and Economic Supplement, Internet site http://www
.census.gov/hhes/www/poverty/data/historical/index.html*

Table 6.21 Poverty Rate by State, 1990 to 2010

(percent of people below poverty level by state, selected years, 1990 to 2010; percentage point change for selected years)

	2010	2000	1990	percentage point change 2000–10	percentage point change 1990–2010
United States	**15.1%**	**11.3%**	**13.5%**	**3.8**	**1.6**
Alabama	17.3	13.3	19.2	4.0	−1.9
Alaska	12.4	7.6	11.4	4.8	1.0
Arizona	18.6	11.7	13.7	6.9	4.9
Arkansas	15.5	16.5	19.6	−1.0	−4.1
California	16.3	12.7	13.9	3.6	2.4
Colorado	12.2	9.8	13.7	2.4	−1.5
Connecticut	8.3	7.7	6.0	0.6	2.3
Delaware	12.1	8.4	6.9	3.7	5.2
District of Columbia	19.9	15.2	21.1	4.7	−1.2
Florida	16.0	11.0	14.4	5.0	1.6
Georgia	18.7	12.1	15.8	6.6	2.9
Hawaii	12.1	8.9	11.0	3.2	1.1
Idaho	14.0	12.5	14.9	1.5	−0.9
Illinois	14.1	10.7	13.7	3.4	0.4
Indiana	16.3	8.5	13.0	7.8	3.3
Iowa	10.3	8.3	10.4	2.0	−0.1
Kansas	14.3	8.0	10.3	6.3	4.0
Kentucky	17.7	12.6	17.3	5.1	0.4
Louisiana	21.6	17.2	23.6	4.4	−2.0
Maine	12.5	10.1	13.1	2.4	−0.6
Maryland	10.8	7.4	9.9	3.4	0.9
Massachusetts	10.6	9.8	10.7	0.8	−0.1
Michigan	15.5	9.9	14.3	5.6	1.2
Minnesota	10.5	5.7	12.0	4.8	−1.5
Mississippi	22.7	14.9	25.7	7.8	−3.0
Missouri	14.8	9.2	13.4	5.6	1.4
Montana	14.0	14.1	16.3	−0.1	−2.3
Nebraska	10.2	8.6	10.3	1.6	−0.1
Nevada	16.4	8.8	9.8	7.6	6.6
New Hampshire	6.6	4.5	6.3	2.1	0.3
New Jersey	10.7	7.3	9.2	3.4	1.5
New Mexico	18.6	17.5	20.9	1.1	−2.3
New York	16.0	13.9	14.3	2.1	1.7
North Carolina	17.4	12.5	13.0	4.9	4.4
North Dakota	12.2	10.4	13.7	1.8	−1.5
Ohio	15.3	10.0	11.5	5.3	3.8
Oklahoma	16.3	14.9	15.6	1.4	0.7
Oregon	14.2	10.9	9.2	3.3	5.0
Pennsylvania	12.2	8.6	11.0	3.6	1.2
Rhode Island	13.6	10.2	7.5	3.4	6.1

	2010	2000	1990	percentage point change	
				2000–10	1990–2010
South Carolina	17.0%	11.1%	16.2%	5.9	0.8
South Dakota	13.2	10.7	13.3	2.5	−0.1
Tennessee	16.7	13.5	16.9	3.2	−0.2
Texas	18.4	15.5	15.9	2.9	2.5
Utah	10.0	7.6	8.2	2.4	1.8
Vermont	10.8	10.0	10.9	0.8	−0.1
Virginia	10.7	8.3	11.1	2.4	−0.4
Washington	11.5	10.8	8.9	0.7	2.6
West Virginia	16.9	14.7	18.1	2.2	−1.2
Wisconsin	9.9	9.3	9.3	0.6	0.6
Wyoming	9.6	10.8	11.0	−1.2	−1.4

Source: Bureau of the Census, Current Population Surveys, Annual Social and Economic Supplement, Internet site http://www .census.gov/hhes/www/poverty/data/historical/index.html

A Growing Share of Poor Lives in the Suburbs

The share of the poor living in nonmetropolitan areas has declined.

As more Americans move to the suburbs of metropolitan areas, the poverty population is becoming increasingly suburban. In 1990, only 31 percent of the poor lived in the suburbs. By 2010, the suburbs were home to 41 percent of the nation's poor. During those two decades, the percentage of the poor who live in the principal cities of metropolitan areas held steady at 42 percent. The percentage who live in nonmetropolitan areas fell from 27 to 17 percent.

Between 2000 and 2010, poverty rates climbed regardless of metropolitan status. The poverty rate of central cities grew from 16.3 to 19.7 percent. In nonmetropolitan areas, the poverty rate climbed from 13.4 to 16.5 percent. The biggest increase in the poverty rate occurred in the suburbs, with the rate growing from 7.8 to 11.8 percent between 2000 and 2010.

■ The largest share of the poor once lived in rural areas. Today, the suburbs are close to overtaking the central cities as home to the largest share of the poor.

The suburbs of metropolitan areas are home to a growing share of poor

(percent distribution of poor people by metropolitan status, 1990 and 2010

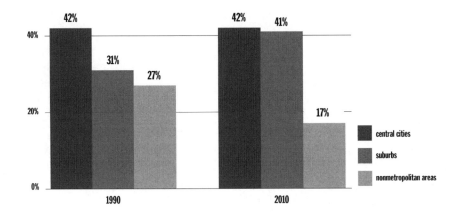

Table 6.22 Distribution of People below Poverty Level by Metropolitan Residence, 1990 to 2010

(number of people below poverty level and percent distribution by metropolitan residence, 1990 to 2010; people in thousands as of the following year)

| | total people in poverty | | metropolitan areas | | | |
	number	percent	total	inside principal cities	outside principal cities	nonmetropolitan areas
2010	46,180	100.0%	83.0%	42.2%	40.8%	17.0%
2009	43,569	100.0	81.8	41.9	39.9	18.2
2008	39,829	100.0	81.8	43.2	38.5	18.2
2007	37,276	100.0	80.3	42.9	37.4	19.7
2006	36,460	100.0	80.3	42.1	38.3	19.7
2005	36,950	100.0	81.5	43.2	38.2	18.5

| | total people in poverty | | metropolitan areas | | | |
	number	percent	total	inside central cities	outside central cities	nonmetropolitan areas
2004	37,040	100.0%	–	–	–	–
2003	35,861	100.0	79.1%	40.6%	38.5%	20.9%
2002	34,570	100.0	78.4	39.9	38.5	21.6
2001	32,907	100.0	77.3	40.7	36.6	22.7
2000	31,581	100.0	77.9	42.0	35.9	22.1
1999	32,791	100.0	77.1	40.9	36.2	22.9
1998	34,476	100.0	78.3	43.3	35.0	21.7
1997	35,574	100.0	76.7	42.2	34.4	23.3
1996	36,529	100.0	77.2	42.8	34.4	22.8
1995	36,425	100.0	77.8	44.7	33.1	22.2
1994	38,059	100.0	77.8	42.3	35.5	22.2
1993	39,265	100.0	75.4	42.8	32.6	24.6
1992	38,014	100.0	74.7	43.0	31.7	25.3
1991	35,708	100.0	75.1	42.9	32.2	24.9
1990	33,585	100.0	73.0	42.4	30.5	27.0

Note: "–" means data are not available.
Source: Bureau of the Census, Current Population Surveys, Annual Social and Economic Supplement, Internet site http://www
.census.gov/hhes/www/poverty/data/historical/index.html

Table 6.23 Number and Percent of People below Poverty Level by Metropolitan Residence, 1990 to 2010

(number and percent of people below poverty level by metropolitan residence, 1990 to 2010; people in thousands as of the following year)

	total people in poverty		metropolitan areas total		inside principal cities		outside principal cities		nonmetropolitan areas	
	number	percent	number	percent	number	percent	number	percent	number	percent
2010	46,180	15.1%	38,325	14.9%	19,465	19.7%	18,860	11.8%	7,855	16.5%
2009	43,569	14.3	35,655	13.9	18,261	18.7	17,394	11.0	7,914	16.6
2008	39,829	13.2	32,570	12.9	17,222	17.7	15,348	9.8	7,259	15.1
2007	37,276	12.5	29,921	11.9	15,983	16.5	13,938	9.0	7,355	15.4
2006	36,460	12.3	29,283	11.8	15,336	16.1	13,947	9.1	7,177	15.2
2005	36,950	12.6	30,098	12.2	15,966	17.0	14,132	9.3	6,852	14.5

	total people in poverty		metropolitan areas total		inside central cities		outside central cities		nonmetropolitan areas	
	number	percent	number	percent	number	percent	number	percent	number	percent
2004	37,040	12.7%	–	–	–	–	–	–	–	–
2003	35,861	12.5	28,367	12.1%	14,551	17.5%	13,816	9.1%	7,495	14.2%
2002	34,570	12.1	27,096	11.6	13,784	16.7	13,311	8.9	7,474	14.2
2001	32,907	11.7	25,446	11.1	13,394	16.5	12,052	8.2	7,460	14.2
2000	31,581	11.3	24,603	10.8	13,257	16.3	11,346	7.8	6,978	13.4
1999	32,791	11.9	25,278	11.3	13,404	16.5	11,874	8.3	7,513	14.3
1998	34,476	12.7	26,997	12.3	14,921	18.5	12,076	8.7	7,479	14.4
1997	35,574	13.3	27,273	12.6	15,018	18.8	12,255	9.0	8,301	15.9
1996	36,529	13.7	28,211	13.2	15,645	19.6	12,566	9.4	8,318	15.9
1995	36,425	13.8	28,342	13.4	16,269	20.6	12,072	9.1	8,083	15.6
1994	38,059	14.5	29,610	14.2	16,098	20.9	13,511	10.3	8,449	16.0
1993	39,265	15.1	29,615	14.6	16,805	21.5	12,810	10.3	9,650	17.2
1992	38,014	14.8	28,380	14.2	16,346	20.9	12,034	9.9	9,634	16.9
1991	35,708	14.2	26,827	13.7	15,314	20.2	11,513	9.6	8,881	16.1
1990	33,585	13.5	24,510	12.7	14,254	19.0	10,255	8.7	9,075	16.3

Note: "–" means data are not available.

Source: Bureau of the Census, Current Population Surveys, Annual Social and Economic Supplement, Internet site http://www .census.gov/hhes/www/poverty/data/historical/index.html

Many of the Poor Have Jobs

More than 2 million poor people work full-time, year-round.

Many people live in poverty despite having jobs. In 2010, a substantial 34 percent of poor people aged 16 or older had jobs. This figure is lower than in previous years because of the high unemployment rate. The number of the poor with jobs climbed from 8.5 million in 2000 to more than 10 million in 2010.

A substantial share of the poor have full-time jobs—yet their incomes remain below the poverty level. In 2010, 8 percent of poor people worked year-round, full-time. This was down from nearly 12 percent in 2000—again, because of the rise in unemployment.

■ Falling wages for uneducated, low-skilled workers have boosted the number of working poor.

The number of poor people who work has grown

(number of poor people who work, 2000 and 2010)

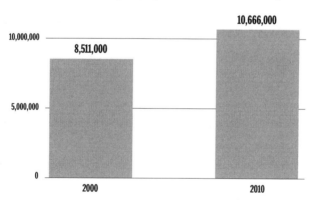

Table 6.24 People below Poverty Level by Work Status, 1990 to 2010

(number of people aged 16 or older below poverty level by work status, and percent of poor who work, 1990 to 2010; people in thousands as of the following year)

	total poor aged 16 or older	worked		worked full-time, year-round	
		number	percent of poor	number	percent of poor
2010	31,383	10,666	34.0%	2,608	8.3%
2009	29,625	10,680	36.1	2,641	8.9
2008	27,216	10,085	37.1	2,754	10.1
2007	25,297	9,089	35.9	2,768	10.9
2006	24,896	9,181	36.9	2,906	11.7
2005	25,381	9,340	36.8	2,894	11.4
2004	25,256	9,384	37.2	2,891	11.4
2003	24,266	8,820	36.3	2,636	10.9
2002	23,601	8,954	37.9	2,635	11.2
2001	22,245	8,530	38.3	2,567	11.5
2000	21,080	8,511	40.4	2,439	11.6
1999	21,762	9,251	42.5	2,559	11.8
1998	22,256	9,133	41.0	2,804	12.6
1997	22,753	9,444	41.5	2,345	10.3
1996	23,472	9,586	40.8	2,263	9.6
1995	23,077	9,484	41.1	2,418	10.5
1994	24,108	9,829	40.8	2,520	10.5
1993	24,832	10,144	40.8	2,408	9.7
1992	23,951	9,739	40.6	2,211	9.2
1991	22,530	9,208	40.9	2,103	9.3
1990	21,242	8,716	41.0	2,076	9.8

Source: Bureau of the Census, Current Population Surveys, Annual Social and Economic Supplement, Internet site http://www.census.gov/hhes/www/poverty/histpov/histpovtb.html

Poverty, 2010

Few Households with Two Earners Are Poor

Single-earner households are much more vulnerable to poverty, especially those headed by blacks or Hispanics.

Increasingly, it takes two incomes to stay out of poverty. Only 2.4 percent of families with two or more workers have incomes that place them below the poverty level, the proportion ranging from just 1.5 percent of non-Hispanic white families to 7.1 percent of Hispanic families. But among families with only one worker, 16.5 percent are poor. An even larger 31.0 percent of families with no workers are poor.

Among married couples, poverty is practically nonexistent for those in which both husband and wife work full-time. But for married couples in which only the husband works full-time and the wife does not work, the poverty rate climbs to 15.2 percent among Hispanics.

Poverty rates are higher for female-headed families because there are fewer workers in the household. Twenty-seven percent of female-headed families with one worker are poor. If the worker has a full-time job, the poverty rate falls to 10.2 percent.

■ Non-Hispanic white and Asian families are less likely to be poor than black families because they have more workers. They are less likely to be poor than Hispanics because of their higher educational level.

Poverty is less likely for families with two or more workers

(percent of families below poverty level by number of workers, 2010)

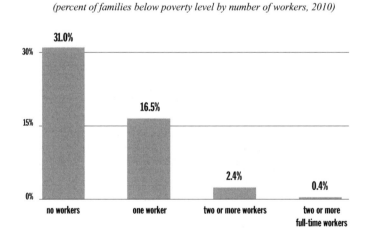

Table 6.25 Families below Poverty Level by Work Status, Race, and Hispanic Origin, 2010

(number and percent of families below poverty level by work status, race, and Hispanic origin, 2010; numbers in thousands)

	total	Asian	black	Hispanic	non-Hispanic white
Number of families in poverty	**9,221**	**340**	**2,355**	**2,557**	**3,922**
With no workers	3,888	152	1,136	791	1,783
With one or more workers	5,333	188	1,219	1,766	2,139
One	4,376	149	1,087	1,401	1,716
Two or more	956	39	131	366	423
With one or more full-time, year-round workers	1,866	81	369	736	683
One	1,782	74	359	705	646
Two or more	84	7	10	31	37
Percent of families in poverty	**11.7%**	**9.1%**	**24.1%**	**24.0%**	**7.3%**
With no workers	31.0	41.3	59.6	61.7	20.0
With one or more workers	8.1	5.6	15.5	18.8	4.8
One	16.5	12.2	25.9	33.1	10.3
Two or more	2.4	1.9	3.6	7.1	1.5
With one or more full-time, year-round workers	3.5	2.7	6.3	10.2	1.9
One	5.4	4.3	8.9	15.1	2.8
Two or more	0.4	0.5	0.5	1.2	0.3

Note: Asians and blacks include those who identify themselves as being of the race alone and those who identify themselves as being of the race in combination with other races. Non-Hispanic whites are those who identify themselves as white alone and not Hispanic. Numbers do not add to total because not all races are shown and Hispanics may be of any race.
Source: Bureau of the Census, 2011 Current Population Survey Annual Social and Economic Supplement, Internet site http://www.census.gov/hhes/www/cpstables/032011/pov/toc.htm; calculations by New Strategist

Table 6.26 Married Couples below Poverty Level by Work Status, Race, and Hispanic Origin, 2010

(number and percent of married couples below poverty level by work status, race, and Hispanic origin, 2010; numbers in thousands)

	total	Asian	black	Hispanic	non-Hispanic white
Number of married couples in poverty	**3,596**	**211**	**390**	**1,152**	**1,812**
With no workers	1,305	80	157	214	829
With one or more workers	2,291	131	233	938	983
Both husband and wife work	453	25	40	157	227
Wife works, husband does not work	414	31	69	91	210
Husband works, wife does not work	1,354	70	112	660	520
With one or more full-time, year-round workers	999	69	90	432	408
Both husband and wife work full-time, year-round	37	4	0	7	26
Wife works full-time, year-round, husband does not	151	13	24	34	78
Husband works full-time, year round, wife does not	784	51	66	373	297
Percent of married couples in poverty	**6.2%**	**7.2%**	**9.0%**	**17.1%**	**4.2%**
With no workers	15.1	31.7	26.2	38.0	11.6
With one or more workers	4.6	4.9	6.2	15.2	2.7
Both husband and wife work	1.4	1.6	1.7	4.7	1.0
Wife works, husband does not work	8.9	13.1	12.2	21.3	6.3
Husband works, wife does not work	10.8	9.0	14.8	29.4	5.9
With one or more full-time, year-round workers	2.4	2.9	2.8	8.7	1.3
Both husband and wife work full-time, year-round	0.2	0.4	0.0	0.4	0.2
Wife works full-time, year-round, husband does not	2.4	4.2	3.5	5.3	1.7
Husband works full-time, year round, wife does not	4.3	4.6	6.1	15.2	2.2

Note: Asians and blacks include those who identify themselves as being of the race alone and those who identify themselves as being of the race in combination with other races. Non-Hispanic whites are those who identify themselves as white alone and not Hispanic. Numbers do not add to total because not all races are shown and Hispanics may be of any race.
Source: Bureau of the Census, 2011 Current Population Survey Annual Social and Economic Supplement, Internet site http://www.census.gov/hhes/www/cpstables/032011/pov/toc.htm; calculations by New Strategist

Table 6.27 Female-Headed Families below Poverty Level by Work Status, Race, and Hispanic Origin, 2010

(number and percent of female-headed families below poverty level by work status, race, and Hispanic origin, 2010; numbers in thousands)

	total	Asian	black	Hispanic	non-Hispanic white
Number of female-headed families in poverty	**4,745**	**100**	**1,712**	**1,167**	**1,770**
With no workers	2,211	54	842	511	815
With one or more workers	2,534	46	870	655	955
One	2,269	44	801	562	849
Two or more	265	2	69	93	107
With one or more full-time, year-round workers	702	11	241	230	218
One	682	10	235	221	214
Two or more	20	0	7	10	4
Percent of female-headed families in poverty	**31.6%**	**20.3%**	**38.4%**	**42.3%**	**24.3%**
With no workers	69.8	61.9	77.7	83.6	58.6
With one or more workers	21.4	11.3	25.8	30.5	16.2
One	27.3	18.1	31.7	39.2	20.8
Two or more	7.5	1.3	8.1	13.1	5.9
With one or more full-time, year-round workers	9.0	3.4	11.1	16.4	5.6
One	10.2	4.5	12.3	19.4	6.3
Two or more	1.8	0.3	2.4	3.6	0.8

Note: Asians and blacks include those who identify themselves as being of the race alone and those who identify themselves as being of the race in combination with other races. Non-Hispanic whites are those who identify themselves as white alone and not Hispanic. Numbers do not add to total because not all races are shown and Hispanics may be of any race.
Source: Bureau of the Census, 2011 Current Population Survey Annual Social and Economic Supplement, Internet site http://www.census.gov/hhes/www/cpstables/032011/pov/toc.htm; calculations by New Strategist

Table 6.28 Male-Headed Families below Poverty Level by Work Status, Race, and Hispanic Origin, 2010

(number and percent of male-headed families below poverty level by work status, race, and Hispanic origin, 2010; numbers in thousands)

	total	Asian	black	Hispanic	non-Hispanic white
Number of male-headed families in poverty	**880**	**29**	**253**	**238**	**339**
With no workers	373	18	137	65	139
With one or more workers	507	12	116	173	201
One	427	6	105	140	172
Two or more	80	5	11	33	29
With one or more full-time, year-round workers	164	1	37	74	57
One	154	0	34	67	57
Two or more	10	1	3	7	0
Percent of male-headed families in poverty	**15.8%**	**10.0%**	**26.5%**	**20.2%**	**11.0%**
With no workers	48.8	–	61.3	60.9	36.3
With one or more workers	10.6	4.4	15.8	16.1	7.4
One	15.1	5.9	21.7	24.7	10.4
Two or more	4.1	3.4	4.4	6.5	2.8
With one or more full-time, year-round workers	4.5	0.5	7.0	9.0	2.8
One	5.6	0.0	8.4	11.8	3.4
Two or more	1.1	1.2	2.6	2.7	0.0

Note: Asians and blacks include those who identify themselves as being of the race alone and those who identify themselves as being of the race in combination with other races. Non-Hispanic whites are those who identify themselves as white alone and not Hispanic. Numbers do not add to total because not all races are shown and Hispanics may be of any race. "–" means sample is too small to make a reliable estimate.
Source: Bureau of the Census, 2011 Current Population Survey Annual Social and Economic Supplement, Internet site http:// www.census.gov/hhes/www/cpstables/032011/pov/toc.htm; calculations by New Strategist

Poverty Rate Is Highest among Families in the South

Families in the Northeast are least likely to be poor.

More than 13 percent of families in the South live in poverty, greater than the 11.7 percent of all families who are poor and higher than the poverty rate in the Northeast, Midwest, or West. Among families with children, the poverty rate in the South climbs to 20.7 percent. In every region, blacks and Hispanics have the highest poverty rates, the rate reaching 41.6 percent among black families with children in the Midwest.

Married couples have lower poverty rates regardless of region, race, or Hispanic origin. Behind their lower poverty rate is the fact that married-couple families are likely to have more earners in the household, which boosts incomes. The importance of a second income is illustrated most starkly in the poverty rate of black families. Among all black married couples, the poverty rate peaks in the Midwest at 11.1 percent. Among all black female-headed families, the poverty rate peaks in the Midwest at a much higher 45.6 percent.

■ Blacks are poor because of their family structure, married couples heading relatively few black families. Hispanics are poor because of their low educational level, unschooled immigrants heading a large proportion of families.

In the South, Hispanic families are most likely to be poor

(percent of families below poverty level in the South, by race and Hispanic origin, 2010)

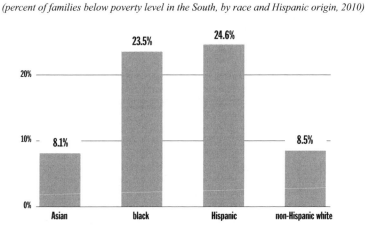

Table 6.29 Families below Poverty Level by Region, Race, and Hispanic Origin, 2010

(number and percent of families below poverty level by region, race, and Hispanic origin, 2010; numbers in thousands)

	total	Asian	black	Hispanic	non-Hispanic white
NUMBER IN POVERTY					
Total families	**9,221**	**340**	**2,355**	**2,557**	**3,922**
Northeast	1,330	83	359	357	580
Midwest	1,845	40	502	231	1,056
South	3,997	71	1,294	988	1,633
West	2,049	148	199	981	653
POVERTY RATE					
Total families	**11.7%**	**9.1%**	**24.1%**	**24.0%**	**7.3%**
Northeast	9.6	11.5	21.9	23.9	5.7
Midwest	10.6	9.1	29.6	26.6	7.4
South	13.4	8.1	23.5	24.6	8.5
West	11.6	8.7	21.5	22.9	6.3

Note: Asians and blacks include those who identify themselves as being of the race alone and those who identify themselves as being of the race in combination with other races. Non-Hispanic whites are those who identify themselves as white alone and not Hispanic. Numbers do not add to total because not all races are shown and Hispanics may be of any race.
Source: Bureau of the Census, 2011 Current Population Survey Annual Social and Economic Supplement, Internet site http://www.census.gov/hhes/www/cpstables/032011/pov/toc.htm; calculations by New Strategist

Table 6.30 Families with Children below Poverty Level by Region, Race, and Hispanic Origin, 2010

(number and percent of families with related children under age 18 at home below poverty level by region, race, and Hispanic origin, 2010; numbers in thousands)

	total	Asian	black	Hispanic	non-Hispanic white
NUMBER IN POVERTY					
Total families with children	**6,997**	**213**	**1,939**	**2,204**	**2,621**
Northeast	988	46	286	295	403
Midwest	1,414	25	432	216	732
South	2,982	48	1,054	841	1,040
West	1,612	95	167	852	446
POVERTY RATE					
Total families with children	**18.3%**	**10.9%**	**33.7%**	**30.6%**	**11.3%**
Northeast	15.2	13.7	30.7	31.4	9.2
Midwest	17.0	9.7	41.6	34.8	11.5
South	20.7	9.7	32.9	31.7	13.1
West	17.8	10.9	28.8	28.6	10.0

Note: Asians and blacks include those who identify themselves as being of the race alone and those who identify themselves as being of the race in combination with other races. Non-Hispanic whites are those who identify themselves as white alone and not Hispanic. Numbers do not add to total because not all races are shown and Hispanics may be of any race.
Source: Bureau of the Census, 2011 Current Population Survey Annual Social and Economic Supplement, Internet site http://www.census.gov/hhes/www/cpstables/032011/pov/toc.htm; calculations by New Strategist

Table 6.31 Married Couples below Poverty Level by Region, Race, and Hispanic Origin, 2010

(number and percent of married couples below poverty level by region, race, and Hispanic origin, 2010; numbers in thousands)

	total	Asian	black	Hispanic	non-Hispanic white
NUMBER IN POVERTY					
Total married couples	**3,596**	**211**	**390**	**1,152**	**1,812**
Northeast	439	53	44	85	261
Midwest	629	20	75	109	426
South	1,574	51	231	471	817
West	954	86	40	487	309
POVERTY RATE					
Total married couples	**6.2%**	**7.2%**	**9.0%**	**17.1%**	**4.2%**
Northeast	4.3	9.1	6.4	11.2	3.2
Midwest	4.8	5.5	11.1	19.2	3.7
South	7.3	7.3	9.1	18.0	5.3
West	7.2	6.7	9.1	17.5	3.7

Note: Asians and blacks include those who identify themselves as being of the race alone and those who identify themselves as being of the race in combination with other races. Non-Hispanic whites are those who identify themselves as white alone and not Hispanic. Numbers do not add to total because not all races are shown and Hispanics may be of any race.
Source: Bureau of the Census, 2011 Current Population Survey Annual Social and Economic Supplement, Internet site http://www.census.gov/hhes/www/cpstables/032011/pov/toc.htm; calculations by New Strategist

Table 6.32 Married Couples with Children below Poverty Level by Region, Race, and Hispanic Origin, 2010

(number and percent of married couples with related children under age 18 at home below poverty level by region, race, and Hispanic origin, 2010; numbers in thousands)

	total	Asian	black	Hispanic	non-Hispanic white
NUMBER IN POVERTY					
Total married couples with children	**2,242**	**124**	**264**	**958**	**888**
Northeast	238	28	22	63	132
Midwest	400	16	58	100	232
South	938	37	156	387	362
West	666	44	28	409	162
POVERTY RATE					
Total married couples with children	**8.8%**	**7.8%**	**12.4%**	**21.6%**	**5.2%**
Northeast	5.4	9.1	6.3	14.2	3.9
Midwest	7.1	7.0	17.6	25.5	5.0
South	10.2	9.2	12.9	23.1	6.2
West	10.6	6.6	11.3	21.3	4.9

Note: Asians and blacks include those who identify themselves as being of the race alone and those who identify themselves as being of the race in combination with other races. Non-Hispanic whites are those who identify themselves as white alone and not Hispanic. Numbers do not add to total because not all races are shown and Hispanics may be of any race.
Source: Bureau of the Census, 2011 Current Population Survey Annual Social and Economic Supplement, Internet site http://www.census.gov/hhes/www/cpstables/032011/pov/toc.htm; calculations by New Strategist

Table 6.33 Female-Headed Families below Poverty Level by Region, Race, and Hispanic Origin, 2010

(number and percent of female-headed families below poverty level by region, race, and Hispanic origin, 2010; numbers in thousands)

	total	Asian	black	Hispanic	non-Hispanic white
NUMBER IN POVERTY					
Total female-headed families	**4,745**	**100**	**1,712**	**1,167**	**1,770**
Northeast	767	23	269	243	269
Midwest	997	13	366	94	513
South	2,093	11	938	443	700
West	887	54	139	386	288
POVERTY RATE					
Total female-headed families	**31.6%**	**20.3%**	**38.4%**	**42.3%**	**24.3%**
Northeast	28.3	27.3	34.7	45.6	19.3
Midwest	32.9	–	45.6	49.0	26.3
South	33.6	11.8	37.5	43.6	26.9
West	29.1	20.2	36.6	37.9	21.6

Note: Asians and blacks include those who identify themselves as being of the race alone and those who identify themselves as being of the race in combination with other races. Non-Hispanic whites are those who identify themselves as white alone and not Hispanic. Numbers do not add to total because not all races are shown and Hispanics may be of any race. "–" means sample is too small to make a reliable estimate.
Source: Bureau of the Census, 2011 Current Population Survey Annual Social and Economic Supplement, Internet site http://www.census.gov/hhes/www/cpstables/032011/pov/toc.htm; calculations by New Strategist

Table 6.34 Female-Headed Families with Children below Poverty Level by Region, Race, and Hispanic Origin, 2010

(number and percent of female-headed families with related children under age 18 at home below poverty level by region, race, and Hispanic origin, 2010; numbers in thousands)

	total	Asian	black	Hispanic	non-Hispanic white
NUMBER IN POVERTY					
Total female-headed families with children	**4,089**	**80**	**1,478**	**1,061**	**1,476**
Northeast	654	16	227	213	231
Midwest	853	8	325	92	419
South	1,798	8	807	395	587
West	783	47	120	361	240
POVERTY RATE					
Total female-headed families with children	**40.7%**	**28.7%**	**47.1%**	**50.3%**	**32.7%**
Northeast	39.2	–	44.6	53.9	29.2
Midwest	41.4	–	54.1	56.5	33.6
South	42.6	–	45.9	51.2	36.1
West	37.6	29.6	44.6	46.1	28.4

Note: Asians and blacks include those who identify themselves as being of the race alone and those who identify themselves as being of the race in combination with other races. Non-Hispanic whites are those who identify themselves as white alone and not Hispanic. Numbers do not add to total because not all races are shown and Hispanics may be of any race. "–" means sample is too small to make a reliable estimate.
Source: Bureau of the Census, 2011 Current Population Survey Annual Social and Economic Supplement, Internet site http://www.census.gov/hhes/www/cpstables/032011/pov/toc.htm; calculations by New Strategist

Table 6.35 Male-Headed Families below Poverty Level by Region, Race, and Hispanic Origin, 2010

(number and percent of male-headed families below poverty level by region, race, and Hispanic origin, 2010; numbers in thousands)

	total	Asian	black	Hispanic	non-Hispanic white
NUMBER IN POVERTY					
Total male-headed families	**880**	**29**	**253**	**238**	**339**
Northeast	124	7	46	29	50
Midwest	218	7	61	28	117
South	330	8	125	74	116
West	208	8	20	108	57
POVERTY RATE					
Total male-headed families	**15.8%**	**10.0%**	**26.5%**	**20.2%**	**11.0%**
Northeast	12.3	–	27.3	13.9	8.3
Midwest	17.9	–	28.3	25.6	13.6
South	16.7	–	27.2	19	11.3
West	15.3	5.1	18.9	22.7	9.7

Note: Asians and blacks include those who identify themselves as being of the race alone and those who identify themselves as being of the race in combination with other races. Non-Hispanic whites are those who identify themselves as white alone and not Hispanic. Numbers do not add to total because not all races are shown and Hispanics may be of any race. "–" means sample is too small to make a reliable estimate.
Source: Bureau of the Census, 2011 Current Population Survey Annual Social and Economic Supplement, Internet site http://www.census.gov/hhes/www/cpstables/032011/pov/toc.htm; calculations by New Strategist

Table 6.36 Male-Headed Families with Children below Poverty Level by Region, Race, and Hispanic Origin, 2010

(number and percent of male-headed families with related children under age 18 at home below poverty level by region, race, and Hispanic origin, 2010; numbers in thousands)

	total	Asian	black	Hispanic	non-Hispanic white
NUMBER IN POVERTY					
Total male-headed families with children	**667**	**10**	**197**	**186**	**256**
Northeast	96	2	37	19	40
Midwest	161	1	49	24	81
South	245	3	91	59	91
West	164	4	19	83	45
POVERTY RATE					
Total male-headed families with children	**24.2%**	**11.1%**	**40.8%**	**28.3%**	**17.2%**
Northeast	23.6	–	48.1	18.8	17.1
Midwest	25.2	–	45.9	–	18.0
South	24.8	–	38.8	28.9	17.6
West	22.9	–	–	29.3	15.2

Note: Asians and blacks include those who identify themselves as being of the race alone and those who identify themselves as being of the race in combination with other races. Non-Hispanic whites are those who identify themselves as white alone and not Hispanic. Numbers do not add to total because not all races are shown and Hispanics may be of any race. "–" means sample is too small to make a reliable estimate.
Source: Bureau of the Census, 2011 Current Population Survey Annual Social and Economic Supplement, Internet site http://www.census.gov/hhes/www/cpstables/032011/pov/toc.htm; calculations by New Strategist

Poverty Rate Is Highest in the Inner Cities

Rate is lowest in the suburbs.

The percentage of families living in poverty is higher in the principal (central) cities of metropolitan areas than outside principal cities (suburbs) or in nonmetropolitan areas. The poverty rate is higher for Hispanic and black families than for non-Hispanic white or Asian families. It is higher for families with children than for those without children.

The poverty rate peaks among Hispanic female-headed families with children living in nonmetropolitan areas, where the rate exceeds 56 percent (56.5). Their black counterparts are not far behind, with a poverty rate of 55.7 percent. The poverty rate among families with children bottoms out among non-Hispanic white married couples living in the suburbs, just 4.2 percent of whom are poor.

■ The poverty rate of families in nonmetropolitan areas is slightly above the national average and well above the poverty rate of families in the suburbs.

Among families with children, the poverty rate peaks among Hispanic female-headed families in nonmetropolitan areas

(highest and lowest poverty rates among families with children by race, Hispanic origin, and metropolitan residence, 2010)

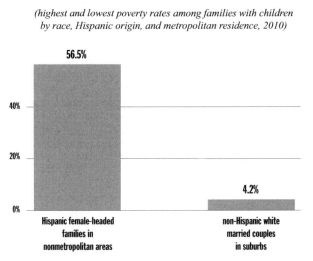

Table 6.37 Families below Poverty Level by Metropolitan Status, Race, and Hispanic Origin, 2010

(number and percent of families below poverty level by metropolitan status, race, and Hispanic origin, 2010; numbers in thousands)

	total families	Asian	black	Hispanic	non-Hispanic white
NUMBER IN POVERTY					
Total families	**9,221**	**340**	**2,355**	**2,557**	**3,922**
Metropolitan	7,569	337	2,068	2,339	2,850
Inside principal cities	3,742	196	1,278	1,387	910
Outside principal cities	3,827	141	790	952	1,939
Not metropolitan	1,652	4	287	218	1,072
POVERTY RATE					
Total families	**11.7%**	**9.1%**	**24.1%**	**24.0%**	**7.3%**
Metropolitan	11.5	9.4	23.8	23.7	6.6
Inside principal cities	15.9	11.0	27.1	27.3	7.6
Outside principal cities	9.1	7.8	19.9	19.8	6.2
Not metropolitan	12.6	2.7	26.7	27.8	10.0

Note: Asians and blacks include those who identify themselves as being of the race alone and those who identify themselves as being of the race in combination with other races. Non-Hispanic whites are those who identify themselves as white alone and not Hispanic. Numbers do not add to total because not all races are shown and Hispanics may be of any race.
Source: Bureau of the Census, 2011 Current Population Survey Annual Social and Economic Supplement, Internet site http://www.census.gov/hhes/www/cpstables/032011/pov/toc.htm; calculations by New Strategist

Table 6.38 Families with Children below Poverty Level by Metropolitan Status, Race, and Hispanic Origin, 2010

(number and percent of families with related children under age 18 at home below poverty level by metropolitan status, race, and Hispanic origin, 2010; numbers in thousands)

	total	Asian	black	Hispanic	non-Hispanic white
NUMBER IN POVERTY					
Total families with children	**6,997**	**213**	**1,939**	**2,204**	**2,621**
Metropolitan	5,734	210	1,700	2,020	1,839
Inside principal cities	2,937	115	1,043	1,194	615
Outside principal cities	2,797	95	658	826	1,224
Not metropolitan	1,263	3	238	185	781
POVERTY RATE					
Total families with children	**18.3%**	**10.9%**	**33.7%**	**30.6%**	**11.3%**
Metropolitan	17.7	11.2	33.1	30.3	9.9
Inside principal cities	24.3	12.9	37.0	34.8	12.4
Outside principal cities	13.8	9.5	28.2	25.5	9.0
Not metropolitan	21.4	–	39.2	34.9	17.3

Note: Asians and blacks include those who identify themselves as being of the race alone and those who identify themselves as being of the race in combination with other races. Non-Hispanic whites are those who identify themselves as white alone and not Hispanic. Numbers do not add to total because not all races are shown and Hispanics may be of any race. "–" means sample is too small to make a reliable estimate.
Source: Bureau of the Census, 2011 Current Population Survey Annual Social and Economic Supplement, Internet site http://www.census.gov/hhes/www/cpstables/032011/pov/toc.htm; calculations by New Strategist

(number and percent of married couples below poverty level by metropolitan status, race, and Hispanic origin, 2010; numbers in thousands)

	total	Asian	black	Hispanic	non-Hispanic white
NUMBER IN POVERTY					
Total married couples	**3,596**	**211**	**390**	**1,152**	**1,812**
Metropolitan	2,994	210	342	1,064	1,367
Inside principal cities	1,271	119	174	581	391
Outside principal cities	1,722	90	167	483	976
Not metropolitan	602	1	49	87	445
POVERTY RATE					
Total married couples	**6.2%**	**7.2%**	**9.0%**	**17.1%**	**4.2%**
Metropolitan	6.2	7.4	8.8	17.1	3.9
Inside principal cities	8.2	8.8	9.3	19.3	4.2
Outside principal cities	5.3	6.1	8.4	15.0	3.8
Not metropolitan	6.0	1.4	10.0	18.0	5.1

Note: Asians and blacks include those who identify themselves as being of the race alone and those who identify themselves as being of the race in combination with other races. Non-Hispanic whites are those who identify themselves as white alone and not Hispanic. Numbers do not add to total because not all races are shown and Hispanics may be of any race.
Source: Bureau of the Census, 2011 Current Population Survey Annual Social and Economic Supplement, Internet site http://www.census.gov/hhes/www/cpstables/032011/pov/toc.htm; calculations by New Strategist

Table 6.40 **Married Couples with Children below Poverty Level by Metropolitan Status, Race, and Hispanic Origin, 2010**

(number and percent of married couples with related children under age 18 at home below poverty level by metropolitan status, race, and Hispanic origin, 2010; numbers in thousands)

	total	Asian	black	Hispanic	non-Hispanic white
NUMBER IN POVERTY					
Total married couples with children	**2,242**	**124**	**264**	**958**	**888**
Metropolitan	1,882	123	233	891	640
Inside principal cities	864	64	112	487	199
Outside principal cities	1,018	58	121	403	441
Not metropolitan	360	1	31	67	248
POVERTY RATE					
Total married couples with children	**8.8%**	**7.8%**	**12.4%**	**21.6%**	**5.2%**
Metropolitan	8.7	8.0	12.2	21.6	4.6
Inside principal cities	12.2	9.2	12.1	24.7	5.7
Outside principal cities	7.0	6.9	12.2	18.7	4.2
Not metropolitan	9.3	–	14.2	22.1	7.7

Note: Asians and blacks include those who identify themselves as being of the race alone and those who identify themselves as being of the race in combination with other races. Non-Hispanic whites are those who identify themselves as white alone and not Hispanic. Numbers do not add to total because not all races are shown and Hispanics may be of any race. "–" means sample is too small to make a reliable estimate.
Source: Bureau of the Census, 2011 Current Population Survey Annual Social and Economic Supplement, Internet site http://www.census.gov/hhes/www/cpstables/032011/pov/toc.htm; calculations by New Strategist

Table 6.41 Female-Headed Families below Poverty Level by Metropolitan Status, Race, and Hispanic Origin, 2010

(number and percent of female-headed families below poverty level by metropolitan status, race, and Hispanic origin, 2010; numbers in thousands)

	total	Asian	black	Hispanic	non-Hispanic white
NUMBER IN POVERTY					
Total female-headed families	**4,745**	**100**	**1,712**	**1,167**	**1,770**
Metropolitan	3,841	98	1,499	1,054	1,231
Inside principal cities	2,091	57	970	670	428
Outside principal cities	1,750	41	529	385	803
Not metropolitan	904	2	212	112	540
POVERTY RATE					
Total female-headed families	**31.6%**	**20.3%**	**38.4%**	**42.3%**	**24.3%**
Metropolitan	30.1	20.9	37.8	41.5	21.1
Inside principal cities	35.1	21.5	41.3	45.8	22.4
Outside principal cities	25.8	20.2	32.8	35.7	20.5
Not metropolitan	39.7	–	43.2	51.1	37.0

Note: Asians and blacks include those who identify themselves as being of the race alone and those who identify themselves as being of the race in combination with other races. Non-Hispanic whites are those who identify themselves as white alone and not Hispanic. Numbers do not add to total because not all races are shown and Hispanics may be of any race. "–" means sample is too small to make a reliable estimate.
Source: Bureau of the Census, 2011 Current Population Survey Annual Social and Economic Supplement, Internet site http://www.census.gov/hhes/www/cpstables/032011/pov/toc.htm; calculations by New Strategist

Table 6.42 Female-Headed Families with Children below Poverty Level by Metropolitan Status, Race, and Hispanic Origin, 2010

(number and percent of female-headed families with related children under age 18 at home below poverty level by metropolitan status, race, and Hispanic origin, 2010; numbers in thousands)

	total	Asian	black	Hispanic	non-Hispanic white
NUMBER IN POVERTY					
Total female-headed families with children	**4,089**	**80**	**1,478**	**1,061**	**1,476**
Metropolitan	3,300	78	1,290	961	1,012
Inside principal cities	1,788	44	833	599	346
Outside principal cities	1,511	34	457	361	666
Not metropolitan	789	2	188	100	464
POVERTY RATE					
Total female-headed families with children	**40.7%**	**28.7%**	**47.1%**	**50.3%**	**32.7%**
Metropolitan	39.0	29.7	46.1	49.7	28.7
Inside principal cities	44.7	30.2	50.7	53.6	30.6
Outside principal cities	34.0	29.1	39.6	44.3	27.9
Not metropolitan	49.9	–	55.7	56.5	47.0

Note: Asians and blacks include those who identify themselves as being of the race alone and those who identify themselves as being of the race in combination with other races. Non-Hispanic whites are those who identify themselves as white alone and not Hispanic. Numbers do not add to total because not all races are shown and Hispanics may be of any race. "–" means sample is too small to make a reliable estimate.
Source: Bureau of the Census, 2011 Current Population Survey Annual Social and Economic Supplement, Internet site http://www.census.gov/hhes/www/cpstables/032011/pov/toc.htm; calculations by New Strategist

Table 6.43 Male-Headed Families below Poverty Level by Metropolitan Status, Race, and Hispanic Origin, 2010

(number and percent of male-headed families below poverty level by metropolitan status, race, and Hispanic origin, 2010; numbers in thousands)

	total	Asian	black	Hispanic	non-Hispanic white
NUMBER IN POVERTY					
Total male-headed families	**880**	**29**	**253**	**238**	**339**
Metropolitan	734	29	227	220	252
Inside principal cities	380	19	133	136	91
Outside principal cities	354	10	93	84	161
Not metropolitan	145	0	26	18	88
POVERTY RATE					
Total male-headed families	**15.8%**	**10.0%**	**26.5%**	**20.2%**	**11.0%**
Metropolitan	15.4	10.2	26.4	20.0	10.1
Inside principal cities	19.0	12.3	27.1	22.7	12.0
Outside principal cities	12.8	7.7	25.4	16.7	9.2
Not metropolitan	18.3	–	27.5	23.4	15.2

Note: Asians and blacks include those who identify themselves as being of the race alone and those who identify themselves as being of the race in combination with other races. Non-Hispanic whites are those who identify themselves as white alone and not Hispanic. Numbers do not add to total because not all races are shown and Hispanics may be of any race. "–" means sample is too small to make a reliable estimate.
Source: Bureau of the Census, 2011 Current Population Survey Annual Social and Economic Supplement, Internet site http://www.census.gov/hhes/www/cpstables/032011/pov/toc.htm; calculations by New Strategist

Table 6.44 Male-Headed Families with Children below Poverty Level by Metropolitan Status, Race, and Hispanic Origin, 2010

(number and percent of male-headed families with related children under age 18 at home below poverty level by metropolitan status, race, and Hispanic origin, 2010; numbers in thousands)

	total	Asian	black	Hispanic	non-Hispanic white
NUMBER IN POVERTY					
Total male-headed families with children	**667**	**10**	**197**	**186**	**256**
Metropolitan	553	10	177	169	187
Inside principal cities	285	7	97	107	71
Outside principal cities	268	3	80	61	116
Not metropolitan	114	0	19	17	69
POVERTY RATE					
Total male-headed families with children	**24.2%**	**11.1%**	**40.8%**	**28.3%**	**17.2%**
Metropolitan	24.0	11.4	41.3	27.7	16.1
Inside principal cities	29.1	–	40.6	31.5	20.2
Outside principal cities	20.2	–	42.3	22.9	14.3
Not metropolitan	25.3	–	–	–	21.2

Note: Asians and blacks include those who identify themselves as being of the race alone and those who identify themselves as being of the race in combination with other races. Non-Hispanic whites are those who identify themselves as white alone and not Hispanic. Numbers do not add to total because not all races are shown and Hispanics may be of any race. "–" means sample is too small to make a reliable estimate.

Source: Bureau of the Census, 2011 Current Population Survey Annual Social and Economic Supplement, Internet site http://www.census.gov/hhes/www/cpstables/032011/pov/toc.htm; calculations by New Strategist

Non-Hispanic Whites Dominate Elderly Poor

Minorities account for the majority of poor under age 45.

Among the nation's 46 million poor in 2010, the 42 percent minority was non-Hispanic white. Twenty-nine percent were Hispanic, 25 percent were black, and 4 percent were Asian.

The non-Hispanic white share of the poor rises fairly steadily with age. Among poor children under age 18, only 30 percent are non-Hispanic white. A smaller 29 percent of poor children are black and a much larger 37 percent are Hispanic. The non-Hispanic white share of the poor becomes the majority in the 45-to-54 age group. Among poor people aged 75 or older, fully 64 percent are non-Hispanic white.

■ As the Hispanic population grows, it is becoming a growing share of the poor.

Non-Hispanic whites account for the majority of poor people aged 65 or older

(percent of people below poverty level who are non-Hispanic white, by age, 2010)

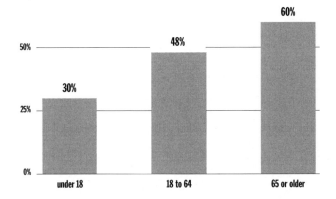

Table 6.45 People below Poverty Level by Age, Race, and Hispanic Origin, 2010

(number of people below poverty level by age, race, and Hispanic origin, and percent distribution of poor by race and Hispanic origin, 2010; numbers in thousands)

	total	Asian	black	Hispanic	non-Hispanic white
Total in poverty	**46,180**	**1,859**	**11,361**	**13,243**	**19,599**
Under age 18	16,401	547	4,817	6,110	5,002
Under age 5	5,467	188	1,689	2,070	1,557
Aged 5 to 17	10,934	360	3,127	4,040	3,445
Aged 18 to 64	26,258	1,100	5,908	6,619	12,481
Aged 18 to 24	6,507	296	1,514	1,547	3,132
Aged 25 to 34	6,333	255	1,485	1,917	2,682
Aged 35 to 44	5,028	223	1,032	1,618	2,129
Aged 45 to 54	4,662	181	1,039	968	2,421
Aged 55 to 59	1,972	89	445	308	1,095
Aged 60 to 64	1,755	56	393	261	1,024
Aged 65 or older	3,520	213	636	514	2,116
Aged 65 to 74	1,737	117	337	296	967
Aged 75 or older	1,784	96	299	218	1,149
PERCENT DISTRIBUTION OF POOR BY RACE AND HISPANIC ORIGIN					
Total in poverty	**100.0%**	**4.0%**	**24.6%**	**28.7%**	**42.4%**
Under age 18	100.0	3.3	29.4	37.3	30.5
Under age 5	100.0	3.4	30.9	37.9	28.5
Aged 5 to 17	100.0	3.3	28.6	36.9	31.5
Aged 18 to 64	100.0	4.2	22.5	25.2	47.5
Aged 18 to 24	100.0	4.5	23.3	23.8	48.1
Aged 25 to 34	100.0	4.0	23.4	30.3	42.3
Aged 35 to 44	100.0	4.4	20.5	32.2	42.3
Aged 45 to 54	100.0	3.9	22.3	20.8	51.9
Aged 55 to 59	100.0	4.5	22.6	15.6	55.5
Aged 60 to 64	100.0	3.2	22.4	14.9	58.3
Aged 65 or older	100.0	6.1	18.1	14.6	60.1
Aged 65 to 74	100.0	6.7	19.4	17.0	55.7
Aged 75 or older	100.0	5.4	16.8	12.2	64.4

Note: Asians and blacks include those who identify themselves as being of the race alone and those who identify themselves as being of the race in combination with other races. Non-Hispanic whites are those who identify themselves as white alone and not Hispanic. Numbers do not add to total because not all races are shown and Hispanics may be of any race.
Source: Bureau of the Census, 2011 Current Population Survey Annual Social and Economic Supplement, Internet site http://www.census.gov/hhes/www/cpstables/032011/pov/toc.htm; calculations by New Strategist

Table 6.46 People below Poverty Level by Age and Sex, 2010: Total People

(number and percent of people below poverty level by age and sex, 2010; numbers in thousands)

	total	females	males
Total people in poverty	**46,180**	**25,167**	**21,012**
Under age 18	16,401	7,947	8,454
Under age 5	5,467	2,602	2,865
Aged 5 to 17	10,934	5,345	5,589
Aged 18 to 64	26,258	14,852	11,406
Aged 18 to 24	6,507	3,676	2,831
Aged 25 to 34	6,333	3,705	2,628
Aged 35 to 44	5,028	2,844	2,184
Aged 45 to 54	4,662	2,588	2,073
Aged 55 to 59	1,972	1,067	905
Aged 60 to 64	1,755	971	784
Aged 65 or older	3,520	2,368	1,153
Aged 65 to 74	1,737	1,094	642
Aged 75 or older	1,784	1,274	510
PERCENT IN POVERTY			
Total people	**15.1%**	**16.2%**	**14.0%**
Under age 18	22.0	21.8	22.2
Under age 5	25.9	25.1	26.5
Aged 5 to 17	20.5	20.5	20.5
Aged 18 to 64	13.7	15.3	12.0
Aged 18 to 24	21.9	25.2	18.8
Aged 25 to 34	15.2	18.0	12.5
Aged 35 to 44	12.6	14.1	11.1
Aged 45 to 54	10.6	11.5	9.6
Aged 55 to 59	10.1	10.6	9.5
Aged 60 to 64	10.1	10.8	9.3
Aged 65 or older	9.0	10.7	6.7
Aged 65 to 74	8.1	9.5	6.5
Aged 75 or older	10.0	12.1	7.0

Source: Bureau of the Census, 2011 Current Population Survey Annual Social and Economic Supplement, Internet site http:// www.census.gov/hhes/www/cpstables/032011/pov/toc.htm; calculations by New Strategist

Table 6.47 People below Poverty Level by Age and Sex, 2010: Asians

(number and percent of Asians below poverty level by age and sex, 2010; numbers in thousands)

	total	females	males
Total Asians in poverty	**1,859**	**1,010**	**850**
Under age 18	547	259	288
Under age 5	188	79	108
Aged 5 to 17	360	180	179
Aged 18 to 64	1,100	624	476
Aged 18 to 24	296	162	134
Aged 25 to 34	255	148	107
Aged 35 to 44	223	134	89
Aged 45 to 54	181	92	89
Aged 55 to 59	89	53	36
Aged 60 to 64	56	34	22
Aged 65 or older	213	126	86
Aged 65 to 74	117	68	49
Aged 75 or older	96	59	37
PERCENT IN POVERTY			
Total Asians	**11.9%**	**12.3%**	**11.4%**
Under age 18	13.6	12.7	14.6
Under age 5	15.1	12.3	18.2
Aged 5 to 17	13.0	13.0	13.0
Aged 18 to 64	10.8	11.7	9.8
Aged 18 to 24	19.8	22.7	17.1
Aged 25 to 34	10.2	11.4	8.8
Aged 35 to 44	8.8	10.0	7.4
Aged 45 to 54	8.7	8.4	9.0
Aged 55 to 59	10.2	11.0	9.3
Aged 60 to 64	8.0	8.9	6.9
Aged 65 or older	14.4	14.9	13.7
Aged 65 to 74	13.0	13.3	12.6
Aged 75 or older	16.4	17.1	15.5

Note: Asians are those who identify themselves as being of the race alone and those who identify themselves as being of the race in combination with other races.
Source: Bureau of the Census, 2011 Current Population Survey Annual Social and Economic Supplement, Internet site http:// www.census.gov/hhes/www/cpstables/032011/pov/toc.htm; calculations by New Strategist

Table 6.48 People below Poverty Level by Age and Sex, 2010: Blacks

(number and percent of blacks below poverty level by age and sex, 2010; numbers in thousands)

	total	females	males
Total blacks in poverty	**11,361**	**6,385**	**4,975**
Under age 18	4,817	2,340	2,476
Under age 5	1,689	785	904
Aged 5 to 17	3,127	1,555	1,572
Aged 18 to 64	5,908	3,603	2,305
Aged 18 to 24	1,514	877	636
Aged 25 to 34	1,485	974	512
Aged 35 to 44	1,032	671	361
Aged 45 to 54	1,039	611	428
Aged 55 to 59	445	237	208
Aged 60 to 64	393	233	160
Aged 65 or older	636	442	194
Aged 65 to 74	337	212	125
Aged 75 or older	299	230	68
PERCENT IN POVERTY			
Total blacks	**27.4%**	**29.0%**	**25.6%**
Under age 18	38.2	37.6	38.7
Under age 5	44.5	42.4	46.5
Aged 5 to 17	35.4	35.5	35.3
Aged 18 to 64	23.3	26.3	19.7
Aged 18 to 24	31.9	35.8	27.7
Aged 25 to 34	25.1	31.1	18.4
Aged 35 to 44	19.8	23.3	15.4
Aged 45 to 54	19.0	20.3	17.4
Aged 55 to 59	20.5	20.4	20.5
Aged 60 to 64	21.2	22.0	20.0
Aged 65 or older	18.2	20.8	14.2
Aged 65 to 74	16.4	17.6	14.6
Aged 75 or older	20.7	24.8	13.4

Note: Blacks are those who identify themselves as being of the race alone and those who identify themselves as being of the race in combination with other races.
Source: Bureau of the Census, 2011 Current Population Survey Annual Social and Economic Supplement, Internet site http://www.census.gov/hhes/www/cpstables/032011/pov/toc.htm; calculations by New Strategist

Table 6.49 People below Poverty Level by Age and Sex, 2010: Hispanics

(number and percent of Hispanics below poverty level by age and sex, 2010; numbers in thousands)

	total	females	males
Total Hispanics in poverty	**13,243**	**6,824**	**6,420**
Under age 18	6,110	2,892	3,218
Under age 5	2,070	992	1,078
Aged 5 to 17	4,040	1,900	2,140
Aged 18 to 64	6,619	3,592	3,027
Aged 18 to 24	1,547	854	693
Aged 25 to 34	1,917	1,065	852
Aged 35 to 44	1,618	853	765
Aged 45 to 54	968	500	468
Aged 55 to 59	308	161	147
Aged 60 to 64	261	158	103
Aged 65 or older	514	340	174
Aged 65 to 74	296	193	103
Aged 75 or older	218	147	71
PERCENT IN POVERTY			
Total Hispanics	**26.6%**	**28.2%**	**25.0%**
Under age 18	35.0	34.1	35.9
Under age 5	37.6	36.8	38.4
Aged 5 to 17	33.9	32.9	34.8
Aged 18 to 64	22.4	25.5	19.5
Aged 18 to 24	26.8	32.3	22.2
Aged 25 to 34	23.6	28.7	19.3
Aged 35 to 44	22.9	25.2	20.8
Aged 45 to 54	18.1	18.7	17.4
Aged 55 to 59	17.1	17.7	16.5
Aged 60 to 64	18.0	20.6	15.0
Aged 65 or older	18.0	20.9	14.2
Aged 65 to 74	17.3	19.9	13.9
Aged 75 or older	19.0	22.4	14.5

Source: Bureau of the Census, 2011 Current Population Survey Annual Social and Economic Supplement, Internet site http://www.census.gov/hhes/www/cpstables/032011/pov/toc.htm; calculations by New Strategist

Table 6.50 People below Poverty Level by Age and Sex, 2010: Non-Hispanic Whites

(number and percent of non-Hispanic whites below poverty level by age and sex, 2010; numbers in thousands)

	total	females	males
Total non-Hispanic whites in poverty	**19,599**	**10,858**	**8,741**
Under age 18	5,002	2,470	2,532
Under age 5	1,557	758	799
Aged 5 to 17	3,445	1,712	1,733
Aged 18 to 64	12,481	6,952	5,529
Aged 18 to 24	3,132	1,768	1,363
Aged 25 to 34	2,682	1,511	1,170
Aged 35 to 44	2,129	1,179	949
Aged 45 to 54	2,421	1,359	1,062
Aged 55 to 59	1,095	597	497
Aged 60 to 64	1,024	537	487
Aged 65 or older	2,116	1,436	680
Aged 65 to 74	967	610	357
Aged 75 or older	1,149	826	324
PERCENT IN POVERTY			
Total non-Hispanic whites	**9.9%**	**10.8%**	**9.0%**
Under age 18	12.4	12.5	12.2
Under age 5	14.6	14.6	14.5
Aged 5 to 17	11.6	11.8	11.3
Aged 18 to 64	9.9	11.0	8.8
Aged 18 to 24	17.8	20.3	15.4
Aged 25 to 34	10.8	12.3	9.3
Aged 35 to 44	8.6	9.5	7.7
Aged 45 to 54	7.9	8.8	7.0
Aged 55 to 59	7.6	8.1	7.0
Aged 60 to 64	7.7	8.0	7.4
Aged 65 or older	6.8	8.3	5.0
Aged 65 to 74	5.8	6.9	4.6
Aged 75 or older	7.9	9.7	5.4

Note: Non-Hispanic whites are those who identify themselves as being white alone and not Hispanic.
Source: Bureau of the Census, 2011 Current Population Survey Annual Social and Economic Supplement, Internet site http://www.census.gov/hhes/www/cpstables/032011/pov/toc.htm; calculations by New Strategist

Poverty Rate Varies by Family Status and Age

The largest share of the poor live in female-headed families.

Among the nation's 46 million poor, the 34 percent plurality lives in female-headed families. A smaller 31 percent live in married-couple families, while 27 percent are what the government terms unrelated individuals—people who live alone or with nonrelatives. Only 6 percent of the poor live in male-headed families.

The family status of the poor varies considerably by race and Hispanic origin. Among poor blacks, the 54 percent majority lives in female-headed families. Only 15 percent of poor blacks live in married-couples families. Among Hispanics, in contrast, 43 percent of the poor live in married-couple families and a smaller 35 percent live in female-headed families. Among poor non-Hispanic whites, those living in married-couple families outnumber those in female-headed families—30 versus 25 percent. Among poor Asians, those living in married-couple families greatly outnumber those in female-headed families, 47 to 19 percent.

The family status of poor Americans varies greatly by age as well. Most of the poor under age 55 live in families, while the most of the poor aged 55 or older are unrelated individuals.

■ The poverty rate of all people aged 65 or older is just 9.0 percent, but among unrelated individuals in the age group the poverty rate is fully 16.8 percent.

People who live alone or with nonrelatives account for a large share of the poor

(percent distribution of people living below poverty level by family status, 2010)

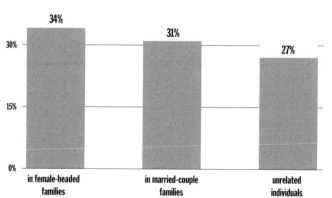

Table 6.51 People below Poverty Level by Age and Family Status, 2010: Total People

(number, percent distribution, and percent of people below poverty level by age and family status, 2010; numbers in thousands)

	total	in families total	married-couple families	female hh, no spouse present	male hh, no spouse present	in unrelated subfamilies	unrelated individuals
Total people in poverty	**46,180**	**33,007**	**14,292**	**15,895**	**2,820**	**751**	**12,422**
Under age 18	16,401	15,796	5,819	8,683	1,294	459	146
Under age 5	5,467	5,313	1,930	2,920	464	154	–
Aged 5 to 17	10,934	10,483	3,890	5,763	830	305	146
Aged 18 to 64	26,258	15,795	7,554	6,796	1,445	287	10,176
Aged 18 to 24	6,507	3,611	1,219	1,994	398	47	2,849
Aged 25 to 34	6,333	4,228	1,968	1,921	339	143	1,963
Aged 35 to 44	5,028	3,485	1,823	1,363	298	76	1,467
Aged 45 to 54	4,662	2,738	1,433	1,034	272	20	1,903
Aged 55 to 59	1,972	896	587	242	67	0	1,076
Aged 60 to 64	1,755	837	523	242	72	0	918
Aged 65 or older	3,520	1,416	919	416	81	5	2,100
Aged 65 to 74	1,737	775	511	225	39	5	957
Aged 75 or older	1,784	641	408	191	42	0	1,143

PERCENT DISTRIBUTION OF PEOPLE IN POVERTY BY FAMILY STATUS

	total	in families total	married-couple families	female hh, no spouse present	male hh, no spouse present	in unrelated subfamilies	unrelated individuals
Total people in poverty	**100.0%**	**71.5%**	**30.9%**	**34.4%**	**6.1%**	**1.6%**	**26.9%**
Under age 18	100.0	96.3	35.5	52.9	7.9	2.8	0.9
Under age 5	100.0	97.2	35.3	53.4	8.5	2.8	–
Aged 5 to 17	100.0	95.9	35.6	52.7	7.6	2.8	1.3
Aged 18 to 64	100.0	60.2	28.8	25.9	5.5	1.1	38.8
Aged 18 to 24	100.0	55.5	18.7	30.6	6.1	0.7	43.8
Aged 25 to 34	100.0	66.8	31.1	30.3	5.4	2.3	31.0
Aged 35 to 44	100.0	69.3	36.3	27.1	5.9	1.5	29.2
Aged 45 to 54	100.0	58.7	30.7	22.2	5.8	0.4	40.8
Aged 55 to 59	100.0	45.4	29.8	12.3	3.4	0.0	54.6
Aged 60 to 64	100.0	47.7	29.8	13.8	4.1	0.0	52.3
Aged 65 or older	100.0	40.2	26.1	11.8	2.3	0.1	59.7
Aged 65 to 74	100.0	44.6	29.4	13.0	2.2	0.3	55.1
Aged 75 or older	100.0	35.9	22.9	10.7	2.4	0.0	64.1

PERCENT IN POVERTY

	total	in families total	married-couple families	female hh, no spouse present	male hh, no spouse present	in unrelated subfamilies	unrelated individuals
Total people	**15.1%**	**13.2%**	**7.6%**	**34.2%**	**17.3%**	**45.5%**	**22.9%**
Under age 18	22.0	21.5	11.6	46.9	28.1	49.8	92.8
Under age 5	25.9	25.4	13.3	58.7	32.2	68.1	–
Aged 5 to 17	20.5	20.0	10.9	42.5	26.2	43.8	92.8
Aged 18 to 64	13.7	10.5	6.6	27.4	13.8	40.2	24.5
Aged 18 to 24	21.9	15.6	8.4	31.8	16.4	58.6	44.4
Aged 25 to 34	15.2	14.0	9.0	32.9	14.2	44.1	17.7
Aged 35 to 44	12.6	10.6	7.1	26.9	15.0	34.6	21.7
Aged 45 to 54	10.6	7.8	5.1	21.0	12.3	–	22.2
Aged 55 to 59	10.1	6.0	4.6	16.3	8.7	–	23.9
Aged 60 to 64	10.1	6.3	4.6	19.4	10.6	–	22.1
Aged 65 or older	9.0	5.3	4.1	13.6	6.7	–	16.8
Aged 65 to 74	8.1	4.9	3.7	15.4	6.3	–	17.1
Aged 75 or older	10.0	5.9	4.7	12.0	7.0	–	16.5

Note: "–" means sample is too small to make a reliable estimate. "hh" stands for householder.
Source: Bureau of the Census, 2011 Current Population Survey Annual Social and Economic Supplement, Internet site http:// www.census.gov/hhes/www/cpstables/032011/pov/toc.htm; calculations by New Strategist

Table 6.52 People below Poverty Level by Age and Family Status, 2010: Asians

(number and percent of Asians below poverty level by age and family status, 2010; numbers in thousands)

	total	in families total	married-couple families	female hh, no spouse present	male hh, no spouse present	in unrelated subfamilies	unrelated individuals
Total Asians in poverty	**1,859**	**1,338**	**878**	**348**	**113**	**20**	**501**
Under age 18	547	529	321	168	40	9	9
Under age 5	188	187	125	58	4	1	–
Aged 5 to 17	360	342	196	110	36	8	9
Aged 18 to 64	1,100	676	455	156	65	11	413
Aged 18 to 24	296	112	61	32	19	0	184
Aged 25 to 34	255	155	114	36	5	6	95
Aged 35 to 44	223	171	120	39	12	3	49
Aged 45 to 54	181	149	97	30	22	2	30
Aged 55 to 59	89	59	44	11	4	0	29
Aged 60 to 64	56	30	20	8	3	0	26
Aged 65 or older	213	134	102	24	8	0	79
Aged 65 to 74	117	78	63	11	4	0	38
Aged 75 or older	96	56	39	12	4	0	40

PERCENT DISTRIBUTION OF ASIANS IN POVERTY BY FAMILY STATUS

Total Asians in poverty	**100.0%**	**72.0%**	**47.2%**	**18.7%**	**6.1%**	**1.1%**	**26.9%**
Under age 18	100.0	96.7	58.7	30.7	7.3	1.6	1.6
Under age 5	100.0	99.5	66.5	30.9	2.1	0.5	–
Aged 5 to 17	100.0	95.0	54.4	30.6	10.0	2.2	2.5
Aged 18 to 64	100.0	61.5	41.4	14.2	5.9	1.0	37.5
Aged 18 to 24	100.0	37.8	20.6	10.8	6.4	0.0	62.2
Aged 25 to 34	100.0	60.8	44.7	14.1	2.0	2.4	37.3
Aged 35 to 44	100.0	76.7	53.8	17.5	5.4	1.3	22.0
Aged 45 to 54	100.0	82.3	53.6	16.6	12.2	1.1	16.6
Aged 55 to 59	100.0	66.3	49.4	12.4	4.5	0.0	32.6
Aged 60 to 64	100.0	53.6	35.7	14.3	5.4	0.0	46.4
Aged 65 or older	100.0	62.9	47.9	11.3	3.8	0.0	37.1
Aged 65 to 74	100.0	66.7	53.8	9.4	3.4	0.0	32.5
Aged 75 or older	100.0	58.3	40.6	12.5	4.2	0.0	41.7

PERCENT IN POVERTY

Total Asians	**11.9%**	**9.8%**	**8.0%**	**21.5%**	**11.1%**	**–**	**25.4%**
Under age 18	13.6	13.3	9.7	32.2	24.9	–	–
Under age 5	15.1	15.1	11.7	46.8	–	–	–
Aged 5 to 17	13.0	12.5	8.8	27.6	32.5	–	–
Aged 18 to 64	10.8	8.0	6.7	16.5	8.7	–	24.3
Aged 18 to 24	19.8	9.8	7.7	17.0	12.0	–	51.5
Aged 25 to 34	10.2	8.1	7.6	14.6	2.9	–	16.0
Aged 35 to 44	8.8	7.8	6.5	20.2	8.2	–	15.4
Aged 45 to 54	8.7	8.0	6.3	15.1	15.5	–	13.9
Aged 55 to 59	10.2	7.9	7.2	–	5.4	–	26.4
Aged 60 to 64	8.0	5.0	4.0	–	–	–	25.0
Aged 65 or older	14.4	11.1	10.7	16.3	7.4	–	29.6
Aged 65 to 74	13.0	10.4	10.0	–	–	–	27.3
Aged 75 or older	16.4	12.2	12.0	15.6	–	–	32.2

Note: Asians are those who identify themselves as being of the race alone and those who identify themselves as being of the race in combination with other races. "–" means sample is too small to make a reliable estimate. "hh" stands for householder.
Source: Bureau of the Census, 2011 Current Population Survey Annual Social and Economic Supplement, Internet site http:// www.census.gov/hhes/www/cpstables/032011/pov/toc.htm; calculations by New Strategist

Table 6.53 People below Poverty Level by Age and Family Status, 2010: Blacks

(number, percent distribution, and percent of blacks below poverty level by age and family status, 2010; numbers in thousands)

| | | in families | | | | | |
	total	total	married-couple families	female hh, no spouse present	male hh, no spouse present	in unrelated subfamilies	unrelated individuals
Total blacks in poverty	**11,361**	**8,711**	**1,715**	**6,186**	**810**	**105**	**2,544**
Under age 18	4,817	4,733	759	3,579	395	68	16
Under age 5	1,689	1,662	272	1,250	141	27	–
Aged 5 to 17	3,127	3,071	487	2,329	254	41	16
Aged 18 to 64	5,908	3,739	869	2,477	392	36	2,133
Aged 18 to 24	1,514	1,049	166	782	101	4	461
Aged 25 to 34	1,485	1,038	187	764	88	22	425
Aged 35 to 44	1,032	729	227	422	80	6	297
Aged 45 to 54	1,039	596	158	352	85	4	439
Aged 55 to 59	445	167	65	76	26	0	279
Aged 60 to 64	393	161	67	82	12	0	232
Aged 65 or older	636	239	86	130	23	1	395
Aged 65 to 74	337	137	58	68	10	1	199
Aged 75 or older	299	102	28	62	12	0	196
PERCENT DISTRIBUTION OF BLACKS IN POVERTY BY FAMILY STATUS							
Total blacks in poverty	**100.0%**	**76.7%**	**15.1%**	**54.4%**	**7.1%**	**0.9%**	**22.4%**
Under age 18	100.0	98.3	15.8	74.3	8.2	1.4	0.3
Under age 5	100.0	98.4	16.1	74.0	8.3	1.6	–
Aged 5 to 17	100.0	98.2	15.6	74.5	8.1	1.3	0.5
Aged 18 to 64	100.0	63.3	14.7	41.9	6.6	0.6	36.1
Aged 18 to 24	100.0	69.3	11.0	51.7	6.7	0.3	30.4
Aged 25 to 34	100.0	69.9	12.6	51.4	5.9	1.5	28.6
Aged 35 to 44	100.0	70.6	22.0	40.9	7.8	0.6	28.8
Aged 45 to 54	100.0	57.4	15.2	33.9	8.2	0.4	42.3
Aged 55 to 59	100.0	37.5	14.6	17.1	5.8	0.0	62.7
Aged 60 to 64	100.0	41.0	17.0	20.9	3.1	0.0	59.0
Aged 65 or older	100.0	37.6	13.5	20.4	3.6	0.2	62.1
Aged 65 to 74	100.0	40.7	17.2	20.2	3.0	0.3	59.1
Aged 75 or older	100.0	34.1	9.4	20.7	4.0	0.0	65.6
PERCENT IN POVERTY							
Total blacks	**27.4%**	**25.9%**	**10.9%**	**40.9%**	**29.0%**	**37.1%**	**33.4%**
Under age 18	38.2	38.1	16.0	52.5	45.1	40.1	–
Under age 5	44.5	44.4	19.0	62.1	46.5	–	–
Aged 5 to 17	35.4	35.3	14.7	48.5	44.4	33.7	–
Aged 18 to 64	23.3	19.7	9.1	32.4	22.6	31.9	33.8
Aged 18 to 24	31.9	27.3	12.2	37.1	27.2	–	51.8
Aged 25 to 34	25.1	24.0	9.7	38.2	21.2	–	27.9
Aged 35 to 44	19.8	17.8	10.1	28.6	21.3	–	26.8
Aged 45 to 54	19.0	14.9	6.9	25.8	24.1	–	30.6
Aged 55 to 59	20.5	11.5	7.0	19.2	20.7	–	38.7
Aged 60 to 64	21.2	13.2	8.1	27.9	12.3	–	36.5
Aged 65 or older	18.2	10.7	6.3	19.0	12.4	–	31.1
Aged 65 to 74	16.4	10.1	6.4	20.2	10.6	–	28.2
Aged 75 or older	20.7	11.7	6.3	17.9	14.5	–	34.7

Note: Blacks are those who identify themselves as being of the race alone and those who identify themselves as being of the race in combination with other races. "–" means sample is too small to make a reliable estimate. "hh" stands for householder.
Source: Bureau of the Census, 2011 Current Population Survey Annual Social and Economic Supplement, Internet site http://www.census.gov/hhes/www/cpstables/032011/pov/toc.htm; calculations by New Strategist

Table 6.54 People below Poverty Level by Age and Family Status, 2010: Hispanics

(number, percent distribution, and percent of Hispanics below poverty level by age and family status, 2010; numbers in thousands)

		in families					
	total	total	married-couple families	female hh, no spouse present	male hh, no spouse present	in unrelated subfamilies	unrelated individuals
Total Hispanics in poverty	**13,243**	**11,188**	**5,654**	**4,643**	**891**	**249**	**1,806**
Under age 18	6,110	5,917	2,763	2,734	420	161	32
Under age 5	2,070	2,005	898	927	180	65	–
Aged 5 to 17	4,040	3,911	1,865	1,807	239	96	32
Aged 18 to 64	6,619	5,004	2,741	1,813	449	88	1,527
Aged 18 to 24	1,547	1,142	479	536	126	21	384
Aged 25 to 34	1,917	1,476	876	488	112	44	398
Aged 35 to 44	1,618	1,292	775	412	105	18	309
Aged 45 to 54	968	724	404	248	71	6	239
Aged 55 to 59	308	218	124	71	22	0	90
Aged 60 to 64	261	153	83	57	13	0	108
Aged 65 or older	514	268	151	95	22	0	246
Aged 65 to 74	296	171	101	64	7	0	125
Aged 75 or older	218	96	50	32	15	0	122
PERCENT DISTRIBUTION OF HISPANICS IN POVERTY BY FAMILY STATUS							
Total Hispanics in poverty	**100.0%**	**84.5%**	**42.7%**	**35.1%**	**6.7%**	**1.9%**	**13.6%**
Under age 18	100.0	96.8	45.2	44.7	6.9	2.6	0.5
Under age 5	100.0	96.9	43.4	44.8	8.7	3.1	–
Aged 5 to 17	100.0	96.8	46.2	44.7	5.9	2.4	0.8
Aged 18 to 64	100.0	75.6	41.4	27.4	6.8	1.3	23.1
Aged 18 to 24	100.0	73.8	31.0	34.6	8.1	1.4	24.8
Aged 25 to 34	100.0	77.0	45.7	25.5	5.8	2.3	20.8
Aged 35 to 44	100.0	79.9	47.9	25.5	6.5	1.1	19.1
Aged 45 to 54	100.0	74.8	41.7	25.6	7.3	0.6	24.7
Aged 55 to 59	100.0	70.8	40.3	23.1	7.1	0.0	29.2
Aged 60 to 64	100.0	58.6	31.8	21.8	5.0	0.0	41.4
Aged 65 or older	100.0	52.1	29.4	18.5	4.3	0.0	47.9
Aged 65 to 74	100.0	57.8	34.1	21.6	2.4	0.0	42.2
Aged 75 or older	100.0	44.0	22.9	14.7	6.9	0.0	56.0
PERCENT IN POVERTY							
Total Hispanics	**26.6%**	**25.6%**	**19.5%**	**44.5%**	**21.1%**	**52.5%**	**31.8%**
Under age 18	35.0	34.6	25.1	57.0	31.5	59.1	–
Under age 5	37.6	37.1	25.9	64.7	35.4	70.5	–
Aged 5 to 17	33.9	33.4	24.8	53.8	29.0	53.4	–
Aged 18 to 64	22.4	20.5	16.5	35.1	16.7	43.7	31.0
Aged 18 to 24	26.8	23.4	17.1	38.4	18.9	–	44.8
Aged 25 to 34	23.6	22.9	20.1	36.4	15.0	48.7	24.8
Aged 35 to 44	22.9	21.7	18.0	37.7	19.3	–	29.0
Aged 45 to 54	18.1	16.0	12.6	28.3	15.8	–	29.6
Aged 55 to 59	17.1	14.7	11.7	28.2	13.3	–	28.4
Aged 60 to 64	18.0	13.1	9.7	27.4	11.9	–	38.1
Aged 65 or older	18.0	12.4	10.2	20.3	10.6	–	35.2
Aged 65 to 74	17.3	13.0	10.7	24.3	6.4	–	31.6
Aged 75 or older	19.0	11.4	9.3	15.3	15.4	–	39.8

Note: "–" means sample is too small to make a reliable estimate. "hh" stands for householder.
Source: Bureau of the Census, 2011 Current Population Survey Annual Social and Economic Supplement, Internet site http://www.census.gov/hhes/www/cpstables/032011/pov/toc.htm; calculations by New Strategist

Table 6.55 People below Poverty Level by Age and Family Status, 2010: Non-Hispanic Whites

(number, percent distribution, and percent of non-Hispanic whites below poverty level by age and family status, 2010; numbers in thousands)

		in families					
	total	total	married-couple families	female hh, no spouse present	male hh, no spouse present	in unrelated subfamilies	unrelated individuals
Total non-Hispanic whites in poverty	**19,599**	**11,740**	**5,965**	**4,802**	**973**	**400**	**7,460**
Under age 18	5,002	4,684	1,983	2,275	426	233	85
Under age 5	1,557	1,492	642	710	140	65	–
Aged 5 to 17	3,445	3,192	1,342	1,565	286	168	85
Aged 18 to 64	12,481	6,301	3,420	2,361	520	163	6,017
Aged 18 to 24	3,132	1,316	505	658	153	24	1,792
Aged 25 to 34	2,682	1,539	801	614	124	78	1,064
Aged 35 to 44	2,129	1,277	681	501	95	50	802
Aged 45 to 54	2,421	1,256	746	410	99	10	1,155
Aged 55 to 59	1,095	436	339	83	14	0	659
Aged 60 to 64	1,024	478	348	96	34	0	546
Aged 65 or older	2,116	755	561	165	28	3	1,358
Aged 65 to 74	967	376	277	82	17	3	588
Aged 75 or older	1,149	379	284	84	11	0	770

PERCENT DISTRIBUTION OF NON-HISPANIC WHITES IN POVERTY BY FAMILY STATUS

Total non-Hispanic whites in poverty	**100.0%**	**59.9%**	**30.4%**	**24.5%**	**5.0%**	**2.0%**	**38.1%**
Under age 18	100.0	93.6	39.6	45.5	8.5	4.7	1.7
Under age 5	100.0	95.8	41.2	45.6	9.0	4.2	–
Aged 5 to 17	100.0	92.7	39.0	45.4	8.3	4.9	2.5
Aged 18 to 64	100.0	50.5	27.4	18.9	4.2	1.3	48.2
Aged 18 to 24	100.0	42.0	16.1	21.0	4.9	0.8	57.2
Aged 25 to 34	100.0	57.4	29.9	22.9	4.6	2.9	39.7
Aged 35 to 44	100.0	60.0	32.0	23.5	4.5	2.3	37.7
Aged 45 to 54	100.0	51.9	30.8	16.9	4.1	0.4	47.7
Aged 55 to 59	100.0	39.8	31.0	7.6	1.3	0.0	60.2
Aged 60 to 64	100.0	46.7	34.0	9.4	3.3	0.0	53.3
Aged 65 or older	100.0	35.7	26.5	7.8	1.3	0.1	64.2
Aged 65 to 74	100.0	38.9	28.6	8.5	1.8	0.3	60.8
Aged 75 or older	100.0	33.0	24.7	7.3	1.0	0.0	67.0

PERCENT IN POVERTY

Total non-Hispanic whites	**9.9%**	**7.4%**	**4.6%**	**24.8%**	**11.9%**	**46.1%**	**19.3%**
Under age 18	12.4	11.7	6.4	34.8	19.1	48.8	96.9
Under age 5	14.6	14.1	7.5	49.1	23.9	70.2	–
Aged 5 to 17	11.6	10.9	5.9	30.7	17.3	43.7	96.9
Aged 18 to 64	9.9	6.5	4.2	21.4	10.0	42.7	21.3
Aged 18 to 24	17.8	9.9	5.4	25.1	12.6	–	41.8
Aged 25 to 34	10.8	8.9	5.7	27.6	11.8	45.3	14.6
Aged 35 to 44	8.6	6.3	4.0	21.8	10.5	40.4	18.8
Aged 45 to 54	7.9	5.1	3.6	16.6	7.9	–	19.2
Aged 55 to 59	7.6	3.9	3.4	11.1	3.5	–	20.0
Aged 60 to 64	7.7	4.7	3.8	14.1	8.6	–	17.6
Aged 65 or older	6.8	3.6	3.1	9.5	4.0	–	13.3
Aged 65 to 74	5.8	3.1	2.5	10.4	5.1	–	13.5
Aged 75 or older	7.9	4.4	3.9	8.7	3.0	–	13.1

Note: Non-Hispanic whites are those who identify themselves as being of the race alone and not Hispanic. "–" means sample is too small to make a reliable estimate. "hh" stands for householder.
Source: Bureau of the Census, 2011 Current Population Survey Annual Social and Economic Supplement, Internet site http:// www.census.gov/hhes/www/cpstables/032011/pov/toc.htm; calculations by New Strategist

Few College Graduates Are Poor

High school dropouts account for a large share of the poor.

In 2010, only 4.3 percent of the nation's college graduates had incomes that placed them below the poverty level. In contrast, 29.2 percent of high school dropouts were poor. Among the 23 million poor Americans aged 25 or older, fully 31 percent were high school dropouts.

A college degree almost guarantees a life free of poverty—regardless of race or Hispanic origin. The proportion of college graduates who are poor ranges from 3.6 percent among non-Hispanic whites to about 7.9 percent among Hispanics.

The story is different for high school dropouts. Among blacks without a high school diploma, 39.2 percent are poor. The poverty rate among Hispanic high school dropouts stands at 32.3 percent. Among poor Hispanics, the 55 percent majority does not have a high-school diploma.

■ If the educational attainment of Hispanics climbs, their poverty rate should fall.

Poverty rate declines as education increases

(percent of people aged 25 or older below the poverty level, by education, 2010)

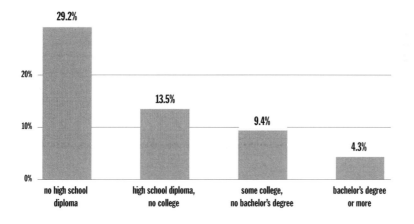

Table 6.56 People below Poverty Level by Education, Race, and Hispanic Origin, 2010

(number and percent of people aged 25 or older below poverty level by educational attainment, race, and Hispanic origin, 2010; numbers in thousands)

	total	Asian	black	Hispanic	non-Hispanic white
Number in poverty	**23,271**	**1,016**	**5,030**	**5,587**	**11,466**
No high school diploma	7,311	281	1,459	3,075	2,477
High school diploma, no college	8,338	328	2,068	1,565	4,319
Some college, no bachelor's degree	4,997	162	1,141	650	2,962
Bachelor's degree or more	2,626	245	363	296	1,708
PERCENT DISTRIBUTION OF PEOPLE IN POVERTY BY EDUCATION					
Total people in poverty	**100.0%**	**100.0%**	**100.0%**	**100.0%**	**100.0%**
No high school diploma	31.4	27.7	29.0	55.0	21.6
High school diploma, no college	35.8	32.3	41.1	28.0	37.7
Some college, no bachelor's degree	21.5	15.9	22.7	11.6	25.8
Bachelor's degree or more	11.3	24.1	7.2	5.3	14.9
PERCENT IN POVERTY					
Total people	**11.5%**	**11.9%**	**20.8%**	**20.9%**	**8.2%**
No high school diploma	29.2	24.8	39.2	32.3	23.4
High school diploma, no college	13.5	14.9	24.8	19.7	10.1
Some college, no bachelor's degree	9.4	9.2	15.8	11.9	7.7
Bachelor's degree or more	4.3	4.8	7.5	7.9	3.6

Note: Asians and blacks include those who identify themselves as being of the race alone and those who identify themselves as being of the race in combination with other races. Non-Hispanic whites are those who identify themselves as white alone and not Hispanic. Numbers do not add to total because not all races are shown and Hispanics may be of any race.
Source: Bureau of the Census, 2011 Current Population Survey Annual Social and Economic Supplement, Internet site http://www.census.gov/hhes/www/cpstables/032011/pov/toc.htm; calculations by New Strategist

Many Young Adult Workers Are Poor

Among 18-to-24-year-olds with jobs, one in seven is poor.

While poverty rates are relatively low for people with jobs, a substantial number of workers are poor despite getting a paycheck. Among all workers aged 16 or older, 7.0 percent had incomes that placed them below poverty level in 2010. The poverty rate among workers is highest in the young-adult age group: 14.9 percent of 18-to-24-year-old workers are poor. Even among young adults who work full-time, 6.2 percent are poor. Many young adults make minimum wage in entry-level jobs.

Among black workers, a substantial 11.7 percent were poor in 2010, including 4.2 percent of those with full-time jobs. Among employed blacks aged 18 to 24, fully 22.5 percent live in poverty. A substantial 10.8 percent of those with full-time jobs were poor.

The poverty rate among Hispanic workers is even higher than the rate among blacks. Fourteen percent of Hispanic workers live in poverty, including 7.0 percent of those with full-time jobs. Among non-Hispanic white workers with full-time jobs, only 1.6 percent are poor.

■ The poverty rate is lower for non-Hispanic white workers than for black workers because the white workers are more likely to live in households with two or more earners.

Among black and Hispanic workers, more than 1 in 10 are poor

(percent of workers aged 16 or older below poverty level, by race and Hispanic origin, 2010)

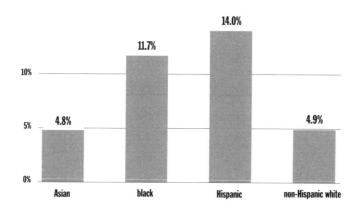

Table 6.57 Number and Percent of Workers below Poverty Level by Sex, Age, and Work Status, 2010: Total Workers

(number and percent of workers aged 16 or older below poverty level by sex, age, and work status, 2010; numbers in thousands)

	total workers		full-time, year-round workers	
	number	percent	number	percent
Total workers in poverty	**10,666**	**7.0%**	**2,608**	**2.6%**
Aged 16 to 17	115	7.5	11	–
Aged 18 to 64	10,392	7.2	2,569	2.7
Aged 18 to 24	2,755	14.9	378	6.2
Aged 25 to 34	3,005	9.0	749	3.3
Aged 35 to 54	3,823	5.7	1,264	2.5
Aged 55 to 64	809	3.3	179	1.0
Aged 65 or older	159	2.0	28	0.8
Male workers in poverty	**5,087**	**6.3**	**1,419**	**2.5**
Aged 16 to 17	43	5.7	3	–
Aged 18 to 64	4,961	6.5	1,399	2.6
Aged 18 to 24	1,176	12.3	159	4.6
Aged 25 to 34	1,493	8.3	407	3.1
Aged 35 to 54	1,918	5.4	734	2.6
Aged 55 to 64	374	2.9	99	1.0
Aged 65 or older	82	1.9	17	0.8
Female workers in poverty	**5,579**	**7.7**	**1,189**	**2.8**
Aged 16 to 17	72	9.2	8	–
Aged 18 to 64	5,430	8.0	1,169	2.8
Aged 18 to 24	1,579	17.8	218	8.4
Aged 25 to 34	1,511	9.9	341	3.6
Aged 35 to 54	1,905	6.0	530	2.5
Aged 55 to 64	435	3.7	80	1.0
Aged 65 or older	76	2.1	12	0.8

Note: "–" means sample is too small to make a reliable estimate.
Source: Bureau of the Census, 2011 Current Population Survey Annual Social and Economic Supplement, Internet site http://www.census.gov/hhes/www/cpstables/032011/pov/toc.htm; calculations by New Strategist

Table 6.58 Number and Percent of Workers below Poverty Level by Sex, Age, and Work Status, 2010: Asian Workers

(number and percent of Asian workers aged 16 or older below poverty level by sex, age, and work status, 2010; numbers in thousands)

	total workers		full-time, year-round workers	
	number	percent	number	percent
Total Asian workers in poverty	**375**	**4.8%**	**111**	**2.1%**
Aged 16 to 17	2	–	0	–
Aged 18 to 64	371	5.0	111	2.1
Aged 18 to 24	67	9.2	9	3.9
Aged 25 to 34	103	5.5	29	2.2
Aged 35 to 54	159	4.2	63	2.2
Aged 55 to 64	42	3.9	10	1.3
Aged 65 or older	2	0.7	0	0.1
Asian male workers in poverty	**169**	**4.2**	**69**	**2.2**
Aged 16 to 17	1	–	0	–
Aged 18 to 64	166	4.3	68	2.3
Aged 18 to 24	24	6.0	2	1.6
Aged 25 to 34	51	5.0	21	2.7
Aged 35 to 54	74	3.8	38	2.3
Aged 55 to 64	18	3.3	7	1.7
Aged 65 or older	1	0.8	0	0.2
Asian female workers in poverty	**206**	**5.6**	**43**	**1.8**
Aged 16 to 17	1	–	0	–
Aged 18 to 64	205	5.8	43	1.9
Aged 18 to 24	43	12.9	7	7.1
Aged 25 to 34	52	6.0	8	1.4
Aged 35 to 54	85	4.7	25	2.0
Aged 55 to 64	25	4.6	3	0.8
Aged 65 or older	1	0.6	0	–

Note: Asians are those who identify themselves as being of the race alone and those who identify themselves as being of the race in combination with other races. "–" means sample is too small to make a reliable estimate.
Source: Bureau of the Census, 2011 Current Population Survey Annual Social and Economic Supplement, Internet site http://www.census.gov/hhes/www/cpstables/032011/pov/toc.htm; calculations by New Strategist

Table 6.59 **Number and Percent of Workers below Poverty Level by Sex, Age, and Work Status, 2010: Black Workers**

(number and percent of black workers aged 16 or older below poverty level by sex, age, and work status, 2010; numbers in thousands)

	total workers		full-time, year-round workers	
	number	percent	number	percent
Total black workers in poverty	**2,065**	**11.7%**	**477**	**4.2%**
Aged 16 to 17	14	8.7	4	–
Aged 18 to 64	2,014	11.9	465	4.2
Aged 18 to 24	551	22.5	90	10.8
Aged 25 to 34	642	14.8	145	5.2
Aged 35 to 54	660	8.4	187	3.2
Aged 55 to 64	161	7.1	42	2.6
Aged 65 or older	37	6.0	8	2.6
Black male workers in poverty	**736**	**9.0**	**152**	**2.8**
Aged 16 to 17	1	–	0	–
Aged 18 to 64	714	9.2	148	2.8
Aged 18 to 24	198	16.8	22	5.6
Aged 25 to 34	204	10.0	39	2.9
Aged 35 to 54	233	6.5	66	2.4
Aged 55 to 64	78	7.8	21	2.9
Aged 65 or older	22	7.5	4	2.6
Black female workers in poverty	**1,329**	**13.9**	**325**	**5.4**
Aged 16 to 17	13	15.4	4	–
Aged 18 to 64	1,301	14.3	316	5.4
Aged 18 to 24	353	27.7	68	15.5
Aged 25 to 34	438	19.1	106	7.4
Aged 35 to 54	427	10.0	122	3.9
Aged 55 to 64	83	6.5	21	2.3
Aged 65 or older	16	4.6	4	2.6

Note: Blacks are those who identify themselves as being of the race alone and those who identify themselves as being of the race in combination with other races. "–" means sample is too small to make a reliable estimate.
Source: Bureau of the Census, 2011 Current Population Survey Annual Social and Economic Supplement, Internet site http:// www.census.gov/hhes/www/cpstables/032011/pov/toc.htm; calculations by New Strategist

Table 6.60 Number and Percent of Workers below Poverty Level by Sex, Age, and Work Status, 2010: Hispanic Workers

(number and percent of Hispanic workers aged 16 or older below poverty level by sex, age, and work status, 2010; numbers in thousands)

	total workers		full-time, year-round workers	
	number	percent	number	percent
Total Hispanic workers in poverty	**3,056**	**14.0%**	**942**	**7.0%**
Aged 16 to 17	36	20.0	4	–
Aged 18 to 64	2,988	14.2	933	7.1
Aged 18 to 24	581	17.5	86	6.8
Aged 25 to 34	970	15.6	318	7.9
Aged 35 to 54	1,289	13.6	489	7.4
Aged 55 to 64	148	7.7	40	3.0
Aged 65 or older	32	5.5	5	1.6
Hispanic male workers in poverty	**1,781**	**14.0**	**635**	**7.6**
Aged 16 to 17	20	24.2	3	–
Aged 18 to 64	1,741	14.1	628	7.7
Aged 18 to 24	275	14.2	52	6.0
Aged 25 to 34	618	16.0	218	8.4
Aged 35 to 54	785	14.3	333	8.4
Aged 55 to 64	63	6.0	26	3.3
Aged 65 or older	20	6.0	3	2.0
Hispanic female workers in poverty	**1,275**	**14.1**	**308**	**6.0**
Aged 16 to 17	16	16.3	1	–
Aged 18 to 64	1,247	14.4	305	6.1
Aged 18 to 24	305	21.9	35	8.3
Aged 25 to 34	352	14.9	100	7.0
Aged 35 to 54	504	12.5	156	5.9
Aged 55 to 64	85	9.7	15	2.6
Aged 65 or older	13	4.7	2	1.2

Note: "–" means sample is too small to make a reliable estimate.
Source: Bureau of the Census, 2011 Current Population Survey Annual Social and Economic Supplement, Internet site http://www.census.gov/hhes/www/cpstables/032011/pov/toc.htm; calculations by New Strategist

Table 6.61 Number and Percent of Workers below Poverty Level by Sex, Age, and Work Status, 2010: Non-Hispanic White Workers

(number and percent of non-Hispanic white workers aged 16 or older below poverty level by sex, age, and work status, 2010; numbers in thousands)

	total workers		full-time, year-round workers	
	number	percent	number	percent
Total non-Hispanic white workers in poverty	**5,151**	**4.9%**	**1,090**	**1.6%**
Aged 16 to 17	62	5.2	3	–
Aged 18 to 64	5,005	5.1	1,075	1.6
Aged 18 to 24	1,550	13.0	195	5.2
Aged 25 to 34	1,297	6.2	267	1.9
Aged 35 to 54	1,702	3.7	526	1.5
Aged 55 to 64	456	2.4	87	0.7
Aged 65 or older	84	1.3	13	0.5
Non-Hispanic white male workers in poverty	**2,417**	**4.3**	**581**	**1.5**
Aged 16 to 17	20	3.4	0	–
Aged 18 to 64	2,358	4.6	573	1.5
Aged 18 to 24	679	11.2	89	4.2
Aged 25 to 34	644	5.8	139	1.7
Aged 35 to 54	819	3.4	298	1.5
Aged 55 to 64	217	2.1	47	0.6
Aged 65 or older	39	1.1	8	0.4
Non-Hispanic white female workers in poverty	**2,734**	**5.5**	**509**	**1.8**
Aged 16 to 17	42	7.1	3	–
Aged 18 to 64	2,647	5.8	501	1.8
Aged 18 to 24	871	15.0	106	6.4
Aged 25 to 34	654	6.8	128	2.1
Aged 35 to 54	883	4.1	227	1.6
Aged 55 to 64	239	2.7	40	0.7
Aged 65 or older	45	1.6	5	0.5

Note: Non-Hispanic whites are those who identify themselves as being white alone and not Hispanic. "–" means sample is too small to make a reliable estimate.
Source: Bureau of the Census, 2011 Current Population Survey Annual Social and Economic Supplement, Internet site http://www.census.gov/hhes/www/cpstables/032011/pov/toc.htm; calculations by New Strategist

More than One-Fourth of the Nonworking Poor Are Ill or Disabled

A large share of the nonworking poor are retired, and many say they are caring for home and family.

Among the 21 million poor people aged 16 or older who were not in the labor force at any time in 2010, illness or disability was one of the most important reasons cited for not working. Twenty-six percent gave this reason, including about half of those aged 55 to 64.

Eighteen percent of the nonworking poor did not work because they are retired, including 78 percent of men aged 65 or older. Another 20 percent of the nonworking poor cited caring for home and family as the reason they did not work in 2010. Among poor women aged 25 to 34 who were not working, 56 percent gave family reasons.

Surprisingly few of the nonworking poor said they did not work in 2010 because they could not get a job—only 18 percent of poor men and 8 percent of poor women gave this as a reason. Among poor men aged 25 to 34, however, a substantial 30 percent say they did not work because they could not find a job.

■ As the population ages, illness and disability may become an even more important reason for keeping the poor out of the labor force.

Many of the poor are too sick to work

(percent distribution of poor people aged 16 or older who did not work, by reason for not working, 2010)

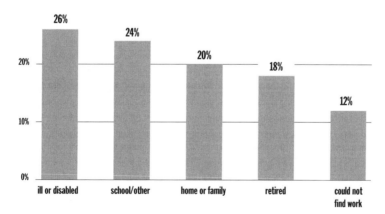

Table 6.62 People below Poverty Level by Reason for Not Working, 2010

(number of people aged 16 or older below poverty level who did not work and percent distribution by reason for not working, by sex and age, 2008; numbers in thousands)

| | did not work at all in 2010 | | | | | | |
| | total | | ill or disabled | retired | home or family | could not find work | school/other |
	number	percent					
Total people in poverty who did not work	**20,717**	**100.0%**	**25.7%**	**18.4%**	**20.3%**	**11.8%**	**23.8%**
Aged 16 to 17	1,488	100.0	1.8	0.6	3.2	1.7	92.7
Aged 18 to 64	15,867	100.0	29.9	7.5	25.5	15.0	22.1
Aged 18 to 24	3,752	100.0	6.8	0.6	20.9	13.8	57.9
Aged 25 to 34	3,329	100.0	18.6	2.0	40.9	17.1	21.4
Aged 35 to 54	5,867	100.0	40.9	5.0	27.1	17.9	9.1
Aged 55 to 64	2,919	100.0	50.2	27.5	10.7	8.5	3.2
Aged 65 or older	3,362	100.0	16.9	77.6	3.2	1.3	0.9
Total men in poverty who did not work	**8,263**	**100.0**	**29.0**	**16.5**	**6.2**	**17.7**	**30.6**
Aged 16 to 17	748	100.0	2.0	0.8	1.5	1.2	94.4
Aged 18 to 64	6,445	100.0	34.0	8.1	7.7	22.1	28.1
Aged 18 to 24	1,655	100.0	8.3	0.7	5.6	17.5	67.9
Aged 25 to 34	1,135	100.0	27.3	2.1	11.5	30.0	29.1
Aged 35 to 54	2,340	100.0	45.4	5.4	9.1	27.2	12.9
Aged 55 to 64	1,315	100.0	51.6	27.3	4.6	12.2	4.3
Aged 65 or older	1,070	100.0	17.6	78.3	0.6	2.1	1.4
Total women in poverty who did not work	**12,454**	**100.0**	**23.6**	**19.6**	**29.7**	**8.0**	**19.2**
Aged 16 to 17	740	100.0	1.5	0.4	5.0	2.2	90.9
Aged 18 to 64	9,422	100.0	27.1	7.0	37.7	10.1	18.0
Aged 18 to 24	2,097	100.0	5.6	0.5	33.0	11.0	50.0
Aged 25 to 34	2,193	100.0	14.0	2.0	56.2	10.4	17.5
Aged 35 to 54	3,528	100.0	38.0	4.7	39.1	11.7	6.6
Aged 55 to 64	1,604	100.0	48.9	27.7	15.8	5.4	2.2
Aged 65 or older	2,292	100.0	16.6	77.2	4.5	0.9	0.7

Source: Bureau of the Census, 2011 Current Population Survey Annual Social and Economic Supplement, Internet site http://www.census.gov/hhes/www/cpstables/032011/pov/toc.htm; calculations by New Strategist

Poverty Is Highest in the South

Poverty rate is lowest in the Northeast.

With 16.9 percent of its residents living below the poverty level in 2010, the South has the highest overall poverty rate. In every age group, poverty rates are highest in the South. The rate peaks at 24.4 percent among children under age 18 in the region. Among people aged 65 or older, the poverty rate is lowest in the West (7.6 percent) and highest in the South (10.5 percent).

Among Asians, the poverty rate is highest in the Northeast at 14.8 percent. Among Hispanics, the poverty rate ranges from 25 to 28 percent regardless of region. Among blacks, the highest poverty rate is in the Midwest, at 33 percent. The poverty rate among non-Hispanic whites is more than 10 percent only in the Midwest and South.

■ The poverty rate is highest in the South in part because of the region's large black and Hispanic populations.

Seventeen percent of people who live in the South are poor

(percent of people below poverty level by region, 2010)

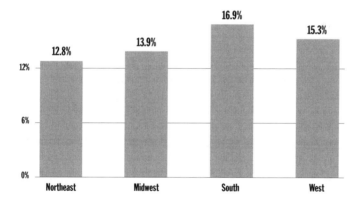

Table 6.63 People below Poverty Level by Age and Region, 2010

(number and percent distribution of people below poverty level and percent of people who are poor, by age and region, 2010; numbers in thousands)

	total	Northeast	Midwest	South	West
NUMBER IN POVERTY					
Total people in poverty	**46,180**	**6,987**	**9,148**	**19,072**	**10,973**
Under age 18	16,401	2,269	3,223	6,858	4,051
Aged 18 to 24	6,507	992	1,343	2,536	1,637
Aged 25 to 34	6,333	969	1,276	2,569	1,519
Aged 35 to 44	5,028	655	980	2,114	1,280
Aged 45 to 54	4,662	759	942	1,926	1,035
Aged 55 to 59	1,972	371	348	830	424
Aged 60 to 64	1,755	292	350	737	376
Aged 65 or older	3,520	680	687	1,503	650
Aged 65 to 74	1,737	335	339	722	340
Aged 75 or older	1,784	345	348	782	310
PERCENT DISTRIBUTION OF POOR BY REGION					
Total people in poverty	**100.0%**	**15.1%**	**19.8%**	**41.3%**	**23.8%**
Under age 18	100.0	13.8	19.7	41.8	24.7
Aged 18 to 24	100.0	15.2	20.6	39.0	25.2
Aged 25 to 34	100.0	15.3	20.1	40.6	24.0
Aged 35 to 44	100.0	13.0	19.5	42.0	25.5
Aged 45 to 54	100.0	16.3	20.2	41.3	22.2
Aged 55 to 59	100.0	18.8	17.6	42.1	21.5
Aged 60 to 64	100.0	16.6	19.9	42.0	21.4
Aged 65 or older	100.0	19.3	19.5	42.7	18.5
Aged 65 to 74	100.0	19.3	19.5	41.6	19.6
Aged 75 or older	100.0	19.3	19.5	43.8	17.4
PERCENT IN POVERTY					
Total people	**15.1%**	**12.8%**	**13.9%**	**16.9%**	**15.3%**
Under age 18	22.0	18.4	20.4	24.4	22.2
Aged 18 to 24	21.9	17.9	21.0	23.9	23.1
Aged 25 to 34	15.2	13.6	14.6	16.6	14.9
Aged 35 to 44	12.6	9.5	11.6	14.2	13.3
Aged 45 to 54	10.6	9.0	9.6	12.1	10.7
Aged 55 to 59	10.1	10.1	8.1	11.5	9.7
Aged 60 to 64	10.1	9.3	9.3	11.3	9.3
Aged 65 or older	9.0	8.9	7.9	10.5	7.6
Aged 65 to 74	8.1	8.4	7.3	9.0	7.1
Aged 75 or older	10.0	9.4	8.5	12.5	8.2

Source: Bureau of the Census, 2011 Current Population Survey Annual Social and Economic Supplement, Internet site http://www.census.gov/hhes/www/cpstables/032011/pov/toc.htm; calculations by New Strategist

Table 6.64 People below Poverty Level by Region, Race, and Hispanic Origin, 2010

(number and percent distribution of people below poverty level and percent in poverty, by region, race, and Hispanic origin, 2010; numbers in thousands)

	total	Asian	black	Hispanic	non-Hispanic white
Total people in poverty	**46,180**	**1,859**	**11,361**	**13,243**	**19,599**
Northeast	6,987	453	1,792	1,837	3,161
Midwest	9,148	211	2,437	1,189	5,251
South	19,072	387	6,098	5,039	7,546
West	10,973	809	1,034	5,179	3,641

PERCENT DISTRIBUTION OF POOR BY RACE AND HISPANIC ORIGIN

	total	Asian	black	Hispanic	non-Hispanic white
Total people in poverty	**100.0%**	**4.0%**	**24.6%**	**28.7%**	**42.4%**
Northeast	100.0	6.5	25.6	26.3	45.2
Midwest	100.0	2.3	26.6	13.0	57.4
South	100.0	2.0	32.0	26.4	39.6
West	100.0	7.4	9.4	47.2	33.2

PERCENT IN POVERTY

	total	Asian	black	Hispanic	non-Hispanic white
Total people	**15.1%**	**11.9%**	**27.4%**	**26.6%**	**9.9%**
Northeast	12.8	14.8	25.0	26.6	8.3
Midwest	13.9	11.5	33.1	28.0	10.1
South	16.9	10.9	26.7	27.9	11.1
West	15.3	11.2	25.0	25.1	9.4

Note: Asians and blacks include those who identify themselves as being of the race alone and those who identify themselves as being of the race in combination with other races. Non-Hispanic whites are those who identify themselves as white alone and not Hispanic. Numbers do not add to total because not all races are shown and Hispanics may be of any race.
Source: Bureau of the Census, 2011 Current Population Survey Annual Social and Economic Supplement, Internet site http:// www.census.gov/hhes/www/cpstables/032011/pov/toc.htm; calculations by New Strategist

More than 29 Percent of Children in the Nation's Principal Cities Are Poor

In the suburbs, a smaller 16.8 percent of children are poor.

Nationally, poverty rates are higher in the principal (central) cities and nonmetropolitan areas than outside the principal cities (suburbs). In 2010, a substantial 19.7 percent of principal city residents were poor. In nonmetropolitan areas the poverty rate was 16.5 percent. In the suburbs, 11.8 percent of people are poor.

Among children under age 18 in principal cities, 29.4 percent are poor. The poverty rate of young adults in the central cities is not far behind, at 28.1 percent. In contrast, the lowest poverty rate is found among 65-to-74-year-olds living in the suburbs—only 9.0 percent were poor in 2010.

Among the nation's 50 largest metropolitan areas, poverty rates were highest in Memphis—19.1 percent in 2010, according to the Census Bureau's American Community Survey. The poverty rate is lowest in the Washington, D.C. metropolitan area, with just 8.4 percent of its residents being poor.

■ Washington, D.C., is the only major metropolitan area in which the poverty rate is not in the double digits.

The poverty rate is highest in the principal cities

(percent of people below poverty level by metropolitan residence, 2010)

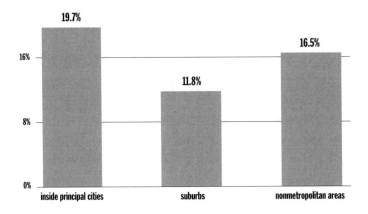

Table 6.65 People below Poverty Level by Age and Metropolitan Status, 2010

(number and percent distribution of people below poverty level and percent who are poor, by age and metropolitan status, 2010; numbers in thousands)

	total	in metropolitan areas			not in metropolitan areas
		total	inside principal cities	outside principal cities	
Total people in poverty	**46,180**	**38,325**	**19,465**	**18,860**	**7,855**
Under age 18	16,401	13,630	7,025	6,604	2,771
Aged 18 to 24	6,507	5,449	2,930	2,519	1,058
Aged 25 to 34	6,333	5,407	2,837	2,570	926
Aged 35 to 44	5,028	4,286	2,138	2,148	742
Aged 45 to 54	4,662	3,754	1,803	1,951	908
Aged 55 to 59	1,972	1,651	806	845	322
Aged 60 to 64	1,755	1,396	676	720	359
Aged 65 or older	3,520	2,753	1,251	1,503	767
Aged 65 to 74	1,737	1,369	603	765	368
Aged 75 or older	1,784	1,384	647	737	399
PERCENT DISTRIBUTION OF POOR BY METROPOLITAN STATUS					
Total people in poverty	**100.0%**	**83.0%**	**42.2%**	**40.8%**	**17.0%**
Under age 18	100.0	83.1	42.8	40.3	16.9
Aged 18 to 24	100.0	83.7	45.0	38.7	16.3
Aged 25 to 34	100.0	85.4	44.8	40.6	14.6
Aged 35 to 44	100.0	85.2	42.5	42.7	14.8
Aged 45 to 54	100.0	80.5	38.7	41.8	19.5
Aged 55 to 59	100.0	83.7	40.9	42.8	16.3
Aged 60 to 64	100.0	79.5	38.5	41.0	20.5
Aged 65 or older	100.0	78.2	35.5	42.7	21.8
Aged 65 to 74	100.0	78.8	34.7	44.0	21.2
Aged 75 or older	100.0	77.6	36.3	41.3	22.4
PERCENT IN POVERTY					
Total people	**15.1%**	**14.9%**	**19.7%**	**11.8%**	**16.5%**
Under age 18	22.0	21.5	29.4	16.8	24.7
Aged 18 to 24	21.9	21.7	28.1	17.1	23.5
Aged 25 to 34	15.2	15.0	17.1	13.2	16.8
Aged 35 to 44	12.6	12.5	16.5	10.1	13.3
Aged 45 to 54	10.6	10.2	14.1	8.1	13.0
Aged 55 to 59	10.1	10.2	14.2	8.0	9.7
Aged 60 to 64	10.1	9.8	13.2	7.9	11.5
Aged 65 or older	9.0	8.7	11.2	7.3	10.4
Aged 65 to 74	8.1	7.9	10.1	6.8	9.0
Aged 75 or older	10.0	9.6	12.6	7.9	12.1

Source: Bureau of the Census, 2011 Current Population Survey Annual Social and Economic Supplement, Internet site http://www.census.gov/hhes/www/cpstables/032011/pov/toc.htm; calculations by New Strategist

Table 6.66 Poor Population by Metropolitan Area, 2010

(number of poor people and poverty rate in the 50 largest metropolitan areas, 2010)

	number of poor	poverty rate
Atlanta–Sandy Springs–Marietta, GA Metro Area	770,629	14.8%
Austin–Round Rock–San Marcos, TX Metro Area	268,740	15.9
Baltimore–Towson, MD Metro Area	291,682	11.0
Birmingham–Hoover, AL Metro Area	188,894	17.0
Boston–Cambridge–Quincy, MA–NH Metro Area	455,773	10.3
Buffalo–Niagara Falls, NY Metro Area	158,695	14.4
Charlotte–Gastonia–Rock Hill, NC–SC Metro Area	252,137	14.5
Chicago–Joliet–Naperville, IL–IN–WI Metro Area	1,267,449	13.6
Cincinnati–Middletown, OH–KY–IN Metro Area	291,328	14.0
Cleveland–Elyria–Mentor, OH Metro Area	306,822	15.1
Columbus, OH Metro Area	282,368	15.7
Dallas–Fort Worth–Arlington, TX Metro Area	918,907	14.6
Denver–Aurora–Broomfield, CO Metro Area	316,367	12.5
Detroit–Warren–Livonia, MI Metro Area	704,937	16.6
Hartford–West Hartford–East Hartford, CT Metro Area	118,453	10.1
Houston–Sugar Land–Baytown, TX Metro Area	975,706	16.5
Indianapolis–Carmel, IN Metro Area	254,204	14.8
Jacksonville, FL Metro Area	202,028	15.3
Kansas City, MO–KS Metro Area	248,177	12.4
Las Vegas–Paradise, NV Metro Area	291,272	15.1
Los Angeles–Long Beach–Santa Ana, CA Metro Area	2,060,008	16.3
Louisville/Jefferson County, KY–IN Metro Area	193,530	15.3
Memphis, TN–MS–AR Metro Area	246,265	19.1
Miami–Fort Lauderdale–Pompano Beach, FL Metro Area	938,750	17.1
Milwaukee–Waukesha–West Allis, WI Metro Area	236,734	15.5
Minneapolis–St. Paul–Bloomington, MN–WI Metro Area	350,972	10.9
Nashville–Davidson–Murfreesboro–Franklin, TN Metro Area	238,764	15.4
New Orleans–Metairie–Kenner, LA Metro Area	202,099	17.4
New York–Northern New Jersey–Long Island, NY–NJ–PA Metro Area	2,569,999	13.8
Oklahoma City, OK Metro Area	195,368	15.9
Orlando–Kissimmee–Sanford, FL Metro Area	309,150	14.7
Philadelphia–Camden–Wilmington, PA–NJ–DE–MD Metro Area	741,531	12.7
Phoenix–Mesa–Glendale, AZ Metro Area	672,299	16.3
Pittsburgh, PA Metro Area	278,824	12.2
Portland–Vancouver Hillsboro, OR–WA Metro Area	295,632	13.4
Providence–New Bedford–Fall River, RI–MA Metro Area	211,253	13.7
Raleigh–Cary, NC Metro Area	143,264	12.9
Richmond, VA Metro Area	141,304	11.6
Riverside–San Bernardino–Ontario, CA Metro Area	714,335	17.1
Sacramento–Arden-Arcade–Roseville, CA Metro Area	317,506	15.1
Salt Lake City, UT Metro Area	145,786	13.1
San Antonio–New Braunfels, TX Metro Area	344,044	16.3
San Diego–Carlsbad–San Marcos, CA Metro Area	446,060	14.8
San Francisco–Oakland–Fremont, CA Metro Area	467,195	10.9
San Jose–Sunnyvale–Santa Clara, CA Metro Area	192,896	10.6
Seattle–Tacoma–Bellevue, WA Metro Area	396,212	11.7
St. Louis, MO–IL Metro Area	368,646	13.3
Tampa–St. Petersburg–Clearwater, FL Metro Area	422,750	15.4
Virginia Beach–Norfolk–Newport News, VA–NC Metro Area	173,071	10.6
Washington–Arlington–Alexandria, DC–VA–MD–WV Metro Area	459,626	8.4

Source: Bureau of the Census, 2010 American Community Survey, Internet site http://factfinder2.census.gov/faces/nav/jsf/pages/searchresults.xhtml?refresh=t; calculations by New Strategist

More than One-Third of Nation's Poor Live in Four States

Thirteen states are home to more than 1 million poor people.

Thirty-six percent of poor Americans live in California, Florida, New York, or Texas. California alone is home to 13 percent, while Texas accounts for another 10 percent, New York an additional 7 percent, and Florida 6 percent. Other states with more than 1 million poor residents are Arizona, Georgia, Illinois, Indiana, Michigan, North Carolina, Ohio, Pennsylvania, and Tennessee. Together, the 11 states with at least 1 million poor residents account for the 65 percent majority of the nation's poor.

Among the 50 states, the poverty rate was highest in Mississippi at 22.7 percent in 2010. The poverty rate was lowest in New Hampshire, at 6.6 percent.

■ The poverty rate is likely to continue to rise in most states during the next few years because of the sluggish recovery from the Great Recession.

The majority of poor Americans live in just eight states

(number of people below poverty level, for states with at least 1 million poor residents, 2010; numbers in millions)

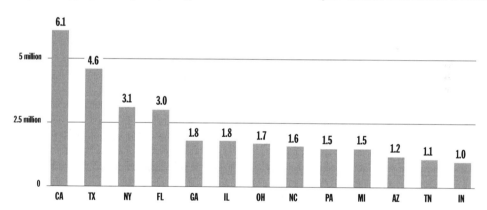

Table 6.67 People below Poverty Level by State, 2010

(number, percent, and percent distribution of people below poverty level by state, 2010; numbers in thousands)

	number in poverty	percent in poverty	percent distribution of poor by state
United States	**46,180**	**15.1%**	**100.0%**
Alabama	808	17.3	1.7
Alaska	86	12.4	0.2
Arizona	1,241	18.6	2.7
Arkansas	445	15.5	1.0
California	6,077	16.3	13.2
Colorado	617	12.2	1.3
Connecticut	292	8.3	0.6
Delaware	106	12.1	0.2
District of Columbia	121	19.9	0.3
Florida	2,962	16.0	6.4
Georgia	1,836	18.7	4.0
Hawaii	152	12.1	0.3
Idaho	214	14.0	0.5
Illinois	1,817	14.1	3.9
Indiana	1,035	16.3	2.2
Iowa	305	10.3	0.7
Kansas	394	14.3	0.9
Kentucky	758	17.7	1.6
Louisiana	958	21.6	2.1
Maine	161	12.5	0.3
Maryland	620	10.8	1.3
Massachusetts	702	10.6	1.5
Michigan	1,511	15.5	3.3
Minnesota	544	10.5	1.2
Mississippi	664	22.7	1.4
Missouri	885	14.8	1.9
Montana	136	14.0	0.3
Nebraska	182	10.2	0.4
Nevada	432	16.4	0.9
New Hampshire	85	6.6	0.2
New Jersey	931	10.7	2.0
New Mexico	376	18.6	0.8
New York	3,086	16.0	6.7
North Carolina	1,609	17.4	3.5
North Dakota	77	12.2	0.2
Ohio	1,739	15.3	3.8
Oklahoma	597	16.3	1.3
Oregon	535	14.2	1.2
Pennsylvania	1,521	12.2	3.3
Rhode Island	142	13.6	0.3
South Carolina	767	17.0	1.7

	number in poverty	percent in poverty	percent distribution of poor by state
South Dakota	106	13.2%	0.2%
Tennessee	1,050	16.7	2.3
Texas	4,635	18.4	10.0
Utah	283	10.0	0.6
Vermont	67	10.8	0.1
Virginia	832	10.7	1.8
Washington	774	11.5	1.7
West Virginia	304	16.9	0.7
Wisconsin	553	9.9	1.2
Wyoming	51	9.6	0.1

Source: Bureau of the Census, 2011 Current Population Survey Annual Social and Economic Supplement, Internet site http://www.census.gov/hhes/www/cpstables/032011/pov/toc.htm; calculations by New Strategist

Glossary

adjusted for inflation Income or a change in income that has been adjusted for the rise in the cost of living, or the consumer price index.

aggregate income The total amount of household income, calculated by multiplying average income by the number of households.

American Community Survey The ACS is an ongoing nationwide survey of 250,000 households per month, providing detailed demographic data at the community level. Designed to replace the census long-form questionnaire, the ACS includes more than 60 questions that formerly appeared on the long form, such as language spoken at home, income, and education. ACS data are available for areas as small as census tracts.

Asian Includes Native Hawaiians and other Pacific Islanders unless those groups are shown separately.

Baby Boom U.S. residents born between 1946 and 1964.

Baby Bust U.S. residents born between 1965 and 1976, also known as Generation X.

black Includes those who identified themselves as "black" or "African American."

Consumer Expenditure Survey The CEX is an ongoing study of the day-to-day spending of American households administered by the Bureau of Labor Statistics. The CEX includes an interview survey and a diary survey. The average spending figures shown are the integrated data from both the diary and interview components of the survey. Two separate, nationally representative samples are used for the interview and diary surveys. For the interview survey, about 7,000 consumer units are interviewed on a rotating panel basis each quarter for five consecutive quarters. For the diary survey, 7,000 consumer units keep weekly diaries of spending for two consecutive weeks.

consumer unit *(on spending tables only)* For convenience, the term consumer unit and household are used interchangeably in the Spending chapter of this book, although consumer units are somewhat different from the Census Bureau's households. Consumer units are all related members of a household, or financially independent members of a household. A household may include more than one consumer unit.

Current Population Survey The CPS is a nationally representative survey of the civilian noninstitutional population aged 15 or older. It is taken monthly by the Census Bureau for the Bureau of Labor Statistics, collecting information from more than 60,000 households on employment and unemployment. In March of each year, the survey includes the Annual Social and Economic Supplement, which is the source of most national data on the characteristics of Americans, such as educational attainment, living arrangements, and incomes.

discretionary income The amount of money households have left over after they pay taxes and buy necessities.

dual-earner couple A married couple in which both the husband and wife are in the labor force.

earnings A type of income, earnings is the amount of money a person receives from his or her job. *See also* Income.

employed All civilians who did any work as a paid employee or farmer/self-employed worker, or who worked 15 hours or more as an unpaid farm worker or in a family-owned business, during the reference period. All those who have jobs but who are temporarily absent from their jobs due to illness, bad weather, vacation, labor management dispute, or personal reasons are considered employed.

expenditure The transaction cost including excise and sales taxes of goods and services acquired during the survey period. The full cost of each purchase is recorded even though full payment may not have been made at the date of purchase. Average expenditure figures may be artificially low for infrequently purchased items such as cars because figures are calculated using all consumer units within a demographic segment rather than just purchasers. Expenditure estimates include money spent on gifts for others.

family A group of two or more people (one of whom is the householder) related by birth, marriage, or adoption and living in the same household.

family household A household maintained by a householder who lives with one or more people related to him or her by blood, marriage, or adoption.

female/male householder A woman or man who maintains a household without a spouse present. May head family or nonfamily households.

foreign-born population People who are not U.S. citizens at birth.

full-time employment Thirty-five or more hours of work per week during a majority of the weeks worked.

full-time, year-round Fifty or more weeks of full-time employment during the previous calendar year.

Generation X U.S. residents born between 1965 and 1976, also known as the baby-bust generation.

Hispanic Because Hispanic is an ethnic origin rather than a race, Hispanics may be of any race. While most Hispanics are white, there are black, Asian, American Indian, and even Native Hawaiian Hispanics.

household All the persons who occupy a housing unit. A household includes the related family members and all the unrelated persons, if any, such as lodgers, foster children, wards, or employees who share the housing unit. A person living alone is counted as a household. A group of unrelated people who share a housing unit as roommates or unmarried partners is also counted as a household. Households do not include group quarters such as college dormitories, prisons, or nursing homes.

household, race/ethnicity of Households are categorized according to the race or ethnicity of the householder only.

householder The person (or one of the persons) in whose name the housing unit is owned or rented or, if there is no such person, any adult member. With married couples, the householder may be either the husband or wife. The householder is the reference person for the household.

householder, age of The age of the householder is used to categorize households into age groups such as those used in this book. Married couples, for example, are classified according to the age of either the husband or wife, depending on which one identified him or herself as the householder.

housing unit A house, an apartment, a group of rooms, or a single room occupied or intended for occupancy as separate living quarters. Separate living quarters are those in which the occupants do not live and eat with any other persons in the structure and that have direct access from the outside of the building or through a common hall that is used or intended for use by the occupants of another unit or by the general public. The occupants may be a single family, one person living alone, two or more families living together, or any other group of related or unrelated persons who share living arrangements.

housing value The respondent's estimate of how much his or her house and lot would sell for if it were for sale.

iGeneration U.S. residents born in 1995 or later.

immigration The relatively permanent movement (change of residence) of people into the country of reference.

in-migration The relatively permanent movement (change of residence) of people into a subnational geographic entity, such as a region, division, state, metropolitan area, or county.

income Money received in the preceding calendar year by each person aged 15 or older from each of the following sources: (1) earnings from longest job (or self-employment); (2) earnings from jobs other than longest job; (3) unemployment compensation; (4) workers' compensation; (5) Social

Security; (6) Supplemental Security income; (7) public assistance; (8) veterans' payments; (9) survivor benefits; (10) disability benefits; (11) retirement pensions; (12) interest; (13) dividends; (14) rents and royalties or estates and trusts; (15) educational assistance; (16) alimony; (17) child support; (18) financial assistance from outside the household, and other periodic income. Income is reported in several ways in this book. Household income is the combined income of all household members. Income of persons is all income accruing to a person from all sources. Earnings are the money a person receives from his or her job.

income fifths or quintiles Where the total number of households are divided into fifths based on household income. One-fifth of households fall into the lowest income quintile, one-fifth into the second income quintile, and so on. This is a useful way to compare the characteristics of low-, middle-, and high-income households.

industry Refers to the industry in which a person worked longest in the preceding calendar year.

job tenure The length of time a person has been employed continuously by the same employer.

labor force The labor force tables in this book show the civilian labor force only. The labor force includes both the employed and the unemployed (people who are looking for work). People are counted as in the labor force if they were working or looking for work during the reference week in which the Census Bureau fields the Current Population Survey.

labor force participation rate The percent of the civilian noninstitutional population that is in the civilian labor force, which includes both the employed and the unemployed.

married couples with or without children under age 18 Married couples with or without own children under age 18 living in the same household. Couples without children under age 18 may be parents of grown children who live elsewhere, or they could be childless couples.

median The amount that divides the population or households into two equal portions: one below and one above the median. Medians can be calculated for income, age, and many other characteristics.

median income The amount that divides the income distribution into two equal groups, half having incomes above the median, half having incomes below the median. The medians for households or families are based on all households or families. The median for persons are based on all persons aged 15 or older with income.

metropolitan statistical area A large population nucleus with adjacent communities having a high degree of social and economic integration with the core. The Office of Management and Budget defines the nation's metropolitan statistical areas. In general, they must include a city or urbanized area with 50,000 or more inhabitants and a total population of 100,000 or more. The county (or counties) that contains the largest city is the "central county" (counties), along with any adjacent counties that are socially and economically integrated with the central county (or counties). In New England, MSAs are defined in terms of cities and towns rather than counties.

Millennial generation U.S. residents born between 1977 and 1994.

National Compensation Survey The Bureau of Labor Statistics' NCS examines the incidence and detailed provisions of selected employee benefit plans in small, medium, and large private establishments, and state and local governments. Each year BLS economists visit a representative sample of establishments across the country, asking questions about the establishment, its employees, and their benefits.

Native Hawaiian and other Pacific Islander The 2000 census identified this group for the first time as a separate racial category from Asians. In most survey data, however, the population is included with Asians.

net migration Net migration is the result of subtracting out-migration from in-migration for an area. Another way to derive net migration is to subtract natural increase (births minus deaths) from total population change in an area.

net worth The amount of money left over after a household's debts are subtracted from its assets.

nonfamily household A household maintained by a householder who lives alone or who lives with people to whom he or she is not related.

nonfamily householder A householder who lives alone or with nonrelatives.

non-Hispanic People who do not identify themselves as Hispanic are classified as non-Hispanic. Non-Hispanics may be of any race.

non-Hispanic white People who identify their race as white alone and who do not indicate an Hispanic origin.

nonmetropolitan area Counties that are not classified as metropolitan areas.

occupation Occupational classification is based on the kind of work a person did at his or her job during the previous calendar year. If a person changed jobs during the year, the data refer to the occupation of the job held the longest during that year.

occupied housing units A housing unit is classified as occupied if a person or group of people is living in it or if the occupants are only temporarily absent—on vacation, example. By definition, the count of occupied housing units is the same as the count of households.

outside principal cities The portion of a metropolitan county or counties that falls outside of the principal city or cities; generally regarded as the suburbs.

own children Sons and daughters, including stepchildren and adopted children, of the householder. The totals include never-married children living away from home in college dormitories.

owner occupied A housing unit is "owner occupied" if the owner lives in the unit, even if it is mortgaged or not fully paid for. A cooperative or condominium unit is "owner occupied" only if the owner lives in it. All other occupied units are classified as "renter occupied."

part-time employment Less than 35 hours of work per week in a majority of the weeks worked during the year.

percent change The change (either positive or negative) in a measure that is expressed as a proportion of the starting measure. When median income changes from $20,000 to $25,000, for example, this is a 25 percent increase.

percentage point change The change (either positive or negative) in a value which is already expressed as a percentage. When a labor force participation rate changes from 70 percent of 75 percent, for example, this is a 5 percentage point increase.

poverty level The official income threshold below which families and people are classified as living in poverty. The threshold rises each year with inflation and varies depending on family size, age of householder, and number of children under age 18 in the household. According to the Census Bureau, poverty thresholds in 2010: for a person under aged 65 who lives alone, $11,344; for a person aged 65 or older who lives alone, $10,458; for a family of four including two children, $22,113.

principal cities The largest cities in a metropolitan area are called the principal cities. The balance of a metropolitan area outside the principal cities is regarded as the "suburbs."

proportion or share The value of a part expressed as a percentage of the whole. If there are 4 million people aged 25 and 3 million of them are white, then the white proportion is 75 percent.

race Race is self-reported and can be defined in three ways. The "race alone" population comprises people who identify themselves as only one race. The "race in combination" population comprises people who identify themselves as more than one race, such as white and black. The "race, alone or in combination" population includes both those who identify themselves as one race and those who identify themselves as more than one race.

regions The four major regions and nine census divisions of the United States are the state groupings as shown below:

Northeast:

—New England: Connecticut, Maine, Massachusetts, New Hampshire, Rhode Island, and Vermont

—Middle Atlantic: New Jersey, New York, and Pennsylvania

Midwest:

—East North Central: Illinois, Indiana, Michigan, Ohio, and Wisconsin

—West North Central: Iowa, Kansas, Minnesota, Missouri, Nebraska, North Dakota, and South Dakota

South:

—South Atlantic: Delaware, District of Columbia, Florida, Georgia, Maryland, North Carolina, South Carolina, Virginia, and West Virginia

—East South Central: Alabama, Kentucky, Mississippi, and Tennessee

—West South Central: Arkansas, Louisiana, Oklahoma, and Texas

West:

—Mountain: Arizona, Colorado, Idaho, Montana, Nevada, New Mexico, Utah, and Wyoming

—Pacific: Alaska, California, Hawaii, Oregon, and Washington

renter occupied *See* Owner Occupied.

Retirement Confidence Survey The RCS, sponsored by the Employee Benefit Research Institute, the American Savings Education Council, and Mathew Greenwald & Associates, is an annual survey of a nationally representative sample of 1,000 people aged 25 or older. Respondents are asked a core set of questions that have been asked since 1996, measuring attitudes and behavior towards retirement. Additional questions are also asked about current retirement issues.

rounding Percentages are rounded to the nearest tenth of a percent; therefore, the percentages in a distribution do not always add exactly to 100.0 percent. The totals, however, are always shown as 100.0. Moreover, individual figures are rounded to the nearest thousand without being adjusted to group totals, which are independently rounded; percentages are based on the unrounded numbers.

self-employment A person is categorized as self-employed if he or she was self-employed in the job held longest during the reference period. Persons who report self-employment from a second job are excluded, but those who report wage-and-salary income from a second job are included. Unpaid workers in family businesses are excluded. Self-employment statistics include only nonagricultural workers and

exclude people who work for themselves in incorporated business.

sex ratio The number of men per 100 women.

suburbs *See* Outside Principal City.

Survey of Consumer Finances A triennial survey taken by the Federal Reserve Board. It collects data on the assets, debts, and net worth of American households. For the 2009 survey, the Federal Reserve Board reinterviewed most of the 4,000-plus households that took part in the 2007 survey.

unemployed People who, during the survey period, had no employment but were available and looking for work. Those who were laid off from their jobs and were waiting to be recalled are also classified as unemployed.

white Includes many Hispanics (who may be of any race) unless the term "non-Hispanic white" is used.

work experience Based on work for pay or work without pay on a family-operated farm or business at any time during the previous year, on a part-time or full-time basis.

Bibliography

Bureau of Labor Statistics
   Internet site http://www.bls.gov
   —2009 Consumer Expenditure Survey, Internet site http://www.bls.gov/cex/home.htm
   —2010 Employee Benefits Survey, Internet site http://www.bls.gov/ncs/ebs/benefits/2010/ownership_civilian.htm

Bureau of the Census
   Internet site http://www.census.gov/
   —2011 Current Population Survey Annual Social and Economic Supplement, Internet site http://www.census.gov/hhes/www/income/dinctabs.html
   —2010 American Community Survey, Internet site http://factfinder2.census.gov/faces/nav/jsf/pages/searchresults.xhtml?refresh=t
   —Historical income data, Current Population Survey Annual Demographic Supplements, Internet site http://www.census.gov/hhes/www/income/data/historical/index.html
   —Historical poverty data, Current Population Survey Annual Demographic Supplements, Internet site http://www.census.gov/hhes/www/poverty/data/historical/index.html
   —*Income, Poverty, and Health Insurance Coverage in the United States: 2010,* Current Population Report P60-239, 2011; Internet site http://www.census.gov/hhes/www/income/income.html

Employee Benefit Research Institute
   Internet site http://www.ebri.org/
   —Retirement Confidence Survey, Internet site http://www.ebri.org/surveys/rcs/

Federal Reserve Board
   Internet site http://www.federalreserve.gov/pubs/oss/oss2/scfindex.html
   —"Surveying the Aftermath of the Storm: Changes in Family Finances from 2007 to 2009," Finance and Economics Discussion Series, 2011-17, Appendix tables, Internet site http://www.federalreserve.gov/pubs/oss/oss2/2009p/scf2009phome.html

Index